Introduction to Business

to the students that will use business as a way to create and protect the future

Sara Miller McCune founded SAGE Publishing in 1965 to support the dissemination of usable knowledge and educate a global community. SAGE publishes more than 1,000 journals and over 600 new books each year, spanning a wide range of subject areas. Our growing selection of library products includes archives, data, case studies, and video. SAGE remains majority owned by our founder and after her lifetime will become owned by a charitable trust that secures the company's continued independence.

Los Angeles | London | New Delhi | Singapore | Washington DC | Melbourne

Introduction to Business

Heidi M. Neck

Babson College

Christopher P. Neck

Arizona State University

Emma L. Murray

Los Angeles | London | New Delhi
Singapore | Washington DC | Melbourne

SAGE Publications, Inc.
2455 Teller Road
Thousand Oaks, California 91320
E-mail: order@sagepub.com

SAGE Publications Ltd.
1 Oliver's Yard
55 City Road
London, EC1Y 1SP
United Kingdom

SAGE Publications India Pvt. Ltd.
Unit No. 323-333, Third Floor, F-Block
International Trade Tower
Nehru Place, New Delhi 110 019
India

SAGE Publications Asia-Pacific Pte. Ltd.
18 Cross Street #10-10/11/12
China Square Central
Singapore 048423

Copyright © 2024 by SAGE Publications, Inc.

All rights reserved. Except as permitted by U.S. copyright law, no part of this work may be reproduced or distributed in any form or by any means, or stored in a database or retrieval system, without permission in writing from the publisher.

All third party trademarks referenced or depicted herein are included solely for the purpose of illustration and are the property of their respective owners. Reference to these trademarks in no way indicates any relationship with, or endorsement by, the trademark owner.

Printed in Canada

Library of Congress Control Number: 2022921772

ISBN (paperback): 978-1-0718-1314-0

ISBN (loose-leaf): 978-1-0718-5808-0

This book is printed on acid-free paper.

23 24 25 26 27 10 9 8 7 6 5 4 3 2 1

Acquisitions Editor: Lily Norton

Content Development Editors:
Adeline Grout, Darcy Scelsi

Production Editor: Rebecca Lee

Copy Editor: Talia Greenberg

Typesetter: diacriTech

Cover Designer: Gail Buschman

Marketing Manager: Jennifer Haldeman

BRIEF CONTENTS

DETAILED CONTENTS

LIST OF CASE STUDIES

Business Impact Case 1.1: Patagonia—Ventura, California

Business Case 1.2: Ordinary Habit—Doylestown, Pennsylvania

Business Impact Case 2.1: Amazon—Seattle, Washington

Business Case 2.2: Reel—Santa Monica, California

Business Impact Case 3.1: Save the Children—Fairfield, Connecticut (Headquarters)

Business Case 3.2: Lovevery—Boise, Idaho

Business Impact Case 4.1: MassChallenge—Boston, Massachusetts

Business Case 4.2: Workday—Pleasanton, California

Business Impact Case 5.1: Imperfect Foods—San Francisco, California

Business Case 5.2: AppHarvest—Lexington, Kentucky

Business Impact Case 6.1: Tesla—Austin, Texas

Business Case 6.2: Microsoft—Redmond, Washington

Business Impact Case 7.1: 4ocean—Boca Raton, Florida

Business Case 7.2: Intuit—Mountain View, California

Business Impact Case 8.1: Mixtroz—Birmingham, Alabama

Business Case 8.2: Merck—Rahway, New Jersey

Business Impact Case 9.1: Zappos—Las Vegas, Nevada

Business Case 9.2: Saltwater Brewery—Delray Beach, Florida

Business Impact Case 10.1: John's Crazy Socks—Melville, New York

Business Case 10.2: Novozymes—Bagsvaerd, Denmark

Business Impact Case 11.1: Little Cocoa Bean—Boston, Massachusetts

Business Case 11.2: Akamae Co-Creation Ethical Fashion—Mae Hong Son, Thailand

Business Impact Case 12.1: JetBlue—Long Island City, New York

Business Case 12.2: BBVA—Bilbao, Spain

Business Impact Case 13.1: Leaf'd—Los Angeles, California

Business Case 13.2: PIPs Rewards—New York, New York

Business Impact Case 14.1: Autodesk—San Rafael, California

Business Case 14.2 Allbirds—San Francisco, California

Business Impact Case 15.1: Starbucks—Seattle, Washington

Business Case 15.2: Hilton Hotels—McLean, Virginia

Business Impact Case 16.1: Walmart—Bentonville, Arkansas

Business Case 16.2: Overstory—Amsterdam, The Netherlands

Business Impact Case 17.1: Portfolia—San Mateo, California

Business Case 17.2: Accenture—Dublin, Ireland

Business Impact Case 18.1: WW International—New York, New York

Business Case 18.2: AgBiome—Research Triangle Park, North Carolina

PREFACE

Introduction to Business explores the fundamental building blocks of business while emphasizing social impact, entrepreneurial thinking, and ethical decision making throughout. Cases on startups, small businesses, corporations, and nonprofits will ignite student interest as they learn from today's most forward-looking organizations. Regardless of their career aspirations, students will develop the mindset and skillset to think critically, act entrepreneurially, and engage ethically in order to succeed in their professional journeys.

In this text, a *business* is defined as an organization that is engaged in commercial, industrial, or professional activities that produce and/or sell goods or services for the creation of economic *and* social value. *Economic value* relates to the profitability of the business and its ability to generate revenue, pay expenses, and generate positive net income. *Social value* encompasses the positive impact a business can have on society including issues related to employee diversity, equity, and inclusion as well as issues related to environmental sustainability and global challenges. As a holistic approach, the text is modern, purpose-driving, inclusive, and entrepreneurial.

INTRODUCTION TO BUSINESS IS MODERN

Gaining business knowledge within a formal education structure requires a new, more relevant approach based on action and practice. This text approaches teaching business as a set of fundamental building blocks (Figure I.1) that constitute business as an integrated enterprise rather than discipline silos. As a result, students achieve a more holistic view of business, understand how the blocks connect, and appreciate the foundation of the entrepreneurial mindset to business building in the modern era.

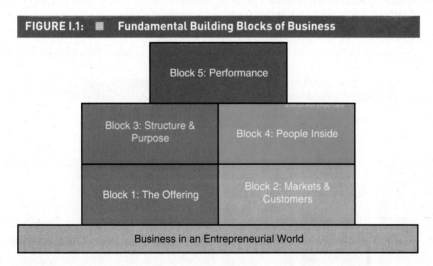

FIGURE I.1: ■ Fundamental Building Blocks of Business

Block 5: Performance

Block 3: Structure & Purpose

Block 4: People Inside

Block 1: The Offering

Block 2: Markets & Customers

Business in an Entrepreneurial World

The text is organized into five blocks, plus a foundational block that introduces students to business in society, the entrepreneurial mindset, and globalization. Chapters connect to each block.

- **Block 1, The Offering,** highlights business creation, business models, and business strategy.

- **Block 2, Markets and Customers,** emphasizes the importance of marketing, sales, customers, and market segments.

- **Block 3, Structure and Purpose,** describes how organizations are designed, the culture they create, and the missions they work to achieve.

- **Block 4, People Inside the Business,** exposes the softer skills of business including leadership, management, human resources, motivation, empowerment, and communication.

- **Block 5, Performance,** addresses operations, data management and analytics, accounting, and financial management.

Together, these blocks and the chapters within each block lead students to the successful completion of the final business impact project.

The *business impact project* encourages students to put their knowledge into action and better understand and connect with a business that they are curious about, admire, want potentially to work for, already work for, want to create—or perhaps they are super fans of its products. Regardless of the business they choose for the project, the business must connect to one or more of the UN Sustainable Development Goals. The project's outcome is a *business impact deck*, which is a PowerPoint (or equivalent) presentation that depicts the five building blocks of the company chosen, its impact related to the UN SDGs, as well as two to four potential entrepreneurial opportunities that company could pursue in the future. These opportunities are uncovered as the student (or student group) researches the five building blocks, learns more about the company, the industry in which it competes, and the customers it currently serves and could serve in the future. These opportunities could be new products, services, processes related to how work is done, new initiatives inside the company, or new projects to benefit the community served by the company. Overall, students see how the business building blocks fit together for one company and the resulting impact of the blocks working together as a whole rather than distinct components or pieces.

INTRODUCTION TO BUSINESS IS PURPOSE-DRIVEN

We execute our purpose-driven premise via the 17 United Nations Sustainable Development Goals (SDGs) adopted by 193 nations. The United Nations SDGs are a blueprint for achieving a thriving, inclusive, and sustainable society. There are 17 goals created to transform our world, goals related to poverty, education, well-being, climate, equality, and hunger, just to name a few (Figure I.2). Meeting

FIGURE I.2 ■ The UN's Sustainable Development Goals

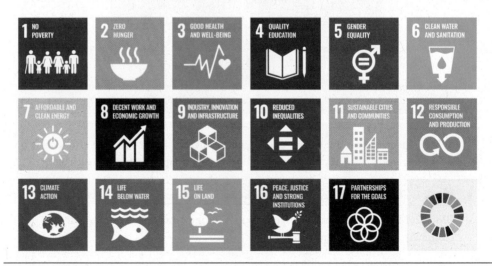

Source: United Nations. (2022). *Sustainable Development Goals*. United Nations Sustainable Development; United Nations. https://www.un.org/sustainabledevelopment/sustainable-development-goals/. The content of this publication has not been approved by the United Nations and does not reflect the views of the United Nations or its officials or member states.

these goals is not just the right thing to do from a social perspective. Economically, the goals represent $12 trillion in business opportunities as well as creating 380 million jobs worldwide.[1] Experts suggest that the greatest impact will be derived from four areas: food and agriculture, cities, energy and materials, and health and well-being.[2] Companies, through a focus on the UN SDGS, are starting to operate in more humane and sustainable ways to drive positive change and protect people and the planet that we inhabit. Students want to work in and build these companies. Seventy percent of Generation Z want their core values, especially values connected to social activism, to align with the values of the organization where they work.[3] Given that students are motivated by these types of companies and the responsibilities of business in society, every company example used in the text relates either directly or indirectly to the pursuit of one or more of the UN SDGs.

INTRODUCTION TO BUSINESS IS INCLUSIVE

An understanding of the fundamentals of modern business is critical for *everyone*—whether you are a CEO, an artist, an entrepreneur, an entry-level employee, a musician, an engineer, anyone who has a desire to offer something of value to the world. This text does not target only "traditional" business students but all students because we believe knowledge of modern business principles can be the difference between long-term success and failure for all majors—not just business majors. Additionally, we celebrate various types of business owners from all around the world to demonstrate that global is local and local is also global. We also emphasize that business is open to all, that is anyone from any gender, race, nationality, or sexual orientation. Celebrations of diversity are found throughout the text, evidence that the modern business world is more accessible than ever before yet acknowledging that constraints, challenges, and bias continue to exist. Given the global nature and diversity of business, ethical dilemmas pepper the landscape, illuminating the complexity of issues and impact of decisions across stakeholder groups. Throughout the text, students will see and feel that ethics is not just a definition to learn, but rather a practice that empowers them to positively impact the world, attack injustice, critically evaluate possible outcomes, and contribute in responsible ways.

INTRODUCTION TO BUSINESS IS ENTREPRENEURIAL

When we say *Introduction to Business* is entrepreneurial we do not mean this is a book specifically for students in entrepreneurship classes. On the contrary, this book is for students who want to learn about today's business world and how to thrive within it. In fact, the term *entrepreneur* is no longer reserved for those starting new businesses. Being entrepreneurial is a way of thinking and acting that combines the ability to find or create new opportunities with the courage to act on them. Being entrepreneurial and acting entrepreneurially is a necessary skillset in today's uncertain business environment. Those who can embrace the uncertainty, navigate the ambiguity, and create value under such conditions are the change makers who are redefining what being an entrepreneur looks like. Not every student of business should be an entrepreneur, but every student should be entrepreneurial, regardless of their career aspirations. Not only do we use examples of all kinds of entrepreneurs, managers, and leaders throughout the text, an entrepreneurial mindset activity in each chapter exists to help students develop their own ability to think and act entrepreneurially.

We highlight our modern, purpose-driven, inclusive, and entrepreneurial approach in each chapter through the inclusion of the following features:

- **Business Impact Case:** A short description of a real business opens each chapter. Each story connects to the content of the chapter but also highlights how the company is working on one or more of the UN Sustainable Development Goals.

- **Entrepreneurial Mindset Activity:** Each chapter includes an entrepreneurial mindset activity that requires students to close the textbook and take action. These activities are designed to help students develop their ability to think and act like an entrepreneur.

- **Ethics in Business:** Peppered with situations faced by real-world entrepreneurs, managers, and employees, the Ethics in Business feature challenges students to address ethical dilemmas, critically evaluate options, and discuss consequences of different decision paths.

- **End-of-Chapter Case Study:** A case study connects to the content of the chapter and also highlights how the company is working toward the UN Sustainable Development Goals (SDGs). The case studies are slightly longer than the business impact stories at the beginning of each chapter.

Overall, we strike a balance between theory and practice. We believe the content of the text reflects the reality of business today and prepares students for the current reality and future possibilities as they get ready for future careers—careers that perhaps don't even exist yet.

CONTENT AND ORGANIZATION

Chapter 1, "The Business of Business," explains the impact of taking an entrepreneurial approach to business, discusses the role business plays in solving complex problems in society, and assesses the importance of social responsibility and ethical decision making in business.

Chapter 2, "Business Without Borders," discusses how the globalization of technology has stimulated global trade, explores how different types of companies compete, and outlines the challenges of working across cultures.

Chapter 3, "The Entrepreneurial Mindset," outlines the effectiveness of an entrepreneurial mindset in business today, describes the differences between a growth and fixed mindset, and discusses the power of practice in developing an entrepreneurial mindset as a habit.

Chapter 4, "Business Creation," describes the importance of entrepreneurship in the world economy, explains the different types of entrepreneurship, and outlines different steps to generate ideas and identify and exploit opportunities.

Chapter 5, "Business Models," examines the core components of a business model, describes the different types of business models in use today, and discusses disruptive business models as a method to create new markets or improve or change an existing business model.

Chapter 6, "Business Strategy for Competitive Advantage," describes the different strategies organizations use to gain market share and competitive advantage, analyzes the internal and external organizational factors to determine strategic resources and competition, and discusses how hypercompetition is used to disrupt markets.

Chapter 7, "Marketing and Sales," explains the differences between marketing and sales, describes the elements of the marketing mix, illustrates the stages of the sales cycle, and investigates different types of modern selling techniques.

Chapter 8, "Customers and Market Segments," describes how customers create markets, identifies the different types of customers, explores consumer behavior, and outlines the main stages of the buying process.

Chapter 9, "Organizational Structure and Design," explores the impact of organizational structure on organizations, outlines the different types and elements of organizational structures, and discusses the factors that influence the design of an organizational structure.

Chapter 10, "Organizational Mission and Culture," explains the importance of mission, vision, and values to a company; describes the impact of organizational culture on business; and discusses the value of employee fit to organizational culture.

Chapter 11, "Management and Leadership," discusses the difference between managers and leaders; identifies the role of managers and the managerial skills needed to be effective in organizations;

explores different leadership styles and theories; and appraises the role of leadership in promoting diversity, equity, and inclusion (DEI).

Chapter 12, "Human Resource Management," explores human resource management (HRM) and the role of talent management within HRM; outlines the recruitment, onboarding, and training processes; and describes the different forms of employee compensation offered by organizations.

Chapter 13, "Motivation and Empowerment," discusses the process of motivation and empowerment and their influence on the workforce, explores the theories of motivation, and evaluates empowerment and self-leadership as strategies for encouraging positive behavior.

Chapter 14, "Communication in Business," describes the different forms of communication, outlines key barriers to effective communication, illustrates the various types of communication networks in organizations, and discusses the importance of cross-cultural communication.

Chapter 15, "Business Operations," explores the critical role played by operations in running an effective business, describes the different types of operations (product operations, service operations, and digital operations), and discusses the importance of supply-chain management in operations.

Chapter 16, "Data Management and Analytics," explains the differences between data and information, evaluates different types of information systems, explores data communication networks, and discusses the various components of business analytics.

Chapter 17, "Accounting and Financial Statements," explains the purpose of accounting in business, identifies the most common branches of the accounting discipline, discusses financial statements, and explores the key ratios used to analyze the financial performance of a company.

Chapter 18, "Financial Management," explores the role of financial management in business, evaluates different aspects of financial planning, discusses equity and debt financing, illustrates the cash conversion cycle, and explains different types of internal financial controls.

AACSB Standards

This book has been written to demonstrate the guiding principles and standards for business accreditation from AACSB, the Association to Advance Collegiate Schools of Business. Throughout this book, you will find several opportunities for students to engage with the AACSB principles, including globalization, diversity, technology, ethics, social responsibility, and sustainability. The test bank that accompanies this text is also correlated to AACSB standards.

ACKNOWLEDGMENTS

The authors are indebted to many people for their support in writing this book and thus would like to give special thanks to some stellar individuals.

Heidi Neck would like to thank Amir Reza, Angelo Santinelli, and Richard Mandell for sharing their expertise for different chapters. She would also like to thank her outstanding research assistants, Alexandra Douglas '23 and Gaurav Khemka, MBA '20, both of Babson College. Most importantly, she thanks the Timmons family and other Babson College donors to the Jeffry A. Timmons endowed chair. This book could not be possible without the resources provided by the Timmons endowed chair that Heidi Neck has held since 2008.

Chris Neck thanks Dean Ohad Kadan and Vice-dean Amy Ostrom at Arizona State (W. P. Carey School of Business), and Wei Shen (department head, Department of Management and Entrepreneurship, Arizona State University) for their encouragement of his teaching and research efforts. He thanks Joanna Grabski (dean of the College of Integrative Sciences and Arts at Arizona State University) for her steadfast support and encouragement to excel in research and teaching. He also thanks Mike Goldsby, Jeff Houghton, and Stuart Mease for their devoted support for the book and other projects over the years. Chris would also like to thank Julia LaRosa and George Heiler for their behind-the-scenes research efforts that helped make this book even better.

While the authors get their names on the cover of this textbook, the truth is that it takes a community to write a textbook. Writing a textbook is a huge undertaking that extends far beyond the author team. We would like to thank the incredibly committed team at SAGE for their constant encouragement, endless patience, and thoughtful suggestions. Their passion and enthusiasm has helped to deliver a textbook of which we are extremely proud.

Maggie Stanley, associate director of College Editorial, and Lily Norton, acquisitions editor, have championed this book every step of the way, and we are enormously grateful for their considerate input and constant support. Content development editor Adeline Grout has been a welcome driving force, encouraging us to explore and consider new ideas. Our talented editor Elsa Peterson helped clarify and refine the material and has significantly contributed to the quality of this textbook. Thanks are due to Kenneth Chapman of Texas Christian University and development editor Shannon LeMay-Finn for contributing to the end-of-chapter case studies in the text. Talia Greenberg, our copy editor, has been meticulous in her work, for which we are very appreciative. Rebecca Lee, our production editor, oversaw the entire production process and, thanks to her, the whole project was kept on track. We'd also like to thank product marketing manager Jennifer Hadelman and senior product specialist Melissa Yokell for their efforts promoting the book, content development editor Darcy Scelsi for handling a number of tasks during development and production of the digital resources, assistant editor Shelly Gupta for her work helping secure permission to use a number of items included in the text, and senior graphic designer Gail Buschman for creating a stunning interior and cover design.

For their thoughtful and helpful comments and ideas on our manuscript, we sincerely thank the following reviewers. Our book is a better product because of their insightful suggestions.

REVIEWERS OF THE FIRST EDITION

Carlynne Allbee, San Diego Mesa College
Judith Allen, Cuyahoga Community College
Vondra Armstrong, Pulaski Technical College
Gene Blackmun, Rio Hondo College

Laurie Breakey, Penn State University–Du Bois
Brenda Canning, Springfield College
Patricia Carver, Bellarmine University
Kenneth Chapman, Texas Christian University
Thomas Collins, Schoolcraft College
Jean Condon, Mid-Plains Community College–McDonald
Erikson Conkling, Trine University
Amy Conley, Genesee Community College
Susan Craver, University of Wisconsin–Green Bay
Kevin De Rosa, River Valley Community College
Rachel Gifford, Harrisburg Area Community College
Robert Gillan, Palm Beach State College–South
Lawrence Hahn, Palomar College
Dale Hartz, Barry University–Miami
Dwight Heaster, Glenville State College
Yundong Huang, St Edwards University
Robin James, William Rainey Harper College
Ryan Kauth, University of Wisconsin–Green Bay
Ilene Kleinman, Bergen Community College
Stephen Konrad, Mt Hood Community College
Steven Levine, Nassau Community College
Mary LoBiondo, Five Towns College
Michael Araujo Moreno, Dutchess Community College
Lorrie Mowry, Mid-Plains Community College–McDonald
Mark Mrowiec, Carthage College
Cynthia Nicola, Carlow University
Barbara Painter, Truckee Meadows Community College
Mark Parfitt, Pennsylvania Highland Community College
Daewoo Park, Hawaii Pacific University
Joseph Patton, Florida Atlantic University–Boca Raton
Daniel Pfaltzgraf, University of Toledo
Veronica Ramsundar, Miami Dade Community College–Wolfson
Jody-Lynn Rebek, Algoma University
Heather Rickgarn, Southwest Minnesota State University
Ryan Roberts, College of the Albemarle
Sonseeahray Ross, Miami University–Oxford
Darrell Smith, North Central Texas College
John Stark, California State University–Bakersfield
Glen Taylor, Paradise Valley Community College
Chris Tingley, Utica College
Shahub Tossi, Mid-Plains Community College–Voc Tech
Amina Valley, Texas Southern University
Randall Wade, Rogue Community College–Redwood
Monica Yang, Adelphi University–Garden City

ABOUT THE AUTHORS

Heidi M. Neck

Heidi M. Neck, PhD, is a Babson College professor and the Jeffry A. Timmons Professor of Entrepreneurial Studies.

Neck has been recognized for teaching excellence at Babson for undergraduate, graduate, and executive education. She has also been recognized by international organizations, the Academy of Management, and USASBE for excellence in pedagogy and course design. For pushing the frontiers of entrepreneurship education in higher education, the Schulze Foundation and the Entrepreneur and Innovation Exchange (EIX) awarded her Entrepreneurship Educator of the Year in 2016. She was again awarded "Entrepreneurship Educator of the Year" in 2022 by USASBE for her distinguished leadership in, and impact on, entrepreneurship education. She is the Academic Director of the Babson Academy, a dedicated unit within Babson that inspires change in the way universities, specifically their faculty and students, teach and learn entrepreneurship. The Babson Academy builds on Neck's work starting the Babson Collaborative, a global institutional membership organization for colleges and universities seeking to increase their capability and capacity in entrepreneurship education, and her leadership of Babson's Symposia for Entrepreneurship Educators (SEE) programs designed to further develop faculty from around the world in the art and craft of teaching entrepreneurship and building entrepreneurship programs. Neck has directly trained over 3,000 faculty around the world in the art and craft of teaching entrepreneurship. She believes how we teach is just as important as what we teach.

She has taught entrepreneurship at the undergraduate, MBA, and executive levels. Neck is a past president of the United States Association of Small Business & Entrepreneurship (USASBE), an academic organization dedicated to the advancement of entrepreneurship education. Her research interests include entrepreneurship education, the entrepreneurial mindset, and entrepreneurship inside organizations. An award-winning educator and author, her textbook *Entrepreneurship: The Practice & Mindset* was awarded the Breakthrough Book of 2018 by SAGE Publishing and the 2018 Most Promising New Textbook Award and 2021 Textbook Excellence Award by the Textbook & Academic Authors Association (TAA). Neck is the lead author of *Teaching Entrepreneurship: A Practice-Based Approach* (Elgar Publishing), a two-volume series written to help educators teach entrepreneurship in more experiential and engaging ways. Additionally, she has published 45+ book chapters, research monographs, and refereed articles.

Neck speaks and teaches internationally on cultivating the entrepreneurial mindset and espousing the positive force of entrepreneurship as a societal change agent. She consults and trains organizations of all sizes on building entrepreneurial capacity. She is the cofounder of VentureBlocks, an entrepreneurship education technology company, and achieved a successful exit with FlowDog, a canine aquatic fitness and rehabilitation center located just outside of Boston. She also serves on the board of a 100% family-owned, seventh-generation land-management company in Louisiana, A. Wilbert's & Sons. Heidi earned her PhD in strategic management and entrepreneurship from the University of Colorado at Boulder. She holds a BS in marketing from Louisiana State University and an MBA from the University of Colorado at Boulder.

Christopher P. Neck

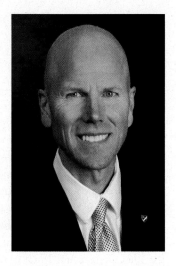

Dr. Christopher P. Neck, PhD, is currently an associate professor of management at Arizona State University, where he held the title "University Master Teacher." From 1994 to 2009, he was part of the Pamplin College of Business faculty at Virginia Tech. He received his PhD in management from Arizona State University and his MBA from Louisiana State University. Neck is author and/or coauthor of 22 books including *Self-Leadership: The Definitive Guide to Personal Excellence* (2017, Sage; 2nd ed., 2019); *Get a Kick Out of Life: Expect the Best of Your Body, Mind, and Soul at Any Age* (2017, Clovercroft Publishing); *Fit to Lead: The Proven 8-Week Solution for Shaping Up Your Body, Your Mind, and Your Career* (2004, St. Martin's Press; 2012, Carpenter's Sons Publishing); *Mastering Self-Leadership: Empowering Yourself for Personal Excellence* (6th ed., Pearson, 2013); *The Wisdom of Solomon at Work* (2001, Berrett-Koehler); *For Team Members Only: Making Your Workplace Team Productive and Hassle-Free* (1997, Amacom Books); and *Medicine for the Mind: Healing Words to Help You Soar,* (4th ed., Wiley, 2012). Neck is also the coauthor of the principles of management textbook *Management: A Balanced Approach to the 21st Century* (2013, Wiley; 2nd ed., 2017, Sage; 2021, 3rd ed., Sage); an introductory to entrepreneurship textbook, *Entrepreneurship,* (2017, Sage; 2nd ed., 2020); and an introductory to organizational behavior textbook, *Organizational Behavior* (2017, Sage; 2nd ed., 2019).

Dr. Neck's research specialties include employee/executive fitness, self-leadership, leadership, group decision-making processes, and self-managing teams. He has over 150 publications in the form of books, chapters, and articles in various journals. Some of the outlets in which Neck's work has appeared include *Organizational Behavior and Human Decision Processes, The Journal of Organizational Behavior, The Academy of Management Executive, Journal of Applied Behavioral Science, The Journal of Managerial Psychology, Executive Excellence, Human Relations, Human Resource Development Quarterly, Journal of Leadership Studies, Educational Leadership,* and *The Commercial Law Journal.*

Neck is the deputy editor of the *Journal of Leadership and Management.* Due to Neck's expertise in management, he has been cited in numerous national publications including *The Washington Post, The Wall Street Journal, The Los Angeles Times, The Houston Chronicle,* and *the Chicago Tribune.*

Dr. Neck was recently voted as a semifinalist (out of 140 nominations) for the prestigious international 2020 Baylor University Cherry Award for Great Teaching. He finished in the top six of all nominations. Neck was also the recipient of the 2007 *Business Week* "Favorite Professor Award." He is featured on *Business Week* as one of the approximately 20 professors from across the world receiving this award.

Dr. Neck has taught over 60,000 students during his career in higher education. He currently teaches a mega section of management principles to approximately 1,000 students at Arizona State University.

Neck was the recipient of the 2020 John W. Teets Outstanding Undergraduate Teaching Award (voted by W. P. Carey students). Neck also received the Order of Omega Outstanding Teaching Award for 2012. This award is granted to one professor at Arizona State by the Alpha Lamda Chapter of this leadership fraternity. His class sizes at Virginia Tech filled rooms of up to 2,500 students. He received numerous teaching awards during his tenure at Virginia Tech, including the 2002 Wine Award for Teaching Excellence. Also, Neck was the 10-time winner (1996, 1998, 2000, 2002, 2004, 2005, 2006, 2007, 2008, and 2009) of the "Students' Choice Teacher of the Year Award" (voted by the students for the best teacher of the year within the entire university). Also, some of the organizations that have participated in Neck's management development training include GE/Toshiba, Busch Gardens, Clark Construction, the United States Army, Crestar, American Family Insurance, Sales and Marketing

Executives International, American Airlines, American Electric Power, W. L. Gore & Associates, Dillard's Department Stores, and Prudential Life Insurance. Neck is also an avid runner. He has completed 12 marathons, including the Boston Marathon, New York City Marathon, and the San Diego Marathon. In fact, his personal record for a single long-distance run is a 48-mile run.

Emma L. Murray

Emma L. Murray, BA, Hdip, completed a bachelor of arts degree in English and Spanish at University College Dublin (UCD) in County Dublin, Ireland, followed by a higher diploma (Hdip) in business studies and information technology at the Michael Smurfit Graduate School of Business in County Dublin, Ireland. Following her studies, Murray spent nearly a decade in investment banking before becoming a full-time writer and author.

Murray has worked on numerous texts, including business and economics, self-help, and psychology. She is the coauthor of the principles of management textbook *Management: A Balanced Approach to the 21st Century* (2013, Wiley; 2nd ed., 2017, Sage; 3rd ed., 2021); the introductory to entrepreneurship textbook, *Entrepreneurship* (2017, Sage; 2nd ed., 2020); and an introductory to organizational behavior textbook, *Organizational Behavior* (2017, Sage; 2nd ed., 2019). She lives in London, UK, with her husband and two children.

BUSINESS IN AN ENTREPRENEURIAL WORLD

Robert Alexander/Archive Photos/via Getty Images

 THE BUSINESS OF BUSINESS

LEARNING OBJECTIVES

1.1   Define business and its role in generating economic and social value.

1.2   Identify the five primary components of business.

1.3   Illustrate how business can play a role in solving the most complex problems facing
society today.

1.4   Relate the evolving practice of business to the changing nature of work.

1.5   Justify that good business is founded on social responsibility and ethical decision
making.

BUSINESS IMPACT CASE 1.1: PATAGONIA—VENTURA, CALIFORNIA

SDG 13: Climate Action

Patagonia is a global brand that specializes in outdoor clothing and gear. The California-based company is a self-proclaimed activist company, and won the prestigious United Nations Champion of the Earth award in 2019, the United Nations' top environmental honor, for its entrepreneurial vision. Patagonia's mission is "We're in business to save our home planet," and this mission guides its business model today.[1]

Patagonia was officially founded in 1973 but has its roots all the way back to 1957. The founder, Yvon Chouinard, was an avid climber and at the age of 19 started forging rock-climbing pitons[2] that he would sell for $1.50 a piece. As the demand for pitons went up, he founded the company Chouinard Equipment. In 1965, Chouinard partnered with Tom Frost, an aeronautical engineer, to help make climbing tools stronger, lighter, and more functional. By 1970, they became the largest supplier of climbing hardware in the United States.

A new opportunity emerged while on a climbing trip in Scotland in 1970. Yvon decided to buy a regulation rugby shirt for climbing. "Overbuilt to withstand the rigors of rugby, it had a collar that would keep the hardware slings from cutting into the neck," Yvon explained.[3] When he returned from Scotland and wore it while climbing in the United States, Yvon's climbing friends asked where they could get one. He ordered a stack of rugby shirts from Umbro in England and sold out immediately. Seeing evidence of demand, Yvon began sourcing the rugby shirts from New Zealand and Argentina. Soon they further diversified into selling waterproof jackets and bivouac sacks (lightweight shelters smaller than tents) from Scotland, boiled-wool gloves and mittens from Austria, and hand-knit reversible "schizo" hats from Boulder, Colorado.

As the business grew, Yvon and Tom decided to name and brand their apparel. Not wanting to use Chouinard Equipment Company, given the narrow association with rock climbing, they chose Patagonia, as it brings to mind "romantic visions of glaciers tumbling into fjords, jagged windswept peaks, gauchos and condors," recalled Yvon. Since 1973, Patagonia has grown its product lines and offers a wide array of general outdoor apparel: equipment for camping, surfing, fly fishing, skiing and snowboarding, mountain biking, climbing; packs and gears such as sleeping bags, laptop bags, and totes and slings for men, women, and kids. In addition to selling through retailers, Patagonia has over 50 stores worldwide, and this number is expected to increase.

Customers, more than ever, appreciate Patagonia's mission to protect the Earth. Yvon always had a focus on the role of businesses in protecting the environment. In the early years, Patagonia realized that the rock-climbing pitons were damaging the rocks. Although the pitons were a very profitable product for Patagonia (then Chouinard), the company decided to phase out the product and introduce aluminum chocks instead, a better alternative that didn't need to be hammered and could be wedged by hand.

Today, Patagonia continues to set the example of how to do big business and good business in the 21st century. Patagonia has built its brand and its business around being an institution that stands for what is right. Here are a few examples:

- It voluntarily imposes a 1% earth tax on its sales and donates proceeds to grassroots environmental organizations. Patagonia has donated approximately $100 million through this initiative.

- It is working toward a goal of ensuring all products are made from recycled materials. Currently, almost 70% of all products are made from recycled materials.

- Patagonia runs an environmental internship program that allows employees to leave their roles and work for an environmental group of their choice for up to 2 months. Employees then return to Patagonia with a renewed commitment to the environment.

- In 2018, the U.S. government lowered tax rates for corporations. While many CEOs of large businesses appreciated the lower rate, Patagonia's CEO, Rose Marcario, called these tax cuts irresponsible and announced that all tax savings would be donated to environmental organizations.

Even in the midst of a global pandemic, Patagonia acted as a role model for other corporations. While working toward protecting the planet as much as it can, it also set benchmarks for taking care of the primary asset of any corporation—its employees. At the end of 2021, Patagonia announced it was giving its employees a paid break. All of its stores closed, and online fulfillment stopped from December 25, 2021, through January 2, 2022.[4] As Patagonia noted on the company's website: "At Patagonia, we do our best to not be bound by convention and to look out for people and the planet. For the last week of this year, we are shutting down our stores, warehouse, and offices in the United States and Canada because our people need a break."

Critical Thinking Questions

1. Why does Patagonia call itself an activist company?

2. How is Patagonia supporting the UN Sustainable Development Goal of Climate Action?

3. How is Patagonia a role model for other corporations?

WHAT IS BUSINESS?

If you are reading this book, we want you to know that the world needs you, and now more than ever. The COVID-19 pandemic has turned the world of work upside down and forced us to think about life and work in different ways. Today's world needs people who can think and act like entrepreneurs by channeling disruption into opportunity and getting comfortable with navigating periods of unprecedented change.

We need *you* to be entrepreneurial and go after something that is meaningful to yourself and to others. To be entrepreneurial requires a way of thinking and acting that combines the ability to find or create new opportunities with the courage to act on them. And we are going to help you work on becoming more entrepreneurial through this book.

Business is the global platform for impact today, which is why it's essential that you understand its foundations.

Business is defined as an organization that is engaged in commercial, industrial, or professional activities that produce and/or sell goods or services for the creation of economic *and* social value. Economic value relates to the profitability of the business and its ability to generate revenue, pay expenses, and generate positive net income. Profit is the amount of money gained after selling goods and services and paying expenses associated with operating the business. Social value encompasses the positive impact a business can have on society including issues related to employee diversity, equity, and inclusion as well as issues related to environmental sustainability and global challenges.

In the Patagonia example, economic value is generated by the sales of its products. For example, if Patagonia sells a winter parka for $250 (called revenue), this is not all profit. Making the product carries a cost that must be deducted, not to mention the cost of just doing business. After costs have been deducted, the profit from that one winter parka may only come to $50, but that profit generates economic value. Patagonia also generates social value through, for example, its 1% earth tax to conduct activities to protect the planet and working to make the most of its products from recycled materials.

Businesses engage in three types of activities: commercial, industrial, or professional.

Commercial indicates the selling of goods or services. In the opening case, Patagonia sells goods in the form of outdoor apparel. Patagonia clothes, however, are made by factories not owned by Patagonia. These factories engage in industrial activities or the manufacturing of goods.

Professional activities are primarily those that require trained or certified skills. For example, a law firm is a business composed of professional lawyers. A medical practice is a business composed of trained and certified doctors and nurses. Even a university is a business composed of academics who are experts in their field.

Types of Business Organizations

We often refer to businesses as organizations, but there is an important difference between the two terms. A business focuses on selling and producing goods, while an organization is a group of people formed and structured in a certain way to achieve goals. In other words, people in organizations engage in business tasks and activities to meet organizational objectives.

In the United States, there are three sizes of organizations: small, mid-size, and large, defined by the number of people they employ. Small businesses have fewer than 100 employees, mid-size businesses between 100 and 500, and large businesses more than 500 employees. Represented in all these size categories are startups, multinational corporations, growth companies, and nonprofit organizations.

Startups

A startup is a newly formed business with limited or no operational history. Some of today's largest and most well-known businesses began as startups, including eBay, Uber, Airbnb, Apple, and Facebook. Many startups are created to solve problems. For example, San Francisco startup fresh food company Afresh, founded in 2016, set out to eliminate food waste (every year, U.S. retailers throw out $18 billion worth of spoiled food) using specialized software that can be accessed by an app.[5] This helps grocery stores monitor their fresh food quantities so they can cut back on waste. Some stores have already reported that their amount of waste has been halved.

Multinational Corporations

A multinational corporation is a business with operations in multiple countries that sells products and services to customers all over the world. Walmart, Exxon Mobil, and Berkshire Hathaway are among the biggest American multinational companies in the world.[6] Multinationals also have many businesses under one umbrella. For example, Proctor and Gamble manages over 60 brands across 10 product categories, including hair care, family care, and skin and personal care.[7]

Growth Companies

A growth company is a business that increases its annual revenue faster than its competitors in the same industry or market. Mattress and bedding brand Bear Mattress is one of the fastest growing companies in the United States.[8] The company differentiates itself from competitors by marketing its mattresses to athletes. Within 3 years from its start in 2014, Bear Mattress made $20 million in revenue. However, as clothing retailer Forever 21 discovered, there is such a thing as growing too fast. It opened more stores during a period when its competitors were closing stores and moving online. In 2019, Forever 21 filed for bankruptcy.[9]

Forever 21 found out the hard way that rapid growth is not always a smart business move. The company filed for bankruptcy protection after opening a large number of stores.

Associated Press/Kiichiro Sato

Nonprofit Organizations

A **nonprofit organization** is a business that is exempt from paying tax, with the expectation that any generated profit will be reinvested in the business and never paid to owners. Religious groups, charities, environmental groups, and cooperatives are all examples of nonprofit organizations. For example, Step Up For Students is a nonprofit organization that raises money for low-income students living in Florida to help pay for school tuition. Goodwill Industries is also an example of a nonprofit, but it seeks to earn revenue by making a profit in its retail stores, which are used to fund other aspects of its operations such as job training and housing.

Regardless of the type of business, each and every organization has the potential to solve some of today's most complex and pressing problems.

THE BUILDING BLOCKS OF A BUSINESS

In this textbook, we have mapped the essential components of business to five blocks. These blocks represent the fundamentals of building and operating a business and are represented in Figure I.1. The five blocks, detailed in the sections that follow, should be thought of as blocks that build a modern business for an increasingly entrepreneurial world.

Block 1: The Offering

Every business offers something to customers who are willing to pay for that something because it is valuable to them in some way. The **offering** includes products (a smartphone), services (haircuts), or a combination of both (grocery delivery). The offering not only addresses the product or service but also the **business model**, which describes the rationale of how a new business venture creates, delivers, and captures value.[10] For example, Naturebox offers healthy snack boxes to promote wellness and nutrition. Its business model is a subscription model, so snacks are delivered monthly.[11]

A business is only successful if its offering can sustain a profit over time, and this requires understanding and outperforming the competition. The **competitive environment** identifies those businesses that compete for customers in the same industry and the different ways in which they compete to outperform each other—something that is called *strategy*. For example, Unilever is a multinational company that owns popular brands such as Dove, Breyers, and Pure Leaf Tea. The company has stiff competition from other large companies, including Procter & Gamble, Johnson & Johnson, and Nestle. Unilever, however, works to differentiate itself at a product level and organization level. On a product level, it differentiates its soap category from competitors by producing Dove, which, unlike most soaps, not only cleans but moisturizes. On the organizational level, its mission statement emphasizes sustainable living and lifelong vitality, claiming, "We meet everyday needs for nutrition, hygiene and personal care with brands that help people feel good, look good and get more out of life."[12]

Block 2: Markets and Customers

Every business works to identify and sell to customers in markets. Businesses don't exist without customers because a business creates value by providing products and services that people need. **Customers** are those willing to buy and use products and services offered by companies. Markets are groupings of similar customers that are entering transactions with businesses. For example, Lime is a micromobility company that offers bike and scooter sharing services. Buyers are younger people who live in urban areas (customers) who need alternative transportation for short commutes (market). Successful companies know how to attract, sell to, and build relationships with customers, which is done through the sales and marketing function of a company.

Block 3: Structure and Purpose

Every business has a structure and a culture. An **organizational structure** determines the flow of work and outlines how tasks are directed to various employees to achieve organizational goals. Think about a job you may have or had. You had a "manager" whom you reported to, and that manager reported to someone else. A **manager** is a person responsible for supervising employees and directing resources in order to achieve those goals. That is part of the structure of a company. The structure is designed to support the purpose of the company—its mission and purpose for existing. The combination of structure and purpose contributes to the corporate **culture**, which are values and beliefs that create an environment that is unique to that business. For example, the culture of Google is known to be flexible, fun, and trusting. Employees are allowed to work when and how they like, encouraged to use video games and ping-pong for fun, and build trusting relationships by coaching each other in the "Googler to Googler" program.[13]

By offering perks like climbing walls and table tennis to its employees, Google demonstrates its fun corporate culture.

MediaNews Group/Boulder Daily Camera via Getty Images

Block 4: People Inside the Business

People are the employees who work in and on a business. From the president of the company to middle managers to entry-level employees and every person in between, businesses comprise people. Essential soft skills such as leadership, management, decision-making, and communication differentiate average employees from top-performing employees. Such soft skills are often overlooked in business textbooks, but their importance in today's workplace should not be underestimated. Leadership relates to influencing, motivating, and empowering others to reach their full potential. Management relates to organizing and facilitating others to get the work of the company done. Effective leadership and management with sound human resource practices create a positive work environment for employees at all levels. Without employees, the business cannot operate or meet the needs of customers.

Block 5: Performance

Business performance relates to efficiency of operations and processes, collecting and recording performance data (such as customer data or financial data) for better decision-making, and sharing recorded data through financial statements to interested parties (such as investors or stockholders).

Business operations is about understanding how all of the above blocks come together to make the organization function. This may include staffing, business processes, location, supply chain, manufacturing, research and development, or use of equipment and technology. Businesses have different operational needs. Hospitals, restaurants, brick-and-mortar retail stores, online stores, hotels, and software companies all have different operational needs. Hospitals have to keep track of patient records, restaurants need systems to keep track of orders, retail stores must track inventory, hotels have systems for cleaning rooms, software companies may need to keep track of a virtual workforce, and so on.

Every business has to manage the money coming into the business (called revenue) and the money leaving the business (called expenses), as well as understanding the implications of financial decisions (such as investments). The accounting function is perhaps the most difficult to understand for students, unless you want to be an accountant. However, do not fear the numbers! Embrace the challenge and work to understand the basics of creating and reading financial statements. Not everyone needs to be an accountant, but a general understanding of the numbers is necessary. All businesses will have financial statements that record and track revenue, expenses, profit, assets, and liabilities (see Chapter 17). The story that numbers can tell can be quite interesting!

THE ROLE OF BUSINESS IN THE WORLD TODAY

The U.S. Business Roundtable (BRT) is a nonprofit association composed of CEOs from major companies that represent every sector of the economy. In 2019, 181 CEOs issued a statement emphasizing the importance of stakeholders, people who have an interest in or are affected by a business such as customers, employees, suppliers, and local communities. Why was this declaration so momentous? Because less than 25 years ago, back in 1997, the BRT stated that the only duty organizations had was to its shareholders, which are individuals or companies that own shares of stock in a corporation. In other words, the primary responsibility of business was to make a profit. The 2019 BRT statement offers a radically different viewpoint of the role of business in today's society.

Larry Fink has a similar view to that of the BRT. You may not have heard of Fink, but he is at the forefront of defining the role of business today. Fink is the CEO of Blackrock, one of the world's largest investment management firms in New York City. In 2018, Fink wrote an open letter to all CEOs imploring them to address the world's most complex social and economic issues, highlighting difficult issues such as environmental protection and racial inequality. Fink stated in his letter:

Companies must ask themselves: What role do we play in the community? How are we managing our impact on the environment? Are we working to create a diverse workforce? Are we adapting to technological change? Are we providing the retraining and opportunities that our employees and our business will need to adjust to an increasingly automated world?[14]

As the BRT and Fink suggest, today's businesses can no longer exist for pure profit. No organization can afford to ignore its social and environmental impact. These viewpoints have become even more important in the wake of the COVID-19 pandemic, which shone a spotlight on the huge divide between the wealthy and the working classes. Many of the people impacted by the virus were those working on the front lines in hospitals, clinics, and grocery stores who often had no health insurance or paid sick leave. Corporations also have a vital role to play in addressing many other social problems, such as climate change, systemic racism, and reevaluating their hiring practices and wage systems to ensure that everybody is given a fair chance and a living wage.

This is why consumers, employees, entrepreneurs, and more and more large corporations—including Patagonia—are existing not only for profit but for purpose. Fink believes that in business, purpose is related to what companies do to create value for their stakeholders, which can and should be positively linked to profit. Purpose-driven companies bring management, employees, and communities together; create a framework for making sound decisions; and deliver long-term financial returns for shareholders.[15] That "purpose" is related to people, planet, and profit.

People, Planet, Profit

Today's organizations must place social and environmental impacts in addition to profit to make a positive difference in the world, something that is called the triple bottom line, or the 3Ps: people, planet, and profit.

People

Every business has a responsibility to take care of its people and the wider community. American insurance company and BRT member Aflac operates on the ethos that taking care of people is the path to business success.[16] Research conducted on great places to work conducted by *Fortune* magazine also demonstrates that companies that give back to the community are associated with higher employee retention, greater employee loyalty to the brand, and more motivated employees.[17]

Planet

Businesses also have a responsibility toward maintaining the health of our planet. Through its Innovation for Good program, Wisconsin-based plumbing fixture company Kohler Co. has invested in clean drinking water and sanitation, clean and affordable energy, and responsible production. When Hurricane Maria devastated Puerto Rico in 2017, Kohler provided 100,000 water filters for schools, houses, and community centers. These contributions allowed more than 270,000 students to go back to school.[18]

Profit

Focusing on people and the planet does not stop organizations from making a profit. In fact, the modern view of business suggests that the highest-performing companies do good for society and the planet while also making money. These are known as dual-purpose companies. Building economic and social value into their core mission helps companies to pay more attention to their employees, customers, communities, and the environment. Outdoor recreation company REI is an example of a dual-purpose company. REI is one of the few retail stores that closes on Black Friday—the annual major shopping event where retailers offer highly promoted sales to customers. Instead, REI has launched an #OptOutside campaign, which encourages people (including REI employees) to spend the day outdoors.[19] Rather than losing money and customers by shutting its doors on a major sales day, REI has actually become even more profitable. It turns out that people are attracted to REI's core values and its eco-friendly philosophy by encouraging outdoor activity in favor of a shopping frenzy.

As another action in support of its core values related to employees, REI adjusted its staff policies in 2020 to ensure that all employees, including those paid by the hour, received income when they tested positive with COVID-19 or cared for ill family members.[20]

Table 1.1 highlights other companies that are doing good while doing well, but there are so many more out there. Look around!

TABLE 1.1 ■ Companies That Do Good for the World While Making a Profit	
Bombas	A sock company whose mission is to help the homeless. Learning that one of the most requested items in a homeless shelter is socks, it donates one pair of socks to homeless shelters for every pair of socks sold. Millions of socks have been donated.
Revolution Foods	The company is driven to provide accessible, healthy meals to school children, and serves millions of chef-crafted meals to schools in over 15 states.
Ben & Jerry's	The purveyor of beloved ice cream, the ingredients used in its products must be fair trade and sustainably farmed.
Subaru	The car company proclaims it "loves the earth," and its actions support the claim. Through partnerships, like with company Terracycle, it is turning hard-to-recycle trash into durable goods. Think park benches, playground equipment, and bike racks!

The UN Sustainable Development Goals (SDGs)

In 2015, 193 nations adopted the United Nations (UN) Sustainable Development Goals (SDGs), which is a blueprint for achieving a thriving, inclusive, and sustainable society by 2030. This involves ending poverty, protecting the planet, and promoting peace. There are 17 goals created to transform our world (see Figure 1.1). The goals address major issues including climate change, chronic health conditions, and aging populations, to name just a few. Every business has the opportunity to do well and to do good by aligning business activities, products sold, manufacturing processes, human resources, and overall impact in support of the UN Sustainable Development Goals (SDGs).

But meeting these goals isn't just the right thing to do: If businesses play their part in addressing these challenges, then $12 trillion could be generated in business opportunities as well as create 380 million jobs worldwide.[21] The major business opportunities that led to the $12 trillion estimate will likely come from four areas: food and agriculture, cities, energy and materials, and health and well-being.[22] Why? Because companies that operate in more humane and sustainable ways drive positive change as well as support such change to protect people and the planet we inhabit. Some companies that align with the SDGs are selling and producing sustainable, Earth-friendly products. Others are minimizing their carbon footprint in manufacturing processes. Still others are changing hiring practices that allow for greater diversity, equity, and inclusion. And many are supporting the SDGs through philanthropic efforts such as supporting reforestation, leading education efforts in developing countries, or partnering with local community organizations to reduce homelessness. These are just a few examples, but one thing is clear: The UN SDGs are an important to-do list for the planet, and many companies are working hard to show that business can make a profit and do good for the planet at the same time. In fact, it is a responsibility for businesses to do so.

The following statement, issued by leading global organizations, private-sector institutions, and networks, emphasizes how important and beneficial the SDGs are to companies all over the world:

> The SDGs provide all businesses with a new lens through which to translate the world's needs and ambitions into business solutions. These solutions will enable companies to better manage their risks, anticipate consumer demand, build positions in growth markets, secure access to needed resources, and strengthen their supply chains, while moving the world towards a sustainable and inclusive development path.[23]

There are many examples in this book of companies working toward the SDGs. For starters, Good Energy, based in the UK, provides renewable energy through wind and solar farms; it has grown over 30% a year by attracting customers interested in combating climate change. Similarly, India-based affordable health care company Narayana was set up to address early heart problems and has since grown to become one of the biggest health care providers in the country.[24] In fact, every single company example we use in this book connects to at least one of the SDGs, and every case at the beginning and ending of each chapter illustrates a company that deeply connects to a particular goal.

FIGURE 1.1 ■ The UN's Sustainable Development Goals

Goal	Description
1 NO POVERTY	End poverty in all of its forms everywhere
2 ZERO HUNGER	End hunger, achieve food security and improved nutrition and promote sustainable agriculture
3 GOOD HEALTH AND WELL-BEING	Ensure healthy lives and promote well-being for all at all ages
4 QUALITY EDUCATION	Ensure inclusive and equitable quality education and promote lifelong learning opportunities for all
5 GENDER EQUALITY	Achieve gender equality and empower all women and girls
6 CLEAN WATER AND SANITATION	Ensure availability and sustainable management of water and sanitation for all
7 AFFORDABLE AND CLEAN ENERGY	Ensure access to affordable, reliable, sustainable and modern energy for all
8 DECENT WORK AND ECONOMIC GROWTH	Promote sustained, inclusive and sustainable economic growth, full and productive employment and decent work for all
9 INDUSTRY, INNOVATION AND INFRASTRUCTURE	Build resilient infrastructure, promote inclusive and sustainable industrialization and foster innovation
10 REDUCED INEQUALITIES	Reduce inequality within and among countries
11 SUSTAINABLE CITIES AND COMMUNITIES	Make cities and human settlements inclusive, safe, resilient and sustainable
12 RESPONSIBLE CONSUMPTION AND PRODUCTION	Ensure sustainable consumption and production patterns
13 CLIMATE ACTION	Take urgent action to combat climate change and its impact
14 LIFE BELOW WATER	Conserve and sustainably use the oceans, seas and marine resources for sustainable development
15 LIFE ON LAND	Protect, restore and promote sustainable use of terrestrial ecosystems, sustainably manage forests, combat desertification, and halt and reverse land degradation and halt biodiversity loss.
16 PEACE, JUSTICE AND STRONG INSTITUTIONS	Promote peaceful and inclusive societies for sustainable development, provide access to justice for all and build effective, accountable and inclusive institutions at all levels
17 PARTNERSHIPS FOR THE GOALS	Strengthen the means of implementation and revitalize the global partnership for sustainable development

Source: United Nations. (2022). *Sustainable Development Goals.* https://www.un.org/sustainabledevelopment/ sustainable-development-goals/. The content of this publication has not been approved by the United Nations and does not reflect the views of the United Nations, its officials, or member states.

ENTREPRENEURIAL MINDSET ACTIVITY

Three Plus Three

The UN Sustainable Development Goals represent $12 trillion in business opportunities. That's huge! To demonstrate further that business can earn profit and do good at the same time, it's time to use your own imagination. Identify three of the 17 goals with which you feel you have a connection. That connection may come from your background, or just curiosity. Learn a little bit more about your three chosen goals by reviewing Figure 1.1 and visiting the United Nations' website. Now it's time to think of new potential business ideas that connect to each of your three goals. So, learn about three UN Sustainable Development Goals and identify one new business idea for each. Write them down. Start talking to others about your favorite idea. You never know what can happen next!

Critical Thinking Questions

1. Why did you choose your three goals?
2. How difficult was it to identify business ideas? Explain why.
3. Did you talk to others about at least one of your ideas? If so, what did they say? If not, why not?

THE FUTURE OF WORK

Not only is the viewpoint of business leaders changing (emphasizing people and planet just as much as profit), but the very nature of work is going through a major evolution. The COVID-19 pandemic first took hold in early 2020, leaving millions of people across the world in lockdown, with over half the global workforce working remotely and forcing them to communicate virtually. The pandemic has also forced people to reevaluate their work and their priorities, leading to millions of Americans leaving their jobs in a trend known as the Great Resignation.

In China, young professionals denounced the pressures of high-stress work with long hours and little reward through a social movement called *tang ping*, or "lying flat"—a lifestyle choice that rejects the culture of overwork by prioritizing health and well-being.[25]

There is no traditional path in business any longer. The idea of getting an entry-level job, climbing the corporate ladder, and retiring with a comfortable pension is completely obsolete. There is no such thing as "lifers" anymore—people who start and end their career with the same company. Instead, more and more people are turning to the gig economy for work.

The Gig Economy

Today, the concept of a career is a bit outdated. Just one generation ago, most employees remained with the same company until retirement. Staying with one company for a long time assumed "a stable and rising income, a steady package of corporate benefits, and a corporate-financed retirement at the end of work."[26] The world of work has undergone a rapid transformation in just a single generation. Today's employees can no longer expect the same job security or financial benefits as before.

Instead, the current generation are looking at their lives as a series of temporary work engagements, a series of projects, or "gigs," which has led to the rise of the gig economy. The **gig economy** is a labor market characterized by picking up short-term, flexible, freelance work known as gigs.

The COVID-19 pandemic has accelerated this trend as millions of employees redefine the nature of work by choosing jobs based on their lifestyle.[27]

The growth of the gig economy is a global trend, with predictions that half the U.S. population will have engaged in gig work by 2027.[28] There are three main components of the gig economy: the workers, the companies, and the consumers.[29]

The Workers

There are two categories of gig workers: labor providers and goods providers. Labor providers are the people who actually do the job. Examples of labor providers might include drivers, delivery people, and freelancers such as journalists, graphic designers, and coders. Goods providers are the people who create the products, such as artists, craftspeople, and clothing makers.

The Companies

Although the concept of gig work isn't new—people have been picking up odd jobs for centuries—the technology platform companies that have emerged over the last few decades have been a major force in the growth of the gig economy. Companies like Uber, Lyft, Etsy, and TaskRabbit have been instrumental in facilitating direct transactions between consumers and workers, providing flexible schedules for workers, and offering a forum for rating both the workers and consumers.

The Consumers

The gig economy also benefits consumers who need a specific service, such as a ride to their workplace, or an item to be delivered. They also benefit from shorter wait times, the huge range of products that can be delivered anywhere at any time, lower transaction costs, the frequent updates on time to arrival, and the power to provide instant feedback on a particular product or service. Overall, the gig economy not only increases access to many different types of services but makes them more affordable and efficient than ever before.

The emergence of the gig economy is not simply driven by platform companies. It's also driven by employees who are dissatisfied with the traditional corporate life and who are looking for something more. In 2018, the Gallup organization reported its highest levels of employee satisfaction since 2000 (see Figure 1.2).

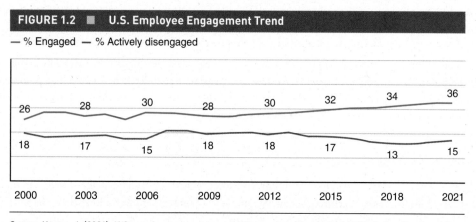

FIGURE 1.2 ■ U.S. Employee Engagement Trend

— % Engaged — % Actively disengaged

26	28	30	28	30	32	34	36
18	17	15	18	18	17	13	15

| 2000 | 2003 | 2006 | 2009 | 2012 | 2015 | 2018 | 2021 |

Source: Harter, J. (2021). U.S. employee engagement holds steady in first half of 2021. *Gallup.* Retrieved from https://www.gallup.com/workplace/352949/employee-engagement-holds-steady-first-half-2021.aspx

It could be argued that the increase in employee satisfaction is also due to the emergence of the gig economy. Despite the uncertainty that comes with giving up the support of a traditional employer (gig workers do not receive health insurance or any other benefits), more and more people believe that satisfying work, quality of life, flexible hours, and more control over their portfolio of gigs is worth the sacrifice. Approximately 150 million workers in North America and Western Europe have left stable, traditional employment to become gig workers. Table 1.2 explains the four strategies gig workers use to cope with the uncertain nature of their work.

TABLE 1.2 ■ The Four Things Gig Workers Do to Thrive in a Gig Economy

1. Place

Gig workers seek out places to work that protect them from outside distractions to give them the best opportunity to create a space they need to be inspired and to get things done.

2. Routines

Daily routines are important to gig workers, as they give them a sense of control and focus when working under uncertain circumstances. These routines could include keeping a schedule, creating a to-do list, meditation, or exercise.

3. Purpose

Gig workers don't just do jobs for money but for the joy of connecting to a broader purpose. Through this sense of purpose comes great satisfaction from being productive, creative, and authentic.

4. People

Despite working for themselves, gig workers still need people around them for social interaction and to exchange thoughts and ideas. These could be friends, family, collaborators, or people who work in similar areas.

Source: Adapted from Petriglieri, G., Ashford, S., & Wrzesniewski, A. (2018). Thriving in the gig economy. *Harvard Business Review*. Retrieved from https://hbr.org/2018/03/thriving-in-the-gig-economy.

AI, Automation, and the Work of the Future

The gig economy is not the only thing that is changing the nature of work. The rise of machine learning, artificial intelligence (AI), and automation is also creating a huge concern for the future of jobs. **Artificial intelligence (AI)** is the capability of a machine to imitate intelligent human behavior.[30] Google Maps and ride-sharing apps such as Lyft or Uber all use AI to tackle complex navigations. **Machine learning** is a branch of AI; it is the science of getting computers to act without being explicitly programmed while also learning and improving with every experience.[31] For example, self-driving cars are a result of machine learning. AI and machine learning are leading us into a new age of automation. According to a McKinsey report published in 2020,[32] two-thirds of senior executives surveyed said that they were increasing their investment in automation and AI.

Desh Deshpande, founder of the Deshpande Foundation, which supports impact through innovations that have significant social and economic impact, said, "The world is split between those that are automating and those that are being automated." In other words, everybody will be affected by automation in the future.

Machines have already replaced the more mundane tasks previously undertaken by humans (think automated self-checkouts in stores) and show no signs of slowing down. Estimates show that 15% of the global workforce, or 400 million workers, could be displaced by automation between 2016 and 2030.[33] But "displaced" does not mean "replaced." Research suggests that technology will create more jobs than it eliminates.[34] Humans have been working alongside machines for many years. Self-checkouts may have been introduced in thousands of stores, but there is still a need for checkout assistants to support customers and troubleshoot the machines when they're experiencing problems. Similarly, former lifters and stackers at Amazon have become robot operators managing the automated arms.[35]

Automation will also increase the need for new workforce skills, which will require training and retraining, not just in technology but in how we think and approach problems. By acquiring the right skills, the possibilities of harnessing automation and AI for the greater good become more attainable. For instance, AI is already having a major impact on SDGs: It is being used to track the progress of re-forestation; to predict war conflict; and to devise smarter traffic signals to minimize pollution and congestion in cities.[36]

A robot capable of giving hugs is just one of many new applications of artificial intelligence. How might AI affect different industries in the future?

Chip Somodevilla/Getty Images News/via Getty Images

Entrepreneurial Thinking and the Future of Business

The future of work as we have discussed here is also giving rise to a whole new generation of entrepreneurs. It's almost impossible not to be entrepreneurial to thrive in the workplace of the future, especially if 50% of today's jobs will disappear in the next two decades.[37] AI, robots, and automation may be making positive changes to how we work, but they could also give rise to unemployment if we don't embrace a different approach to business in this new world.

More than ever, we need to be in a position to create our own jobs—to be entrepreneurial. One thing that separates the human species from computers is our ability to imagine, create, and see the world in different and unique ways.[38] And entrepreneurs are especially good at imagining and executing on the ideas that move us forward, solving complex problems, and creating new jobs and wealth. An entrepreneurial approach to business is not just about making money, but an opportunity to make a real impact on the world. It means being creative, courageous, and energetic—and having a sense of purpose and being that will guide you to do great things. The journey starts here.

SOCIAL RESPONSIBILITY AND ETHICAL DECISION MAKING

By now, you should have a good understanding of what business is, the role it plays in solving complex business problems, and how it relates to the changing nature of work. This new workforce needs entrepreneurs of all kinds to navigate uncertainty, create new opportunities, and build or contribute to innovative businesses that do good and do well by aligning their mission with the UN SDGs.

The ability of business to do good and do well—to positively impact society and earn a profit—is at the core of **corporate social responsibility (CSR)**. By definition, CSR relates to how companies conduct business in a way that is sensitive to social, cultural, economic, and environmental issues.[39] Being socially responsible in business is about accountability, transparency, and understanding the impact business decisions have on the welfare of societies.

Though the UN SDGs are encouraging CEOs, entrepreneurs, managers, and employees of all types to pay more attention to the responsibility of business at the local, state, national, and international levels, social responsibility is just one aspect of doing good business today.

Ethical Decision Making

Ethical practice and decision making is the other side of the responsibility coin. General ethics is defined as the moral principles that guide our behavior, and those behaviors are based on accepted standards of what actions are right and wrong.[40] Similarly, business ethics relates to behaviors based on accepted standards in the business context and often relates to such issues as corporate governance, bribery, discrimination, and improper use or reporting of financial resources.[41]

The question of right versus wrong is not absolute; it's not as simple as red means stop and green means go. There are so many shades of colors in between. Because what is right or wrong is often unclear, ethical dilemmas abound in business. An ethical dilemma is "a situation in which a difficult choice has to be made between two courses of action, either of which entails transgressing a moral principle."[42] For example, an entrepreneur can keep costs down by manufacturing their new, hip T-shirts in a developing country. Costs can be kept down by doing so, which is great. But they quickly learn the T-shirts are being manufactured in a facility that is violating human rights—young women below the age of 15 are sewing the hipster-designed patches on the T-shirts. The entrepreneur is under pressure to grow the business by cutting costs and earning more profit. What's the right call? Should the entrepreneur do everything possible to keep the business alive? Should the entrepreneur feel responsible for human rights violations? If the entrepreneur doesn't go with this manufacturer, will they need to fire their employees in the United States in order to cut costs, given manufacturing costs will be too high? The list of questions can go on, but the answer is not simple. The complexity of business is peppered with many such ethical dilemmas, some more difficult than others to handle. And every chapter of this book will pose to you one of these dilemmas so you can try to feel what it's like to be in these situations and reflect on what you would do.

ETHICS IN BUSINESS

Holding Business to a Higher Standard

Milton Friedman, a 20th century economist, questioned in 1970 how a corporation, a collection of individuals with varying beliefs, could in fact be responsible for social change. He stated that the sole purpose of a business is to increase its profits, and that focus was important to economic prosperity. Fast-forward to 2018 and Larry Fink, as discussed in this chapter, who said, "Companies must ask themselves: What role do we play in the community? How are we managing our impact on the environment?"

Society is increasingly holding businesses socially responsible. Take McDonald's lawsuit as an example, in which the fast-food company was sued on account of making two teenagers obese; or Walmart's pair of lawsuits accusing the retail company of gender discrimination. On the other hand, companies like Patagonia and Ben & Jerry's are holding themselves accountable to stricter guidelines for being internally ethical while also being beneficial to the surrounding community and environment.

Corporations and their products are often the most visible examples of social ills (as well as social good), as their turning a profit can compete with (or complement) ethical social interests.

Critical Thinking Questions

1. Do companies have an ethical responsibility to be socially responsible?
2. Could an increased focus on people and planet issues increase revenue?
3. Should companies only attempt to be socially responsible in order to respond to consumer demands?

Sources: Friedman, M. (1970). A Friedman doctrine. *New York Times*. Retrieved from https://www.nytimes.com/1970/09/13/archives/a-friedman-doctrine-the-social-responsibility-of-business-is-to.html; Weinreb, S. (2018). Mission-driven business? Here's why to become a B Corp, according to four certified companies. *Forbes*. Retrieved from https://www.forbes.com/sites/saraweinreb/2018/04/30/mission-driven-business-here-are-six-reasons-to-consider-b-corp-certification/#21ed97d47def

1.1 Define business and its role in generating economic and social value.

Business is an entity that is engaging in commercial, industrial, or professional activities that produce and/or sell goods or services for profit. **Commercial** indicates the selling of goods or services; *industrial activities* are the manufacturing of goods; and *professional activities* are primarily those that require trained or certified skills. A business focuses on selling and producing goods, while an **organization** is a group of people formed and structured in a certain way to achieve goals. Different types of organizations include: startups, multinational corporations, growth companies, and nonprofit organizations.

1.2 Identify the five primary components of business.

In this textbook, we have mapped the five essential components of business to specific blocks. These blocks represent the fundamentals of business activity. The five components include: the offering, markets and customers, structure and purpose, people inside the business, and performance.

1.3 Illustrate how business can play a role in solving the most complex problems facing society today.

Today's organizations must place social and environmental impacts before profit to make a positive difference in the world, something that is called the triple bottom line, or the 3Ps: people, planet, and profit. Every organization has the opportunity to do well and to do good by following the *UN Sustainable Development Goals* (SDGs), which are a blueprint for achieving a thriving, inclusive, and sustainable society by 2030. This involves ending poverty, protecting the planet, and promoting peace. There are 17 goals created to transform our world, including climate change, chronic health conditions, and aging populations.

1.4 Relate the evolving practice of business to the changing nature of work.

The very nature of work is going through a major evolution. There are two main factors influencing these changes: the gig economy and AI. The *gig economy* is a labor market characterized by picking up short-term, flexible, freelance work known as gigs.

Artificial intelligence (AI) is the capability of a machine to imitate intelligent human behavior, and *machine learning* is a branch of AI; it is the science of getting computers to act without being explicitly programmed. AI and machine learning are leading us into a new age of automation.

1.5 Justify that good business is founded on social responsibility and ethical decision making.

Corporate social responsibility (CSR) relates to how companies conduct business in a way that is sensitive to social, cultural, economic, and environmental issues. Social responsibility is just one aspect of doing good business; the other is ethical practice and decision making. *Ethics* are the moral principles that guide our behavior, and those behaviors are based on accepted standards of what actions are right and wrong. Business ethics relates to behaviors based on accepted standards in the business context and often relates to such issues as corporate governance, bribery, discrimination, and improper use or reporting of financial resources. Because what is right or wrong is often unclear, ethical dilemmas abound in business. An *ethical dilemma* is a situation in which a difficult choice has to be made between two courses of action, either of which entails transgressing a moral principle.

BUSINESSES DISCUSSED IN THIS CHAPTER

Organization	UN Sustainable Development Goal
Aflac	11. Sustainable Cities and Communities
Afresh	12. Responsible Consumption and Production
Bear Mattress	12. Responsible Consumption and Production
Ben & Jerry's	8. Decent Work and Economic Growth 11. Sustainable Cities and Communities 12. Responsible Consumption and Production 17. Partnerships to Achieve the Goals
Berkshire Hathaway	7. Affordable and Clean Energy
Blackrock	9. Industry, Innovation, and Infrastructure
Bombas	10. Reduced Inequality
Deshpande Foundation	9. Industry, Innovation, and Infrastructure
Exxon Mobil	1. No Poverty 3. Good Health and Well-Being 4. Quality Education 5. Gender Equality 7. Affordable and Clean Energy 8. Decent Work and Economic Growth 12. Responsible Consumption and Production 13. Climate Action
Goodwill Industries	8. Decent Work and Economic Growth
Kohler	6. Clean Water and Sanitation 7. Affordable and Clean Energy 12. Responsible Consumption and Production
Lime	11. Sustainable Cities and Communities
Naturebox	3. Good Health and Well-Being
Patagonia	13. Climate Action
Proctor & Gamble	8. Decent Work and Economic Growth 12. Responsible Consumption and Production 13. Climate Action
REI	15. Life on Land
Revolution Foods	3. Good Health and Well-Being 12. Responsible Consumption and Production
Subaru	9. Industry, Innovation, and Infrastructure 13. Climate Action 17. Partnerships to Achieve the Goals
Unilever	3. Good Health and Well-Being 12. Responsible Consumption and Production
Walmart	8. Decent Work and Economic Growth 12. Responsible Consumption and Production 13. Climate Action 14. Life Below Water

KEY TERMS

Artificial intelligence (AI) (p. 15)

Business ethics (p. 17)

Business model (p. 7)

Business (p. 5)

Commercial (p. 6)

Competitive environment (p. 7)

Corporate social responsibility (CSR) (p. 16)

Culture (p. 8)

Customers (p. 8)

Dual-purpose (p. 10)

Economic value (p. 5)

Entrepreneurial (p. 5)

Ethical dilemma (p. 17)

Ethics (p. 17)

Gig economy (p. 13)

Growth company (p. 6)

Industrial activities (p. 6)

Large businesses (p. 6)

Machine learning (p. 15)

Manager (p. 8)

Mid-size businesses (p. 6)

Multinational corporation (p. 6)

Nonprofit organization (p. 7)

Offering (p. 7)

Operations (p. 9)

Organization (p. 6)

Organizational structure (p. 8)

People (p. 9)

Professional activities (p. 6)

Profit (p. 5)

Shareholders (p. 9)

Small businesses (p. 6)

Social value (p. 6)

Stakeholders (p. 9)

Startup (p. 6)

Sustainable Development Goals (SDGs) (p. 11)

BUSINESS CASE 1.2: ORDINARY HABIT—DOYLESTOWN, PENNSYLVANIA

SDG 12:   Responsible Consumption and Production

Unprecedented challenges, from pandemics to war to economic instability, have forced many companies to rethink or reinvent their entire business models. Ordinary Habit is an example of one company that has managed not only to survive but to thrive in the face of unpredictable and continuous business change.

Founded in 2019 by mother–daughter duo Teresa and Echo Hopkins, Ordinary Habit began with a simple purpose: "to create artful objects, designed to be both fun and functional, that would help people access habitual moments of calm and connectedness."

Armed with a strong belief in the transformative nature of "daily play," Teresa and Echo set out to create a debut product that would be beautiful, sustainably produced, simple to use, and easy to transport. They decided to develop a series of limited-edition jigsaw puzzles that would function both as a reason to get together with friends and as a means to have a moment of "peace and time away from the digital world."

They launched their first puzzle during a time in the pandemic when people were looking for fun things to do at home. In fact, Google searches for puzzles saw a 671% increase during March 2020, the start of the COVID-19 shutdown. One of the world's top puzzle manufacturers, Ravensburger, reported that its puzzle sales increased by 370% in March 2020 from March 2019.

By using strikingly beautiful images and puzzle boxes designed to look like pieces of art, Ordinary Habit achieved early success, and has since expanded its collection to include matching cards and "on the go" games.

At first, Ordinary Habit struggled to find a manufacturer that understood its vision to produce its products in a sustainable way. Many manufacturers failed to take the mother–daughter team seriously and didn't fully understand Ordinary Habit's vision for a unique product—a vision of producing all Ordinary Habit products made with recycled materials. After many meetings, Teresa and Echo finally struck up a relationship with a female-owned European manufacturing business in Poland that provided them with exactly such a puzzle, artfully designed, and made only from recycled materials.

With a manufacturer secured and product samples in hand, the next step was to market and ship their products. As the business became increasingly successful, the team learned quickly how to market and sell their products, resolve shipping and handling issues, and navigate the changing business terrain.

This company that Teresa and Echo built is based on the belief that cultivating mindfulness is essential to bring about change. As a result, the duo have pledged to donate a percentage of their profits to groups that support emotional health and well-being, such as the Loveland Foundation, which supports Black women and girls. Ordinary Habit anticipates continued growth and plans to introduce new products that inspire a love of puzzles and celebrate daily play while fostering small moments of mindfulness.

Critical Thinking Questions

1. Consider this chapter's discussion of the five primary components of business. How have the Ordinary Habit founders ensured that their offering stands out from others?

2. Who do you think are Ordinary Habit's primary customers? Explain your response.

3. This chapter discussed the triple bottom line of people, planet, and profit. In what specific ways does Ordinary Habit "do good while also doing well"? How else can a small company like Ordinary Habit support such goals?

References

Chin, M. (2021). Ordinary Habit spotlights female artists with eco-friendly puzzles. https://settingmind.com/ordinary-habit-spotlights-female-artists-with-eco-friendly-puzzles/

Hello, A. (2022). Inside the not-so-puzzling success of Ordinary Habit. https://helloalice.com/blog/ordinary-habit/

Kelley, D. (2020). Where have all the puzzles gone? Here are ones still available. https://www.yahoo.com/lifestyle/puzzle-shortage-180633776.html?guccounter=1

Mark, L. A. (2021). Meet the women-owned companies behind the most beautiful and fun puzzles. https://www.10best.com/interests/travel-gear/beautiful-puzzles-women-owned-companies-pandemic/

Miller, H. (2020). Demand for jigsaw puzzles is surging as coronavirus keeps millions of Americans indoors. https://www.cnbc.com/2020/04/03/coronavirus-sends-demand-for-jigsaw-puzzles-surging.html

Ordinary Habit. (2022). Our story. https://ordinaryhabit.com/pages/about-us

Ordinary Habit. (2022). Frequently asked questions. https://ordinaryhabit.com/pages/faq

Jane Barlow/PA Images/via Getty Images

2 BUSINESS WITHOUT BORDERS

LEARNING OBJECTIVES

2.1   Explain why all business today is global.

2.2   Describe the various types of trade restrictions and implications for business advantage.

2.3   Explore how startups to multinational corporations compete globally.

2.4   Appreciate the challenges of working across cultures.

2.5   Compare different models to help build cultural awareness.

BUSINESS IMPACT CASE 2.1: AMAZON—SEATTLE, WASHINGTON

SDG 8: Decent Work and Economic Growth

Everyone has heard of Amazon, but have you heard of Amazon Accelerate and how it helps launch global e-commerce entrepreneurs? Amazon Accelerate is an annual conference for vendors currently selling their products on Amazon as well as for those wanting to.[1] Today, sales on Amazon from third-party providers accounts for up to 50% of sales. Amazon provides the tools to help aspiring entrepreneurs build an e-commerce business, professionally brand the products, facilitate customer service, and build robust domestic and international sales and distribution channels. Amazon helped launched 200,000 new U.S. businesses on its platform in 2020 alone.[2] The company reports that close to 30,000 small and medium-sized businesses surpassed $1 million in sales in 2021 and created over 1.8 million jobs in the United States.[3]

In late 2021, Amazon Accelerate announced new tools to help U.S.-based businesses to grow their export sales internationally through Amazon global stores. An Amazon "store" may not be what you think it is. Yes, Amazon is starting to enter the world of physical Amazon stores, such as its new store concept called Amazon 4-Star that curates some of the highest-reviewed nonfood, nonperishable products on Amazon in particular locations such as London and New York.[4] A global Amazon store, however, is simply the Amazon.com platform that you would type into your browser from the U.S., but in another region of the world. For example, if you are living in the UK you would reach Amazon by typing in Amazon.co.uk, or in Japan you would go to Amazon.co.jp.

Now, a small business selling on Amazon in the United States can expand its business globally by reaching customers in Europe, Asia-Pacific, Middle East, and other parts of the Americas including Canada, Mexico, and Brazil. Amazon projects that over 6 million products from U.S. sellers have potential for growth in the international stores.[5] According to Eric Broussard, vice president of International Selling Partner Services, "Global Selling helps small businesses leverage Amazon's scale and reach to easily expand into countries around the world, while maintaining control of their brand and not having to worry about global logistics."[6] The new Amazon tools to help entrepreneurs go global include customer service handled by Amazon in foreign markets, assistance in what types of products should be sold internationally, a global inventory viewer so sellers can easily manage their supply and meet demand, and a global listing that allows sellers to list their product once and reach all international stores seamlessly and with just a few clicks.

Vermont-based family business Ann Clark Cookie Cutters is a manufacturer of cookie cutters in the United States.[7] Using Amazon's global selling services, its international revenue has grown to 20–30% of total sales, depending on time of year. Ben Clark, Ann Clark Cookie Cutters CEO, said, "Expanding to international locations without Amazon would have been more difficult because we'd have had to get a distributor in every country to manage our products. Amazon has made this process much easier and taken a lot of the guesswork out of which products will be successful."[8]

Amazon's size is helping the smaller entrepreneurs grow in ways that may not have been possible. The global market is much easier to reach than ever before.

Critical Thinking Questions

1. Research how to start selling on Amazon. Does this seem easier than you expected, or far more complicated?

2. If you buy on Amazon, review your order history and see how many of your orders are from third-party sellers. Any insights?

3. While Amazon has enjoyed much praise for its growth and innovation, it has also experienced criticism related to poor treatment of employees working in its warehouses. Would the treatment of Amazon warehouse employees limit your participation as a third-party seller on Amazon?

GLOBAL BUSINESS TODAY

As the Amazon case demonstrates, the world is getting smaller. By providing access to global markets, small businesses can expand to international stores that would have been considered beyond their reach. Over the last couple of decades, the globalization of technology has led to a new "flattened" world where greater collaboration and competition can flourish without boundaries. In *The World Is Flat*, Pulitzer Prize–winning author and journalist Thomas L. Friedman described his flat world theory as a level playing field between industrial and emerging markets where entrepreneurs and big and small businesses have become part of a global supply chain that allows them to compete across entire continents.[9] As a result, in a flat world large corporations and small businesses compete side by side in global markets—markets previously only accessible to the largest multinationals.

This explosion of global trade, the exchange of goods and services between countries, has led to an exponential rise in the value of goods exported throughout the world. For instance, in 2000 the global trade value of goods amounted to just over $6 trillion. In 2019, it rose to approximately $19 trillion—a 217% increase. This substantial increase in the value of goods in just under two decades reflects the huge development in international trade, technological advances, entrepreneurship, and mass globalization.[10]

The fact is that no national economy can produce all the goods and services required by its people. The harsh weather conditions prevent bananas from growing in Alaska, for example. Climate change is even changing some of the world's oldest and richest markets. Wines from grapes traditionally grown in France's highest-producing areas—Champagne, for example—are not growing as they once were. Higher temperatures and changes in weather patterns have decimated crops. In 2021, France recorded the smallest grape harvest since 1957.[11] The new fine wine market is beginning to come out of England, where the temperatures have become just right for grape growing; England was once too cold. By 2030, experts predict that winemakers will be exporting 20 million bottles a year.

You may not think of England when you think of winemakers, but with warming temperatures, vineyards like this one in East Sussex are becoming more common.

GLYN KIRK /AFP/via Getty Images

Countries import and export goods to meet the needs of their people. **Importing** is the buying of products overseas and reselling them in one's own country; and **exporting** is the sale of domestic products to foreign customers. Importing and exporting are the oldest and most prevalent forms of international trade. In 2020, China, the United States, and Germany were the biggest merchandise exporters in the world. All businesses, big or small, must abide by trade restrictions when trading across borders.

Common Challenges of Global Business

A big challenge of doing business globally is understanding different legal and regulatory environments in each country. Typically, every country has established laws and regulations that must be followed by businesses operating within its borders. Companies doing business internationally often face laws and regulations that are inconsistent among different countries, and some have fallen afoul of certain foreign laws. For example, in 2014, Airbnb was forced to pay a significant fine for failing to comply with housing rental laws in Barcelona, Spain, which requires rentals to be registered on the Catalonia tourism registry.[12] In 2021, Barcelona introduced a new law banning short-term private rentals, the first European country to do so.[13]

Approaches to Managing Legal and Regulatory Obligations

Companies must prepare for expanding into new markets in different countries by assessing the legal and regulatory obligations and the overall risks involved in operating within a new jurisdiction. Seeking advice from local lawyers and liaising with local businesspeople who are familiar with the legal landscape can help companies comply with regulations and deal with bureaucratic obstacles. There are five main areas businesses need consider before expanding internationally.

Choose the Right Business Structure

One of the most important parts of expanding internationally is choosing the type of business structure and ensuring it is compliant with local laws. This involves assessing whether the business will be operated from one central location or if there will be branches set up abroad. If a business wants to set up an office in a different country, it must be registered as a legal entity by a local representative in that country. Businesses that set up branches in different foreign locations will need to consider how teams are managed and organized and how they can work efficiently across different time zones. Coca-Cola is controlled from central headquarters, but its business structure is divided into different subdivisions in each country, with each group overseen by a president.

Be Mindful of Local Employment Laws

When setting up a branch in a different country, businesses must decide whether they will staff their offices with local talent or expats. Both types of employees will require compliance with local employment laws. Most countries do not have the same labor laws as the U.S. For instance, many countries pay employees on a monthly basis rather than week or biweekly, which is often the case in the U.S., and most European countries offer a minimum of 14 weeks' paid maternity leave, unlike the United States, which is under no obligation to do the same. In addition, other countries, such as Belgium, France, and Saudi Arabia, require employment agreements to be translated into the local language before they are deemed valid.[14]

Understand the Impact of Tax Implications

Different tax systems in foreign countries can have serious implications for businesses expanding internationally. Breaking taxation laws can incur huge fines and penalties. In addition, setting up in a country with high corporate tax rates will have a big impact on the bottom line. Saudi Arabia, Brazil, and Germany are among the countries with the highest corporate taxes in the world. Some businesses deliberately choose countries with low tax rates for foreign expansion. MNCs such as Google, Facebook, and Intel have set up operational headquarters in the Republic of Ireland because of its low corporate taxes.

Assess Pricing Challenges

Companies must assess the price of products and services when doing business overseas. The costs of production, shipping, marketing, and labor must be viable for the company to succeed. Swedish furniture manufacturer IKEA originally struggled entering the Chinese market because its prices, considered low in Europe, were regarded as high in China. Local competitors were able to offer lower prices than IKEA because the costs of labor and production were much cheaper. IKEA was able to successfully cut prices by setting up production in China and using locally sourced materials, which led to a significant boost in sales.[15]

The Swedish company IKEA originally found that its prices were higher than local competitors in China. However, it was able to lower its prices by producing and sourcing its products in China, enabling it to be competitive.

LIU JIN/AFP/via Getty Images

Research Political and Cultural Considerations

It is essential for companies entering new markets to be mindful of a country's political and cultural environment and to carefully consider how a country's history, traditions, language, and political landscape impact the business. For instance, foreign governments have the power to make political decisions in relation to changes in tariffs, tax regulations, and foreign trade policies that can seriously impact how companies do business. Cultural differences can also impact the success of a business. For example, Starbucks did not succeed in Australia because the country already had a thriving café culture populated with local, independent coffee shops. The demand for a large café chain just wasn't there.

ENTREPRENEURIAL MINDSET ACTIVITY

It's a Small, Small World

Think of the products you use daily. Chances are good that many if not most of these products were manufactured in a country different from your country of origin.

Your mindset activity is to list all the products you use daily from the moment you wake up until the time you go to sleep. Do this every day for 3 days. Your daily list should include the clothes you wear, the items you use for personal hygiene, the food you consume, etc. After 3 days of logging products, look at all the items you noted in your list. What percentage of these items were manufactured in a country different from your country of origin? This will require you to do a bit of online research.

Critical Thinking Questions

1. How many products that you used were created in countries different from your home country? Were you surprised by this? Why or why not?
2. What are the benefits of having such a global economy where products are manufactured all over the world? Is there a downside?
3. Does the country in which a product is manufactured impact your purchasing decision of this product? Why or why not?

TRADING ACROSS BORDERS

When trading across borders, there are different types of trade restrictions that countries must abide by when importing and exporting goods. A **trade restriction** is a government policy that limits the flow of goods and services between countries. For example, trade restrictions created by the United States are used to protect the U.S. economy from competition created by companies from other countries. Think of a trade restriction as a barrier to entry and often seen as a way to protect domestic jobs and industries. The more formal term is *protectionism.*

Protectionism is a set of government policies designed to defend domestic industries against foreign competition. For example, sports footwear company New Balance, which produces sneakers in the U.S., is protected by a 20% tariff or tax on foreign shoe imports. This means that major competitors, such as Nike and Adidas, that tend to create their products outside the U.S. need to pay that tariff before selling their shoes to U.S. consumers. Typically, the cost of the duty is passed on to the customer by pricing the footwear higher than domestic footwear brands.[16]

Types of Trade Restrictions

There are five main types of trade restrictions: trade surplus, balance of payments, tariffs, embargoes, and quotas.

A **trade surplus** occurs when a nation imports more than it exports. This means that more money is flowing into the country than out and shows that it can afford to pay domestic wages and support business expansion. Most countries strive to maintain a trade surplus and a positive **balance of payments,** a record of international trade and the flow of financial transactions made between a country's residents and the rest of the world. For instance, while American dollars may flow to Japan when purchasing video game console Nintendo, Japanese investors may return the investment when purchasing American golf courses.[17]

A **tariff** is a tax or duty paid on imported goods. There are two types of tariffs. A "unit" or specific tariff is a tax paid as a fixed charge for each unit of imported goods—for instance, $300 per ton of imported steel. Tariffs are typically paid to the government of the country that is receiving the good, but the added cost is often passed on to consumers. An **"ad valorem" tariff** is a tax paid based on a proportion of the value of imported goods. For example, there might be a 20% tariff on the value of cars that are being imported into the country.

The use of tariffs dates back to the 18th century, when the purpose was to raise revenue. Today, tariffs are used not only for raising revenue but to protect certain domestic industries from foreign competition.

The impact of tariffs depends on the resources of a country and the power it has to influence world prices. For example, Ghana, a small country in West Africa, is the world's leading exporter of cocoa beans. The Netherlands, a small country in Europe, is the biggest importer of cocoa in the world.[18] If, hypothetically, the Netherlands' government decided to start a homegrown cocoa bean industry, it might impose a tariff on imports of Ghanaian cocoa to protect the Dutch cocoa bean growers against foreign competition. The consequences of imposing this tariff are mixed. On the one hand, the price of the imported cocoa would rise due to tariff, leading to higher costs for cocoa butter makers and Dutch chocolatiers making chocolate from the cocoa, not to mention consumers buying the chocolate.

On the other hand, buying from Dutch farmers growing their own produce is cheaper than the cost of importing the cocoa, which would encourage more chocolatiers to buy local rather than investing in the more expensive, imported variety. Although this is good news for the Netherlands in terms of gaining a new source of revenue, the Ghanaian economy would suffer as there would be less volume of trade between the two countries, leading to less income for the Ghanaian growers and producers.

Although it has been suggested that some countries are better off imposing tariffs, there is always a danger that the trade partners will retaliate by responding with tariffs of their own. This sort of "tit-for-tat" approach can lead to political conflict and trade wars between countries. For example, the trade war between the United States and China that began in 2018 under former U.S. president Donald Trump has caused tension between the world's biggest superpowers. Trump imposed a series of tariffs on a range of Chinese goods, including meat and musical instruments, to encourage consumers to buy American products by making these goods more expensive. China retaliated with tariffs on U.S. products.[19] As of 2022, the trade war is still ongoing, with neither side taking steps to remove the tariffs.

Tariffs on items such as steel can sometimes lead to trade wars between two countries.

AFP/via Getty Images

An **embargo** is a trade restriction imposed by the government of the exchange of goods or services with a particular country or countries. Embargoes tend to be created as a result of strained economic, diplomatic, or political relationships between the countries involved.

There are several different types of embargoes:

- A **trade embargo** is a trade restriction that bans the exports or imports of certain goods and services to or from one or more countries. The United States has a trade embargo against Syria in response to its position as a sponsor of terrorism.[20]

- A **strategic embargo** is a trade restriction that forbids the exchange of military goods with a country. In 2020, Britain imposed an arms embargo on Hong Kong that prohibits potentially lethal weapons and crowd control equipment such as tear gas, which could be used for internal repression.[21]

- A **sanitary embargo** is a trade restriction enforced to protect people, animals, and plants. For example, the World Health Organization (WTO) places sanitary embargoes on certain countries to prevent them from importing and exporting endangered animals and plants.[22]

Historically, embargoes have not succeeded in bringing any major economic wins to the countries involved. For instance, the ongoing U.S. trade embargo against Cuba, in place for over six decades, has done very little to overturn the policies of Castro's repressive regime and has not generated any real economic gains for either country.[23]

An **import quota** is a type of trade restriction that sets a limit on the quantity of particular goods being imported into a country during a given period of time.[24] The goal of import quotas is to protect domestic markets from being flooded by foreign goods, which tend to be cheaper than those produced by local businesses due to lower production costs or greater efficiency in the overseas market. For example, the United States may limit the quantity of Japanese cars to 3 million a year to protect the U.S. automotive manufacturers. Although import quotas may sound similar to tariffs, there is an important difference. A tariff is a tax on the imports of a particular commodity, while an import quota restricts the quantity of imported goods. There are two main types of import quotas: absolute quota and tariff rate quota.

An **absolute quota** is the maximum number of specific goods permitted to enter a country during a specific time period. Once the quota has been fulfilled, no additional goods are allowed to enter the country. Certain countries may be allowed to selectively set an absolute quota. For example, suppose the government sets an absolute quota of 50 million bottles of hand sanitizer. This would mean that no more than 50 million are allowed to be imported into the U.S. However, with a selective absolute quota, that figure could be divided among exporting countries, meaning that several different countries would be able to export different quantities of bottle sanitizer between them (i.e., Country A, 10 million; Country B, 15 million; Country C, 25 million) as long as the total amounted to 50 million.

A **tariff rate quota** is a two-tiered quota system that allows a specified quantity of product to be imported at a lower tariff rate. When the quota has been met, further goods may be imported, but at a higher tariff rate. For example, under a tariff-rate quota system, a country may allow 80 million bottles of hand sanitizer to be imported at the first-tier lower tariff rate of $1 each. Any bottles of hand sanitizer imported after this quota has been reached would be charged a second-tier higher tariff rate, such as $3 each.

Apart from giving local goods manufacturers a boost by protecting local business, import quotas provide stability in domestic markets because the volume of the imports entering the country is determined by the government rather than fluctuations in demand or changes in exchange rates.

However, import quotas also have negative effects. Large companies may bribe officials in an attempt to circumvent quotas, leading to widespread corruption in which bigger companies profit and small companies are unable to compete. In addition, quotas can create a black market when consumers use illegal means to acquire the goods they desire.

Absolute and Comparative Advantage

As we have explored, international trade is essential for economic growth in the United States and around the world. To further understand the benefits of trade and why countries import some products and export others, it is important to learn the concepts of absolute and comparative advantage.

Absolute advantage is the ability of a country or business to produce certain products more efficiently than its competitors.[25] A nation has an absolute advantage if it's the only source of a particular product or it can make more of a product using the same amount of or fewer resources than other countries. An example of a nation with absolute advantage is Saudi Arabia because of its ability to produce oil more cheaply than any other nation.

Comparative advantage is the ability of a nation to produce a product at a lower opportunity cost compared to another nation.[26] China, for example, has a comparative advantage over the United States because of cheap labor. An American company may choose to produce its product in China because the lower costs of labor and production are so significant that choosing to produce the product in the U.S. would be less efficient and profitable. Opportunity costs, in this scenario, are the products that a country must decide not to make in order to produce other goods and services. In others words, when a country decides to specialize in a particular product, it must sacrifice the production of another product and the opportunity it could have created.

When a nation has absolute advantage, it is considered to be efficient at creating products at a lower cost; whereas countries with a comparative advantage can produce a particular product at a lower opportunity cost, meaning it needs to give up manufacturing less of one product to get more out of another product to compete with other nations. Table 2.1 outlines the differences between comparative advantage and absolute advantage.

The following example illustrates the concept of absolute advantage, comparative advantage, and opportunity cost. In Figure 2.1, the United States makes 30 million cars and 10 million trucks, while

TABLE 2.1 ■ Absolute Advantage Versus Comparative Advantage	
Absolute Advantage	**Comparative Advantage**
The ability of a country or business to produce certain products more efficiently than its competitors	The ability of a nation to produce a product at a lower opportunity cost compared to another nation
Trading is not mutual and only benefits one country	Trading is mutual and benefits both countries
Allows a country to produce higher quantities of goods by using the same amount or fewer resources than other countries	Allows a country to produce goods better than other countries by selecting one product over another
Creates products at a lower production cost	Creates products at a lower opportunity cost

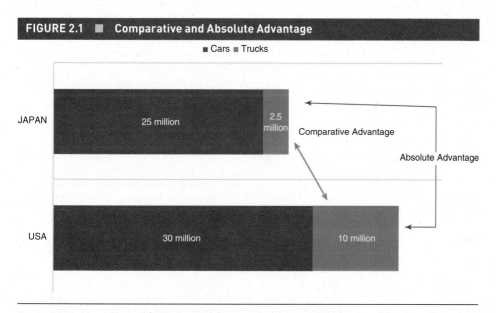

FIGURE 2.1 ■ Comparative and Absolute Advantage

■ Cars ■ Trucks

JAPAN: 25 million / 2.5 million — Comparative Advantage
USA: 30 million / 10 million — Absolute Advantage

Source: Adapted from Boyce, P. (2022, April 25). *Comparative advantage definition.* BoyceWire. https://boycewire.com/comparative-advantage-definition/

Japan makes 25 million cars and 2.5 million trucks.[27] As the U.S. produces more cars and trucks than Japan, it has an *absolute advantage*. It also has a *comparative advantage* in trucks because it is four times better than Japan in producing them. Although it might seem as though Japan should produce more cars than trucks because of the higher output, it has a *comparative advantage* in the production of cars. This is because it is less efficient at producing trucks and so the opportunity cost is much higher. Overall, Japan is more efficient at producing cars than trucks compared to the U.S.

Consider the concept of comparative advantage using a real-world perspective. Soccer star Cristiano Ronaldo is regarded as one of the best players in the world, so it's reasonable to say that he has greater ability on the soccer field than the average person. Let's say Ronaldo also has a wonderful musical ability, but he can't pay equal attention to both soccer and music without a drop in standards. Because of his world-renowned soccer skills, it wouldn't make sense for him to sacrifice soccer for music. This means he has a comparative advantage in soccer over music.[28]

FROM MULTINATIONAL CORPORATIONS TO STARTUPS IN A FLAT WORLD

A company that operates in its own country as well as other, different countries around the world is known as a **multinational corporation (MNC)**. An MNC usually maintains a central office (also known as headquarters) in its home country, which coordinates the management of all its other operations in other countries such as suppliers, factories, other branches, etc. For example, American retail giant Walmart is one of the biggest multinational corporations in the world. It is headquartered in

Arkansas, but has operations in 24 different countries.[29] Table 2.2 lists the top five MNCs in the world. Each of these companies has connections to the UN Sustainable Development Goals. The last column in Table 2.3 identifies the primary goals each MNC is working on, yet most are working on even more goals than those identified in the table.

TABLE 2.2 ■ Top Five Multinational Companies in the World, 2021 (based on market capitalization and revenue)				
Company	**Industry**	**Revenue**	**Employees**	**Primary Connections to UNSDGs**
Walmart	Retail	$559 B	2.2 M	Focus on reducing hunger (goal 2), gender equality (goal 5), affordable and clean energy (goal 7), responsible consumption and production (goal 12), climate action (goal 13)
Amazon	Retail	$386 B	1.3 M	Focus on clean energy (goal 7), sustainable cities and communities (goal 11), reduced inequalities (goal 10)
Royal Dutch Shell	Petroleum	$334 B	86,000	Focus on affordable and clean energy (goal 7); industry, innovation, and infrastructure (goal 9); decent work and economic growth (goal 8); and climate action (goal 13)
Volkswagen	Automotive	$282,760,000	304,174	Focus on affordable and clean energy (goal 7); industry, innovation, and infrastructure (goal 9); climate action (goal 13); responsible consumption and production (goal 12)
BP	Oil and gas	$282,610,000	70,100	Focus on industry, innovation, and infrastructure (goal 9); responsible consumption and production (goal 12); climate action (goal 13); and reduced inequalities (goal 10)

Source: Data for columns 1–3 sourced from MNC definition with a list of multinational corporations—in detail. (2021, March 8). List Bay website: https://listbay.org/multinational-corporation/#Top_Multinational_Companies_in_the_World. Column 4 of table sourced from: United Nations Sustainable Development Goals. (2021). Retrieved January 16, 2022, from 2021 ESG website: https://corporate.walmart.com/esgreport/reporting-data/unsdg; Governance. (2020). Sustainability—US website: https://sustainability.aboutamazon.com/governance; Sustainable, U. (2020). UN Sustainable Development Goals. Retrieved January 16, 2022, from Shell.com website: https://www.shell.com/sustainability/our-approach/un-sustainable-development-goals.html#iframe=L3dlYmFwcHMvc2hlbGwtc2RnLw; Volkswagen Sustainability Report (2020). Volkswagen website: https://www.volkswagenag.com/presence/nachhaltigkeit/documents/sustainability-report/2020/Nonfinancial_Report_2020_e.pdf; bp global. (2021). UN Sustainable Development Goals | Sustainability | Home. Bp global website: https://www.bp.com/en/global/corporate/sustainability/data-and-how-we-report/un-sustainable-development-goals.html

Many MNCs strive to "think globally and act locally," meaning that they incorporate environmentally conscious and community-minded initiatives into their operations to fit the location they occupy. The Coca-Cola brand is global, but it is also supports each individual market it serves. For instance, during COVID-19, Coca-Cola sourced and distributed personal protective equipment (PPE) for front-line workers in Kenya, and when there was an urgent shortage of hand sanitizer in France, Coca-Cola used its French facilities to provide the gel to the French government.

Benefits and Criticisms of MNCs

Multinational companies are growing every day as global brands enter emerging markets to seek revenue and profit from a wider customer base. The following sections outline some benefits and criticisms of MNCs.

Benefits of MNCs

- Provide better, cheaper products for customers: MNCs that expand into developing economies spend less on labor, land, premises, manufacturing, and production, which results in lower-priced goods and services for customers. For example, Apple designs its products in the U.S. but manufactures them in China, where the cost of labor is cheaper.[30]

- Create wealth and jobs: MNCs create jobs in the countries in which they operate through direct employment of locals. Providing employment raises wages, which increases the standard of living for many, particularly for those in developing countries. German motor manufacturer Volkswagen manufactures cars in Kaluga, Russia, thereby creating 3,500 jobs for local workers.[31]

- Provide skills and expertise: MNCs improve the skills of the workforce in different countries through the introduction of new tools and technology. French personal care company L'Oreal runs a global youth program that provides young people all over the world with tools they need to enter the workforce.[32]

- Increase cross-cultural understanding: MNCs raise intercultural awareness by regularly engaging and collaborating with people across borders from different cultural backgrounds through an in-depth understanding of local business practices. For example, in Japan, junior employees rely on senior employees to approve decisions and delegate responsibilities, whereas in Western countries such as the U.S., employees are encouraged to make decisions independently.[33]

- Help entrepreneurs to go global: MNCs can enable entrepreneurs to go global by facilitating expansion into international locations. Tech MNC Amazon provides a range of tools and services to enable third-party sellers sell and promote their products in Amazon's worldwide stores to millions of customers.

Some multinational corporations have been criticized for employing children in developing countries. Here, a young Ivory Coast boy carries cocoa melon seeds, which are used to create chocolate products.

Benjamin Lowy/Reportage Archive/Getty Images

Criticisms of MNCs

- Destroy livelihoods: MNCs have been accused of destroying the livelihoods of workers in their home countries by sending their jobs overseas, where labor is cheaper. For example, in 2021, merchandise store Bed Bath and Beyond, which operates in the U.S., Canada, Mexico, and Puerto Rico, closed its call center in Utah and outsourced the jobs to the Philippines through a contractor, laying off more than 200 employees.[34]

- Exploit the workforce: In some developing countries, workers can work long hours, for below minimum wage, in unsafe working conditions. In the 1990s, Nike was exposed for using sweatshops and child labor and spent over a decade trying to repair its reputation by changing its company practices. In 2021, chocolate companies Hershey and Mars were among the companies accused of exploitation by eight former child workers who claimed they were used as slave labor on cocoa plantations in West Africa.[35] Exploitation can also occur in developed countries. During the COVID-19 pandemic, fashion brand Boohoo, based in the UK, was criticized for exploiting its garment factory workers by paying them below the minimum wage, failing to enforce social distancing, and instructing employees to attend work even when they had tested positive for COVID-19.[36]

- Damage traditional and local customs: MNCs can dilute traditional and local customs by forcing their own views and culture on the host country, a concept called "McDonaldization" by American sociologist George Ritzer.[37] Ritzer believed that the fast-food chain was homogenizing global society by providing cheaper, easier, and unhealthy alternatives to traditional foods.

- Harm physical environments: The environment can be negatively impacted by the expansion of businesses worldwide. For example, global drinks giants Coca-Cola, PepsiCo, Nestle, and Unilever were recently reported as being responsible for more than half a million metric tons of plastic pollution in six developing countries where waste collection is poorly managed.[38] The plastic waste often ends up burned or dumped, leading to harmful emissions and scarred landscapes. This is a paradox, given that these same companies actively support and take actions related to the UN Sustainable Development Goals.

- Susceptible to corruption: Some MNCs have been prosecuted for their involvement in corrupt practices such as foreign bribery to win business in foreign markets. For example, in 2020, aerospace company Airbus agreed to pay $4 billion in fines for bribing key decision makers in a number of countries, including Malaysia, Sri Lanka, Indonesia, and Ghana, to land high-value contracts.[39] Foreign bribery erodes public trust, wastes millions of dollars, and fosters corrupt regimes. Each year, Transparency International, a German-based company focused on combating corruption, ranks countries perceived to be the most likely and least likely to accept bribery and other forms of corruption (see Table 2.3).

TABLE 2.3 ■ Corruption Perceptions Ranked by Country in 2020	
Most Corrupt Countries in the World	**Least Corrupt Countries in the World**
Somalia	Denmark
South Sudan	New Zealand
Syria	Finland
Yemen	Singapore
Venezuela	Sweden

Source: Transparency International. (2020). Corruption Perceptions Index 2020. Transparency International. https://www.transparency.org/en/cpi/2020/index/nzl

Although MNCs have been heavily criticized for inflicting harm on the environment and society, they do have the potential to do good. The sheer scale and size of these companies and the revenue they bring in give MNCs the power to invest profits for public good by improving the social and environmental processes in the developing countries in which they operate.[40]

ETHICS IN BUSINESS

Stay in Russia or Leave?

Ball Corporation is the world's leading provider of innovative, sustainable aluminum packaging for beverage, personal care, and household products. Though its headquarters are in Broomfield, Colorado, Ball Corporation is a multinational company with business in many countries, including Russia. The company's presence in Russia is important to note, given Russia's full-scale military invasion of Ukraine in early 2022. Proceeding this invasion in an emergency United Nations session, 141 of 193 member states voted to condemn Russia's invasion of Ukraine because Russia's actions arguably violated the UN Charter and involved war crimes and crimes against humanity. The UN demanded that Russia immediately cease its use of force in Ukraine. Russia ignored this condemnation. While many global companies ceased operations in Russia as a show of Ukrainian support, Ball Corporation decided to maintain full business operations in the Russian territory.

Critical Thinking Questions

1. If you were the CEO of Ball Corporation, would you maintain operations in Russia? Why or why not?
2. Is there an ethical argument in favor of ceasing business operations in Russia?
3. Is there an ethical argument against ceasing business operations in Russia?

WORKING ACROSS CULTURES

Developing cultural awareness in the country in which a business operates is as important as understanding the legal and regulatory environments. While plenty of companies are embracing cultural differences across their entire workforce (Virgin Group, Disney, and PricewaterhouseCoopers, among others), there are challenges when working across different cultures and languages. For example, French luxury goods company LVMH's acquisition of American jeweler Tiffany in 2021 resulted in a culture clash following an unofficial memo circulated by Tiffany staff outlining some tips on "Franco-American cultural nuances and etiquette." One of these tips stated that French people were more likely to provide negative feedback, were "less warm and fuzzy," and were not inclined to use excessively positive comments such as "amazing" and "fabulous."[41] Although the memo was denounced by Tiffany, it highlighted the cultural differences between the two companies that led to internal conflict and likely misunderstandings.

Cultural Misunderstandings

Cultural misunderstandings are one of the most common causes of friction between employees. But bridging the divide is not easy, especially when research shows that traditional cultural training based on business etiquette isn't particularly effective. Associate professor Yunxia Zhu, an expert in cross-cultural management and strategy at the University of Queensland Business School, believes anyone can learn to overcome cultural barriers as long as they have the right approach.

According to Dr. Zhu, this involves learning through experience by adopting her situated cultural learning approach (SiCuLA), which focuses on observing and reflecting on the behavior of others before exposing them to the culture—for instance, mixing with people from different cultures in the workplace and watching videos that educate people about different cultures.[42] Traditional cultural training is based on identifying cultural patterns which can only ever be generalisations at the national cultural level," Dr. Zhu explains. "Real life situations are much more complex. So for example, people are often told that Eastern cultures are collectivist and Western ones are individualist, yet people visiting China are often surprised to find that this isn't necessarily true."[43]

Dr. Zhu offers seven ways in which we can manage cross-cultural differences:[44]

1. *Expect the unexpected.* Be careful not to overgeneralize; not all Italians eat pasta, and not all French people wear berets! It is also worth taking into account that different cultures can exist within one country. For instance, there are over 50 different ethnic groups in China, with different ways of behaving in different contexts and with different groups of people.

2. *Study people and cultures.* Anybody can take the time to learn more about different people and their cultures. As Dr. Zhu says, "We learn about our own culture by following the cues from our family and the wider community, so we can do the same with other cultures. We need to develop the skills to observe and reflect on everyday practices, checking our own assumptions, and interpret situations."

3. *Learn the basics.* With over 3,000 languages spoken throughout the world today, it won't be possible to learn them all, but it is important to be able to greet someone and thank them. With a bit of extra effort, you can learn enough to show your understanding of cultural etiquette; for example, in China, it is a cultural custom to ask someone whether they have eaten.

4. *Take an objective view.* While you might think other cultures are strange, the chances are others will be thinking the same about your customs and behaviors. For instance, U.S. workers are known for working long hours, taking little vacation time, and eating at their desks—factors that may appear odd from another culture's perspective.[45]

5. *Seek advice from an "insider."* If you are struggling to understand the different customs of another culture, it is useful to find someone from that culture to help bridge the gap. For instance, Dr. Zhu arrived in Australia as a Chinese student. She has spent over 20 years in Australia but still keeps in touch with old friends about cultural practices in China.

6. *Remove the focus from yourself.* Many of us have a tendency to feel self-conscious when immersed in unfamiliar cultures. But making an effort to join in with different cultures and customs by learning a new language, socializing, and reading publications are all positive ways to increase our knowledge and understanding of others.

7. *Keep an open mind.* Even when you think you're getting nowhere with someone else, try to keep an open mind and always strive for a positive outcome. Dr. Zhu says, "Above all we are living in an increasingly multicultural world, and we all have to work with people from different cultures. So we need to develop our cultural awareness and the competencies required for effective collaboration across cultures. There is no such thing as a bigger pie unless we all work together to create it."[46]

Cultural Competence

Research shows that people who are culturally competent tend to share certain characteristics (see Table 2.4). **Cultural competence** is the set of values, behaviors, attitudes, and practices that enables individuals and organizations to interact effectively with people across different cultures.[47]

We need to be aware of and develop these competencies in order to excel in cross-cultural situations. Dr. Milton Bennett's developmental model of intercultural sensitivity (DMIS) is composed of six developmental stages of cultural competence.[48] The six stages start from least complex and sophisticated to the most. As we become more culturally aware and have more global experiences, we can grow our cultural competence. The six stages are:

1. *Denial*: When people don't believe or recognize that cultural differences exist.

2. *Defense/reversal*: When people recognize cultural differences exist but feel threatened by these differences (defense). In contrast, reversal takes place when people criticize their own culture in favor of another culture; for example, people who have immersed themselves in a different culture may prefer the new culture over their own.

TABLE 2.4 ■ Characteristics of Culturally Competent People
Openness to cultural diversity
Flexibility and adaptability
Emotional resilience
Curiosity
Tolerance and respect for differences
Patience
A nonjudgmental attitude
Global identity
Cultural intelligence
Global leadership behaviors
Multicultural experiences, such as being multilingual and having lived in more than one country

Source: Adapted from Society for Human Resource Management. (2015, November 30). Understanding workplace cultures globally. *SHRM*. https://www.shrm.org/resourcesandtools/tools-andsamples/toolkits/pages/understandingworkplacecul-turesglobally.aspx

3. *Minimization*: When people are aware of cultural differences but focus on the similarities between them rather than the differences.

4. *Acceptance*: When people have a deep understanding and appreciation of their own and others' cultural identities and perceptions.

5. *Adaptation*: When people change their reasoning, behavior, and actions to new and different cultures.

6. *Integration*: When people have a deep understanding of one or more cultures and successfully integrates them into their own identity.

Business professionals also need to be culturally aware to build relationships with foreign colleagues. This could be as simple as pronouncing employees' names correctly and ensuring others do the same, learning cultural differences, or assigning a new foreign colleague a mentor to help navigate the organization and cultivate relationships.

The best way to learn about another culture and develop a relationship with a foreign colleague is to ask questions and show authentic curiosity. Because the biggest obstacle to successful cross-cultural diversity is communication. Being concise, listening better, and demonstrating respect for cultural and religious differences help to improve communications between multicultural teams (see Chapter 14: Communication).

MODELS TO HELP IMPROVE YOUR CULTURAL AWARENESS

People with little exposure to other cultures often assume that most of their values and assumptions about how the world works are universal. For example, someone in the "denial" stage of the DMIS model discussed above might think that people in the United States, China, New Zealand, and Sweden all have similar ideas about what it means to be successful and the ways that businesses and customers should interact. In reality, there is a great deal of variety among cultures about what is valuable and how to interact with each other.[49]

In a global economy, being unaware of such differences can lead to embarrassment, lost business, and legal troubles. For example, berating somebody in public in Indonesia is a cultural mistake that may lead to real offense.[50] Organizations that develop cultural awareness have a higher chance of navigating cultural differences and are less likely to encounter cultural mishaps.

Cultural awareness is the understanding that our own culture (customs, social behaviors, attitudes, and values) differs from others. Most often used in the context of different countries, cultural awareness can pertain to any group of people. It can facilitate stronger and more profitable business relationships with companies and clients in other countries and a more diverse, flexible, and creative workforce within a single company.

Because of the impact of globalization, businesspeople need to have a good understanding and working knowledge of cultural differences and influences when operating in a business environment. The following models can help to improve your cultural awareness when either working with international team members or in international contexts.

Hofstede Model of Cultural Dimensions

Over 30 years ago, Dutch sociologist and IBM psychologist Geert Hofstede created the Hofstede model of cultural dimensions research identifying five dimensions that vary across different cultures.

Based on research from more than 100,000 IBM employees in 53 countries, Hofstede identified five dimensions that varied among different cultures: [51]

1. *Individualism versus collectivism.* Individualism is a social view that values individual freedom and self-expression and assumes that individuals are responsible for their own welfare. Collectivism, on the other hand, values the welfare of the group over any one individual and emphasizes the responsibilities of individuals and groups (families and organizations) to each other.

2. *Power distance.* A high ranking on the power distance dimension means that people from a particular culture accept an unequal distribution of power. A low ranking means that people expect a more equal distribution of power.

3. *Uncertainty avoidance.* The higher the ranking on the uncertainty avoidance dimension, the more uncomfortable people are with uncertainty and ambiguity. They are more at ease with conformity and with events that follow an expected structure. Societies with low uncertainty avoidance are more comfortable with a lack of structure and the unexpected.

4. *Competition versus cooperation. Competitive* and *cooperative* refer to whether the society as a whole places greater value on performance, achievement, material success, and contest or on quality of life, collaboration, personal relationships, and group decision making. This dimension is also referred to as "masculine versus feminine."

5. *Long-term versus short-term orientation.* Countries that tend toward long-term orientation are more concerned about the future than the present and value thrift and perseverance. Countries that tend toward short-term orientation, on the other hand, are more concerned with the present and past and value tradition and social obligations.[52]

As depicted in Figure 2.2 below, different countries are high and low across the dimensions. The differences can help explain operational differences among companies and people around the world.

Given that Hofstede's dimensions, though still widely used, were created by Hofstede and his colleagues at IBM working across dozens of different countries, many have disagreed with the universal aspect of the dimensions, arguing that the model focuses too much on one company. Since the emergence of Hofstede's work, other researchers have developed more current frameworks to help us increase and develop our cultural awareness.

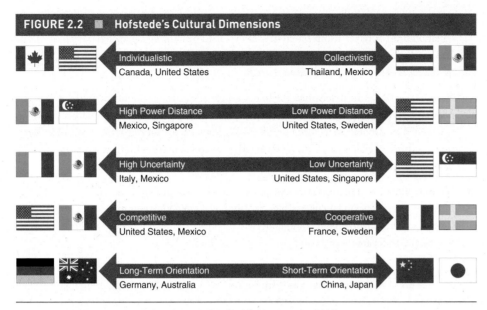

FIGURE 2.2 ■ Hofstede's Cultural Dimensions

Individualistic — Canada, United States ←→ Collectivistic — Thailand, Mexico

High Power Distance — Mexico, Singapore ←→ Low Power Distance — United States, Sweden

High Uncertainty — Italy, Mexico ←→ Low Uncertainty — United States, Singapore

Competitive — United States, Mexico ←→ Cooperative — France, Sweden

Long-Term Orientation — Germany, Australia ←→ Short-Term Orientation — China, Japan

Source: Neck, C. P., Houghton, J. D., & Murray, E. L. (2021). *Management.* SAGE.

Meyer's Cultural Map

Erin Meyer, INSEAD professor and author, created a culture map composed of eight scales showing the most common cultural gaps between countries.[53] Figure 2.3 compares the U.S. and Indian business cultures based on eight behavior scales, detailed below:

1. The Communication Scale measures the differences in communication between low-context and high-context cultures, a method created by anthropologist Edward T. Hall. In *low-context cultures,* communication is explicit, clear, and precise, and conveyed through the spoken or written word. Most of what is communicated is understood at face value. Many European countries (Denmark, Germany, Sweden, and Norway) and Western countries such as the U.S. and Canada are regarded as low-context cultures. In contrast, in *high-context cultures,* communication is more subtle and nuanced, with most messages conveyed through body language, nonverbal cues. Japan, China, and Arab countries are considered to be high-context cultures.[54]

2. The Evaluating Scale measures how receptive different cultures are to constructive criticism in the context of straightforward versus diplomatic feedback. For example, the French tend to be quite direct in their criticism, using more forthright language to express their thoughts, whereas Japanese people are more inclined to use softer, gentler language to share their feedback.

3. The Persuading Scale determines the different approaches used by different cultures to persuade others. For instance, people from southern European and Germanic cultures tend to share an idea or concept before presenting their argument, whereas American and British people are more likely to begin their message with a fact or a statement to persuade others.

4. The Leading Scale measures the cultural differences in leading styles, ranging from egalitarian (the belief that all people should be treated equally), and hierarchical (where treatment is determined by societal rank). The Netherlands and Denmark are examples of egalitarian cultures, whereas Nigeria and China tend to follow more hierarchical structures.[55]

5. The Deciding Scale assesses the degree of group decision making in different cultures. Although Germans are more hierarchical than Americans, they are more likely to engage in group decision making and build group consensus before making decisions.

6. The Trusting Scale gauges the degree to which trust is task-based (trust built through work collaboration) or relationship-based (trust developed by making a personal connection). In the U.S., trust tends to be task-based, while in countries such as Russia and Israel, trust is formed on the basis of shared personal experience.

7. The Disagreeing Scale determines the tolerance for open disagreement and whether it is perceived as helpful or harmful to relationships. Countries such as France and Israel are considered confrontational cultures where disagreements do not impact relationships, but other cultures like Japan and Indonesia avoid open confrontation for fear of disrupting the harmony within the group.

8. The Scheduling Scale gauges the value placed on linear schedules (completing one task before moving on to the next task) or flexible schedules (working on two or more tasks at the same time). Germany, Switzerland, and Japan tend to work to a linear schedule, whereas Saudi Arabia and India are more flexible with their timelines.

Meyer's culture map is an effective guide for businesspeople to understand different cultural characteristics, bridge cultural gaps, and adjust their communication style and create better working relationships within global teams. Figure 2.3 compares the U.S. and Indian business cultures based on seven out of Meyer's eight behavior scales. As you examine the figure, think less about where each node is for the U.S. or India; rather, focus on the distance between each node. Longer distances between nodes signal significant cultural gaps that may lead to misunderstandings, conflict, or difficulties conducting business.

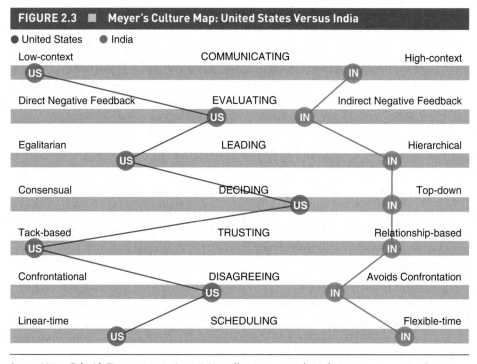

FIGURE 2.3 ■ Meyer's Culture Map: United States Versus India

● United States   ● India

Low-context — COMMUNICATING — High-context
US ... IN

Direct Negative Feedback — EVALUATING — Indirect Negative Feedback
US ... IN

Egalitarian — LEADING — Hierarchical
US ... IN

Consensual — DECIDING — Top-down
US ... IN

Tack-based — TRUSTING — Relationship-based
US ... IN

Confrontational — DISAGREEING — Avoids Confrontation
US ... IN

Linear-time — SCHEDULING — Flexible-time
US ... IN

Source: Meyer, E. (n.d.). *The country mapping tool.* https://erinmeyer.com/tools/culture-map-premium/

Molinsky's Six-Dimension Framework for Global Dexterity

Andy Molinsky, author and professor of international management and organizational behavior at Brandeis University's International Business School, developed a six-dimension framework for global dexterity to capture differences across cultures. **Global dexterity** is the ability to adapt your behavior to be effective when interacting with other cultures without losing your sense of self in the process.[56] The framework is composed of the following questions:

1. Directness: How directly do people communicate in that particular culture?

2. Enthusiasm: How much positivity and energy do people demonstrate?

3. Formality: How much deference and respect do people show each other?

4. Assertiveness: How passionately do people express their opinions?

5. Self-promotion: How appropriate is it for people to speak about their achievements?

6. Self-disclosure: How willing are people to divulge information about themselves?[57]

Molinsky's dimensions can be used to compare any two cultures within a workplace context. Table 2.5 outlines comparisons of two cultures: India and the United States, based on three of the dimensions.[58]

TABLE 2.5 ■ United States versus India Using Molinsky's Framework		
	United States	**India**
Dimensions		
Enthusiasm	*Moderately high* Expectation to show excitement for work accomplishments.	*Low* Inappropriate in formal, professional settings.
Assertiveness	*Moderately high* Strong inclination to be perceived as a "go getter."	*Low* Considered too aggressive. Preference for deference and composure.
Self-Promotion	*Moderately high* Expectation for people to promote themselves.	*Low* Openly speaking about achievements is regarded as arrogant and distasteful.

Molinsky's framework is a useful way to gain more knowledge and understanding about the cultural rules in different countries while also helping to relieve the discomfort and anxiety some people may experience when they are trying to communicate in an unfamiliar cultural setting. To address these cultural challenges, Molinsky suggests learning the rules of how to behave, trying out new behaviors (as long as they fall within your comfort zone), rehearsing and practicing these behaviors to gauge people's reactions to them, and adjusting these behaviors where necessary.[59]

As Molinsky notes, "I want people to know that this isn't rocket science. You don't need to have lived in five countries and learned five languages to be successful across borders. You do need to be thoughtful and self-aware, and you need to be willing to take the leap into the unknown."[60]

IN REVIEW

2.1 Explain why all business today is global.

The globalization of technology has led to a new "flattened" world where greater collaboration and competition can flourish without boundaries. This explosion of *global trade,* the exchange of goods and services between countries, has led to an exponential rise in the value of goods exported throughout the world. *Importing* the buying of products overseas and reselling them in one's own country and *exporting* the sale of domestic products to foreign customers are the oldest and most prevalent forms of international trade. Today's businesses face many global challenges such as navigating different legal and regulatory environments, and understanding political and cultural considerations.

2.2   Describe the various types of trade restrictions and implications for business advantage.

There are five main types of trade restrictions: trade surplus, balance of payments, tariffs, quotas, and embargoes. A *trade surplus* occurs when a nation imports more than it exports. *Balance of payments* is a record of international trade and the flow of financial transactions made between a country's residents and the rest of the world. A *tariff* is a tax or duty paid on imported goods, and an *"ad valorem" tariff* is a tax paid based on a proportion of the value of imported goods. An *embargo* is a trade restriction imposed by the government of the exchange of goods or services with a particular country or countries. An *import quota* is a type of trade restriction that sets a *limit* on the quantity of particular goods being imported into a country during a given period of time. An *absolute quota* is the maximum number of specific goods permitted to enter a country during a specific time period, and a *tariff rate quota* is a two-tiered quota system that allows a specified quantity of product to be imported at a lower tariff rate. *Absolute advantage* is the ability of a country or business to produce certain products more efficiently than its competitors. *Comparative advantage* is the ability of a nation to produce a product at a lower opportunity cost compared to another nation.

2.3   Explore how startups to multinational corporations compete globally.

A company that operates in its own country as well as other different countries around the world is known as a *multinational corporation (MNC)*. An MNC usually maintains a central office in its home country, which coordinates the management of all its other operations in other countries such as suppliers, factories, other branches, etc. Although MNCs have been heavily criticized for inflicting harm on the environment and society, they do have some benefits, including the potential to do good.

2.4   Appreciate the challenges of working across cultures.

It is essential for businesses to gain a deep insight into cultural differences in order to work effectively across different cultures and languages and avoid cultural misunderstandings. A level of *cultural competence*—the set of values, behaviors, attitudes, and practices that enables individuals and organizations to interact effectively with people across different cultures—is required to understand cultural differences and influences when operating in a business environment.

2.5   Compare different models to help build cultural awareness.

There are several different models that help improve cultural awareness: *Hofstede model of cultural dimensions* research that identifies five dimensions that vary across different cultures; *Meyer's culture map* research composed of eight scales showing the most common cultural gaps between different countries; and *Molinsky's six-dimension framework for global dexterity*—a six-dimension framework for global dexterity to capture differences across cultures.

BUSINESSES DISCUSSED IN THIS CHAPTER

Organization	UN Sustainable Development Goal
Airbnb	7. Affordable and Clean Energy 11. Sustainable Cities and Communities
Airbus	4. Quality Education 5. Gender Equality 8. Decent Work and Economic Growth 9. Industry, Innovation, and Infrastructure 12. Responsible Consumption and Production 13. Climate Action 16. Peace, Justice, and Strong Institutions 17. Partnerships to Achieve the Goals

Organization	UN Sustainable Development Goal
Amazon	7. Affordable and Clean Energy 8. Decent Work and Economic Growth 9. Industry, Innovation, and Infrastructure 13. Climate Action
Apple	7. Affordable and Clean Energy 12. Responsible Consumption and Production
BP	9. Industry, Innovation, and Infrastructure 10. Reduced Inequality 12. Responsible Consumption and Production 13. Climate Action
Coca-Cola	6. Clean Water and Sanitation 11. Sustainable Cities and Communities 12. Responsible Consumption and Production 13. Climate Action
Facebook	13. Climate Action
Google	12. Responsible Consumption and Production 14. Life Below Water 15. Life on Land
IKEA	3. Good Health and Well-Being 11. Sustainable Cities and Communities 12. Responsible Consumption and Production
Intel	5. Gender Equality 11. Sustainable Cities and Communities 12. Responsible Consumption and Production
L'Oreal	7. Affordable and Clean Energy 12. Responsible Consumption and Production
LVMH	12. Responsible Consumption and Production 13. Climate Action
New Balance	7. Affordable and Clean Energy 12. Responsible Consumption and Production 13. Climate Action
Shell	3. Good Health and Well-Being 5. Gender Equality 6. Clean Water and Sanitation 7. Affordable and Clean Energy 8. Decent Work and Economic Growth 9. Industry, Innovation, and Infrastructure 10. Reduced Inequality 12. Responsible Consumption and Production 14. Life Below Water 15. Life on Land 16. Peace, Justice, and Strong Institutions 17. Partnerships to Achieve the Goals
Starbucks	6. Clean Water and Sanitation 11. Sustainable Cities and Communities
Volkswagen	7. Affordable and Clean Energy 9. Industry, Innovation, and Infrastructure 12. Responsible Consumption and Production 13. Climate Action
Walmart	2. Zero Hunger 5. Gender Equality 7. Affordable and Clean Energy 12. Responsible Consumption and Production 13. Climate Action

BUSINESS CASE 2.2: REEL—SANTA MONICA, CALIFORNIA

SDG 17:   Partnership for the Goals

All business today is global in our increasingly interconnected world. Although there are challenges to doing business globally, there are also opportunities for significant impact. This is what spurred entrepreneurs Derin Oyekan and Livio Bisterzo to start Reel, a company dedicated to creating environmentally sustainable, eco-friendly paper products while also improving the health and livelihoods of people living in underresourced communities around the world.

Launched in 2019, Reel focuses on two main paper products: toilet paper and paper towels. Toilet paper might not be the first thing that comes to mind when considering innovative business ideas that support a safer, healthier planet, but it happens to be one of the biggest drivers of global climate change. Because toilet paper is one of the largest consumer product categories, it requires vast environmental resources to manufacture. Conventional toilet paper is created from harvesting trees—lots of them, which contributes to greater rates of deforestation. For decades, paper production industry leaders have been using machine-intensive, clear-cutting techniques that contribute heavily to this deforestation. Deforestation leads to climate change because lack of trees can lead to significant changes in weather patterns. Clear-cutting trees not only destroys fragile and vital forested ecosystems, leaving barren land in its wake, but it also further harms the planet through carbon emissions. The National Resource Defense Council reported that approximately 26 million metric tons of carbon are emitted each year through logging practices in Canada's Boreal Forest alone. This is immense, given that one metric ton is as big as a telephone pole or weighs as much as 400 bricks, and that is just one metric ton of carbon.

Reel's solution to this problem is to completely change the manufacturing process by going tree-free. Reel paper products are made with bamboo, a renewable grass, rather than the wood from trees, making the process and the product far more eco-friendly and environmentally sustainable. The company's products are also free of inks, dyes, and BPA (a potentially harmful chemical); are septic safe; and use only sustainable, plastic-free packaging. The company has already sold millions of rolls of toilet paper online and exclusively through Target. According to Reel, each purchase of its specialty pack helps save 27,000 trees that are currently cut down every day for the conventional manufacturing of toilet paper.

Reel has a very strong online business as well as an exclusive relationship with Target. You would think founders Derin and Levio would be thrilled with their early success, but they have a vision of broader global impact. Sanitary bathroom conditions, such as flushable toilets and access to toilet paper, are often an assumed everyday staple in many developed countries, but these conditions are nonexistent in many of the underdeveloped parts of the world. Over 2.4 billion people worldwide lack access to toilets and sanitary waste disposal, and Reel has launched the Reel Change platform to address this health crisis. A percentage of every package of Reel toilet paper sold goes toward helping to improve sanitary waste disposal conditions around the world.

It has also partnered with SOIL, a nonprofit organization located in Haiti dedicated to implementing safe and sustainable solutions for waste management. Only 30% of the Haitian population has access to sanitary waste facilities, and less than 1% of waste is treated safely, giving rise to diseases such as cholera. Reel's partnership with SOIL has resulted in the creation of over 1,200 toilets and access to clean sanitation for over 7,300 people in Haiti. "Ultimately, the goal is to have impact," said

Reel cofounder Derin. "With Reel right now, just knowing that we are literally changing lives with our partnership with SOIL is incredibly rewarding and continues to fuel our drive to do better."

Reel emphasizes the role of community and collaboration in improving the lives of everyone: "We're all connected—by the earth, by the way we treat each other, and by the world we leave behind for the next generation."

Critical Thinking Questions

1. Why is bamboo a more sustainable raw material for making toilet paper?

2. Are larger companies that produce toilet paper (e.g. Procter & Gamble that makes Charmin) likely to start using bamboo? If yes, what will this do to Reel?

3. Reel founders Derin and Livio targeted a small segment of the paper market to help improve the planet. Can you think of other markets or products that could be targets for aspiring entrepreneurs?

References

Ceniza-Levine, C. (2020, September 5). How one entrepreneur trusted his gut and direct-to-consumer brand Reel enters retail with Target partnership.*Yahoo! Finance*. (2021, June 5). https://finance.yahoo.com/finance/news/direct-consumer-brand-reel-enters-120700971.html

MIT. (2020, December 2). How much is a ton of carbon dioxide? *MIT Climate Portal*. https://climate.mit.edu/ask-mit/how-much-ton-carbon-dioxide#:%7E:text=A%20metric%20ton%20is%202%2C204.6,this%20is%20literally%20a%20ton

Reel. (n.d.). *About us*. https://reelpaper.com/pages/our-story-is-your-story

Skene, J. (2020, June 24). Toilet paper is driving the climate crisis with every flush. *National Resource Defense Council*. https://www.nrdc.org/experts/jennifer-skene/toilet-paper-driving-climate-crisis-every-flush

SOIL. (n.d.). *About us*. https://www.oursoil.org/who-we-are/about-soil/

A Save the Children staff member talks with children playing in the ruins of a kindergarten school that was destroyed by Typhoon Ketsana.

Chau Doan/LightRocket/via Getty Images

 3   THE ENTREPRENEURIAL MINDSET

BUSINESS IMPACT CASE 3.1: SAVE THE CHILDREN— FAIRFIELD, CONNECTICUT (HEADQUARTERS)

SDG 2: Zero Hunger

Can an entrepreneurial mindset help reduce childhood malnourishment in Vietnam? Although this might seem like a complex problem, the solution turned out to be quite simple.

In 1990, Jerry Sternin[1] went to Vietnam to help fight malnutrition as part of his job with Save the Children. Save the Children is a worldwide organization working to improve the lives of disadvantaged, vulnerable children. The organization also provides emergency aid in natural disasters, war, and other conflicts.[2]

When Jerry visited in 1990, Vietnam had one of the highest rates of childhood malnutrition in the world, with 41% of children suffering from malnourishment.[3] The problem was attributed to widespread poverty, limited sanitation, and lack of clean drinking water. However, solutions to each of these problems were expensive and took time to implement, and Jerry didn't have either. Instead of looking for a big solution to an enormous problem, Jerry did the entrepreneurial thing.

He traveled to a local village, where he involved all the village mothers in the process of finding ways to improve the nourishment of their kids. Like many successful entrepreneurs, he wanted to involve those affected in the creation of a solution. He learned from the village mothers that the typical eating habits of malnourished children included high-quality rice two times per day. But he also learned that some children in the same impoverished village were not malnourished at all. Jerry wanted to better understand what the healthy children were doing. Jerry then sought to answer the type of question that an entrepreneur would ask: *"What's working and how can we do more of it?"*

He learned that mothers of healthier children were feeding their kids four meals a day with proportionately smaller portions, which allowed the stomach to process the food better. Secondly, while most children were allowed to choose the food they would like to eat, the healthier kids were more actively fed by their parents—even by hand, if necessary. Third, he also noticed that healthy children were eating crab and shrimp—foods that were usually considered "adult food." Finally, Jerry observed that healthy children ate sweet potato greens, food that was considered "low-class." All of these small differences, combined, added the necessary nutrients to a child's diet.[4]

Armed with these insights, Jerry facilitated the development of a community kitchen where the village mothers cooked meals with shrimp, crab, and sweet potato greens, which empowered them to solve the problem. Six months after Jerry's visit, 65% of the children were better nourished and, more importantly, they stayed that way. Soon, the community kitchen program was replicated across Vietnam, reaching over 2.2 million people in 265 villages and becoming a nationwide model.

Jerry didn't tackle sanitation or clean drinking water; rather, he used what was already working in the community to solve the malnutrition epidemic. The entrepreneurial mindset requires using what you have in order to take action and solve problems. Through Save the Children, Jerry did just that.

Critical Thinking Questions

1. What lesson can we learn from Jerry about tackling complex problems?

2. Save the Children is a nonprofit organization. Would Jerry's mindset work in a larger, for-profit company?

3. What does having an entrepreneurial mindset mean to you?

THE ENTREPRENEURIAL MINDSET

Remember, the definition of *entrepreneurial* introduced in Chapter 1 was "a way of thinking, acting, and being that combines the ability to find or create new opportunities with the courage to act on them." "Thinking" comes first in the definition because the entrepreneurial mindset is needed not only during times of action, but it's also needed to better prepare ourselves for the action. The **entrepreneurial mindset** is the ability to quickly sense, take action, and get organized under uncertain conditions in order to find or create opportunities. In the opening case, Jerry demonstrates an entrepreneurial mindset by finding out what was already going on in the community to create a unique solution to the malnutrition problem in one village that could then be replicated throughout the country.

The entrepreneurial mindset is also about sensing when to pivot, or change directions, as the competitive environment evolves or transforms. For example, former *Shark Tank* contestant and entrepreneur David Zamarin used the $200,000 investment from the judges to invest in his startup, Detrapel, a company that manufactures nontoxic stain repellent sprays and protectors. When COVID-19 struck, David used his entrepreneurial mindset to create a set of new products such as hand sanitizers and cleaning products to meet demand. Many more businesses, big and small, pivoted in a similar way: vacuum company Dyson produced a medical ventilator for COVID-19 patients; hockey gear company Bauer manufactured personal protective equipment (PPE) for medical professionals; and handbag startup Rafi pivoted to making resusable, stylish, and sustainable face masks for children and adults.[5]

Business is both complicated and simple. The simple part is understanding that businesses earn profit by selling something at a price that is higher than what it costs to produce. The complicated part is that today's companies are faced with complex problems in an increasingly uncertain world. Technology has increased the pace of change, and it's becoming harder for people who work in business to keep up. However, respected futurist Gerd Leonhard advises against competing with machines. Rather, people should focus on the factors that machines cannot imitate, such as creativity and compassion.[6] This is where entrepreneurship and the entrepreneurial mindset become center stage.

Although the future of the traditional workplace is unpredictable, the climate is ripe for entrepreneurship. Entrepreneurship is so much more than launching new businesses. It is a vital life skill that prepares individuals to deal with an ambiguous and uncertain future. In other words, you don't have to build your own company to think and act like an entrepreneur.

Entrepreneurship encompasses skillset, mindset, and toolset. You need to identify and act on opportunities and solve problems while also managing change, adapting to new conditions, realizing your personal goals, making an impact, and even creating the future. Through entrepreneurship, you will learn a whole new range of skills and abilities—financial, social, communication, marketing, problem solving, and creative thinking, to name a few—that you will be able to apply across many fields. Developing an entrepreneurial mindset will not only help you start your own venture, but it can also set you on a life path that is certain to deviate from the traditional. Being entrepreneurial empowers you to create and identify all types of exciting opportunities for yourself.

GROWTH MINDSET VERSUS FIXED MINDSET

The ability to use your imagination and create new ideas is directly related to how you view yourself and how you see the world—and how you see the world is essentially your mindset. **Mindset**, in general, is a set of beliefs and attitudes that help you make sense of the world around you. It's a lens from which you view *your* world. Our mindset, however, is not "set" at all, so it is essential to understand the type of mindset we have to figure out if we are in need of a mindset change. Stanford University psychologist Carol Dweck proposes that there are two different types of mindset: a fixed mindset and a growth mindset (see Figure 3.1).

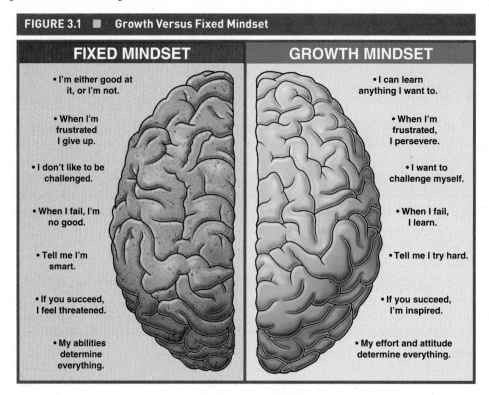

FIGURE 3.1 ■ Growth Versus Fixed Mindset

FIXED MINDSET

- I'm either good at it, or I'm not.
- When I'm frustrated I give up.
- I don't like to be challenged.
- When I fail, I'm no good.
- Tell me I'm smart.
- If you succeed, I feel threatened.
- My abilities determine everything.

GROWTH MINDSET

- I can learn anything I want to.
- When I'm frustrated, I persevere.
- I want to challenge myself.
- When I fail, I learn.
- Tell me I try hard.
- If you succeed, I'm inspired.
- My effort and attitude determine everything.

With a **fixed mindset**, people believe their talents and abilities are set traits and often avoid challenging situations in order to maintain some perceived sense of intelligence and competence. In other words, those using a fixed mindset fear failure because they feel others might think less of them. People with a fixed mindset get defensive when they are given constructive feedback and attribute others' success to luck or some sort of unfair advantage. They would rather tell themselves they can't do something rather than face the prospect of failure or looking stupid.

In contrast, people with a **growth mindset** believe that their abilities can be developed through dedication, effort, and hard work. To them, having brains and talent is just the beginning of a journey of lifelong learning, training, and practice. Unlike people with fixed mindsets, they embrace challenge and perceive failure as an opportunity to improve performance and learn from their mistakes. This means that they persevere rather than give up. Dweck found that a growth mindset is present in successful athletes, writers, musicians, and businesspeople—In fact, she found such a mindset exists within anyone who challenges themselves, accepts and adapts with feedback, and puts in the hard work and practice. She also discovered that people with growth mindsets tend to be more successful and happier than those with fixed mindsets.[7]

The impact of fixed or growth mindset is highlighted in Dweck's research with middle school students. She asked fifth graders to complete a series of increasingly difficult puzzle tests.[8] Over time, she realized that the children who were praised for their hard work and effort on the first test were far more likely to choose the more difficult puzzle the next time—demonstrating a growth mindset. In contrast, the children who were praised for being smart or intelligent after the first test chose the easy puzzle the second time around—demonstrating a fixed mindset. This led Dweck to conclude that the children who had been praised for being smart wanted to keep their reputation, so they avoided the challenge of a more complex test for fear of losing their "smart" reputation if they didn't do as well as the first time. Yet the children who had been praised for how hard they had worked, rather than how smart they were, felt more confident in their abilities to tackle more challenging tests and to learn from any potential mistakes.

Research indicates that achievement and motivation increase with a growth mindset, but it is incredibly hard to practice a growth mindset all the time. Yet, knowing the difference between the growth and fixed mindsets can help us make sense of how we are thinking, acting, feeling, responding, and just showing up.

Developing a Growth Mindset

Most of us demonstrate either a fixed or a growth mindset. But the most important thing to realize is that it is possible to change a mindset from fixed to growth. How does this happen? By listening to that "voice" you have in your head that speaks up whenever you're about to face a new challenge. The ability to recognize that voice, interpreting what it is telling you, responding to it, and taking action is the key to developing a growth mindset.

For example, let's say you just landed a new job with the eyeglass company, Warby Parker. You are excited by the company because for every pair of eyeglasses the company sells, a pair is distributed to someone in need.[9] However, you will be on a team focusing on designing a new store concept for Warby Parker, and the team-lead has put you in charge of developing a social media campaign to generate buzz around the new store concept. Following are some messages you might hear from the "voice" in your head and some responses you might make based on your mindset.[10]

How could adopting a growth mindset help improve your chances of success at a job at a company such as Warby Parker?

Interim Archives/Archive Photos/via Getty Images

FIXED MINDSET: "OMG social media has destroyed my life. I was always the one with the least amount of friends and followers. I should not be the one assigned to this part of the team."

GROWTH MINDSET: **"Given that I didn't use a lot of social media growing up, my perspective may add value to the project because we need to generate buzz for social media influencers but also the average user."**

FIXED MINDSET: "If I fail, I will get fired."

GROWTH MINDSET: **"If I get stuck, I'll ask for help and take initiative to learn new stuff on my own. I'll share my new ideas with colleagues to get early feedback."**

FIXED MINDSET: "Why are they putting me in charge of the social media campaign? I'm the youngest person on the team."

GROWTH MINDSET: **"Wow, what a cool gig! This is going to look great on my résumé having such a responsibility at a young age."**

You might feel different emotions when you read the statements above—the negativity of the fixed mindset statement and the positivity or energy of the growth mindset. Take note of these feelings, because a fixed mindset will limit you in business. The growth mindset will help you overcome challenges, acquire confidence, and act more entrepreneurially.

Keep in mind that our mindset is changeable. It's not permanent or forever fixed. The first step is to understand our own mindset, assess if change is needed, and if it is, then practice a new mindset with intention.

THE ENTREPRENEURIAL MINDSET IN DEPTH

The growth mindset is a necessary foundation for developing an entrepreneurial mindset. Earlier, we defined the entrepreneurial mindset as the ability to quickly sense, take action, and get organized under uncertain conditions *in order to find or create opportunities*. But we need to explore the "ability" part of the definition to get a more in-depth understanding of the entrepreneurial mindset. In this context, ability is a combination of motives and skills that can encourage us to think and act more entrepreneurially. We can look at this as a combination of behaviors and beliefs in ourselves. Table 3.1 lists the common behaviors and attitudes associated with an entrepreneurial mindset.

TABLE 3.1 ■ Common Behaviors and Attitudes Related to Entrepreneurial Mindset	
Behaviors and Attitudes	**Description**
Independence	The desire to work with a high degree of independence
Preference for limited structure	A preference for tasks and situations with little formal structure
Nonconformity	A preference for acting in unique ways; an interest in being perceived as unique
Risk acceptance	A willingness to pursue an idea or a desired goal even when the probability of succeeding is low
Action orientation	A tendency to show initiative, make decisions quickly, and feel impatient for results
Passion	A tendency to experience one's work as exciting and enjoyable rather than tedious and draining
Need to achieve	The desire to achieve at a high level
Future focus	The ability to think beyond the immediate situation and plan for the future
Idea generation	The ability to generate multiple and novel ideas and to find multiple approaches for achieving goals
Execution	The ability to turn ideas into actionable plans and implement those plans
Self-confidence	A general belief in one's ability to leverage skills and talents to achieve important goals
Optimism	The ability to maintain a generally positive attitude about various aspects of one's life
Persistence	The ability to bounce back quickly from disappointment and to remain persistent in the face of setbacks
Interpersonal sensitivity	A high level of sensitivity to and concern for the well-being of those with whom one works

Source: Adapted from Davis, M. H., Hall, J. A., & Mayer, P. S. (2016). Developing a new measure of entrepreneurial mindset: Reliability, validity, and implications for practitioners. *Consulting Psychology Journal: Practice and Research, 68*(1), 1–28. What we call behaviors and attitudes about ourselves, Davis et al. call traits and skills. Our view is that traits are fixed and are not easily developed; therefore, behaviors and attitudes are used in this text.

ENTREPRENEURIAL MINDSET ACTIVITY

How Entrepreneurial Are You?

Take a look at the entrepreneurial mindset behaviors and attitudes list in Table 3.1. Score yourself on each row in the table using a scale from 1 to 10, with 1 meaning that the behavior or attitude does not describe you or how you think at all, to 10 meaning the behavior or attitude completely describes you.

Next, identify your lowest five scores and develop an action plan to increase those scores. What is an action plan in this context? You need to commit to taking three actions to increase each of your lowest five scores. For example, if you scored yourself low on idea generation, maybe you could read a book on creativity or force yourself to only look for problems for 2 hours and then develop ideas to solve those problems.

Critical Thinking Questions

1. What were your three highest-scored behaviors and attitudes? Think about examples in your life that highlight these three.
2. It's not realistic for someone to score a 10 on all of the behaviors and attitudes listed in Table 3.1, so what do you think are the most important to the entrepreneurial mindset?
3. Have a friend, colleague, or family member score you on the behaviors and attitudes. Were the scores different?

Tolerance for Failure

One thing that is missing in Table 3.1 is tolerance for failure. We all fail at one time or another, but entrepreneurs have an expectation of failure. They look at failure as a learning opportunity and try again, but in a better or newer way.

By definition, **fear of failure** is the disposition to avoid failure and/or the capacity for experiencing shame or humiliation as a result of failure.[11] Fear of failure is an emotional state that leads to performance anxiety and goal avoidance. In other words, fear of failure can prevent us from taking action in entrepreneurial ways; to be innovative, creative, and boundary pushing. Fear of failure is an impediment to the entrepreneurial mindset and a major part of the fixed mindset we talked about earlier. Table 3.2 illustrates five types of fear of failure.

TABLE 3.2 ■ Five Fears in Fear of Failure	
Fear	**Example**
Fear of experiencing shame and embarrassment	"When I am failing, it is embarrassing if others are there to see it."
Fear of devaluing one's self-estimate	"When I am failing, it is often because I am not smart enough to perform successfully."
Fear of having an uncertain future	"When I am failing, my future seems uncertain."
Fear of important others losing interest	"When I am not succeeding, people are less interested in me."
Fear of upsetting important others	"When I am failing, I lose the trust of people who are important to me."

Sources: Wilt, K. M. (2016). The role of fear of failure in competitive anxiety and the mediating role of 2 x 2 achievement goals in female high school and collegiate runners. *Ithaca College Digital Commons.* Retrieved from https://digitalcommons.ithaca.edu/cgi/viewcontent.cgi?article=1318&context=ic_theses; and Conroy, D. E. (2001). Progress in the development of a multidimensional measure of fear of failure: The Performance Failure Appraisal Inventory (PFAI). *Anxiety, Stress and Coping, 14*(4), 431–452.

Fear of failure is not necessarily a bad thing. It's two-fold. It can motivate people to succeed, like athletes; or it can prevent someone from acting because the anxiety is too high. The role of fear of failure in the entrepreneurial mindset is somewhere in the middle of these two extremes. Fear of failure keeps our guard up, but no one ever said failure was fun. We do need to anticipate, accept, and learn from failure. Not facing this reality in business can lead to more failure!

Developing Grit

Developing grit is also a good way to overcome some elements of our fear of failure. Grit is the quality that enables people to work hard and sustain interest in their long-term goals. Grit is related to resilience, not just in the face of failure, but in our perseverance to stick to long-term commitments and goals.[12] The concept of grit was developed by Angela Lee Duckworth, a psychologist at the University of Pennsylvania. Through her research, Duckworth discovered that people with higher levels of grit were more effective and achieved more than people with lower levels of grit.

Duckworth's research on grit connects to the growth and fixed mindset, which we explored earlier. People with a growth mindset tend to have higher levels of grit. Table 3.3 outlines several attributes associated with building grit.

TABLE 3.3   ■   Building Grit
Courage: Understanding that failure is part of the learning process rather than something to fear takes courage.
Conscientiousness: Being conscientious means working tirelessly in the face of challenges and toward the achievement of long-term goals.
Perseverance: Committing to long-term goals through practice and pushing through fear of failure requires high levels of perseverance.
Resilience: Having the strength to recover from failure and overcome obstacles in order to persevere toward the achievement of long-term goals. Gritty people believe "everything will be all right in the end, and if it is not all right, it is not the end."
Excellence: Striving for excellence means committing to activities and highlighting opportunities that enhance skills, and prioritize improvement over perfection.

Source: Perlis, M. (2013, October 29). 5 characteristics of grit—How many do you have? *Forbes.* Retrieved from http://www.forbes.com/sites/margaretperlis/2013/10/29/5-characteristics-of-grit-what-it-is-why-you-need-it-and-do-you-have-it/

Successful entrepreneurs have a high tolerance of failure and use grit to cope with missteps and uncertainty. They have this ability because of their entrepreneurial mindset enabling them to think differently about the world.

HOW ENTREPRENEURS REALLY THINK

It has been scientifically proven that entrepreneurs think differently.[13] Take serial entrepreneurs, for instance. A serial entrepreneur is an individual who has started multiple businesses. They typically love coming up with the idea and starting the business but then often get tired of managing it. So they hand the management of the day-to-day to someone else and then go find another business to start. Sir Richard Branson, founder of the Virgin Group, is a good example of a serial entrepreneur. The Virgin Group owns over 200 companies ranging from trains, planes, and spaceships. However, not everything bearing the Virgin brand has been successful, like Virgin Cola, Virgin Brides, Virgin Vodka, and Virgin Clothing. Despite some failures along the way, Branson's perseverance has made Virgin into one of the most successful businesses operating today.[14] Media mogul Oprah Winfrey is also a serial entrepreneur. She established Harpo Productions in the 1980s, before cofounding cable station Oxygen, the Oprah Winfrey Network (OWN), in addition to publishing several magazines and authoring five books.[15]

Theory of Effectuation

It's not just serial entrepreneurs who think differently; all successful entrepreneurs have the ability to look at the world in a unique way. Researcher and Darden School of Business professor Saras Sarasvathy developed the theory of **effectuation**, which is the idea that the future is unpredictable yet controllable.[16] Entrepreneurs look at what's around them and determine what they can achieve with the resources available. They reduce risk and uncertainty by taking small actions to learn and collect information. These actions tend to lead to other actions and further resources, which enable them to grow their ideas and create their own venture.

There are four principles of effectuation theory.[17] These principles are indicative of how the entrepreneurial mind works and explain how entrepreneurs have the ability to take action under conditions of uncertainty and even fear:

- Bird-in-hand principle: You have to create solutions with the resources available here and now.

- Lemonade principle: Mistakes and surprises are inevitable and can be used to look for new opportunities. Think, "when life gives you lemons, make lemonade."

- Crazy quilt principle: Entering into new partnerships and connecting to new people can bring the project new funds, new resources, and new directions, as well as get traction faster.

- Affordable loss principle: You should only invest as much as you are willing to lose.

Sustainable fertilizer company TerraCycle is a good example of effectuation in action. Founder Tom Szasky demonstrated the *bird-in-hand* principle when he used the resources around him, in this case worm poop, to create a fertilizer. He also packaged it in used bottles to save the cost of packaging and reduce environmental impact.

Szasky learned the *lemonade* principle the hard way, when he was ridiculed pitching for investment as a 19-year-old with no clients or retail history. But the rejections only spurred him on to pitch bigger, eventually landing orders from The Home Depot and Walmart. As TerraCycle expanded, Szasky finally attracted attention from investors and entertained the possibility of entering into new partnerships, illustrated by the *crazy quilt* principle. However, the investors wanted to drop TerraCycle's eco-friendly approach and change some of the management. Szasky turned them down and instead redoubled his efforts with the companies with whom he already had a good relationship: Walmart and Home Depot. Finally, Szasky applied the principle of *affordable loss* when he started TerraCycle by only investing as much as he could afford in the business ($20,000 from his personal bank accounts and credit cards).[18]

One principle of effectuation theory is "bird-in-hand"—creating solutions with resources available here and now. TerraCycle's Worm Poop is made from worm waste and packaged in used plastic bottles.

Associated Press/Mel Evans

As TerraCyle grew, it started to partner with companies, manufacturers, retailers, and even individuals in 20 countries to recycle the "nonrecyclable," creating new products from trash ranging from coffee capsules, old pens, or plastic gloves. Today, TerraCycle has successfully recycled over 7 billion pieces of waste, donated $44 billion to charity, and diverted millions of pounds of waste from landfills every month.[19]

Sarasvathy's effectuation theory might show us how entrepreneurs think, but all of us are capable of adopting an entrepreneurial mindset and changing how we think if we are willing to practice.

Deliberate Practice

Developing an entrepreneurial mindset requires practice, and practice leads to habit formation. A habit is a sometimes unconscious pattern of behavior that is carried out often and regularly. Acquiring habits through practice is important; developing an entrepreneurial mindset is not like studying all night only not to remember anything after you take the exam. A mindset develops over time through consistent and deliberate practice.

Higher performers engage in a specific type of practice called deliberate practice, defined as carrying out carefully focused efforts to improve performance.[20] There is evidence of deliberate practice everywhere, from sport, chess, and music, to economics, business, and medicine. People who engage in deliberate practice learn *how* to learn. You may not realize it, but you have probably used deliberate practice in your own activities. Maybe you are a basketball player and you are trying to improve your free throw completion percentage. You set a goal of shooting 100 completed free throws per day for 2 weeks. Your coach videotapes you and shows differences in your form from shots made and shots missed. You make adjustments and then increase your goal to 200 shots made per day. Soon, you develop muscle memory and your free throw percentage increases. You've practiced so much that how you shoot becomes habit! Table 3.4 lists the components of deliberate practice. By the way, the entrepreneurial mindset activities in the book are designed to help you deliberately practice and develop an entrepreneurial mindset as a habit.

TABLE 3.4 ■ Components of Deliberate Practice
● Requires high levels of focus, attention, and concentration.
● Strengthens performance by identifying weaknesses and improving on them.
● Must be consistent and be maintained for long periods of time.
● Must be repeated to produce lasting results.
● Requires continuous feedback on outcomes.
● Involves setting goals beforehand.
● Involves self-observation and self-reflection after practice sessions are completed.

Source: Baron, R. A., & Henry, R. A. (2010). How entrepreneurs acquire the capacity to excel: Insights from research on expert performance. *Strategic Entrepreneurship Journal, 4,* 49–65. Reprinted with permission from John Wiley & Sons.

How Deliberate Practice Shapes the Brain

Deliberate practice not only helps boost our performance, it also has a positive effect on our brain.[21] For instance, neurological changes take place in response to frequent episodes of a repeated activity. When certain brain cells sense this activity, they release myelin, a fatty white tissue that increases the speed, strength, and fluidity of neural impulses. Regular practice does not have the same effect. This is because it lacks the same level of focused effort and only reinforces mindless, automatic habits. Think of something you do every day, like driving a car. In the beginning, you would have worked hard to focus on learning how to drive, but once you got the hang of it, you probably did it without even thinking about it. In other words, you do it out of habit. Deliberate practice is the best way to build expertise and achieve superior performance. Expert entrepreneurs who engage in deliberate practice are generally more skilled at perceiving situations, understanding the meaning of complex patterns, and recognizing the differences between relevant and irrelevant information. Table 3.5 illustrates some more benefits of deliberate practice for entrepreneurs.

TABLE 3.5   ■   Why Deliberate Practice Is Important to Entrepreneurs

- Boosts the capability to maintain effort, concentration, and focus, all of which have important cognitive benefits such as enhancing perception, memory, and the way in which we understand our own performance (or metacognition).

- Improves the ability to store new information and retrieve it when needed, which supports planning, adapting, and quick decision making.

- Gives entrepreneurs a better sense of knowing what they know and don't know, which helps to prevent the potential to become blindsided by passion, which often leads to unnecessary risk and failure.[22]

- Enhances intuition, which allows entrepreneurs to make decisions more speedily and accurately based on prior knowledge and experience.

- Allows any skills developed through deliberate practice (e.g., by playing a musical instrument or sport, creative writing, or anything else that requires strong focus and effort) to be applied to entrepreneurship.

- Gives everybody the opportunity to enhance their skills and become a lifelong learner (entrepreneurs demonstrate these skills by creating their own entrepreneurship portfolio).

Strengthening the entrepreneurial mindset through continuous deliberate practice can help you navigate a VUCA world.

BUSINESS IN A VUCA WORLD

Entrepreneurs take action to identify and act on opportunities. The mindset is an important precursor to action but also needed while acting—thus emphasizing its importance to entrepreneurs. It gives you that "courage" part of the entrepreneurial definition we discussed earlier. Entrepreneurial action encompasses such activities as creating new products or services, new processes, and new ventures. To be an entrepreneur, you need to take action to start something new.[23] This is why there are so many examples of entrepreneurial action in all types of organizations.

Fundamentally, entrepreneurship is about taking action when you don't have all the pieces of the puzzle. How do you act when you are not really sure what to do? How do you start a business when you've never started one before? How do you start a project without the requisite knowledge and skills? How do you bring a product to market that customers have never seen? Understanding something called "VUCA" may help.

VUCA and Entrepreneurs

VUCA is an acronym that stands for volatility, uncertainty, complexity, and ambiguity.[24]

Volatility relates to the pace of change. Because of technology, the pace of change today is increasingly exponential, which means we as humans are having trouble keeping up with it.[25] The faster the pace of change, the more volatility.

Uncertainty relates to the degree that the future is unknown. The amount of uncertainty in business can either prevent us from taking action or can create new opportunities to pursue. This means that uncertainty can be a barrier or motivator.[26] Part of uncertainty is our human ability (or lack thereof) to understand what is going on.

Complexity means there are a lot of moving parts involved. The more moving parts or variables involved, the harder it is to get from point A to point B in a logical way that can easily be planned. The more complex an environment, business, industry, or situation, the harder it is to rationally analyze the situation.[27]

Ambiguity relates to the future being unknowable, very unclear, and vague. Ambiguity can create both complexity and uncertainty.[28]

Uncertainty is a part of any business, but the COVID-19 pandemic created a whole host of uncertainties that restaurants had not dealt with before. Restaurants adapted in numerous ways, such as offering private outdoor dining domes.

Alexi Rosenfeld/Getty Images Entertainment/via Getty Images

VUCA was first used at the U.S. Army War College to describe the environment after the Cold War ended around 1991.[29] In the matter of just a few years, the Berlin Wall crumbled, democratic regimes ousted communist ones, and the Soviet Union dissolved. The speed with which the Cold War ended after 45 years of tensions and conflict created a turbulent environment that was characterized as VUCA. After the 9/11 attacks and the subsequent 2008 financial crisis, the VUCA acronym became popular among business leaders to describe business environments around the world.[30] The global business environment and definitely the environment for entrepreneurs is still very VUCA today. It's not uncommon to hear business leaders talk about how they are managing in a "VUCA world." Consider the recent COVID-19 pandemic. It doesn't get much more VUCA than that. Table 3.6 applies the VUCA framework to the pandemic.

TABLE 3.6 ■ VUCA Framework and the COVID-19 Pandemic	
Volatility	The World Health Organization announced on January 9, 2020, the presence of a novel Coronavirus in Wuhan, China. The spread was so fast that the first cases in the United States were confirmed by January 21. By March, lockdowns started to be implemented around the world and the race to develop a vaccine began.
Uncertainty	In the beginning, it was unclear exactly how the virus spread. It was also unclear when it would end, given the different variants that have emerged, like Delta and Omicron.
Complexity	Every decision made has created new problems. Working from home, school closures, hospitals working at capacity, shortage of ICU beds, testing availability, businesses failing, layoffs, and supply chain issues are just a handful of the problems that emerged.
Ambiguity	COVID-19 has infected 364 million people worldwide and killed 5.6 million.[31] This is an unprecedented epidemic that has lasted longer than any in history, leaving many wondering if it will ever go away.

The Known-Unknown Matrix

The key to tackling VUCA is figuring out what you know and don't know about a particular problem (see Figure 3.2). The concept of knowns and unknowns was made popular in a speech made by then–U.S. Secretary of Defense Donald Rumsfeld prior to the start of the Iraq War in 2002. Rumsfeld said, "Reports that say that something hasn't happened are always interesting to me, because as we know, there are known knowns; there are things we know we know. We also know there are known unknowns; that is to say, we know there are some things we do not know. But there are also unknown unknowns—the ones we don't know we don't know. And if one looks throughout the history of our country and other free countries, it is the latter category that tend to be the difficult ones. The absence of evidence is not evidence of absence, or vice versa."[32]

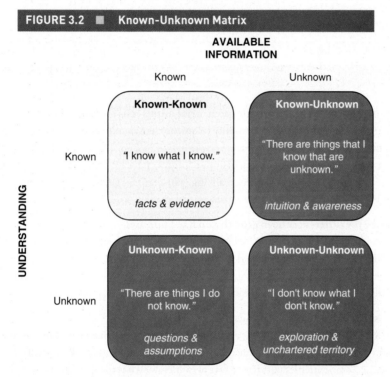

FIGURE 3.2 ■ Known-Unknown Matrix

All the elements of VUCA connect to the blue boxes to varying degrees. For example, ambiguity and volatility are at their highest in unknown-unknown. Complexity is very present in known-unknown, while uncertainty is highlighted in unknown-known. The degree to which VUCA is present, however, is less important than simply knowing it is present.

And when you know VUCA is present, you will know that an entrepreneurial mindset is needed to handle it!

ETHICS IN BUSINESS

When Entrepreneurial Becomes Unethical

Research suggests that 90% of people first check out online reviews before making a purchase. If you are a business owner trying to sell a product or service, the importance of these reviews to your success is not debatable. It could be tempting to sway the reviews in your favor. In fact, Harvard Business School recently published a research article estimating one in five Yelp reviews is fake. How does such a thing occur? Many businesses trying to create an online brand are approached by third parties offering positive online reviews in exchange for cash. As an entrepreneur, it could be very enticing to work with these third parties to help you garner positive reviews. Is there a downside? Indeed, consumers are getting smarter at identifying fake reviews.

Critical Thinking Questions

1. Is it unethical for a company to hire third-party companies to generate fake positive reviews for their product/service?
2. What is the downside for a business that has fake positive reviews?
3. If you realize a review is fake, do you immediately stop your interest in that product or service? Why or why not?

Sources: Willas, S. (2020, January 10). 7 reasons online reviews are essential for your brand. *Mention.* Retrieved from https://mention.com/en/blog/online-reviews/; Erkskine, R. (2018, September 19). 20 online reputation statistics that every business owner needs to know. *Forbes.* Retrieved from https://www.forbes.com/sites/ryanerskine/2017/09/19/20-online-reputation-statistics-that-every-business-owner-needs-to-know/#4155077bcc5c

IN REVIEW

3.1   Explain the importance of an entrepreneurial mindset in business today.

The entrepreneurial mindset is the ability to quickly sense, take action, and get organized under uncertain conditions *in order to find or create opportunities*. It provides a skillset, mindset, and toolset you need to identify and act on opportunities and solve problems while also managing change, adapting to new conditions, realizing your personal goals, making an impact, and even creating the future.

3.2   Describe the differences been growth and fixed mindset.

Drawing from the studies conducted by Carol Dweck, the growth mindset represents a belief that abilities can be developed through dedication, effort, and hard work; while the fixed mindset represents the belief that talents and abilities are set traits leading one to avoid challenging situations in fear of looking less than.

3.3   Discuss the entrepreneurial mindset in greater depth.

There are many common behaviors and attitudes associated with an entrepreneurial mindset, including the desire for independence, a willingness to accept risk, and the ability to generate new ideas. Some entrepreneurs have a fear of failure, which is the disposition to avoid failure and/or the capacity for experiencing shame or humiliation as a result of failure. Developing grit, the quality that enables people to work hard and sustain interest in their long-term goals, helps to overcome fear of failure.

3.4   Assess the role of practice in changing how we think.

Successful entrepreneurs have the ability to look at the world in a unique way. Saras Sarasvathy calls this *effectuation*, which is the idea that the future is unpredictable yet controllable. Higher performers engage in deliberate practice by making carefully focused efforts to improve performance.

3.5   Connect the elements of VUCA to the entrepreneurial mindset.

Entrepreneurs today operate in a VUCA environment. VUCA is an acronym that stands for volatility, uncertainty, complexity, and ambiguity. Navigating VUCA requires an analysis of what you know and don't know about a particular problem. An entrepreneurial mindset is essential when VUCA is present.

BUSINESSES DISCUSSED IN THIS CHAPTER

Organization	UN Sustainable Development Goal
Bauer	2. Zero Hunger 3. Good Health and Well-Being

Organization	UN Sustainable Development Goal
Detrapel	8. Decent Work and Economic Growth 12. Responsible Consumption and Production 13. Climate Action
Dyson	3. Good Health and Well-Being 8. Decent Work and Economic Growth 15. Life on Land
Harpo Productions	3. Good Health and Well-Being 4. Quality Education 5. Gender Equality 16. Peace, Justice, and Strong Institutions
Rafi	8. Decent Work and Economic Growth 12. Responsible Consumption and Production
Save the Children	2. Zero Hunger
TerraCycle	12. Responsible Consumption and Production 13. Climate Action
Virgin Group	1. No Poverty 12. Responsible Consumption and Production
Warby Parker	3. Good Health and Well-Being

KEY TERMS

Ambiguity (p. 57)

Complexity (p. 57)

Deliberate practice (p. 56)

Effectuation (p. 55)

Entrepreneurial mindset (p. 49)

Fear of failure (p. 53)

Fixed mindset (p. 50)

Grit (p. 54)

Growth mindset (p. 50)

Habit (p. 56)

Mindset (p. 49)

Serial entrepreneur (p. 54)

Uncertainty (p. 57)

Volatility (p. 57)

VUCA (p. 57)

BUSINESS CASE 3.2: LOVEVERY—BOISE, IDAHO

SDG 4:   Quality Education

Entrepreneurship is one of the great economic engines of society. It's not only integral to generating jobs, but it also plays a fundamental role in identifying opportunities that help us grow, evolve, and improve as a society. The purest form of the entrepreneurial spirit is, as Benjamin Franklin said, "to do well by doing good." And what better way to do good than to help foster and promote the cognitive growth of the next generation? This is exactly what the company Lovevery aspires to do.

Founded by Jessica Rolph and Roderick Morris in 2017, Lovevery creates toys specifically designed to help children learn at their own pace through play. It's what they call "stage-based play." Lovevery sells play kits for every stage of a child's early development through the first 4 years of life. For example, the "Looker" play kit is designed for a baby 0–12 weeks old. Open the kit and the parents will find such items as a colorful mobile for visual exploration, a black-and-white card set for vision development, tiny mittens to promote body awareness and hand control, among other items all designed to help a baby build new brain connections. Overall, the play kits foster cognitive development in children aged 0–4 while helping to calm stressed parents who are constantly trying to do what's best for their children.

Parents have an endless selection of toys available to them, along with an infinite stream of information on parenting do's and don'ts. When it comes to play and optimizing cognitive development in the first 4 formative years, Lovevery takes the guesswork out of the equation because its stage-based products were developed through consultation with a team of specialists in early childhood development including psychologists, neuroscientists, and educators. The company's philosophy of learning through play is based on the Montessori approach to education, emphasizing that the child's natural curiosity and love of learning is best fostered through independence, choice, and the ability to explore at their own pace. Some of the world's greatest entrepreneurs are outspoken advocates of this educational approach. The cofounders of Google, Larry Page and Sergei Brin; the founder of Amazon, Jeff Bezos; and Wikipedia founder Jimmy Wales were all brought up with Montessori educations. Bezos, for example, recently donated $2 billion for the creation of Montessori-style preschools in underrepresented and underresourced communities.

Lovevery works as a monthly subscription service. Parents sign up for the subscription by providing their child's date of birth and then receive play kits in the mail based on the child's age and stage of development. Because infants (0–52 weeks) grow rapidly in the first year of life, Lovevery offers six play kits to align with each stage of development. In the years that follow, development is not quite as fast as the first year, so four play kits per year are provided instead. Parents have the option to skip a kit or cancel at any time. In all, parents receive 18 kits over the life of their subscription during the first 4 years of their child's life.

Since starting in 2017, Lovevery has gained over 200,000 subscribers and distributes approximately 1 million play kits a year. The company, based in Boise, Idaho, now boasts more than 200 employees and is currently valued at $800 million. Some of its largest investors include the Chan Zuckerberg Initiative and GV (formerly Google Ventures).

As Lovevery grows, its research-based products and services are becoming more accessible. It has recently launched a line of developmental toys at select Target locations and is offering parenting courses through the Lovevery website. An initial public offering (IPO) may also be a possibility in the next few years. As cofounder Morris said, "To realize the full potential of this business, it needs to be a public company."

Critical Thinking Questions

1. How important do you think entrepreneurship is in helping to better society?

2. In what ways do you see an entrepreneurial mindset in action in the creation of Lovevery.?

3. Review the Lovevery website, what other products could they introduce? ?

References

Bhattarai, A., & Davenport, C. (2018, September 13). Bezos pledges $2 billion to help homeless families and launch a network of preschools. *Washington Post.* https://www.washingtonpost.com/business/2018/09/13/bezos-pledges-billion-help-homeless-families-launch-network-preschools/

Day, D. (2021, October 28). Boise's Lovevery lands large funding round & hopes for IPO with growing revenue, product line. *Boise Dev.* https://boisedev.com/news/2021/10/28/lovevery-tcg-ipo/

Driebusch, C. (2021, October 28). Trendy baby-toy maker Lovevery gets $800 million valuation. *The Wall Street Journal.* https://www.wsj.com/articles/trendy-baby-toy-maker-lovevery-gets-800-million-valuation-11635418802

Lovevery. (n.d). Our story. https://lovevery.com/pages/about-us

Sims, P. (2011, April 5). The Montessori mafia. *The Wall Street Journal.* https://www.wsj.com/articles/BL-IMB-20 34?mod=article_inline

BLOCK 1
THE OFFERING

The Boston-based company Freight Farms repurposes shipping containers as mobile farms.
Freight Farms was a 2012 startup in MassChallenge.

Associated Press/Steven Senne

 4 **BUSINESS CREATION**

LEARNING OBJECTIVES
4.1   Recognize the importance of entrepreneurship in the world economy.
4.2   Expose the common myths related to entrepreneurship.
4.3   Explore the different types of entrepreneurship.
4.4   Identify the four pathways of idea generation.
4.5   Discuss the IDEATE method of opportunity recognition.

BUSINESS IMPACT CASE 4.1: MASSCHALLENGE— BOSTON, MASSACHUSETTS

SDG 10: Reduced Inequality

"*We believe great ideas are everywhere, but opportunity is not. We envision a creative and inspired society in which everyone is empowered to turn their brilliant ideas into game-changing businesses.*"—MassChallenge

MassChallenge is a startup accelerator launched in 2010 in Boston, Massachusetts, by cofounders John Harthorne and Akhil Nigam. An *accelerator* is a program that provides a fast-paced, learn by doing education for a class or cohort of young startups.[1] The notion of an accelerator is very common in the world of entrepreneurship. The goal of any accelerator is to speed up the startup process from years to months.

MassChallenge was founded with a single purpose—to make it as easy as possible for entrepreneurs to launch and grow new ventures. John and Akhil envisioned MassChallenge as a global movement, set up to accelerate and support high-potential startups by giving entrepreneurs better access to capital, expertise, and other resources.

There are close to 200 accelerator programs in the United States alone. MassChallenge's popularity and differentiation as a leading accelerator are due to its zero cost and zero equity model. This means that there are no sign-up fees for MassChallenge programs, nor an obligation to give away equity or a stake in your startup. They simply select high-potential ventures across all industries and guide founders through an intensive curriculum that includes mentoring, access to experts, seed funding, and free collaboration space.

Today, MassChallenge has expanded its vision beyond Massachusetts with accelerators in Rhode Island, Texas, New Mexico, Israel, and Switzerland. Its global impact is impressive. Since its launch in 2010, it has accelerated 2,344 startups, which together have raised $5 billion in startup capital, generated revenues in excess of $2.7 billion, and created 136,000 jobs.[2]

Many of MassChallenge startups focus on solving significant social problems. For example, Freight Farms, a former participant of the program in 2012, is now the world's leading manufacturer of container farming, empowering anyone to grow food in their community.[3] Furthermore, 2010 alumnus Ginkgo Bioworks has a valuation of $4.2 billion and is considered one of the most promising biotech companies in the U.S. Ginkgo Bioworks specializes in synthetic biology—a process of programming cells like you would program a computer to make products.[4]

Whatever the location, MassChallenge is helping to build communities that celebrate entrepreneurship, introduce innovations, generate new jobs, solve big problems, and benefit the world both economically and socially.

Critical Thinking Questions

1. How do accelerators, like MassChallenge, help entrepreneurs reduce their time to start and grow their business?

2. What do you think is the most important benefit MassChallenge provides founders?

BUSINESS CREATION THROUGH ENTREPRENEURSHIP IS THE ECONOMIC ENGINE OF SOCIETY

When we think of business, we might think of the big ones: Facebook, Amazon, Google, Walmart, Home Depot, Marriott. But most of business is small. Without small businesses and startup entrepreneurs, our economy would crumble. For instance, there are over 30 million small businesses in the United States, comprising 99% of businesses in total.[5] Small businesses employ nearly 60 million people and create close to 2 million jobs annually.[6] They stimulate the economy by driving growth and innovation to the communities in which they are operating. Startup accelerators like MassChallenge play a vital role in business creation by providing support to emerging startups to get them up and running as quickly as possible. But entrepreneurship is not just flourishing in the U.S.; it has taken off on a global scale, with a reported 500 million entrepreneurs worldwide.

Yet small business and entrepreneurship are not impervious to crisis. The COVID-19 pandemic stalled or killed many small businesses around the world. Up to 34% of small businesses closed during the pandemic[7] with restaurants and brick-and-mortar retail hit the hardest. Some waited to reopen, but many were not able to survive and permanently shut their doors. But it's not just the entrepreneurs and small-business owners who endured this harsh reality—employees also bore the brunt. Job loss or fear of job loss during the pandemic proved to be paralyzing for many.

Global Entrepreneurship

The Global Entrepreneurship Monitor (GEM) is a global research study founded by Babson College and the London Business School in 1999. Today, the study is conducted by a consortium of universities around the world and measures the total entrepreneurial activity (known as TEA) across 114 economies.[8] TEA is the percentage of the population of each country between the ages of 18 and 64 who are either an early entrepreneur (setting up a business) or owner-manager of a new business (up to 3 years old).

For example, as Figure 4.1 illustrates, the early-stage TEA in the United States was just over 15.4% in 2020, down from 17.4% in 2019.[9] This means that just over 15% of the U.S. adult population from 18 to 64 years old was involved in some type of entrepreneurial activity, such as being in the process of starting a new business or owning and managing a business that was less than 3 years old. The decrease in entrepreneurial activity for the United States, and other nations as well, was attributed to the global pandemic.

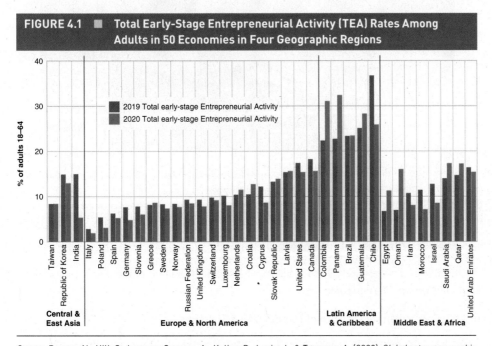

FIGURE 4.1 ■ Total Early-Stage Entrepreneurial Activity (TEA) Rates Among Adults in 50 Economies in Four Geographic Regions

Source: Bosma, N., Hill, S., Ionescu-Somers, A., Kelley, D., Levie, J., & Tarnawa, A. (2020). *Global entrepreneurship monitor: 2020/2021 global report.* Global Entrepreneurship Research Association: London Business School, 42.

As you can see from Figure 4.1, in the Latin America and Caribbean region, Ecuador and Chile have the highest TEA rate, while in the Europe and North America regions, countries like Italy and Poland appear to have some of the lowest rates. Not every early startup will succeed, but the ones that do play a huge role in contributing to their country's economy by providing employment, and producing products and services that people want to buy. Although it is commonly reported that more than half of new businesses fail in the first year, this isn't necessarily true. Data from the U.S. Bureau of Labor Statistics show that 20% of new businesses fail in the first year, 45% in the first 5 years, and 65% in the first 10 years. Approximately 25% of new businesses survive 15 years or more. The data do paint a more positive picture than the more commonly held belief, but there is still no denying that plenty of new businesses close every year in the U.S.

THE TRUTH ABOUT ENTREPRENEURSHIP

To truly understand what it takes to be an entrepreneur, it is worth debunking some of the myths, many of which have been perpetuated by the media. Contrary to some sensationalist reports, Bill Gates (Microsoft), Oprah Winfrey (Harpo Productions), and Elon Musk (Tesla) are not overnight successes, nor were they "born" entrepreneurs. Their successes came from years of hard work, commitment, and constant iteration. Although the likes of Bill Gates and his peers are certainly inspirational, they do little to represent the reality of entrepreneurship. The following section exposes the myths about entrepreneurship by exploring seven truths and explains how entrepreneurship can be a path for many, rather than just a chosen few.

Oprah Winfrey built an empire that has included a television talk show, a magazine, a production company, and a television network. Here she is with author Ta-Nehisi Coates after choosing his book *The Water Dancer* for her book club, a discussion segment of her talk show.

Michele Crowe/CBS/via Getty Images

The Seven Truths About Entrepreneurship

The following seven truths (see Table 4.1) help to separate fact from fiction and dispel some of the misconceptions surrounding entrepreneurs.

Truth #1: Entrepreneurship Is Not Reserved for Startups

Entrepreneurs are commonly associated with startups. Traditionally, they create businesses from an idea, and grow the business using funds from family members, investors, or themselves. If the business is successful, the startup develops into a formal organization, or merges with another organization, or may even be bought by another company. Yet this is not the only path for entrepreneurs. The truth is that entrepreneurs go way beyond the startup; they can be found in big corporations, family businesses, franchises, and nonprofit organizations. Section 4.3 explores these different types of entrepreneurs in more detail.

Truth #2: Entrepreneurs Do Not Have a Special Set of Personality Traits

Contrary to what is reported in the media, there is no scientific evidence to suggest that entrepreneurs are born with a special set of personality characteristics that distinguishes them from the rest of us. Early research identified four main traits that are commonly ascribed to entrepreneurs: a desire for achievement, the ability to influence events, a tendency to take risks, and a tolerance for ambiguity.[10] Yet nothing has been proven to confirm these traits, especially in diverse populations that include women and people of color. Over the last couple of decades, researchers have shifted the focus from "who" the entrepreneur is to how entrepreneurs think and act.

Through a study involving serial entrepreneurs—entrepreneurs who start several businesses, either simultaneously or consecutively—researcher Saras Sarasvathy discovered that there are patterns in how entrepreneurs think, and this thinking can be changed and altered. She developed a theory, introduced in Chapter 3, called effectuation, which is the idea that the future is unpredictable yet controllable. This means that entrepreneurs use a particular mindset, an entrepreneurial mindset, to create and obtain control by taking actions to learn, collecting information, reducing risk and uncertainty, and using available resources. Entrepreneurs start off small and make the most of what they have; as time goes on, their actions lead to more results and new resources.[11] Armed with this mindset, Sarasvathy believes that effectual entrepreneurs have the power to create the future rather than predict it by building relationships, accepting and moving on from failure, and identifying new opportunities when they arise. They use their own initiative and resources to fulfill their vision of the future.

Truth #3: Entrepreneurship Can Be Taught Because It's a Way of Thinking

If it were true that entrepreneurs are born with a certain set of personality traits, then it would follow that entrepreneurship could not be taught. What has been proven, instead, is that entrepreneurs exhibit common patterns in how they think, and our thinking can be changed and altered.[12] This means that entrepreneurship can absolutely be taught. So how do entrepreneurs think? Generally, entrepreneurs use what they have to start new things rather than waiting until they get all the resources they think they need. They take quick, smart action to test new ideas, especially when they are not fully baked, in order to learn and even fail fast and cheap. They leverage their networks for help and guidance and are constantly working to develop new relationships because they know entrepreneurship is more collaborative than competitive. They tend to be proactive rather than reactive—working to create the future rather than respond to it. Through education and practice we can train ourselves to think and act more entrepreneurially.

TABLE 4.1 ■ The Truths About Entrepreneurship	
Truth #1	Entrepreneurship is not reserved for startups.
Truth #2	Entrepreneurs do not have a special set of personality traits.
Truth #3	Entrepreneurship can be taught because it's a way of thinking.
Truth #4	Entrepreneurs are not extreme risk takers.
Truth #5	Entrepreneurs collaborate more than they compete.
Truth #6	Entrepreneurs act more than they plan.
Truth #7	Entrepreneurship is a life skill.

Truth #4: Entrepreneurs Are Not Extreme Risk Takers

There is a popular viewpoint that entrepreneurs are big risk takers who like to gamble when the stakes are high. However, there is no evidence to suggest that entrepreneurs take more risks than anyone else. On the contrary, entrepreneurs who are considered to be big risk takers are usually not successful, simply because they are leaving too much to chance.[13] In fact, most entrepreneurs are very calculated risk takers and gauge what they are willing to lose with every step taken. They practice a cycle of act-learn-build that encourages taking small actions in order to learn and build that learning into the next action (see Figure 4.2).[14] Entrepreneurship should never be a zero-sum game; it's never an all-or-nothing decision. Also, every entrepreneur has a different threshold of what they are willing to lose, which is why entrepreneurs seem rebellious and enjoy risk.

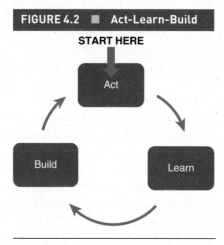

FIGURE 4.2   ■   Act-Learn-Build

Source: Neck, H. M., Neck, C. P., & Murray, E. L. (2020). *Entrepreneurship: The practice and mindset* (2nd ed.). SAGE.

Truth #5: Entrepreneurs Collaborate More Than They Compete

The media often perpetuate the myth of the solitary entrepreneur hiding away in the family garage or basement, guarding their secrets from their competition. But the truth is that entrepreneurs are more likely to collaborate and build strong relationships with other like-minded entrepreneurs, willing to help one another out with a "pay it forward" attitude—collaborating for the greater good.[15]

Not only do successful entrepreneurs collaborate with other entrepreneurs, they also collaborate with their target customers to test new ideas, potential investors to build trust, and family and friends for support. In fact, recent studies have shown that entrepreneurs who collaborate and share information can be a more valuable behavior and skill than the ability to identify new opportunities.[16]

Truth #6: Entrepreneurs Act More Than They Plan

Traditionally, entrepreneurs draft a business plan, a lengthy written document that articulates the entrepreneur's vision for the future by outlining the core business objectives and how they are to be achieved over a certain period of time. But not every entrepreneur needs a business plan. Research shows that fewer than half of Inc. 500 founders wrote formal business plans prior to launching their companies, and nearly 30% had only basic plans.[17] So what did they do instead? They took action by talking to other people about their vision, connected with their customers, generated buzz about their product or service, and built a strong network. The business, and the opportunity, took shape through action, testing, and validating that a market existed for what it was selling and enough customers are willing to pay.

Although planning and research are important, the creation of a formal business plan is not because it doesn't prove that customers exist and will buy. Entrepreneurs that spend too much time writing a business plan lose sight of the importance of taking action on their idea to really learn whether it has potential.

Truth #7: Entrepreneurship Is a Life Skill

The meaning of entrepreneurship has transcended into something more than just the ability to start a new business. Entrepreneurship has become a life skill that helps people to think, act, identify opportunities, approach problems in a specific way, adapt to new conditions, and take control of personal goals and ambitions. It also provides people with a set of skills that can be applied to many other fields. Being entrepreneurial empowers us to create opportunities and reach our goals.[18]

Now that we have separated the truths from the myths, it is time to understand more about the different types of entrepreneurship in practice today.

TYPES OF ENTREPRENEURSHIP

As we discussed in the previous section, entrepreneurship is not just reserved for startups. Let's take a look at the types of entrepreneurship (see Table 4.2) most commonly in practice today.

Corporate Entrepreneurship

Corporate entrepreneurship (also known as intrapreneurship) is a process of creating new products, ventures, processes, or renewal within large corporations.[19] It is typically carried out by employees working in areas separate from the mainstream corporation who create and test innovations that are then absorbed into the broader corporation.

Corporate entrepreneurs tend to explore new possibilities and seek ways in which the company's current structure and process can enable innovation. They also identify opportunities, build teams, and create something of value in order to enhance competitive positioning and profitability. For example, Dutch science company DSM specializes in solutions for nutrition, health, and sustainable living. In 2001, it set up an arm called DSM Venturing, which invests in entrepreneurs by helping them to move from the idea stage to running a new business. Entrepreneurs are provided with funding, resources, and mentoring, as well as the freedom to create without too much corporate interference. Today, DSM has invested in 75 startups in the field of nutrition, health, and sustainable living and has 35 companies in its portfolio.[20]

Entrepreneurship Inside

Entrepreneurs inside are employees who think and act entrepreneurially within different types of organizations. Although this might sound similar to corporate entrepreneurs (employees who work for large corporations), there is an important difference. Entrepreneurs inside can exist and function in any type of organization, big or small, including government agencies, nonprofits, religious entities, self-organizing entities, and cooperatives.[21] Like other entrepreneurs, inside entrepreneurs build new businesses, products, services, and processes that create value and drive growth for the organization. For example, multinational technology company IBM has a long history of encouraging entrepreneurial thinking inside its organization. Chief Innovation Officer Dr. Bernard Myerson is a good example of an inside entrepreneur who has been involved in some of the most important cutting-edge innovations today, including integrated circuits and Wi-Fi.[22]

Franchising

A franchise is a type of license purchased by an individual (franchisee) from an existing business (franchisor) that allows the franchisee to trade under the name of that business.[23] In this type of entrepreneurship, both the franchisor (the founder of the original business) and the franchisee are entrepreneurs. A franchise is often referred to as a "turnkey operation." In other words, the franchisee turns the key to open the door and is ready for business. A franchisee not only pays the franchisor a lump sum to buy the franchise but also has to pay royalties, which are calculated as a percentage of monthly sales revenue. According to results of *Entrepreneur* magazine's annual Franchise 500, announced in 2019, McDonald's, Dunkin' Donuts, and Kumon Math & Reading Centers are among the most popular franchises in the United States.[24] Today, there are more than 770,000 franchise establishments in the United States.[25]

Buying a Small Business

Buying a small business is another way to enter the world of entrepreneurship. In this arrangement, the entrepreneur is buying out the existing owner(s) and taking over operations. For some entrepreneurs this is a less risky approach than starting from scratch.[26] For instance, some entrepreneurs presume that buying an existing business involves substantial capital. However, there are many benefits to buying a small business that can make the cash investment worthwhile. By having the product or service, branding, and customer and supplier list already in place, entrepreneurs have a great opportunity to use their ideas to quickly scale the business. Examples of small-business owners who bought rather than started their own business include former U.S. Army officer Greg Ambrosia, who acquired Dallas-based window-cleaning specialist company City Wide Building Services; engineer-turned-entrepreneur Jennifer Braus, who owns Systems Design West, a company that manages billing for emergency services near Seattle; and Tony Bautista, who left his career in investment management to run Fail Safe Testing, a company that tests equipment for fire departments.[27] Entrepreneurs can check out the listings of small businesses to buy on sale exchange marketplace BizBuySell. The site allows you to put in a location such as Boston, Massachusetts, and then provides you with a list of available businesses.

Clothing brand Eileen Fisher is one example of a B Corp member. The company supports environmental causes and other sustainability initiatives.

Jessica Antola/Contour/Getty Images

Social Entrepreneurship

Social entrepreneurship is the process of sourcing innovative solutions to social and environmental problems.[28] Every year, thousands of initiatives are launched by social entrepreneurs to improve social problems such as water shortages, lack of education, poverty, and global warming. A subcategory of social entrepreneurship is the benefit corporation, or B Corp. This is a form of organization certified by the nonprofit B Lab for for-profit companies that ensures that strict standards of social and environmental performance, accountability, and transparency are met.[29] To be certified as a B Corp, the organization is rated on how its employees are treated, its impact on the environment, and how it benefits the community in which it operates.[30] Household and personal care company Seventh Generation was one of the first to achieve B Corp status.[31] Its eco-friendly, plant-based products help protect human health and the environment.[32] Clothing brand Eileen Fisher is another example of a B Corp member. Eileen Fisher takes a socially responsible approach to clothing design through a range of initiatives focused on empowering women-owned businesses and supporting environmental causes.[33]

Family Enterprise

A family enterprise is a business that is owned and managed by multiple family members, typically for more than one generation. Family enterprising is considered a type of entrepreneurship because each generation has an opportunity to grow and change the organization in new, innovative ways.[34] Of the 30 million small businesses in the U.S., almost 20% are family owned. Family-owned businesses are incredibly important to the U.S. economy and account for 60% of employment, 78% of new jobs, and 65% of total wages. An entrepreneurial approach focused on innovation and adaptation is extremely important for business survival—fewer than 12% of family businesses survive into the third generation of ownership, and only 13% remain in the family for more than 60 years.[35]

Many leading family businesses are successful because of their history, experience, and their ability to inspire commitment and loyalty from their employees and family members. To continue their cycle of growth, innovation, and continuity, family members need to pass on their entrepreneurial wisdom to the next generations. It is this mindset that ensures the survival of the family business for many years to come. For example, global clothing and outdoor recreation company L.L. Bean is one of the longest surviving and successful privately held family businesses in the U.S. Headquartered in Maine. It was founded in 1912 by Leon Leonwood (L. L.) Bean as a one-man operation and subsequently transformed into a global brand by his grandson Leon Gorman. L.L. Bean credits much of its success to its commitment to outstanding customer service, which is to "sell good merchandise at a reasonable profit, treat customers like human beings and they'll always come back for more."[36]

Serial Entrepreneurship

Serial entrepreneurs, also known as habitual entrepreneurs, are people who come with continuous ideas and start several businesses, either simultaneously or consecutively. Not satisfied with just focusing on one business, serial entrepreneurs are constantly looking out for the next big thing before handing over the responsibility to someone else, and moving on to the next idea or business. Media leader and philanthropist Oprah Winfrey is a good example of a serial entrepreneur. She began her career as a local TV anchor before moving on to *The Oprah Winfrey Show* in the 1980s, and establishing Harpo Productions soon afterward. She is also the cofounder of cable station Oxygen; the founder of the Oprah Winfrey Network (OWN); the founder of *O, The Oprah Magazine*; and the author of five books.[37]

Regardless of the different types of entrepreneurship discussed, every successful entrepreneur has something important in common—the ability to identify unique opportunities to create new businesses.

TABLE 4.2 ■ Types of Entrepreneurship	
Corporate entrepreneurship	Employees working in separate units within a corporation who create and test innovations to generate profit for the organization.
Entrepreneurship inside	Employees who work in any type of organization, big or small, and build new products and services to create value.
Franchising	Entrepreneurs (franchisee) who purchase a license, pay a lump sum and royalties run an existing business (franchisor).
Buying a small business	Entrepreneurs who buy a small business from an existing owner and take over operations.

(Continued)

TABLE 4.2 ■ Types of Entrepreneurship (*Continued*)	
Social entrepreneurship	Entrepreneurs who create innovations to solve social problems (such as water scarcity, poverty, and climate change).
Family enterprise	Family members who own and run a business and focus on innovation and adaptation to ensure its continuity.
Serial entrepreneurship	Entrepreneurs who develop continuous ideas and start several businesses at the same time or consecutively.

OPPORTUNITIES—NOT IDEAS—CREATE BUSINESSES

Opportunities start with thousands of ideas. In entrepreneurship, an **opportunity** is a way of generating value through unique, novel, or desirable products, services, and even processes that have not been previously exploited in a particular context. A new idea that constitutes an opportunity, whether it is a product, service, or technology, must be something people need, desire, find useful or valuable. Most importantly, they need to be willing to pay for it. An idea may be good, but if there is not a market for it—customers who are willing to purchase—then it's not an opportunity.

The Idea Classification Matrix

Opportunities spring from ideas, but not all ideas are opportunities, which is why entrepreneurs must be able to choose the ones with the most potential. The **idea classification matrix** (see Figure 4.3) helps entrepreneurs to identify and rate the ideas that can be converted to innovations or significant improvements as sources of new business opportunities. The matrix is divided into four quadrants along two dimensions. Based on the dimensions of value and usefulness and degree of novelty (think new and unique), an idea can be considered an innovation, invention, improvement, or as irrelevant. Of these, innovations and inventions are high in novelty, while improvements and irrelevant ideas are low in novelty.

A successful idea scores highly as an *innovation* if the product or service is novel, useful, and valuable. Today's smartphone and GPS (Global Positioning Systems) are both good examples of innovative products.

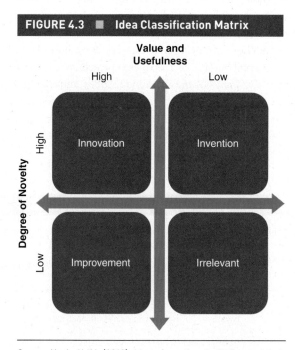

FIGURE 4.3 ■ Idea Classification Matrix

Source: Neck, H. M. (2010). Idea generation. In B. Bygrave & A. Zacharakis (Eds.), *Portable MBA in entrepreneurship* (pp. 27–52). John Wiley & Sons.

Inventions, by definition, score highly for novelty, but if an invention does not reach the market or appeal to consumers, then it will be rendered useless. This was the case for "wink glasses," a product invented by Japanese manufacturer Masunaga, that monitored the number of times you blink while staring at a screen.[38] If you don't blink enough, one of the lenses fogs up, forcing your blinking to return to a normal rate. The novel glasses were expensively priced at $350 and never really established a foothold in the market. As the wink glasses example shows, the success of inventions depends on demand. When products in the early stages find a market, they move to the innovation stage. The Post-It is an example of an invention that developed into an innovation— although it scored high on novelty and usefulness, it only became valuable when it reached the market.

Ideas do not always need to be unique or novel to appeal to customers. There are many ideas that focus on *improvement*. These improvements are based on enhancing existing products and may result in new customers or increased value and benefits for existing customers. While the products may not be high in novelty, there is still a strong market for these products, as many people will find them useful. For example, Logitech, a manufacturer of computer peripherals such as keyboards, mouse, and headsets, has a washable keyboard. A cap is provided to cover the USB cable, and you submerge the keyboard in your favorite dishwashing liquid and scrub away.

Finally, there are ideas that fall into the *irrelevant* category, scoring low on both novelty and usefulness. Yet the problem with ideas is that it's difficult to predict whether something is irrelevant, given that someone else might find it appealing. For example, the world may not need or want shoe umbrellas, but where would we be today without personal computers? In 1977, Ken Olsen, founder of one of the top computer companies at the time, Digital Equipment Corporation, said, "There is no reason anyone would want a computer in their home."[39] What seems irrelevant may actually prove to be one of the greatest innovations by humankind.

A washable keyboard is considered an improvement on the idea classification matrix.

Associated Press/Bruce Lipsky

Every one of us has the capability to generate a huge range of ideas, but turning an idea into a business opportunity requires a huge amount of commitment in terms of work, time, and resources, which doesn't appeal to everyone. As the idea classification matrix illustrates, most opportunities in entrepreneurship demand high value and some degree of novelty. Finding solutions to problems and meeting customer needs are the essence of opportunity recognition.

ETHICS IN BUSINESS

When is taking someone else's idea stealing?

You are on a public internet forum or social networking site and someone has posted an idea for a really innovative new product. You see huge potential in this idea; you run with it and turn the idea into a very successful business. Here's a quick ethical test: If your photo is plastered one day on the front page of *The Wall Street Journal* with your successful business, would you feel a sense of pride and accomplishment?

Critical Thinking Questions

1. What are some ways you might be able to safely share an idea without fear of idea theft?
2. Does the different execution of another's idea still count as idea theft?
3. Is there value in an idea, or is the value in the execution of the idea?

Four Pathways to Opportunity Recognition

As discussed throughout this chapter, developing new ideas is one thing, but transforming those ideas into valuable opportunities and a business is quite a different process. Entrepreneurs can use four different pathways or steps to identify and exploit opportunities (Figure 4.4).

As you move from step to step on the staircase, you may experience greater levels of complexity and uncertainty, which results in even more valuable opportunities. Furthermore, *how* the opportunity is discovered through a particular pathway is often done with hindsight rather than planned or premeditated.

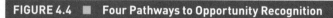

FIGURE 4.4   ■   Four Pathways to Opportunity Recognition

I wanted to create something innovative. I started looking around, observed, and talked to some people and identified new, unmet needs. Then I created something to meet those needs.

I thought about what I knew, my skills, experiences, and abilities and developed an idea that matched "me." I created something and just started testing it.

I knew I wanted to start a business but was unsure what business to start. I intentionally searched for different opportunities.

I saw a clear problem and developed a solution.

Source: Neck, H. (2019). *Beyond the entrepreneurial mindset.* Keynote presentation for the Kern Engineering Network Annual Conference. January 5, 2019. Dallas, TX.

The find pathway is the least complicated and perhaps most common form of identifying new opportunities. It focuses first on identifying a problem and developing a business to solve that problem. For example, the COVID-19 health crisis in 2020 inspired former Babson student Helena Dweck to come up with a solution to make social distancing and quarantining from loved ones more bearable. Helena launched AirHugger, a company that sells pins and apparel through a website and Instagram to send messages of warmth to others while socially distancing.[40]

The search pathway is used when entrepreneurs are not quite sure what type of venture they want to start but engage in active searching to discover new opportunities.[41] We all possess certain information sets, or knowledge bases, established by our existing knowledge.[42] By actively searching what we already know, we can access a wealth of information and uncover new opportunities. Through this process, entrepreneurs are able to uncover areas of interest that allow them to start searching for business opportunities. For example, John Lee Cronin, a young man with Down syndrome, and his father, Mark Cronin, uncovered an idea for their business John's Crazy Socks (featured in Chapter 10: Organizational Mission and Culture) by designing crazy, colorful socks to commemorate World Down Syndrome Day, and later on, other charities too.[43] Today, John's Crazy Socks recognizes and celebrates disabilities by selling more than 2,000 styles of socks from about 20 suppliers.

The effectuation path involves using what you have (skills, knowledge, abilities) to uncover an opportunity that uniquely fits with the entrepreneur. Unlike finding and searching, effectuating is more about *creating* opportunities rather than simply uncovering them through finding or searching. To identify opportunities, this approach advocates using what you know, whom you know, and who you are. Your role as an entrepreneur is to take action and see how the market responds, recognize patterns, and learn from iteration to define the opportunity as it evolves.

Former Babson student Jim Poss, founder of Bigbelly, the company that designs solar-powered, sensor-equipped trash compactors to help reduce waste, is a good example of an entrepreneur who effectuated opportunities.[44] When he was first starting out, he first factored in what he knew already—his background in geology, environmental science, and engineering gave him a good foundation for this innovation. Next, he identified who he knew to help him bring his idea to reality. Two of those experts were engineering students Jeff Satwicz and Bret Richmond, from the Franklin W. Olin School of Engineering, and the other was Alexander Perera, a fellow Babson student at the time with a background in renewable energy use and energy efficiency. When Poss had an early prototype of the trash compactor, he took action and sold the concept to a ski resort in Vail, Colorado, where collecting trash was expensive and timely, given the remote locations of some of the ski lodges. The feedback from that first sale helped Poss and the team to iterate their invention by changing the one-bin system to two-bin, adding a wireless function to alert the operator when the bin was full, and to attach wheels to the cart inside. As a consequence, Poss started to sell more and more compactors to companies looking for more sustainable environmental solutions to waste collection. Today, BigBelly has over 60,000 solar-powered trash compactors in over 50 countries.[45]

The final approach at the top of the staircase, **the design pathway**, is one of the most complex but can be the most value-creating. In this approach, entrepreneurs can uncover high-value opportunities by focusing on unmet needs of customers—specifically, latent needs (needs we have but don't know we have). In this path, opportunities are created using a process called **design thinking**—a nonlinear problem-solving method that requires talking with and observing customers to identify needs, quickly developing prototypes to test new ideas, and get ongoing feedback from those you are designing for to ensure you are meeting the needs identified. It takes practice and imagination to uncover true unmet needs, but by identifying them, the entrepreneur has a chance to create an entirely new market. For example, we didn't know we needed an iPhone until Apple created it. Today, many of us might say that we couldn't live without it—a true example of a latent need being a source of a huge opportunity.

BigBelly solar trash compactors help reduce waste and are a good example of a product from an entrepreneur who effectuated an opportunity.

Associated Press/Matt Rourke

THE IDEATE METHOD OF OPPORTUNITY RECOGNITION

It's really hard to develop new opportunities if you don't have a lot of life experience. Young, aspiring entrepreneurs tend to focus on novelty products and services but don't have the experience or knowledge to prove that their ideas have potential. As a consequence, they end up wasting a lot of time and resources on ideas that are simply not viable. In contrast, more seasoned entrepreneurs start off from a place of knowledge by using their experience to assess the potential for profit and the number of people likely to purchase their offering. This allows them to experiment with their ideas and make changes where necessary. Remember: The best ideas are the ones based on knowledge that you can transform into an opportunity. The IDEATE method, an acronym that stands for identify, discover, enhance, anticipate, target, and evaluate, is a useful way for students to begin building a skillset for identifying and selecting high-potential ideas that can be converted to new business opportunities (see Table 4.3).[46]

TABLE 4.3 ■ The IDEATE Method for Opportunity Recognition	
Identify	Identifying problems that customers are currently trying to solve, are spending money to solve, but are still not solved to the customers' satisfaction. Also identifying the underlying cause of the problem.
Discover	Actively searching for ideas in problem-rich environments where there is social and demographic change, technological change, political and regulatory change, and/or change in industry structure.

(Continued)

TABLE 4.3 ■ The IDEATE Method for Opportunity Recognition (*Continued*)	
Enhance	Taking ideas and expanding to new applications, adding innovative twists, or simply enhancing existing ideas.
Anticipate	Studying and analyzing future scenarios as they relate to social, technological, and other global changes and trends.
Target	Defining and understanding a particular target market, and validating new ideas with early adopters.
Evaluate	Evaluating ideas generated from the approaches above by analyzing market size, feasibility, and willingness of customers to pay.

Source: Cohen, D. A., Pool, G., & Neck, H. M. (2021). *The IDEATE method: Identifying high-potential entrepreneurial ideas.* SAGE.

Applying the IDEATE Method

Using the example of the modern-day gourmet food truck, let's apply each acronym of the IDEATE method.

The mobile food industry has been around for many years: Fast-food products such as hotdogs, ice-cream, and burgers have long been sold from kiosks, trucks, and food carts. Yet, in the past decade, the mobile food industry has been undergoing something of a revolution. People are looking for a quick, healthy alternative to traditional fast food, which is giving rise to a new type of street food that is becoming increasingly upscale.

The first step in the IDEATE method is to *identify* the problem in need of solving. In this mobile food example, it is clear that although traditional fast food is still popular, people are looking for a healthier alternative. One potential solution might be to operate a food truck that serves seasonal salads and healthy grain bowls.

The second step in the IDEATE method is the *discover* stage, where entrepreneurs can explore social, demographic, political, or other environmental changes. This is the stage where an opportunity could change into an entirely different concept. For instance, food trucks are notorious for using disposable plastic tableware, which is destructive to the environment. An eco-friendly solution would be to use biodegradable tableware. Now the food truck is healthy both for its customers and for the environment. To make the food truck even more eco-friendly, it could be run on clean energy, such as solar power, or biofuel. For example, Amsterdam's two-wheeled pastry food cart Pief Paf Pofferje is operated by bicycle.[47]

The *enhance* stage allows you to change the food truck opportunity even further by expanding the idea or adding new, innovative twists. Maybe the food truck could offer classes on healthy cooking and composting. Now the food truck not only serves healthy food in an environmentally friendly way but also educates its customers in how to do the same.

During the *anticipate* stage, entrepreneurs have the opportunity to consider future scenarios, which might instigate another change in the original food truck concept. One scenario involves food deserts—areas with little to no access to affordable, healthy, fresh food. It is estimated that more than 23 million people in the U.S., including 6.5 million children, live in food deserts, causing severe health problems.[48] Most of these deserts are in rural, low-income areas where corner stores selling junk food are the only main sources of food. How can food trucks help this bleak situation? Perhaps the trucks can go to these low-income areas and sell healthy food at more affordable rates while also educating the public on how to eat healthy on small budgets.

In the *target* stage, you could test your healthy food truck idea on potential customers by trying out your menu on people in your local downtown area. If you'd like to explore the food deserts concept further, you could choose a low-cost urban area to test the idea before investing in trucks. The idea here is to find a market of early customers that will help validate your idea and give you the proof you need to convert it into a viable business.

Finally, the *evaluate* stage encourages you to take all of the ideas and assess the size of the problem:

1. food truck with salads and bowls

2. food truck (same as #1) that only uses compostable packaging and utensils

3. food truck offering classes on healthy cooking and composting

4. fleet of trucks offering lower-cost healthy food in food deserts

Now you can evaluate whether there is a big enough market for your food truck ideas, or if you have the ability to reach customers, or even if you have the skills to execute your ideas. It will also enable you to think about who you know that can help you make this idea a reality, or even if you want to run a food truck at all.

ENTREPRENEURIAL MINDSET ACTIVITY

Identifying Headache Problems

Consumers don't buy products; they buy solutions to what is termed a *headache problem*. A person with a headache needs immediate relief, and that is usually aspirin. A lot of people have headaches, so that means a lot of people buy aspirin. Nearly 6 million people in the United States take aspirin daily—that's a lot of aspirin![49]

The goal in the IDEATE method is to identify a migraine headache problem to solve because the bigger the headache, the larger the market and opportunity. In the IDEATE method, it's important to focus first on the headache problems before coming up with new business ideas. Small headache equals very small business or probably no business at all. So take time to look for the big, migraine headaches.

For this activity, identify three products or services *that you have paid for* recently. What's the headache problem being solved by each?

Critical Thinking Questions

1. On a scale of 1 to 5 with 1 being small and 5 being large, how big is the headache problem for each product or service? What is the basis for your evaluation?
2. What products or services today solve migraine headache problems? How and why?

IN REVIEW

4.1   Recognize the importance of entrepreneurship in the world economy.

Entrepreneurship has taken off on a global scale, with a reported 500 million entrepreneurs worldwide. Not every early startup will succeed, but the ones that do play a huge role in contributing to their country's economy by providing employment, and producing products and services that people want to buy.

4.2   Expose the common myths related to entrepreneurship.

There are seven truths about entrepreneurship that help to separate fact from fiction: (1) Entrepreneurship is not just for startups; (2) entrepreneurs do not have a special set of personality traits; (3) entrepreneurship can be taught because it's a way of thinking; (4) entrepreneurs are not extreme risk takers; (5) entrepreneurs collaborate more than they compete; (6) entrepreneurs act more than they plan; (7) entrepreneurship is a life skill.

4.3   Explore the different types of entrepreneurship.

There are many different types of entrepreneurship in practice today. Corporate entrepreneurship (also known as intrapreneurship) exists inside large corporations. Similar to corporate entrepreneurs, entrepreneurs inside also work in big organizations, but they are also found in other organizations including government agencies, nonprofits, religious entities, self-organizing entities, and cooperatives. Franchising and buying existing businesses are good ways to enter a business without the need to start from scratch. Social entrepreneurship is the process of finding solutions to some of the world's most pressing problems. Benefit Corporations, or B Corp, is a form of social entrepreneurship that rates organizations on social and environmental performance. Family enterprises, businesses owned and managed by multiple family members, are the dominant form of businesses in the United States and beyond. Serial entrepreneurs are constantly looking out for the next big thing, before handing over the responsibility to someone else, and moving on to the next idea or business.

4.4   **Identify the four pathways of idea generation.**

Entrepreneurs can use four different pathways or steps to identify and exploit opportunities: finding, searching; effectuating, and designing. Each pathway is characterized by different levels of complexity and uncertainty with designing being the most complex and uncertain.

4.5   **Discuss the IDEATE method of opportunity recognition.**

The IDEATE method—identify, discover, enhance, anticipate, target, and evaluate—is a useful way for students to begin building a skillset for identifying and selecting high-potential ideas that can be converted to new opportunities.

BUSINESSES DISCUSSED IN THIS CHAPTER

Organization	UN Sustainable Development Goal
BigBelly	11. Sustainable Cities and Communities 12. Responsible Consumption and Production 13. Climate Action 17. Partnerships to Achieve the Goals
DSM	2. Zero Hunger 3. Good Health and Well-Being 7. Affordable and Clean Energy 12. Responsible Consumption and Production 13. Climate Action
Dunkin' Donuts	5. Gender Equality 7. Affordable and Clean Energy 10. Reduced Inequality 11. Sustainable Cities and Communities 12. Responsible Consumption and Production
Eileen Fisher	5. Gender Equality 12. Responsible Consumption and Production
IBM	Contributes to all 17 goals
John's Crazy Socks	3. Good Health and Well-Being 10. Reduced Inequality
Kumon	3. Good Health and Well-Being 4. Quality Education
L.L. Bean	12. Responsible Consumption and Production
Logitech	7. Affordable and Clean Energy 12. Responsible Consumption and Production 13. Climate Action
Mass Challenge	10. Reduced Inequality
McDonald's	4. Quality Education 13. Climate Action
Oprah Winfrey	4. Quality Education 5. Gender Equality 10. Reduced Inequality 13. Climate Action
Seventh Generation	10. Reduced Inequality 11. Sustainable Cities and Communities 12. Responsible Consumption and Production 13. Climate Action

KEY TERMS

Benefit corporation, or B Corp (p. 72)

Business plan (p. 70)

Corporate entrepreneurship (also known as intrapreneurship) (p. 67)

Design pathway (p. 73)

Design thinking (p. 77)

Effectuation pathway (p. 72)

Effectuation (p. 69)

Entrepreneurs inside (p. 71)

Family enterprise (p. 73)

Find pathway (p. 76)

Franchise (p. 71)

Idea classification matrix (p. 74)

Opportunity (p. 74)

Search pathway (p. 76)

Serial entrepreneurs (p. 69)

Serial entrepreneurs (also known as habitual entrepreneurs) (p. 69)

Social entrepreneurship (p. 72)

TEA (p. 67)

BUSINESS CASE 4.2: WORKDAY—PLEASANTON, CALIFORNIA

SDG 7: Affordable and Clean Energy

Workday is everywhere, but it is likely you've never heard of it because the company is a tech powerhouse helping companies with financial and human resources functions—functions you don't really see. Workday is a SaaS company, meaning it offers "Software as a Service," and human resource and financial data are maintained and stored for its customers, which are other companies, in Workday's cloud. Today, Workday is one of the largest tech businesses in the world, servicing the needs of approximately 60 million users in 9,500 organizations globally, including more than 50% of the Fortune 500 and 23% of Global 2000 companies. The company was founded in 2005 by former CEO David Duffield and current CEO Aneel Bhusri, who previously worked for PeopleSoft, a direct competitor to Workday. Interestingly, David was a former CEO of PeopleSoft. Today, Workday is a publicly traded company worth over $60 billion.

David and Aneel, with a strong entrepreneurial mindset and significant industry experience, recognized that most businesses were investing lots of money into building hardware and software systems to manage human resources, financial services functions, and day-to-day business activities (such as payroll, expense management, accounting, employee benefits, and budgeting), or outsourcing these functions to other companies. Unlike many competitors at the time, they decided to set up an easily accessible system designed to manage finance, HR, and planning by offering companies cloud-based subscriptions rather than selling solutions that were maintained on-site, allowing for quick updates and customization. Companies are able to choose the subscriptions that best meet their budget and company needs, thereby eliminating the need for multiple or expensive software systems.

The idea of Workday seems complicated because it crosses many business functions, yet the power of the cloud-based software is that it offers an all-in-one product for medium-to-large companies to manage payroll, vacation and time tracking, human resources, accounting, procurement, expense reporting, budgeting, and other customizable features to meet the needs of Workday customers. Given the all-in-one nature, data are centralized and allow for better reporting and decision making.

Workday seeks to improve the lives of those the company touches. The SaaS solution resolves many data challenges facing larger companies, but Workday pays significant attention to its carbon footprint through its environmental sustainability plan that commits to:

● Achieving net-zero carbon emissions across all locations

● Using 100% renewable electricity across all locations—a goal it achieved in 2020

● Adhering to e-Steward standards for e-waste disposal

● Setting science-based emissions reduction targets

Workday is also one of the first companies to achieve a "lifetime net-zero carbon footprint," mitigating its historical carbon emissions. In addition, senior sustainability manager Erik Hansen oversees a Workday "Green Team" program, which helps to create sustainability projects in Workday offices worldwide. In fact, in its 2021 Global Impact Report, Workday outlined all the company initiatives that were directly aligned with UN SDG goals, further emphasizing the company's focus on sustainability.

Workday is also focused on diversity. Perhaps the company says it best: "From cultivating a culture where all employees can bring their best selves to work to deploying diversity initiatives that support all, we're doing what it takes to build a more equitable workplace and world." The company has signed the White House Equal Pay Pledge, put its name on the Business Statement for Transgender Equality, and signed the CEO Action for Diversity & Inclusion Pledge. *Fortune* ranks Workday as #5 on its "100 Best Companies to Work For" list, and 93% of people report Workday as being a "great place to work," compared to 57% at typical U.S.-based companies.

Critical Thinking Questions

1. Based on what you're read about Workday, with what form of entrepreneurship does the company most closely align?

2. What opportunity did Workday founders David and Aneel capitalize on when they started their business?

3. Where would you place the product that Workday offers on the idea classification matrix (Figure 4.3)?

References

Clark, D. (2012, October 12). *Cloud-computing firm workday's IPO soars. The Wall Street Journal.* https://www.wsj.com/articles/SB10000872396390444799904578052411733809482

Fortune. (2022). *100 best companies to work for.* https://fortune.com/best-companies/2020/workday/

Great place to work. (2019, August). *Workday.* https://www.greatplacetowork.com/certified-company/1269734

Lauchlan, S. (2022, March 2). *Workday accelerates into fiscal 2023 with a strong year end as cloud adoption gets a COVID-bounce.* https://diginomica.com/workday-accelerates-fiscal-2023-strong-year-end-cloud-adoption-gets-covid-bounce

Macrotrends. (2022, March 4). *Workday net worth 2011–2021.* https://www.macrotrends.net/stocks/charts/WDAY/workday/net-worth

Weir, M. H. (2018, April 20). *An inside look at the Workday green team leadership program.* https://blog.workday.com/en-us/2018/an-inside-look-at-the-workday-green-team-leadership-program.html

Workday. (2021). *Inspiring a brighter work day for all: 2021 Global Impact Report.* https://www.workday.com/content/dam/web/en-us/documents/other/workday-2021-global-impact-report.pdf

Workday. (2022). Workday.com.

Richard Levine / Alamy Stock Photo

BUSINESS MODELS

5.1   Define business model.

5.2   Discuss the most common components in a business model.

5.3   Explore different types of business models most used in business today.

5.4   Illustrate the Business Model Canvas as a tool for business model development.

5.5   Examine entrepreneurship as disrupting existing business models.

BUSINESS IMPACT CASE 5.1: IMPERFECT FOODS— SAN FRANCISCO, CALIFORNIA

SDG 15: Life on Land

Imperfect Foods delivers groceries on a mission. Cofounder Ben Simon, while attending the University of Maryland, was shocked to see how much food was being thrown away in his college dining hall. He recalls, "I was shocked to see someone buy a full sandwich, eat half of it, and throw the other half out. It was not the values I grew up with."[1]

Ben, along with three of his classmates, started the Food Recovery Network (FRN) in 2011. They recovered good dining hall food at the end of the night and provided meals to homeless shelters. By the end of the school year, they had recovered 30,000 meals for Washington, D.C.– area hunger-fighting nonprofits. During the spring semester of 2012, the second chapter of the FRN was started at Brown University, which was cofounded by Benjamin Chesler. In 2013, the Sodexo Foundation provided FRN with funds to hire full-time staff and turn it into a professional nonprofit. Today, FRN has 230 chapters in 44 states.

Given their early success with FRN, Ben, Benjamin, and Ron Clar founded a new business in 2015 called Imperfect Produce—a service that delivers seasonal produce that is cosmetically imperfect or deformed but perfectly okay to consume. "We wanted to think bigger about how to fight this food waste and create a more sustainable food system that was scalable," Ben said during a CNN interview.[2] Later, in 2019, Imperfect Produce changed its name to Imperfect Foods in order to expand its offerings.

The origin of Imperfect Foods was a reaction to daunting waste statistics. Approximately 20 billion pounds of produce on farms go to waste every year simply because "ugly" or "imperfect" produce does not match the aesthetic standards of grocery stores in the United States.[3] These aesthetic standards require uniform sizing and symmetry as well as being free from too many blemishes and scars. As a result, farmers are unable to sell a large portion of their crops—anywhere from 5 to 30%. This has a trickle-down impact on critical resources such as the loss of labor, land, and water that are needed to grow the unsalable produce.

At the start of Imperfect Foods, the founders wanted to sell their produce through grocery stores, but they quickly learned that grocery stores had little interest given the beauty standards they wanted. So the business model changed, and Imperfect Foods became an online store, selling its not-so-pretty and imperfect produce at a 30% reduced cost directly to consumers using a subscription model.[4] The company operates six distribution centers across the United States (as of June 2020) in Los Angeles, San Francisco, Portland, San Antonio, Baltimore, and Chicago, where it supplies food to its 200,000+ subscriber base across 43 states.[5] It sources its produce from 250 local producers all across the country and currently offers 50 to 60 produce items, plus 200 grocery items to its customers.

According to Ben in his CNN interview, "The important part of running a company founded by Millennials is to use the role of business to look out for people and the planet. As much as it's about making a profit, we hope to elevate the conversation about food waste, climate change and creating an equitable food system."[6]

Critical Thinking Questions

1. What is the business model of Imperfect Foods?

2. Who do you think is the company's primary customer?

3. Are there other ways to tackle the problem of food waste?

WHAT IS A BUSINESS MODEL?

Successful businesses meet customer needs by offering something of value. A *business model* describes the rationale of how a new venture creates, delivers, and captures value. Imperfect Foods provides value to the customer by selling heavily discounted produce, and its business rationale to fight food waste also benefits farmers, families with low incomes, and the planet.[7] It includes a network of activities and resources that interact to deliver value to customers.

The term *business model* was rarely in use before the 1990s, but the advent of the personal computer and the growing popularity of spreadsheets and modeling made it possible for people to strategically design the businesses they wanted before they were launched.[8] This meant they were able to create a roadmap that captures what the business is, how it works, and how it is financially sustainable. In other words, the business model is a roadmap that helps entrepreneurs to better understand how the pieces of their business fit together in relation to what they are doing, how they are doing it, for whom, and why.[9] Business models are relevant to both startup and existing businesses. For startups, thinking about the overall business model is a way to test the feasibility of a new opportunity. For existing businesses, it's a way to articulate how you are doing business as well as think about new spaces for innovation or growth. Business models are constantly evolving to reflect changing business environments and customer needs. The very idea of calling it a "model" shows that it's temporary, subject to change, adjustable, and flexible. Companies need to ensure and continuously reassess that their products and services both offer value to customers and generate the level of profit needed to sustain the business in the long term.

The Four Parts of a Business Model

A business model consists of four main interlocking parts that together create "the business": the *offering*, the *customers*, the *infrastructure*, and the *financial viability*.[10] No business is able to survive without these four parts. Each part has the potential to give the organization advantage over the competition. In other words, competitive advantage doesn't always come from the product or service you are offering; it can come from the other areas of the business as well. Let's apply the four parts to our opening case, Imperfect Foods.

The Offering

The first part of the business model is the offering, which identifies what you are offering to a particular customer segment, the value generated for those customers, and how you will reach and communicate with them. The offering includes the customer value proposition (CVP), which explains how your products and services can help customers do something more inexpensively, easily, effectively, or quickly than before. Imperfect Foods' CVP is to deliver seasonal produce to consumers that costs 30% less than produce they would buy at the grocery store. Not only does it save customers money, but it also adds value by saving its customers the time they would have spent going to the grocery store to buy this produce.

The Customers

Customers are the people who populate the segments of a market that your offering is serving. They are the individuals or businesses willing to pay for what you are offering. As you won't be able to serve everyone, you will need to choose the customers you most want to target, determine how you will reach them, and figure out how you will build and maintain a relationship with them. The majority of

Imperfect Foods' customers are people in their 20s, 30s, and 40s who want to play their part in tackling climate change by eliminating food waste. Imperfect Foods supplies food to over 200,000 subscribers in over 40 states and reaches its customers through its online store.[11]

The Infrastructure

The **infrastructure** generally includes all the key resources (people, technology, products, suppliers, partners, facilities) that an entrepreneur must have to drive the value proposition. Imperfect Foods' infrastructure comprises customer data infrastructure, employees (office staff and delivery drivers), an office based in San Francisco, and local producers from across the country who supply the produce.

Financial Viability

Financial viability defines the revenue and cost structures a business needs to meet its operating expenses and financial obligations. It helps entrepreneurs to assess how much it will cost to deliver the offering to their customers and the amount of revenue that can be generated from customers. Imperfect Foods generates revenue by running a subscription-based model that offers its customers a 30% discount on produce.

But the business model is more than just about how to make money; it is a fundamental way for entrepreneurs to assess why customers would give the business money in the first place: What's in it for them? This is where the most common components of a business model come in.

THE MOST COMMON COMPONENTS OF A BUSINESS MODEL

The components of a business model enable the entrepreneur to explore in greater depth how the company will create real value for customers, employees, and prospective partners, in addition to assessing the degree of competition in the marketplace and many other important factors. There are 11 common components of a business model.[12] Let's apply these components to global outdoor clothing company Patagonia (featured in Chapter 1: The Business of Business).

The Problem

Every new business begins with a problem. Successful entrepreneurs uncover what target customers need, provide solutions to meet those needs, and relieve the pain points—persistent or recurring problems (as with a product or service) that frequently inconvenience or annoy customers. Patagonia addressed pain points by first designing lighter, more functional climbing tools (heavy, less functional tools were a pain point for customers) before going on to offer high-quality general outdoor clothing and equipment.

The Solution

The **solution** outlines how the company intends to meet the customers' needs. Patagonia not only uncovered a solution to climbing gear and outdoor apparel but did so with a focus on protecting the environment—a factor that appeals greatly to its target customer base.

Key Resources

Key resources consist of the physical, intellectual, human, and financial assets at a company. Patagonia's key resources include the fiber and materials used for clothing and equipment, its employees, partners, technology, offices, retail stores, distribution centers, and intellectual property. **Intellectual property** is a category of property created by human intelligence that includes ideas, inventions, slogans, logos, designs, and symbols.

Customer Segments

Customer segments involve identifying the company's target customers. Dividing customers into particular groups helps companies to market to each group more effectively. Patagonia's customer segments include environmentally conscious consumers, climbers, surfers, snowboarders, camping and fishing enthusiasts, and hunters.

Value Proposition

The **value proposition** explains the uniqueness of a company's offering suggesting why a customer should choose your company over the competition. For example, Patagonia's value proposition is attractive to customers because it provides long-lasting, high-quality, sustainable products that cause no unnecessary harm to the environment. It also donates 1% of company proceeds to grassroots environmental initiatives, which appeals to socially conscious consumers.

Competitive Advantage

Every company has to deal with a certain amount of competition in its industry. Continuously assessing the competitive landscape is necessary to maintain a competitive advantage. For instance, Patagonia's main competitors include The North Face and L.L. Bean. Companies gain **competitive advantage**, a position of superiority or top performance, by showcasing characteristics that are not easily copied or bought elsewhere. Patagonia's greatest competitive advantage is maintaining high standards of product quality as well as ethical and environmental commitments that many of its rivals have found difficult to replicate to the same degree. It has also cultivated a strong corporate culture where employees want to work.

Sales Channels

A company's **sales channels** determine how the company reaches its customers. Patagonia's sales channels include its website, brick-and-mortar stores, and selected retail stores. Patagonia also engages with its customers by launching initiatives such as the Worn Wear Wagon—a mobile repair shop that travels around the country teaching people how to mend their own gear to save them from buying new apparel unnecessarily.[13] Customers are also able to resell secondhand Patagonia clothing through the Patagonia website and trade in their old garments at a Patagonia store for store credit.

Revenue Model

A company's **revenue model** identifies how the company will make money and generate profits. Patagonia's revenue model is based on revenue streams from manufacturing and selling high-quality outdoor apparel online and in physical stores.

Cost Structure

The **cost structure** represents all the expenses required to run the company and how those costs impact pricing. Patagonia's cost structure includes employees, raw materials, store rentals, donations, taxes, suppliers, distributors, and manufacturers.

Key Partners

Companies compete with others in their industry, but they also collaborate with key partners to get the work done. Using **key partners** such as suppliers, distributors, and other business associates can help the company grow and operate more efficiently, and these relationships may become a source of competitive advantage. Patagonia's partners include selected retailers, distributors, suppliers, and manufacturers.

Key Metrics

A company's **key metrics** show how the company measures success by tracking its overall performance. Patagonia founder Yvon Chouinard explains how Patagonia uses its key metrics: "At the end of the year, we measure success by how much good we've done and what impact we're having on society, not by profit."[14]

Now that we have explored the different components of business models, let's take a look at the different types of business models used in today's companies.

TYPES OF BUSINESS MODELS

There are different types of business models used for different businesses. Each type determines how the company makes its profits and who its customers will be. For example, a traditional car manufacturer's business model is mostly based on generating income from selling to retailers rather than selling the finished product directly to the customer. Let's take a look at 12 main types of business models (see Table 5.1).

Distributor

A **distributor** buys products from manufacturers and resells them to retailers or the public. For example, wholesale food company UNFI is a distributor that sources high-quality organic, natural, and specialty products locally and around the globe from producers and resells them to selected stores, which then sell the items on to their customers.

Retailer

A **retailer** is a person or business that sells products directly to the public either from a store or a website. For example, retail company Target sells general merchandise to customers through its stores and online.

Franchising

Recall from Chapter 4 that a *franchise* is a type of license purchased by an individual (franchisee) from an existing business (franchisor) that allows the franchisee to trade under the name of that business. The **franchising business model** is based on the franchisor helping the franchisee by providing support in marketing, operations, and financing. In return, the franchisee pays the franchisor royalties based on an agreed percentage of sales. The Mathnasium Learning Center based in Los Angeles, California, is a franchise that was set up to help children understand and master math using certain instructional techniques.

Eight-year-old Travis Maag-Brown studies math with Lisa Iguchi, co-owner of Mathnasium, after school. The tutoring franchise helps students in Grades 2–12 with math only.

Marty Caivano/Digital First Media/Boulder Daily Camera/Getty Images

Subscription

The subscription business model involves charging customers to gain continuous access to a product or service and earns money through repeat purchases. Before the internet took off, this type of model had been traditionally applied to magazines and newspapers that charged customers a subscription fee to receive each issue of the publication. Although these types of subscriptions still exist today, a growing number of online businesses also use the subscription revenue model. TV and movie–streaming on-demand service Hulu operates a subscription-based model whereby customers may sign up for a variety of subscription plans to gain access to their favorite shows.

Aggregator

The aggregator business model is a model whereby the company connects vendors and buyers on the same platform and sells its services under its own brand. Customers make purchases through the aggregators, which in turn collect a commission on each transaction. Online hospitality marketplace Airbnb operates an aggregator business model as it connects customers with owners who offer lodging or tourism experiences. It also makes a social impact by extending its services to house refugees and people who have been affected by natural disasters. Airbnb earns revenue by taking a commission on every booking.

Advertising

The advertising business model relies on the amount of revenue gained through advertising products and services. In the past, the advertising model was based on magazines and newspapers accepting advertisements and charging by the space or by the word; early radio and television did something similar by charging by the minute or second to broadcast ads. Today, advertising business models are most relevant in the digital world, where information is provided for free but ads are paid for by recognized sponsors. Google relies on advertising for most of its revenue. Vendors are charged for ad placement or sponsored search results. Google AdWords service charges the advertiser a fee every time a user clicks on the ad. AdWords also includes the cost-per-action (CPA) advertising model, whereby advertisers pay only when the click converts to an actual sale of a product or service.

Data Licensing/Data Selling

Companies use the data licensing/selling model when they generate revenue by selling or licensing high-quality, exclusive, valuable information to other parties. Some technology companies sell or license user data to third parties that use the data for advertising and analysis. There are more than 120 data brokers operating in the United States that buy and sell third-party data. However, some companies use data for different reasons altogether. Canadian digital company Bluedot uses data to help prepare the world for infectious diseases by gaining insight into the location of the outbreaks. By analyzing the data, Bluedot is able to figure out the best approach to combat the outbreaks.[15]

Software as a Service (SaaS)

Software as a Service (SaaS) is a distribution model in which companies offer their applications, software, and platforms to customers over the internet. The SaaS model operates on the basis of "pay as you go," where customers only pay for the services they are using. Multinational computer technology corporation Oracle uses an SaaS model that includes a wide range of cloud-based applications to meet the business needs of other organizations.

Utility and Usage

The utility and usage business model charges customers fees on the basis of how often goods or services are used. It operates in a similar way to the SaaS model, as it also offers a pay-as-you-go system. Mobile phone carriers may use this model by charging users a fee for the number of minutes used on calls or for the volume of text messages sent. Hotels use this model by charging customers by the night, and car rental companies also generate revenue through this model by charging per unit of time.

Professional

The **professional business model** provides professional services on a time and materials contract. For example, consultants, lawyers, and accountants often charge by the hour for their services. Websites like Get a Freelancer, PeoplePerHour, and Elance also use this model by allowing freelancers to charge a fixed fee for projects posted online by other companies.

People gather around a speaker during a lunchtime seminar on Elance, an online site for hiring freelancers, at a co-operative coworking space in Washington, D.C.

Mandel Ngan/AFP/Getty Images

Licensing

The **licensing business model** is a way of earning revenue by giving permission to other parties to use protected intellectual property (copyrights, patents, and trademarks) in exchange for fees. In the technology industry, the software we use on our computers is often under license from the developer of that software. Similarly, people who design the apps we use on our smartphones sell them to companies, such as Apple, that have the capability to market them to a wider audience. Global research organization Battelle, headquartered in Ohio, is another example of a company that licenses its technology to other organizations.

Freemium

The **freemium business model** involves mixing free (mainly web-based) basic services with premium or upgraded services. In this model, businesses create at least two versions or tiers of products or services. The company gives away the basic low-end version of the service, which comes with limits on usage, storage, and functionality, but charges certain premiums for higher-end versions that offer more storage, functionality, and performance. Professional networking service LinkedIn offers its core features for free but charges recruiters and job seekers for enhanced features that support job search.

TABLE 5.1   ■   Types of Business Models

Distributor	A model based on buying products from manufacturers and reselling them to retailers or the public
Retailer	A business that sells products directly to the customer either from a store or a website
Franchising	The process whereby franchises are sold by an existing business to allow another party to trade under the name of that business
Subscription	The amount of revenue generated by charging customers payment to gain continuous access to a product or service
Aggregator	A model whereby the company connects vendors and buyers on the same platform and sells its services under its own brand
Advertising	A model that generates revenue by selling ads for products and services
Data Licensing/ Selling	The revenue generated by selling or licensing high-quality, exclusive, valuable information to other parties
Software as a Service (SaaS)	A type of distribution model in which companies offer their applications, software, and platforms to customers over the internet
Utility and Usage	The amount of revenue generated by charging customers fees on the basis of how often goods or services are used
Professional	The amount of revenue generated by providing professional services on a time and materials contract
Licensing	A way of earning revenue by giving permission to other parties to use protected intellectual property (copyrights, patents, and trademarks) in exchange for fees
Freemium	The amount of revenue gained by mixing free (mainly web-based) basic services with premium or upgraded services

ETHICS IN BUSINESS

Can a Product Offering Be Unethical?

Running has always been a passion of yours and your "go-to" exercise for fitness and stress reduction. You decide to turn your passion into a business of making and selling running shoes. But you are faced with a quandary in terms of your product, which is central to your overall business model. In terms of your product offering, you could follow one of two options: (1) You could design your running shoes to last only 6 months to a year; or (2) you could design your running shoes to last double that time, and you know this is possible and doable given the materials available on the market. Yet you know if you go with Option 1, you may make more revenue, given runners will have to buy shoes more often. What would you do?

Critical Thinking Questions

1. Why is the product offering above so important to the overall business model? How does each option impact the business model?
2. Is choosing Option 1 unethical? Why or why not?
3. What if you went with Option 2? Could success be achieved?

THE BUSINESS MODEL CANVAS TOOL

Earlier in the chapter, we described the four major parts of the business model—the offering, the customers, the infrastructure, and the financial viability—and identified the most common components. In this section, we further explore how a company creates, delivers, and captures value for customers through the **Business Model Canvas (BMC)**. Introduced in 2008 by Swiss business theorist Alexander Osterwalder, the BMC is a one-page plan that subdivides the business model's four parts to further understand how to create, capture, and deliver value.[16] When the four parts are divided into nine components, the result looks like this:

- The offering constitutes the (1) value proposition.

- Customers relate to (2) customer segments, (3) channels, and (4) customer relationships.

- Infrastructure includes (5) key activities, (6) key resources, and (7) key partners.

- Financial viability includes (8) cost structure and (9) revenue streams.

Figure 5.1 illustrates the BMC's nine components using ride-sharing company Uber. As you can see from the figure, Uber's main *value proposition* is to connect riders with drivers—both of whom function as its main *customer segments*. It builds *customer relationships* through a rating system accessed by the *channel*, the Uber App. Uber's *key activities* include refining the Uber platform, recruiting drivers, and marketing and advertising, drawing from *key resources* such as its talented employee pool and driver network. *Key partners* such as payment processors, map tech companies, and investors enable Uber to adapt and grow as a business and help manage its *cost structure*, largely associated with paying employees, drivers, and legal fees. Uber's *revenue streams* include taking a cut of the fares and surge pricing (charging higher fares at peak times). Over the last few years, Uber has added UberEATS to its services—an app that allows people to order food from restaurants remotely for either pickup or delivery. For the purposes of this example, we have focused solely on the ride-sharing side of the business.

FIGURE 5.1 ■ The Business Model Canvas: Uber

BUSINESS MODEL CANVAS: UBER

Key Partners	Key Activities	Value Proposition	Customer Relationship	Customer Segment
• Payment processors • Map tech companies • Investors	• Platform development and maintenance • Marketing and ads • Hiring drivers • Operations	• Platform to connect riders with drivers • Easiest way around • Anywhere, anytime • Low-cost luxury • Various levels of service • Earn money when you want	• Rating system	• Riders: People who need a ride • Drivers: People who want to earn money driving
	Key Resources • Tech platform • Driver network • Talented employees • Brand		**Distribution Channels** • Uber app	

Cost Structure	Revenue Streams
• Employee payroll • Driver payouts • Legal fees • Marketing and ads • Tech platform costs	• $/km or mile • Surge pricing

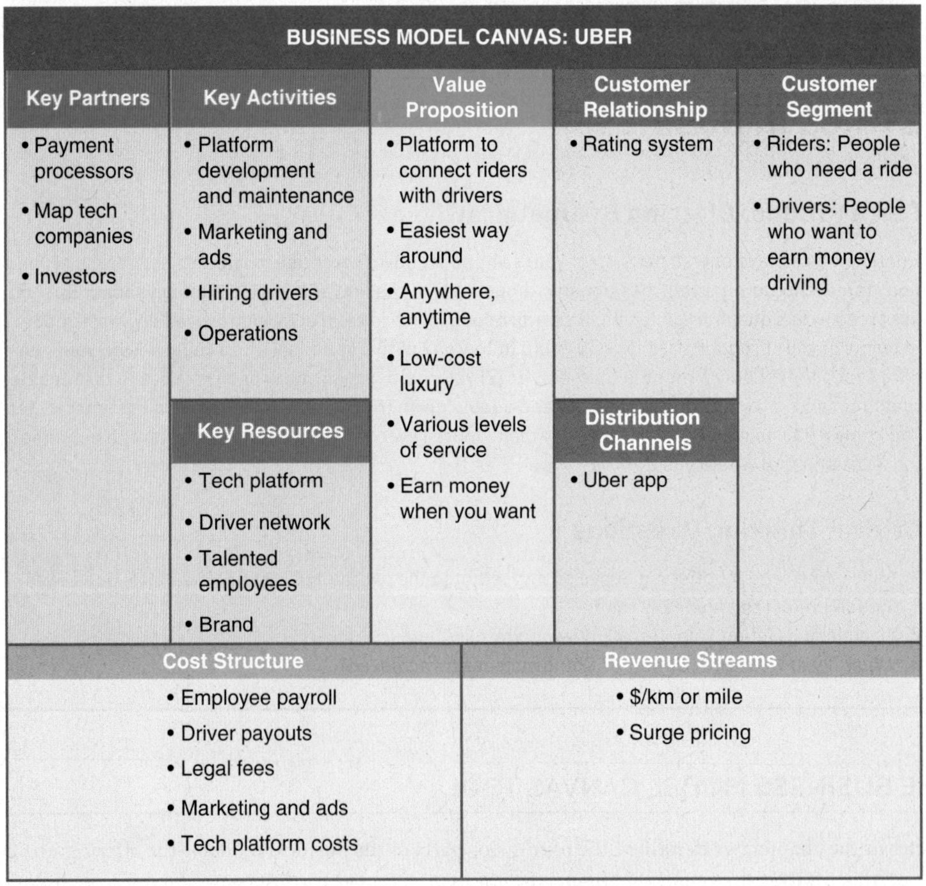

Source: Lokitz, J. (2017, November 2). *How to use the Business Model Canvas for innovation.* Design a Better Business. https://designabetterbusiness.com/2017/11/02/how-to-use-the-business-model-canvas-for-innovation/

Using the BMC for Ideation and Innovation

The BMC is a useful tool for inspiring creativity (ideation) and innovation, but there are several techniques that help to tell the "story" of what a company does and how it works. The following methods help to kickstart the ideation process when applied to an existing business model.

Freshwatching

The term *freshwatching* originated in the Netherlands. Freshwatching involves focusing on other companies, often from outside your own business or industry, to ignite new ideas:[17] in other words, looking at your company through the lens of another company. Applying other business models to your own allows you to think more deeply about how your company operates and may provide you with different ideas about how to make money. For example, your BMC for a traditional house-cleaning business overlaid by the Uber BMC (Figure 5.1) might inspire you to think about enhancing your business by offering an app that matches your customers with cleaners. On the face of it, a cleaning business has nothing to do with a ride-sharing business, yet looking at both together can provide you with some interesting opportunities and ideas.

Remove the Core

Removing the core is another ideation technique that involves taking the core value proposition out of your business model.[18] Figure 5.2 illustrates the Business Model Canvas for high-end car manufacturer

FIGURE 5.2 ■ Business Model Canvas: BMW

BUSINESS MODEL CANVAS: BMW

Key Partners	Key Activities	Value Proposition	Customer Relationship	Customer Segment
• Visionaries • Supply chain partners • Other car companies (e.g., Toyota) • IT companies	• Sales, marketing, and production • Innovation for a better driving experience • Develop future of mobility • Accelerating the pulse of the time (iVisions)	• Ultimate driving experience • 1, 2, 3, 4, 5, 6, 7, X, M series • Connected drive: Reach destination on time and relax • Remote services (find car, lock, comfort) • Active cruise control with stop and go • Full-electric i3, i8 (hybrid) • Connected drive, parking and charging included	• Always by your side, at your service • Love brand (car for life) • Co-pilot driver assistance	• Performance-driven, quality-minded people • Urbanites
	Key Resources • Efficient dynamics (fuel down, pleasure up) • Agile manufacturing system • BMW brand • Talented people		**Distribution Channels** • Online rental booking • Dealers • 3rd-party mobility service providers	

Cost Structure	Revenue Streams
• Research and development • Innovation and explorations • Production • Sales and marketing • People training	• Car sales • Service and maintenance • Leasing fees • Rental fees

Source: Lokitz, J. (2017, November 2). *How to use the Business Model Canvas for innovation.* Design a Better Business. https://designabetterbusiness.com/2017/11/02/how-to-use-the-business-model-canvas-for-innovation/

BMW. BMW's core value proposition is offering its customers the "ultimate driving experience." What happens if you were to remove this value proposition? What would the company look like without it? How would you fix it? Imposing constraints leads to new ideas.

Epicenters

Every part of the Business Model Canvas is dependent on the other parts. In other words, changing a component in one block will automatically impact another component in a different block. *Epicenter-based ideation* involves removing all the components apart from one.[19] Using the BMW example, what would happen if you removed everything but its key resources? Everything else might be gone, but you are still left with the BMW brand, a large pool of talented employees, a sophisticated manufacturing system, and efficient dynamics. The epicenter technique encourages us to think about what else we could do if we were left with such resources. Some of the answers could then be incorporated into the original Business Model Canvas.

Follow Patterns

Because each part of the Business Model Canvas is dependent on the others, they tend to create a pattern whereby one part depends on the other part to perform a number of activities, such as addressing new customer needs, creating new revenue streams, and so on. Recall from earlier in the chapter that some business model patterns follow subscription models to generate revenue, while others might use the freemium model to attract new customers. Following patterns on an existing Business Model Canvas helps to establish the type of business model for your new venture.

Ask Trigger Questions

Asking trigger questions such as "what if?" is a powerful way to inspire new, creative ideas. This method works best with a team. You could apply "what if?" questions to each part of the Business Model Canvas and make a list of the ideas with the most potential. Let's take the "channels" component from the BMW model, for instance. BMW's channels include car dealers and car rentals. What if those cars were sold online, instead? What would this mean for the business? What would it take to make such a significant change?

View of a BMW car for sale at a dealership in Shanghai, China. China is the main growth driver for the German luxury car maker.

Imagine China/Newscom

These five techniques are a great starting point for ideation and innovation. Some of the ideas you generate may fall into the scrap heap, but some could easily shift your perspective, helping you to see your existing Business Model Canvas in an entirely new light. Remember, a business model is really about how a business captures and delivers value, and sometimes the business model itself can be new and never seen before. In the next section, we will explore how some of today's most successful startups created a business model that not only captures and delivers value but also disrupts existing markets by displacing big, established companies.

ENTREPRENEURIAL MINDSET ACTIVITY

Identify a company you admire that also connects to one of the UN Sustainable Development Goals. For more information on the goals, refer to Figure 1.1 in Chapter 1. Once you identify the company, complete a Business Model Canvas on this company. You can use the template for a Business Model Canvas provided in Figure 5.3. Read about and research the company, and work to fill in the components of the business model. If you want to take this activity a little further, try completing a canvas on a business idea you have!

FIGURE 5.3 ■ Create Your Own Business Model Canvas

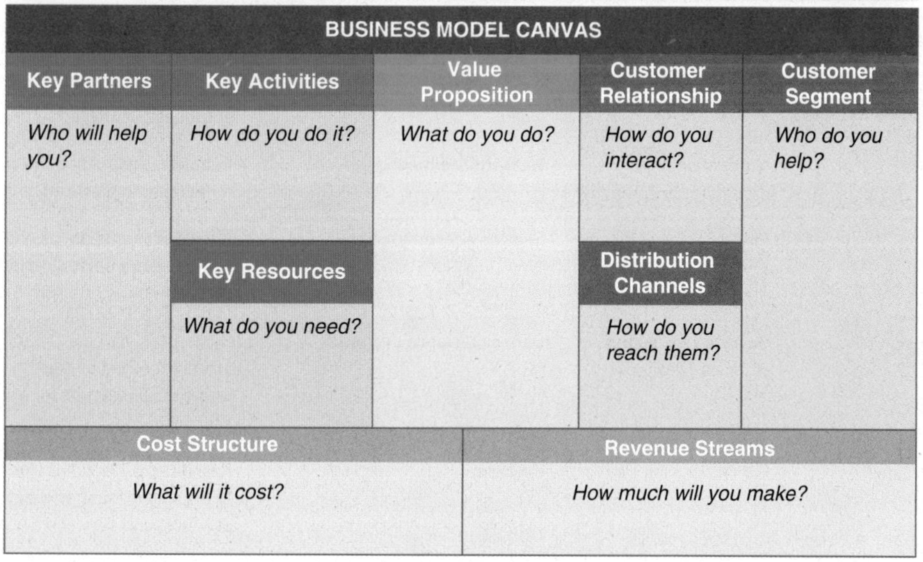

BUSINESS MODEL CANVAS

Key Partners	Key Activities	Value Proposition	Customer Relationship	Customer Segment
Who will help you?	How do you do it?	What do you do?	How do you interact?	Who do you help?
	Key Resources		**Distribution Channels**	
	What do you need?		How do you reach them?	

Cost Structure	Revenue Streams
What will it cost?	How much will you make?

Critical Thinking Questions

1. What information was most difficult to find about the company you admire most?
2. Can you identify the part of the canvas that really separates the company from others in its industry?
3. What type of business model is used by the company you chose? (See Table 5.1.)

BUSINESS MODEL DISRUPTION

A vast number of new technologies over the last few decades have changed either industry behavior (how businesses compete) or human behavior (how we live and work). This type of business model is called a **disruptive business model**, which is a model that creates new markets by addressing unmet needs by significantly improving or changing an existing business model.[20] Companies doing this (known as "disrupters") tend to start off by focusing on small or niche markets rather than immediately trying to compete with the bigger organizations. Unlike more established organizations, disrupters have more freedom to pursue opportunities, test their ideas, and take risks without suffering any major blows to their bottom line or their reputation. In other words, they have less to lose and are incredibly entrepreneurial. A classic example of a successful disruption is the failure of movie rental company Blockbuster.[21] Although Netflix was on the horizon, Blockbuster stuck to its retail business model, focusing on its rental stores. Netflix disrupted Blockbuster's business model by providing mail-based video rental and, later, on-demand access to movies, TV shows, and documentaries. When Netflix started to become successful, Blockbuster tried to make some changes, but by that time it was too late. Today, Netflix is one of the most successful startups in the world, while Blockbuster is operating with just one store in Bend, Oregon. Table 5.2 lists some more companies with disruptive business models.

TABLE 5.2 ■ Companies With Disruptive Business Models			
Company	What It Does	Disruptive Business Model	How It Works
LinkedIn	Professional networking site	Freemium	Offers basic options for free and charges for premium options
Netflix	Leading internet entertainment service	Subscription	Customer signs up and benefits from improvements or extensions to the service
Google	Multinational technology company	Free offerings	Provides free access to search engine but charges for advertising and personalized offers
eBay	Multinational e-commerce company	Marketplace model	Connects sellers and buyers on a common platform
Lyft	Ride-sharing company	Sharing economy	Allows access to goods and services for a limited period of time
Tesla	Electric vehicle and clean air company	User experience premium	Customers are charged a premium based on their levels of satisfaction for a product
Dropbox	File hosting service	Pyramid	Recruits people connected to the organization to resell products and services
Apple	Multinational technology company	Ecosystem	Designs a "lock-in" system where people can only use hardware or software from that particular company
Uber	Multinational ride-hailing company	On-demand	Provides immediate access to services that save customers time and money

Source: Talin, V. B. (2019, December 30). 9 disruptive business models for 2020—New opportunities for companies. *More than digital.* Retrieved from https://morethandigital.info/en/9-disruptive-business-models-new-opportunities-for-companies/

Disruptive Innovation

Disruptive business models are powered by **disruptive innovation**, a term coined by American academic and business consultant Clayton Christensen, which means an innovation that either disrupts the existing market by displacing established companies or creates an entirely new market segment.[22] Over the last few decades, many products and services have succeeded in shaking up the market: reference services like Wikipedia have disrupted traditional encyclopedias, video-streaming services like

Netflix have disrupted movie rental stores and cable channels, and cell phone cameras have disrupted photography companies, to name just a few.

Often a disruptive innovation starts off as a low-cost, simple solution initially launched in a small market. Because these innovations are typically overlooked by more established companies and tend to operate under the radar, disrupters do not face any challenges from competitors, at least at first. Because of this, the disrupters are able to move quickly and gain traction in the market, often throwing existing industries into disarray and toppling existing market leaders.

That's not to say that established companies don't innovate. In fact, most of them are innovating all the time. However, this level of innovation usually applies to modifications and improvements to existing products and services based on the demands of their current customer base, rather than the creation of new innovations. On the face of it, this might seem like a sensible move—to continue satisfying top-tier customers—but often taking the "safe" path puts the company at risk of being disrupted. Table 5.3 outlines some characteristics of disruptive innovators.

TABLE 5.3 ■ Characteristics of Disruptive Innovators
Low-cost, affordable, and accessible
Serve the small, niche market first (and then expand to a bigger market)
Go largely unnoticed by more established companies
Provide innovations that make life easier and are more accessible to people
Create new value rather than just improving on what already exists
Address the unmet or repressed needs of customers who want a new way of doing things
Provide products and services that are convenient, and have the ability to be personalized and customized.

Source: Wood, M. (2020, January 31). Why your company needs a disruptive business model. *Fundera*. Retrieved from https://www.fundera.com/blog/disruptive-business-model

How Companies Can Develop a Disruptive Business Model[23]

As Table 5.3 shows, many of today's most successful companies operate with disruptive business models. Here's what it takes to achieve this level of disruption.

Disruption Requires Research

Successful disruption involves a great deal of research. Disrupters need to take the time to identify the customer pain points that lead to viable opportunities. This involves focusing on the areas that are being neglected by other companies and working on some ideas and solutions that will go toward filling these gaps. Digital writing tool Grammarly uncovered some repressed demands of users to successfully check articles, emails, and dissertations for grammatical errors. Its digital tool allows you to check your writing for contextual grammatical errors, incorrect spellings, and more.

Unmet Needs

During your research, you may uncover some unmet needs. You might come across customers who are using existing products but are not fully happy with them, or you could discover a product that isn't doing enough to make the customer's life easier. For example, Airbnb discovered that the existing hospitality industry wasn't capitalizing on the unused properties available from owners to rent or lease to guests. It was also able to create more affordable service for a larger amount of people.

Innovation Is Key

Disruptive business models cannot exist without innovative ideas. Innovative products and ideas will only become disruptive when they have the ability to make people's lives easier at an affordable cost.

Sony is a good example of an established company that consistently explores innovative ideas. When Sony released its portable cassette player the Walkman in the late 1970s, the company succeeded in creating an entirely new market of young people who were keen to listen to music while on the move.

Sony introduced the first model of its Walkman in the summer of 1979. The Walkman was the first product that allowed individuals to listen to music whenever and wherever they wanted.

Thomas Graal/Alamy Stock Photo

Market Creation

Creating a new market isn't easy. The pain point is identified, the disruptive business model is developed, and then you can start attracting people to your innovation. Instagram created a whole new market by providing a social network where people could share their lives visually.

IN REVIEW

5.1 Define *business model.*

A *business model* describes the rationale of how a new venture creates, delivers, and captures value. It includes a network of activities and resources that interact to deliver value to customers. The business model consists of four main interlocking parts that together create "the business": the *offering*, the *customers*, the *infrastructure*, and the *financial viability*.

5.2 Discuss the most common components in a business model.

There are 11 common components of a business model: the problem, the solution, key resources, customer segments, value proposition, competitive advantage, sales channels, revenue model, cost structure, key partners, and key metrics.

5.3 Explore different types of business models most used in business today.

There are different types of business models used for different businesses. Each type determines how the company makes its profits and who its customers will be. There are 12 main types of business models: distributor, retailer, franchising model, subscription model, aggregator model, advertising model, data licensing/selling model, software as a service (SaaS), utility and usage model, professional model, licensing model, and freemium model.

5.4 Illustrate the Business Model Canvas as a tool for business model development.

Companies create, deliver, and capture value for customers through the *Business Model Canvas (BMC),* which is a one-page plan that divides the business model's four parts into nine components. The offering constitutes the (1) value proposition. Customers relate to (2) customer segments, (3) channels, and (4) customer relationships. Infrastructure includes (5) key activities, (6) key resources, and (7) key partners. Financial viability includes (8) cost structure and (9) revenue streams.

5.5 Examine entrepreneurship as disrupting existing business models.

Many of today's successful companies have developed a *disruptive business model* to address unmet needs by improving or changing an existing business model. Companies using this model (known as "disrupters") tend to start off by focusing on small or niche markets rather than immediately trying to compete with the bigger organizations. Unlike more established organizations, disrupters have more freedom to pursue opportunities, trial their ideas, and take risks without suffering any major blows to their bottom line or their reputation.

Disruptive business models are powered by *disruptive innovation*, which means innovations that either disrupt the existing market by displacing established companies or create an entirely new market segment.

BUSINESSES DISCUSSED IN THIS CHAPTER

Organization	UN Sustainable Development Goal
Airbnb	7. Affordable and Clean Energy 11. Sustainable Cities and Communities
Apple	7. Affordable and Clean Energy 12. Responsible Consumption and Production
Batelle	7. Affordable and Clean Energy 11. Sustainable Cities and Communities 12. Responsible Consumption and Production
Bluedot	3. Good Health and Well-Being
BMW	12. Responsible Consumption and Production
Dropbox	4. Quality Education
eBay	7. Affordable and Clean Energy 8. Decent Work and Economic Growth 12. Responsible Consumption and Production 13. Climate Action 17. Partnerships to Achieve the Goals
Google	12. Responsible Consumption and Production 14. Life Below Water 15. Life on Land
Grammarly	4. Quality Education
Hulu	7. Affordable and Clean Energy
Imperfect Foods	15. Life on Land
Instagram	4. Quality Education

(Continued)

Organization	UN Sustainable Development Goal
LinkedIn	5. Gender Equality 10. Reduced Inequality 13. Climate Action 17. Partnerships to Achieve the Goals
Lyft	11. Sustainable Cities and Communities 13. Climate Action
Mathnasium	4. Quality Education
Netflix	12. Responsible Consumption and Production
Oracle	3. Good Health and Well-Being 4. Quality Education 7. Affordable and Clean Energy 8. Decent Work and Economic Growth 9. Industry, Innovation, and Infrastructure 11. Sustainable Cities and Communities 12. Responsible Consumption and Production 13. Climate Action
Patagonia	12. Responsible Consumption and Production 13. Climate Action
Sony	13. Climate Action
Target	5. Gender Equality 6. Clean Water and Sanitation 8. Decent Work and Economic Growth 11. Sustainable Cities and Communities 12. Responsible Consumption and Production 13. Climate Action
Tesla	12. Responsible Consumption and Production 13. Climate Action
Uber	11. Sustainable Cities and Communities 13. Climate Action
UNFI	3. Good Health and Well-Being

KEY TERMS

Advertising business model (p. 89)

Aggregator business model (p. 89)

Business Model Canvas (BMC) (p. 92)

Competitive advantage (p. 87)

Cost structure (p. 87)

Customer segments (p. 86)

Customer value proposition (CVP) (p. 85)

Customers (p. 85)

Data licensing/selling model (p. 89)

Disruptive business model (p. 95)

Disruptive innovation (p. 96)

Distributor (p. 88)

Financial viability (p. 86)

Franchising business model (p. 88)

Freemium business model (p. 90)

Freshwatching (p. 93)

Infrastructure (p. 86)

Intellectual property (p. 86)

Key metrics (p. 87)

Key partners (p. 87)

Key resources (p. 86)

Licensing business model (p. 90)

Offering (p. 85)

Professional business model (p. 90)

Retailer (p. 88)

Revenue model (p. 87)

Sales channels (p. 87)

Software as a Service (SaaS) (p. 89)

Solution (p. 86)

Subscription business model (p. 89)

Utility and usage business model (p. 89)

Value proposition (p. 87)

BUSINESS CASE 5.2: APPHARVEST—LEXINGTON, KENTUCKY

SDG 1:   No Poverty

AppHarvest, an agricultural technology company based in Kentucky, has created a business model that not only focuses on customers but uplifts and empowers its workers. AppHarvest's business model reshapes the economy of an entire region of the United States as it revolutionizes the way farming is done. As AppHarvest founder and CEO Jonathan Webb puts it, "We are taking on the monumental task of redefining American agriculture."

AppHarvest was founded in 2017 as a public benefit corporation and a certified B corporation, which means it performs to the highest social and environmental standards in addition to performing a public good. Jonathan came up with the idea for AppHarvest in the hope of providing two public goods: to create a more environmentally friendly, sustainable way to produce crops and also to revitalize the local economy of the Appalachian region where he grew up—an economically depressed area that has been hit particularly hard in recent decades as coal is increasingly phased out in favor of greener energy sources. Jonathan's goal is to replace closed coal mines with high-tech greenhouses, making Kentucky and the wider Appalachian region the epicenter of agricultural technology (ag-tech).

An AppHarvest greenhouse isn't a regular greenhouse. The AppHarvest greenhouse is a massive, 60-acre facility (about 60 football fields) that uses cutting-edge technology to maximize productivity, conserve energy, and reduce environmental waste. The process brings together data analytics, robotics, and artificial intelligence. Hydroponic technology allows produce to grow up, literally, from floor to ceiling, rather than out, which allows for the growth of more fruits and vegetables while only using a fraction of the land.

An AppHarvest greenhouse is equipped with irrigation systems that only use 10% of the water that would normally be used in a traditional farming operation, and the climate-controlled greenhouse means that a vertical crop can grow all year long. These measures mitigate two huge farming challenges: the restrictions of seasonal planting and harvesting, and the increasingly extreme weather swings of drought and flood brought on by climate change.

Perhaps just as important as the innovations AppHarvest is bringing to the agricultural industry is the good it's doing by shifting away from fossil fuels that have decimated Kentucky and the entire Appalachian region in recent decades as a result of its reliance on the coal industry for job creation. Approximately 15% of Kentucky residents live below the poverty line. Jonathan is hoping to transform the region and the economy with new ag-tech jobs that will uplift current residents and improve the quality of life of generations to come.

AppHarvest has created hundreds of jobs through its first greenhouse, and the company will continue to create quality jobs as it expands from one greenhouse location to three. AppHarvest reports that 1,500 jobs will be created by the end of 2022. And the jobs AppHarvest creates are living-wage jobs—that is, they pay well enough for a family to live comfortably. The starting pay at AppHarvest is 41% higher than that offered by comparable jobs in the state of Kentucky. In addition to higher pay, the company offers what it calls "whole-family" benefits packages that include "100% company-paid medical, dental, and life insurance options."

Such comparably generous pay and benefits are part of Jonathan's broader strategy to help break the cycle of poverty and drug addiction in the region. AppHarvest is committed to hiring individuals who have suffered addiction and gone through rehab because, according to Jonathan, rehab isn't enough. "We've got to have a robust economy," he says, "where people can enter into, feel like they're a part of something, have purpose." And to ensure that these aren't just short-term remedies, AppHarvest is partnering with local schools and summer camps to introduce the next generation to agricultural technology. To end poverty in the area for good, Jonathan and AppHarvest are, in a very real sense, trying to plant the seeds early.

Critical Thinking Questions

1. With which type of business model that you learned about in this chapter does AppHarvest best align?

2. Think of another company that is trying to revolutionize an industry. In what ways is AppHarvest similar and different to this company?

3. As noted in the case, AppHarvest is a public benefit company and a certified B corporation. Do you think this is a beneficial corporate model for businesses? Why or why not?

References

Brand B. (2022, January 12). How AppHarvest is regrowing Applachia. *Allnewsbuzz*. https://www.allnewsbuzz.com/how-appharvest-is-regrowing-appalachia/

AppHarvest. (n.d). Impact. *AppHarvest*. https://www.appharvest.com/impact/

Farmer, B. M. (2019, March 17). Opioids and unemployment: Stopping the cycle. *CBS News*. https://www.cbsnews.com/news/opioids-and-unemployment-stopping-the-cycle-60-minutes/

Mullins, J. (2021, July 20). AppHarvest partners with Pike County Extension Office to teach children about AgTech opportunities and more. *WKYT*. https://www.wkyt.com/2021/07/20/appharvest-partners-with-pike-county-extension-office-teach-children-about-agtech-opportunities-more/

Spencer Platt/Getty Images News/via Getty Images

6 BUSINESS STRATEGY FOR COMPETITIVE ADVANTAGE

LEARNING OBJECTIVES

6.1   Define business strategy and explain its central role in business.

6.2   Describe four generic strategies and their connection to competitive advantage.

6.3   Analyze external factors to determine how competitive and attractive an industry is.

6.4   Assess internal organizational factors that help identify strategic resources, opportunities, and threats.

6.5   Discuss how hypercompetition is used to disrupt markets and even change how companies compete in industries.

BUSINESS IMPACT CASE 6.1: TESLA—AUSTIN, TEXAS

SDG 7:   Affordable and Clean Energy

When you hear "Tesla" you may think high-end, high-performing electric cars, and that's exactly what its brand is meant to convey. In a small but fast-growing electric car market, Tesla has risen to the top of the industry for consumers who want an electric car that drives like a fun, gasoline-powered luxury sports car—and even better. Tesla is working to redefine and reimagine what a car is, and today Tesla is considered the world's most valuable automaker. Yet it's really more than an automaker.

Founded in 2003 by two engineers, Martin Eberhard and Mark Tarpenning, with Elon Musk joining shortly thereafter, Tesla began with a vision that electric cars could be faster, better, and more fun than gasoline cars. Tesla now offers numerous car models but also builds large-scale clean energy generation and storage products for homeowners and businesses. Tesla believes "the faster the world stops relying on fossil fuels and moves toward a zero-emission future, the better."[1]

Not only does Tesla differentiate its cars by look, performance, and being 100% electric, Tesla has also reimagined the car buying experience. There are only two ways to buy a Tesla: online or through one of its 200 in-person showrooms or galleries around the world.[2] You won't see a traditional car dealership; you're more likely to buy a Tesla at a mall. Further, not all Tesla stores offer test drives, because some U.S. states don't allow them to due to dealership laws that have existed for years.

Tesla's entry strategy in 2008 with the introduction of the Model S was a type of strategy that we will discuss in this chapter called "differentiation focus." This involved targeting a product to a niche market of high-end buyers who wanted a luxury, high-performing electric car. As Tesla has gained market share and introduced a lower-cost model, the Model 3, it has moved to a broad differentiation strategy (another strategy we will discuss in this chapter), targeting more of a mass market who were willing to pay $38,000.[3] Think about it: You see a lot more Teslas on the road today than 10 years ago. Both in the beginning and now, Tesla outcompetes its rivals because few automakers, if any, match the product and unique features that Tesla offers. However, the competition is heating up as more and more automakers increase their electric car offerings.

The company also competes on levels that the average consumer doesn't see but that the industry does. Tesla designed an entirely new way to build an electric car. For example, other car builders use up to five different software systems rather than one, integrated system like Tesla does.[4] The result is a major performance advantage. Tesla also provides a solution rather than a product. Tesla provides the car, automatic software upgrades, charging, and insurance. It seems Tesla took all the problems or pain points out of car ownership—buying at a dealership and haggling over price, shopping for insurance, environmental effects of using fossil fuels, performance of an electric car.[5] As you will learn in this chapter, Tesla has also created a state of hypercompetition, which keeps its competitors guessing, watching, innovating, and wondering what CEO Elon and his team will do next.

According to Tesla's website, "With Tesla building its most affordable car yet, Tesla continues to make products accessible and affordable to more and more people, ultimately accelerating the advent of clean transport and clean energy production. Electric cars, batteries, and renewable energy generation and storage already exist independently, but when combined, they become even more powerful—that's the future we want."[6]

Critical Thinking Questions

1. How will Tesla's strategy change as electric cars become more mainstream and competition increases?

2. In what ways has Tesla disrupted the auto industry?

3. What do you think is the future of Tesla? Do some research on your own. What is the company up to now?

THE IMPORTANCE OF BUSINESS STRATEGY

Every business, big or small, needs a strategy to compete. Tesla, featured in our case, has developed a strategy that captures the attention of a growing market by creating uniquely designed electric cars with luxury brand recognition that can't be easily matched by competitors—at least not yet. A **business strategy** is a plan of action that helps companies develop a path to compete in an industry. During COVID-19, companies were forced to rapidly adapt their business strategies to provide innovative solutions for their customers. For example, fast casual Mexican food chain Chipotle opened its first digital-only restaurant to allow customers to pre-order online and pick up rather than engage directly with workers in the store. Chipotle's new strategy has resulted in a huge increase in online sales, and the chain is considering opening more digital-only restaurants.[7]

An **industry** is a grouping of similar companies based on their primary business activities. For example, car manufacturing companies like Toyota, Ford, Lexus, Chevrolet, Tesla, BMW, and Mercedes are all competing in the same industry. An industry is different than a market, which is a grouping of similar consumers who are often characterized by their buying habits.[8]

The discipline of strategy is more about industry analysis and competition, whereas marketing, as discussed in Chapter 5 and in the upcoming Chapter 7, is more about market analysis and customer acquisition. Using the car industry as an example, we could say there are different markets for electric vehicles (Tesla, Toyota Prius), high-end luxury (Lexus, BMW, Mercedes), economical (Ford Fusion or Toyota Corolla), and so on. In sum, strategy focuses more on how each business competes in an industry, whereas marketing focuses on markets or consumers.

Connecting Strategy to Mission and Vision

It is impossible to create a strategy without first aligning your mission and vision with your business goals. A mission is a brief description that articulates the purpose of an organization, and a vision is a forward-facing view of what an organization wants to become; but we will have a deeper discussion of these concepts in Chapter 10. The important consideration here is that strategy helps align all of these components for a cohesive business operation, purpose, and direction. As Figure 6.1 illustrates, mission relates to *what* will be achieved; stakeholders represent *who* is involved in creating value and direction; strategy establishes *how* resources should be allocated to achieve the mission and direction established by stakeholders; and vision connects to *why* people in the company should feel motivated to perform at the high level needed to accomplish company goals.[9] Taken together, the mission, stakeholders, strategy, and vision provide the what, who, how, and why required to stimulate action and execute strategy in organizations.

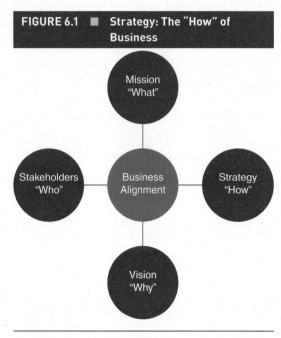

FIGURE 6.1 ■ Strategy: The "How" of Business

Source: Watkins, M. D. (2007, September 10). Demystifying strategy: The what, who, how, and why. *Harvard Business Review.* Retrieved from https://hbr.org/2007/09/demystifying-strategy-the-what

How Strategy Connects With Competitive Advantage

Strategy is really about how companies execute their business models (see Chapter 5). Strategy connects the what and how of the business model; it is the pathway to create and deliver value for customers, taking into account the level of competition in the industry and the strategic resources available inside the business. When strategy is used to outperform the competition, it's called competitive advantage. **Competitive advantage** refers to those factors that lead to a business outperforming its rivals and competitors. All strategies are based on getting a competitive advantage for a period of time over the competition. Sources of competitive advantage are extensive but can be grouped into three broad categories—cost, focus, and differentiation.

1. Cost refers to producing products and services at the lowest cost possible and thus charging the lowest price with no frills.

2. Focus refers to a narrow market, often termed a "niche." A niche market is a focused or smaller segment of a broader market where the product meets a very specific need.

3. Differentiation refers to offering elements of product uniqueness when compared to the competition. Companies can differentiate their offerings in many ways, including level of quality, design, features, brand, customer service, delivery, and more.[10]

These three categories of cost, focus, and differentiation lead to four generic strategies, which will be discussed in the next section.

Lefty's: The Left Hand Store in San Francisco is an example of a company gaining a competitive advantage by having a very narrow market focus.

Khim Hoe Ng/Alamy Stock Photo

THE FOUR GENERIC STRATEGIES AND COMPETITIVE ADVANTAGE

The most well-known academic in strategy, Harvard Business School professor Michael Porter, created what are commonly known today as the four generic strategies (see Figure 6.2).[11]

1. **Cost leadership strategy** is a strategy used by organizations to seek competitive advantage and gain market share by offering low-priced products. The market scope with this strategy is very broad as a company attempts to sell its product or service to all markets in the industry. Getting to a low-selling price can be a result of dramatically cutting expenses in the making of the product or reducing any type of frills associated with the product. Retailers such as Aldi and Walmart often use this strategy by offering reduced prices that compete against their rivals and win new customers.

Aldi uses a cost leadership strategy, offering reduced prices to compete for customers.

Daniel Acker/Bloomberg/via Getty Images

2. **Differentiation strategy** is a strategy used by organizations to seek competitive advantage by providing goods and services that are significantly different from the competition. This might include differentiation in design, functionality, brand image, customer service, mode of delivery, and other unique attributes. Apple is a good example of a company that makes unique products utilizing cutting-edge technology to attract customers. Once again, the market scope for this strategy is broad in that the company is going after most markets in an industry.

3. **Cost focus strategy** is a strategy used by organizations to gain competitive advantage by keeping costs and prices lower than their rivals while targeting a narrow market where products meet a very specific need, often referred to as a *niche* market. It is similar to cost leadership strategy, but the focus is on a narrow market. This is one of the more difficult strategies to implement because it can be difficult to target a niche market and also compete on lower price. For example, Old Navy targets working moms between the ages of 25 and 34 with low-cost clothing for kids from children to young adult with a niche focus on denim and inexpensive accessories. It carries everything The Gap carries, but at a lower price and expected lower quality.

4. **Differentiation focus strategy** is a strategy used by organizations to achieve competitive advantage by providing better-value products or services to a narrow or niche target market. As the opening case discussed, Tesla started with a differentiation focus strategy by offering a premium electric car to a high-end market (luxury car buyers). As time went on and Tesla was able to offer a unique car at a lower cost, Tesla used more of a differentiation strategy as it targeted a broader market rather than just the high-end luxury car market.

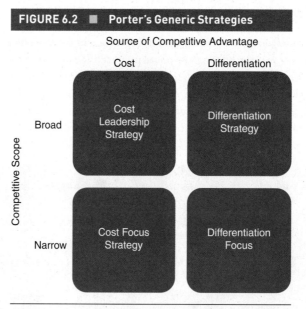

FIGURE 6.2 ■ Porter's Generic Strategies

Source: Porter, M. E. (1985). *The competitive advantage: Creating and sustaining superior performance*. Free Press. (Republished with a new introduction, 1998).

Figure 6.2 illustrates the different types of strategies that businesses can follow. These strategies help to define where a company fits within an industry in relation to competitive advantage and competitive scope. For competitive advantage, a company might compete on cost or differentiation, and for competitive scope, a company might compete in a narrow or broad market. These choices determine your overall competitive strategy and create organizational focus and direction. According to Porter, companies that make these choices will have a greater opportunity to achieve competitive advantage. But if a company lacks focus and chooses to play in multiple boxes, the risk, according to Porter, is being "stuck in the middle."

Stuck in the Middle

While Porter's four strategies may be useful to many organizations, they are not necessarily compatible with each other, which is why he cautions against using more than one at the same time. There are different risks inherent in each generic strategy, but being "all things to all people" is a sure recipe for mediocrity—getting "stuck in the middle." Organizations that are stuck in the middle lose focus on the direction of the organization, which results in a failure to establish a core market base, typically because products and services aren't unique enough to attract customers and their prices are too high to effectively compete based on price or the company assumes "everyone" is a customer.[13]

Roast beef sandwich chain Arby's is a good example of a company that became stuck in the middle: Its roast beef sandwiches were not any cheaper than other forms of fast food; nor was the flavor of the sandwiches a real differentiator, either. Parent company Wendy's sold Arby's in 2011 due to its poor performance. Since then, Arby's has made a big comeback by focusing on quality meats and innovative marketing strategies.[14] With its now-famous "We Have the Meats" campaign, which highlights quality products sold at a fair price, Arby's was able to become "unstuck" enough to compete with the other major players in the fast-food industry.

ETHICS IN BUSINESS

Is Cheaper Better?

As CEO of Hot Hats, a fashionable hats company, you are in charge of setting the strategic direction of your company. As such, you are responsible for deciding which strategy your company should adopt from a myriad of different options. One particular business strategy you are considering is a *cost focus* strategy so you can sell hats at an affordable price to young, urban, hip consumers. One idea you are pondering is contracting out the production of your hats to a factory in a developing country. This would save your company tons of money, given that the labor and materials in this developing country are cheaper than they would be in the United States. The downside to this strategy, however, involves negative social impact. In other words, your company's brand could suffer because the workers in these factories would be receiving very low wages and working in horrible conditions. Is the cost savings to employ this strategy worth it to your company in the long run?

Critical Thinking Questions

1. As CEO of your company, is it ethical to have your company's products produced in a country where the workers are making very low wages and working within very poor environments?
2. As a customer, would you buy products from a company that produces its products in countries where workers are treated poorly? Why or why not?
3. If you were an employee of Hot Hats, and it followed the strategy discussed above, would you say anything if you disapproved of how the hats were being manufactured?

EXTERNAL STRATEGIC ANALYSIS

A useful way to analyze the competition and understand where your company is positioned in a particular industry is to carry out an **external strategic analysis**, which is an objective evaluation of the environment in which a business operates. Michael Porter created the **five forces model** (Figure 6.3) as an external strategic analysis tool to help companies analyze the potential attractiveness of an industry as whole and establish whether it is worth entering or remaining in. If the analysis shows that the industry is not attractive, then it's unlikely to benefit a new company entering and competing with existing companies.

The five forces model highlights five industry forces that, when analyzed as either positive or negative, help a company better understand how competitive the industry will be and how likely it is that the entering company will succeed in the long term. The five forces include: competitive rivalry, the

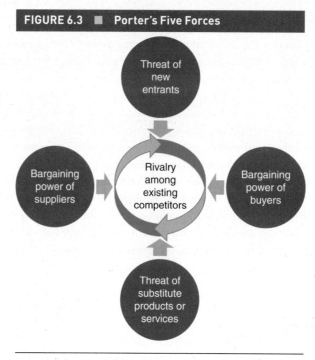

FIGURE 6.3 ■ Porter's Five Forces

Source: Adapted from Porter, M. E. (1985). *The competitive advantage: Creating and sustaining superior performance.* Free Press. (Republished with a new introduction, 1998).

bargaining power of suppliers, the bargaining power of customers, the threat of new entrants, and the threat of substitute products and services.[15]

1. **Competitive Rivalry**

   This force analyzes the intensity of competition in an industry. Rivalry competition is high when just a few competitors offer the same products and services in a growing industry and customers have the benefit of switching from one to the other. Fierce competition for market share can result in price wars, which can have a negative impact on the company's bottom line. Performance apparel company Under Armour is experiencing intense competitive rivalry from other sports giants such as Nike and Adidas, which have entered the performance apparel market to gain market share.[16] Nike and Adidas, as well-established companies, have the resources to make a serious impact in the performance apparel industry in the future.

2. **Bargaining Power of Suppliers**

   All companies need suppliers to provide them with the products and services they need to operate a business. This force analyzes the level of power suppliers hold and how easily they could raise their prices. Suppliers become powerful negotiators when only a limited number of them specialize in a particular area or when switching suppliers is considered to be a lengthy, costly process. Using different types of multiple suppliers is a good way to limit suppliers' bargaining power. For example, Under Armour uses dozens of manufacturers (suppliers) in many different countries to produce its products, which diminishes the degree of power any one supplier may have over Under Armour. In other words, if one supplier did not perform and tried to raise its prices, Under Armour would likely just drop that supplier and move more business to another supplier with which it works.

3. **Bargaining Power of Customers**

   Powerful buyers can heavily influence an industry and impact price and quality. Fewer consumers with the opportunity to easily switch sellers tend to have the most power. In contrast, consumers have less buying power when they are unable to get similar products from other sellers, when the switching costs are too high, or when the seller's product is heavily differentiated from those of other competitors. Under Armour's wholesale customers such as Dick's Sporting Goods have a degree of bargaining power, as they could choose to substitute Under Armour's products with similar products from competitors to gain higher profits. However, Under Armour's end users have less bargaining power because of Under Armour's clever marketing strategies, which have successfully boosted brand recognition.

4. **Threat of New Entrants**

New entrants into an industry put pressure on prices and costs as competitors try to maintain their customer base. The easier it is for new competitors to enter an industry, the greater threat it is for established businesses' market share. Huge costs are involved in entering the performance apparel market, which means that companies like Under Armour may not have to deal with the threat of too many new competitors. However, the entrance of existing sports companies like Nike and Adidas in the performance apparel market has posed a serious threat to Under Armour, and now, Under Armour is offering shoes in addition to apparel.

5. **Threat of Substitute Products and Services**

Certain industries can be threatened by new products and services that meet the same need in a different way. The demand for performance apparel is predicted to grow, which means that this force does not impact Under Armour as much because it is difficult for a competitor to create the same number of substitute products across such a wide range of sports with the same quality and material technology that Under Armour has.

If you were thinking of starting a new company offering performance sports apparel, you could use the five forces model to conclude that the industry is somewhat attractive. Although competition exists from some very large companies, an abundance of suppliers is available to manufacture products offshore at a low cost. Customer demand is increasing because the millennial and Gen Z populations are very large markets and most likely to buy performance wear, especially as they earn more income. Because competition is strong, consumers may choose from many options for athletic apparel, but if you have a unique fabric with new performance technology (say, 100% odorless), you might be a very attractive new entrant in the industry.

Keep in mind that the five forces model is just one analytical framework. It's not perfect, and there are other analysis tools, as you will see next. Always remember that it's not about using just one tool or framework to make decisions in business. It's about using multiple tools, getting lots of information from different perspectives, and then making decisions.

PESTLE Analysis

PESTLE analysis is another external strategic analysis tool for assessing the business environment based on six factors external to the business: political, economic, social, technological, legal, and environmental (see Figure 6.4). You have to look at not only the current situation for each of the six factors but also how they are changing. When analyzing industries, it's more important to look ahead than to look at the present. Let's apply a PESTLE analysis to soft-drink giant Coca-Cola.[17]

1. **Political**

Coca-Cola must comply with rules set by the governments in every country in which it operates and be prepared for changes in the law that may impact its manufacturing and distribution.

2. **Economic**

Coca-Cola is impacted by several economic factors that are out of its control. Some of these factors include changes in exchange rates, inflation, global economic and financial crises, and the rising cost of labor and raw materials.

3. **Social**

   Approximately 70% of Coca-Cola's income is derived from countries outside the U.S. This means that Coca-Cola needs to cater to the different customs, cultures, tastes, and preferences of its overseas customers. For instance, Coca-Cola created 30 flavors of soft drinks to appeal to its customers in Japan. In the U.S., as the demand for a healthier lifestyle grows, Coca-Cola has reduced the amount of sugar in some of its drinks to cater to the needs of its customer base.

4. **Technological**

   Coca-Cola uses the latest technologies in its manufacturing equipment to boost production and increase speed of delivery. It also uses social media technology to connect with audiences by running unique social media campaigns. One of Coca-Cola's most successful campaigns is the Share a Coke campaign, where the logos on the labels of Coke bottles were replaced with popular names. Consumers were encouraged to share photos of their personalized Coke bottles on social media through the #ShareaCoke hashtag. The result? More than 500,000 people shared their photos, and Coca-Cola gained 25 million new Facebook followers—all in just 1 year.[18]

6. **Legal**

   As Coca-Cola is a global company, it must adhere to the local laws of the countries in which it operates. For instance, it must abide by laws relating to labor practices and ensure that it meets the required standards for ingredients in its drinks. Following the highest ethical guidelines is key to preserving the Coca-Cola brand and reputation.

Share a Coke campaign, where the logos on the labels of Coke bottles were replaced with popular names.

Barry Tuck/Stockimo/Alamy Stock Photo

7. **Environmental**

   Coca-Cola needs to take certain environmental factors into consideration that might impact its ability to operate. Water scarcity brought about by climate change is a very real problem for a drinks manufacturer. If Coca-Cola doesn't have access to water, then it cannot operate. Equally, Coca-Cola must ensure that its own water processing operations are environmentally responsible, especially when operating in countries suffering from severe water shortages.

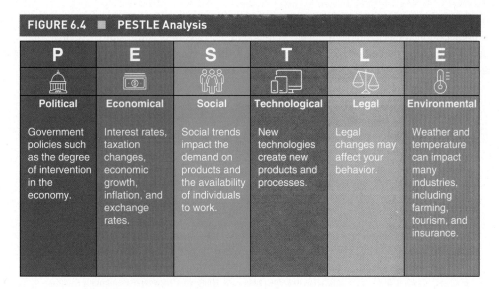

FIGURE 6.4 ■ PESTLE Analysis

P	E	S	T	L	E
Political	**Economical**	**Social**	**Technological**	**Legal**	**Environmental**
Government policies such as the degree of intervention in the economy.	Interest rates, taxation changes, economic growth, inflation, and exchange rates.	Social trends impact the demand on products and the availability of individuals to work.	New technologies create new products and processes.	Legal changes may affect your behavior.	Weather and temperature can impact many industries, including farming, tourism, and insurance.

By conducting a PESTLE analysis, companies like Coca-Cola will have a better chance of looking ahead, analyzing the factors that might impact their operations, and creating a strategy to cope with these changes if or when they arise. Output of a PESTLE analysis can feed into Porter's five forces as well as a SWOT analysis, which will be discussed a little later in this chapter.

Scenario Planning

Scenario planning is a strategic planning method for managing uncertainty that makes assumptions and predictions about different future circumstances (called scenarios) that could occur and then identifies responses and creates contingency plans for when or if such scenarios actually happen.[19] The military uses scenario planning to identify the range of possible outcomes of every event and puts a plan in place to manage both positive and negative consequences. Forward-thinking companies are using scenario planning to help them prepare for an uncertain future in a post–COVID-19 world. One of these scenarios involves identifying what happens should vaccines become ineffective against new strains. Although you may think of a multitude of different scenarios for your business, the goal is to create four different scenarios that are most likely to happen (Figure 6.5).[20]

1. **Identify your driving forces**

    The first step is to analyze the major external factors in the business environment. What societal shifts will impact your business? Are there any future changes in the world of economics, technology, or politics that will affect your company? Using PESTLE analysis could help here.

2. **Identify your critical uncertainties**

    Once the driving forces have been identified, choose the two critical uncertainties that will affect your business the most.

3. **Develop a range of plausible scenarios**

    Draw a quick matrix sketch with your two options as the axis. This will enable you to create four possible scenarios for the future, depending on what direction each of these uncertainties takes.

4. **Discuss the implications**

    Finally, take some time to discuss the impacts of each scenario and apply those findings to your overall business strategy and goals.

Multinational oil and gas company Shell uses scenario planning to engage in an uncertain future.[21] Early on, it identified certain global shifts including the impact of climate change on energy companies, the critical nature of energy efficiency, and changes in consumer behavior in relation to clean energy. Shell's scenario planning has highlighted the urgency of addressing these environmental issues, emphasized the importance of collaboration with government and society, and promoted the development and use of clean energy sources such as wind and solar power.

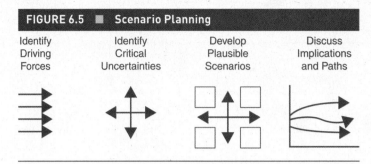

FIGURE 6.5 ■ Scenario Planning

Identify Driving Forces | Identify Critical Uncertainties | Develop Plausible Scenarios | Discuss Implications and Paths

Source: Adapted from Mariton, J. (2020, March 9). *What is scenario planning and how to use it.* SME. https://www.smestrategy.net/blog/what-is-scenario-planning-and-how-to-use-it

INTERNAL STRATEGIC ANALYSIS

Where an external analysis focuses on the industry environment, an internal strategic analysis is an objective evaluation of an organization's internal environment to identify its strengths and weaknesses. One of the most effective ways of assessing a company's internal environment is to conduct a SWOT analysis, which is a method of assessing an organization's strengths, weaknesses, opportunities, and threats (abbreviated as SWOT).[22] SWOT is a useful way for business people to define the current internal environment of the company, identify insights, and make strategic decisions.

Though opportunities and threats apply to the external environment, they can also relate to the internal environment. Once the SWOT analysis is completed, you can leverage and capitalize on strengths, improve weaknesses or minimize their impact on the business, look for opportunities that can help further develop the business, and consider threats—those factors that can harm the business. Table 6.1 lists a number of questions to ask in a SWOT analysis.

TABLE 6.1 ■ SWOT Analysis

Strengths	Weaknesses
● What are we known for?	● What is always causing us problems?
● What resources do we have available?	● What do customers not like about our product(s)?
● What do customers like most about our product(s)?	● What complaints do we hear most often from customers? From employees? From other stakeholders?
● Does our brand have value to customers?	● What resources do we lack?
● Do we have strong relationships with customers? Suppliers?	● What skills are our employees missing?
● What are we doing differently from competitors?	● Do we have enough employees? Do we have too many?
● What assets do we have in terms of people, technology, infrastructure?	● Do we have too much debt that is difficult to pay off?
● Do our employees have specialized skills?	● Is any of our equipment or software outdated?
● Do we have proprietary technology?	
● Does our location give us an advantage?	

Opportunities

- What are the new things happening in the industry?
- What are our customers asking for?
- What would be an ideal opportunity for us?
- What is the competition ignoring that we should go after?
- What are the weaknesses of our competitors?
- Are there opportunities for geographic expansion?
- Are there any trends we should pay attention to?
- Is there emerging technology we can utilize?

Threats

- What competitors are we not paying attention to, and what are they doing?
- Has there been an increase in competition lately?
- Are our competitors growing faster than us?
- Can we afford new resources we need? If not, what will happen?
- Are there any new competitors entering the industry?
- Are we losing customers to competitors? Why?
- Can technology make us obsolete?
- How can the current state of the economy hurt us?

Sources: Frue, K. (2017, September 12). The best 20 questions to ask in SWOT analysis. *PESTLE Analysis.* Retrieved from https://pestleanalysis.com/20-questions-about-swot-analysis/; 48 questions to ask in your SWOT analysis. (2017, July 12). *SCORE.* Retrieved from https://www.score.org/resource/48-questions-ask-your-swot-analysis

Let's apply a SWOT analysis to a California diner called Friendly Burgers that sells meatless burgers made from plant products. In addition to burgers, the diner sells frozen takeout options and provides a variety of fresh salads and healthy beverages such as smoothies and juices made from natural ingredients. The company is in the process of opening its first location in downtown Riverside, California, and intends on expanding quickly to offer franchising opportunities in the future. Table 6.2 lists Friendly Burgers' SWOT analysis.

TABLE 6.2 ■ SWOT Analysis: Friendly Burgers

Strengths	Weaknesses	Opportunities	Threats
Location: The downtown location will attract more traffic from visitors and shoppers.	Lack of capital: To date, all the funds have come from loans and investors.	Area growth: The population of Riverside is growing by 8% every year, which might help to attract more customers.	Competition: There is one other competitor in the area that also sells meatless burgers made from a similar recipe. This diner also has an established customer base.
Uniqueness: The meatless burger is a unique alternative to fast food and will appeal to environmentally conscious diners.	Lack of reputation: This is a new business that hasn't yet established a reputation.	Working families with children: The diner could appeal to two-income families who have less time to cook but want to provide their children with healthier meal options.	Being unprepared for opening numbers: Poor preparation could lead to bad service and compromised product quality, which may put off first-time customers.
Strong management: The team members each have the skills to run this sort of business, from experience in running restaurants, to accountancy, to people management.	Skeptical customers: It might take time to convince customers to change their dietary habits and become regular visitors to the diner.		

ENTREPRENEURIAL MINDSET ACTIVITY

Your Personal SWOT Analysis

Strategy is often seen as a "corporate" activity where a company is trying to figure out how to out-compete its rivals. But as individuals, especially entrepreneurial individuals, we should be able to apply some of the strategic tools introduced in this chapter to our own lives. In this mindset activity, you are challenged to do a SWOT analysis on YOU! What are your strengths, weaknesses, opportunities, and threats? Use one sheet of paper; draw two lines so you have four squares similar to the table below.

| Strengths | Weaknesses |
| Opportunities | Threats |

Look back at the questions in the table and ask yourself similar questions. For example, for strengths ask yourself: What am I known for? What resources do I have available? What are my top three skills? What do I do differently from others?

For weaknesses, you could ask yourself: What do I always struggle with? What do my friends criticize me the most for? What resources do I lack? What skills do I lack?

For opportunities, you could ask yourself: What new trends are happening around me that excite me? Are there opportunities for me to move someplace new to advance my career? What will I do with my college degree? What would be an ideal opportunity for me?

Finally, for threats, you could ask yourself: Am I pursuing a career that could be replaced by robots? Are there too many people doing what I want to do? Do I not have enough education to get to the next level?

You can answer the above questions or create your own to better help you record your strengths, weaknesses, opportunities, and threats to complete your personal SWOT analysis. Upon completion, answer the critical thinking questions below:

Critical Thinking Questions

1. How can you capitalize on your strengths?
2. Are you doing things that play to your weaknesses when you should be engaging in activities that play to your strengths?
3. Is there a weakness that you would like to make a strength, and how might you do that?
4. Is there an opportunity that you really want to pursue? How might you do that?
5. Are there any threats that could be turned into opportunities?

Resource-Based View

A **resource-based view** is a theoretical framework that helps businesses identify sources of competitive advantage.[23] It's considered an internal analysis tool because it requires the organization to "look inside" to find the source of competitive advantage rather than looking outside, as with some of the external analysis tools described in the previous section. The resource-based view uses **VRIO analysis**, which is a four-question framework to assess whether a resource is valuable, rare, inimitable, and if the business is organized enough to capture value from that resource.[24] The framework can also be used on products, services, and entire organizations. Figure 6.6 illustrates the four-question framework in greater detail.

According to the resource-based theory, long-term competitive advantage is achievable when these conditions (valuable, rare, inimitable, organized) are met, in which case the resource is considered a strategic resource. A **resource** is something that adds value. Inside a company, resources include human resources (employees, knowledge, skills), financial resources (money, shares), material resources (machinery, equipment), and nonmaterial resources (informational, capital). A bundle or grouping of resources is called a **capability,** which can be used to do something new, innovative, or strategic. For example, Apple has a capability in smartphone design, but that capability is a function of talented

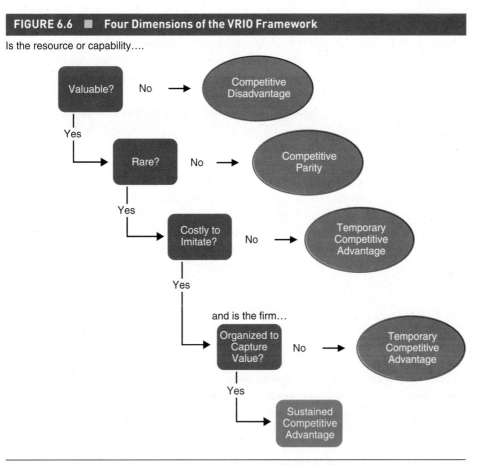

FIGURE 6.6 ■ Four Dimensions of the VRIO Framework

Is the resource or capability....

Source: Jerevicius, O. (2021, November 11). VRIO framework explained. *Strategic Management Insight.* https://strategicmanagementinsight.com/tools/vrio/

designers, programmers, and research and development—all of which are resources. Apple's design capability is something that makes many of the company's products valuable, rare, and inimitable, while also aligning with the organization's skills, knowledge, and even culture. Figure 6.6 also mentions **competitive parity**, which describes the average capabilities of a company in a particular area as compared to other companies in the same industry. In competitive parity, the company is maintaining a competitive position similar to others.[25] For example, two cars in the same class, such as two compact crossover SUVs like a Honda CRV and Ford Escape, have competitive parity. Let's explore the four dimensions of the VRIO framework, using Google as an example.[26]

Valuable

The first question asks whether a resource is valuable. A resource is valuable when it adds value by enabling the company either to take advantage of opportunities or defend against threats. However, even if a resource is valuable, if it doesn't fit into the other dimensions of the VRIO framework, it will not achieve competitive advantage. A resource will only add value if it is considered rare and costly to imitate. Google's most valuable resource is its people. It hires people based on human capital management data to find the most innovative and productive employees. High levels of talent mean that Google's employees consistently develop some of the most popular products and services in the world.

Rare

A resource is considered rare when it is uncommon and can only be acquired by very few other companies. Rare and valuable resources can achieve competitive advantage, but only temporarily, as they will likely be imitated by competitors. Google's data-based talent management strategy is considered to be rare, as no other companies seem to following the same approach so extensively.

Costly to Imitate

Resources are difficult to imitate if they are expensive for another organization to acquire or if they are protected by legal means. Although a resource may be valuable, rare, and costly to imitate, it will not gain competitive advantage if the organization isn't organized enough to capture that value. Data-based human capital management is expensive and very difficult to imitate, as companies need to invest in building their own sophisticated platform and finance the cost of training their staff on the new technology.

Organized to Capture Value

Companies can get organized to capture value by putting the right systems, processes, policies, and structures in place to realize the potential of the resource. Only businesses that are capable of exploiting resources that are considered valuable, rare, and costly to imitate will be able to gain sustained competitive advantage. Google is organized to capture value from its data-based human capital management because of the high level of trained staff: The information technology (IT) department is populated with people who have the right skills to collect and maintain the data, and human resources (HR) teams have been trained to use the data to hire, promote, and manage employees.

Competitive Profile Matrix

A **competitive profile matrix (CPM)** is a tool that allows you to compare your business to competitors so that your strengths and weaknesses (and theirs) are revealed.[27] The CPM requires an understanding of critical success factors in a particular industry, and every industry is different. **Critical success factors** are internal and external factors required by businesses to perform at the highest levels in an industry.[28] Table 6.3 lists some general critical success factors that are commonly used, but this list is certainly not exhaustive.

TABLE 6.3 ■ Common Critical Success Factors		
Market share	Power over suppliers	Product quality
Skilled employees	Access to key suppliers	Clear strategic direction
Location of facilities	Production capacity	Sales capacity
Ability to reach customers easily	Customer service (after sale)	Product features
Brand reputation	Price competitiveness	Strong online presence
Effective social media management	Employee satisfaction	High level of corporate social responsibility
Variety of products	Profit margin	Entrepreneurial culture
Fast inventory turnover	R&D spending	Product design
Positive cash flow	New patents per year	Income per employee
Superior marketing capabilities	Quality operations	Effective supply chain

Source: Jurevicius, O. (2013). Competitive profile matrix. *Strategic Management Insight.* Retrieved from https://strategicmanagementinsight.com/tools/competitive-profile-matrix-cpm.html

Once the most important key success factors in your industry have been identified and applied to particular competitors, you can start creating the matrix. Each critical success factor should be assigned a weight ranging from 0.0 (low importance) to 1.0 (high importance), and the sum of all factors should add up to 1. The more important a critical success factor, the higher the weight will be. Next, you assign each company a score for every critical success factor, which can range from 4 to 1—where 4 means major strength, 3 means minor strength, 2 means minor weakness, and 1 means major weakness.

The total score is calculated by multiplying the weight of each critical success factor by the rating. Companies with the highest score are considered to perform better than their competitors. Table 6.4 lists the weights, ratings, and scores of three main competitors and their smartphone operating systems: Google's Android OS, Apple's iOS, and Microsoft's Windows Phone. The CPM analysis shows strengths and weaknesses across all three systems. For example, Android scores highly in several critical success factors including distribution channels, company brand reputation, and customization. However, iOS scores better than Android for frequency of updates, marketing capabilities, and the rate of OS crashes.

Overall, Android is the strongest player but has less market share than iOS. Windows is clearly the poorest performing in the industry, which makes sense. In 2019, Microsoft stopped offering the Windows Phone. Maybe it should have done a CPM earlier on!

TABLE 6.4 ■ CPM Analysis

CPM Example

Critical Success Factor	Weight	Android OS		iOS		Windows Phone	
		Rating	Score	Rating	Score	Rating	Score
Market share	0.13	4	0.52	2	0.26	2	0.26
Number of apps in store	0.10	4	0.40	4	0.40	2	0.20
Frequency of updates	0.06	3	0.18	4	0.24	2	0.12
Design	0.07	3	0.21	3	0.21	3	0.21
Product brand reputation	0.05	3	0.15	3	0.15	2	0.10
Distribution channels	0.11	4	0.44	2	0.22	3	0.33
Usability	0.11	3	0.33	3	0.33	3	0.33
Customization features	0.04	4	0.16	2	0.08	2	0.08
Marketing capabilities	0.04	2	0.08	4	0.16	2	0.08
Company brand reputation	0.10	4	0.40	4	0.40	3	0.30
Openness	0.02	4	0.08	2	0.04	2	0.04
Cloud integration	0.12	4	0.48	2	0.24	2	0.24
Rate of OS crashes	0.08	1	0.08	4	0.32	3	0.24
Total	1.00	-	3.51		3.05	-	2.53

Source: Jurevicius, O. (2013). Competitive profile matrix. *Strategic Management Insight.* Retrieved from https://strategicmanagementinsight.com/tools/competitive-profile-matrix-cpm.html

HYPERCOMPETITION

Many of the frameworks introduced in this chapter were built to help companies develop long-term competitive advantage. Though the tools are still relevant and useful, the concept of long-term competitive advantage is more of an anomaly than an expectation. And when a company believes its competitive advantage can't be taken away, it may be in for a big surprise. Kodak is a good example, here. Kodak was synonymous with film and cameras, but it ignored the coming revolution of digital photography.

It's not that the company wasn't aware of it. In fact, it was a Kodak engineer who invented the first digital camera in 1975, but the corporate response was, "That's cute, but given that it's filmless, we are not interested."[29] Today's companies, large and small, are constantly in search of the next competitive advantage. The companies that we thought were once invincible—IBM, Microsoft, Walmart—are sometimes one big innovation away from being knocked off the top of the mountain, especially when they do not acknowledge the presence of hypercompetition.

Hypercompetition is characterized by intense competitive action and rapid innovation in an industry that forces competitors to respond quickly. Companies that create their own competitive advantages are more likely to eliminate the benefits of their rivals. According to Richard d'Aveni, the researcher who developed the concept of hypercompetition, the best-performing companies disrupt the market by behaving as if there are no entry barriers or boundaries to prevent them from toppling their rivals.[30]

D'Aveni also believes that the traditional approach to competition, which involved defining an industry, reducing competition, and avoiding competition, no longer works. Instead, it's all about disruption. Companies are shortening product life cycles, entering markets they were never previously in, and making competitive moves that were once regarded as incredibly risky, but in hypercompetitive industries, like computers, smartphones, and e-commerce, aggressive competition is the new normal.[31] If Kodak had acknowledged its industry was becoming hypercompetitive and responded quickly, it might not only have survived but thrived and excelled in digital photography.

As previously mentioned, the pace of business is changing so quickly today that stable and ongoing competitive advantage is almost impossible to maintain. Industry lines are blurring, which makes it very difficult to set strategy and compete in the long term. The most successful companies realize that competitive advantages are short-lived and defending one position and only one position no longer works.[32] Today, you have a company like Amazon that is competing against Walmart in retail while starting to compete in health care against hospitals and pharmaceutical companies.[33] Operating in a hypercompetitive environment does not mean creating a sustainable competitive advantage in a particular industry and striving to maintain the status quo, like Kodak, but rather engaging in a cycle of finding and building temporary advantage by disrupting markets. This is called *transient advantage*. According to Rita McGrath, a world-renowned researcher of competitive strategy, transient advantages require starting new strategic initiatives and exploiting many short-term competitive advantages at the same time.[34]

By definition, transient advantage is a strategy that assumes competitive advantages are temporary and requires continuous innovation to maintain any type of competitive positioning.[35] Transient advantage has a life cycle of launch, ramp up, exploitation, and reconfigure.[36] *Launch* is recognizing a new opportunity and mobilizing resources, *ramp up* is about scaling and proving the opportunity is viable and has a market, and *exploitation* is when the product is brought to market and profits are realized, requiring competitors to react. Finally, *reconfigure* is when the competitive advantage starts to weaken, so the company has to reconfigure resources to do something differently.

Sounds very entrepreneurial, doesn't it? In modern business today, even the largest companies are acting more entrepreneurial in order to achieve transient advantage. The smartphone competition between Apple and Samsung is a clear example of this. Each launch of a new phone offers new features, new design, or better technology. Samsung's introduction of the Galaxy Z Fold phone is creating a transient advantage for the company. Apple has yet to introduce a foldable version of its iPhone.

Kodak failed to engage in hypercompetition and saw its industry disrupted by digital cameras.

iStock.com/Baiploo

The 7S's Hypercompetition Model

McGrath's concept of transient advantage connects to D'Aveni's **7S's hypercompetition model**, which is a framework that guides companies to continuously create competitive advantage in disruptive environments (Figure 6.7). The 7S's framework includes: stakeholder satisfaction, strategic soothsaying, speed, surprise, signals, shifting the rules, and simultaneous strategic thrusts.

1. Stakeholders include anyone directly or indirectly impacted by the company (employees, suppliers, customers, community members, and investors, just to name a few). As a result, stakeholder satisfaction is important to gaining competitive advantage. Customers are the most critical stakeholders, but employees are also important because they are the people who will be creating new products, services, and processes for the customer. Universally accessible language learning platform Duolingo, based in Pittsburgh, has attracted over 300 million active monthly users worldwide. Its website section allows its users and employees to suggest improvements for projects and initiatives that are in development.[37] By involving its stakeholders in the development process, Duolingo is able to build products that appeal to its target market.

2. Strategic soothsaying is the process of finding out information that enables companies to predict what customers will want in the future. Ohio-based multinational consumer goods corporation Procter & Gamble operates a GrowthWorks program to create products that address pain points and satisfy customer needs. First, consumer research is conducted to identify the problem, then a small team creates prototypes and carries out experiments to test the viability of the ideas. By assessing customer needs and going through this process of experimentation, Procter & Gamble has a higher chance of providing products that customers will want in the future.[38]

3. Speed enables companies to disrupt the status quo, destroy advantages gained by other companies, and create new advantages before those companies can react. Videoconferencing platform Zoom quickly became the most important app in the world during the COVID-19 pandemic. In December 2019, Zoom had 10 million daily meeting participants. By June 2020, that number had grown to 300 million.[39] Millions of people used Zoom to stay connected to their families and work colleagues. Many universities started using Zoom to teach online learning activities, and doctors used it to remotely diagnose patients and conduct online consultations.[40] Zoom has outpaced its competitors Google, Webex, Skype, and others by providing better features and improved functionalities. For instance, it offers limited services for free and ensures that the program can be accessed on any device, including laptops, iPads, iPhones, desktops, and Androids.[41]

4. Surprise allows a company to create a competitive advantage by immobilizing its competitors before they can launch a counterattack. Ride-sharing startup Firefly has taken its competitors Uber, Lyft, and others by surprise by working directly with drivers to place digital ads on top of their cars. The digital screens will display ads based on driver routes and area demographics.[42] Firefly drivers also earn an additional $300 from the ads, which boosts the notoriously low wages earned by drivers with rival ride-sharing companies.

5. Signals are the verbal announcements of a new product or service intended to throw the competitor off balance. For instance, when companies hear a new product being announced, it forces them to assess their own products and consider whether they need to be redesigned. For example, Tesla announced that it is planning to launch a new low-cost battery pack that lasts 1 million miles before it needs to be replaced.[43] The announcement has sparked automakers such as Toyota and General Motors to develop and build their own long-lasting battery packs to power their electric vehicles.[44]

6. Shifting the rules means transforming the rules of the market, which can be incredibly disruptive for competitors. For example, the Gillette Company shifted the rules in shaving

by creating a premium version of the disposable razor called the Sensor.[45] This new product transformed the market by focusing on high quality, price, and convenience, rather than just the previous priority of convenience and price.

7. Simultaneous strategic thrusts take place when companies carry out several strategic moves at the same time or in quick succession—such as making a series of product announcements or entering multiple geographic markets at once—all with the goal of confusing the competition. For example, many years ago when people started to buy personal computers for home use, Dell stunned IBM and the rest of the computer industry when it launched several simultaneous strategic moves including successful direct mail, telephone sales, and direct-to-consumer shipping from new distribution centers. Though commonplace today, this distribution model had never been done before.[46] Dell's competitors were forced to scramble to compete with Dell as they fought to reclaim market share.

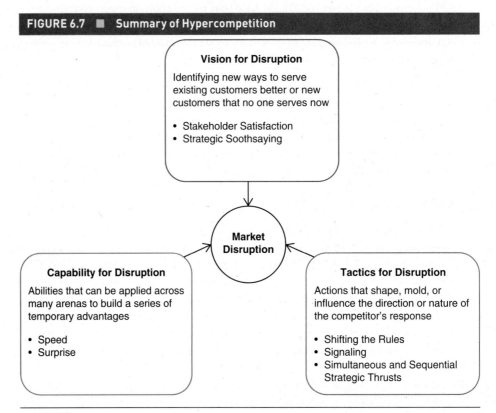

FIGURE 6.7 ■ Summary of Hypercompetition

Vision for Disruption

Identifying new ways to serve existing customers better or new customers that no one serves now

- Stakeholder Satisfaction
- Strategic Soothsaying

Market Disruption

Capability for Disruption

Abilities that can be applied across many arenas to build a series of temporary advantages

- Speed
- Surprise

Tactics for Disruption

Actions that shape, mold, or influence the direction or nature of the competitor's response

- Shifting the Rules
- Signaling
- Simultaneous and Sequential Strategic Thrusts

Source: Smith, T. J. (2012). Strategically escaping price compression: A summary of D'Avenis's Hyper-Competition. *Wiglaf Journal.* Retrieved from https://wiglafjournal.com/strategically-escaping-price-compression-a-summary-of-davenis-hyper-competition/

IN REVIEW

6.1   Define business strategy and explain its central role in business.

Every business, big or small, needs a strategy to compete. A business strategy is a plan of action that helps companies develop a path to compete in an industry. An industry is a grouping of similar companies based on their primary business activities. Strategy focuses more on industry, whereas marketing focuses on markets or consumers.

6.2   Describe four generic strategies and their connection to competitive advantage.

Harvard Business School professor Michael Porter created the four generic strategies: Cost leadership strategy is a strategy used by organizations to seek competitive advantage and gain market share by producing a product or service at the lowest cost possible and thus offering low-priced products; differentiation strategy is a strategy used by organizations to seek competitive advantage by providing goods and services that are significantly different from the competition; cost focus strategy is a strategy used by organizations to gain competitive advantage by keeping costs and prices lower than their rivals while targeting a narrow market where products meet a very specific need, often referred to as a "niche" market; and differentiation focus is a strategy used by organizations to achieve competitive advantage by providing better-value products or services to a narrow or niche target market.

6.3   Analyze external factors to determine how competitive and attractive an industry is.

An external strategic analysis is an objective evaluation of the industry environment in which a business operates. Michael Porter's five forces model includes competitive rivalry, the bargaining power of suppliers, the bargaining power of customers, the threat of new entrants, and the threat of substitute products and services. PESTLE analysis is another external strategic analysis tool for assessing the environment based on six factors external to the business: political, economic, social, technological, legal, and environmental. Scenario planning is a strategic planning method that makes assumptions about different future circumstances and identifies a set of uncertainties that may impact your business.

6.4   Assess internal organizational factors that help identify strategic resources, opportunities, and threats.

An internal strategic analysis is an objective evaluation of an organization's internal environment, which is a method of assessing an organization's strengths, weaknesses, opportunities, and threats (abbreviated as SWOT). VRIO analysis uses a four-question framework to assess whether a resource is valuable, rare, inimitable, and if the business is organized enough to capture value from that resource. Businesses can also use a competitive profile matrix (CPM), which is a tool that allows them to compare their business to competitors to reveal strengths and weaknesses.

6.5   Discuss how hypercompetition is used to disrupt markets and even change how companies compete in industries.

Hypercompetition is characterized by intense competitive action and rapid innovation to which competitors must respond quickly. D'Aveni's 7S's hypercompetition model is a framework created to enable companies to continuously create competitive advantages in a disruptive environment. The 7S's framework includes: stakeholder satisfaction, strategic soothsaying, speed, surprise, signals, shifting the rules, and simultaneous strategic thrusts. Connected to D'Aveni's 7S's model is the concept of transient advantage, a strategy that assumes competitive advantages are temporary and requires continuous innovation to maintain any type of competitive positioning.

BUSINESSES DISCUSSED IN THIS CHAPTER

Organization	UN Sustainable Development Goal
Apple	7. Affordable and Clean Energy 12. Responsible Consumption and Production
Arby's	2. Zero Hunger 4. Quality Education 10. Reduced Inequality
Coca-Cola	6. Clean Water and Sanitation 8. Decent Work and Economic Growth 12. Responsible Consumption and Production 14. Life Below Water 17. Partnerships to Achieve the Goals

(Continued)

Organization	UN Sustainable Development Goal
Duolingo	10. Reduced Inequality
Firefly	9. Industry, Innovation, and Infrastructure 11. Sustainable Cities and Communities
Google	12. Responsible Consumption and Production 14. Life Below Water 15. Life on Land 17. Partnerships to Achieve the Goals
IBM	All goals
Old Navy	12. Responsible Consumption and Production
Procter & Gamble	8. Decent Work and Economic Growth 12. Responsible Consumption and Production 13. Climate Action
Shell	7. Affordable and Clean Energy 8. Decent Work and Economic Growth 13. Climate Action
Tesla	7. Affordable and Clean Energy
Under Armour	8. Decent Work and Economic Growth 12. Responsible Consumption and Production 13. Climate Action
Zoom	3. Good Health and Well-Being

KEY TERMS

7S's hypercompetition model (p. 127)

Business strategy (p. 111)

Capability (p. 122)

Competitive advantage (p. 112)

Competitive parity (p. 123)

Competitive profile matrix (CPM) (p. 124)

Cost focus strategy (p. 114)

Cost leadership strategy (p. 113)

Critical success factors (p. 124)

Differentiation focus strategy (p. 114)

Differentiation strategy (p. 114)

External strategic analysis (p. 115)

Five forces model 115

Hypercompetition (p. 126)

Industry (p. 111)

Internal strategic analysis (p. 120)

PESTLE analysis (p. 117)

Resource-based view (p. 122)

Resource (p. 122)

Scenario planning (p. 119)

SWOT analysis (p. 120)

Transient advantage (p. 126)

VRIO analysis (p. 122)

BUSINESS CASE 6.2: MICROSOFT—REDMOND, WASHINGTON

SDG 10: Reduced Inequality

There are few companies as well known as Microsoft, the world's largest technology company. Headquartered in Redmond, Washington, Microsoft employs 181,000 people worldwide, with subsidiaries in over 100 countries. Today, the company operates in three segments of the technology industry: productivity and business processes, intelligent cloud, and personal computing.

Microsoft was founded in 1975 by Bill Gates and Paul Allen, two friends who foresaw the power of putting computers into the hands of everyday users. Since its inception, Microsoft has remained a leader in the ever-changing technology industry, where former giants like Netscape and Compaq did not survive. Under the leadership of CEO Bill, Microsoft's suite of Windows and Office products became the de facto standard all over the world.

When Bill stepped down in 2000, incoming CEO Steve Ballmer continued Bill's vision for Microsoft's dominance in the tech industry. Microsoft gained a reputation for being hostile to competitors—a trait that won Microsoft few friends in the highly collaborative, open-source culture of Silicon Valley. However, in the early 2000s, when other tech firms were focused on the internet, cloud computing, and smartphones—very open-sourced spaces—Microsoft was stuck in its devotion to desktop computers. Though still very profitable, this decision to maintain its focus on PCs led to stagnating shareholder value. As Bill noted, "Sometimes we get taken by surprise. For example, when the Internet came along, we had it as a fifth or sixth priority."

When Satya Nadella became CEO in 2014, he changed the strategic direction of the company. First, he refocused the company by revising its mission statement to "empower every person and every organization on the planet to achieve more." Next, he unveiled a three-tiered strategy to encourage innovation in the company: (1) invest in cloud computing and target Microsoft services to iPhone, Android, Linux, and Mac users; (2) focus on technological growth areas like AI, quantum computing, and mixed reality; and (3) promote a collaborative culture of empathy and inclusion that encourages risk-taking.

For example, in 2019, Microsoft took its collaborative culture outside of its Redmond campus by partnering with competitors like Oracle. By integrating Microsoft's Azure cloud computing service with Oracle's Cloud Infrastructure, customers enjoy a seamless integration of the two leading cloud service providers in tech. Another example of a successful tech partnership is with software company Adobe. When Microsoft integrated Adobe's PDF capabilities into Microsoft 365, it was a win-win for customers. Microsoft also partnered with companies like Topcoder and WiPro. These companies expanded the number of testers to give feedback and document errors on Microsoft devices and in its operating systems. Under Satya's leadership, Microsoft earned 95% of its revenue through relationships with partners in 2017.

Microsoft's growth in market share is a result of strategic acquisitions. In 1987, Microsoft made its first acquisition of the company Forethought, which had pioneered a presentation program that would later become PowerPoint. When Steve was CEO, Microsoft continued to make about 10 acquisitions deals annually. But under Satya's leadership, the acquisitions signaled Microsoft's interest in taking bigger risks. Take, for instance, Steve's acquisition of cell phone company Nokia and compare it to Satya's future acquisition of Activision Blizzard, a video game developer. One might characterize the Nokia acquisition as reactive, an attempt to catch up to Apple and Google in the early 2000s, whereas the Activision Blizzard acquisition demonstrates Microsoft's intent to be on the cutting edge of gaming and "a building block to the metaverse." If the FTC approves the merger for 2023, the Activision Blizzard deal will be Microsoft's biggest investment yet at $68.7 billion.

Microsoft, from its entrepreneurial roots in 1975, continues to practice an entrepreneurial mindset today. From a new product development perspective, the company has been at the forefront of modeling the importance of inclusivity and equity. CEO Satya told *Fortune* in 2017, "Empathy makes you a better innovator. If I look at the most successful products we [at Microsoft] have created, it comes with that ability to meet the unmet, unarticulated needs of customers." He focused the company's investment in AI to make technology more accessible to people with disabilities. Key innovations in this area include Eye Gaze, which allows people with ALS to type by using just their gaze, and Seeing AI, an app that uses a phone camera to describe objects to visually impaired users (including text and handwriting).

Critical Thinking Questions

1. How has Microsoft's acquisition strategy helped the company's growth?

2. Identify at least 10 companies that Microsoft has acquired that are not mentioned in the case. Why did Microsoft buy these companies?

3. How has Microsoft's strategy changed from Steve as CEO to Satya as CEO?

References

Agnihotri, A., & Bhattacharya, S. (2021). Satya Nadella: Leading Microsoft's growth. In *SAGE business cases*. SAGE. https://dx.doi.org/10.4135/9781529764314

Bedingfield, W. (2022, January 19). Microsoft's activision blizzard deal is a move toward the post-console world. *Wired*. https://www.wired.com/story/microsoft-activision-blizzard-post-console-world/#:~:text=%22The%20fantastic%20franchises%20across%20Activision,devices%20you%20already%20own.%22%20This

Frank, B. H. (2015, June 25). Satya Nadella's new mission for Microsoft: Help people achieve more. *PCWorld*. https://www.pcworld.com/article/2940912/satya-nadellas-new-mission-for-microsoft-help-people-achieve-more.html

Lev-Ram, M. (2017, October 3). Microsoft CEO Satya Nadella says empathy makes you a better innovator *Fortune*. https://fortune.com/2017/10/03/microsoft-ceo-satya-nadella-says-empathy-makes-you-a-better-innovator/; Yale School of Management (2022, March 17, 2022). Over 400 companies have withdrawn from Russia—but some remain.

Loomis, C. J. (2013). *Tap dancing to work: Warren Buffett on practically everything, 1966—2013*. Penguin.

Microsoft. (2019, October 16). Microsoft: Annual Report 2019 https://www.microsoft.com/investor/reports/ar19/index.html

Microsoft. (2022a). Facts bout Microsoft. https://news.microsoft.com/facts-about-microsoft/

Naughton, J. (2019, May 12). How Microsoft reinvented itself. *The Guardian*. https://www.theguardian.com/commentisfree/2019/may/12/how-microsoft-was-resurrected-as-the-third-most-valuable-tech-company-1-trillion-dollars

Oracle. (n.d.). Cloud partner: Oracle and Microsoft strategic alliance. *Oracle*. https://www.oracle.com/cloud/partners/microsoft/

PART

BLOCK 2
MARKETS AND CUSTOMERS

Jonas Gratzer/LightRocket/via Getty Images

7 MARKETING AND SALES

LEARNING OBJECTIVES

7.1   Explain the differences between marketing and sales functions in business.

7.2   Describe the elements of the marketing mix: product, promotion, price, place.

7.3   Distinguish between B2B and B2C sales.

7.4   Illustrate the seven stages of the sales cycle.

7.5   Explore modern selling techniques.

BUSINESS IMPACT CASE 7.1: 4OCEAN—BOCA RATON, FLORIDA

SDG 14: Life Below Water

4ocean, with headquarters in Boca Raton, Florida, is on a mission to clean up waste in our oceans and on our beaches. While on a surfing trip in Bali, Indonesia, founders Alex Schulze and Andrew Cooper were shocked to see the beaches covered with waste and "trash-filled waves delivering more garbage with each break."[1] That surfing vacation turned into a mission. They saw the magnitude of the problem and decided to do something about it. Alex and Andrew started with hiring boat captains and local workers to remove plastic from the ocean full-time, and then repurposing the plastic coming out of the water into bracelets. The average price of a bracelet to the consumer is $25, and the company claims to remove 1 pound of plastic waste from the ocean for every bracelet sold.

The company has created an extremely strong core mission that is not only important to employees but also the 4ocean brand. A customer doesn't just buy a bracelet; they buy into a cause. The mission that 4ocean focuses on is easy to connect with and buy into—everyone wants to "walk along the beaches—in Bali, in Haiti, in Florida, and around the world—and see nothing but warm sand and rolling waves," and everyone wants to help reduce plastic pollution.[2]

Currently, the company sells over 30 kinds of bracelets, most of which are named after different animals that the company is focused on protecting such as sharks, whales, penguins, and sea turtles. The company offers its customers the option to buy a monthly subscription that enables them to receive one bracelet per month. Customers can buy directly online, or through 4ocean's retail partners that sell its bracelets in their stores. In order to be approved as a 4ocean partner, the retailer must have a mission that aligns with 4ocean's.

Since its founding in 2017, 4ocean has expanded its product line to include water bottles, cleanup kits, single-use alternatives, and reusable straws. The company has so far removed over 9 million pounds of plastic waste from the ocean. According to its website, "We are a purpose-driven business, founded to help end the ocean plastic crisis. Today, our ocean cleanup and advocacy mission is funded primarily by your 4ocean product purchases."[3]

Given the importance of cleaning up oceans to its overall brand, 4ocean's marketing efforts focus on keeping customers informed about the impact their purchases are making around the world. The company invests heavily in documenting its efforts, and posts regular updates and compelling content on Facebook (1.2 million followers), Instagram (more than 2 million followers), YouTube (more than 100,000 subscribers), Twitter (more than 250,000 followers), Pinterest (more than 16,000 followers), and Vimeo (more than 1,000 followers). Its marketing efforts have resulted in drawing increased attention to the plastic problem in our oceans and how customers are helping to solve the problem one bracelet at a time.[4] More recently, the company is focusing on cleaning up rivers because rivers are the source of most of the plastic that is ending up in our oceans.

Critical Thinking Questions

1. Is 4ocean selling a bracelet or a feeling?

2. How would you describe the 4ocean brand? What does it stand for? What do customers think about when they see the brand?

3. Can 4ocean, as a single company, really solve the massive problem of plastic polluting our oceans? Search the internet and describe in greater detail the impact this company is making.

THE ROLE OF MARKETING AND SALES IN BUSINESS

Marketing and sales are two different functions, but they coexist and collaborate to identify, reach, and attract customers in order to generate revenue for businesses. It can be argued that sales is part of the overall marketing process. Without marketing, companies would collapse due to lack of customers, which leads to lack of sales, resulting in zero or loss of profit. Marketing is the process of attracting people to the goods and services on sale. Marketers conduct research to analyze needs of potential customers and launch campaigns, sometimes over the course of several months, to spark interest in a company's brand, goods, and services.[5] Marketers work to identify a group of specific people who are most likely to buy the company's products and services, which is called a target market. Marketers also conduct research to analyze needs of potential customers and launch advertising campaigns, sometimes over the course of several months, to ignite curiosity in a company's brand, products, and services. For example, 4ocean has built its entire marketing strategy around its environmental mission to reduce the amount of plastic in the ocean. Even during the pandemic, 4ocean created and sold face masks made from 100% recycled plastic as a way to meet a new need while still drawing attention to the plastics problem. 4ocean's environmentally friendly masks proved to be one of its best-selling products.

While marketing is about building and communicating a brand to a target market, sales is more about creating relationships and converting a potential customer into a paying customer. Sales refers to all the activities that lead to the selling of products and services with particular emphasis on convincing customers to purchase. Salespeople manage relationships with customers and work to provide product solutions that meet their needs. For instance, 4ocean sells bracelets and other merchandise made of repurposed plastic to fund trash removal from the ocean. Its salespeople likely work with current and potential partner retailers that promote and sell 4ocean products in stores. Generally, salespeople have shorter-term goals than marketers, typically focusing on achieving sales goals on a monthly basis.

Think of marketing as more strategic—bigger view—and sales as more tactical—getting the customer to actually pay for a product or service. Table 7.1 outlines the differences between sales and marketing.

TABLE 7.1 ■ The Differences Between Sales and Marketing

	Marketing	Sales
Goals	Communicating product, service, brand	Reach sales quotas, build customer base, sell product
Time frame	Longer-term view	Shorter-term view
Focus	Build pipeline of interest	Convert pipeline to sales revenue
Connection to customer	Communicating brand	Building a relationship

The process of marketing is facilitated by the different elements of the marketing mix, which is described in the following section.

THE MARKETING MIX

Marketing requires ongoing research and commitment to ensure the business's products are in line with the overall company vision. Using an established marketing framework is essential when it comes to developing marketing strategy.

The basic principles of marketing are grounded in the marketing mix, a framework that helps define the brand and differentiate it from the competition. The marketing mix is made up of four main elements, known as the 4 Ps: product, price, promotion, and place (see Figure 7.1). Each of the 4 Ps should be considered in relation to the others, in order to build the best overall marketing strategy for a company's offering.

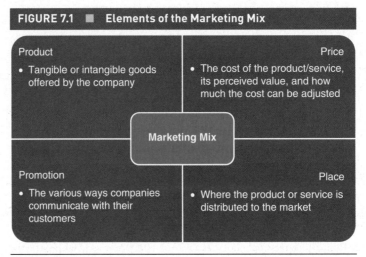

FIGURE 7.1 ■ Elements of the Marketing Mix

Product
- Tangible or intangible goods offered by the company

Price
- The cost of the product/service, its perceived value, and how much the cost can be adjusted

Marketing Mix

Promotion
- The various ways companies communicate with their customers

Place
- Where the product or service is distributed to the market

Source: Neck, H. M., Neck, C. P., & Murray, E. L. (2019). *Entrepreneurship: The practice and mindset.* SAGE.

Product

The product is anything tangible or intangible (such as a service) offered by the company. This includes the features, the brand, how it meets customer needs, how and where it will be used, and how it stands out from competitors. For instance, the product in the 4ocean case is a bracelet made out of plastic removed from the ocean. A good way of assessing your product is to ask critical questions (see Table 7.2). By repeatedly asking these questions, you will have a better understanding of your product or service and how it fits into the marketplace.

TABLE 7.2 ■ Critical Questions to Ask When Developing a Product

- What does the customer want from the service or product?
- How will the customer use it?
- Where will the customer use it?
- What features must the product have to meet the customer's needs?
- Are there any necessary features that you missed out?
- Are you creating features that are not needed or wanted by the customer?
- What's the name of the product?
- Does it have a catchy name?
- What are the sizes or colors available?
- How is the product different from the products of your competitors?
- What does the product look like?

Source: The marketing mix 4P's and 7P's explained. *The Marketing Mix.* Retrieved from https://marketingmix.co.uk/

Price

Price is the amount that the customer is expected to pay for the product. Price is determined by understanding its perceived value (what customers think it's worth), market demand, and the price of competing products. Pricing a product is one of the most difficult yet important factors of your marketing strategy. The price of a 4ocean bracelet is approximately $25, but how did the company settle on this price? It's likely one or more of the pricing strategies below was used.

Types of Pricing Strategies

There are five common pricing strategies used in marketing: cost-plus pricing, competitive pricing, value-based pricing, price skimming, and penetration pricing.

1. **Cost-plus pricing** is a pricing strategy that involves determining the costs of making your product and adding a markup to determine a selling price.[6] This is one of the simplest and most common price strategies used by companies, particularly retailers. Online clothing company Everlane uses cost-plus pricing to justify its commitment to transparency by detailing the reasons behind the markup, such as costs associated with materials, labor (including fair wages), transport, and so on.[7] Everlane's approach attracts customers who want to buy from sustainable companies that pay fair wages to the workers manufacturing their garments.

2. **Competitive pricing** is a pricing strategy that involves setting prices based on what the competition is charging. However, not every customer will want to buy a product just because it's cheaper than another. For example, activity tracker smartwatch company FitBit can charge a higher price than competitors such as Delvfire because it has already built an established brand with a loyal customer base.[8]

3. **Value-based pricing** is a pricing strategy based on the customers' perceived value of the product or service. For example, Starbucks uses value-based pricing to maximize profits by conducting extensive research into its customer base to establish the amount they are willing to pay for its products.[9] Over the years, Starbucks has built a loyal, higher-income customer following who are more likely to accept a price increase in their gourmet coffee than more price-sensitive customers.

4. **Price skimming** is a pricing strategy that involves setting a product at a high price when it enters the market before gradually lowering it as the market evolves. Apple is a good example of a company that uses price skimming. For instance, Apple prices its new product high when it first enters the market, which helps to establish its luxury brand image and attracts early adopters who are keen to be among the first to try out a new innovation. However, dropping the price too soon after a product reaches the market can upset early adopters. In 2007, Apple experienced a backlash when it reduced the price of the iPhone by $200 only 2 months after its release—a move that angered early adopters who had paid the significantly higher price.[10]

5. **Penetration** is a pricing strategy that initially uses low prices to attract customers to a new product or service in an effort to tempt customers away from the competition. For example, television and internet providers such as Comcast and DirectTV offer low introductory prices on services during a limited period, such as the first year. When the period is over, the price increases.[11] The main goal for companies using the penetration pricing strategy is to entice customers to move from an existing provider to its own, like moving from DirectTV to Comcast. The penetration strategy also includes mixing free (mainly web-based) basic services with premium or upgraded services. Some companies give away the low-end version, services with limits on usage and functionality, for free to entice people to pay for the higher-end versions that offer more functionality and performance. For example, LinkedIn gives members free access to build a profile and maintain a professional network. It charges a fee for

its premium service, which further benefits job seekers and recruiters with added functions such as search filtering, sending personalized messages, and tracking visits to the member's profile. Similarly, meditation app Calm provides some meditation sessions for free but offers enhanced services to paying subscribers, which include a bigger range of meditation lessons, videos, and Sleep Stories often narrated by actors such as British actor and author Stephen Fry.[12] When used successfully, penetration pricing can attract new customers, increase market share, and build customer loyalty.

Promotion

The third element of the marketing mix is promotion, which refers to any type of marketing communication used by companies to inform target customers about their offering. Promotion has become a core function of marketing and is used by big and small businesses to publicize products, build brand awareness, and attract a broader customer base. A promotional tactic that works one day may not work the next, so continuous development of new strategies is essential to retaining and increasing your customer base. Promotions online, through social media, direct mail, in the press, or on TV, are all channels for promotion. 4ocean promotes its bracelets through social media (Facebook, Instagram, Twitter, Pinterest, and Vimeo) and TV advertising.

Promotion is vast and includes advertising, specialty promotion, sales promotion, public relations, and content marketing—we discuss these in greater depth next.

Types of Advertising

Online advertising involves advertising through the internet. Companies use digital marketing strategies such as placing ads on popular websites or social media sites to spread awareness of their products and services. Companies can use AdWords from Google to pay for ads placed within the search engine results page. The business pays Google if someone clicks on the ad, something that is called "cost per click." Google AdSense allows companies to place ads on other company websites, blogs, and forums, and those outlets get paid when people click on those ads. Websites with a lot of traffic tend to benefit the most from this form of advertising. For example, cat-lover community catforum.com monetizes its website by using AdSense. With almost 50,000 members, catforum is likely to see the benefits of Google AdSense, given the high number of visitors to its site.[13]

Social media advertising is a specific form of online advertising that allows companies to attract target audiences while they are engaging with posts or stories on their preferred social media platforms.[14] Facebook, which is popular across many demographics, enables companies to create photo and video ads in different formats to showcase their products and demonstrate how to use them. Instagram, owned by Facebook, offers the same advertising capabilities as Facebook, and is more popular with millennials and Gen Z. Companies can place ads on their Instagram feed, Instagram Stories, Instagram Reels, in addition to posting longform videos on IGTV. Many companies choose to advertise on fast-growing Chinese video-focused social networking platform TikTok. Unlike Facebook and Instagram, which offer many different advertising formats, TikTok offers video-only advertising, and companies use and pay customers to show their products in use. Although TikTok is a relative newcomer to social media, it has gained huge traction, initially with younger audiences but now across all age groups, and is growing in popularity with companies looking to promote their brands. Other commonly used social media platforms include LinkedIn, YouTube, Twitter, and Snapchat. Social media advertising has taken off over the last 5 years, with studies showing that more than 90% of U.S. companies use it for quick and effective brand-building. In 2020, U.S. companies spent $40 billion on paid advertising on social media, a figure that is expected to rise in the coming years.[15]

In-app advertising is a form of advertising where companies place ads or run campaigns inside mobile apps to attract new app users and maximize revenue. People spend an average of 3 hours a day on mobile apps, which is why this form of advertising has become an increasingly popular medium for targeting smartphone users, particularly in the music, gaming, and entertainment industries.[16]

Examples of in-app advertising in the gaming world include ads that take over the screen between levels of a mobile game, banner ads that appear at the top or bottom of a screen, or reward ads where players are offered rewards such as an extra life, or coins in exchange for watching an ad. Successful in-app advertising can engage customers and create a better user experience, but ineffective in-app advertising can serve as an annoyance, leading users to stop using the app altogether. It's a balancing act.

Print advertising is a type of advertising that is printed in hard copy such as ads in magazines, newspapers, or use of catalogs, brochures, leaflets, postcards, and flyers mailed directly to consumers. Although digital advertising is a great way to reach a huge audience, print advertising still has the power to attract consumers, especially when the ads are placed in publications with a wide circulation or can be inexpensively mailed to a very targeted audience. For example, a painter can send a postcard advertising their services to new home buyers that just moved into an area. A list of recent home buyers and their physical address can easily be purchased or obtained from the town. Sometimes it is a lot easier to get physical addresses than email addresses!

Guerilla advertising is a form of advertising that focuses on personally interacting with a target group by promoting products and services through surprise or other unconventional means. A successful guerrilla marketing campaign enhances the customer's perception of value, inspires word of mouth, and increases sales. For example, paper towel brand Bounty installed a gigantic popsicle and a huge knocked-over coffee cup on the streets of New York to advertise its product and its cleaning properties; a simple message delivered in a unique, effective way.[17]

Broadcast advertising is a form of advertising that includes television and radio. Although broadcast advertising has the potential to reach millions, it can be very costly. For instance, the average cost of a 30-second ad during the Super Bowl is over $5 million.[18] Yet the cost for TV ads can vary wildly; for example, the cost of advertising during the Women's World Cup Finals in 2018 was just over $500,000 for a 30-second ad—a higher figure than the cost of the 30-second ad during the men's final.[19] However, small businesses on a budget can also place short ads on local television stations for around $5,000—still a lot of money but a lot less expensive than advertising nationally during major sporting events!

Outdoor advertising, also known as out-of-home, is a type of advertising that targets customers when they are away from home. Billboards, bus shelter posters, digital boards, and fly posters are all examples of outdoor advertising.

Public service advertising (PSA) also referred to as a public service announcement, is a type of advertising intended to inform or educate rather than sell a product or service. Traditionally, PSAs have been broadcast on television or radio, but they can also appear online. For example, dozens of celebrities including Arnold Schwarzenegger have made PSAs online in an effort to educate people about the dangers of the coronavirus and how to prevent people from spreading it to one another.[20]

Product placement advertising is the promotion of brands and products within the context of a TV show or a movie. Companies pay to position their products in this form of media in order to reach their target demographic. For example, the Starbucks cup appears frequently in the movie *Fight Club*, and Utz potato chips have been heavily featured in the hit U.S. series *The Office*—both of which attract specific audiences most likely to consume these products.[21] With the rise of Netflix and other streaming platforms, product placement is becoming more sophisticated, with plans to position products based on who is watching. For example, viewers known to be whiskey drinkers might see a billboard advertising a liquor brand in a particular scene.[22]

This unique outdoor advertisement calls attention to the need for more facilities for people with disabilities.

Photo of "American Disability Association" by Arturo de Albornoz via Flickr. Licensed under CC BY-SA 2.0 https://creativecommons.org/licenses/by-sa/2.0/.

Product placements such as these Pop-Tarts in the movie *Elf* are commonplace in the film industry.

AA Film Archive/Alamy Stock Photo

Specialty Promotion

Specialty promotion uses merchandise "giveaways" to celebrate or promote a company, brand, or product. A T-shirt with your college logo given to you during orientation, a frisbee with a radio station name thrown out to the audience at a local concert, free hand sanitizer with a tour company's logo available to you as you board the tour bus, or a 4ocean sticker given to you when you purchase a bracelet are all examples of specialty promotion. The word "specialty" is used simply because it is a customized product printed with a company's logo.

Sales Promotions

Sales promotions are a great way for companies to attract customer interest in their products and services and increase revenue. There are 10 sales promotion strategies commonly used by companies.[23]

1. **Limited-Time Offers**

   A limited-time offer is a type of sales promotion strategy that involves providing products or services at a discount, deal, or for free over a limited period. Limited-time offers initiate a sense of urgency and scarcity of availability, which ignites a fear-of-missing-out (FOMO). For example, Pura Vida Bracelets, based in California, offers a 15% discount to customers on their second purchase through a pop-up on its website. The pop-up has a countdown timer to encourage hesitant visitors to make a quick decision by driving a sense of urgency.

2. **Daily Deals**

   A daily deal (also known as a flash sale) is a type of sales promotion strategy that offers products at a discount from anywhere between 24 and 72 hours. Daily deals are a great way to boost revenue in a short amount of time in addition to shifting excess inventory and "out of season" stock. Like limited-time offers, daily deals create a buzz, trigger FOMO, and grow brand awareness by driving a sense of urgency. One of the biggest flash sales of the year is Black Friday Cyber Monday (BFCM), when brands promote new products at a discount for a limited time. In 2019, BFCM generated $28 billion in online sales, most of which happened during a 4-hour window on Cyber Monday.[24]

3. **Mystery Offers**

   Mystery offers are special offers that evoke curiosity by including a surprise. Lifestyle, clothing, and accessories company American Eagle uses mystery offers in its email marketing by sending discount codes with phrases intended to spark excitement such as "click below to reveal an offer—you can ONLY get it here" before adding a "Reveal Your Offer" button. By simulating the act of opening a present, American Eagle manages to successfully convert visitors to customers.

4. **Cross-Selling Campaigns**

   Cross-selling is the practice of selling an extra product in conjunction with a primary product. One of the most common cross-selling promotions is "buy 2, get 1 free." Combining free shipping with cross-selling is also a powerful way to attract customers. For example, Tarte Cosmetics, based in New York City, promotes its cross-selling strategy through its email subject line "1 + 1 = Free shipping." In other words, customers need to buy two products (typically complementary products) before they qualify for free shipping. Successful cross-selling builds customer loyalty and satisfaction, and boosts revenue for the company.

5. **Subscriber Specials**

   Subscriber specials are discounts given to subscribers. However, there are different types of subscribers, and each group should be treated in a certain way. Long-term subscribers may be offered better discounts and rewards than first-time visitors. For example, Swedish clothing company Monki invites its longtime subscribers to a "VIP Sale" to access special offers if they sign up for its newsletter, something that would not be available to first-time visitors.

6. **Clearance Sales**

   Clearance sales are a type of sales promotion where goods are sold at a discount to get rid of surplus stock. Clearance sales are a useful way to sell off seasonal stock, such as winter clothing, Christmas decorations, etc., and also promote scarcity and urgency since the products are set at a limited time. U.S. clothing company American Eagle Outfitters often promotes clearance sales in its emails with the subject heading, "Up to 70% off clearance: THIS. NEVER. HAPPENS." The company also triggers FOMO by telling customers that the sale is "3 days *only*" and "online *only*."

7. **Seasonal Deals**

   Seasonal deals is a sales promotion strategy that involves selling off company stock at a discount. Attracting attention to their seasonal products can be difficult for small companies—especially during the Christmas or Black Friday holidays, when bigger companies tend to dominate. However, not all holidays are as busy and some can be a unique selling day. For example, the company Barkbox celebrates National Dog Day to create demand for its products by sending out emails with fun instructions for dog owners such as "Dress your pup in their National Dog Day Outfit (It's nude. Glorious nude!)" before advertising the seasonal deals.

8. **Free Samples**

   Free samples is a sales promotion strategy where small portions of new products are introduced to customers for free.[25] Costco provides free food samples such as pizza squares, yogurt, smoothies, and much more to customers regardless of whether they purchase anything or not. Free samples not only attract customers but encourage them to buy the product, thereby increasing sales. This method can also work with lotions, perfumes, or aromatherapy products. People like to try before they buy.

9. **Social Media Contests and Giveaways**

   A social media contest is a sales promotion strategy that involves running an online contest to attract a larger audience.[26] These contests are often used to promote or give away products and come in many different formats, including raffles, photo and video contests, Like to Win (where people are invited to "Like" a Facebook page or Twitter post to win a certain product), and more. For example, Texas-based sock subscription company Sock Club runs contests in the "Stories" feature of Instagram to build brand awareness and give away products for free.[27] Successful social media contests engage a larger audience, increase brand awareness, and build a community around the brand.

10. **Joint Promotions**

Joint promotions is a promotional strategy whereby two companies join together to promote their products and services.[28] Successful joint promotions raise awareness of both brands, build business, and provide an opportunity to break into new markets. For instance, although online mattress and bedding company Caspar ran a hugely popular series of unboxing videos on YouTube, it still needed to find a way for its customers to try out its mattresses. So Caspar partnered with high-end furniture company West Elm to allow shoppers to test the mattress in West Elm stores. Although Caspar doesn't sell furniture and West Elm doesn't sell mattresses, this joint promotional strategy allowed both companies to highlight their products to a broader group of customers and promoting the mattress (from Casper) and the bed frame (from West Elm) as a possible one stop purchase.[29]

Public Relations

Public relations is a type of communication process used to protect, enhance, or build reputations through the media.[30] Public relations specialists generate positive publicity for their clients by writing and distributing press releases, speech writing, managing the firm's messaging, blogging for the web, and creating responses to negative opinions online. It can also be used to spread powerful messages. For example, New York City–based PR agency Ogilvy worked with the Hellman's brand to launch "The Restaurant With No Food" campaign to highlight food waste, which is often driven by lack of inspiration. People were asked to bring their unused food to a local restaurant, where chefs transformed the produce into 5-star meals. Not only did the campaign publicize the problem of food waste, but it also took over social media, and received an endorsement from the United Nations.[31]

Although public relations is often confused with advertising, they are not the same thing. While advertising is paid media, public relations is earned media; it uses persuasion to convince third parties such as magazines, newspapers, TV stations, or websites to publish positive stories about their clients. Table 7.3 outlines the differences between advertising and public relations.

TABLE 7.3 ■ Differences Between Advertising and Public Relations	
Advertising	**Public Relations**
Pay for advertising	Earn credibility
Builds exposure	Builds trust
Skeptical audience	Trusted third-party validation
Guaranteed ad placement	Must persuade media to place articles, etc.
Complete creative control	Media control the final version
Ads are mostly visual	PR uses text
More expensive	Less expensive and sometimes free
Used for selling	Used for informing

Source: Adapted from Wynne, R. (2016, January 22). Five things everyone should know about public relations. *Forbes.* Retrieved from https://www.forbes.com/sites/robertwynne/2016/01/21/five-things-everyone-should-know-about-public-relations/?sh=1b722b2b2a2c

Content Marketing

Content marketing is the process of planning, creating, distributing, sharing, and publishing content to engage, attract, and retain a target audience.[32] It is a nonpushy way for businesses to educate and build relationships with their audience by showing them how their products and services can help solve their challenges. Content marketing is really the new "advertising," with over 92% of businesses using it to promote their products and services.

The key to good content is quality. If you can create content that is meaningful to your audience, they will share it through their own social networks—think tweets, retweets, likes, comments, reviews. Recent data show that in just 1 minute, 300 hours of new video are uploaded to YouTube; 350,000 tweets are sent; and 250,000 posts are "liked" by Instagrammers.[33] This proves that getting the content right is key to attracting a wide audience. It also helps to get in touch with people in a similar market who already have a large number of followers, and build a relationship with them by linking to various posts, or sharing their links to your social media pages.

The most successful content marketers maintain a loyal following by publishing content regularly through blogs, infographics, videos, tweets, and taking part in conversations. Let's explore the six main types of content marketing.[34]

1. **Social Media Content Marketing**

   With over 3.7 billion users, social media is a powerful medium to share and distribute content. Through platforms like Facebook, Instagram, Pinterest, LinkedIn, and Snapchat, content marketers can create and share content such as photos, videos, and stories. For example, UK cosmetics retailer Lush uses Instagram to showcase its product line, providing information on how each product meets the specific needs of people from different ethnicities, genders, and backgrounds.

2. **Infographic Content Marketing**

   Infographics are visual images of information and data designed to present an easy-to-understand overview of a particular topic. They are an excellent way to communicate to simplify a complex topic for the benefit of a wider audience. Facebook or Twitter are good places to post an infographic. For example, California-based education technology website Course Hero uses a variety of infographics to simplify different types of learning and connect readers to the material. Course Hero's literature infographics detail characters and themes in a visual way that support comprehension and help to bring the works of literature to life.[35]

3. **Blog Content Marketing**

   Blogs are a powerful way to share information with customers and a target audience. Longform articles that provide helpful information to users are ideal for blog posts. Connecting with other bloggers is also a great way to boost visibility, build relationships, and improve brand awareness. For example, online shopping company Expedia uses blog content marketing to include a wide range of topics such as hotel recommendations, unique destinations to visit, and different types of activities all over the globe in which travelers can engage.

4. **Podcast Content Marketing**

   A podcast is a digital audio file that can be downloaded from the internet or streamed over your favorite podcasting app. Over 6 million people listen to podcasts in the United States, which is why so many businesses have started to create podcasts of their own. Podcasts are an excellent way for companies to promote their products and services, engage their audience, and increase brand awareness. For example, journalist Guy Raz hosts a popular podcast called "How I Built This" where he narrates fascinating stories about innovators, entrepreneurs, and idealists and how they built their companies.

5. **Video Content Marketing**

   Video marketing is the use of videos to market or promote a product or service. A recent survey of over 3,000 consumers in Europe, the United States, and Latin America shows that

50% of people would prefer to see videos posted by a brand or a company. Videos can attract a wider audience, especially when they are shared across different social media platforms. California-based grooming products company Dollar Shave Club, bought by Unilever in 2017, has run hugely successful video marketing campaigns by being humorous, likeable, and totally on-brand. Through its online video content, Dollar Shave Club has managed to experience enormous business growth and brand recognition. As previously mentioned, you can see a lot of examples of video content marketing on Instagram, YouTube, and TikTok.

6. **Mission-Driven Content Marketing**

   Mission-driven content marketing is a type of marketing that incorporates the company's core values that align with its audience's interests.[36] Some of these values include putting environmental and social initiatives front and center. For example, Vermont-based creamery Ben & Jerry's, owned by Unilever, uses its vast platform for supporting core social issues such as racial justice, LGBTQ equality, climate justice, and fair trade. It also releases limited editions of ice cream flavors to further highlight these issues, such as the "I Dough, I Dough" ice cream to support marriage equality, and the "Empower Mint" flavor to encourage people to vote. Mission-driven companies like Ben & Jerry's can achieve powerful results. Research shows that 55% of consumers are more likely to spend more on products and services that drive positive social and environmental impact. Why? Because it makes people feel good knowing that some of the money they spend is supporting a good cause.

Place

Finally, **place** is where the product is actually distributed and sold to buyers: trade fairs, retail stores, catalogs, mail order, online, and so forth. 4ocean distributes and sells its bracelets online and through select retailers. There are two types of distribution channels available to companies: direct and indirect (see Figure 7.2). **Direct distribution channels** involve the distribution of the product directly from the manufacturer to the consumer. For example, Dell Computers sells directly to its target customers, which gives it total control over its product. **Indirect distribution channels** involve the distribution of products through the use of an intermediary, such as a wholesaler, before they are sold through a retailer.

Companies can also use several types of distribution strategies to sell their products and services: intensive distribution, selective distribution, and exclusive distribution.

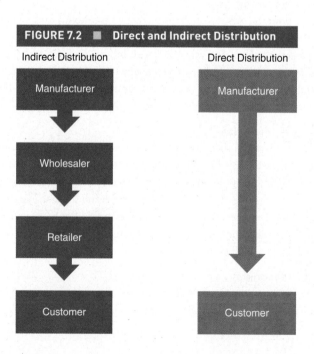

FIGURE 7.2 ■ Direct and Indirect Distribution

Indirect Distribution

Direct Distribution

Manufacturer → Wholesaler → Retailer → Customer

Manufacturer → Customer

- **Intensive distribution** is a distribution strategy under which a company sells through as many locations or outlets as possible, including supermarkets, drug stores, gas stations, etc. This type of strategy is usually used for low-priced products or impulse purchases, such as chewing gum, snacks, soft drinks, and so on.

- **Selective distribution** is a distribution strategy under which a company sells through just a few select businesses who specialize in more expensive products. This strategy is typically used for selling high-quality products such as computers, household appliances, and televisions.

- **Exclusive distribution** is a distribution strategy under which a company sells its products through just one outlet. A good example of exclusive distribution would be cars that are sold through dealers who usually have the sole rights to sell the product.

It is also possible to change your strategy regarding where you sell your product. For example, if you're selling retail products, you might start off selling online and then also decide to rent a retail space in order to make your company more visible to your target market. Wherever you choose to sell, it is essential that your customers receive the best buying information on your product or service to help them make a buying decision.

B2B AND B2C SALES

You might think all sales approaches are the same, but there are vast differences between businesses selling to other businesses (B2B) and businesses selling to consumers (B2C). **B2B businesses** sell their products and services directly to the decision makers in another business.[37] For example, Oregon-based BulkBookStore is a B2B business that sells books in bulk to other businesses for big conferences, large meetings, and promotions. **B2C businesses** sell their products and services to consumers for personal use, such as food, clothing, cars, jewelry, cruises, and so on.[38] The marketing mix discussed in this chapter plays a more prominent role in B2C sales than B2B sales. For example, American food company Chobani, which specializes in yogurt, promotes its product through colorful photos posted on Instagram, which showcase how yogurt can enhance particular meals such as Caesar salad, flatbread pizza, and peach cheesecake.[39] This type of visual promotion would not typically be used in B2B sales. Table 7.4 highlights the differences between the two forms of sales.

DocuSign is a B2B app sold to certain businesses such as law firms and real estate agencies, to enable their clients to sign documents electronically.

Tiffany Hagler-Geard/Bloomberg/Getty Images

Generally, B2B selling is a longer selling process than B2C selling. In B2B sales, you need to appeal to the decision makers in another company. These people will take a longer amount of time to purchase because they need to carry out research, assess budgets, and check out the competition before they agree to buy. In other words, the sales cycle is long and, because the products usually come with a higher price tag, the stakes are higher. Building a trusting relationship with a buyer is paramount at this stage to ensure the sale goes through and to secure repeat orders in the future.

On the other hand, B2C customers want to know everything as soon as possible and are more likely to make quick purchasing decisions based on "social proof" such as product reviews, referrals, and recommendations. Unlike B2B customers, who are driven by the need to purchase with a goal of enhancing their business and improving the bottom line, B2C customers are motivated to buy from a desire for a particular product that they believe improves their lives in some way.

TABLE 7.4 ■ Differences Between B2B and B2C Selling

	B2B	B2C
Decision maker	Committee or multiple people	Consumer
Length of sales cycle	Long	Short
Relationship between buyer and seller	Consultative and requires trust building	Transactional and quick
Purchase is based on ...	Budget and planned purchase	Emotion and/or need
Order size	Larger price tag (e.g., bulk orders, large equipment)	Smaller (e.g., a pair of jeans or even a car)

Adapted from Gotter, A. (2018). B2B and B2C marketing: What's the difference? *Disruptive Advertising.* https://www.disrup-tiveadvertising.com/marketing/b2b-and-b2c/#:~:text="B2B"%20stands%20for%20"business,makers%20in%20any%20particular%20business.&text=B2C%20businesses%20sell%20products%20and%20services%20to%20customers%20for%20personal%20use.

Although there are many differences between B2B and B2C sales and marketing, there are some similarities, too. You may be selling to businesses on the one hand, or customers on the other, but it is important to remember that you're still selling to real people who share the same emotions. For instance, in a B2C real estate transaction, the higher price tag may lead to a selling cycle and relationship that appears more like B2B—think buying a house or a car, where relationship with the salesperson is a bit more important than buying a pair of jeans! Overall, regardless of what you are selling, it is essential to understand your target market and what they need.

ETHICS IN BUSINESS

The Ethics of Fake Reviews

A new athleisure apparel company, Lulugrapefruit, plans to sell all of its products online, directly to the consumer. Lulugrapefruit's first major product is a fashionable, comfortable, and technologically advanced yoga pant. The entrepreneur who founded Lulugrapefruit knows from marketing research and her own, personal shopping experience that potential buyers strongly consider online reviews when determining whether to make a purchase. They identify 50 people to receive a free pair of Lulugrapefruit yoga pants in exchange for a positive online review delivered before the new pant goes live online. You were one of the lucky 50 people selected. What do you do? Do you accept the product and give the positive review?

Critical Thinking Questions

1. Would you be willing to provide a positive review for a company's product/service in exchange for a sample of the free product/service even if you didn't like the product? Do you think this is ethical on your part? The company's part?
2. Does giving a product away in exchange for a positive online review constitute a fake review?
3. Would you feel differently about a company if you purchased the company's product/service based on fake reviews?

Source: Fake reviews? Ethical business practices. (2018) *Steerpoint.* https://www.steerpoint.com/fake-reviews-ethical-business-practices-digital-marketing

THE SALES CYCLE

As we have learned, marketers must also be educators—ready to provide easy-to-understand, engaging content that appeals to their target audience and ultimately translates into sales. For many of us, the word "sales" has a negative connotation in business because of long-used, high-pressure sales tactics. But sales is an essential skill of every business person and entrepreneur. Think of sales not as high-pressure tactics but as a relational transaction because you are providing value to a customer who is willing to pay for that value.

Regardless of the type of selling, salespeople follow a set of specific actions to close a sale, called a **sales cycle**. Figure 7.3 illustrates the seven stages in a sales cycle: 1. sales prospecting, 2. making contact, 3. qualifying the lead, 4. nurturing the lead, 5. making an offer, 6. handling objections, 7. closing the sale.[40]

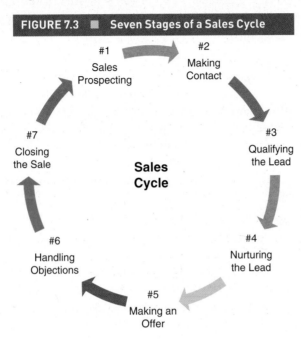

FIGURE 7.3 ■ Seven Stages of a Sales Cycle

1. **Sales Prospecting**

   The sales cycle begins with the prospecting process, which involves leveraging information from various channels to identify people who might be a good fit for your products or services. Salespeople can find *prospects* (potential customers) by calling existing and past clients, cold calling, emailing, attending industry events, and engaging in online business groups like LinkedIn.

2. **Making Contact**

   As soon as the prospects have been identified, it's time to start contacting them. Try and find a mutual acquaintance to introduce you to reach out over social media, email, or phone. During this initial period of contact, it is important that you communicate the value of what you have to offer. For example, you could say something like, "Hello, Maria. My name is Jaden, and I'm with Food Connection. Is food waste a problem in your grocery story? I help stores like yours reduce waste by taking your expiring food and connecting with local food banks and soup kitchens. Is this something you'd like to learn more about?"

3. **Qualifying the Lead**

   After contact has been made, then it's time to verify (or qualify) if they are the right fit for your business, and vice versa. You can do this by setting up a call to learn more about the business and its needs and identify whether you can meet those needs. At this stage, you may discover that you're not a good fit for each other, or you might find that there is a strong case for working together. If the outlook is positive, then you can move on to the next stage of the sales cycle.

4. **Nurturing the Lead**

   Although your prospect may be showing interest in your company's products and services, they may not be ready to buy immediately. Rather than trying to force the sale, start nurturing your prospects gradually in a way that helps them make a decision. This might include sending them useful information such as eBooks, articles, or case studies to gently encourage them to make an informed decision.

5. **Making an Offer**

   All going well, the prospect will have enough information to show an intent to purchase your product or service. This is where you might be asked to give a presentation to the key decision makers that might include a demo of your product and how it can solve their pain points and challenges. Following the presentation, you are in a good position to make a relevant and targeted offer.

6. **Handling Objections**

   You've made your pitch, but be prepared for some pushback. It is likely that they will have some questions and concerns about your product. They might be checking out another competitor, or show reluctance about committing to a contract, or raise other issues around the product's features. It is your job to listen carefully to these objections and do as much as you can to persuade them that your company is the right choice for them. For example, if there are concerns raised about the product's features or fears that it might be too complex, then you can reassure them by informing them about your training strategies and excellent support channels.

7. **Closing the Sale**

   Once all objections have been addressed, then it's time for the final stage in the cycle: closing the sale. This means asking whether the prospect is ready to buy and pay. If they say "yes," then you will need to take payment, or if for a house or likely a B2B sale, create a formal contract and send it to them for review and eventual signing. But if they say "no," then there is more work to be done. Remind them of how your product can address all their pain points and what you are prepared to do to help them through the transition. If they still remain unconvinced, then you might have to walk away for the moment. When this happens, don't close the door completely; make sure to stay in touch with the prospect in case their circumstances change in the future.

MODERN SELLING TECHNIQUES

As we have explored, the old-school, pushy sales technique no longer works in modern times. Thanks to the internet, customers are more knowledgeable and educated than ever, and salespeople need to adopt the right types of sales techniques to appeal to a savvy digital audience and meet the demands of customers living in this post-pandemic world. This section explores some of these techniques.

SPIN Selling

SPIN selling is a sales technique based on four stages of questions designed to engage prospects with a goal of making a sale. The acronym SPIN stands for Situation, Problem, Implication, and Need-payoff.[41]

Situation

Situation questions help you to understand the prospect and their current situation and ascertain whether your offering fits their needs. For example, if you're in the website development business, one of your questions could be: "How often are you updating your website with fresh content?"

Problem

Problem questions help to raise awareness of a problem that your prospect may not have noticed before and identify other problems that have been overlooked. For example, "What's the biggest complaint you have about your website from employees or customers?"

Implication

Implication questions uncover the issue and focus on the depth of the pain point. Not only do these questions bring the matter to the prospect's attention, but they help instill a sense of urgency to resolve it. For example, "If you don't update your website consistently, what will the impact be on your business?"

Need-Payoff Questions

Need-payoff questions help the prospect to understand the value of the solution you are offering. Ideally, prospects will be able to identify these benefits in their own words. For example, "If you could cut the amount of time spent on website development and maintenance, how would that impact your business?"

These four questions are a useful way for salespeople to figure out what their prospects need and how they can help them. By asking the right questions in the right order, listening to what the prospect has to say, and incorporating those needs into your product's features, you have every chance of generating positive sales results.

SNAP Selling

SNAP selling is a sales technique that focuses on how customers make decisions and influences them positively to encourage them to feel as though they have made a decision by themselves.[42] By responding to their thoughts, priorities, and business objectives, you will have a better chance of gaining their trust and highlight the value of your product or service. SNAP is an acronym for Simple, iNvaluable, Align, and Prioritize and these components are described below.

Keep It Simple

In the fast-paced world of work, people have less time than ever before, which is why it is important to keep your sales message concise and simple enough for people to immediately grasp. Ways to do this include condensing information into a 30-second phone message, 90-word emails, or one-page emails.

Be iNvaluable

Every day, modern buyers are bombarded with information. You will be able to stand out from the crowd by becoming experts in your field, ready to showcase your product's value and differentiate your business.

Always Align

Being in alignment with customers means understanding their needs, issues, and objectives, and supporting them in achieving their organizational goals. When people want to work with you, you automatically gain access to the main decision makers.

Raise Priorities

Tapping into a buyer's priorities is essential to how you align your product. The key is to position your product as the solution to achieving their priorities. For instance, if saving costs is a top priority, then make sure you emphasize this aspect during the sales process.

FIGURE 7.4 ■ What Is SNAP Selling?			
S	**N**	**A**	**P**
Keep it **S**imple	Be i**N**valuable	Always **A**lign	**R**aise Priorities
Make things easy and clear.	Be the person your customers can't live without.	Sync up with your customers' objectives, issues, and needs.	Keep the most important decisions at the forefront.

N.E.A.T. Selling

N.E.A.T. Selling is a sales technique acronym that stands for Needs, Economic impact, Access to authority, and Timeline.[43]

Needs: The first stage involves focusing on the needs of the prospects and understanding their particular pain points. Putting yourself in the prospect's shoes to truly understand the core issues is important to finding a solution to the problem. A good question to ask yourself here is: What is the core need of your prospect?

Economic impact: Every decision made by a company to buy a new product or service will have a financial impact. Calculate the economic impact of their current situation by measuring their current solution against your own solution and show them the benefits of choosing your company. A good question to ask here is: How do these needs impact them financially?

Access to authority: Gaining access to the main decision maker is key to a successful sale. It is essential to find out who has the authority to sign off on a deal, early in the sales process. Ask yourself: Who is authorized to make financial decisions, and how do I reach that person?

Timeline: All sales professionals need to create a timeline of their sales process to ensure that the deal is closed in a timely manner. Both sellers and buyers must have a compelling reason to close the sale by a certain deadline; for instance, negative consequences such as loss of money. Ask yourself: What's a realistic time frame for closing the deal?

Inbound Selling

Inbound selling is a sales technique that prioritizes the needs, challenges, goals, and interests of individual buyers to help guide them through the decision-making process.[44] This is also referred to as pull selling to bring customers to you. A good example would be Tesla. Electric car manufacturer Tesla has "stores" where customers can go in and design their own car. Given the high demand for Tesla as a modern iconic brand, customers go to Tesla and buy rather than Tesla advertising and pushing sales on customers. Inbound sales is the direct opposite of outbound sales, a traditional sales approach that involves pushing your sales message onto people who may or may not be interested in your product. For example, a lot of outbound sales happen through cold calls or trade shows.

Unlike outbound sales, where closing the deal as soon as possible is the main goal, inbound sales focuses on educating, informing, nurturing, and guiding prospects to encourage them to take an active interest in the products or services offered. This is why it is crucial to know more about the buyer before you approach them. A good way to do this is to analyze the level of interaction they have with your company website, product, or blog posts. For example, they might have commented on a blog or filled out a form to receive an eBook. LinkedIn, Twitter, and Instagram can also be useful for additional knowledge. Once you have captured all this information, you are in a good position to understand more about what your prospects are looking for and start a meaningful conversation. Thanks to these insights, you will be able to craft a personalized sales strategy based on the buyer's wants and needs.

Inbound sales involves educating prospective customers about a product or service to increase interest.

Albert Shakirov/Alamy Stock Photo

Customer-Centric Selling[45]

Customer-centric selling is a sales technique that uses empathy through every stage of the sales process. This means elevating your customers and prioritizing their needs, challenges, and goals with the goal of helping them improve their lives and making the world a better place in the process. Software company Help Scout, based in

Boston, builds empathy among its employees by practicing an initiative called Whole Company Support, where everyone takes part working in customer support for a week. This gives all team members an insight into specific pain points and helps them to develop empathy for the customer.

Customer-centric selling also involves being curious. Successful salespeople ask questions to determine whether they are the right fit for the customer. They must also be willing to walk away if they cannot help them make the changes they require. Author Daniel Pink suggests that salespeople ask themselves two questions to figure out whether they are a good fit for a potential customer: 1. If the person you're selling to agrees to buy, will their life improve? 2. When your interaction is over, will the world be a better place than when you began? If the answer is no, then walk away.

When customer-centric selling works, word spreads. Your customers will likely suggest your product or service and excellent customer experience to their business contacts. As former consultant Frederick F. Reichheld said, "The only path to profitable growth may lie in a company's ability to get its loyal customers to become, in effect, its marketing department."

ENTREPRENEURIAL MINDSET ACTIVITY

Interacting With Strangers

Many people say they don't like sales because they don't want to cold-call or talk to strangers. This exercise will get you a bit more comfortable approaching strangers and asking them for things. To make this activity a little less scary and a bit more fun, identify one or two other people to work with, but there should be no more than three to a group. To make this even more fun, it could be a group competition in your class.

As a group, you will practice approaching strangers with small talk and try to get something (see list below) called a "memento" from them. A memento is some type of keepsake, record, or souvenir. Record the memento given to you by strangers with a photo or video using your phone. Your job as a team is to collect as many mementos and points as you can in 60 minutes.

Here's what you can ask for with corresponding points:

Memento (what you will ask the stranger for)	Points
Selfie	10 points
Piece of candy, gum, or equivalent	10 points
Biographical information (work, age, etc.)	10 points
Sing their favorite song to you	20 points
Favorite memory from childhood	20 points
Share favorite quote	20 points
A hug (but don't be creepy)	30 points
Participate in mini flash mob with the group	40 points
Get $100 (but make sure to give it back later)	50 points
Share a meal	100 points

Critical Thinking Questions

1. What was the difference between asking for lower-point and higher-point mementos?
2. Were you ever treated as invisible or unwelcome? How did this make you feel?
3. What was your mindset coming into the activity and did it change in any way after the activity? How?

Sources: Stark, K. (2016). How to talk to strangers. *IDEAS.TED.COM.* Retrieved from https://ideas.ted.com/how-to-talk-to-strangers/; 7 sales training games that actually boost your skills. (2017). *Userlike.* Retrieved from https://www.userlike.com/en/blog/sales-training-games

IN REVIEW

7.1 Explain the differences between marketing and sales functions in business.

Marketing is the process of attracting people to the goods and services on sale. Marketers conduct research to analyze needs of potential customers and launch campaigns, sometimes over the course of several months, to spark interest in a company's brand, goods, and services. Sales refers to all the activities that lead to the selling of goods and services. Salespeople have shorter-term goals than marketers, typically focusing on achieving sales goals on a monthly basis.

7.2 Describe the elements of the marketing mix: product, promotion, price, place.

The marketing mix is a framework that helps define the brand and differentiate it from the competition. It is made up of four main elements, known as the 4 Ps: product, price, promotion, and place. The product is anything tangible or intangible (such as a service) offered by the company; the price is the amount that the customer is expected to pay for the product; promotion refers to any type marketing communication used by companies to inform target customers about their offering; and place is where the product is actually distributed to your target market.

7.3 Distinguish between B2B and B2C sales.

B2B businesses sell their products and services directly to the decision makers in another business, and B2C businesses sell their products and services to customers for personal use.

7.4 Illustrate the seven stages of the sales cycle.

Salespeople follow a set of specific actions to close a sale, called a sales cycle. There are seven stages in a sales cycle: 1. sales prospecting, 2. making contact, 3. qualifying the lead, 4. nurturing the lead, 5. making an offer, 6. handling objections, 7. closing the sale.

7.5 Explore modern selling techniques.

SPIN selling is a sales technique based on four stages of questions designed to engage prospects with a goal of making a sale. The acronym SPIN stands for Situation, Problem, Implication, and Need-payoff. SNAP selling focuses on how customers make decisions and influences them positively to encourage them to feel as though they have made a decision by themselves. N.E.A.T. selling is a sales technique based on a particular framework. The acronym N.E.A.T. stands for Needs, Economic impact, Access to authority, and Timeline. Inbound selling is a sales technique that prioritizes the needs, challenges, goals, and interests of individual buyers to help guide them through the decision-making process. Customer-centric selling is a sales technique that uses empathy through every stage of the sales process.

BUSINESSES DISCUSSED IN THIS CHAPTER

Organization	UN Sustainable Development Goal
4ocean	14. Life Below Water
American Eagle	6. Clean Water and Sanitation 7. Affordable and Clean Energy 12. Responsible Consumption and Production
Apple	7. Affordable and Clean Energy 12. Responsible Consumption and Production
Barkbox	12. Responsible Consumption and Production 15. Life on Land
Bounty	11. Sustainable Cities and Communities 12. Responsible Consumption and Production

Organization	UN Sustainable Development Goal
BulkBookStore	4. Quality Education 12. Responsible Consumption and Production
Caspar	8. Decent Work and Economic Growth 9. Industry, Innovation, and Infrastructure 12. Responsible Consumption and Production
Chobani	3. Good Health and Well-Being 8. Decent Work and Economic Growth 9. Industry, Innovation, and Infrastructure 11. Sustainable Cities and Communities 12. Responsible Consumption and Production
Costco	11. Sustainable Cities and Communities 12. Responsible Consumption and Production
Course Hero	4. Quality Education
Dell	12. Responsible Consumption and Production 13. Climate Action 17. Partnerships to Achieve the Goals
Everlane	8. Decent Work and Economic Growth 10. Reduced Inequality 12. Responsible Consumption and Production
Expedia	1. No Poverty 13. Climate Action
Facebook	13. Climate Action
Fitbit	3. Good Health and Well-Being
Help Scout	8. Decent Work and Economic Growth 13. Climate Action
Instagram	11. Sustainable Cities and Communities
LinkedIn	8. Decent Work and Economic Growth 13. Climate Action
Monki	12. Responsible Consumption and Production
Ogilvy	12. Responsible Consumption and Production
Pura Vida	8. Decent Work and Economic Growth 11. Sustainable Cities and Communities 12. Responsible Consumption and Production 17. Partnerships to Achieve the Goals
Sock Club	11. Sustainable Cities and Communities 12. Responsible Consumption and Production
Starbucks	6. Clean Water and Sanitation 11. Sustainable Cities and Communities
Tarte Cosmetics	12. Responsible Consumption and Production
Tesla	12. Responsible Consumption and Production 13. Climate Action
TikTok	1. No Poverty 12. Responsible Consumption and Production 13. Climate Action
Unilever	9. Industry, Innovation, and Infrastructure 11. Sustainable Cities and Communities 13. Climate Action

KEY TERMS

B2B businesses (p. 141)

B2C businesses (p. 141)

Broadcast advertising (p. 135)

Clearance sales (p. 137)

Competitive pricing (p. 133)

Content marketing (p. 139)

Cost-plus pricing (p. 133)

Cross-selling (p. 137)

Customer-centric selling (p. 146)

Daily deal (p. 136)

Direct distribution channels (p. 140)

Exclusive distribution (p. 141)

Free samples (p. 137)

Guerilla advertising (p. 135)

In-app advertising (p. 134)

Inbound selling (p. 146)

Indirect distribution channels (p. 140)

Infographics (p. 139)

Intensive distribution (p. 141)

Joint promotions (p. 138)

Limited-time offer (p. 136)

Marketing mix (p. 132)

Marketing (p. 131)

Mission-driven content marketing (p. 140)

Mystery offers (p. 137)

N.E.A.T. selling (p. 146)

Online advertising (p. 134)

Outbound sales (p. 146)

Outdoor advertising (p. 135)

Penetration (p. 133)

Place (p. 140)

Podcast (p. 139)

Price skimming (p. 133)

Price (p. 133)

Print advertising (p. 135)

Product (p. 132)

Product placement advertising (p. 135)

Promotion (p. 134)

Public relations (p. 138)

Public service advertising (PSA) (p. 135)

Sales (p. 131)

Sales cycle (p. 143)

Seasonal deals (p. 137)

Selective distribution (p. 141)

SNAP selling (p. 145)

Social media advertising (p. 134)

Social media contest (p. 137)

Specialty promotion (p. 136)

SPIN selling (p. 144)

Subscriber specials (p. 137)

Target market (p. 131)

Value-based pricing (p. 133)

Video marketing (p. 139)

BUSINESS CASE 7.2: INTUIT—MOUNTAIN VIEW, CALIFORNIA

SDG 11:   Sustainable Cities and Communities

Imagine a software that would allow you to manage and pay all your bills in one place. The idea may seem old-fashioned now, but in the early 1980s, Scott Cook found a way to do just that. Scott, together with computer programmer Tom Proulx, launched the global technology company Intuit in 1983. The first product was Quicken, a software application that helped users manage their budgets and pay bills. The company experienced rapid growth and went public in 1993, and currently has 14,200 employees worldwide in 20 offices located in nine different locations.

While you may not have heard of Intuit, you've most likely heard of its products. Its suite of products today includes TurboTax, Credit Karma, QuickBooks, Mint, and Mailchimp. Most of its products provide financial services directly to customers (B2C); Turbotax, CreditKarma, and Mint are marketed to the general public as free services to help individuals with their finances, be it filing their taxes, check their credit scores, or budget planning, respectively. Its other products, Quickbooks and Mailchimp, however, are marketed toward small businesses (B2B). Quickbooks is a bookkeeping software system and Mailchimp is an email marketing campaign service. According to Intuit's website, "between 2015 and 2020, Intuit's marketing strategy was evolving, moving from a 'house of brands' to a 'connected brand ecosystem' in support of its new mission, 'powering prosperity around the world,' and customer promise of 'no work, more money, complete confidence.'"

Intuit owes its success to strong marketing campaigns, which showcase how Intuit products can change customers' lives by solving some of their significant problems. Its flagship offering today is QuickBooks, a financial and business management tool that offers payroll solutions, merchant payment processing solutions, and financing for small businesses. Because small businesses are a huge target market for the company, Intuit also invests in mission-driven marketing campaigns that encourage and support entrepreneurs. In 2017, the company created the "BACKING YOU" campaign demonstrating how QuickBooks helped small businesses achieve prosperity. During the COVID-19 pandemic, a time when small businesses were struggling to stay in the black, it partnered with baseball legend and investor Alex Rodriguez on a video marketing campaign called "Journey to Success," which showed the ups and downs that business owners experienced on their path to success.

An Intuit survey in November 2021 of 8,000 U.S. employees projected as many as 17 million new small businesses could be set up in 2022. In response, it created an "early start" campaign in 2022 aimed at new entrepreneurs. This campaign marketed educational content resources and advice from clinical psychologist Dr. Sherry Walling, an expert in helping entrepreneurs stay focused, gain clarity, and find joy in the opportunities and challenges of owning a business. It also launched a social media campaign aimed to inspire new businesses, and even aired a 2022 Super Bowl commercial showing how Quickbooks helps creatives manage their finances.

Intuit is working to meet the needs of diverse racial and ethnic groups. In 2022, the company announced an integrated marketing campaign for TurboTax that targeted Latino taxpayers. Says Cathleen Ryan, VP of marketing for Intuit TurboTax: "As one of the fastest-growing segments in the U.S. economy, the Latino community continues to be a key driver and priority for our business. It is important for us not only to educate the Latino community around taxes in their language of preference but also understand their overall needs so we can better serve them with tools and services so they can feel confident their taxes are done right."

Marketing, at times, can have unintended consequences. For example, Intuit ran a campaign for TurboTax using the tagline, "Free, free, free." Turbotax customers assumed the tax filing program was free but, in fact, users had to pay. The lawsuit claimed that the "free" campaign lured in customers with misleading advertising. After a lawsuit settlement in 2022, Intuit will pay $141 million to customers across the United States who were deceived by misleading promises of free tax-filing services through TurboTax.

Today, Intuit is a successful company and recorded $9.63 billion in revenue in 2021 (a 25.45% increase from 2020). The company is making efforts to invest back into the community through mission-driven content marketing. In 2019, Intuit announced its "50x by 30 strategy," which focuses on sustainability initiatives inside and outside the company. Specifically, the 50x by 30 strategy aims to reduce global carbon emissions by 2 million metric tons, which is 50 times the company's 2018 carbon footprint, by the year 2030. In 2021, the company committed to helping 1 million small businesses reduce their own carbon emissions by 50% by 2030. Any small business owner in the United States and United Kingdom can go to the "Intuit Climate Action Marketplace," a website that provides information about products and services from 12 initial solution-providers across the energy, travel, food waste, commuting, and packing and shipping sectors. Examples include Copia, which allows businesses to safely donate their excess food, and Aspiration, which plants trees by rounding up the change on customer purchases. The company also plans to abide by the United Nations Global Compact emissions reduction targets, thus joining over 12,000 other companies across the world.

Critical Thinking Questions

1. What are examples of "good" marketing and "bad" marketing in this case?

2. Why does a company like Intuit, a software company, care about environmental sustainability?

3. Should social issues, like climate change and sustainability, be a part of a company's marketing campaign? Are you more likely to buy from a company that invests back into the community?

References

Associated Press. (2022, May 4). Intuit to pay $141 million for "free" ad campaign PBS. https://www.pbs.org/newshour/economy/inuit-to-pay-141-million-for-free-ad-campaign

Business Wire. (2022, February 28). Intuit TurboTax empowers Latino taxpayers to do their taxes "a su manera" through integrated bilingual efforts. Businesswire.com. https://www.businesswire.com/news/home/20220228005483/en/Intuit-TurboTax-Empowers-Latino-Taxpayers-to-Do-Their-Taxes-%E2%80%9CA-Su-Manera%E2%80%9D-Through-Integrated-Bilingual-Efforts

Intuit. (2020, December 21). Intuit QuickBooks debuts new campaign to spotlight small businesses' "journey to success." Intuit. https://investors.intuit.com/news/news-details/2020/Intuit-QuickBooks-Debuts-New-Campaign-to-Spotlight-Small-Businesses-Journey-to-Success/default.aspx

Intuit. (2021, November 2). Intuit commits to helping 1 million US small businesses cut emissions in half by 2030. Intuit Press Release. https://www.intuit.com/company/press-room/press-releases/2021/intuit-commits-to-helping-1-million-us-small-businesses-cut-emissions-in-half-by-2030/

Intuit. (2022). https://www.intuit.com/

Intuit. (2022, January 5). Intuit QuickBooks kicks off integrated campaign spotlighting "early start" entrepreneurs. Intuit Press Release. https://www.intuit.com/company/press-room/press-releases/2022/intuit-quickbooks-kicks-off-integrated-campaign-spotlighting-early-start-entrepreneurs/

Smart Energy Decisions. (2019, September 23). Intuit commits to 50x climate positive by 2030. Smart Energy Decisions. https://www.smartenergydecisions.com/energymanagement/2019/09/23/intuit-commits-to-50x-climate-positive-by-2030

Mixtroz founders Ashlee Ammons (left) and Kerry Schrader (right)

Courtesy of Ashlee Ammons

8 CUSTOMERS AND MARKET SEGMENTS

LEARNING OBJECTIVES

8.1   Explain how customers create markets.

8.2   Identify the five different types of customers.

8.3   Define consumer behavior and explore its role in understanding purchasing decisions.

8.4   Explore the five steps in the buying process.

8.5   Discuss different ways to segment markets to better reach customers.

BUSINESS IMPACT CASE 8.1: MIXTROZ—BIRMINGHAM, ALABAMA

SDG 9:   Industry, Innovation, and Infrastructure

Mother and daughter dynamic duo Kerry Schrader and Ashlee Ammons attended a lot of networking events only to walk away disappointed with the lack of real connections made and opportunities lost. Ashlee recalls the awkward experience of showing up at an event and the organizer telling her to find someone with the same-colored dot as on her nametag and talk to them. Her mother had similar experiences, and the duo soon learned that many people had those same wasted, awkward, unfulfilling experiences at networking events. To solve this problem and revolutionize the event management industry, Kerry and Ashlee founded Mixtroz, an online platform that groups and connects event attendees through real-time surveying.[1] It's designed to get people's eyes away from their smartphone and onto real people face to face.

In a recent interview in her home state with Alabama.com, Ashlee explained how Mixtroz works:

> It's a tool where if you have 50 or more people coming together, you can use Mixtroz to help increase the engagement among attendees, and also to collect data. We figured out how to make a survey with an algorithm actionable. And by having people complete a survey in real time, you're getting a live data set. For example, I give the welcome address at my alma mater (Baldwin Wallace University) for all the new students each year. So the students will launch the Mixtroz app and get a Baldwin Wallace branded experience. They'll make a name tag, which includes their name, their email, and a selfie. And then they answer 10 questions that Baldwin Wallace has customized—anything from "what major are you" to "what will you do after class." Our algorithm will figure out who among this group of 700 are the best matches for one another. Students will get a notification that shows them whom they've been grouped with, and where to meet that group in real time. Once they get there, we give them things to do, be it a group activity or questions to kick off the conversation. And then the school gets access to all of that data immediately.[2]

Mixtroz targets three customer segments. The event segment is designed for all types of conferences and large gatherings where people want to connect with like-minded people they don't already know. The education segment uses Mixtroz to connect and orient new students (as in the example above), break down faculty silos, and even amplify alumni engagement. Finally, the enterprise segment is targeting the use of Mixtroz in business. It can be used for team building, employee orientation, and breaking down the silos across business departments. Though the segments are different, the purpose is the same—to connect people in real time based on real data.

As COVID-19 shut down all face-to-face networking events and conferences, Mixtroz showed its agility to quickly adapt and speed up new product development. Though the company was planning to release a version of Mixtroz for virtual meetings, the pandemic caused it to accelerate product development from 6 months to 45 days! What was an initial drop in revenue in early 2020 resulted in revenue growth of 300% in the later parts of 2020. The pandemic exacerbated the need to create community and engagement online, and Mixtroz answered the call. As Ashlee noted in a Google Startups interview, "A profound shift in the market and user behavior created a watershed moment for us. People everywhere are looking for solutions to make our digital-first world more connected. We're delighted that we can help with that."[3]

Critical Thinking Questions

1. Consider the three customer segments targeted by Mixtroz. Are the customers more similar or different?

2. What is the core part of the marketing message across all the segments?

3. In the early days of Mixtroz, Kerry and Ashlee would go to tech conferences to talk about their app. They would wear T-shirts that said "Black Female Founder Fund Me" because conference attendees would automatically identify them as event staff rather than founders. Look up the concept of "unconscious bias." How do stereotypes perpetuate these types of reactions?

HOW CUSTOMERS CREATE MARKETS

In the Mixtroz case, Kerry and Ashlee managed to revolutionize the event management industry by creating an app to make networking a less awkward, more efficient, and more fulfilling experience. By connecting different people through an app-based, real-time survey, Mixtroz is able to create groups of people who share common interests to amplify engagement at events. Kerry and Ashlee's solution to poor networking experiences created a new market of customers wanting to reignite their personal networking.

Businesses don't exist without customers, and companies have realized that they must treat customers almost like members of their family through every stage of the customer journey to create a sustainable business. That means understanding and nurturing customers, both existing and potential, from the very first interaction to long after the first purchase has been made. Acquiring, servicing, valuing, listening, and responding to customers is a core function of business.

The truth is that no matter how great you think your product or service is, nobody will buy it unless you really understand what your customers want and need and you are providing more value than your competition. Once you have this knowledge, you can use it to attract more customers.

Customers and Markets

In Chapter 7 we defined marketing as the process of attracting people to the goods and services on sale. We also talked about how marketers sell to a target market, a group of specific people who are most likely to buy the company's products and services. In this chapter, we are going deeper on who those customers are, how they are identified, and how they are segmented in order to sell to them. First, let's explore what is meant by customers and markets.

Although we tend to use the terms customer and consumer interchangeably, they do not mean the same thing. A **customer** is someone who pays for a product or service. Customers become **consumers** when they actually use the product or service.

There can also be some confusion over the definition of a market.[4] Some people consider market to mean customers or customer demand, but that is only one part of it. A **market** is a place where people can sell goods and services (the supply) to people who wish to buy those goods and services (the demand). **Supply** refers to the sellers who compete for customers in the marketplace, while **demand** implies the prospective customers' desire for the goods and services available. When supply meets demand, millions of successful exchanges take place every day.

A market also has different segments. These segments are the markets within the larger market, often referred to as **micromarkets**.[5] For example, Proctor and Gamble is a company that serves the hair care market with brands such as Head & Shoulders, Herbal Essences, and Pantene. A micromarket was created when it introduced Pantene Relaxed & Natural shampoo for Black women.[6] Similarly, there is a micromarket for women who have chemically colored hair—the Pantene Color Adapt collection. We will explore market segmentation in further detail later in the chapter.

Finally, market is not the same as industry (see Chapter 6). Markets are composed of people who buy similar products. Industries are composed of companies that manufacture and/or sell similar products and are typically broader in size and scope. For example, cosmetics is an industry where L'Oreal, Estee Lauder, and Clinique compete. But within that industry there are customers for skin care, makeup, hair care, and fragrances—these are markets. Similarly, The Gap competes with Uniqlo and Zara in the retail clothing industry, but within this industry there are markets for women's jeans, outdoor apparel, footwear, etc. Understanding the customers inside markets is central to building, growing, and sustaining a profitable business. Remember, if you can't access customers, then there is no business. In the next section, we will explore the five different types of customers that are encountered in markets.

TYPES OF CUSTOMERS

People often think of businesses having one type of customer, but instead of looking for a single customer, companies should identify the "chain of customers" composed of users, influencers, recommenders, buyers (purchasers), and decision makers.[7] Depending on the type of business you are in, the customer may play more than one of these roles. For instance, consider a video game production company producing games for Xbox owners targeting children between the ages of 9 and 13. Although 9- to 13-year-olds might certainly be the "users" of the product, they might not necessarily be the purchasers; the "buyers" and "decision makers" are likely the parents. Similarly, the kids' "recommenders" need to be taken into account, who could be close friends or family members or even "influencers"—those on TV or social media. Identifying how customer types overlap is important when building a target base for your product or service because buying behavior and marketing messages may be different. Table 8.1 illustrates five different types of customers in the video game scenario with the company GameStop, a large gaming retailer.[8] Let's take a closer look at each of these types.

TABLE 8.1 ■ Five Types of Customers	
Customer	**Example**
End user	Teen playing a video game
Influencer	Celebrity endorsing the video game in a commercial
Recommender	Blogger writing positive reviews for the video game on a website
Economic buyer	Buyer for GameStop who decided to stock the video game in the company's stores
Decision maker	Parent buying video game for child; CEO, or other high-level decision maker at GameStop, responsible for approving what games the entire company sells in its 4,500+ stores around the world

Source: Neck, H. M., Neck, C. P., & Murray, E. M. (2020). *Entrepreneurship: The Practice & Mindset.* SAGE, p. 130.

End users: The customers who will actually use your product. They will buy it (or not), touch it, operate it, use it, and tell you whether they love it or hate it. Gaining a deeper insight into the needs and motivations of end users is essential, as their feedback will help you refine and tweak the product.

Influencers (or opinion leaders): Customers with a large following who have the power to influence our purchase decisions. Sometimes the biggest influence on the success of a service or product comes from "customers" who have no involvement in it all. Celebrities, journalists, industry analysts, YouTubers, and bloggers have the power to influence our purchase decisions. For example, best-selling music artist Taylor Swift is considered one of the world's most powerful influencers. Swift uses her social media platform to highlight injustices in the music industry. For instance, in 2015 Swift used her influence to take a public stand against Apple Music's policy for offering a free 3-month trial to subscribers, arguing that artists deserved to be paid for their music. Thanks to her protest, Apple changed its policy and artists are now paid for any music streamed during this period.[9] Yet, increasingly, it is social media influencers—those without star status who have managed to establish credibility through their online platforms—who are becoming the new face of marketing. YouTubers in particular are considered to be even more powerful influencers than celebrities because they are perceived to be more authentic and relatable.

Influencers like YouTube fashion and beauty influencer Dulce Candy Ruiz (left) have the power to influence customers' purchase decisions.

Randy Shropshire/Getty Images Entertainment/via Getty Images

Recommenders: People who may evaluate your product and tell the public about it, such as bloggers or experts in an industry. Their opinions have the power to make or break your reputation. For example, a gaming blogger who recommends a new game or a YouTuber showing gamers tips on how to successfully play a game could do wonders for a new product. YouTuber Leah Ashe has amassed over 4 million subscribers to her YouTube channel by creating videos to demonstrate online game platform and game creation system Roblox to children and young adults.

Economic buyers: The customers who have the ability to pay for the purchase. In the case of a B2B transaction (see Chapter 7), the economic buyer may be the one to approve large-scale purchases, such as buyers for retail chains, corporate office managers, and corporate VPs. In the case of a B2C transaction, the buyer is simply the one that pays for the product or service. In our earlier example, the parent would buy the video game for the child (user).

Decision makers: Customers that are similar to economic buyers but who have the highest level of authority to make purchasing decisions, as they are positioned higher up in the hierarchy. The ultimate decision makers do not need to be CEOs—they could also be "Mom" or "Dad," who have the power to approve purchases for their family. For example, Roblox users need to pay to upgrade their avatars by buying a Roblox subscription. Younger children require approval from their parents to make these purchases.

In addition, entrepreneur and educator Steve Blank suggests that we do not ignore one other customer type: the *saboteurs*.[10] Saboteurs are anyone who can veto or slow down a purchasing decision—from top managers, to friends, to spouses, and negative online reviews (that may or may not be real). Identify those saboteurs and find out what's putting them off. You might learn a lot from their feedback.

Now that we understand who customers are, let's turn our attention to how they behave and what influences their buying decisions.

CONSUMER BEHAVIOR AND BUYING DECISIONS

Have you ever gone shopping and just spent lots of your cash on products without really thinking about it? It's true that many of us will make impulse purchases, but most of us tend to think about what we're going to buy before we buy it, why we're buying it, and what kind of value it will add to our day-to-day lives. This process is called consumer behavior, the actions and decision-making processes people go through when purchasing a product or service that they believe will satisfy some need or want.

Gaining insight into consumer behavior allows companies to understand why customers value certain products or services over others, how they view competitors' offerings, where they prefer to buy from, how much they want to pay, and the factors that influence their decision to buy.[11] When companies have this knowledge, they are better able to increase customer retention, predict future trends, enhance customer service, and design marketing strategies that align with their customers' buying behavior.

Customers Seek Functional and Emotional Value

Customers buy because a product gives them functional value and/or emotional value. Functional value is value derived from the problem it solves. For example, the functional value of WD 40 spray includes protecting metal from rusting and corroding, but it can solve many more problems, such as removing bird poop from cars, ink from carpet, gum from shoes, and crayon from walls.[12]

Emotional value is value derived from how a product makes the customer feel. For example, you might feel a sense of pride or coolness when you purchase the latest model of the iPhone because you feel you have the latest and greatest. Similarly, you might feel a sense of gratification when Amazon Prime delivers your package on the day you ordered it. Or even the sense of authority you may feel when gyms like 24 Hour Fitness offer you the opportunity to work out any time you like.[13] These are the types of emotions that many companies tap into to connect with their customers when designing new products and services.

Consider the following true story of a marketing professor who walked into his class on a cold, snowy day. He noticed that half of his students were wearing popular, yet very expensive, Canada Goose–branded jackets. A Canada Goose jacket can cost anywhere from $500 to $1,500. At the beginning of his class, he asked one of the students wearing the Canada Goose jacket why he purchased the jacket. The student responded, "Because it keeps me warm." The professor then turned to another student who came in with a similar-looking jacket but not Canada Goose and asked why she purchased the jacket she was wearing. The student also replied, "Because it keeps me warm." The professor then turned to the class and asked: If both jackets provide the same functional value, why is one student buying a jacket for $1,500 and the other is buying theirs for $250? This example really gets to the heart of emotional value and how the Canada Goose jacket makes the customer feel. Warm? Yes, but also perhaps "hip," "wealthy," and "successful." Because emotional value is so important let's go deeper and examine recent research in this area.

Why do some people choose to wear expensive Canada Goose jackets like this one when less expensive alternatives are available? The answer may lie in the emotional value of Canada Goose products.

Rich Fury/Getty Images Entertainment/via Getty Images

Connecting With Customers on an Emotional Level

A big part of consumer behavior is the ability to connect with customers on an emotional level. Researchers Scott Magids, Alan Zorfas, and Daniel Leemon suggest that connecting with the emotions of customers is integral to building sales, brand recognition, and customer loyalty. They researched hundreds of brands across a diverse group of product categories to identify "emotional motivators" that help companies connect more deeply with their customers in order to drive sales.

The researchers suggest that if companies can identify the most powerful emotional motivators for their customers, they are likely to have a competitive advantage:

> "Our research stemmed from our frustration that companies we worked with knew customers' emotions were important but couldn't figure out a consistent way to define them, connect with them, and link them to results. We soon discovered that there was no standard lexicon of emotions, so 8 years ago, we set out to create one, working with experts and surveying anthropological and social science research. We ultimately assembled a list of more than 300 emotional motivators (p. 68)." [14]

It's complicated to measure emotion. The researchers used big customer data sets and applied extensive data analytics (see Chapter 16) to identify emotional motivators. Though motivators change based on industry, brand, and customer touchpoints, the researchers were able to uncover 10 emotional motivators that crossed all the product categories and brands studied (see Table 8.2).

The research also suggests that customers who are both satisfied with the product and emotionally connected to the company or brand are 52% more valuable to the company than customers who are only highly satisfied. The satisfied and emotionally connected customers are likely to be loyal and repeat customers and are also likely to be a recommender to friends, family, and others.

TABLE 8.2 ■ High-Impact Emotional Motivators

Emotional Motivator	How Businesses Can Leverage the Motivator
Stand out from the crowd	Project a unique social identity; be seen as special
Have confidence in the future	Perceive the future as better than the past; have a positive mental picture of what's to come
Enjoy a sense of well-being	Feel that life measures up to expectations and that balance has been achieved; seek a stress-free state without conflicts or threats
Feel a sense of freedom	Act independently, without obligations or restrictions
Feel a sense of thrill	Experience visceral, overwhelming pleasure and excitement; participate in exciting, fun events
Feel a sense of belonging	Have an affiliation with people they relate to or aspire to be in life; feel part of a group
Protect the environment	Sustain the belief that the environment is sacred; take action to improve their surroundings
Be the person I want to be	Fulfill a desire for ongoing self-improvement; live up to their ideal self-image
Feel secure	Believe that what they have today will be there tomorrow; pursue goals and dreams without worry
Succeed in life	Feel that they lead meaningful lives; find worth that goes beyond financial or socioeconomic measures

Source: Magids, S., Zorfas, A., & Leemon, D. (2015, November). The new science of customer emotions: A better way to drive growth and profitability. *Harvard Business Review*, 66–76.

ETHICS IN BUSINESS

Excluding People From Receiving Ads

Targeting different segments with different messages is a popular marketing strategy. Criticism has been mounting over the years, however, when companies target more vulnerable populations such as elderly, children or marginalized ethnic groups. Critics believe that companies that exploit vulnerable populations are acting unethically. But as social media advertising has grown exponentially, the concept of "dark ads" has emerged. A dark ad is when part of the population receives the ad and others don't. Facebook has been criticized for this practice. Facebook was accused by the U.S. Department of Housing and Urban Development for violating the Fair Housing Act. An investigation found that Facebook could create housing ads where posters could exclude Black people—a practice called *discriminatory targeting*. In another lawsuit, the American Civil Liberties Union claimed Facebook was excluding women from receiving a particular set of job postings. While social media has allowed advertisers to better target and create compelling messages for customers, excluding protected groups (based on race, sex, and sexual orientation) is creating ethical debates in marketing circles.

Critical Thinking Questions

1. Should advertisers be able to exclude reaching people based on traits they cannot change?
2. What are some societal implications of dark ads?
3. Can you find other examples of how dark ads have been used?

Sources: Cui, G., & Choudhury, P. (2003). Consumer interests and the ethical implications of marketing: A contingency framework. *The Journal of Consumer Affairs*, 37(2), 364–387; Concick, H. (2019, March 21). The ethics of targeting minorities with dark ads. *American Marketing Association*. Retrieved from https://www.ama.org/marketing-news/the-ethics-of-targeting-minorities-with-dark-ads/

THE BUYING PROCESS

Before customers complete a purchase, they take a number of actions to find the solution that meets their needs. This is called the **buying process**, which refers to the sequential steps a customer follows to find the right product or service. Although most people tend to follow a similar trajectory, not everyone behaves the same way: Some people might take longer to make a purchasing decision than others. For example, a person buying a new car may wish to test drive it a number of times and conduct extensive research before making the decision to buy, while another may have loyalty to a particular manufacturer and buy the car pretty quickly. Additionally, the length of the buying process is determined by the amount of money being spent. What fast-food restaurant to visit for lunch is a different buying process than what laptop to buy or what apartment to rent or what college to attend. Overall, the buying process depends on the type of product being purchased and the personal preferences of the customer. However, there are five main steps in most buying situations (see Figure 8.1).

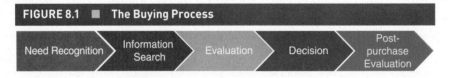

FIGURE 8.1 ■ The Buying Process

Need Recognition → Information Search → Evaluation → Decision → Post-purchase Evaluation

1. **Need Recognition**

   Need recognition (also called problem recognition) occurs when a customer identifies an unmet need and recognizes the need for a product or a service. For example, you might have a cough and cold (problem), so you buy Sudafed, a popular decongestant and cough suppressant. This first step in the buying process is commonly considered the most important for companies. Not only do successful companies produce products and services that solve customer problems, but they may also meet latent needs. Latent needs are needs we have that have yet to surface. Many companies have created products that are based on the ability to identify latent needs of customers. The iPhone, personal computer, calculator, even the old telephone served latent needs. Users of these products were not saying, "I really need an iPhone or a PC." It wasn't until after it was created that we tend to say, "This is a real problem-solver and has made my life better. I can't imagine my life without it!" Generally, a company needs to understand why a customer is buying, and it's usually to solve a problem or meet a need.

2. Information Search

In the second step of the buying process, customers conduct an information search, which involves collecting information on the products or services identified in the need recognition stage. Customers might do some research online by reading reviews or ask friends and family about their experiences. Perusing social media sites and asking for opinions on these sights is commonplace. Additionally, companies that identify themselves as an industry leader have a better chance of increasing their credibility and providing security to the customer. Given the amount of information available today, however, it's hard to know what is fact or fiction. Watching a TikTok video could be a commercial and you don't even know it! A nonprofit company, Consumer Reports, has been around since 1936 and still provides consumers with unbiased evaluations to this day. It is known for its rigorous, independent testing of products and works "to create a marketplace built on credible information, greater transparency, and fairness."[15] Consumer Reports tests everything from cleaning products to electronics to cars and has 63 labs and over 140 testing experts to collect testing data.

Consumer Reports is a nonprofit organization that provides independent testing of products, helping customers engaging in information search.

NetPhotos/Alamy Stock Photo

3. Evaluation

After customers have identified a need and carried out an information search, they will reach a stage where they may have a few options from which to choose. This is called evaluation, the third step in the buying process, whereby customers consider and compare alternative possibilities to ensure they are making the right decision. During this stage, customers may compare the product's attributes with other, similar offerings on the market and evaluate the price of each product. Leading auto insurance provider Geico, based in Maryland, makes it easier for customers to compare its rates with other insurers by offering a comparison tool on its website, even when the competition is less expensive.[16] This transparent approach is a valuable way to building trust and loyalty with customers.

4. **Purchase Decision**

Having evaluated different alternatives, the customer reaches the purchase decision stage, the point in the buying process at which they decide to move forward with the purchase. Today, companies can track what users do on retail websites. For example, you may place a new pair of shoes in your online shopping cart but choose not to purchase just yet. Then you might get an email reminding you that they are there waiting for you to buy and that, of course, inventory is running low! You also may start seeing advertisements on your Facebook or news feeds for those orange Chuck Taylor Converse sneakers you were thinking about buying!

5. **Post-Purchase Evaluation**

Post-purchase evaluation is the final stage of the buying process, where the customer considers the value and usefulness of the purchase and how satisfied they are with the product or service. If the customer is happy with the purchase, then they will likely recommend it to others or perhaps post a positive review on social media or write a blog about their experience online, which is good news for the company as favorable endorsements help to drive sales and boost a company's reputation. This is why it is important for companies to send follow-up surveys and thank-you emails to ensure that the customer buys from them in the future. However, in a situation where the customer is not happy with the purchase, companies must ensure that they have a skilled customer service team in place to ensure the returns or exchange process goes as smoothly as possible so that the customer won't be put off from buying from them in the future. Zappos is a great example of retaining customers even after purchase. It was one of the first companies to offer free returns for shoes purchased online, and the process to do so was quite easy. This enabled customers to reduce the risk of what marketers term buyer's dissonance—a condition of remorse or regret shortly after buying a product. Though buyer's dissonance most often occurs with high-ticket items, shoe fit and look is very important. Without the ability to try on shoes, walk in them, and return them, the Zappos business model could not have worked because customers would think the purchase was too risky.

The Technology Adoption Life Cycle

Although the buying process gives companies insight into the steps customers take toward purchasing a product or service, it is equally important to understand the different ways that people respond to new products, particularly in relation to new technology, when they enter the marketplace.

The success or failure of your product or service depends on the response of potential customers in the marketplace. Customers tend to adopt new products at different times, and understanding how people adopt or accept new innovations is key to success.

The technology adoption life cycle, introduced by communications professor Everett Rogers, is a model that describes the acceptance process of a new innovation over time, according to defined adopter groups. The model divides the customers into five categories: innovators, early adopters, early majority, late majority, and laggards. As Figure 8.2 illustrates, innovators will start their buying process early when a new product is introduced, but a late majority will not enter the buying process until much later. For example, have you bought a virtual reality headset yet? If yes, you would be classified as an early adopter! Let's explore each category of customer in the technology adoption life cycle in further detail.

1. **Innovators (2.5% of customers):** These are the first customers to try a new product. They are people who are enthusiastic about new technology and are willing to take the risk of

product flaws or other uncertainties that may apply to early versions. In general, innovators are wealthier than other adopters; in other words, they can afford to take a risk on a new innovation. Companies often get buy-in from this group by involving them in early user trials.

2. **Early adopters (next 13.5% of customers):** This is the second group to adopt a product. Like innovators, they tend to buy new products shortly after they hit the market. However, unlike innovators, they are not motivated by their enthusiasm for new technology and prefer to consult reviews before they make a purchase. Early adopters are usually people who make reasoned decisions about product purchases. Companies may provide this group with technical insights to encourage them to support the innovation.

3. **Early majority (next 34% of customers):** People in this category tend to take interest in a new product as it begins to have mass market appeal. They are both practical and extremely risk averse, preferring to wait and see how others view the technology before they buy it themselves. As a consequence, they look for opinions from their peers, thought leaders, or professional contacts to support them in their decision to invest. Companies may cater to the early majority by enhancing their products and offering improvements.

4. **Late majority (next 34% of customers):** These customers are typically skeptical, pessimistic, risk averse, and less affluent than the previous groups. However, because this group makes up such a large portion of the life cycle, they cannot be ignored. Companies can appeal to this group by providing special offers and promotions and creating simpler products or systems at an affordable cost.

5. **Laggards (final 16% of customers):** People in this final category are the last to adopt a new innovation, sometimes taking years after its release. They tend to have a negative attitude toward technology in general and have a strong aversion to risk and change. Despite their best efforts, companies may never be able to persuade this group that their innovation is worth a first glance, never mind going so far as to purchase it.

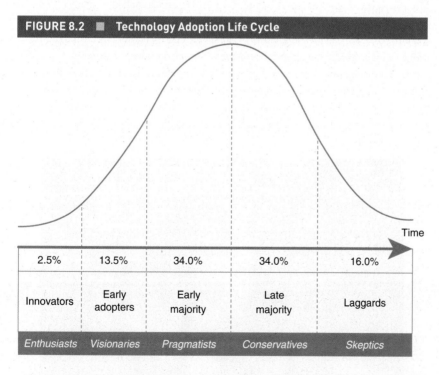

FIGURE 8.2 ■ Technology Adoption Life Cycle

In an ideal world, all five categories of customers in the adoption life cycle would eventually adopt the new product, but of course, this is not the case. As the model shows, a product tends to go through differ-ent stages of adoption over time. Some customers may rush to purchase a product as soon as it comes on the market, while others may not. Understanding this concept is essential to understanding the buying process and also explains why some products never really take off. Think about some of your recent purchases of new products and identify where you are on this curve. For example, do you own a smartwatch like an Apple watch? If yes, when did you buy, and how would you classify yourself on the adoption curve?

MARKET SEGMENTATION

In Chapter 7 we discussed how marketers sell to a target market—a group of specific people who are most likely to buy the company's products and services. Target markets can be grouped into subsets through market segmentation, which is the process of dividing a target market into approachable groups based on wants, needs, common interests, common behaviors, and demands.[17] Mixtroz is a good example of a company that segmented its market by dividing its customers into specific groups to facilitate the networking experience. Segmenting the market allows you to target your products and services to the right people in the right way so they are more likely to be your customer.

Types of Segments

There are four types of market segmentation used by marketers: demographic segmentation, geographic segmentation, psychographic segmentation, and behavioral segmentation (see Table 8.3). Combined these methods of segmentation help companies better understand who their customers are, what their lives are like, and how to reach them.

1. **Demographic Segmentation**

   Demographic segmentation divides a market by demographic factors such as age, education, income, gender, occupation, ethnicity, family size, and nationality. For example, luxury goods manufacturer most known for high-end writing pens Montblanc worked with London-based ecommerce company Yieldify to target customers based on their income.[18] As Montblanc customers are typically high earners, Yieldify launched a variety of promotions for Father's Day on the Montblanc website. The Father's Day deal offered a free gift to customers spending over $275, which aligned with the spending expectations of its market. As a result, Montblanc received a greater number of conversions from those targeted.

   Although demographics are useful in identifying target customers, they don't provide an entirely accurate representation of your customers. For instance, segmenting your market by location or age doesn't tell you much about your customer preferences, so you will need to consider the other types of segmentation analyses to build a more detailed picture of your target customers.

It is clear from the way the Montblanc store in Beverly Hills, California, is designed that the company typically targets customers with high incomes.

Patrick T. Fallon/Bloomberg/via Getty Images

2. **Geographic Segmentation**

Geographic segmentation divides the market based on geographical location, climate, or population density. A good knowledge of where customers are located helps companies to better understand the needs, preferences, and interests of customers, which allows them to be more specific with their ads and messaging. For example, a swimwear brand that segments its market by climate would not focus on Alaskan residents in January, as Alaska has an Arctic climate.[19] Geographic segmentation also allows focus on a particular service area. For example, when trying to project the number of potential patrons that may visit a new restaurant, you can look at a 10-mile radius (geographic segment) and see if there are enough potential customers that fit your anticipated demographic profile of a likely restaurant customer.

3. **Psychographic Segmentation**

Psychographic segmentation takes into account the psychological aspects of behavior such as values, opinions, personality traits, attitudes, lifestyle, hobbies, beliefs, fears, and interests. This information is useful for finding out the likes and dislikes of different customers, how they live and work, and what their needs may be. For example, a fitness company may use psychographic segmentation to search for people who care about healthy living and exercise; whereas a dance club may not target customers who show a strong preference for quiet pursuits like reading.[20]

Although psychographic data are useful, they are difficult to find and even harder to analyze for accuracy. For instance, Facebook may be able to provide some information about customers' likes and dislikes, but it is not easy to pinpoint in-depth details like fears without conducting expensive market research such as focus groups, observation, interviewing, and surveying.

4. **Behavioral Segmentation**

Behavioral segmentation divides markets based on customer behaviors and decision-making patterns. These behaviors include online purchasing habits, how often they use a product or service, previous products, the actions they take on a website (time spent on the site etc.), or their loyalty to a certain brand. For example, family restaurant Ladles, based in South Carolina, rewards customers for their loyalty by offering a $2 discount on their next purchase.[21] By using behavioral segmentation, companies can understand how customers interact with their products and services and target them more effectively.

TABLE 8.3 ■ Four Main Types of Market Segmentation

Demographic	Geographic	Psychographic	Behavioral
Age	Location	Values	Purchasing habits
Education	Climate	Opinions	Consumption
Income	Needs	Personality traits	Brand loyalty
Gender	Preferences	Attitudes	Lifestyle
Occupation	Interests	Lifestyle	Product usage
Ethnicity		Hobbies	
Family size		Beliefs	
Nationality		Fears	
		Interests	

Benefits of Segmenting a Market[22]

With hundreds of millions of people in the U.S. alone with countless different needs and demands, it would be impossible for any company to cater to such a vast market. This is why market segmentation is so vital for companies, as it allows them to limit the field of customers and tailor their offerings to better meet their needs as well as earn revenue more efficiently. It's too expensive to market to *everyone*. A company must decide who is most likely going to buy its products and develop its marketing plan accordingly. In general, there are five main benefits to customer segmentation:

1. **Increase Brand Loyalty**

    By identifying specific market segments, companies are better able to serve customers' wants and needs. This allows them to build a better relationship with their customers, leading to brand loyalty and higher customer retention. In the U.S., Amazon is often cited as the company with the greatest brand loyalty in online retail. Table 8.4 shows customer loyalty leaders in 2020—the year of the COVID-19 pandemic.

TABLE 8.4 ■ **Top 10 Most Loyal Customer Brands in 2021**

Rank	Brand	Category
1	Amazon	Online retail
2	Apple	Smartphones
3	Netflix	Video streaming
4	Domino's	Pizza
5	Amazon	Video streaming
6	Disney	Video streaming
7	Google	Search engines
8	WhatsApp	Instant messaging
9	Instagram	Social networking
10	Nike	Athletic footwear

Source: Adapted from Brand Keys Customer Loyalty List 2021. Retrieved from https://thewisemarketer.com/research/brand-keys-2021-annual-loyalty-leaders-list-unveiled/

2. **Stronger and Clearer Marketing Message**

    When a company focuses on a specific group it is able to target those segments with clear, specific marketing communications. Communication happens between company and customer through social media, email, and other forms of advertising. A common way to send a clear message is by adopting a tagline. A **tagline** is often an easy way to send a strong, clear message. By definition, a tagline is a short, memorable phrase or motto to convey the purpose or value of a brand or product. Think Nike's *Just Do It*. Recollect your own experience in applying for college. What grabbed your attention? What message stood out to you? Even colleges and universities are targeting different segments of students. Check out some of the college taglines (without associated names) in Table 8.5. Do any of them speak to you?

TABLE 8.5 ■ **Taglines Used by Colleges**

A foundation for life.	Building a road for tomorrow.
Courage to act.	Dream big.
Faster, better, stronger.	Full of good ideas.
Be the change.	Going farther.
Giving you the choice.	Infinite possibilities.
Making the world a better place.	Open minds. Creating futures.
The power of ideas.	The future awaits.
The revolution starts here.	Uncommon leadership.

Source: Gaille, B. (2017). List of 101 catchy college campaign slogans. *Brandon Gaille small business & marketing advice.* Retrieved from https://brandongaille.com/list-30-catchy-college-campaign-slogans/

3. **Differentiates the Brand from the Competition**

   Targeting specific customer segments enables companies to have a deeper understanding of the customer and market more effectively to them to build that brand loyalty previously discussed. This approach elevates companies above their competitors through differentiation (see Chapter 6). During the COVID-19 pandemic the use of video conferencing software surged and kept the world connected and perhaps even sane. Zoom differentiated itself quickly and became a market leader even though alternatives existed including Skype, Google Hangouts, Microsoft Teams, Webex, and many others. Zoom was able to differentiate itself because it was extremely easy to use, offered 40 free minutes with up to 100 attendees, and didn't require any unusual or timely downloads.[23] Additionally, it is incredibly adaptive to change and responds quickly to customer needs.[24]

4. **Better Opportunities for Growth and Expansion**

   Brand loyalty, clear messaging, and differentiation lead to more customers, and those customers are keen to experience new products from these same companies. Having strong relationships with customer segments means a company really understands the customer and is in a better position to identify new needs, solve new problems, and innovate. Having a strong customer following also gives a company more marketing power to break into new markets and expand into another locations. Zoom is very transparent with its customer base and stakeholders. It is constantly communicating with stakeholders about its video conferencing software, including enhancements and issues, but it's also talking about new products such as hardware solutions for working at home and accelerating the launch of its new product called Zoom Phone.[25] Zoom Phone is a cloud phone system that allows users to make and receive calls from Zoom.

5. **Enhanced Profits**

   Targeting everyone or thinking that everyone in the world can be your customer rarely works. Choose a core segment to target, really focus on doing well for that segment, and then expand. Even Facebook started with its core segment of students at Harvard and then saw expansion after early success and working out the kinks. Companies that initially focus on a narrowly defined market, often termed a "niche market," tend to receive a better return on investment. The price of customer acquisition is high and wasting money on a diluted message that is going to get lost in an already noisy marketplace is an inefficient use of resources. Think about Patagonia, which we introduced in Chapter 1. Its target is clear—outdoor enthusiasts who care for the environment. It has focused on this segment since its inception. Does it have other customers outside of this target? Yes, but it only has those customers because they are attracted to the message and want to be perceived as outdoor enthusiasts who care about the environment.

ENTREPRENEURIAL MINDSET ACTIVITY

Creating a Buyer Persona

Even when a business has a target market and a clear understanding of its potential market segments, it is important to create a buyer persona. A buyer persona is a fictional representation of the ideal customer. In the case of an existing business, this can be a persona based on sales data that you already have on who is buying and why. Building personas takes you beyond demographic and geographic segmentation with more attention given to psychographics and behaviors. As an example, let's consider a company that is producing a podcast related to the "gig economy." The gig economy relates to individuals working and earning income from a series of projects rather than a single career. When the podcast company analyzes the data from its listeners, it realizes that many listeners are in search of their next career move. When the company thinks of its ideal listener (customer), it creates the following persona (see Figure 8.3).

FIGURE 8.3 ■ Cooper, the Stay-at-Home Dad

©istockphoto.com/gradyreese

LIFESTYLE

- Cooper is married to Jessica and they have three kids—2 boys (ages 8 and 10) and 1 girl (age 4).
- Jessica has a very demanding job as a lead research scientist with a biotechnology company and often works long hours.
- There are some financial pressures given that the family is living on one salary, but they live in an area with strong public schools.
- Cooper gets the boys to school every day but also stays at home with his daughter. The boys are starting to do more activities after school, which also requires a lot of scheduling and carpooling.
- Cooper, once a chef for a restaurant, also cooks all the meals.
- Cooper and Jessica love the outdoors and find themselves hiking and camping with the kids more often.

BACKGROUND

- Graduated from culinary school.
- Traveled through Italy after school to learn about Italian cuisine.
- Jessica, his wife, has a PhD in biology.
- They currently live in a suburb of Boston, Massachusetts, given that Boston is the hub of many biotech companies.

CHALLENGES/PAIN POINTS

- Jessica makes a good salary, but the Boston area is expensive.
- Their youngest daughter will be in school soon, so Cooper is considering getting a job again, but being a chef is not conducive to raising children given long work hours.
- Cooper is considering alternative lines of work but worries he may need to go back to school.

VALUES

- Cooper values family first. He was an acclaimed chef but when they had their first child, he knew he had to focus on the family.
- Values education and was very much attracted to Jessica because of her PhD.
- Has raised his kids to value diversity and be kind to all types of people.
- Both Cooper and Jessica are strong advocates of protecting the environment and educating their kids to do the same.

How does the company then use this persona? Whenever it is brainstorming new podcast episodes or even potential new podcast series, it will use "Cooper" as a sounding board. Would Cooper listen to this episode? What else does Cooper need? How can we create a better relationship with Cooper?

In this Mindset activity, you are to create a persona for one of the branded products in Table 8.6. Do some research on typical customers to justify what to include in your persona. Follow the template set forth in Figure 8.3 above, with Cooper.

Once you complete your persona, next identify three new business ideas to serve that type of customer!

TABLE 8.6 ■ Branded Products to Choose From

Mixtroz online platform	Free Bird camper van
Weight Watchers mobile app	Apple watch
Peloton fitness bike	Sony PlayStation gaming console

Critical Thinking Questions

1. How can personas be used to build better relationships with customers?
2. How can personas be used by new companies just getting started?
3. Was it difficult or easy to identify new business ideas for the persona you created?

IN REVIEW

8.1 Explain how customers create markets.

Businesses don't exist without customers, so gaining a deep understanding of your customers is absolutely essential to early business success. Companies must work hard toward understanding and nurturing customers, both existing and potential, from the very first interaction to long after the first purchase has been made. A customer is someone who pays for a product or service.

Customers become consumers when they actually use the product or service. A market is a place where people can sell goods and services (the supply) to people who wish to buy those goods and services (the demand).

8.2   Identify the five different types of customers.

Typically, there are different types of customers: end users, influencers, recommenders, economic buyers, and decision makers. End users are the customers who will actually use your product; influencers (or opinion leaders) are customers with a large following who have the power to influence our purchase decisions; recommenders are the people who may evaluate your product and tell the public about it, such as bloggers or experts in an industry; economic buyers are the customers who have the ability to approve large-scale purchases, such as buyers for retail chains, corporate office managers, and corporate VPs; and decision makers are customers similar to economic buyers who have even more authority to make purchasing decisions, as they are positioned higher up in the hierarchy.

8.3   Define consumer behavior and explore its role in understanding purchasing decisions.

Consumer behavior is the actions and decision-making processes people go through when purchasing a product or service that they believe will satisfy some need or want. Gaining insight into consumer behavior allows companies to understand why customers value certain products or services over others, how they view competitors' offerings, where they prefer to buy from, how much they want to pay, and the factors that influence their decision to buy.

8.4   Explore the five steps in the buying process.

The buying process refers to the number of sequential steps a customer follows to find the right product or service. There are five main steps in the buying process: need recognition, information search, evaluation, decision, and post-purchase evaluation. The technology adoption life cycle provides further insight into the buying process by dividing the market into five categories of potential customers: innovators, early adopters, early majority, late majority, and laggards.

8.5   Discuss different ways to segment markets to better reach customers.

Target markets can be grouped into subsets through market segmentation, which is the process of dividing a target market into approachable groups based on wants, needs, common interests, common behaviors, and demands. There are four main types of market segmentation used by companies: demographic segmentation, geographic segmentation, psychographic segmentation, and behavioral segmentation.

BUSINESSES DISCUSSED IN THIS CHAPTER

Organization	UN Sustainable Development Goal
Canada Goose	12. Responsible Consumption and Production
Geico	7. Affordable and Clean Energy 11. Sustainable Cities and Communities
Ladles	3. Good Health and Well-Being
Mixtroz	9. Industry, Innovation, and Infrastructure
Montblanc	11. Sustainable Cities and Communities
Proctor & Gamble	8. Decent Work and Economic Growth 12. Responsible Consumption and Production 13. Climate Action
WD40	8. Decent Work and Economic Growth
Zappos	12. Responsible Consumption and Production
Zoom	9. Industry, Innovation, and Infrastructure

KEY TERMS

Behavioral segmentation (p. 165)

Buyer persona (p. 167)

Buyer's dissonance (p. 162)

Buying process (p. 160)

Consumer behavior (p. 158)

Consumers (p. 155)

Customer (p. 155)

Decision makers (p. 157)

Demand (p. 155)

Demographic segmentation (p. 164)

Economic buyers (p. 157)

Emotional value (p. 158)

End users (p. 156)

Evaluation (p. 161)

Functional value (p. 158)

Geographic segmentation (p. 165)

Influencers (or opinion leaders) (p. 156)

Information search (p. 161)

Latent needs (p. 161)

Market segmentation (p. 164)

Market (p. 155)

Micromarkets (p. 155)

Need recognition (p. 160)

Post-purchase evaluation (p. 162)

Psychographic segmentation (p. 165)

Purchase decision (p. 162)

Recommenders (p. 157)

Supply (p. 155)

Tagline (p. 166)

Target market (p. 164)

Technology adoption life cycle (p. 162)

BUSINESS CASE 8.2: MERCK—RAHWAY, NEW JERSEY

SDG 3:   Good Health and Well-Being

Markets can often be segmented into demographic characteristics such as age, gender, marital status, and income. But for the multinational pharmaceutical giant Merck, market segments are based on diseases and illnesses. With more than 50 pharmaceutical products in its product portfolio, the company specializes in addressing a range of health issues, including type 2 diabetes, cancer, nervous-system disorders, and cardiovascular, respiratory, and infectious diseases. Customers with these disorders represent market segments where different products (drugs) are developed for each segment.

Merck rose from humble beginnings as a drug store in Darmstadt, Germany, in 1668 to the pharmaceutical giant it is today, with profit of more than $13 billion, ranking 71st on the 2022 Fortune 500. Throughout its history, Merck has been at the forefront of patient health: In 1898, it sold the first commercially used smallpox vaccine in the U.S., manufactured the first measles vaccine in 1963, and made the first mumps vaccine in 1967. Recently, it released a COVID-19 treatment pill called Molnupiravir, which is currently being used to treat COVID patients who are unable to take antibody drugs. The company also announced this year that its new drug, Keytruda, reduces the risk of early lung cancer returning in patients who had undergone lung surgery by 24%.

The pharmaceutical industry is a series of complex marketplaces, as the user of the drug is not always the buyer of the drug, who also may not be the decision maker agreeing to prescribe the drug. First, health care providers can recommend or block certain drugs and treatments. Second, there is added complication in the buying process, as insurance coverage can dictate availability or greatly influence purchase decisions of patients.

Interestingly, the United States and New Zealand are the only two countries that allow drug companies to advertise prescription drugs directly to consumers. There was much debate around the positive and negative effects on direct-to-consumer (DTC) advertising for pharmaceuticals, but in the 1980s, the FDA ruled in favor of DTC advertisements because they were concerned about public health. In 1981, Merck debuted the first DTC print advertisement, promoting its pneumonia vaccine. Today, pharmaceutical agencies have to follow rigid rules for disclosing side effects and other information, explaining the television and print advertisements you see.

After Oprah Winfrey's famous televised 2021 interview of Prince Harry and Meghan Markle aired in the United Kingdom, many viewers were shocked to see these drug TV advertisements from the United States that read a long list of side effects. "American adverts make me feel like I'm in some post-apocalyptic world," one tweet read. Pharma ads are still controversial in the U.S. In 2015, the

American Medical Association, the country's largest physician trade group, called for a ban on drug advertising, but did not succeed.

The United States' pharmaceutical advertising affects consumer behavior, as it puts more responsibility into consumers' hands to manage their health care and ask their health care providers about drugs and treatments. Many believe that consumers need to be motivated to seek treatment for an illness or to ask their doctor about therapy options, potential outcomes, and costs. Health care consumers are more educated today than ever before because of their access to information on the internet.

Customer trust drives business in health care. In a 2021 Deloitte Centers for Health Solutions survey, about half of U.S. consumers said they don't trust biopharma companies. The top three reasons cited were focus on profit-making, high prices for medicines, and doctors overprescribing drugs. "For biopharma, maintaining reputational integrity within the health care ecosystem among all stakeholders—consumers, health care providers, regulators, NGOs—is critical. . . . In general, trust drives customer loyalty; 62% of people who report highly trusting a brand buy almost exclusively from that brand over competitors in the same category."

Critical Thinking Questions

1. Who is Merck's primary customer?

2. Pick one drug offered by Merck. What are examples of the five types of customers discussed in the chapter?

3. What is the impact of drug advertising on customer loyalty and product use?

4. What is your opinion of drug advertising in the United States and New Zealand versus the rest of the world?

References

Akhtar, A. (2021, March 8). Brits are calling out the "dystopian" and "post-apocalyptic" American pharma ads that aired during Oprah's interview with Meghan Markle and Prince Harry. *Business Insider.* https://www.businessinsider.com/brits-call-american-pharmaceutical-ads-post-apocalyptic-2021-3

Drugwatch. (n.d.). Merck & Co. https://www.drugwatch.com/manufacturers/merck/

Fortune. (2022). Merck company profile: Fortune 500. *Fortune.* https://fortune.com/company/merck/fortune500/

Hopkins, J. S. (2022, March 15). Merck's COVID-19 pill heavily used so far despite concerns. *The Wall Street Journal.* https://www.wsj.com/articles/mercks-covid-19-pill-heavily-used-so-far-despite-concerns-11647250200

Kimball, S. (2022, March 17). Merck's Keytruda reduced risk of disease recurrence or death in early lung cancer patients by 24%. *CNBC News.* https://www.cnbc.com/2022/03/17/mercks-keytruda-reduced-risk-of-recurrence-or-death-in-early-lung-cancer-patients-by-24percent.html

Merck. (n.d.). Research and products. https://www.merck.com/research-and-products/

Reh, G., Gupta, L., Ronte, H., & Varia, H. (2021, May 6). Overcoming biopharma's trust deficit. *Deloitte.* https://www2.deloitte.com/us/en/insights/industry/life-sciences/trust-in-biopharmaceutical-companies-covid.html

Statistica. (2022, February). Top selling products of Merck & Co. based on revenue from 2019 to 2021. *Statistica.* https://www.statista.com/statistics/272367/revenues-of-merck-and-co-top-selling-drugs/

Ventola, C. L. (2011). Direct-to-consumer pharmaceutical advertising: Therapeutic or toxic?. *P & T: A Peer-Reviewed Journal for Formulary Management, 36*(10), 669–684. https://www.ncbi.nlm.nih.gov/pmc/articles/PMC3278148/

BLOCK 3
STRUCTURE
AND PURPOSE

Liz Gregersen works at the offices of Zappos.com, Inc.

Ronda Churchill/Bloomberg/via Getty Images

9 ORGANIZATIONAL STRUCTURE AND DESIGN

BUSINESS IMPACT CASE 9.1: ZAPPOS—LAS VEGAS, NEVADA

SDG 3:   Good Health and Well-Being

When you consider buying shoes online, you might go to Zappos. Founded in 1999 by entrepreneur Nick Swinmurn with $2 million, later sold to Amazon in 2009 for $2 billion, and consistently recognized as a great place to work, Zappos is hailed as a company that cares about its 1,500 employees' happiness. The company's core values, listed below, give insight into what it feels like to work at Zappos.[1]

1. Deliver WOW through service

2. Embrace and drive change

3. Create fun and a little weirdness

4. Be adventurous, creative, and open-minded

5. Pursue growth and learning

6. Build open and honest relationships with communication

7. Build a positive team and family spirit

8. Do more with less

9. Be passionate and determined

10. Be humble

In order to build and support the "innovative and quirky" culture at Zappos, the structure of the company is important. After Zappos grew from a small startup to a much larger corporation, its rapid growth had the potential to threaten everything that made Zappos exceptional—the employees and culture.

To address this issue, in 2013 Zappos made the controversial move to organize the company as a holacracy, an alternative way of structuring, rning, and operating a company where power is distributed and structure is flexible while easy to change.[2] Within a holacracy, people do not have job titles and are able to create their own guidelines. Zappos desired a structure that would give employees more freedom and autonomy but also encourage growth and productivity. Rather than following the more common hierarchical structure populated with top management, middle managers, supervisors, and direct reports, the organization was divided into small pods/groups/teams represented as "circles" in the company.[3] Prior to the transition, Zappos had 150 departments that eventually evolved into 500 circles. Within these circles, the employees would come together to decide what work they felt the most connected to and were given the freedom to design the guidelines they would use to rn themselves. John Bunch, a lead organizational designer at Zappos, explained the new model:

We're classically trained to think of "work" in the traditional paradigm. One of the core principles is people taking personal accountability for their work. It's not leaderless. There are certainly people who hold a bigger scope of purpose for the organization than others. What it does do is distribute leadership into each role. Everyone is expected to lead and be an entrepreneur in their own roles, and Holacracy empowers them to do so.[4]

The transition to a holacracy was not without challenge; it quickly turned out that not everyone was comfortable working in such an environment. Employees who didn't embrace the new holacracy structure were offered severance packages; 18% of the employees accepted the offer and subsequently left.

It might not have been easy to create a holacracy at Zappos, but the company continues to operate with this same structure today. Every employee is empowered to make changes and decisions in their roles as long as the changes embrace the purpose and values of Zappos.

Critical Thinking Questions

1. Review the core values of Zappos. What three values are most attractive to you? What does your choice say about the type of company you would like to work for?

2. Can you see yourself performing at a high level in a holacracy, or do you need more structure?

3. Why is a holacracy considered a more entrepreneurial way of organizing a company?

ORGANIZATIONAL STRUCTURE

An organizational structure is a system that coordinates the people, tasks, and activities necessary to carry out a particular purpose. Organizational structures help companies to function at their best because they improve the flow of communication between employees, establish clear responsibilities and reporting relationships, provide opportunities for company growth and expansion, and facilitate the successful completion of tasks and activities. As you will learn in this chapter, there are different types of organizational structures. The Zappos case features one type of organizational structure called a holacracy, which is a company structure that distributes decision-making authority to self-managed, "boss-less" teams or "circles." Zappos chose this structure to give employees the ability to choose the work that matches their skills and interests, set their own guidelines around how that work gets done, and make decisions based on the company's goals.

Just as the holacracy structure was an experiment for Zappos, the shift to remote working during the COVID-19 pandemic forced many companies to redesign their organizational structures by devising ways to adapt to different working conditions. Some of these initiatives involve creating an agile decision-making approach that promotes greater levels of inclusion, developing ways to accommodate flexible working and work–life balance, and designing new innovations to meet the demands of customers and markets.

In the following sections, we will explore the evolution of organizational structures and how they continue to develop in order to enhance business performance and maintain a competitive edge.

Organizational Charts

All organizations, big or small, need an organizational chart, which is a graphic representation of a company's structure that communicates how a company is organized.[5] Organizational charts are important because they list the roles and responsibilities of every single person in the company, thereby eliminating any confusion over accountability, which enables smoother communication. Figure 9.1 provides a general example of an organizational chart.

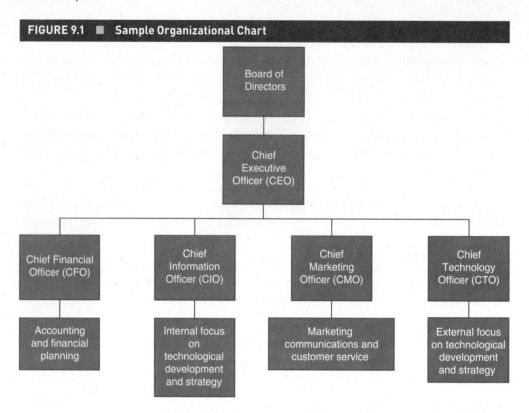

FIGURE 9.1 ■ Sample Organizational Chart

An organization's structure affects how successfully it can coordinate and accomplish its work activities. Structures vary from company to company and depend on a number of factors, such as size of company, the degree of specialization for a particular job, and the number of people who report to an individual manager, of which there are several types.

Types of Managers

Managers are usually classified by type, to help people inside and outside the organization to better understand each manager's decision-making power and scope of authority. Traditional organizations are formed hierarchically (like a pyramid), with a few senior managers at the top and a greater number of lower-level managers below who are responsible for daily tasks and overseeing employee development and performance. This structure is designed to ensure that lines of communication, authority, and reporting responsibilities are clear to everyone. There are three main types of managers: *top managers, middle managers, and first-line managers.* Each type makes decisions based on different time scales, spanning days to decades.

Top managers set the organization's direction and make decisions that affect everybody. For example, a top manager of a manufacturing plant might make the decision to use a different supplier, which could make an impact on the company for months or even years.

Middle managers report to upper management and direct the work of first-line managers; they are also responsible for divisions or departments. Middle managers regularly monitor performance and ensure lower-level employees carry out their assigned duties.

First-line managers direct daily activities for producing goods and services. A first-line manager at a restaurant might settle on how to schedule employee work hours most effectively over a holiday season, which could impact the organization for 2 to 3 weeks.[6] Table 9.1 provides a breakdown of types of managers, their typical titles, the kinds of decisions they make, and the time frames of those decisions.

TABLE 9.1 ■ Types of Managers

Types	Titles	Decisions
Top managers *Set the organization's direction and make decisions that affect everyone.*	CEO President Executive director Director General manager Executive vice president	Establish partnerships Approve significant purchases Approve strategic plans Commit resources for new opportunities
Middle managers *Direct the work of first-line managers and are responsible for divisions or departments.*	Vice president Assistant vice president Manager	Assign financial and human resources Allocate budget resources Set production and service offerings
First-line managers *Direct daily activities for producing goods and services.*	Associate director Project manager Coordinator Assistant manager Team leader	Set employee schedules Hire and promote staff Change processes to improve daily tasks and actions

Source: Adapted from Bonoma, T. V., & Lawler, J. C. (1989). Chutes and ladders: Growing the general manager. *MIT Sloan Management Review, 30*(3), 27–37.

Organizational structures vary from company to company, but typically they are based on a number of building blocks, which we will explore in the next section.

ELEMENTS OF ORGANIZATIONAL STRUCTURE

When developing an organizational structure, managers take into account the following elements: division of labor, departmentalization, chain of command, span of control, authority, responsibility and delegation, centralization or decentralization, and formalization.

Division of Labor

Division of labor is the level to which jobs are divided into specific tasks.[7] When work is specialized, employees who work in a certain department carry out only the tasks that relate to their roles. For example, at the theater, there might be someone taking money for tickets, another person checking tickets and showing people to their seats, or another person selling ice cream during the interval.

Departmentalization

Departmentalization is a process of grouping activities into different types of departments within the overall organizational structure.[8] Many mid-sized and large organizations are structured in this way. Starbucks is one example of a large company that groups its business functions into different departments including an HR department, a finance department, and a marketing department.

Chain of Command

Many organizations devise a chain of command, a flow of authority and power from the highest to the lowest levels of the organization.[9] The conventional top-down, chain-of-command structure begins with executive-level officers followed by department managers and employees (see Figure 9.2).[10] Each executive officer reports to the CEO, who in turn reports directly to the board of directors, which is a group of people elected by company shareholders to monitor the actions of the organization. The following is a brief description of the five main types of executive officers, also known as the C-suite:

Chief executive officer (CEO): The highest-ranking person of a company, the CEO is responsible for making major decisions, creating a corporate vision, and communicating with the board of directors about company strategy. Ramon Laguarta is the chair and chief executive officer of PepsiCo. Laguarta is the first Spanish CEO of a large U.S. multinational company.[11]

Chief financial officer (CFO): An executive officer who is responsible for the financial operations of a company and is responsible for cash flow, financial risk, and financial strategy. CEO of Oracle, Safra Ada Catz is one of the most well-paid CFOs in the world, earning over $35 million per year.[12]

Chief marketing officer (CMO): An executive officer who is responsible for marketing strategies in relation to the company's products and offerings that are designed to deliver value for target customers, clients, or other businesses. Seth Farbman, CMO of international media services provider Spotify, has boosted user engagement through clever marketing campaigns using memes in witty billboard ads.[13]

Chief information officer (CIO): An executive officer who oversees the planning, development, and implementation of technology inside the organization. Tim Crawford, an adviser to CIOs, explains how CIOs use their responsibilities to transform organizations: "The transformational CIO is a business leader first that has responsibility for technology. They're aligned closely with the CEO, rest of the C-suite, and objectives of the board of directors. But they're looking at ways to bring technology to the forefront. Instead of tech for tech's sake, it's business first."[14]

Chief technology officer (CTO): An executive officer who is responsible for technology creation and design, anticipating customer needs, and focusing on emerging technologies. Bridget Frey is the CTO of real estate brokerage RedFin. Frey and her team of software engineers are responsible for building technologies designed to simplify the buying and selling of houses.[15]

Until recently, former Starbucks chief operating officer (COO) Rosalind Brewer was responsible for overseeing the day-to-day functioning of the business. Today, Brewer is the CEO of Walgreens Boots Alliance.

JASON REDMOND/AFP/via Getty Images

FIGURE 9.2 ■ Chain of Command

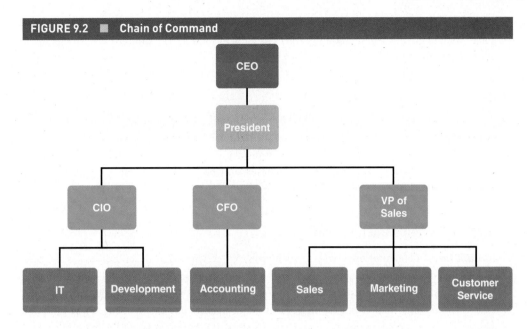

Another example of a senior executive is the chief operating officer (COO), who is responsible for overseeing the day-to-day functioning of the business. Although COOs used to be common to most businesses, the role of the COO has declined steadily over the past decade, with many of the original duties being taken over by other executive officers and departments. The COO role may be fading out in some industries, but it seems to be more important than ever in select industries where structure and process are a priority.[16] For example, Facebook's Sheryl Sandberg (before leaving), CBS's Joe Ianniello, and Starbucks's Rosalind Brewer are among some of the most recognized COOs in the world.

Span of Control

Span of control refers to the number of subordinates for whom managers are directly responsible.[17] For example, a manager with five subordinates has a span of control of five. The type of span of control is influenced by the size of the company and how it is structured. For instance, organizations that operate a tight chain of command will usually have a narrow span of control because senior leaders will be responsible for middle management and team leaders. In contrast, companies with highly trained employees operate with a wide span of control, as these employees do not need to be as closely supervised.

Authority, Responsibility, and Delegation

Most successful organizational structures are made up of people working together to achieve goals. Building the right structure involves understanding three key drivers: authority, responsibility, and delegation.

Authority

Authority is the legitimate right to give orders and make decisions. Within the limitations of company policies, rules, and the law, managers have the authority to carry out certain duties on behalf of the organization such as firing, hiring, and making decisions about resources.

Responsibility

The more authority a manager possesses, the greater the level of responsibility. Responsibility is the personal obligation to perform tasks and reach specified goals. People can have responsibility without much authority. For example, in a restaurant the waiting staff may be responsible for bringing meals to the table, but it might be the restaurant manager's decision to authorize a refund to the customer in the event of a food complaint.

Delegation

Delegation is the process of transferring authority and responsibility to others to carry out certain tasks and activities. Successful delegators choose the right person for the task, equip people with the appropriate resources to complete the job, and view mistakes as learning opportunities rather than failures. One recent study shows that companies run by leaders who delegate well tend to experience rapid growth, high revenue, and increased levels of job creation.[18]

Centralization and Decentralization

Centralization is an organizational structure that gives top-level managers the authority to make decisions on behalf of the entire company.[19] Although it is more common for very small companies with few employees carrying out routine duties to operate a centralized structure, some larger companies also use this type of structure. For example, fast-food companies like Burger King, Pizza Hut, and McDonald's rely on a predominantly centralized structure to ensure that control is maintained over their many thousands of outlets.

Decentralization is an organizational structure where middle managers and lower-level employees are permitted to make decisions and suggestions, rather than just top-level management.[20] In other words, the power is distributed throughout the organization. In decentralized organizations, people are assigned more responsibility, encouraged to take initiative, and empowered to be more independent, all of which relieve senior management from having sole decision-making authority. Pharmaceutical goods company Johnson & Johnson is a decentralized organization.[21] It operates over 200 individual business units that are allowed to function autonomously. Table 9.2 lists the differences between centralization and decentralization.

Formalization

Formalization is the process of determining an organization's policies, procedures, and rules, usually in writing.[22] An employee handbook or training guide is an example of formalization. For example, a

TABLE 9.2 ■ Differences Between Centralization and Decentralization	
Centralization	**Decentralization**
Decisions made by top management	Decisions made by mid-level or lower-level management
Employees must comply with management decisions	Employees have the authority to make decisions and contribute feedback and suggestions
Communication goes up the chain of command	Communication flows freely between groups
Typically found in a smaller organization	Typically found in a larger organization
Works best in a stable work environment	Works best in a complex, unpredictable work environment
Exists in companies where employees may not have much decision-making experience	Exists in companies where employees have decision-making experience
Decision-making slower as the power is in the hands of one person	Faster decision-making by multiple people working closely to the task

customer service operator working in a call center might turn to a handbook or written procedure for guidelines when dealing with a complex complaint. One of the tenets of Amazon's customer service is to "Anticipate customer needs and treat their time and attention as sacred."[23] In other words, address customer problems quickly and efficiently, and treat customers well by respecting the time they are taking to make the call.

All of the elements discussed in this section can be found in most types of organizational structures from traditional to contemporary.

ETHICS IN BUSINESS

Breaking the Chain

Imagine this scenario. You work for a company and feel that your manager is not being fair to all employees with respect to awarding bonuses. The manager seems to be favoring the men in the department over the women. You go to your manager and air your disapproval, yet nothing changes. What do you do? Do you go above your manager's head and complain to their manager? According to a 2009 article by Jeffrey Kassing, the most common break in the chain of command comes when a supervisor ignores complaints.

Critical Thinking Questions

1. Is it ethical to break the chain of command and go above a manager's head?
2. What should a higher-up executive do when an employee breaks the chain of command and brings a complaint to them instead of the employee's direct manager?
3. In what situations would you be compelled to break the chain of command? How do you think your manager would react?

Source: Kassing, J. W. (2009). Breaking the chain of command: Making sense of employee circumvention. *The Journal of Business Communication* (1973), 46(3), 311–334.

TRADITIONAL ORGANIZATIONAL STRUCTURES

Traditional organizations are usually quite fixed and rigid, and most operate within a hierarchical structure where power flows vertically and upward to senior management.

There are five main types of traditional organizational structures: simple structures, functional structures, divisional structures, vertical structures, and horizontal structures.

Simple Structure

Simple structure (see Figure 9.3) is a common organizational structure used in small businesses where decision making is centralized with one single person. For example, the owner of a small sports store might only have to manage a cashier and a couple of sales staff. Because there are no layers of management, decisions can be made rapidly and implemented instantly.

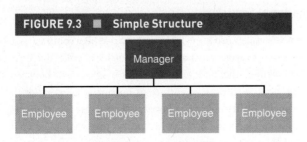

FIGURE 9.3 ■ Simple Structure

Disadvantages: With only one person—often the business owner—making decisions that person is at risk of becoming overwhelmed. Alternatively, the business owner may struggle to delegate properly which leads to slow decision making and getting tasks completed.

Functional Structure

Functional structure is an organizational structure that groups employees according to the tasks they perform for the organization, such as marketing, finance, and human resources (Figure 9.4). Here, employees are managed by clear levels of authority. In general, this structure works well for smaller organizations, where people tend to sit more closely together.

Disadvantages: Risk of lack of communication between the departments in large organizations because groups work separately from each other.

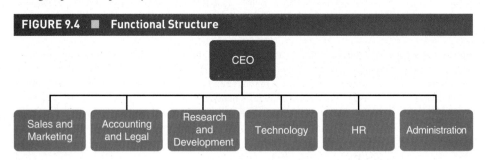

FIGURE 9.4 ■ Functional Structure

Divisional Structure

The **divisional structure** is an organizational structure that groups employees by products and services, markets, geographic regions, or customers (see Figure 9.5). Global companies benefit from this structure because each division has a degree of independence. PepsiCo is an example of a company with a divisional structure. It is made up six divisions, each positioned in different locations with its own way of doing business: PepsiCo Beverages North America; Frito-Lay North America; Quaker Foods North America; Pepsico Latin America; Pepsico Europe Sub-Saharan Africa; and Pepsico Asia, Middle East, and North Africa.[24]

Disadvantages: Divisions that perform similar tasks may risk duplicating work with other divisions in separate locations. They may also become too embedded in their own ways of doing business and compete with other divisions for resources.

Vertical Organizational Structure

A **vertical organizational structure**[25] is a traditional company structure based on a chain of command where leaders sit at the top of the hierarchy and pass down orders to lower-level workers. The vertical organizational structure typically works well for companies that require fast decision making and a clear line of command such as the U.S. Marine Corps.

Disadvantages: Employees at the bottom of the chain of command may feel devalued, and the multiple layers of management could cause bureaucracy. In addition, weak leadership at the top could result in poor decision making, lack of productivity, and low morale.

Horizontal Organizational Structure

Horizontal organizational structure (also known as flat structures) is a company structure that focuses on teamwork and collaboration to work on shared tasks to achieve collective goals (see Figure 9.6). Compared with vertical structures, there are fewer layers of management between senior executives and lower-level employees, often leading to a culture of openness, cooperation, and collaboration. Social media software company Buffer operates a horizontal structure where employees are given the autonomy to choose their own projects and decide which teams they want to be a part of.[26]

Disadvantages: Lack of close supervision from management might lead to poor decision making, reduced productivity, and employee dissatisfaction.

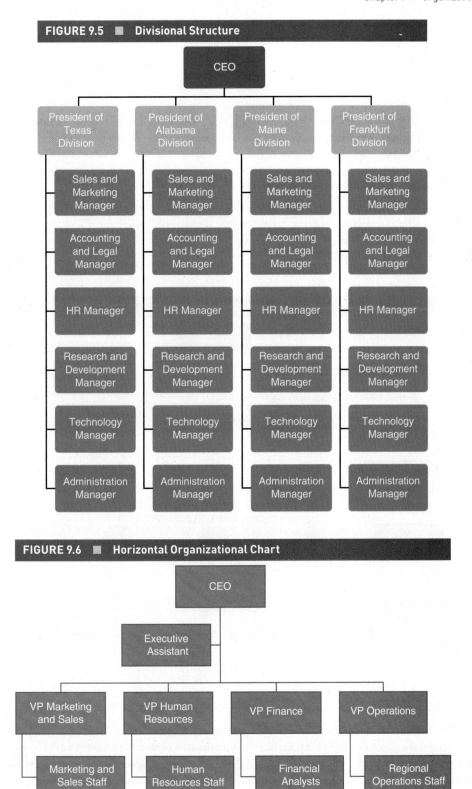

FIGURE 9.5   ■   Divisional Structure

FIGURE 9.6   ■   Horizontal Organizational Chart

CONTEMPORARY ORGANIZATIONAL STRUCTURES

A changing business environment and the desire for current generations to have more meaning and purpose in their work has led to flatter organizations. While some organizations still use traditional structures, others have adopted different types of structures designed to improve communication and collaboration. Some of these structures are called: matrix, network, holacratic, process-based, virtual, and circular.

Matrix Organizations

A **matrix organizational structure** is a company structure that combines functional and divisional reporting lines to create a grid, or matrix (see Figure 9.7). Within the matrix structure, employees tend to have dual reporting relationships to both *functional managers*, the people who have authority over specific departments, and *product managers*, the people responsible for the development of products in an organization. This type of structure provides employees with opportunities to collaborate and innovate with coworkers across different departments, thereby facilitating the acquisition of new skills and knowledge. For example, high-technology firms like aerospace company Boeing use a matrix structure, which reflects its flexible working environment.

Disadvantages: Reporting to two or more managers can lead to poor communication, which may slow down decision making, efficiency, and productivity. Multiple managers could also create conflict in loyalty.

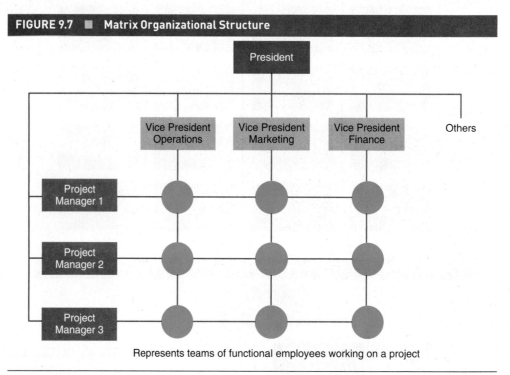

FIGURE 9.7 ■ Matrix Organizational Structure

Represents teams of functional employees working on a project

Source: Lussier, R. N. (2020). *Management fundamentals: Concepts, applications, and skill development* (9th ed.). SAGE.

Network Structure

A **network structure** is an organizational structure in which organizations work together to provide goods and services (see Figure 9.8). This structure is particularly beneficial to businesses that outsource to other companies around the world. For example, from its head office in Stockholm, Swedish multinational retail clothing company Hennes & Mauritz (H&M) uses a network structure (see Figure 9.8) to outsource the production and processing of goods to companies in countries such as Australia, Singapore, and Malaysia.[27]

Disadvantages: Because the network is so spread out, it can be difficult to control, especially when problems arise. Communication can also be an issue when business partners are in different countries.

Holacratic Organizational Structure

As featured in our Zappos case, a holacratic organizational structure is a company structure that distributes decision-making authority to self-managed, "boss-less" teams or "circles" (see Figure 9.9). The

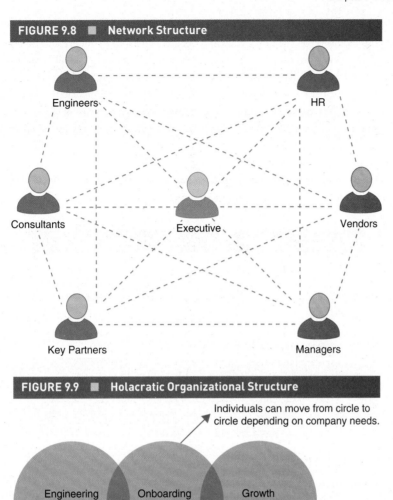

FIGURE 9.8 ■ Network Structure

Engineers   HR   Consultants   Executive   Vendors   Key Partners   Managers

FIGURE 9.9 ■ Holacratic Organizational Structure

Individuals can move from circle to circle depending on company needs.

Engineering Circle   Onboarding Circle   Growth Circle

One employee can fill multiple roles if they have the skills.

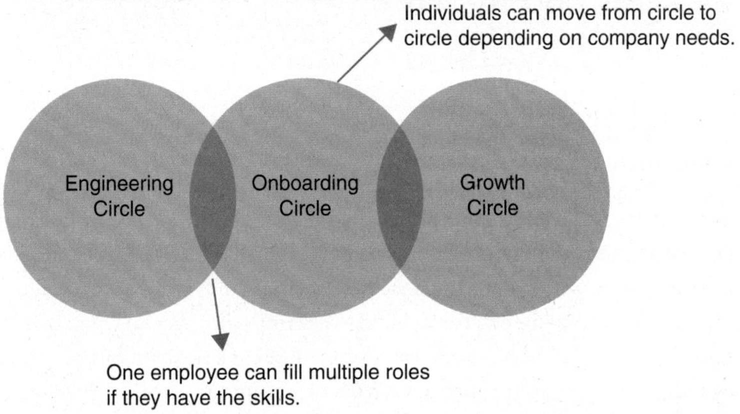

structure focuses on roles rather than individual job descriptions, which allows employees to experience several roles within the organization rather than just one. The main goal of this structure is to provide employees with freedom to choose what they would like to work on and make those decisions based on what they do best. Although Zappos was one of the early adopters of a holacracy, many others have since followed suit, including French pharmaceutical company Sanofi and online lodging marketplace Airbnb. However, the holacratic structure is typically more common in smaller companies; Zappos is the largest company to date to adopt the style.[28]

Disadvantages: Not everybody feels comfortable working in a leaderless environment where they are expected to make their own rules and take on full responsibility for their actions. In addition, because of the focus on their own tasks, there is a danger of teams becoming too inward-looking, thereby losing sight of the overall company vision.

Process-Based Organizational Structure

A process-based organizational structure is a company structure designed around systems, processes, tasks, and knowledge. Unlike traditional structures, which are typically organized around departments, functions, and roles, the process-based structure is aligned by systems and processes involving people who do the work. Employees are encouraged to share and distribute their knowledge throughout the organization to boost transparency. They are also expected to view the organization as a whole (rather than solely focusing on their own roles and departments) and to understand that the work they do has a direct impact on the company. When processes are properly aligned and working efficiently, organizations have the capability to streamline their business and deliver higher levels of customer service. For example, software companies that constantly redevelop and create new products tend to use process-based organizational structures. They start with research and development, then focus on acquiring customers, and finally fulfill the order. Figure 9.10 illustrates a process-based structure: The product needs to be developed before it can be advertised to customers; equally, the order cannot be filled until customers have been acquired.

Disadvantages: In some companies, a process-based structure can sometimes erect boundaries between different process groups, which tends to hamper communication.

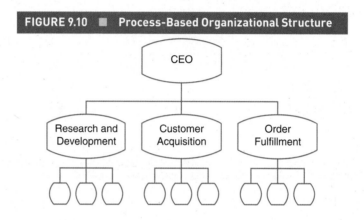

FIGURE 9.10 ■ Process-Based Organizational Structure

Virtual Organizational Structure

A **virtual organizational structure** is a company structure where employees are geographically spread and tend to communicate by phone, email, and the internet (see Figure 9.11). Virtual structures depend on smooth collaboration between diverse teams and geographies, which is enabled by email and tools such as Slack (instant messaging), Zoom (videoconferencing), and Trello (project management), to name just a few. Software company Basecamp is a good example of a virtual company. It is headquartered in Chicago, but its team of 50 are located across 32 different cities worldwide. Basecamp believes that supporting individual work habits through virtual communication is the key to quality work performance and a productive company culture. During COVID-19, many companies shifted to remote operations, moving toward a flatter, more decentralized way of working. Software company Red Hat has been praised by employees for adopting an equality-based approach during the pandemic. As one Red Hat employee said, "The executive team holds video conference meetings from home and maintains the same casual, honest, down-to-earth reputation."[29]

Disadvantages: The success of a virtual organization depends on multiple technologies, which can be quite costly to maintain. Lack of real face-to-face (not Zoom) interactions and cultural clashes can also impede communication. Remote collaboration may not be as impactful as in-person collaboration, particularly for new hires or employees without a prior working relationship. Finally, some people might feel isolated, disconnected, and disengaged working in a virtual environment, which could lead to low mood and increased stress.

Circular Structure

A **circular structure** is an organizational structure that depicts higher-level employees at the center of the circle and lower-level employees on the outer rings. This structure is designed to encourage a free flow of information between all parts of the organization by illustrating that all divisions are part of the same whole. Figure 9.12 demonstrates the circular organizational structure used by Apple when it was under the direction of the late CEO Steve Jobs.

FIGURE 9.11 ■ Virtual Organizational Structure

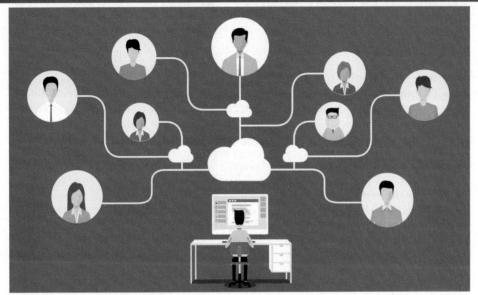

Source: iStockphoto.com/TCmake_photo

FIGURE 9.12 ■ Circular Organizational Structure

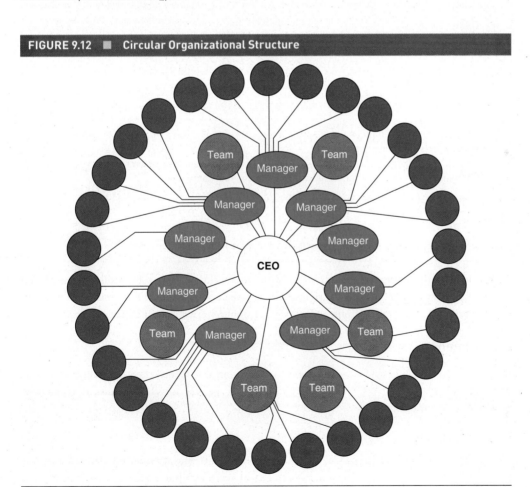

Source: Adapted from Lee, K. (2019, May 13). 10 org charts we admire. *Buffer Open Blog.*

Disadvantages: Employees accustomed to more traditional, hierarchical organizational structures may find the circular structure confusing, particularly in relation to where they fit in the organization and to whom they are supposed to be reporting.

ENTREPRENEURIAL MINDSET ACTIVITY

Draw It!

This chapter talks about the way organizations are structured, and includes a common tool for visualizing the order of employment among leaders, managers, and employees called an organizational chart. It is important for all members of an organization to have a clear understanding of seniority and reporting structures to ensure that confusion and abuse of power are limited. Sometimes there are "dotted line" relationships where an employee has a second or third manager who they report to indirectly, but it is generally good practice to give every employee a single supervisor with whom they can build trust and a great working relationship.

Your activity will be to draw up a mock organizational chart for three hypothetical companies, all related but different sizes. Using simple job titles and a tree with connections branching down to one another, draw the first organizational chart for a hypothetical food truck that sells tacos. This includes anyone who works on or for the food truck, and shouldn't have very many employees. Next, draw one for a restaurant that sells tacos—it should have more complexity and more levels of employment in the organizational chart. Lastly, make an organizational chart for a large, complex taco restaurant chain with 150 locations across the United States; for this final chart, feel free to abbreviate where there may be many employees with the same job title by only drawing out one or two of them, but give an estimate of how many employees there are with that title. Consider that there may be a true corporate board and executive team for a national chain that size. Using your charts, compare and contrast them and discuss how complexity and structure evolve with the size of an organization. Count the number of job levels in all three companies to get a sense for how many leadership and managerial positions are created as companies grow to the size of the 150-location chain.

Critical Thinking Questions

1. Reviewing your organizational charts, why is this a useful tool for employees and for managers?
2. How many levels of employment did you have at each of the three companies? Compare and discuss this with your classmates.
3. Have you ever worked in a position where you felt confused about which person was your manager? If so, what types of issues arose in the chain of command?

PRIMARY FACTORS IN DETERMINING STRUCTURAL TYPE

With so many different types of organizational structures to choose from, those leading the company need to make sure they are making the right choices for their organizations. This involves taking several factors into account: the environment, strategy, technology, financial condition, and size.

Environment

Organizational structures tend to be either mechanistic or organic. When choosing an organizational structure, managers need to take into consideration which type best suits the business environment in which the company operates.

Mechanistic Structure

The mechanistic model is a formalized structure based on high centralization and departmentalization.[30] Mechanistic organizations tend to run as a bureaucracy, which refers to a system characterized by formalized rules and regulations, specialized routine tasks, division of labor, and centralized authority.[31] It represents a traditional top-down approach to organizational structure where employees work within a definite chain of command, and very little communication and collaboration exists between lower-level employees and upper-level management. Mechanistic structures work best in times of stability.

Although the mechanistic structure is relatively easy to implement, and ensures everybody knows their role and place in the organization, it can be repetitive and difficult to adapt in times of rapid change given the number of layers and depth of reporting structure.

Organic Structure

The **organic model** is a less formalized structure based on decentralization and cross-functional teams.[32] In contrast with the mechanistic model, employees across the organization are encouraged to participate in decision making, empowered to try new things, and provided with opportunities to be creative. Typically, communication is open and frequent, and employees are more likely to accept and adapt to the inevitable changes that arise from operating in fast-moving industries such as fashion or technology. Table 9.3 illustrates the differences between mechanistic and organic structures, and Table 9.4 lists the types of mechanistic and organic structures. Interestingly, mechanistic structures are more traditional and organic structures are more contemporary, which reflects the changing nature of work in modern business today.

TABLE 9.3 ■ The Differences Between Mechanistic and Organic Structures

Mechanistic Structures	Organic Structures
Employees work separately and specialize on one particular task	Employees collaborate and work together on a variety of tasks
Clear chain of command	Free flow of information
Based on a centralized, hierarchical structure	Based on a decentralized, flatter structure
Narrow spans of control	Wide spans of control
High formalization	Low formalization
Vertical communication	Lateral communication
Lots of rules and bureaucracy	Fewer rules and less bureaucracy

TABLE 9.4 ■ Types of Mechanistic or Organic Structures

Types of Mechanistic Structures	Types of Organic Structures
Horizontal	Holacratic
Vertical	Virtual
Divisional	Matrix
Functional	Network
Simple	Process-based
	Circular

Company Size

The size of a company influences the type of organizational structure. Research shows that larger organizations (more than 2,000 employees) tend to follow a mechanistic structure, with employees expected to follow company rules, procedures, and regulations. In contrast, smaller companies tend to follow more organic structures, with fewer rules and regulations. However, a small startup that starts off with an organic structure may end up applying some elements of mechanistic structure as the business grows.

Strategy

The type of organizational structure should also be aligned with the company's vision, strategy, and goals, concepts we discussed previously in Chapter 6. The structure should also be flexible enough to change if the company's strategy adapts. For example, Microsoft CEO Satya Nadella changed the organizational structure in line with Microsoft's new strategy to become cloud-first and mobile-first. As a result, Microsoft moved away from the old functional structure that had been the cause of some internal friction and power play to a divisional structure that divides groups into business functions. Since moving to the new structure, Microsoft has become one of the biggest leaders in cutting-edge cloud computing services.[33]

Microsoft CEO Satya Nadella adapted the structure of the company so that it was in line with the company's new strategy, focusing on cutting-edge cloud and mobile computing services.

Grant Hindsley/Bloomberg/via Getty Images

Technology

Technology has a major influence over the type of organizational structure to implement. In many cases, automated systems have replaced more mundane tasks such as data entry and filing, which removes the number of people needed to fill those roles. However, the IT department may need more hires to maintain and grow the technology. As technology continues to evolve, the organizational structure will continue to develop, driving more companies to invest in technology designed to streamline work processes. San Francisco–based company Braidio enables organizations to create a structure that connects people to real-time information, knowledge, and insights while boosting efficiency and productivity.[34]

Financial Condition

Financial condition influences both the company size and the structure. A new startup without much financing to begin with will likely be made up of just a few people. With less people and expenses to pay, the structure will be flatter. As the startup receives financing, starts earning revenue, and grows its number of employees, the structure will become more formalized to ensure employees follow the company's rules, procedures, and guidelines. When it was founded in 2011, global remote web application company Zapier began as a three-person company before evolving into a remote company with a workforce of over 200 people based in more than 20 countries all over the world. By hiring trustworthy people, implementing the right software to enable smooth communication, and providing processes that everybody complies with, Zapier has managed to build an organizational structure based on trust and accountability.[35]

The Organizational Life Cycle

The organizational life cycle also has an impact on organizational structure. As the organization goes through these stages it can become more mechanistic and bureaucratic, shaping the overall structure of an organization. There are four stages of the life cycle: birth, youth, midlife, and maturity (see Figure 9.13).[36]

1. Stage 1: The birth stage (nonbureaucratic): Also referred to as the startup stage, this is the stage in which the organization is first created. Typically, there is very little staff, no written rules or procedures to follow, and very few formalized processes. Facebook founder Mark Zuckerberg famously began working informally on his social networking website in a dorm room in Harvard University before eventually growing it into one of the most influential social networking companies in the world.[37]

2. Stage 2: The youth stage (prebureaucratic): This is the stage of the organization where growth and expansion take place. More people have joined the company, a new product or service has been launched, and rules and guidelines are being established. For example, Chinese videosharing social networking company TikTok, which provides the technology to make short lip-sync, comedy, and talent videos, moved from the birth stage to the youth stage when it grew in popularity in other major countries around the world, including the U.S.[38]

3. Stage 3: The midlife stage (bureaucratic): In the midlife stage, the organization is growing in the marketplace and becoming larger in size thanks to additional new hires, giving rise to a more decentralized structure with many more rules and procedures. Media services provider and production company Netflix is an example of an organization in the midlife stage. It continues to grow but remains equipped to adapt to changes in the market through its commitment to creativity and innovation.

4. Stage 4: The maturity stage (very bureaucratic): In the maturity stage, the organization becomes very bureaucratic and mechanistic. During this stage, there is a risk that companies will become more stagnant and flexibility and innovation will be stifled. Not everyone agrees, but some experts have suggested that Apple is losing its innovation edge—especially when it comes to the latest iPhones, which have been criticized for their lack of new features.[39]

FIGURE 9.13 ■ Four Stages of the Organizational Life Cycle

Birth Stage (Nonbureaucratic) → Youth Stage (Prebureacratic) → Midlife Stage (Bureaucratic) → Maturity (Very Bureaucratic)

Designing organizational structures is a complex task that needs to take into consideration a wide variety of factors and elements to provide growth opportunities without sacrificing creativity and innovation.

IN REVIEW

9.1   Explain the impact of organizational structure on the organization.

An organizational structure is a system that coordinates the people, tasks, and activities necessary to carry out a particular purpose. Organizational structures help companies to function at their best because they improve the flow of communication between employees, establish clear responsibilities and reporting relationships, provide opportunities for company growth and expansion, and facilitate the successful completion of tasks and activities. An organizational chart is a graphic representation of a company's structure that communicates how a company is organized.

9.2   Describe the different elements of organizational structure.

When developing an organizational structure, managers take into account the following elements: division of labor, departmentalization, chain of command, span of control, authority, responsibility and delegation, centralization or decentralization, and formalization. **Division of labor**, also known as work specialization, is the degree to which jobs are divided into specific tasks. **Departmentalization** is a process of grouping people with related job duties, skills, and experiences into the same area within the overall organizational structure. A **chain of command** is the flow of authority and power from the highest to the lowest levels of the organization. There are five main types of executive officers: CEO, CTO, CMO, CFO, and CIO. **Unity of command** is a management strategy where employees report to only one designated manager. **Span of control** refers to the number of direct reports for whom managers are directly responsible. **Authority** is the legitimate right given to managers to give orders and make decisions. **Responsibility** is the personal obligation to perform preset tasks and reach specified goals, and **delegation** is the process of transferring authority and responsibility to others to carry out certain tasks and activities. **Centralization** refers to an organizational structure that is designed to give top-level managers the authority to make decisions on behalf of the entire company. **Decentralization** refers to an organizational structure that is designed to allow all employees to make decisions and recommend changes. **Formalization** is the process of determining an organization's policies, procedures, and rules, usually in writing.

9.3   Discuss the traditional types of organizational structures.

Traditional organizational structures tend to be grouped into five main types: simple structures, functional structures, divisional structures, vertical structures, and horizontal structures. **Simple structure** is a common organizational structure used in small businesses where decision making is centralized with the business owner. **Functional structure** is an organizational structure that groups employees according to the tasks they perform for the organization, such as marketing, finance, and human resources. The **divisional structure**—sometimes called multidivisional structure—is an organizational structure that groups employees by products and services, by geographic regions, or by customers. A **vertical organizational structure** is a traditional company structure based on a chain of command where leaders sit at the top of the hierarchy and pass down orders to lower-level workers. A horizontal organizational structure (also known as a flat structure) is a company structure that focuses on teamwork and collaboration to achieve collective goals.

9.4   Discuss the different types of contemporary organizational structures.

A **matrix organizational** structure is a company structure in which the reporting lines are set up as a grid, or matrix. A flatter structure is a company structure where some layers of management are removed but a degree of hierarchy remains. **Flatarchies** are types of organizational structures that share characteristics of hierarchies and flat organizations. A **holacratic organizational structure** is a company structure that distributes decision-making authority to self-managed, "boss-less" teams or "circles." A virtual organizational structure is a company structure where employees are geographically spread and tend to communicate by phone, email, and the internet. A circular structure is an organizational structure that borrows from a hierarchical structure by depicting higher-level employees at the center of the circle and the lower-level employees positioned on the outer rings.

9.5   Discuss the factors that influence the design of an organization's structure.

To make the right decisions, managers need to take the following factors into account: the environment, strategy, technology, financial condition, and size. The **mechanistic model** is a formalized structure based on centralization and departmentalization. The **organic model** is a less formalized structure based on decentralization and cross-functional teams. The organizational life cycle also has an impact on organizational structure. As the organization goes through these stages, it becomes more mechanistic and bureaucratic, shaping the overall structure of an organization. There are four stages of the life cycle: birth, youth, midlife, and maturity.

BUSINESSES DISCUSSED IN THIS CHAPTER

Organization	UN Sustainable Development Goal
Airbnb	7. Affordable and Clean Energy 11. Sustainable Cities and Communities
Amazon	8. Decent Work and Economic Growth 13. Climate Action
Apple	7. Affordable and Clean Energy 12. Responsible Consumption and Production
Basecamp	8. Decent Work and Economic Growth
Boeing	12. Responsible Consumption and Production 13. Climate Action 14. Life Below Water 15. Life on Land
Braidio	9. Industry, Innovation, and Infrastructure
Buffer	12. Responsible Consumption and Production
CBS	5. Gender Equality 10. Reduced Inequality
Facebook	13. Climate Action
H&M	6. Clean Water and Sanitation 7. Affordable and Clean Energy
Johnson & Johnson	3. Good Health and Well-Being 13. Climate Action
McDonald's	4. Quality Education 13. Climate Action
Microsoft	4. Quality Education 8. Decent Work and Economic Growth 16. Peace, Justice, and Strong Institutions
Netflix	12. Responsible Consumption and Production
Oracle	7. Affordable and Clean Energy
PepsiCo	5. Gender Equality 6. Clean Water and Sanitation 8. Decent Work and Economic Growth 12. Responsible Consumption and Production 13. Climate Action
Red Hat	11. Sustainable Cities and Communities 12. Responsible Consumption and Production
Redfin	3. Good Health and Well-Being 11. Sustainable Cities and Communities
Sanofi	12. Responsible Consumption and Production
Spotify	8. Decent Work and Economic Growth 10. Reduced Inequality 12. Responsible Consumption and Production
Starbucks	6. Clean Water and Sanitation 11. Sustainable Cities and Communities
U.S. Marine Corps	6. Clean Water and Sanitation 7. Affordable and Clean Energy

Organization	UN Sustainable Development Goal
Zapier	8. Decent Work and Economic Growth 9. Industry, Innovation, and Infrastructure 11. Sustainable Cities and Communities
Zappos	12. Responsible Consumption and Production

KEY TERMS

Authority (p. 181)

Birth stage (p. 193)

Board of directors (p. 179)

Bureaucracy (p. 190)

Centralization (p. 182)

Chain of command (p. 179)

Chief executive officer (CEO) (p. 180)

Chief financial officer (CFO) (p. 180)

Chief information officer (CIO) (p. 180)

Chief marketing officer (CMO) (p. 180)

Chief technology officer (CTO) (p. 180)

Circular structure (p. 188)

Decentralization (p. 182)

Delegation (p. 182)

Departmentalization (p. 179)

Division of labor (p. 179)

Divisional structure (p. 184)

First-line managers (p. 178)

Formalization (p. 182)

Functional structure (p. 184)

Holacracy (p. 177)

Horizontal organizational structure (p. 184)

Matrix organizational structure (p. 186)

Maturity stage (p. 193)

Mechanistic model (p. 190)

Middle managers (p. 178)

Midlife stage (p. 193)

Network structure (p. 186)

Organic model (p. 191)

Organizational chart (p. 177)

Organizational structure (p. 177)

Process-based organizational structure (p. 187)

Responsibility (p. 181)

Simple structure (p. 183)

Span of control (p. 181)

Top managers (p. 178)

Vertical organizational structure (p. 184)

Virtual organizational structure (p. 188)

Youth stage (p. 193)

BUSINESS CASE 9.2: SALTWATER BREWERY—DELRAY BEACH, FLORIDA

SDG 14:   Life Below Water

Founded in 2013 by a team of Florida beach-lovers, Saltwater Brewery in Delray Beach, Florida, brews sustainably sourced beer by using natural ingredients and biodegradable packaging. Cofounder Chris Gove went to college in San Diego and was inspired by the microbrew culture of the area. He wanted to bring that culture and craft beer lifestyle back home to Delray Beach. Together with three friends, Chris started Saltwater Brewery, the first microbrewery in Delray Beach.

The small company, characterized by a simple organizational structure, uses ocean-inspired names for its products such as Screamin' Reels and Sea Cow Milk Stout, and supports ocean-based organizations such as The Ocean Foundation, Mote Marine Laboratory & Aquarium, and the Billfish Foundation. It was also the first brewery to use biodegradable, animal-friendly, and compostable six-pack rings (what the company calls "Eco Six Pack Rings"). The six-pack rings are constructed of a by-product waste called spent grain that is left over from the brewery process plus other compostable materials. According to Chris, "It all started with a seaweed six pack ring and from there, it snowballed into this kind of global movement. We've been all over the world, kind of telling about this circular economy, and that's giving back via our waste. We're just trying to help out with what we know." Chris hopes that other, larger breweries start to use similar six-pack rings.

It appears the big brewers are indeed taking note and have begun to focus more on sustainability in their production processes. Recently, Danish beer brewery Carlsberg announced it would use glue instead of plastic to hold its six-packs together, while American–Canadian company Molson Coors announced it would invest $85 million to move from plastic six-pack rings to sustainable cardboard wrap carriers. Molson Coors also announced a goal for cardboard packaging to be used in all of its products distributed in the United States by 2025, thereby eliminating 1.7 million pounds of plastic waste each year.

These sustainability initiatives are desperately needed. Consider these statistics:

- 14 million tons of plastic find their way into oceans every year.

- Scientists estimate that half of the world's sea turtles have eaten plastic, causing intestinal blockages that lead to starvation.

- Some plastics take as long as 400 years or more to break down.

- It is predicted that there will be more plastic in the ocean than fish by weight by 2050.

- Plastic rings have been linked to an increase in ocean pollution.

Saltwater Brewery is a business designed to raise awareness and promote action regarding the global challenges related to protecting our oceans. "From the beginning, it's been about giving back to the ocean," Chris said. "It's like the why behind the business as Saltwater Brewery. It's about not only the lifestyle of the saltwater and what not . . . it's about the environment it entails. We want to give back what's giving back to us our whole life."

Critical Thinking Questions

1. How does keeping its organization small and local help Saltwater Brewery to achieve its goals?

2. How might a larger organizational structure impact the business?

3. How might a company's organizational structure reflect a sustainability focus?

References

Feltman, R. (2015, September 15). More than half the world's sea turtles have eaten plastic, new study claims. *Washington Post*. https://www.washingtonpost.com/news/speaking-of-science/wp/2015/09/15/more-than-half-the-worlds-sea-turtles-have-eaten-plastic-new-study-claims/

Galanty, H. (2016, May 13). Saltwater Brewery creates edible six-pack rings. *Craft Beer*. https://www.craftbeer.com/editorspicks/saltwater-brewery-creates-edible-six-pack-rings

Lolo, S. (2018, July 20). Saltwater Brewery not only brews craft beer, but helps marine life with eco-six pack rings. *CBS News*. https://cbs12.com/news/local/saltwater-brewery-not-only-brews-craft-beer-but-helps-marine-life-with-eco-six-pack-rings

Parker, L. (2019, June 7). The world's plastic pollution crisis explained. *National Geographic*. https://www.nationalgeographic.com/environment/article/plastic-pollution

Saltwater Brewery. (2021). *Community*. https://saltwaterbrewery.com/pages/community

Sorrentio, L. M. (2022). A solution package for plastic pollution—from measurement to action. *IUCN*. https://www.iucn.org/resources/solution-package-plastic-pollution-measurement-action

Valinsky, J. (2022, March 1). Coors Light is ditching those nasty plastic six-pack rings. *CNN*. https://www.cnn.com/2022/03/01/business/plastic-rings-molson-coors/index.html

World Economic Forum. (2016, January 16). More plastic than fish in the ocean by 2050: Report offers blueprint for change. World Economic Forum. https://www.weforum.org/press/2016/01/more-plastic-than-fish-in-the-ocean-by-2050-report-offers-blueprint-for-change/

John Cronin donates a percentage of John's Crazy Socks sales to charities that help people with disabilities.

REUTERS/Alamy Stock Photo

10 ORGANIZATIONAL MISSION AND CULTURE

10.1   Define organizational mission, vision, and values, and explain their importance to the company.

10.2   Define culture and its impact on organizations.

10.3   Describe the four dimensions of organizational culture.

10.4   Discuss the importance of employee fit to organizational culture.

10.5   Compare and contrast the various clues to organizational culture.

BUSINESS IMPACT CASE 10.1: JOHN'S CRAZY SOCKS—MELVILLE, NEW YORK

SDG 16:   Peace, Justice, and Strong Institutions

Can a pair of socks create happiness? Well, John Lee Cronin, a young man with Down syndrome[*][1] and his father certainly think so, and they are doing a good job showing it's possible with their company, John's Crazy Socks. The business does exactly what it sounds like. From a small warehouse in Melville, New York, it sells socks with "crazy" patterns and colors. The "crazy" socks are based on almost everything imaginable, from flowers, to superheroes, to patriotic themes. Additionally, socks are sold to raise awareness for different causes such as Down syndrome, autism, literacy, antibullying, and many more.

John's Crazy Socks started in 2016, when John found himself with limited opportunities after graduating from high school. In an interview with CNBC, John's father, Mark Cronin, said, "There are not many options open to people with disabilities. All job training programs and workshop programs had waiting lists and not many employers offer jobs for people like John."[2] John also didn't like the options available, so he decided to go into business with one of the people he loved the most—his father.

John and his father came up with the idea of John's Crazy Socks during a brainstorming session. They thought about creating a food truck business, but neither could cook. Then they had a better idea: selling socks for World Down Syndrome Day.

World Down Syndrome Day takes place every year on March 21. The day is traditionally celebrated by wearing crazy, colorful socks with different patterns. John himself loved wearing crazy socks, so they began looking for socks to sell that commemorated the day, but none could be found. John decided to make his own. He sketched a design of a purple sock with hearts, adding the numbers 3-21, not only to signify the date of World Down Syndrome Day but to symbolize the triplication of the 21st chromosome that causes Down syndrome.

From then on, the duo started designing and selling all types of crazy socks through their website. Their inspirational story is matched by an equally inspiring mission. As their website states, "John's affinity for crazy socks paired with his love of making people smile made our mission clear: we want to spread happiness. This mission supports everything they do." One way John spreads happiness is by wrapping the sock orders in red paper, writing a hand-written thank-you note, and placing the note and candy inside the box. This has been a source of joy among his customers from day one. In the beginning, John hand-delivered the orders to his early customers; videos of those deliveries went viral on social media. Being so mission-focused

---

[*]Down syndrome is a chromosomal condition with symptoms that include low muscle tone, small stature, and an upward slant to the eyes, as well as cognitive delays, according to the National Down Syndrome Society.

and really working to spread happiness led to 452 orders that equated to $13,000 in revenue in their first month.

Today, they sell more than 2,000 styles of socks from about 20 suppliers. Their bestselling socks are charity awareness socks, which are designed by the company. For every pair of awareness socks sold, $2 goes to the charity partner. Additionally, 5% of the total annual profit is donated to the Special Olympics.

The mission doesn't only guide sales; it guides organizational culture as well. John's Crazy Socks employs people of differing abilities, such as people who have been diagnosed with autism and Down syndrome. John and Mark believe in equal rights and have been advocating for employment opportunities for people with differing abilities, even testifying before the U.S. House Committee on Small Business. They are working to lower barriers to employment and also changing mindsets so that employers will hire people with differing abilities. As Mark Cronin notes, "Too often when we have discrimination in the workplace, it's because we focus on things that don't matter. We need people working in our warehouse. I don't need them to show me all these other skills. Employers can't find enough good workers, and yet we have this great national resource of people with differing abilities who are ready, able and willing to work, and all you have to do is give them a chance, right?"[3]

John's official title is Chief Happiness Officer, and he's a man on a mission. Though business is booming and his profile is growing (John and Mark recently won the New York Entrepreneurs of the Year Award), he still makes time for personal deliveries to local customers.

Critical Thinking Questions

1. What is the mission of John's Crazy Socks, and in what ways does it guide how the company operates?

2. In what way is John's Crazy Socks working to reduce inequality?

3. How would you describe the culture of John's Crazy Socks? Is this a company you would like to work for? Why or why not?

ORGANIZATIONAL MISSION, VISION, AND VALUES

In the opening case, one of the key parts of John's Crazy Socks' mission is to spread happiness, something that influences everything the company does, from how employees are treated to how buying socks makes its customers feel. A mission is a brief description that defines the purpose of an organization. It may reflect the types of products or services it produces, who its customers tend to be, and its core beliefs. Dutch chocolate manufacturer Tony's Chocolonely is another company on an important mission: to make the manufacturing of chocolate 100% free from child labor, and with no exploitation of farmers.[4] Its products include chocolate made up of wildly different flavors such as "dark milk pretzel toffee," and its customers are people who hold the same values and want to support the mission. Thanks to its mission, Tony's Chocolonely is the most successful chocolate brand in the Netherlands, with a goal to expand further into countries in Europe, and in the United States.

Mission Statement

Many companies articulate their mission in a **mission statement**, which is usually a short statement defining what an organization is, why it exists, and its reason for being. The most impactful mission statements consist of three main components: contribution, emotion, and differentiation. Let's apply these different elements to John's Crazy Socks.

1. **Contribution:** What impact does your organization make?

    John's Crazy Socks makes a social impact by providing work opportunities to people with differing abilities and makes a financial impact by donating to charities and events such as the Special Olympics. During the COVID-19 pandemic, John's Crazy Socks created a line of Healthcare Superhero Socks to celebrate the heroic work carried out by front-line workers and donated 10% of the sale of those socks to the Good Samaritan Hospital Medical Center in Long Island, New York, raising nearly $1,000. John's father and cofounder, Mark Cronin, said: "Our social mission is just as important as our business mission and they are indivisible. Giving back is an essential part of that mission."[5]

2. **Emotion:** Why does your company do it?

John's Crazy Socks raises awareness of people with differing abilities while fighting for equal employee rights.

3. **Differentiation:** How does your company do it? How is it unique?

John's Crazy Socks fulfills its mission to spread happiness by hand-delivering its products to local customers, but also sharing its story with those customers that buy online. Customers feel happy when they purchase John's Crazy Socks.

Mission as a Guide for Strategic Decisions

Just about every company has a mission statement. They come in all shapes and sizes. There is one thing they all have in common—each statement indicates a sense of purpose and reason for existing. The mission also acts as a guide indicating the direction and focus of the company. For example, U.S. retail company Dick's Sporting Goods is a good example of a company guided by its mission "to be the No. 1 sports and fitness specialty retailer for all athletes and outdoor enthusiasts through the relentless improvement of everything we do." This mission statement emphasizes the importance of market position for the company and how committed it is to becoming a top sporting retailer in the United States.

An important part of its mission is to serve communities. Following a school shooting in Florida in 2018, Dick's stopped selling assault-style rifles at all of its stores.[6] This move was supported by a part of Dick's mission to better serve local communities by promoting a gun-free culture.

In another example, U.S. children's media company GoldieBlox uses its mission to attract more girls to STEM (Science, Technology, Education, and Math), thereby challenging gender stereotypes. Not only does GoldieBlox's mission guide its overall strategy, but it has attracted millennial and Gen Z employees that resonate with their focus on making a profound impact in the toy space. Part of this contribution is participating in activities designed for children such as running the booth at the annual video tech conference VidCon, and acquiring feedback from the GoldieBlox kids council. GoldieBlox founder Debbie Sterling said, "It's these moments of getting to see how our work lights up a kid's face that reminds everyone, in the most visceral way, why we show up to work every day."[7]

Vision

Although the two terms are often used interchangeably, a mission is different from a vision. A **vision** is a mental image that describes what an organization wants to become. In other words, a vision extends the mission from "what is our reason for being?" to "what do we want to become?" Many companies promote their vision through a **vision statement**, which is a short statement that describes the current and future organizational goals. A big part of being a business leader is to bring the organization's vision to life by continuously reminding employees so it becomes an integral part of their daily working life. Indeed, Zappos's vision to provide the best customer service possible is

Debbie Sterling, founder of GoldieBlox, started her company to teach girls engineering principles using toys. That mission still guides the strategy of the company today.

Laura A. Oda/MCT/Newscom

reinforced throughout the organization with fun rewards.[8] For example, when a Zappos employee delivers excellent customer service, someone rings a bell and everybody congratulates that person. Other acknowledgments include a public word of thanks, a handwritten note, a gift card, and even Zappos dollars (known as Zollars), which can be spent in the Zappos company store. Celebrating the effort to contribute to the company vision is a powerful way to motivate employees and encourage them to do the best job they can.

Values

Values are underlying desires and core beliefs that shape an identity of an organization, and act as a good guide for how employees are expected to behave. Values show others what your company stands for. Many companies promote their core values to inform employees and customers about their priorities and goals.

The most successful companies demonstrate their core values every day. One of American Express's (Amex) core values is customer commitment: "We develop relationships that make a positive difference in our customers' lives".[9] In fact, Amex card holders are called "members" to make them feel like they are part of a special club. Amex really goes the extra mile for customers even when there is no protocol in place. In one case, a hotel café manager called up the Amex team to inform them that he had accidentally sold a cake to an Amex card member that was only supposed to be for display. The cake had harmful chemicals in it, and he was concerned about the health impact on the customer. The Amex team had no guidelines for this sort of request, but they analyzed the number of people who used the card at the café at around the same time as the cake was sold and eventually tracked down the customer before the cake was consumed. This story is a good example of a company that lives by its values even when there is no real protocol in place. Table 10.1 outlines examples of missions, visions, and core values from different organizations.

TABLE 10.1 ■ Mission, Vision, and Core Values			
	Mission Statement	**Vision Statement**	**Core Values**
Lululemon	To elevate the world from mediocrity to greatness	To be the experimental brand that ignites a community of people living the sweat life through sweat, grow and connect	Nurturing entrepreneurial spirit, taking personal responsibility, valuing connection, honesty and courage, and choosing fun
Patagonia	We're in business to save our home planet	Use of all its resources to protect life on Earth	Building the best products, causing no unnecessary harm, using business to protect nature, and not bound by convention
Coca-Cola	To refresh the world in mind, body, and spirit, to inspire moments of optimism and happiness through our brands and actions, and to create value and make a difference	Inspiring each other to be the best we can be by providing a great place to work	Leadership, collaboration, integrity, accountability, passion, diversity, and quality
Microsoft	To empower every person and every organization on the planet to achieve more	To help people and businesses throughout the world realize their full potential	Innovation, trustworthy computing, diversity and inclusion, corporate social responsibility, philanthropies, and environment

(Continued)

TABLE 10.1 ■ Mission, Vision, and Core Values (*Continued*)			
	Mission Statement	**Vision Statement**	**Core Values**
Starbucks	To inspire and nurture the human spirit—one person, one cup and one neighborhood at a time	To establish Starbucks as the premier purveyor of the finest coffee in the world while maintaining our uncompromising principles while we grow	Teamwork, integrity, respect for culture, and perseverance
Uber	Transportation as reliable as running water, everywhere for everyone	We ignite opportunity by setting the world in motion	We build globally, we live locally, we are customer obsessed, we celebrate differences, we do the right thing, we act like owners, we persevere, we value ideas over hierarchy, we make big bold bets
Disney	To entertain, inform and inspire people around the globe through the power of unparalleled storytelling, reflecting the iconic brands, creative minds and innovative technologies that make ours the world's premier entertainment company.	To be one of the world's leading producers and providers of entertainment and information	Make everyone's dreams come true, you better believe it, never a customer, always a guest, all for one and one for all, share the spotlight, dare to dare, practice, practice, practice, make your elephant fly and capture the magic with storyboards
Facebook	To give people the power to share and make the world more open and connected	To stay connected with friends and family, to discover what's going on in the world, and to share and express what matters to them	Focus on impact, move fast, be bold, be open, and build social value

Source: Data retrieved from Mission Statement Academy. (n.d.). https://mission-statement.com/

Great missions, visions, and values are just the beginning in communicating to employees, customers, and other stakeholders why a company exists, but without an organizational culture to support the mission, vision, and values, everything kind of falls short. In other words, organizational culture is evidence that the company is walking its talk.

ORGANIZATIONAL CULTURE

When you're considering working for a particular company, you're bound to have lots of questions, such as: What do they pay? What hours am I expected to work? What kind of benefits do they offer? One of the important questions to ask about a company is: What's the culture like? Some people link culture to the fun perks offered by some companies such as open and free cafés and ping-pong tables. But culture is more than just free drinks and games. Organizational culture is a pattern of shared norms, rules, values, and beliefs that guide the attitudes and behaviors of its employees. In other words, it describes the personality of the organization. Every organization has a personality, and some employees fit into some cultures better than others. There is no one-size-fits-all type of culture because not every company or industry is the same.

The COVID-19 pandemic has triggered employees to question their value to the organization and their purpose in life. As a result, many workers are leaving the workforce. Accordingly, this has forced a renewed focus on organizational culture and how culture can keep and attract employees. Recent studies show that companies that prioritize a flexible working culture, value employee health and well-being, celebrate recognition, embrace advanced technology, and foster people-focused initiatives such as diversity, equity, and inclusion strategies, experience higher levels of retention, engagement, and job satisfaction.[10]

Strong and Weak Organizational Cultures

Organizational culture has a direct impact on business. Recent research shows that almost 90% of business leaders believe work culture to be important.[11] This is not surprising, given that studies show that ineffective work cultures lead to disengaged employees, poor customer service, high turnover, and falling company profits. Weak organizational cultures have been the cause of some of the biggest company scandals over the past decade. For example, multinational financial services company Wells Fargo is still recovering from a huge scandal where Wells Fargo employees opened millions of fake bank accounts to meet overly aggressive sales targets.[12] The pressurized work culture led employees to take extreme measures to keep up with daily goals. Ride-sharing company Uber is another example of a company with a weak company culture characterized by sexual harassment, discrimination, and aggressive behavior between employees.[13]

Ride-sharing company Uber's company culture has been criticized by many for promoting an environment rife with aggressive behavior.

Krisztian Bocsi/Bloomberg/via Getty Images

In contrast, strong working cultures are connected with some of the most successful and desired to work for companies in the world. Table 10.2 lists some of the best places to work in 2022, which is indicative of strong corporate cultures. An additional strong culture example is workforce management solutions company TCWGlobal, formerly TargetCW, based in San Diego. It attributes happy employees to its positive work culture and cultivates the culture by supporting employees through the good times and the hard times.[14] Samer Khouli, founder and CEO of TCWGlobal, said, "We are all about people. We have people go through tragedies, cancers, death, and we are there for them. TargetCW is a place where life is lived, not just work." Samer also believes there is a direct link between culture and profit; as long as employees are happy, then the profits will follow. He added, "When you have someone fully engaged, they will be more productive. And I'll be happier because I'll have less stress. Dealing with turnover is miserable. Dealing with unhappy employees is miserable. To me, it's a no brainer."

TABLE 10.2 ■ Top 10 Best Companies to Work For
1. Cisco
2. Hilton
3. Wegmans Food Markets
4. Salesforce
5. Nvidia
6. Accenture
7. Rocket Companies
8. American Express
9. David Weekley Homes
10. Capital One Financial

Source: Fortune. (2022). 100 best companies to work for. *Fortune Magazine.* https://fortune.com/best-companies/

ETHICS IN BUSINESS

Boys Will Be Bros

In 2017, new Uber CEO Dara Khosrowshahi set out to dramatically change the company's culture. Uber had a long-standing reputation for having a "bro" culture. A bro culture is one that is dominated by younger "macho men" who tend to be obnoxious, arrogant, and overconfident. Uber had multiple accusations of unreported or underreported sexual assault from customers and employees, alike.

In an interview, founder and former CEO Travis Kalanick discussed a running joke told within Uber at the time involving a variation of the Uber business model. Instead of rides on demand, the joke involved women on demand, with the resulting company called "Boober" instead of "Uber."

Investors forced Kalanick to resign in 2019. He later sold 90% of his shares in Uber. In Khosrowshahi's first public statement at the helm of the post-Kalanick company, he stated that "culture needs to be written from the bottom up."

Critical Thinking Questions

1. Do you think a "Bro" culture is an ethical concern?
2. How can a hypermasculine culture affect the company's bottom line?
3. Do some more research on this issue. Does your research suggest that Khosrowshahi's statement was strong enough to amend for the faults in Kalanick's company culture?

Sources: Benstead, S. (2018, October 18). "Bro culture" and why it's an issue for startups. *Breathehr.com.* https://www.breathehr.com/en-gb/blog/topic/company-culture/bro-culture-and-why-its-an-issue-for-startups; Khosrowshahi, D. (2017, November 7). Uber's new cultural norms. Retrieved from LinkedIn: https://www.linkedin.com/pulse/ubers-new-cultural-norms-dara-khosrowshahi/; Lee, B. (2017, February 20). An engineer says she suffered repeated misogyny at Uber, and few are surprised. Retrieved from Vox: https://www.vox.com/new-money/2017/2/20/14664736/uber-travis-kalanick-sexism

DIMENSIONS OF ORGANIZATIONAL CULTURE

Different types of cultures influence the behavior of people and cultures. Professors Robert Quinn and Kim Cameron provide a useful classification of different types of corporate cultures through the **competing values framework (CVF)**, which helps to identify, measure, and change culture.[15]

This model highlights two main value dimensions: the internal-external dimension and the stability-flexibility dimension. For the internal-external dimension, an organization might look inwards, meaning a focus on employee development, well-being, and collaboration (internal) or outwards (external), meaning a focus on the market, competitors, and customers. Organizations require a combination of both internal and external attention to achieve long-term success.

For the stability-flexibility dimension, organizations that focus on stability believe the outside world is predictable, and value planning, budgeting, efficiency, and reliability. In contrast, organizations that operate with flexibility perceive reality to be unpredictable, therefore ensuring measures are put in place to adapt quickly to changing circumstances. Because of the competing nature of stability and flexibility, organizations are unable to do both at the same time.

These two dimensions combined result in four different types of culture: clan, hierarchy, adhocracy, and market (see Table 10.3).[16]

The **clan culture** falls under internal focus and values flexibility dimension. It is a family-like or tribe-like type of corporate environment that emphasizes consensus, teamwork, collaboration, participation, and the commonality of goals and values. Southwest Airlines is a good example of a clan culture, as it promotes a sense of a family working together, motivated by loyalty to achieve shared objectives.

TABLE 10.3 ■ Competing Values Framework

Culture Type	Assumptions	Beliefs	Values	Behaviors	Results
Clan	Human relationships	People are more likely to be loyal and committed when they have trust in an organization	Collaboration, trust, loyalty, and support	Teamwork, engagement, open communication	Loyalty, commitment, and job satisfaction
Hierarchy	Stability	People behave appropriately in formal organizations governed by rules and procedures	Communication, consistency, and formalization	Obedience and probability	Efficiency, productivity, and timeliness
Market	Accomplishment	People are more motivated to reach goals when they are rewarded for their achievements	Communication, capability, and achievement	Goal-setting, competitiveness, planning, researching the competition	Increasing market share and profit, productivity
Adhocracy	Change	People create and innovate when they understand the need for change	Growth, inspiration, attention to detail	Creativity, flexibility, adaptability	Innovation

Source: Adapted from Quinn, R. E., & Kimberly, J. R. (1984). Paradox, planning, and perseverance: Guidelines for managerial practice. In J. R. Kimberly and R. E. Quinn (Eds.), *New futures: The challenge of managing corporate transitions* (pp. 295–313). Dow Jones–Irwin.

The hierarchy culture exhibits a combination of stability and an internal focus. In contrast with the clan cultures, hierarchical cultures are based on clearly defined corporate levels and structures where employees are primarily guided by processes, rules, and procedures. The U.S. Navy has a hierarchical culture based on maximizing compliance and minimizing mistakes. However, overly rigid organizations are slower to adapt to change.

Like the hierarchy culture, the market culture is also positioned under the control and stability dimension but emphasizes competitiveness not only between the organization and its market competitors but also between employees. Google uses competition to bring out the best in its employees. Yet too much emphasis on results means that market culture can also be aggressive and high-pressured, which can lead to unhealthy competition, stress, and burnout.[17]

The adhocracy culture focuses on flexibility and discretion with an external emphasis. This type of corporate culture is based on the ability to adapt quickly to changing conditions by challenging assumptions and taking risks. Facebook and many other tech companies are adhocracy companies that continuously innovate to stay competitive.[18]

In the current business environment, clan and adhocracy cultures, companies with an emphasis on strong relationships based on mutual respect built inside and outside the workplace, are particularly successful in a workplace that nurtures creativity and innovation.[19]

Different Types of Culture

Although the adhocracy, clan, hierarchy, and market cultures described within the competing values framework provide a good overview of different cultures, many more types of cultures exist in today's workplace, such as positive organizational cultures, communal cultures, fragmented cultures, mercenary cultures, networked cultures, ethical cultures, and spiritual cultures. It should also be noted that a single company can have more than one culture at the same time.

Positive Organizational Culture

Organizations with positive organizational cultures focus on supporting employees' strengths, increasing morale, and providing rewards for good work.[20] In this type of culture, employees are active in decision making, encouraged to collaborate, rewarded for achieving goals, and kept informed of the organization's vision and direction. A positive organizational culture increases morale, raises productivity and efficiency, enhances work performance, and reduces turnover and stress. Prior to the pandemic, frictionless communications provider Zoom nurtured a positive work culture by providing its employees with competitive pay and benefits, unlimited time off, free meals, and monthly office parties.[21] Working from home during the pandemic impacted Zoom's strong in-office culture, but the company managed to maintain its positive working culture by hosting virtual meetups; providing benefits to support working from home such as food delivery, gym equipment, and home office equipment; and offering wellness benefits such as monthly allowances for online exercise classes. In 2021, Zoom was named one of the best places to work by the Glassdoor Employees' Choice Awards.[22]

Communal Culture

Organizations that nurture a communal culture environment are home to employees who tend to think alike, are happy to share knowledge, and have a clear focus on the direction of the task.[23] They are sociable, responsive, and work well together to achieve goals. Healthy restaurant chain Sweetgreen draws from the communal nature of college campus life when creating its work cultures. Communal spaces are designed for the whole team to come together, thereby providing opportunities for swapping ideas, forming bonds, and being creative.[24]

Fragmented Culture

Fragmented culture is found in companies where employees tend to keep to themselves, avoid socializing, and work as individuals rather than as part of a team.[25] For example, computer programmers often spend long periods of time working alone, which may cause distance and disconnection from the rest of

Sweetgreen is an example of a company with a communal culture, where the focus is on sociable and responsive teams working together to accomplish goals.

Adam Glanzman/Bloomberg/via Getty Images

the group. This type of culture often occurs on a group level when people work in silos, meaning teams that work separately from other teams. As a consequence, there is little communication, collaboration, and teamwork between the silos. A fragmented culture characterized by a silo mentality was thought to be one of the reasons for the 2014 General Motors (GM) ignition switch crisis.[26] Employees worked in silos where they had the mindset of being responsible for their part only, and had little communication with people working in the other silos. This lack of collaboration led to faulty ignition switches, which resulted in the recall of 30 million cars worldwide, and linked to over 100 deaths. GM has since overhauled its company culture, obliterating the silos in favor of a more open culture where people are encouraged to work together and share their safety concerns.

Mercenary Culture

As the name suggests, mercenary cultures exist in organizations where making money is the top priority.[27] Employees are measured by their levels of performance and productivity, and are expected to have a high commitment to achieving organizational goals. Because the culture is task driven, they do not tend to socialize, which can sometimes result in an unfriendly working environment. Media services provider Netflix is a good example of a company with a mercenary culture. Constant expectations for high performance put enormous pressure on employees, many of whom live in fear of getting fired. When employees are fired, emails are sent to hundreds of employees specifically explaining the reasons for the dismissal. Although Netflix appears to operate a cutthroat culture, survival is possible, but only when employees consistently demonstrate high levels of performance.[28]

Networked Culture

A networked culture is characterized by a high degree of trust between employees and a willingness to communicate and share information.[29] Employees may work independently of each other, but they come together on an informal basis to swap and exchange ideas. Highly creative organizations such as space exploration company SpaceX, in which people are encouraged to think differently, tend to have networked cultures.

Ethical Culture

There have been dozens of well-documented ethical scandals during the past few years, which have led many organizations to build more ethical cultures.[30] In companies with ethical cultures, senior people lead by example by behaving in an ethical manner and ensuring, through clear communication and training workshops, that their employees do the same. Many organizations reinforce their ethical cultures by rewarding ethical behavior and punishing unethical behavior. Nonprofit health care provider Blue Shield of California was included in the 2021 World's Most Ethical Companies by the Ethisphere Institute.[31] Blue Shield strives to bring affordable health care to the people and communities who need it the most.

Spiritual Culture

Spiritual culture focuses on opportunities for employees to grow and find purpose in the workplace by carrying out meaningful tasks that contribute to the good of society as a whole.[32] Organizations with a spiritual culture prioritize caring, compassion, and support for others over profit. Natural-ingredients personal care company Tom's of Maine embraces a spiritual culture by giving away 10% of pretax profits to charitable organizations while also giving employees 4 paid hours per month for community service.[33]

TABLE 10.4 ■ Types of Organizational Cultures	
Culture	**Attributes**
Positive Organizational Culture	• Employees' strengths supported • High morale • Good work is rewarded
Communal Culture	• Employees think alike • Employees share knowledge • Have clear focus on goals • Goals achieved as a team
Fragmented Culture	• Little socializing • Work as individuals
Mercenary Culture	• Employees measured by level of performance and productivity • High commitment expected • Financial goals are top priority • Little socializing
Networked Culture	• High degree of trust • Employees communicate openly and share information • Mostly work independently, but come together to share ideas • Highly creative
Ethical Culture	• Managers act as ethical role models • Ethical standards communicated clearly • Employees trained to behave ethically
Spiritual Culture	• Focus on tasks that contribute to the good of society • Prioritize caring, compassion, and support over profit

Despite the different types of cultures within organizations today, some cultures will suit some people more than others—it all really depends on how well your personality matches with the culture of the organization.

EMPLOYEE FIT WITH ORGANIZATIONAL CULTURE

"The people make the place" is a common expression, but what does this mean for the workplace? Based on the four organizational cultures described earlier—clan, hierarchy, market, and adhocracy, researcher William Gardner and colleagues set out to uncover how different kinds of personalities fit into different types of organizations—something called the person-organization fit (P-O fit).[34] They discovered that certain types of personalities fit better with particular cultures. For example, people who tended to be more agreeable and extroverted had a better fit with the clan culture; people who were more conscientious and reserved suited the hierarchy culture; people who were less agreeable fit better with the market culture; and people who scored highly on openness worked better in an adhocracy culture.

The research also showed that when the right personality is matched to the right company culture, many positive outcomes arise, such as improved job performance, higher job satisfaction, and greater organizational commitment—all of which leads to less turnover.

When it comes to workplace cultures, not everybody is a good fit, but that doesn't mean you won't find the right place to work. The most important thing is to make sure your personality fits your chosen job or career. For example, if you tend to get bored or are easily distracted, then you might be better off looking for a job that provides variety and unpredictability, such as entrepreneurship. Or if you're the type of person who is constantly "on," then a media or PR career might work best, where reacting quickly to events is part of the job description. If you like meeting and interacting with people, and finding solutions to different problems, then consulting might be the right fit. Understanding your own personality is the first step to identifying the best cultural match for you. The second step is finding a company culture that fits your personality. Table 10.5 illustrates some tips for job seekers to find the best cultural fit.

TABLE 10.5 ■ How to Find Your Cultural Fit
● Avoid accepting a new job without finding out more about the culture and how it fits in with your personality.
● Do your homework by talking to people who already work there or by reading reviews online (think Glassdoor).
● During an interview, ask the interviewer to describe the company culture to see if it matches what you have learned in your research.
● Ask your recruiters about people they have already placed in the organization. (Are they still there? Are they happy? Have they experienced any problems?)
● Make an effort to secure a temporary work placement (like an internship) if the opportunity arises. This is the best way to get a preview of the role and the working culture.
● If you're on an internship, ask existing employees about what it's like to work there, and pay attention to the way they interact with each other.
● Ask about expectations of work hours. Do people stay past 5 pm or work on weekends? This will illuminate the work–life balance at the company.
● Find out if there are hybrid work options when some days are spent in the office or at home online.
● How does the company use technology for working remotely? This will signal how current the organization is.
● Look around the office space. Does it feel exciting to you? Or does it feel draining? Do you work in offices or shared space, and what is your preference?
● Is there signage or artwork on the walls? What does it say, and do you agree with it?

Sources: Lublin, J. (2020, January 15). Considering a new job? Beware a culture misfit. *The Wall Street Journal.* https://www.wsj.com/articles/considering-a-new-job-beware-a-culture-misfit-11579084201; and Ryan, R. (2021, September 8). Interview questions you should ask the employer in the Covid era. *Forbes.* https://www.forbes.com/sites/robinryan/2021/09/08/interview-questions-you-should-ask-in-the-covid-era/?sh=aa3a5366c312

Although a good P-O fit has positive consequences for the individual and the company, cultures cannot afford to remain static; instead, they should constantly be evolving to ensure that the needs of employees are being addressed. This is particularly important for mental health.

Culture and Mental Health

A positive culture supportive of mental health is essential to the functioning of an organization. A recent study showed that 76% of full-time U.S. workers reported a mental health condition during 2021, and more than 80% of Gen Zers and nearly 70% of millennials have left their jobs for mental health reasons. Kelly Greenwood, founder and CEO of Mind Share Partners, said, "The future of workplace mental health demands culture change. . . . We can't afford to go back to 'business as usual.' Now is the time to be intentional and imagine what work could be—with more vulnerability, compassion, and sustainable ways of working."[35]

When people don't feel comfortable sharing their experiences, both the individual and the company feel the impact. The individual continues to suffer in silence, unwilling to seek the right treatment, which leads to unhappiness and absenteeism; and the company suffers a huge blow to the bottom line. For instance, sick days (200 million every year), lost productivity (costing companies more than $16 billion), and mental health treatment (for depression, stress, and anxiety) have a big impact on income and profits. It is more important than ever for companies to build a culture of acceptance that encourages employees to be honest and open about their mental health conditions, and to provide the support they need.

By applying the steps illustrated in Table 10.6, companies can create work cultures where employees will feel comfortable, protected, and cared for.

TABLE 10.6 ■ Building a Culture of Acceptance

- **Change starts at the top:** Managers, leaders, and senior employees must share their own experiences with their staff and model vulnerability as a strength, rather than a weakness. They can also build deeper connections with employees by checking in with them regularly with a simple "How are you?" and using empathy and authenticity to address any concerns.

- **Invest in training:** Managers need to be trained in how to spot an employee who might be suffering with mental health problems, to treat every employee as an individual, and to respect each person.

- **Provide support:** At the very least, companies need to provide mental health benefits and ensure that employees are aware of these benefits during employee orientations and communications throughout the year.

- **Invest in DEI:** Companies must invest in Diversity, Equity and Inclusion (DEI) to support mental health and address the issues of systemic racism and violence to foster a culture of acceptance (see Chapter 11). A recent study showed that companies that offer a platform to workers to discuss social and political topics at work help to build a more mentally healthy culture.

Source: Greenwood, K., Bapat, V., & Maughan, M. (2019, November 22). Research: People want their employers to talk about mental health. *Harvard Business Review.* https://hbr.org/2019/10/research-people-want-their-employers-to-talk-about-mental-health; and Greenwood, K., & Anas, J. (2021, October 4). It's a new era for mental health at work. *Harvard Business Review.* https://hbr.org/2021/10/its-a-new-era-for-mental-health-at-work

American multinational technology company Cisco is a good example of a company establishing a culture of acceptance. It incorporates mental health services as part of its overall health care coverage and introduced #SafetoTalk, a virtual community that encourages employees to share their struggles and connect with others.

In a note to employees, Cisco CEO Chuck Robbins said, "Each of us has a role to play in making sure that those suffering feel less afraid to ask for support in the moments they need it most. No one needs to go it alone."[36]

CLUES TO HELP DECIPHER ORGANIZATIONAL CULTURE

Whether you're on a job interview or doing an internship, there are several clues to a company's culture that will help you to understand if it is the right workplace for you. These clues include symbols, practices, rituals, and myths. Values, which we explored earlier, can also be considered a type of clue.

Symbols

Symbols are objects that convey meaning to others about an organization's culture. For example, multilevel marketing company Mary Kay rewards its employees with "career cars" including a pink Cadillac or Mini Cooper for meeting sales quotas, thereby demonstrating a culture that acknowledges hard work and commitment. As the sales quotas are extremely tough, the cars are perceived as a symbol of success. VP of sales at Mary Kay, Laura Beitler, stated: "When you see a sales force member driving a Mary Kay career car, you know these women are very successful. . . . It's a way of rewarding them and having that symbol of success out in the world."[37]

A pink Mary Kay vehicle conveys meaning to others about the organization's culture and acknowledges the hard work and commitment of the women who drive it.

George Rose/Getty Images News/via Getty Images

Practices

Practices are activities within an organization that occur frequently and give an indication of the type of organizational culture in an organization. At San Diego–based protein bar company Perfect Snacks, employees are expected to comply with clear, written policies designed to ensure they take plenty of breaks and have a healthy work–life balance. For instance, from Monday to Thursday, meetings are not permitted before 9 am or after 4 pm. On Fridays, not only are meetings not permitted, but staff are encouraged to go home at 2 pm. Finally, staff are instructed to set an out-of-the-office automated message when they are off sick or on vacation. Bill Keith, CEO of Perfect Snacks, explained the reasoning behind the company's practices: "We want to make sure that when folks come in here, we're breaking any bad habits they have, and creating those boundaries for their professional and personal lives." [38]

Rituals

Rituals are activities and ceremonies that celebrate important occasions and accomplishments within an organization. For example, when new hires first join Starbucks, they take part in a ritual tasting of their store manager's favorite coffee. During this ritual, new hires learn about the origins of the coffee, how it is grown, and how it is brewed, thereby reinforcing Starbucks's key mission: to serve the highest-quality coffee to its customers.[39]

Myths

Myths are narratives based on true events that are repeated to emphasize an important component of an organization's culture. For example, a popular story at upscale retailer Nordstrom describes a customer who went into Nordstrom in Anchorage, Alaska, with the intention of returning a set of snow tires. Nordstrom sells a lot of different products such as clothes, shoes, and accessories, but it does not sell snow tires. It turned out that the customer had previously bought the snow tires at the store that had occupied the same space before Nordstrom came along. After some thought, the Nordstrom store manager agreed to allow the customer to return the snow tires.[40] This story is a useful way of reminding employees of Nordstrom's commitment to going the extra mile for its customers.

Clues are a powerful driver of an organization's culture. The more positive the company clues, the more likely it is to be successful. Culture is all around us and evolving every day. The most successful organizations tend to continuously nurture cultures that achieve significantly higher levels of financial performance, customer satisfaction, productivity, and employee engagement.

ENTREPRENEURIAL MINDSET ACTIVITY

What's Your School's Culture?

Every organization has a culture, whether by accident or through intentionally promoting the types of items described in this chapter: symbols, rituals, values, and practices. Developing a clear and consistent mission is also an important task for leaders, so that employees across divisions and geographic locations can all agree on the same core mission and work together in unison.

To complete this entrepreneurial mindset activity, simply observe and analyze the culture that exists and is promoted at your university. Walk across campus and through buildings, take note of everything, from the posters on the walls to the recurring rituals and practices. Are there rituals around sports, holidays, and other widely recognized events? Read closely the emails and other communication on social media provided by the university.

Also find a formal mission statement and statement of values. The senior leadership most likely references these often, and they can usually be found on the school's website.

Does your school have a mascot? If so, research the symbol and learn how it fits with the school, its history, and its broader culture.

Using your findings and your data, describe a clear picture of the mission and culture at your university and discuss it with classmates.

Critical Thinking Questions

1. What did you find during this exercise? Does the university culture support its mission? Why or why not?

2. Do the mission and values of your university fit your own? Explain.

3. Did you and your classmates come to any notably different conclusions about the university's mission and culture? If yes, what are the differences? If no, how do you feel about having a similar view?

IN REVIEW

10.1 Define organizational mission, vision, and values and explain their importance to the company.

A mission defines the purpose of an organization. It reflects the types of products or services it produces, who its customers tend to be, and its core beliefs. A vision describes what an organization wants to become. Values are underlying desires and core beliefs that shape an identity of an organization, and act as a good guide for how employees are expected to behave. Great missions, visions, and values are an essential foundation for company longevity and success.

10.2 Define culture and its impact on organizations.

Organizational culture is a pattern of shared norms, rules, values, and beliefs that guides the attitudes and behaviors of its employees. The type of organizational culture has a direct impact on business. Weak company cultures have been blamed for the downfall of many organizations, while strong company cultures have been connected with some of the most successful companies in the world.

10.3 Describe the four dimensions of organizational culture.

The competing values framework (CVF) is a way to identify, measure, and change culture. This model highlights two main value dimensions: internal-external dimension and stability-flexibility dimension. These two dimensions combined result in four different types of culture: clan, hierarchy, adhocracy, and market. The *clan* culture is a family-like or tribe-like type of corporate environment that emphasizes consensus, teamwork, collaboration, participation, and the commonality of goals and values. The hierarchy culture is based on clearly defined corporate levels and structures where employees are primarily guided by processes, rules, and procedures. The market culture emphasizes competitiveness not only between the organization and its market competitors but also between employees. The adhocracy culture is based on the ability to adapt quickly to changing conditions by challenging assumptions and taking risks.

10.4 Discuss the importance of employee fit to organizational culture.

Different kinds of personalities fit better into different types of organizations—something called the person-organization fit (P-O fit). When the right personality is matched to the right company culture, then many positive outcomes arise, such as improved job performance, higher job satisfaction, and greater organizational commitment—all of which leads to less turnover.

10.5 Compare and contrast the various clues to organizational culture.

There are several clues to a company's culture that give people a better understanding of the type of workplace. These clues include values, symbols, practices, rituals, and myths. Symbols are objects that convey meaning to others about an organization's culture; practices are activities within an organization that occur frequently and give an indication of the type of organizational culture in an organization; rituals are activities and ceremonies that celebrate important occasions and accomplishments within an organization; and myths are narratives based on true events that are repeated to emphasize an important component of an organization's culture.

BUSINESSES DISCUSSED IN THIS CHAPTER

Organization	UN Sustainable Development Goal
American Express	12. Responsible Consumption and Production 13. Climate Action
Blue Shield of California	11. Sustainable Cities and Communities 12. Responsible Consumption and Production
Cisco	13. Climate Action 15. Life on Land
Coca-Cola	6. Clean Water and Sanitation 11. Sustainable Cities and Communities 12. Responsible Consumption and Production 13. Climate Action
Dick's Sporting Goods	3. Good Health and Well-Being 12. Responsible Consumption and Production

(Continued)

Organization	UN Sustainable Development Goal
Disney	12. Responsible Consumption and Production 13. Climate Action 14. Life Below Water 15. Life on Land
Facebook	13. Climate Action
General Motors	12. Responsible Consumption and Production
GoldieBlox	5. Gender Equality
Google	12. Responsible Consumption and Production 14. Life Below Water 15. Life on Land
John's Crazy Socks	3. Good Health and Well-Being 10. Reduced Inequality 16. Peace, Justice, and Strong Institutions
Lululemon	10. Reduced Inequality 11. Sustainable Cities and Communities 12. Responsible Consumption and Production
Mary Kay	3. Good Health and Well-Being 12. Responsible Consumption and Production
Microsoft	3. Good Health and Well-Being 4. Quality Education
Netflix	12. Responsible Consumption and Production
Nordstrom	12. Responsible Consumption and Production
Patagonia	12. Responsible Consumption and Production 13. Climate Action
Perfect Snacks	3. Good Health and Well-Being
Southwest Airlines	12. Responsible Consumption and Production 13. Climate Action
SpaceX	12. Responsible Consumption and Production
Starbucks	6. Clean Water and Sanitation 11. Sustainable Cities and Communities
Sweetgreen	8. Decent Work and Economic Growth 12. Responsible Consumption and Production
TCWGlobal	4. Quality Education 5. Gender Equality
Tom's of Maine	8. Decent Work and Economic Growth 9. Industry, Innovation, and Infrastructure 12. Responsible Consumption and Production 13. Climate Action
Tony's Chocolonely	8. Decent Work and Economic Growth 10. Reduced Inequality 16. Peace, Justice, and Strong Institutions
Uber	11. Sustainable Cities and Communities 13. Climate Action
U.S. Navy	7. Affordable and Clean Energy 13. Climate Action
Wells Fargo	11. Sustainable Cities and Communities 13. Climate Action

Organization	UN Sustainable Development Goal
Zappos	12. Responsible Consumption and Production
Zoom	9. Industry, Innovation, and Infrastructure

KEY TERMS

Adhocracy culture (p. 208)

Clan culture (p. 207)

Communal culture (p. 208)

Competing values framework (CVF) (p. 207)

Ethical culture (p. 210)

Fragmented culture (p. 208)

Hierarchy culture (p. 208)

Market culture (p. 208)

Mercenary culture (p. 209)

Mission statement (p. 201)

Myths (p. 213)

Networked culture (p. 209)

Organizational culture (p. 204)

Person-organization fit (P-O fit) (p. 211)

Positive organizational culture (p. 208)

Practices (p. 213)

Rituals (p. 213)

Spiritual culture (p. 210)

Symbols (p. 213)

Values (p. 203)

Vision statement (p. 202)

Vision (p. 202)

BUSINESS CASE 10.2: NOVOZYMES—BAGSVAERD, DENMARK

SDG 13: Climate Action

Novozymes is a Danish global biotechnology company that produces industrial enzymes and micro-organisms. Its mission statement is: "Together we find biological answers for better lives in a growing world. Our purpose looks ahead to what we can achieve together with customers, consumers, governments, academia, and others around us in terms of finding the sustainable answers that our world needs."

So what exactly are enzymes and microorganisms, and how do they help to provide sustainable answers? Enzymes are proteins that are used in industrial processes instead of chemicals and are frequently used in beer and bread-making. Novozymes works to find natural enzymes and enhance them so they can be used in other products manufactured by different industries. For instance, Novozymes's enzymes can be used in laundry and dishwashing detergent, where they improve stain removal and help the products work more effectively at lower temperatures. These enzymes are also used to produce biofuels, where they turn starch or cellulose from biomass into sugars that are fermented to ethanol. Like enzymes, microorganisms such as bacteria, algae, and fungi can be used in a number of different processes. Novozymes supplies microorganisms to its industrial customers for use in animal health and nutrition, agriculture, industrial cleaning, and wastewater treatment.

By replacing potentially harmful chemicals with natural materials and speeding up chemical reactions, Novozymes helps industrial customers to produce less waste and use less energy. In 2020, its customers saved an estimated 49 million tons of carbon dioxide emissions by applying Novozymes products, the equivalent of taking approximately 20 million cars off the road. In 2021, Novozymes was awarded the Terra Carta Seal, for sustainability, by the Prince Charles Sustainable Markets Initiative. This award is important, given "it recognizes those organizations which have made a serious commitment to a future that is much more sustainable, and puts Nature, People and the Planet at the heart of the economy."

In 2021, the company entered into a strategic collaboration with the global agricultural sciences company FMC to "research, co-develop, and commercialize novel enzyme-based crop protection solutions for farmers around the world." The goal of this partnership is to replace chemical pesticides used by farmers with biological solutions. In that same year, Novozymes North America was selected as a Safer Choice Partner of the Year award winner by the U.S. Environmental Protection Agency "for achievement in the design, manufacture, selection, and use of products with safer chemicals." The company also set self-imposed emissions goals: "We . . . recognize the urgent need for action and are raising our commitment on climate change to include all emissions from our supply chain . . . and we will now strive for a 50% reduction in absolute emissions from operations & supply chain . . . by 2030."

Novozymes's willingness to create partnerships and collaborate with others in its quest to carry out its mission to provide biological solutions to improve industrial performance is key to its rapid growth and financial success. In 2021, Novozymes generated $2.1 billion in revenue with a market value of $18.1 billion.

Critical Thinking Questions

1. How does Novozymes seem to be fulfilling its mission?

2. How often do you think a company should review its mission statement? Explain your response.

3. Should a business change its organizational mission if the business is not successful? Or should other changes be made first? Explain your response.

References

EPA. (2021, September 22). Novozymes North America recognized as one of EPA's 2021 safer choice partners of the year. U.S. Environmental Protection Agency. https://www.epa.gov/newsreleases/novozymes-north-america-recognized-one-epas-2021-safer-choice-partners-year#:~:text=News%20Releases%3A-,Novozymes%20North%20America%20Recognized%20as%20one%20of%20EPA's,Choice%20Partners%20of%20the%20Year&text=RALEIGH%20(Sept.,of%20the%20Year%20award%20winner

Forbes. (2022). Novozymes. https://www.forbes.com/companies/novozymes/?sh=4f75d2622237

Novozymes. (2020). The Novozymes Report 2020. https://report2020.novozymes.com/PDF/The_Novozymes_Report_2020.pdf

Novozymes. (2021). The Novozymes Report 2021. https://report2021.novozymes.com/?_ga=2.174230945.2021551744.1647872939-930179551.1647872939#last-section-

Novozymes. (2022). About us. https://www.novozymes.com/en/about-us

Persio, S.L. (2021, November 3). Amazon, Salesforce, among 45 companies awarded Terra Carta seal from Prince Charles. *Forbes*. https://www.forbes.com/sites/sofialottopersio/2021/11/03/amazon-salesforce-among-45-companies-awarded-terra-carta-seal-from-prince-charles/?sh=1596f143752d

Reed, S. (2018, January 1). Fighting climate change, one laundry load at a time. *The New York Times*. https://www.nytimes.com/2018/01/01/business/energy-environment/climate-change-enzymes-laundry.html?auth=login-email&login=email

Singh, R., Kumar, M., Mittal, A., & Mehta, P. K. (2016, August 19). Microbial enzymes: Industrial progress in 21st century. *3 Biotech*, 6(2), 174. https://doi.org/10.1007/s13205-016-0485-8

Sustainable Markets Initiative. (2020). The Terra Carta Seal. *Sustainable Markets Initiative*. https://www.sustainable-markets.org/terra-carta-seal/intro/

BLOCK 4
PEOPLE INSIDE THE BUSINESS

11 MANAGEMENT AND LEADERSHIP

LEARNING OBJECTIVES

11.1   Discuss the meaning of management and its importance in the workplace.

11.2   Describe a manager's four major tasks—planning, organizing, leading, and controlling.

11.3   Outline the skills managers need in organizations.

11.4   Explain leadership styles to identify the difference between leaders and managers.

11.5   Explore the role of leadership in promoting diversity, equity, and inclusion (DEI).

BUSINESS IMPACT CASE 11.1: LITTLE COCOA BEAN—BOSTON, MASSACHUSETTS

SDG 3:   Good Health and Well-Being

Tracy Skelly, entrepreneur and mother of 3-year-old Sophia, identified a significant problem in a large and growing market. Culturally relevant, healthy baby and toddler food for Black, Indigenous, and People of Color does not exist. Walk down the baby food aisle of any grocery store and you primarily see overly processed, Eurocentric food. Tracy looked around and noticed that the healthy, nutrient-dense foods that she grew up eating as an Afro-Latina were not present. "Where was the papaya, collards, chayote, and tamarind?" she thought. And even if, for example, jarred plantains could be found in the baby food aisle, the manufacturing process turned a nutrient-dense food into an overly boiled, less healthy version of its whole food self.[1]

Being a new mother and making baby food from scratch for Sophia, she started to do more research. She quickly learned that during the first 1,000 days of life the brain grows more in that time period than in any other period of life. Additionally, two-thirds of the calories consumed by babies are metabolized through their brain, which feeds overall brain growth and brain development. "The consumption of healthy and diverse food in the first few years of life is a social determinant of health," says Tracy. "In communities of color, Black and Latinx die from health-related disease at a higher rate than their white counterparts. Research supports that this is connected to early food consumption and access to healthy options." She reminds all of us, "What you eat in the early years of life impacts what you eat throughout life, and whole foods matter."

Inspired by the market gap and social need, Tracy founded Little Cocoa Bean in late 2019 with a mission "to show parents how to increase their child's consumption of healthy and diverse foods by highlighting and celebrating the food that our ancestors have eaten for centuries around the globe." Tracy's original plan to produce and sell nutritional, ready-made baby foods representing African American culture and heritage was quickly stalled when the COVID-19 pandemic stifled the U.S. economy, hitting small businesses particularly hard. As many entrepreneurs were required to do, she quickly pivoted from her original plan and started offering Instagram and Facebook Live sessions sharing and showing recipes. Rather than selling ready-made food, she began selling the tools needed for her viewers to make their own, such as storage jars, bamboo plates, microwavable sanitizing bags, and reusable food pouches. In addition to healthy foods, Tracy also focuses on sustainable packaging.

In early 2022, Tracy went back to her original concept. She found a producer and copacker for her tested recipes. She will soon open a physical storefront in the Boston neighborhood of Jamaica Plain that will sell her ready-made foods for infants and toddlers as well as fresh food that can be consumed on site by young children and their families. She will continue to sell directly online utilizing her social media following and will work to scale the brand and sell through grocery stores in the future.

In the early days of a venture, the entrepreneur wears many hats. Tracy is a leader, manager, salesperson, and involved in every aspect of the business. Her leadership role, however, is one with which she deeply connects. Tracy says, "Leadership is being the first person willing to do the hard thing and the hard thing changes often." For example, Little Cocoa Bean is partnering with a local women's shelter that provides job training. Many of Tracy's employees for the new store will likely come from this shelter. Many don't have extensive résumés, and some may have been formerly incarcerated. As Tracy notes, "My core values require me to give people an opportunity that they might not otherwise get elsewhere. And to accept the responsibility and the consequences that come with making that choice. I'm willing to be the leader—to do the hard thing and willing to except the risk. This holds true in all areas of my business."

Critical Thinking Questions

1. How would you describe Tracy's leadership style? Are there other leaders in your life who use a similar style?

2. What is the connection between core values and leadership? How do your own core values intersect with your own leadership style?

3. Entrepreneurs are leaders and managers. Does this statement hold true for Tracy?

WHAT IS MANAGEMENT?

The Little Cocoa Bean case demonstrates the impact of positive leadership on the community and the environment. Tracy's commitment to providing healthy, diverse baby food for Black, Indigenous, and People of Color helps ensure that babies get the best start in life, and her focus on sustainable packaging demonstrates her efforts to minimize environmental waste. Tracy is also making a real impact on the community by partnering with a women's shelter to offer employment opportunities. As an early entrepreneur and founder of a growing business, Tracy is both leader and manager—sometimes influencing others to act and other times organizing and planning what needs to be done.

Management is the process of working with people and organizational resources to achieve goals efficiently and effectively. Management styles have evolved over the decades. In the past, managers were expected to give orders, closely monitor their workforce, and punish those who did not obey. Although some managers still behave this way today, most managers tend to work more collaboratively, with an emphasis on teamwork and culture. For instance, they provide opportunities for employees to learn and grow, encourage communication, build an environment that nurtures creativity, invite feedback, openly share information with workers, and support, motivate, and guide employees through training and coaching.

Today's most successful organizations are run by managers who display these behaviors and more. When Google carried out its own internal research, named Project Oxygen, to understand what makes a great manager, it discovered 10 main qualities (Table 11.1).

TABLE 11.1 ■ The 10 Behaviors of a Great Manager According to Google
1. Is a good coach
2. Empowers team and does not micromanage
3. Creates an inclusive team environment, showing concern for success and well-being
4. Is productive and results-oriented
5. Is a good communicator—listens and shares information
6. Supports career development and discusses performance
7. Has a clear vision/strategy for the team
8. Has key technical skills to help advise the team
9. Collaborates across Google
10. Is a strong decision maker

Source: Friedman, Z. (2018). Google says the best managers have these 10 qualities. *Forbes.* Retrieved from https://www.forbes.com/sites/zackfriedman/2018/08/30/best-managers-google/#4ff118a14f26

Alongside the skills and behaviors described above, managers also need the ability to adapt to rapid change and navigate uncertainty, challenge the status quo, and continuously learn new skills to meet the demands of a constantly evolving workplace. Let's explore what managers do.

What Managers Do

Management researcher, strategy theorist, and author of *The Nature of Managerial Work* Henry Mintzberg describes a manager's work in terms of managerial roles, or organizational expectations that determine the actions of managers, including *interpersonal, informational,* and *decisional* roles (see Table 11.2).

In interpersonal roles, managers build relationships with the people they work with and act as a public symbol for the many people they represent. Informational roles require managers to gather, assess, and communicate information to individuals and teams in support of the organization's values, mission, vision, and goals.

And in decisional roles, managers are responsible for making judgments and decisions based on available information and analysis of the situation.[2]

Laureen Asseo, founder of Fresh N Lean, an organic meal delivery company started in 2010, is a good example of a manager who fits well into Mintzberg's theory of management roles. Laureen motivates and empowers her employees by being positive and showing them what they are capable of (interpersonal role); she constantly gathers data and feedback to improve the customer experience (informational); and focuses on the learning aspect of mistakes rather than the mistake itself (decisional).[3]

TABLE 11.2 ■ Henry Mintzberg's Management Roles		
Categories	**Roles**	**Example Actions**
Interpersonal *Manager's actions that include symbolic, public-facing activities*	Figurehead Leader Liaison	● Speaking or being present at ceremonial events, hosting guests (e.g., vendors, clients, or potential employees) ● Motivating and influencing employees' behaviors, train and mentor employees ● Keeping up information links internally and externally to the organization
Informational *Manager's actions relating to gathering, assessing, and communicating information*	Monitor Disseminator Spokesperson	● Gathering data and information, studying industry papers, reading reports, maintaining interpersonal relationships ● Sending messages (email, text, and voice), writing memos, forwarding relevant information ● Making speeches, citing the organization's position on a subject
Decisional *Manager's actions that include making judgments and decisions based on situations and information gathered*	Entrepreneur Disturbance handler Resource allocator Negotiator	● Identifying new business opportunities, nurturing new projects or initiatives, selling new business ● Working through employee conflict, conducting efforts during a crisis, interpreting and responding to internal and external change ● Approving and setting budgets, deciding the beneficiaries of internal resources, setting priorities ● Mediating discussions with unions, protecting the organization's interests, bargaining and agreeing to supplier deals

Source: Adapted from Mintzberg, H. (1973). *The nature of managerial work.* Prentice Hall.

Regardless of the type of business or organization you work for, all managers need to perform the four basic functions of management and understand their importance in achieving organizational goals and objectives.

THE FOUR FUNCTIONS OF MANAGEMENT

Mintzberg's management roles embrace the following four main management functions to help managers tackle business challenges: planning, organizing, leading, and controlling, commonly known as the POLC framework (see Figure 11.1).

Planning

Planning is a type of management function that first involves setting the purpose or mission of the company (the company's reason for being in existence). Next, planning involves developing goals for the future, designing appropriate strategies, and acquiring the right resources in order to achieve the mission and related goals and objectives. Planning is an essential part of management, mainly because the other functions are unlikely to succeed without it. Even the most careful planning can have unexpected consequences; for example, in 2018, Domino's Pizza in Russia launched a "Domino's Forever" promotional campaign offering 100 free pizzas per year to loyal customers who tattooed the Domino's logo onto their skin. The company had not anticipated that hundreds of people would fulfill the request and was forced to cap the number of people eligible for the deal, and end the campaign soon after it began.[4]

Domino's Pizza had not planned for the overwhelming response to its "Domino's Forever" campaign. After just 5 days, over 350 people had posted images of their Domino's tattoos, prompting the chain to end its campaign early.

PA Images/Alamy Stock Photo

Types of Plans

Plans can be broad and long-term or narrow and short-term. There are several main types of plans managers use to achieve goals in an organization: strategic, tactical, operational, directional, business, and action.

A strategic plan is a broad, long-term plan that helps to define the entire organization's strategic mission and goals, and the actions needed to achieve them. Executive management such as CEOs and their teams tend to design strategic plans to assess industry, competitor, and customer trends. For example, as part of its customer service strategy, web hosting service provider SiteGround connects with its customers by providing the opportunity for them to provide feedback 24/7 through three different channels: tickets, live chat, and phone.[5]

A tactical plan supports a strategic plan by transforming it into a specific plan by applying it to particular parts of the organization. A tactical plan ensures adequate resources and assigns responsibility to each section and individuals involved in the strategy. Tactical plans are usually short-term plans, plans that cover 1 year or less, and are used to achieve short-term goals.

An **operational plan** focuses on particular procedures and processes required to keep the organization running smoothly. Front-line or lower-level managers are most likely to make operational plans. These plans might involve designing a staff schedule, creating a monthly budget, or outlining performance goals for employees.

A **directional plan** is a general, flexible plan that provides guidelines for an organization's long-term goals. Directional plans provide focus but do not include specific objectives or allocate responsibility. They are used to educate employees about where the organization is going and what it hopes to achieve in the future.

A **business plan** is a written document that describes the actions and goals needed to support organizational strategy. New businesses commonly use business plans to outline their goals and objectives. Airbnb founder Brian Chesky is famous for his one-page business plan for global domination.[6]

An **action plan** is the specific action, people, and resources needed to accomplish a goal. For example, the World Health Organization (WHO) has created a global action plan to strengthen collaboration between organizations working toward the health-related UN Sustainable Development Goals.[7]

Action plans like the 2030 Development Agenda list specific people, actions, and resources needed to accomplish a goal. The 193 countries in the UN General Assembly adopted the 2030 Development Agenda, which outlines an action plan for 17 Sustainable Development Goals.

Anadolu Agency/Getty Images

Organizing

Organizing is the process of orchestrating people, structure, actions, resources, and decisions to achieve goals. Organizing involves deciding what is going to be done to achieve an organization's mission and goals, as well as how is it going to be done and by whom. A key part of the organizing function is to offer employees the opportunities for further learning and development. For example, outdoor clothing company The North Face encourages its employees to learn more about its core mission by offering opportunities for them to go on hiking, skiing, and climbing trips led by professional athletes.[8]

Leading

Managers can ensure that activities go as planned through leading: the process of influencing people to achieve goals. Understanding what motivates employee behavior and communicating effectively with a diverse team is a critical leadership skill for managers. HubSpot, a developer and marketer of software products, has been rated highly by its employees for its leadership team: "HubSpot's leaders are truly remarkable. They care about your personal and professional growth and are passionate about solving for the customer."[9]

Controlling

The last of the four functions, controlling, is the process of monitoring activities such as financials, policies, measuring results, comparing them with goals, and correcting performance when necessary. The main aim of controlling is to ensure that performance meets the objectives of goals and plans. For example, Detroit-based financial services company Quicken Loans has a company policy of returning every customer phone call or email on the same day that it was received. If an employee is unable to do this, they are instructed to call Dan Gilbert, the company's founder, who does it instead. Controlling this process is an essential part of management at Quicken Loans.[10]

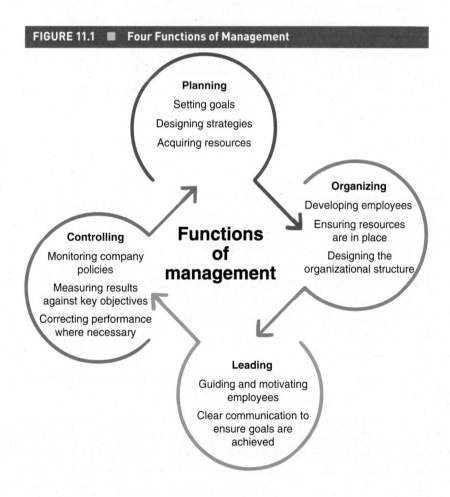

FIGURE 11.1 ■ Four Functions of Management

Different Types of Managers

Typically, organizations are divided into different areas such as finance, operations, marketing, human resources, and administration. Each department needs managers with the right skills to specialize in these areas to ensure everything runs smoothly.

Financial Managers

Financial managers maintain the financial health of an organization by providing financial guidance and support. Duties might include preparing financial reports, monitoring cash flow and payroll, and finding ways to improve profitability.

Operations Managers

Operations managers oversee day-to-day operations and ensure processes and procedures are being applied by employees. They support people in the achievement of tasks and goals, and make sure everybody is working to the highest levels of productivity and efficiency.

Marketing Managers

Marketing managers are responsible for helping the organization promote and sell its products and services to customers. Their duties involve creating and coordinating marketing campaigns, developing marketing strategies, and overseeing the department's marketing budget.

Human Resources Managers

Human resources managers oversee the human resources department and ensure HR teams carry out their functions and tasks. This might involve developing compensation plans, organizing employee training and development, and preparing strategic solutions for recruitment and selection.

Administrative Managers

Administrative managers oversee the day-to-day management of operations and workers. They provide support, guidance, and leadership to employees; develop and improve administrative systems, policies, and procedures; and plan office events such as meetings, conferences, and interviews.

Regardless of the different areas of specialization, managers will need to display certain skills, all of which are dependent on the type of organization for which they work.

ESSENTIAL MANAGEMENT SKILLS

To carry out their duties efficiently and effectively, managers of every type need to master a variety of essential skills and strengths. Skills are talents or abilities that enable a person to complete a particular task, interaction, or process effectively and efficiently. Focusing on your strengths is considered to be more productive than agonizing over your weaknesses. In 2021, 18-year-old Emma Raducanu became the youngest British player to win a Grand Slam title at the U.S. Open. Emma's intensive training regime includes a high-level focus on both mental and physical strength, and she uses those skills to great effect when facing formidable opponents on the court. Raducanu credits the power of sport and tennis for her inner strength. She says:

> Through playing sport, and having to be bold on the court and fearless and fight, it's given me inner strength. If you have that . . . then you can really achieve whatever you want.[11]

There are three types of skills essential for top managers, middle managers, and first-line managers: *conceptual, technical,* and *relational skills* (see Figure 11.2).

Conceptual or abstract skills are the ability of a manager to visualize the entire organization and think through complex systems and problems. These skills allow managers to look beyond their own department to make decisions that positively impact organizational goals. Top managers are likely to use conceptual skills to observe the world around them to find creative ways to make connections and resolve problems.

Technical skills are the abilities and knowledge to perform job-specific tasks. These skills are more important for first-line managers or those in their first professional roles. Common technical skills in today's high-tech environment are coding, security, and cloud computing.[12]

Emma Raducanu, the 2021 U.S. Open champion, employs an aggressive baseline strategy, meaning she relies on the strength of her groundstrokes to move her opponents around the court.

Al Bello/Getty Images Sport/Getty Images

Relational skills help managers collaborate and communicate with others. Managers across all three levels of management need to master relational skills to interact well with others. Daniel Springer, CEO of DocuSign, and his management team were rated highly by employees in a recent survey conducted by anonymous company review site Glassdoor for truly caring about their staff and outside work.[13] The TV show *Undercover Boss*, where the CEO or president of a company is placed in a lower-level position to work undercover alongside their staff, is also a good example of managers making an effort to better understand and develop empathy for their employees.[14]

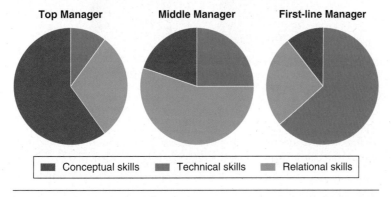

FIGURE 11.2 ■ Skills Required by Types of Managers

Top managers need a higher level of conceptual skills than middle or first-line managers; middle managers require a greater degree of relational skills; and first-line managers need to possess more technical skills.

Top Manager   Middle Manager   First-line Manager

■ Conceptual skills   ■ Technical skills   ■ Relational skills

Source: Neck, C. P., Houghton, J. D., & Murray, E. L. (2022). *Management* (3rd ed.). SAGE.

Other Important Management Skills

Critical thinking is the use of intelligence, knowledge, and skills to question and carefully explore situations and arrive at thoughtful conclusions based on evidence and reason.[15] It involves questioning and learning with an open mind. Critical thinking is one of the most in-demand skills for job candidates.[16] You don't need to be an expert in critical thinking to get a job. Many of these skills can be learned in the workplace. However, employers look for candidates who have a questioning mind, a willingness to embrace change, and a keen desire to learn.

Communication skills are the ability to give and receive information. Effective communication skills are essential to everybody in the workplace. Being able to express yourself in formal and informal situations and in writing is key to getting your message across to the right people. According to a study by online learning platform Udemy, communication skills are among the most practiced by employees.[17] Chapter 14 provides more information on communication.

Time-management skills are the ability to manage time effectively. As a manager, you will likely face being bombarded with emails, phone calls, instant messages, and other forms of communication methods. Good time management leads to less stress and anxiety, greater work performance and productivity, and a higher quality of work. Managers can manage their time effectively by prioritizing tasks, freeing up part of the day to respond to calls and emails, and eliminating unnecessary paperwork.

Decision-making skills are the ability to choose between possible solutions to a problem to select the best outcome. Managers often use a five-step model of decision making (also called the classical model of decision making) to help them make good decisions and find solutions to complex problems (see Figure 11.3). For example, say you're working as a manager of a large call center and your staff keep leaving their jobs.

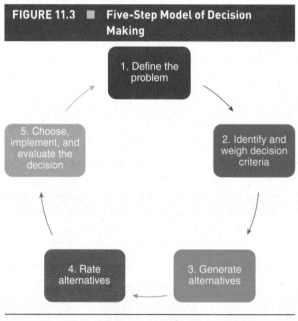

FIGURE 11.3 ■ Five-Step Model of Decision Making

Source: Neck, C. P., Houghton, J. D., & Murray, E. L. (2020). *Organizational behavior* (2nd ed.). SAGE.

- *Define the Problem*

  The first step is to identify the problem that needs to be solved. Figuring out the roots of the problem and why it needs a solution is the first important step to making good decisions. In this example, the problem is lack of staff commitment, and the goal is to find ways to encourage staff to stay.

- *Identify and Weigh Decision Criteria*

  Now that the problem has been defined, you will need to identify and weigh the criteria in the decision. For example, the reasons why your employees are leaving.

- *Generate Multiple Alternatives*

  Next, you may think of possible solutions to the defined problem. Perhaps if you discover that your employees are not happy with their salaries, you could consider a financial incentive, like a raise or a bonus. Alternatively, if you find out that they are simply frustrated with their role, you could arrange for them to learn new skills that could be applied to a different role.

- *Rate Alternatives on the Basis of Decision Criteria*

   During this step, it is important to take the time to weigh the two possible solutions against each other. For example, if you analyze the figures and realize that you can't afford to offer any more financial awards. Similarly, though you might provide your employees with the opportunities for further training, they might be reluctant to learn new skills.

- *Choose, Implement, and Evaluate the Best Alternative*

   Once the first four steps have been completed, it is time to make a decision on the basis of the information you have gathered. If financial rewards are not possible, then you might be able to create more meaningful benefits that could appeal to your staff, such as working from home for a portion of the week, flexible working hours, or more vacation time. To encourage further learning, you could explain to each of your team members why they need to gain new skills, the training tools available to them, and the type of support they will receive during the process.

So far, you have explored how managers operate in the workplace, the four main functions they need to embrace to help them tackle business challenges, and the skills they need to carry out their roles effectively. In the following section, you will learn more about leadership and the important role leaders play in organizations.

ETHICS IN BUSINESS

Balancing Compassion and Business

All employees come into the workplace with emotions; it's human nature. Is it ethical for managers to ignore the emotions of their employees? How does a manager walk the line of compassion for employees and the need to get work done, especially when our emotions and mental well-being can limit us from performing at our highest levels? Let's consider one of the most relevant workplace issues today—employee mental health. If an employee is experiencing mental health issues such as anxiety or depression, what is a manager to do? Consider this example.

   Baxter recently graduated from college and started a new job as financial analyst for a large investment bank. Having been challenged by anxiety and depression through college, Baxter was not surprised that some of the challenges he faced in school carried over to his new job. After 6 months of working, he started taking more sick days than the average employee and began to fall behind on his work. When he missed a few important deadlines, Baxter's manager, Imani, called a meeting. During the meeting, Baxter informed Imani that he had been diagnosed with moderate anxiety and depression a few years prior, which was the cause for his recent low job performance.

Critical Thinking Questions

1. What should Imani do as a manager?
2. How does Imani balance the need to be compassionate and understanding with the need to get very important work done?

Sources: Goudreau, J. (2013, January 9). From crying to temper tantrums: How to manage emotions at work. *Forbes.* Retrieved from https://www.forbes.com/sites/jennagoudreau/2013/01/09/from-crying-to-temper-tantrums-how-to-manage-emotions-at-work/#3d02a6c4bdff; Lukens, M. (2016, March 9). How leaders can balance logic and emotion to make better decisions. *Fast Company.* Retrieved from https://www.fastcompany.com/3057568/how-to-balance-logic-and-emotion-in-order-to-make-better-d; Sherman, F. (2018, June 29). Is your boss allowed to yell at you? *Chron.* Retrieved from https://work.chron.com/boss-allowed-yell-you-15384.html

LEADING VERSUS MANAGING OTHERS

Leadership is the process of influence aimed at directing behavior toward the accomplishment of goals and objectives.[18] The topic of leadership has been the subject of much fascination for researchers over the centuries, but despite numerous studies, there is no proven "right" way to be a leader, nor are there any identifiable characteristics, behaviors, or traits that describe a leader.

This is mainly because leadership has evolved over many years, helping us to function in different situations. For instance, in hunter-gatherer times, leaders were chosen for their physical strength, whereas in more recent times, leaders are more likely to be admired for their intellectual ability and interpersonal skills.

Effective leaders today are most likely to lead from a position of influence rather than power, and use their decision-making, motivational, and communication skills to inspire others with their vision in order to generate results.

What Leaders Do

Effective leaders create a vision and motivate others to follow, empower others by providing a sense of autonomy, and lead by example to establish appropriate ethics, values, and culture. Successful leaders succeed in bringing out the best in others. They share their vision with their workers on a daily basis. This helps to remind people of where the organization is going and keeps them motivated toward achieving organizational goals. Successful leaders constantly work toward changing things for the better and empower others by allowing them to take responsibility for decisions, hold themselves accountable for outcomes, and let them experience the consequences of their actions.

The Differences Between Managers and Leaders

People often use the terms *managers* and *leaders* interchangeably, but they are not the same. You can be a good manager but not be a good leader; equally, you might be a good leader but not be a good manager. Although both leaders and managers work with people, set goals, and influence others in order to achieve those goals, several distinctions separate the two functions. For instance, leaders tend to create the vision for organizations, and managers are responsible for implementing that vision. A leader might decide to introduce e-learning into the company's training program, but the manager will be expected to set goals to realize this vision.

Leaders are also responsible for creating value while managers track value. Leaders create value by looking for ways to grow the business, improve processes, and empower employees to suggest ideas and handle certain tasks without interference. Managers track value by monitoring the amount of work carried out by the team, reporting on progress, and ensuring that goals are being achieved. However, sometimes counting value can impede productivity if it is taken too far. For example, managers who expect call center employees to report every 15 minutes on how many sales they have made are distracting them from doing their job, which subtracts value. Table 11.3 outlines more differences between managers and leaders.

TABLE 11.3 ■ The Differences Between Managers and Leaders

1. *Managers create circles of power; leaders create circles of influence.* Managers have a certain number of people who report to them, while leaders generate followers by influencing their behaviors and reactions. The more people that come to you for advice, the more likely it is for people to perceive you as a leader.

2. *Managers manage work; leaders lead people.* Managers are responsible for controlling a group to achieve specific goals, while leaders are primarily expected to motivate, influence, and inspire people to contribute to the success of an organization.

3. *Managers promote stability; leaders promote change.* Managers tend to maintain the status quo, sticking to what works. Leaders embrace change and create waves where they need to.

4. *Managers create a culture of rationality and control.* Managers are problem solvers who encourage people to work efficiently to contribute to the organization. Leaders influence the thoughts and actions of people by creating new ideas, visions, and goals and motivating them to strive for desirable outcomes and objectives.

5. *Managers balance opposing views; managers coordinate conflicting views between people to reach acceptable compromises.* Leaders do the opposite. Instead, they create new approaches to problems and develop new solutions.

Sources: Nayar, V. (2013, August). Three differences between managers and leaders. *Harvard Business Review.* Retrieved from https://hbr.org/2013/08/tests-of-a-leadership-transiti; Zalenzik, A. (2014). Managers and leaders: Are they different? *Harvard Business Review.* Retrieved from https://hbr.org/2004/01/managers-and-leaders-are-they-different

Although it is useful for leaders to have managerial skills, it is not essential. Of course, it is beneficial for leaders to understand the management functions, but they don't necessarily need to be managers as well as leaders. Their primary strength lies in the ability to influence the behaviors and work of others in order to realize their vision and achieve goals. They do this by following a variety of leadership styles.

ENTREPRENEURIAL MINDSET ACTIVITY

When are managers leaders?

Your mindset activity involves further exploring this difference between leaders and managers. Within your circle of friends, family, and colleagues, there are probably a number of people you know who are in a management position in an organization. Your job is to interview them. Ask them a series of questions about their jobs, what they do daily, and what they think are the most important aspects of their roles. After the interview, ask the person you have interviewed if you can "shadow" them for a day (or even a few hours) so you may observe their work in action.

After completing the interview, look at your notes, or listen to the recording of the interview, and ask yourself: Is this manager also a leader? Why or why not? Then, if you were able to observe the manager for a day, did they practice what they said in their interview? In what ways?

Various Leadership Styles

Although there is no one ideal set of identifiable characteristics of effective leaders, nor one style of leadership for every situation, it is worth learning about some of the most distinct leadership approaches and styles identified by leadership theorists, and how they can be effective (see Table 11.4).

Directive leadership is a style of leadership in which leaders provide specific, task-focused directions, giving commands, assigning goals, implementing guidelines, closely supervising employees, and ensuring individuals follow rules. Directive leaders tend to focus more on the technical or task aspects of the job and make decisions without asking for suggestions from others. This leadership style is often depicted in popular movies about the military where a commander's orders are expected to be followed through and if not punitive consequences result. Directive leaders may also use their power to command, reprimand, or intimidate in order to spark fear to get the desired results from their subordinates. However, research shows that employees ruled by fear are less creative, have a diminished ability to think clearly, and only comply because they are forced to, not because they want to.[19]

Transactional leadership is a style of leadership in which leaders use rewards and punishment as motivation. Types of rewards include bonuses and salary raises, while punishment could be low or no bonus, withdrawing support, or giving a bad review. The transactional leader sets goals for followers who are expected to carry out the leader's requests.

Transformational leadership is a style of leadership in which leaders create visions to motivate, inspire, and stimulate employees. Transformational leaders trust their followers to make decisions in their jobs and give them the freedom to be creative. *Huffington Post* CEO Arianna Huffington is a transformational leader who leads by prioritizing her employees' well-being to generate high performance and productivity.[20] Marriott follows a transformational leadership style by cultivating an inclusive environment that supports the well-being and growth of its employees.

Empowering leadership is a style of leadership in which leaders encourage followers to take ownership of their own behaviors and work processes and provide them with the support and resources to achieve their goals. In other words, empowering leaders encourage their employees to be self-leaders—that is, to lead themselves to achieve their goals. Dr. Hossein Rahnama, CEO and founder of digital experience platform Flybits, empowers his employees by giving them the freedom to grow.[21] Referring to Rahnama's leadership style, team member Justin Cheung said, "His 'you're in charge from day one, but I'm here if you need me' style of leadership creates a genuine feeling of autonomy and empowerment among our team."[22]

Dr. Hossein Rahnama (right) and student Damyan Petkov (left) demonstrate Flybits's new Way Finder, which uses augmented reality to help people find things based on context awareness.

David Cooper/Toronto Star/Getty Images

In addition to the four types of leaders, **situational leadership** suggests that leaders should adapt their leadership style based on the skills and abilities of the people they are leading and the requirements of the job or task to be done.[23] Situational leaders do not rely on one particular leadership style, and they might use many different styles based on the people and situations they are dealing with. These styles include directing, coaching, supporting, and delegating. For example, in the event of an emergency, they might use a "directing" style where leaders provide followers with clear instructions on how to deal with the situation as quickly and safely as possible. The choice of leadership style depends on how ready and able followers are to get the job done.

TABLE 11.4 ■ Four Basic Types of Leaders	
Directive Leaders ● Implement guidelines ● Provide expectations ● Set performance standards ● Ensure rules are followed	**Transactional Leaders** ● Set goals for followers ● Motivate with rewards
Transformational Leaders ● Create vision to motivate followers ● Utilize charisma to gain support ● Expect commitment from followers	**Empowering Leaders** ● Develop followers' skills ● Encourage followers to take ownership of their work ● Lead others to lead themselves

Source: Neck, C. P., Houghton, J. D., & Murray, E. L. (2020). *Organizational behavior* (2nd ed.). SAGE.

So far, we have described the different types of managers and leaders and the challenges and opportunities they face every day. The most successful managers and leaders lead by example to establish appropriate ethics, values, and culture, and continuously strive to make a positive difference in the world.

They also infuse their leadership and workplace culture with diversity, equity, and inclusion (DEI) through better business practices. In the next section, we will explore DEI and the role it plays in leadership.

DIVERSITY, EQUITY, AND INCLUSION (DEI)

Modern leaders today embrace diversity, equity, and inclusion (DEI) and view it as essential for building and operating organizations that support and value people from various backgrounds. The globalization of business has led to diverse customer populations in addition to cross-cultural work teams. Many organizations are working to address systemic racism, sexual harassment, and other forms of discrimination, to fulfill both moral and legal imperatives. As Figure 11.4 depicts, DEI is synergistic—each element works in harmony together, which is why it is so important for organizations to pay attention to all three. An organization that embraces DEI is one that supports the full potential of the individual, where innovation thrives and employee views, beliefs, and values are integrated.

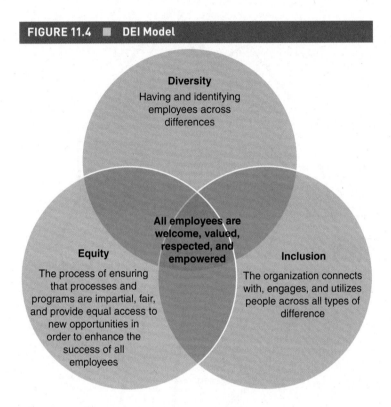

FIGURE 11.4 ■ DEI Model

Diversity
Having and identifying employees across differences

All employees are welcome, valued, respected, and empowered

Equity
The process of ensuring that processes and programs are impartial, fair, and provide equal access to new opportunities in order to enhance the success of all employees

Inclusion
The organization connects with, engages, and utilizes people across all types of difference

Why is DEI in the workplace so important to leaders? Because today's workforce is composed of more people from diverse backgrounds and experiences than ever before, and the benefits of leveraging their value are tremendous. For example, studies have shown that companies that champion DEI are more likely to outperform companies with a more homogeneous workforce (those that share cultural similarities and norms) in areas such as profitability (up to 36% more profitable), innovation (up to 20% higher innovation), and risk (up to 30% more capable of spotting and reducing risk). The same research has also shown that DEI-focused organizations are statistically more likely to have higher rates of employee engagement and retention.[24] The following sections explore DEI in greater depth.

Diversity is the presence of differences within a given setting and is expressed in many types of forms including race and ethnicity, gender and gender identity, sexual orientation, socioeconomic status, language, culture, national origin, religion, age, ability, and political standpoint.[25] Diversity of skills, thinking, and experiences also add to a richer fabric that can lead to more creative solutions to problems. For instance, research focusing on the impact of diversity in the workplace shows that teams composed of people with different backgrounds and ethnicities tend to have a higher rate of productivity, experience less conflict, have lower levels of turnover, and tend to be more creative than their competitors.[26]

As Figure 11.5 illustrates, diversity is mostly composed of what we don't see, which is why it is so important to look below the surface.

There is no doubt that leaders must work hard to push back against systems and people that have marginalized underrepresented groups in the workplace. They must not only fight history but create a more inclusive future for all. But in the past, so much attention had been paid to diversity with little regard to equity and inclusion. DEI is not just about overcoming injustice. When organizations focus on all three, they will have a greater chance of attaining greater levels of performance.

FIGURE 11.5 ■ Dimensions of Diversity

The iceberg model relates to organizational culture, identity, and diversity. It has also been applied to systems thinking and problem solving to encourage looking at the whole problem or environment rather than just the obvious. As a result, there is a lot we don't see that creates each of our identities.

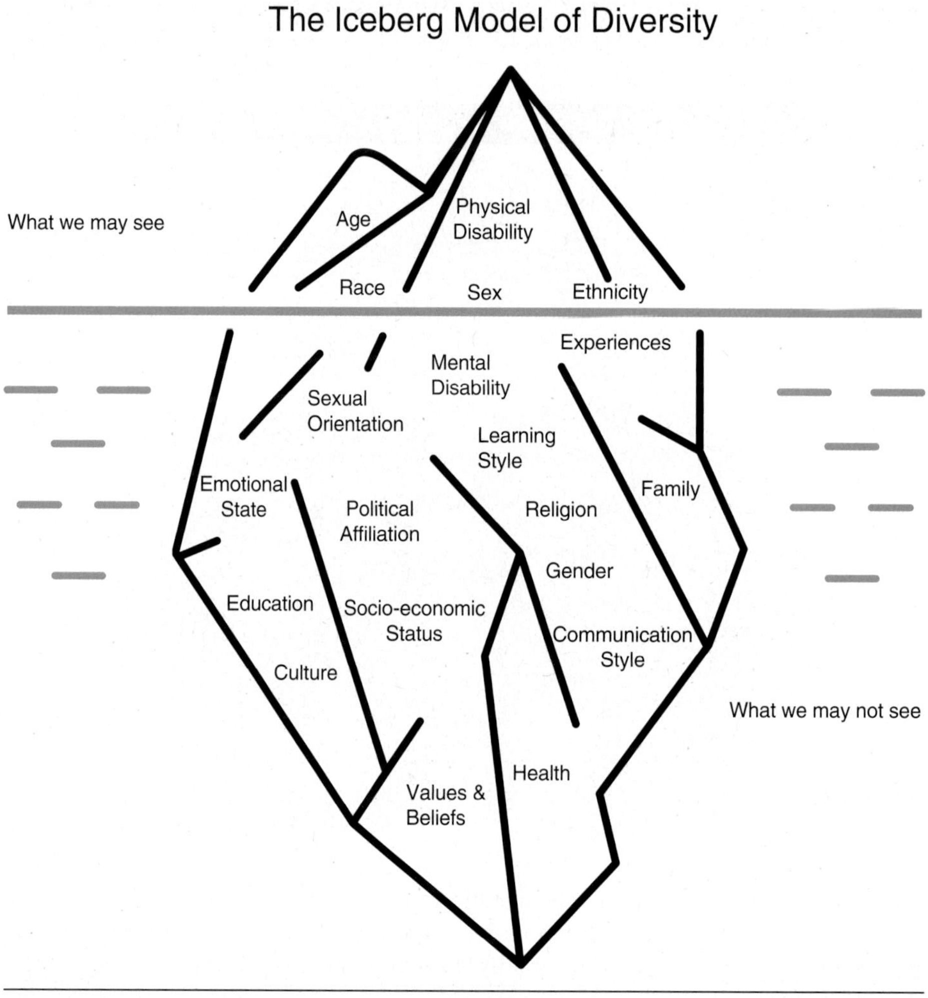

The Iceberg Model of Diversity

What we may see

Age
Physical Disability
Race   Sex   Ethnicity

Experiences
Mental Disability
Sexual Orientation
Learning Style
Emotional State
Political Affiliation
Religion
Family
Education
Socio-economic Status
Gender
Communication Style
Culture
Values & Beliefs
Health

What we may not see

Sources: Schein, E. H. (2004). *Organizational culture and leadership* (3rd ed.). Jossey-Bass; Hall, E. (1976). *Beyond culture*. Doubleday; *The Iceberg Model explained*. (n.d.). Retrieved from https://www.systemsinnovation.io/post/iceberg-model-explained; World Economic Forum. (2020). *Diversity, Equity and Inclusion 4.0: A toolkit for leaders to accelerate social progress in the future of work*. Retrieved from https://www.weforum.org/reports/diversity-equity-and-inclusion-4-0-a-toolkit-for-leaders-to-accelerate-social-progress-in-the-future-of-work

Equity ensures that processes and programs are impartial, fair, and provide equal access to new opportunities in order to enhance the success of all employees. While many organizations have made great strides in fostering a fair and equal workplace, high levels of inequality still remain. Women are often treated unfairly at work through sexual harassment or pay discrimination. Gender discrimination has also been found in hiring practices. For example, researchers found that when the highest-ranking (and male-dominated) symphony orchestras in the country began to hold "blind" auditions in their hiring processes, the likelihood of female musicians being selected increased by 30%.[27] Not only does this research highlight the problem of gender-based hiring, but it also shows the presence of a significant gender pay gap—issues that still need to be addressed in all types of organizations around the world.

Inclusion is the practice of ensuring that people feel a sense of belonging in the workplace and are welcomed. Inclusion is about feeling you are truly part of the team and can be involved in decision-making processes—that one is both visible and valuable.[28] Inclusion also relates to how well the organization connects with, engages, and utilizes people across all types of difference.[29] Where diversity is about having and identifying employees across differences, as illustrated in Figure 11.5, inclusion relates to true integration of the differences into the overall organization—into its culture.[30]

How Leaders Can Promote DEI in Organizations

One way that leaders can promote DEI in their companies is by implementing DEI training. This type of training is an important way to break down any barriers to DEI and eliminate prejudices or psychological barriers among those who resist attempts to make their organizations more diverse, equitable, and inclusive. In 2018, Starbucks closed thousands of its cafés to conduct DEI-related training when an employee called the police after two Black men asked to use the bathroom. The men were then arrested for trespassing.[31] This DEI program was designed to tackle **implicit bias**, which is a set of positive or negative stereotypes someone may unconsciously hold toward a person or group. An example of implicit bias is the inclination to believe that younger workers are more productive than senior workers (over age 50), or people who wear glasses are smarter than those who don't. Table 11.5 lists some more examples of implicit bias.

TABLE 11.5 ■ Types of Implicit Bias

- **Affinity bias**: When people are drawn to others because they share similar interests, experiences, and backgrounds (for example, growing up in the same town).

- **Confirmation bias**: The tendency to seek out information to support our views while dispensing information that does not (for instance, a manager who dislikes an employee may view their work performance more negatively than others).

- **Attribution bias**: When people negatively interpret the behaviors of others based on prior interactions rather than making an effort to understand that person (for example, an employee late to meetings may be perceived as "lazy").

- **The halo effect**: The tendency to ascribe positive attributes to a person after learning something impressive about them (for example, an employee who has been promoted to a senior position at an unusually young age).

- **The horns effect**: The tendency to view another person negatively after learning something "unsavory" about them (for example, their school is a rival of your school).

- **Gender bias:** The tendency to prefer one gender over another gender.

- **Ageism**: When negative feelings toward others are based on their age.

- **Name bias**: When people prefer certain types of names over others—typically Anglo-sounding names.

- **Beauty bias:** When attractive people are treated more favorably because they are perceived to be more successful, competent, and qualified.

- **Height bias**: The tendency to judge a person who is significantly shorter or taller than the "normal range."

- **Anchor bias**: When people hold on to a preexisting piece of information to make decisions (such as hiring a candidate because they went to the same college as you).

- **Nonverbal bias**: When nonverbal communication attributes such as body language (e.g., a weak handshake) negatively influences our perception of others.

Source: Reiners, B. (2021, September 21). 16 unconscious bias examples and how to avoid them in the workplace. *Built In.* Retrieved from https://builtin.com/diversity-inclusion/unconscious-bias-examples

Leaders have to be prepared for possible feelings of resentment when DEI programs are created and employees are required to participate. Peter Cappelli, management professor and director of Wharton's Center for Human Resources, believes people should be told what to do, rather than be told what to think, by explaining the appropriate behaviors they need to demonstrate in the workplace, and why these behaviors are so important to the success of the business. In other words, changing behaviors is a precursor to changing mindsets.[32] One of the best ways to address bias in the long term is to ensure that each level of an organization is as diverse as possible. As Harvard organizational sociology professor Frank Dobbin says, "We all have positive and negative biases against all types of groups, but if you work next to somebody in that group as co-equals, you'll start to individuate members of the group instead of generalize them."[33]

Positive Ways to Promote DEI

Many organizations today are doing various things to promote DEI in the workplace. For example, Ring Central conducts compensation equity audits to ensure that it is paying employees equitably, and Hollister Staffing has established metrics for hiring diverse talent and identifying ways to ensure its company is representative of the diversity within the community it serves.[34] Organizations can also follow the seven methods outlined below to promote DEI in the workplace:

1. **Perform the Three Cs (collect, count, and compare) of Diversity Data:** Organizations can collect and count data on diversity and compare these data to the numbers at other organizations. By doing this, companies can increase accountability and transparency involving DEI.[35]

2. **Use Diverse Job Platforms:** Organizations can find top talent from marginalized talent pools by using job platforms designed to promote underrepresented workers. These platforms include Hire Autism, Recruit Disability, and 70 Million Jobs, a job platform for people with criminal records.[36]

3. **Hire for DEI at Top Levels of Organization:** DEI begins at the top of the organization. A lack of diversity across senior management can result in inadequate decision making as well as send a poor message to the rest of its employees. Thus, it is imperative that the top decision makers in a company represent a wide variety of different opinions, views, and perspectives.[37]

4. **Examine and Rectify Biased Hiring and Recruiting Practices:** Biased recruiting can unravel an organization's DEI efforts. Hiring managers should be trained in understanding, recognizing, and avoiding bias during the recruitment process. This is essential for the prevention of discriminatory recruiting.[38]

5. **Create Transparency Involving Wages:** Organizations should be entirely transparent about how salary ties into job performance in order to avoid biased pay gaps.[39]

6. **Accommodate All Holidays:** There is a tendency for certain widely celebrated religious holidays to be overlooked by many U.S. companies. This can cause workers to feel alienated, especially when organizations recognize one religious tradition while ignoring other religious beliefs. Organizations can support inclusion by allowing flexible time off to allow employees to observe the customs that are most important to them.[40]

7. **Use Inclusive Pronouns:** Companies that respect the identity of its employees create a more welcoming and inclusive environment. Use of binary pronouns in the workplace has become outdated and hinders inclusion, particularly for those who are trans or nonbinary. Companies should consider replacing "his/her" with "theirs" in all workplace communications.[41]

IN REVIEW

11.1   Discuss the importance of management and its importance in the workplace.
Management is the process of working with people and organizational resources to achieve goals efficiently and effectively. *Managers* are the people responsible for controlling employees and those resources. Today's managers place social and environmental impacts before profit to make

a positive difference in the world, something that is called the triple bottom line, or the 3Ps: people, planet, and profit.

11.2 Describe a manager's four major tasks—planning, organizing, leading, and controlling.
There are four main management functions to help managers tackle business challenges: planning, organizing, leading, and controlling, commonly known as the POLC framework. *Planning* is a type of management function that involves developing the mission or purpose of the business, setting goals for the future, designing appropriate strategies, and choosing the right resources to achieve the mission and the related organizational goals and objectives. There are several main types of plans managers use to achieve goals in an organization: strategic, tactical, operational, directional, business, and action. Organizing is the process of orchestrating people, structure, actions, resources, and decisions to achieve goals. *Leading* is the process of motivating and communicating with people to achieve goals. *Controlling* is the process of monitoring activities such as company and regulatory policies, measuring results, comparing them with goals, and correcting performance when necessary.

11.3 Outline the skills managers need in organizations.
Managers need three types of skills to be effective in organizations: conceptual, technical, and relational. *Conceptual or abstract skills* are the ability of a manager to visualize the entire organization and think through complex systems and problems; *technical skills* are the abilities and knowledge to perform job-specific tasks; and *relational skills* are the ability to help managers collaborate and communicate with others. Managers across all three levels of management need to master relational skills to interact well with others. Other important management skills include critical thinking, communication skills, time-management skills, and decision-making skills.

11.4 Explain leadership styles to identify the difference between leaders and managers.
Leadership is the process of influence aimed at directing behavior toward the accomplishment of objectives. Some differences between managers and leaders include the following: Leaders create the vision and management implements it; managers promote stability while leaders support change; and managers manage work while leaders lead people. There are four basic leadership styles: directive leadership, transactional leadership, transformational leadership, and empowering leadership. In addition to the four types of leaders, *situational leadership* is a style of leadership where leaders adapt their leadership style based on the types of people they are leading and the requirements of the task.

11.5 Explore the role of leadership in promoting diversity, equity, and inclusion (DEI).
Diversity, equity, and inclusion (DEI) is increasingly important to leaders because today's workforce is composed of more people from diverse backgrounds and experiences than ever before, and the benefits of leveraging their value are tremendous. *Diversity* is the presence of differences within a given setting. *Equity* is the process of ensuring that processes and programs are impartial, fair, and provide equal possible outcomes for every individual. *Inclusion* is the practice of ensuring that people feel a sense of belonging in the workplace and are welcomed. Leaders can promote DEI in their companies by implementing DEI training to break down any barriers to DEI.

BUSINESSES DISCUSSED IN THIS CHAPTER

Organization	UN Sustainable Development Goal
Docusign	15. Life on Land
Domino's	11. Sustainable Cities and Communities
Flybits	5. Gender Equality 11. Sustainable Cities and Communities

(Continued)

Organization	UN Sustainable Development Goal
Fresh N Lean	3. Good Health and Well-Being 6. Clean Water and Sanitation 8. Decent Work and Economic Growth 12. Responsible Consumption and Production 15. Life on Land
Hollister Staffing	8. Decent Work and Economic Growth 10. Reduced Inequality 13. Climate Action
Hubspot	5. Gender Equality 8. Decent Work and Economic Growth
Little Cocoa Bean	3. Good Health and Well-Being
North Face	11. Sustainable Cities and Communities
Quicken Loans	15. Life on Land
RingCentral	8. Decent Work and Economic Growth 10. Reduced Inequality 13. Climate Action
Siteground	15. Life on Land
Udemy	11. Sustainable Cities and Communities

KEY TERMS

Action plan (p. 226)
Administrative managers (p. 228)
Affinity bias (p. 237)
Ageism (p. 237)
Anchor bias (p. 237)
Attribution bias (p. 237)
Beauty bias (p. 237)
Business plan (p. 226)
Communication skills (p. 230)
Conceptual or abstract skills (p. 228)
Confirmation bias (p. 237)
Controlling (p. 227)
Critical thinking (p. 229)
Decision-making skills (p. 230)
Decisional roles (p. 224)
Directional plan (p. 226)
Directive leadership (p. 233)
Diversity (p. 235)
Empowering leadership (p. 233)
Equity (p. 236)
Financial managers (p. 228)
First-line managers (p. 228)
Gender bias (p. 237)
Height bias (p. 237)
Human resources managers (p. 228)
Implicit bias (p. 237)
Inclusion (p. 237)

Informational roles (p. 224)
Interpersonal roles (p. 224)
Leadership (p. 231)
Leading (p. 227)
Management (p. 223)
Managerial roles (p. 224)
Marketing managers (p. 228)
Middle managers (p. 228)
Name bias (p. 237)
Nonverbal bias (p. 237)
Operational plan (p. 226)
Operations managers (p. 228)
Organizing (p. 226)
Planning (p. 225)
Relational skills (p. 229)
Situational leadership (p. 234)
Skills (p. 228)
Strategic plan (p. 225)
Tactical plan (p. 225)
Technical skills (p. 228)
The Halo effect (p. 237)
The Horns effect (p. 237)
Time-management skills (p. 230)
Top managers (p. 228)
Transactional leadership (p. 233)
Transformational leadership (p. 233)

BUSINESS CASE 11.2: AKAMAE CO-CREATION ETHICAL FASHION—MAE HONG SON, THAILAND

SDG 10:   Reduced Inequality

More than 1 million people work in Thailand's garment and textile industry, one of the country's most lucrative exports. Much of the garment production work is concentrated in Tak, a province on the border of Thailand and Burma (Myanmar). The region is home to many economic migrants, who are employed in the industry under oppressive conditions and low wages. The workers are also disproportionately female. It is estimated that over 70% of these migrant workers in the garment and textile industry are women.

In addition to economic migrants, Thailand is a major destination for asylum seekers and refugees from Burma, which is home to one of the longest ongoing conflicts in the world. The conflict results in the forced migration of marginalized ethnic groups from resource-rich areas of the country. These refugees are placed in camps and villages where the Thai government restricts their freedom of movement, access to resources, and ability to work. It is estimated that 111,000 refugees live in camps along the Burma–Thailand border.

The camps in Thailand are extremely isolated in the mountains and have no electricity or phone service. Health care and educational opportunities are scarce. The people rely on weekly food distributions from international NGOs or community-based charities, and they cannot leave the camps to gain employment to improve their conditions. If they leave, they risk arrest by the Thai police.

Cara Boccieri aims to transform the oppressive conditions of Thailand's garment and textile industry and improve opportunities for artisans in refugee camps. After completing an MA in International Peace and Conflict Resolution from the United Nations University for Peace, Cara began her career researching solutions for humanitarian disasters. Cara's 2014 book, *We Don't Know Our Future: A Holistic Approach to Refugee Settlements*, was foundational research about creating self-reliant refugee communities. She found that empowering refugees is both environmentally sustainable and produces long-term benefits to host communities and governments.

When Cara lived in a refugee camp on the Burma–Thailand border, she noted, "People were saying to me over and over again, 'We have traditional skills, we don't have access to a marketplace because we're in these camps, but we'd like to be using these skills to move towards self-reliance. Can we create something together?'" The people who live in Thailand's refugee camps have artisanal skills, many of which are fashion-related, and Cara saw an opportunity to collaborate with the artisans on a textile business. Her vision would also provide employment opportunities for refugees in an environment that honored their culture and unique skillset.

Cara's venture into the garment and textile business is well timed. The demand for sustainable and ethical fashion has been growing steadily around the world. Increasingly, consumers care about where their clothing is sourced, and they want to know their purchase goes to organizations that pay their employees a fair wage. Experts at ResearchAndMarkets predict that global ethical fashion will become a $15.2 billion market by 2030.

With her humanitarian research and strategic market knowledge, Cara founded the ethical fashion brand Akamae in 2018. Akamae, which means "freedom," offers co-creation fashion opportunities. Her business is in Mae Hong Son, Thailand, which has a strong influence of the Shan people from the Shan State of Burma. The Shan people include several different ethnic groups, which adds to the diversity of the jewelry and textiles Akamae produces. Akamae connects refugee artisans to fashion brands and designers, either through one-on-one collaborations or by facilitating creative retreats. Fashion brands and designers collaborate with artisans on a capsule garment or jewelry collection. Akamae also offers training programs for students, entrepreneurs, and investors to learn more about its business model. The refugees in the camps name their own prices, and Akamae offers the support to ensure they are confident in pricing their products.

As a leader at Akamae, Cara's priority was encouraging the artisans to follow their design instincts. As people affected by trauma, some of the refugee artisans on her team appeared hesitant to take creative risks or provide collaborative feedback. She knew it was important to empower the artisans and help build confidence in their work. "I communicated to people how valuable I see them, that I also see myself as valuable, and together we can create things," Cara said in an interview. Not long afterward, she says she saw once-quiet artisans collaborating and producing creative pieces.

Cara developed and championed the vision for the business—to create "a future for the fashion industry that values our individual choices and honors the spaces of creativity where products are created." This mission would not be possible without empowering individual artisans.

Back in her initial days as a researcher in refugee camps, Cara listened when the refugee artisans said they wanted more responsibility and ownership over their lives. They wanted to contribute to the economy, to create art, and to make a livelihood, but they were limited by the oppressive conditions of the camp. Cara cultivated a team of artisans, helped them develop their skillset, and connected them to the global marketplace. "I tell the women I work with every day—'I am not a charity. I am a business. And I am here because I value your skills and experiences.'" Her story demonstrates how an empowering leadership style benefits both business and the world at large.

Critical Thinking Questions

1. Would you classify Cara as an effective manager or an effective leader? Or both?

2. Revisit Table 11.4 on the four basic types of leaders. Cara is an example of which of the four leadership types?

3. Consider your answer to question 2. How does Cara empower the artisans?

References

Akamae. (n.d.). Akamae co-creation ethical fashion. https://akamae.com/

Boccieri, C. (2012). *We don't know our future: A holistic approach to refugee settlements: A case study of the Thailand Burma border.* LAP LAMBERT Academic Publishing.

Humanity & Inclusion. (n.d.). Refugees in Thailand. *Humanity & Inclusion US.* https://www.hi-us.org/refugees_in_thailand

Jones, M. (2021, May 20). Sustainable and ethical fashion: Market overview and latest trends. *Entrepreneur.* https://www.entrepreneur.com/article/372548

O'Malley, M. (2018, October 23). How Akamae uses fashion co-creation to support refugee communities. *Eco Warrior Princess.* https://ecowarriorprincess.net/2018/10/how-akamae-uses-fashion-co-creation-support-refugee-communities/

Patrick T. Fallon/Bloomberg/via Getty Images

12 HUMAN RESOURCE MANAGEMENT

BUSINESS IMPACT CASE 12.1: JETBLUE—LONG ISLAND CITY, NEW YORK

SDG 4: Quality Education

Great employees are attracted to companies who invest in their future, and American airliner JetBlue is attracting some of the best because it prioritizes improving the education and skill-sets of its employees. JetBlue, which has nearly 20,000 employees and annual revenues of $8 billion, has created a unique talent management environment that emphasizes the growth and educational development of its "crew members" (JetBlue employees). In 2016, JetBlue created the JetBlue Scholars undergraduate pathway program, an award-winning employer-sponsored college degree program open to any crew member wanting a degree. JetBlue provides access to quality degree-granting institutions and covers most of the tuition costs for its crew members. Over 500 crew members have received a college degree since the Scholars program started. According to its press release: "The JetBlue Scholars undergraduate pathway gives crew members the accessibility and flexibility to learn at their own pace. The program provides a clearer path and converts aviation and military training and other professional certificates into college credit, helping reduce the time and cost for crew members to obtain their undergraduate degrees".[1,2] This program involves a partnership between JetBlue and colleges and universities where JetBlue employees take online classes toward a college degree, and JetBlue pays for it. On average, it takes crew members about 13 months to complete an associate degree and 16 months to complete a bachelor's degree through JetBlue's model.

While JetBlue helps employees obtain formal collegiate education, the company also provides internal education on the company's values and mission as part of employee orientation. Learning new skills through universities is important, but being able to apply them in a specific workplace is the next step, and the orientation process is an important step in a company's talent management process. Orientation includes the activities involved in introducing new employees to the organization and their jobs. Companies can attract the best talent in the world, but without great orientation protocols, also called onboarding, the new employees may never fully grow into their roles and contribute to their personal success and the company's overall success.

In Orlando, Florida, JetBlue runs a program called JetBlue University designed specifically for the orientation and onboarding of its 1,500 new employees each year. At a minimum, employees spend 2 days doing a company culture orientation, but pilots and select other new employees spend up to 2 months at JetBlue University. It is easy to see why orientation is especially important for airline pilots: Every day they fly large planes with hundreds of people on board, and it is of the utmost importance that pilots are fully aware of every detail about their aircraft and their company's policies. At the JetBlue orientation, new pilots go through a rigorous four-part onboarding, which includes learning the company's systems, procedures, maneuvers, and flight training.[3] They simulate the most difficult conditions and situations and train all their pilots on how to handle the many complexities of flying and landing safely. Though not all companies have pilots and large airplanes, education and orientation is a key aspect of preparing employees for success. Solid talent management strategies and strong human resource management are core to the people side of business.

Critical Thinking Questions

1. In your opinion, does JetBlue stand out among large companies as a great employer, or do most companies do a good job of talent management?

2. How does JetBlue promote business and economic sustainability through quality education?

3. Have you ever had a strongly positive or strongly negative experience with the human resource management department in a company you worked for? If you are able to discuss it, describe the situation and some key takeaways.

HUMAN RESOURCE MANAGEMENT AND TALENT MANAGEMENT

Human resource (HR) policies affect every aspect of your job in a business, including your salary, training, behavioral conduct, promotions, performance reviews, compensation, and benefits. Without the Human Resource Management (HRM) function, employees would be left without any support. **Human resource management** is the practice of recruiting, hiring, deploying, and managing an organization's employees. It is the part of a business that focuses on people in organizations—all the employees.[4] Effective HRM leads to more satisfied employees. Organizations with more satisfied employees have lower turnover, higher productivity, increased profits, and greater employee loyalty.[5] Within HRM, there is **talent management**, which is the processes involved in managing the flow of well-qualified employees into an organization and through various positions within the organization.[6] Through talent management systems, corporations seek to keep and retain their best people. JetBlue, featured in the opening case, operates a rigorous talent management program as part of HRM by investing in quality education through its JetBlue Scholars program.

Managers know that the success of an organization depends on the quality of its employees. They also know that the right talent can give companies an enormous competitive and strategic advantage over rival institutions. Yet today's organizations struggle to fill positions because they cannot find the right people to match the skills they are looking for. In a survey conducted by Gartner, the world's leading research and advisory company, over 60% of global senior executives indicated that talent shortage was the greatest risk to organizations. The survey highlighted financial services, industrial and manufacturing, consumer services, government and nonprofit, and retail and hospitality sectors as some of the sectors impacted by the talent shortage.[7]

Grocery store chain Trader Joe's is another example of a company that runs an effective HRM program. Employees are not only given a great deal of autonomy in how they interact with customers, but they are also provided with comprehensive customer service training, and above average compensation and benefits.[8] Because of its HRM strategy, Trader Joe's has become hugely successful in finding and retaining great employees, which has led to a more satisfied and productive workforce.

Main Challenges for HRM

The HRM function is increasingly being woven into all aspects of a business. HR professionals are expected to be well versed in economics, politics, education, technology, labor laws, health care, sociocultural trends, and many other issues affecting organizations today. In an increasingly complex legal environment, HR managers are challenged with maintaining ethical and financial standards, which involves monitoring employees from the top down to ensure that they are in compliance with government laws and regulations. Let's explore some of the challenges facing HR leaders today.

Trader Joe's is known for its HRM strategy. In fact, Glassdoor recently named the grocery store chain one of the best places in the U.S. to work.

Jeenah Moon/Bloomberg/via Getty Images

Rise in Flexible Working

HR plays a pivotal role in managing work–life balance to fit the needs of employees' lifestyles. With the rapid growth of technology and changing customer expectations, more and more companies are supporting flexible work schedules, especially when millennials have proven time and again that the flexible model often works, even before the onset of the COVID-19 pandemic. Ana Recio, executive vice president of global recruiting at Salesforce, said, "This generation is single-handedly paving the way for the entire work force to do their jobs remotely and flexibly."[9]

Growth in Gig Workers

In Chapter 1, we explored the global growth of the gig economy and the impact it has on workers, companies, and consumers. Although many workers are attracted to the flexible lifestyle associated with gigs, the gig economy presents a number of challenges for HR professionals. As people come and go, HR needs to build a culture that supports speedy recruitment and onboarding, rapid training, and discover ways to engage talented gig workers so they feel more incentivized to return. Global head of talent acquisition at digital solutions provider Avanade, Paul Philips, said: "In the end, I don't think we have a choice about whether to embrace a gig approach to HR. It's a bit like artificial intelligence or machine learning: It is one of those new fads that has quickly become a reality."[10]

Reskilling/Upskilling

The Great Resignation that took place during the COVID-19 pandemic has put companies under even more pressure to retain workers. Reskilling or **upskilling** is the process of equipping workers with the necessary skills or abilities to move into a new role within the organization rather than terminating workers and recruiting new people with a different skill set.[11] Research shows that upskilling empowers workers and increases engagement and staff retention.[12] Boston-based insurance company John Hancock upskills its employees by giving them two afternoons of paid time every month to participate in an online self-service learning program that offers a variety of courses designed to contribute to employees' professional development.[13]

Increasingly Diverse Workforce

HR leaders face challenges when dealing with an increasingly diverse workforce related to gender, race, sexual orientation, and religion; diverse geographical locations with remote workers choosing to work in more rural areas; not to mention managing four different generations (baby boomers, Generation X, millennials, Generation Z) expected to work in harmony together. Overall, the role of HR is to drive diversity initiatives through training and targeted recruitment efforts, and establish strong policies to protect employees from harmful behaviors such as prejudice, stereotyping, harassment, and discrimination. In addition, the impact of having a diverse workforce full of people from different backgrounds, experiences, and perspectives is undeniable. A study from McKinsey shows that companies with a diverse workforce are 35% more likely to have greater financial returns than those that do not.[14] The following section explores diversity and inclusion in more detail.

RECRUITMENT AND SELECTION FOR DIVERSITY AND INCLUSION

The HR talent management process begins with planning and defining what the company needs. To ensure that the organization is properly staffed, talent managers engage in **strategic human resource planning**, which is the process of developing a plan for satisfying the organization's human resource needs to help the company achieve its mission and related goals.[15] To develop an HR plan, managers must organize information about a certain role by performing a **job analysis**, which is the process of gathering and analyzing information about the content and the human requirements of jobs, as well as the context in which jobs are performed.[16] The job analysis is then used to prepare two documents: a **job description** listing the duties and responsibilities of a position and a **job specification**, which lists the qualifications—skills, knowledge, and abilities—needed to perform the job.[17]

Talent managers must also ensure that they are recruiting with diversity and inclusion in mind. **Recruiting** is the process of identifying suitable candidates and encouraging them to apply for openings in the organization.[18] Once suitable candidates have been identified, they undergo several rounds of interviews and, in many cases, complete assessment tests.

Today's workplace is composed of more people from diverse backgrounds and experiences than ever before. **Workplace diversity** refers to the degree to which an organization values the differences and similarities between people in relation to age, gender, religion, race, ethnicity, sexual orientation, skills, and backgrounds, and effort made by those organizations to promote an inclusive culture.[19] Diversity and inclusion are often perceived as the same thing, but there is an important difference: While *diversity* recognizes the differences between people, *inclusion* involves making people feel welcome. Recruiting a diverse workforce is critical for every type of organization. Table 12.1 outlines the main advantages of diversity and inclusion in the workplace.

TABLE 12.1 ■ Benefits of Diversity and Inclusion in the Workplace
● Better organizational financial performance
● Increased problem-solving capabilities and productivity
● Improved creativity and innovation due to differing individual perspectives
● More cohesive company culture
● Stronger, more empathetic leadership at the top
● Increased likelihood of attracting and retaining diverse talent

Source: Eswaran, V. (2019, April 29). The business case for diversity in the workplace is now overwhelming. *World Economic Forum.* https://www.weforum.org/agenda/2019/04/business-case-for-diversity-in-the-workplace/

Levels of Diversity

There are two main types of diversity: surface-level diversity and deep-level diversity.[20] (See Figure 12.1.) **Surface-level diversity** describes the more obvious differences between us, such as age and generation, race and ethnicity, gender and sexual orientation, and physical and/or mental ability. In contrast, **deep-level diversity** describes verbal and nonverbal behaviors that lie beneath the surface. Deep-level diversity may include attitudes, values, beliefs, and personality traits. This section explores the different types of surface-level diversity.

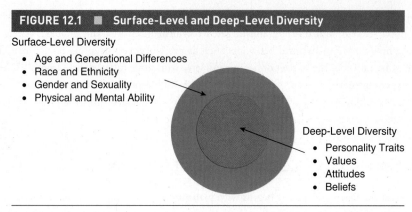

Source: Huszczo, G., & Endres, M. (2013). Joint effects of gender and personality on choice of happiness strategies. *Europe's Journal of Psychology*, 9(1), 136–149. https://doi.org/10.5964/ejop.v9i1.536. Licensed by Creative Commons Attribution (CC BY) 3.0 International License.

Age Diversity

With workforce demographics shifting and the number of mature people in the workplace rising, managers need to find ways to leverage age diversity, which is the inclusion of people of all different ages within the workplace.[21]

Although the number of older people in the workforce is rising, ageism, a type of discrimination based on someone's age, is one of the most common forms of discrimination at work. According to Glassdoor's 2020 Diversity and Inclusion study survey polling more than 2,000 U.S. adults aged between 50 and 80, nearly 50% of respondents said they had experienced ageism.[22] British multinational insurance company Aviva is combating ageism by hiring more employees over age 50 and developing and training its aging workforce. The results of these efforts have been positive: Not only has Aviva attracted more talent, but it has also experienced higher retention, production, and performance rates.[23]

Race and Ethnicity Diversity

The U.S. population is becoming more racially and ethnically diverse, with the non-Hispanic white population declining and other racial groups such as Asian and African American growing.[24] Sometimes the terms *race* and *ethnicity* are used interchangeably, but race is related to factors of physical appearance such as skin, hair, or eye color, whereas ethnicity is associated with sociological factors such as nationality, culture, language, and ancestry.[25]

To attract new talent, organizations must build a sense of group harmony in the workplace, by treating every person with whom they work as an individual rather than a collection of predetermined labels. Sixty percent of health care organization Kaiser Permanente's workforce is made up of people from different races and ethnicities.[26]

Gender Diversity

Gender diversity is the equal representation of both men and women in the workplace.[27] Though many businesses have gender diversity, issues still remain related to gender equality. Despite a growing number of women advancing into senior management positions, the gender pay gap still exists. According to a 2021 report conducted by PayScale, women only make 82 cents for every dollar made by a man.[28] This pay disparity also occurs outside the workplace; for instance, the U.S. women's soccer team sued the U.S. Soccer Federation for paying women soccer players less per game than male soccer players. In 2022, the U.S. women's soccer team won $24 million in an equal pay settlement, thereby advancing equality in the soccer world.[29] Organizations can fight gender discrimination and develop talent by ensuring more women are represented at board level, increasing the level of diversity of new hires, and including women in important company-wide decisions.[30]

In May 2022, U.S. Soccer became the first sports league to offer equal pay to both the men's and women's teams.

Associated Press/PA Wire

Sexual Orientation

Sexual orientation refers to a person's sexual identity and the gender(s) to which a person is attracted, including people who identify as lesbian, gay, bisexual, and transgender (LGBT). LGBT often becomes LGBTQ, for people who are unsure about their sexual orientation (the "Q" stands for "Questioning" but can also stand for "Queer"). To retain talent and create a cohesive environment, managers must make every effort to promote inclusiveness in the workplace and protect employees against discrimination. Hotel group Hyatt supports the LGBTQ community by providing employees with spousal and partner benefits and transgender-inclusive health coverage.[31] In 2020, the U.S. Supreme Court issued a federal ban prohibiting employers from discriminating against workers on the basis of sexual orientation or gender identity.[32]

Ability Diversity

Ability diversity is the representation of people with different levels of mental and physical abilities within an organization. In 1990, Congress passed the Americans with Disabilities Act (ADA) to address discrimination against people with disabilities—physical or mental impairments that substantially limit one or more of an individual's major life activities.[33] A study conducted by Accenture shows that companies that cultivate an inclusive culture for people with diverse abilities will regularly achieve higher revenue and profit margins, yet organizations can still do more to recruit talented people who may have physical and mental impairments.[34] More than 15 million people in the U.S. have some sort of disability, with over 10 million unemployed—a significant talent pool for companies willing to embrace ability diversity. For example, Bank of America has recruited 300 people with intellectual disabilities to work in its support function.[35]

Legal Framework for Diversity and Inclusion

HRM must comply with certain laws when going through the recruitment and selection process to avoid discrimination. Following the 1964 Civil Rights Act, which made racial and sex discrimination illegal, successive presidents issued executive orders requiring affirmative action, proactive steps taken by organizations to counteract discrimination against marginalized populations, including women.[36] In 2020, sexual orientation and gender identity discrimination were also deemed illegal. In addition to the Civil Rights Act, Congress passed the Americans with Disabilities Act (ADA) in 1990 to address discrimination against people with disabilities—physical or mental impairments that substantially limit one or more of an individual's major life activities.

Photographer Simon Smith is just one of many talented people who have a physical disability. Smith is also a painter and a musician.

Homer Sykes/Alamy Stock Photo

The U.S. Equal Employment Opportunity Commission (EEOC) is the government agency charged with "enforcing federal laws that make it illegal to discriminate against a job applicant or an employee because of the person's race, color, religion, sex (including pregnancy), national origin, age (40 or older), disability, or genetic information"[37] (see Table 12.2).

TABLE 12.2 ■ A Legal Framework for Recruitment and Selection		
Job advertisements	It is illegal for an employer to publish a job advertisement that shows a preference for or discourages someone from applying for a job because of their race, color, religion, sex (including pregnancy), national origin, age (40 or older), disability, or genetic information.	For example, a "Help Wanted" ad that seeks "females" or "recent college graduates" may discourage men and people over 40 from applying and may violate the law.
Recruitment	It is illegal for an employer to recruit new employees in a way that discriminates against them because of their race, color, religion, sex (including pregnancy), national origin, age (40 or older), disability, or genetic information.	For example, an employer's reliance on word-of-mouth recruitment by its mostly Hispanic workforce may violate the law if the result is that almost all new hires are Hispanic.
Job referrals	It is illegal for an employer, an employment agency, or a union to take into account a person's race, color, religion, sex (including pregnancy), national origin, age (40 or older), disability, or genetic information when making decisions about job referrals.	For example, an employer cannot show preference for candidates who go to a certain church.
Job assignments and promotions	It is illegal for an employer to make decisions about job assignments and promotions based on an employee's race, color, religion, sex (including pregnancy), national origin, age (40 or older), disability, or genetic information.	For example, an employer may not give preference to employees of a certain race when making shift assignments and may not segregate employees of a particular national origin from other employees or from customers.

TABLE 12.2 ■ A Legal Framework for Recruitment and Selection

Pay and benefits	It is illegal for an employer to discriminate against an employee in the payment of wages or employee benefits on the basis of race, color, religion, sex (including pregnancy), national origin, age (40 or older), disability, or genetic information. Employee benefits include sick and vacation leave, insurance, access to overtime and overtime pay, and retirement programs.	For example, an employer may not pay Hispanic workers less than African American workers because of their national origin, and men and women in the same workplace must be given equal pay for equal work.
Discipline and discharge	An employer may not take into account a person's race, color, religion, sex (including pregnancy), national origin, age (40 or older), disability, or genetic information when making decisions about discipline or discharge.	For example, if a white employee and an Asian employee commit a similar offense, an employer may not discipline them differently.
Employment references	It is illegal for an employer to give a negative or false employment reference (or refuse to give a reference) because of a person's race, color, religion, sex (including pregnancy), national origin, age (40 or older), disability, or genetic information.	When an employer is contacted for a reference for a female worker, it may not cite pregnancy or having children as a negative trait.
Reasonable accommodation and disability	The law requires that an employer provide reasonable accommodation to an employee or a job applicant with a disability, unless doing so would cause significant difficulty or expense for the employer. A reasonable accommodation is any change in the workplace (or in the ways things are usually done) to help a person with a disability apply for a job, perform the duties of a job, or enjoy the benefits and privileges of employment.	Reasonable accommodation might include, for example, providing a ramp for a wheelchair user or providing a reader or an interpreter for a blind or deaf employee or applicant.
Reasonable accommodation and religion	The law requires an employer to provide reasonable accommodation for an employee's religious beliefs or practices, unless doing so would cause difficulty or expense for the employer.	Reasonable accommodation might include, for example, providing structured breaks during the day for prayer or to attend religious services.
Training and apprenticeship programs	It is illegal for a training or apprenticeship program to discriminate on the basis of race, color, religion, sex (including pregnancy), national origin, age (40 or older), disability, or genetic information.	For example, an employer may not deny training opportunities to African American employees because of their race.
Terms and conditions of employment	The law makes it illegal for an employer to make any employment decision because of a person's race, color, religion, sex (including pregnancy), national origin, age (40 or older), disability, or genetic information.	An employer may not discriminate when it comes to such things as hiring, firing, promotions, and pay. It also means, for example, that an employer may not discriminate when granting breaks, approving leave, assigning work stations, or setting any other term or condition of employment, however small.

Source: U.S. Equal Employment Opportunity Commission. (n.d.). Prohibited Employment Policies/Practices. *EEOC.* http://www1.eeoc.gov//laws/practices/index.cfm?renderforprint=1

By promoting diversity and inclusion, companies will be better able to increase the degree of contact between diverse groups of people in the workplace to build relationships and work alongside each other as equals. Table 12.3 describes some positive ways to promote diversity and inclusion.

TABLE 12.3   ■   Positive Ways to Promote Diversity and Inclusion
Develop Permanent Training Programs and Policies Escalating racial tensions have caused many companies to evaluate the degree of inclusion and diversity within their teams. Racial trauma and mental health therapist Ashley McGirt believes that every organization should develop programs and policies around antiracism. She also suggests that these policies should be ingrained in the company culture to see long-term change. Companies can promote diversity and inclusion by involving people from diverse backgrounds in creating training as well as being involved in the training itself.
Expand the Network Many organizations tend to hire from the same talent pools every year, such as the same schools or job fairs, which limits the potential for diversity and inclusion. Venture capitalist Abyah Wynn suggests that organizations broaden their networks by connecting with more diverse universities to source new talent.
Create a Safe Space It is fundamental that organizations create an environment and culture where all employees feel safe and protected from negative attitudes. Many employees have spoken up against injustices in the workplace by sharing stories about being bullied and mistreated. To make employees feel safe, companies could form a committee where people can share any concerns about poor treatment experienced by themselves or others without fear of retribution.
Be Held Accountable Over the last few years, many big brands have been called out on social media for their lack of diversity, forcing them to be held accountable for choices they have made. In response, many of these brands have issued apologies for their actions, publicly promising to do better in the future. In 2020, Christine Barberich, cofounder of digital media entertainment website Refinery29, stepped down after a number of employees complained about the lack of diversity at the company. Barberich admitted that she had personally failed to build a diverse culture "to the detriment of Black women and women of color in particular."[38]

Source: Robert, Y. (2020, June 11). 4 ways to actually create diversity and inclusion in the workplace. *Forbes.* https://www.forbes.com/sites/yolarobert1/2020/06/11/4-ways-to-actually-create-diversity-and-inclusion-in-the-workplace/#5a2682ea3fcd

Finding Strong Talent

Talent managers assess whether they need to recruit internal (employees working from inside the company) or external (people from outside the company) candidates to fill available roles. There are benefits and disadvantages to each approach. For instance, hiring internally is good for morale, as it signals to employees an opportunity to move to different roles in the organization. Studies also show that it is less expensive to hire internally because there are less recruitment fees—on average, it costs 1.7 times more to hire people from outside the organization.[39] However, there are some benefits to hiring externally, too: External candidates bring new skills and fresh ideas, and can also increase diversity in the workplace.

Finding Internal and External Candidates

There are several ways for companies to find the candidates they need. For internal candidates, jobs might be posted on the company website, or they might be nominated by a manager. For external candidates, companies may also advertise the role internally, conduct on-campus recruiting, and might partner with a recruitment agency to support their search. More and more of today's companies use social media as part of their recruitment strategy. A recent study reported that 73% of workers between ages 18 and 34 discovered their last job through social media recruiting.[40] Furthermore, application rates can rise by up to 50% if the company's job openings are posted on social media. Table 12.4 demonstrates the most common types of social media used by companies to attract talent.

TABLE 12.4 ■ Recruiting Through Social Media

- **LinkedIn:** LinkedIn has an online employment service used by companies to find talent. Talent managers join relevant LinkedIn groups, list job postings in target industries, and engage with group members by answering questions, contributing to conversations, or sharing industry news.

- **Facebook:** Talent managers can use their own company's Facebook page to post information about available roles and invite potential candidates to contact the company through Facebook Messenger with any questions.

- **Instagram:** Photo and videosharing social media platform Instagram is one of the most popular forms of social media for young professionals, so it pays for organizations to participate. Organizations can share photos and videos of company events to showcase the company culture, demonstrate what a typical working day looks like, or highlight employees' achievements.

- **Twitter:** Talent managers can use Twitter to post job openings using the relevant hashtags and describe (in 140 characters) the basic requirements of the role and its location. Like Instagram, Twitter is also a good platform for sharing photos, and useful for sharing messages from teams and reaching out to people.

Source: SmartBrief. (2019). HR recruiting on social media: HR best practices. https://www.smartbrief.com/original/2019/11/hr-recruiting-social-media-hr-best-practices?utm_source=brief&utm_medium=FC&utm_campaign=SEO2019;

Hiring Nontraditional Candidates

For the most part, companies tend to hire on the basis of experience and 4-year college degrees, yet some companies are opening up their talent search to nontraditional candidates, which include people without degrees, people from different educational backgrounds, people with no employment experience, and people with criminal records. Ohio-based Nehemiah Manufacturing Company is a good example of a company that has benefited from hiring nontraditional candidates, particularly by recruiting people from criminal backgrounds. Since taking this recruitment approach, Nehemiah Manufacturing has created a workforce of loyal, hardworking employees with a turnover rate of less than 15%.[41]

British skincare and beauty products company The Body Shop is also trying out a new recruitment strategy called "open hiring" where job posts are filled on a first-come, first-served basis.[42] Unlike traditional recruitment processes, there are not any screening or background checks. Candidates merely have to answer three questions to get a job: "Are you authorized to work in the U.S.?" "Can you stand for up to 8 hours?" and "Can you lift over 50 pounds?" If candidates say "yes" to all three questions, then they have the opportunity to work in The Body Shop distribution center. The results? Monthly turnover fell by 60%, productivity increased, and the company easily found the staffing it needed.

The Selection Process

The traditional selection process involves gathering information on candidates, evaluating their qualifications, and choosing the best candidate for the job.[43] This might include assessing application forms and résumés, following up on references, and carrying out background checks. The selection process might also involve an interview (in person or by phone, or video) to enable the employer to find out more about the candidate, and vice versa. Table 12.5 outlines some interviewing tips.

Some companies are moving away from the traditional interviewing approach by adopting the latest technology to streamline the early hiring process. For example, hundreds of companies in the finance and hospitality services, including Hilton, Unilever, and Goldman Sachs, use an AI face-scanning system that analyzes the job candidates' hireability based on facial movements, eye contact, word choice, and speaking voice. However, the system has been criticized by some AI researchers for penalizing non-native English speakers or visibly nervous or anxious applicants.

When candidates are successful during the interviewing process and have passed all the checks carried out by HR, they will receive a job offer and an employee contract. If candidates accept the role, they will experience onboarding and training during their first weeks of employment.

TABLE 12.5 ■ Best Practices When Interviewing for a Job

● **Listen More Than You Speak**

   According to a study by the Harvard University Social Cognitive and Affective Neuroscience Lab, people spend 60% of conversations talking about themselves or thinking about what they're going to say next. However, it is much more impactful to make a conscious effort to listen rather than dominating the conversation. By listening more than you talk, you will more likely be perceived by the interviewer as someone who is very interested in the role and what the company can offer.

● **Keep Your Answers Short**

   The National Center for Biotechnology Information has reported that the average attention span of human beings is now 8 seconds, so if you want to keep your interviewer engaged, it pays to keep your answers short and to the point. A good way of keeping your listener focused is to call out each point with a number such as "First . . . Second . . . Third . . ." or to use words such as "To begin with . . . Next . . . Finally." This is a useful way to ensure your interviewer's attention doesn't drift off while you're talking.

● **Avoid Using Too Many "I's"**

   In an interview situation, it's tempting to take the credit for all our achievements, but too many "I statements" (such as "I did this" or "I did that") can give the impression that you're more interested in yourself than working with others. Of course, it's important to share your accomplishments, but make sure you also honor the efforts of your team, leaders, and mentors. This will show that you are good at working with and collaborating with others.

● **Show Gratitude**

   It is also important to recognize others for getting you where you are today by showing gratitude. For example, "Thanks to a great leader in my previous role, I am skilled at managing large teams." Acknowledging the contributions of others shows that you have valuable interpersonal skills such as good values and a collaborative mindset.

Source: Humphrey, J. (2019, October 10) How to sell yourself in an interview without seeming too promotional. *Fast Company.* https://www.fastcompany.com/90414705/how-to-sell-yourself-in-an-interview-without-seeming-too-promotional

ENTREPRENEURIAL MINDSET ACTIVITY

Your Ideal Job

When searching for a suitable job or career, one of the most important parts of the process is reviewing job descriptions. While it is difficult to ascertain every detail about a company role by reading a description, it can help college graduates with filtering job possibilities they find fulfilling and those they wish to avoid.

For your mindset activity, your task is to draft a brief job description of your ideal position. You should write short responses to the following fields: Job Location—this should be a geographic region in which you would love to work; Job Title—this can be a very general title indicating the type of role or specialty you would enjoy; Job Description—this should be a paragraph listing some specific activities included in the job, and the things you enjoy doing, things in which you believe you are proficient or skilled, and things that attract you about a job; Compensation—this can be used to try to set a range of compensation that would be enough to excite you about entering the professional world, and can include policies about salary growth or bonus pay that improves with time or performance. None of your responses will be perfect, and you can't be expected to know exactly what you want to do without having spent some time in different jobs, but this exercise will assist you in finding the best possible starting place.

Once you have completed your job description, your final task is to spend a few minutes browsing job posting websites and searching for roles with some of the parameters and descriptions you wrote down. You can use CareerBuilder.com, ZipRecruiter.com, and many others. These sites allow for filtering things like location, salary, title, and even key-word searches for job descriptions.

Critical Thinking Questions

1. What did you discover new about yourself in this activity? Were you surprised by the job you developed in any way?

2. Do you think online job search websites like the ones mentioned are an advantage or disadvantage to people seeking a career today?
3. Do you have a particular skill or two that you think should play an important role in your career? If so, describe them. These are your superpowers!

ONBOARDING AND TRAINING EMPLOYEES

Successful onboarding programs positively influence a new hire's decision to stay at a company. Onboarding is the process of equipping workers with the skills, knowledge, and behaviors to transition into an organization.[44] Onboarding is often confused with orientation. While orientation is a one-time event involving the completion of routine tasks such as paperwork, onboarding is an ongoing process that can last up to 12 months, designed to encourage new hires to progress through management support and on-the-job training. As up to 20% of people leave during the first 45 days of joining a new company, a positive onboarding experience is essential to retain employees and integrate them into the organization successfully.[45]

Onboarding goes much further than simply taking care of the basics, such as desks, computer access, and ID badges for new hires. Research shows that almost 70% of employees will remain at a company if they have a positive onboarding experience. Smooth onboarding has also been linked to higher staff retention, engagement, and productivity.

Some companies have taken a unique approach to onboarding. For example, prior to Elon Musk buying Twitter, former CEO Dick Costolo introduced an onboarding process called "Yes-to-Desk," which involved the 75 steps it took from an employee saying yes to a job offer to sitting at their desk. The whole process lasted a month, during which the new hire met Costolo, toured the offices, had lunch with the team, learned about the company history, and absorbed information about their new role.

Remote Onboarding

As remote working is on the rise, companies need to find ways to onboard their new remote workers. Social media tools provider Buffer consists of a distributed team of 79 employees. Like Twitter, Buffer's onboarding program begins as soon as the new hire says yes to a job offer. The whole process lasts 6 weeks, when new hires are assigned three buddies: the Leader whose role is to teach them about the company values, a Role Buddy to provide them with information about their role, and a Cultural Buddy who educates them about company culture and assesses whether they are good fit.

Regardless of how smooth a company's onboarding process is, there is no doubt that being the newcomer to an organization can be daunting, to say the least. Overall, companies will be more successful in their onboarding if they offer well-structured, carefully planned onboarding processes that are designed to communicate company culture, build internal bonds, and provide employees with the tools, skills, and knowledge to hit the ground running.

The Training Process

Onboarding does not stop after the first few weeks. To continue the integration, new hires will need to be provided with a degree of formal training, which is the process of teaching new or existing employees the skills necessary to carry out their roles and improve current job performance. Training is big business in the U.S. In 2020, organizations spent more than $40 billion on training internal staff.[46] The goal of training is to enhance employee development, where managers help employees learn the skills necessary to carry out future roles.[47] Investment in employee training and development is one of the top priorities for HR professionals.[48] Why the urgency to invest in training? Because digitization and automation are changing the skills companies require to successfully compete in an ever-changing business landscape. According to the McKinsey Global Institute report, by 2030, there will be 375 million workers (14% of the global workforce) who will face the prospect of switching careers.[49] Table 12.6 describes the different types of training methods used by organizations.

TABLE 12.6 ■ Types of Training Methods

- **Training by an Instructor:** An instructor presents to a group of employees using visual aids such as PowerPoint.

- **Interactive Training:** Similar to instructor-led training, this also involves adding interactive and group activities to the training experience, such as case study reviews, role playing, and quizzes.

- **Hands-on Training:** Workers practice the skills they will need to perform in their role.

- **E-learning Training:** Online training in particular areas to support professional development. Can be in the form of watching videos or simulations that prepare employees for real-world situations.

- **Video Training:** How-to videos dedicated to educating employees about complex topics.

- **Coaching and Mentoring:** Employees receive more focused attention from their leaders who help them with career goal-setting and skills development.

- **Cross-Training:** Employees are given the opportunities to experience other roles across departments and learn the skills required to perform other tasks.

- **Peer-to-Peer Learning:** When employees learn from each other by sharing information, feedback, and ideas.

Source: Ferguson, S. (2022, January 27). 13 methods for insanely effective employee training. *Wyzowl.* https://www.wyzowl.com/employee-training-methods/

ETHICS IN BUSINESS

Posting a Job That Does Not Exist

You are the founder and CEO of your new protein bar company, Fuel Your Body, Inc. As an entrepreneur, you have to wear a number of hats and one of those hats is managing your new company's talent. At the current time, you have enough employees to do the work that is needed. However, you want to build a pipeline of talent to make it easier for you to hire more employees in the future. Your idea is to post a job online for a position that does not yet exist in your company to create this pipeline and to give the impression that your company is growing. One of your employees remarks that this is an unethical thing to do. What do you do now?

Critical Thinking Questions

1. Is posting a fictitious job an ethical action? Why or why not?
2. How do you respond to your employee?
3. Are there other ways to create a pipeline of future talent?

Source: What are some common ethical dilemmas that HR professionals face during the recruiting process? (n.d.). *SHRM.* https://www.shrm.org/resourcesandtools/tools-and-samples/hr-qa/pages/ethicaldilemmashrprofessionalsface.aspx

EMPLOYEE PERFORMANCE

Most companies will conduct performance appraisals for employees at least once a year. A **performance appraisal** is an assessment of an employee's performance that provides the employee with feedback necessary to improve performance.[50] The performance appraisal is a component of the overall performance management process. There are four stages of a traditional performance management process: planning, acting, tracking, and reviewing. During the planning stage, managers will set a number of goals together with the guidance and requirements they need to accomplish their objectives. The act and track stages take place throughout the year with employees taking the action they need to achieve their goals, with managers tracking and monitoring their progress along the way. The final stage, review, normally takes place at the end of the year in the form of an **annual performance review** that identifies goal achievements, areas for improvement, performance issues, and opportunities for career progression. Typically, annual bonuses are tied to ratings based on employee performance.

Although performance appraisals present a great opportunity for managers and employees to get together to discuss performance expectations, future goals, and career-development opportunities, many employees and managers find them uncomfortable and awkward. According to a Gallup study, only 14% of employees believe that performance appraisals inspire them to improve their work performance.[51] Additionally, a recent PayScale survey reported that 95% of managers don't like the way they are conducted.[52] To make performance appraisals more effective, Gallup suggests they should comprise three main qualities: achievement-oriented, fair and accurate, and developmental.[53]

Achievement-Oriented

Sometimes employees feel demotivated by performance appraisals because they come across as punitive rather than constructive. Managers should focus on achievements made during the year such as goals met, new ideas put into action, sales quota exceeded, contributions to a team project, and leading a project, just to name a few. The key is to focus more on the positives than the negatives to boost morale and motivate employees to constantly strive for performance improvements.

Fair and Accurate

Gallup reported that less than 50% of employees receive annual performance reviews, with only about half agreeing that the reviews are fair and accurate. Regular performance reviews that discuss goals, priorities, expectations, and progress in a fair and accurate manner are key to encouraging employee development. Holding ongoing open dialogue where managers involve employees in decision making and goal setting is another powerful method that managers can adopt to engage and motivate their employees.

Developmental

Although most employees today are looking to work for a company that will nurture their career growth and development, only three out of 10 employees agree that their development is being encouraged at work. For employees to feel satisfied at work, managers should create reviews with a career path in mind that aligns with employees' overall life, work, and aspirations. Additionally, employees should be offered ways to help them improve such as taking an outside or inside training course, participating in workshops on various topics, or even offering a subscription to such platforms as LinkedIn Learning or MasterClass. By prioritizing developmental needs, employees will feel more valued, and better able to visualize their future with the company.

The Importance of Feedback

Giving feedback to employees is a fundamental part of being a manager. However, Gallup research shows that almost 80% of employees who come out of performance reviews feeling criticized and deflated will start seeking a job elsewhere.[54] Feedback should be given regularly and in a way that motivates employees to improve rather than causing them to experience negative feelings. There are four ways managers can provide effective feedback:[55]

1. **Start with the positives**

   Managers can begin the review by asking the employees about their achievements from their point of view. This approach helps to start the discussion on a positive note and boosts employees' confidence from the outset. Edward Mady, general manager of the Beverly Hills Hotel, believes that appraisals should start off on a human note and be treated like a dialogue, not a lecture.[56]

2. **Focus on specifics**

   Feedback should be specific, rather than general. For instance, telling an employee that her performance is "mediocre" doesn't give her much information without providing specific details about what her role should look like. Employees will only learn from their mistakes or failures when they are given specific and focused feedback that helps them to learn and plan for the future.

3. Provide constructive feedback

The reality is that in many cases employees will make mistakes that require correction, but when managed in the right way, mistakes can be important learning experiences. When giving constructive feedback, managers can ask employees what they learned from the mistake and offer advice to help them avoid doing the same thing again in the future. Hardware company Screwfix is a good example of a company that encourages honest feedback from both managers and employees. Not only do managers provide feedback to their direct reports, but employees are also encouraged to give feedback to their managers on a biweekly basis. Screwfix's commitment to transparent feedback has led to higher productivity, increased profitability, and better staff retention.[57]

4. Hold regular conversations

Weekly conversations are a powerful way for managers to stay in touch with employee performance and needs. They also give the employees the opportunity to ask questions, clarify certain issues, and discuss any performance obstacles. Google and Amazon Music recruiter Jon Volk believes that frequent check-ins about career goals is the key to retaining employees and reducing turnover: "I think that just communication with your employees is massive," Volk said. "It seems like such a simple thing."[58]

In a performance appraisal, employees are provided with feedback about their performance.
iStock.com/fizkes

While the traditional performance model is still in use, it is regarded as ill-suited to today's fast-paced work environment where organizational goals tend to change more regularly as companies strive to adapt to new market changes in an effort to keep up with the competition. Many organizations prefer to provide feedback through more frequent and informal performance assessments to meet the changing needs and requirements of employees.

RETAINING EMPLOYEES THROUGH COMPENSATION

Offering competitive pay and benefits helps organizations attract qualified employees. Typically, companies that pay their employees more than their competitors generally have lower turnover.[59] This is particularly important, given that a survey by career-oriented platform iHire showed 75% of employees do not stay in their jobs longer than 5 years.[60] But it's not all about the pay. Insurance company Aflac reported that more than 50% of employees are likely to choose a job with lower pay but with better benefits.[61] One of the biggest benefits for employees are programs that offer personal and professional growth through **employee development programs**.

Retaining Employees Through Development Programs

Research has found that employees need more than just a paycheck to commit to a company for the long term. For instance, 80% of employees polled by recruitment agency The Execu Search Group said they would be tempted to leave their current roles and go to other companies if they were offering better development programs.[62] Gen Zers, in particular, are attracted to companies that offer professional development and career planning as part of their programs. Table 12.7 outlines five reasons why employment development programs are an essential way to retain talent.

TABLE 12.7 ■ Five Key Benefits of Development Programs

1. **Reduce turnover**

   Employee development programs reduce turnover because employees feel committed to a company that invests in their personal growth. American e-commerce website Etsy keeps its staff engaged through its Etsy Learning and Development program, which provides employees with a clear career map of their future at Etsy.[63]

2. **Enhance confidence**

   When employees are engaged with new learning opportunities, their self-confidence increases. Mentorship programs are a particularly powerful way to encourage employee development and support employees from different backgrounds. For example, in addition to its regular mentoring programs, top consultancy Bain & Company offers specialized mentoring services for different marginalized groups, including Blacks at Bain, Latinos at Bain, BGLAD (an LGBTQ+ group), Women at Bain, and Veterans at Bain.

3. **Increase commitment through outside partnerships**

   Not all development programs are in-house. Some organizations partner with higher education institutions that offer employees online courses in addition to their daily work tasks and activities. This arrangement is a great way to support employees completing a degree or taking a short course or seminar or working on new, innovative projects. For example, in 2017, open-source solutions provider Red Hat launched an "open innovation lab" near Boston and partnered with Boston University to connect students and faculty with open-source industry experts. The initiative provided an opportunity for researchers and students to collaborate to drive new ideas and new technologies.[64]

4. **Boost commitment to care**

   Employee development programs not only offer valuable ways to increase commitment, confidence, and engagement, but they are also a good way for companies to show appreciation for employees. When companies care about their workforce, their employees are more likely to make their customers feel the same way. Fast-food chain Chick-fil-A offers plenty of opportunities for its employees to grow and develop by offering leadership roles, educational scholarships, and the option of becoming franchise operators themselves. Happy, fulfilled employees tend to treat their customers better, and is one of the reasons why Chick-fil-A has been praised time and again for its excellent customer service.[65]

5. **Attract top talent through reputation**

   When the word spreads about companies investing in their people through employee development programs, it becomes easier for talent managers to find the talent they are looking for. People will always be attracted to a company that has a great reputation for taking care of its workforce. Bonobos, men's clothing ecommerce retailer and subsidiary of Walmart, offers a "Managing for Success" program that teaches management skills by training employees how to navigate relationships with senior managers. It also provides a "Know Your Customer" program that helps employees to better understand their customers and their shopping experience. Tiff Poppa, senior director of employee experience, said, "The goal is to help our employees become better workers and to equip them with the skills they need to manage themselves and their teams."[66]

Additional Benefits To Compensation Packages

Companies employ a variety of different ways to increase staff retention by offering additional benefits to their compensation packages. Here are some examples:

College Tuition Assistance

Some organizations attract talent by providing college tuition assistance and helping with student loans. For example, fast-food chain Chipotle Mexican Grill covers the cost of college tuition at certain universities to help employees acquire business and technology degrees.

Flexible Working Hours

More and more companies are putting a more flexible work schedule in place to attract employees. According to the Gartner 2021 Digital Worker Experience Survey, 43% of respondents said that flexibility in working hours helped them achieve greater productivity, and 30% of respondents said that less or no time commuting enabled them to be more productive.[67]

Sales executive Sara Martlage works to a flexible working schedule at Arizona-based training company Trainual: "It's empowering to have authority over your schedule," she says. "It makes me want to work harder, be available to take calls and answer email some nights and weekends to go above and beyond to keep my work integrity intact with the rest of my teammates."

Shorter Working Week

Although flexible working hours are becoming more common, a growing group of companies are going one step further by offering their employees a 4-day work week. In the summer of 2019, Microsoft Japan introduced a new initiative called the "Work Life Choice Challenge," which closed its offices every Friday for the month of August. Thanks to the additional day off, employees worked even harder during the 4 days, which led to a 40% rise in productivity.[68] The company also saved on other resources such as electricity. Pilot programs run by organizations in other countries across the globe show that shorter working weeks can lead to less sick days, higher productivity, better work–life balance, and increased morale.[69]

Financial Wellness Programs

Financial wellness programs provide employees with the knowledge and expertise to advise them on certain financial issues such as handling money, making good financial decisions, and planning for the future. According to recent John Hancock research, financial stress such as debt is one of the leading causes of absenteeism, poor productivity, and weak performance.[70] Bank of America is a good example of a company that offers its employees help securing their financial future through a variety of financial wellness programs, including a financial wellness tracker, a tool that provides employees an overview of their own financial behaviors. Employees answer questions about their financial habits and the tool then suggests some options to improve their financial situations.[71]

Leave Policies

Leave policies allow employees to take time off, usually with pay. Leave policies include vacation leave, sick leave, and often parental leave for when a couple has a child. Trending as of late, some companies now offer unlimited vacation, though this is still quite rare. In a recent survey of close to 650 companies, only 4% offered unlimited vacation. The most well-known companies offering this benefit include Netflix, LinkedIn, Zoom, Vimeo, and Adobe. Netflix CEO Reed Hastings shared an employee comment in his book, *No Rules Rules,* that led to the unlimited vacation policy. The employee said,

> "We are all working online some weekends, responding to emails at odd hours, taking off an afternoon for personal time. We don't track hours worked per day or week. Why are we tracking days of vacation per year?"

Trust that employees will not take advantage of the benefit says a lot about the culture of Netflix. To date there is no evidence that the benefit has been abused, which is really cool!

On a more sorrowful note, most people will experience the death of a loved one, and millions have been left grieving following the devastating impact of COVID-19. While the majority of companies offer bereavement leave, the amount of leave may not support the time needed to manage the logistics of a death or to grieve. For instance, the traditional bereavement leave lasts 1 to 4 days. Studies show that grief costs companies approximately $75 billion a year in lost productivity leading more companies to revise their bereavement policies. In 2017, Facebook's then COO Sheryl Sandberg doubled the company's bereavement leave to 4 weeks following the sudden death of her own husband in 2017,[73] and other companies have followed suit. Airbnb, Mastercard, Adobe, General Mills, and U.S. Steel are among the companies that have recently revised their bereavement-leave policies, offering up to 20 days for employees depending on their relationship to the deceased. Other leave policies include vacation leave, sick leave, and parental leave.

Organizations that offer additional benefits such as flexible working hours, financial health programs, mental health programs, college tuition, generous leave policies, and more, have a greater chance of attracting top talent and retaining staff.

Well-being Programs

Some organizations offer well-being programs such as on-site gyms for physical fitness as well as programs that focus on employee mental health. These latter programs, also known as mental health programs, are a way that businesses can help their employees manage stress, anxiety, and depression and otherwise protect and improve their mental health.[74] In 2019, the World Health Organization (WHO) classified "burnout" as a medical diagnosis, leading many companies to create a culture that promotes wellness and work–life balance.[75] The rate of burnout escalated during COVID-19, particularly among health care workers, with nearly 50% of health professionals reporting burnout and more than 25% struggling with high levels of stress and anxiety. Several organizations have implemented well-being programs to include physical, emotional, financial, career, and social wellness. For example, technology company Hewlett Packard, based in California, offers the HP Spirit Program, which provides health and well-being apps, career information, and advice and guidance for working parents. Research shows that nearly 70% of Gen Zers view well-being programs as a priority when considering job offers, with an emphasis on financial well-being and emotional/mental health well-being.[76]

IN REVIEW

12.1 Explore human resource management (HRM) and the role of talent management within HRM.

Human resource management is the field of study and practice that focuses on people in organizations. HR policies affect every aspect of your role in an organization, including your salary, training, behavioral conduct, promotions, performance reviews, compensation, and benefits. Talent management is a function of HRM and can be defined as the processes involved in managing the flow of well-qualified employees into an organization and through various positions within the organization.

12.2 Describe how managers recruit talent for diversity and inclusion.

Talent managers must also ensure that they are recruiting with diversity and inclusion in mind. Workplace diversity refers to the degree to which an organization values the differences and similarities between people in relation to age, gender, religion, race, ethnicity, sexual orientation, skills, and backgrounds, and effort made by those organizations to promote an inclusive culture. While diversity recognizes the differences between people, inclusion involves making people feel welcome.

12.3 Discuss the onboarding and training process.

Onboarding is the process of equipping workers with the skills, knowledge, and behaviors to transition into an organization. A positive onboarding experience is essential to retain employees and integrate them into the organization successfully. Training is the process of teaching new or existing employees the skills necessary to carry out their roles and improve current job performance.

12.4 Explain how companies conduct employee appraisals.

A performance appraisal is an assessment of an employee's performance and provides the employee with feedback necessary to improve performance. There are four stages of a traditional performance management process: planning, acting, tracking, and reviewing.

12.5 Compare and contrast various forms of employee compensation.

Offering competitive pay and benefits helps organizations attract and retain qualified employees. Companies employ a variety of different ways to increase staff retention by offering additional benefits to their compensation packages such as college tuition assistance, flexible working hours, financial wellness programs, and mental health programs.

BUSINESSES DISCUSSED IN THIS CHAPTER

Organization	UN Sustainable Development Goal
Adobe	12. Responsible Consumption and Production 13. Climate Action
Aflac	12. Responsible Consumption and Production 13. Climate Action
Airbnb	7. Affordable and Clean Energy 11. Sustainable Cities and Communities
Amazon	8. Decent Work and Economic Growth 13. Climate Action
Avanade	3. Good Health and Well-Being
Aviva	10. Reduced Inequality
Bain & Company	10. Reduced Inequality 12. Responsible Consumption and Production 13. Climate Action
Bank of America	7. Affordable and Clean Energy 13. Climate Action
Beverly Hills Hotel	11. Sustainable Cities and Communities 13. Climate Action
Boston University	4. Quality Education 13. Climate Action
Chick-fil-A	7. Affordable and Clean Energy 13. Climate Action 14. Life Below Water
Chipotle	13. Climate Action
Etsy	13. Climate Action
Facebook	13. Climate Action
General Mills	13. Climate Action
Goldman Sachs	13. Climate Action
Google	12. Responsible Consumption and Production 14. Life Below Water 15. Life on Land
Hewlett Packard	12. Responsible Consumption and Production 13. Climate Action
Hilton	12. Responsible Consumption and Production 13. Climate Action 14. Life Below Water
Hyatt	10. Reduced Inequality
Instagram	11. Sustainable Cities and Communities
JetBlue	4. Quality Education
Kaiser Permanente	3. Good Health and Well-Being 6. Clean Water and Sanitation 7. Affordable and Clean Energy
LinkedIn	8. Decent Work and Economic Growth 13. Climate Action

Organization	UN Sustainable Development Goal
Mastercard	10. Reduced Inequality 11. Sustainable Cities and Communities 12. Responsible Consumption and Production
Microsoft	3. Good Health and Well-Being 4. Quality Education
Nehemiah Manufacturing	10. Reduced Inequality 16. Peace, Justice, and Strong Institutions
Red Hat	11. Sustainable Cities and Communities 12. Responsible Consumption and Production
Refinery29	3. Good Health and Well-Being 12. Responsible Consumption and Production
Salesforce	6. Clean Water and Sanitation 7. Affordable and Clean Energy 11. Sustainable Cities and Communities 13. Climate Action
The Body Shop	12. Responsible Consumption and Production 13. Climate Action 14. Life Below Water
Trader Joe's	2. Zero Hunger 3. Good Health and Well-Being 6. Clean Water and Sanitation 7. Affordable and Clean Energy
Trainual	3. Good Health and Well-Being
Twitter	10. Reduced Inequality 11. Sustainable Cities and Communities
Unilever	9. Industry, Innovation, and Infrastructure 11. Sustainable Cities and Communities 13. Climate Action
U.S. Steel	7. Affordable and Clean Energy 10. Reduced Inequality 13. Climate Action

KEY TERMS

Ability diversity (p. 249)

Affirmative action (p. 249)

Age diversity (p. 248)

Ageism (p. 248)

Annual performance review (p. 256)

Deep-level diversity (p. 247)

Disabilities (p. 249)

Employee development programs (p. 259)

Employee development (p. 255)

Gender diversity (p. 248)

Human resource management (p. 245)

Job analysis (p. 247)

Job description (p. 247)

Job specification (p. 247)

Nontraditional candidates (p. 253)

Onboarding (p. 255)

Performance appraisal (p. 256)

Performance review (p. 256)

Recruiting (p. 247)

Selection process (p. 253)

Sexual orientation (p. 249)

Strategic human resource planning (p. 247)

Surface-level diversity (p. 247)

Talent management (p. 245)

Training (p. 255)

Upskilling (p. 246)

Workplace diversity (p. 247)

BUSINESS CASE 12.2: BBVA—BILBAO, SPAIN

SDG 15: Life on Land

BBVA—short for Banco Bilbao Vizcaya Argentaria—is the 39th-largest bank in the world. With its global headquarters in Bilbao, Spain, BBVA presence is mainly seen in Europe, South America, and North America and is leading the industry in its transformation from a traditional bank to a cutting-edge, digital global financial institution. Becoming a digital bank may evoke images of all transactions being completed on a mobile phone and never having to walk into a bank branch ever again. This is certainly true, but moving to a more digital company also requires shifts in *how* work is done in which spaces and under what conditions. With over 110,000 employees around the world, organizing how work is done for a digital transformation is a human resource challenge.

BBVA has been listed in the top 10 multinational workplaces by Great Place to Work. The bank attracts talented employees by offering attractive compensation packages and a corporate culture that fosters "leadership without hierarchies." Donna DeAngelis, director of talent and culture at BBVA, said, "We are creating a culture where our employees embrace a new way of working, immerse themselves in the customer experience and feel empowered to ask the right questions and do the right thing. It's not only transformational for our business, it's transformational for our employees. We are becoming a more fulfilling place to work." In support of being an attractive place to work, BBVA created the "Work Better, Enjoy Life" plan, an initiative that creates a more flexible work environment and emphasizes productivity and results over hours worked. It's not about being in the office, but the work produced and results achieved. BBVA piloted "Work Better, Enjoy Life" in 2019 *before* the COVID-19 pandemic and has since expanded the program to many of the bank's other locations.

In 2015, BBVA constructed new headquarters in Spain for a workforce of the present and the future—a new headquarters that emphasizes creativity, collaborative work, product and service innovation, employee experience, and environmental sustainability. As part of BBVA's internal digital transformation, it initiated the "New Approaches to Work" project that sought to reimagine the employee on-the-job experience by evaluating work environments, use of technology, and people management. In an examination of how employees work and prefer to work, BBVA found that the physical environment impacts motivation and mindset, technology impacts productivity as well as communication with one another, and the overall corporate culture supports a shared vision. As such, BBVA was challenged to create collaborative work spaces and invite employees to interact toward common goals.

The outcome of "New Approaches to Work" was transformational, and all BBVA buildings around the world provide the exact same employee experience. All physical spaces are designed to promote collaboration. Specifically, the redesign included enhanced meeting rooms, informal lounges, and workbench-style workstations rather than closed offices.

According to BBVA:

As a result all our buildings around the world provide a uniform experience. There is no need for corporate logos or colors—as soon as you walk into one of our sites you immediately sense the BBVA "character." Any of our employees, regardless of their place of origin, will feel at ease in any of our buildings. They will recognize the entry systems, the elevators, the transparent meeting rooms, the open plan workstations, the brainstorming sessions. They won't need extra time to adapt, or special guidance—they'll fit right in straight away. Pathways within buildings are identical across all headquarters, from entry points, workstations, meeting rooms, and lounges to other communal areas.

The digital customer experience and the collaborative employee experience are two pieces of a three-piece pie. The third piece relates to environmental sustainability and the communities in which they operate. All new buildings adhere strictly to guidelines related to sustainability, energy efficiency, carbon emission, and accessibility for all employees and visitors.

The bank's recent innovation relates to sustainable finance by "providing innovative solutions to help customers transition to a low-carbon economy and driving sustainable finance; and . . . systematically incorporating social and environmental risk into their decision-making processes." In fact, BBVA was awarded the 2021 award for Most Responsible Investment Management Team (Spain) from Capital Finance International. It was also awarded the prize for the best global sustainable strategy from CFI in 2022 and was named the best bank in Latin America in the development category of the sustainability accolades awarded by *Latin Trade* magazine. Not bad for a bank you may never have heard of.

Critical Thinking Questions

1. What role does human resources and culture play in a global company like BBVA? How does culture impact human resources and vice versa?

2. Why is BBVA considered a great place to work? What do you find most attractive?

3. What is the role of space in work satisfaction, productivity, and overall happiness?

References

Baeza, C. (2021, June 22). Work life balance, more important than ever. *News BBVA*. https://www.bbva.com/en/sustainability/work-life-balance-more-important-than-ever/

BBVA. (2022). Action and investments ODS plan. https://www.bbva.com/en/sustainability/bbva-reports-on-its-progress-in-sustainability-by-releasing-its-third-tcfd-disclosure/

BBVA. (2022). Awards. *BBVA*. https://www.bbva.com/en/sustainability/bbva-asset-management-wins-cfi-award-for-best-global-sustainable-strategy/

BBVA. (2022). Career opportunities. *BBVA*. https://bbva.csod.com/ux/ats/careersite/15/home?c=bbva

BBVA. (2022). Commitment. *BBVA*. https://www.bbva.com/en/sustainability/bbva-wins-latin-america-sustainability-accolade-awarded-by-latin-trade/

BBVA. (2022). Corporate information. *BBVA*. https://www.bbva.com/en/corporate-information/#responsible-banking-model

CFI. (n.d). BBVA asset management: Most responsible investment management team Spain 2021. *Capital Finance International*. https://cfi.co/awards/europe/2021/bbva-asset-management-most-responsible-investment-management-team-spain-2021/

Global, Brands. (2022). BBVA one of the top 25 global companies to work for, says Great Place to Work. *Global Brands Magazine*. https://www.globalbrandsmagazine.com/bbva-one-of-the-top-25-global-companies-to-work-for-says-great-place-to-work/

Great Place to Work. (2015). World's best workplaces 2015. *Great Place to Work*. https://www.greatplacetowork.com/best-workplaces-international/world-s-best-workplaces/2015

LexisNexus Risk Solutions. (2021, September 20). Top 50 banks in the world. *LexisNexis*. https://risk.lexisnexis.com/insights-resources/article/bank-rankings-top-banks-in-the-world

OpenMind. (2015). New workplaces for BBVA: Promoting a culture of collaborative work. *BBVA*. https://www.bbvaopenmind.com/en/articles/new-workplaces-for-bbva-promoting-a-culture-of-collaborative-work/

13

MOTIVATION AND EMPOWERMENT

LEARNING OBJECTIVES

13.1   Compare and contrast motivation and empowerment and discuss the roles of both in business today.

13.2   Explain the meaning of intrinsic motivation and detail various intrinsic theories of motivation.

13.3   Describe the concept of extrinsic motivation and explore various extrinsic theories of motivation.

13.4   Explore how intrinsic and extrinsic motivation can be combined to achieve superior results in businesses.

13.5   Evaluate how empowerment helps to motivate others and how encouraging self-leadership is a key empowerment strategy for managers.

BUSINESS IMPACT CASE 13.1: LEAF'D—LOS ANGELES, CALIFORNIA

SDG 12:   Responsible Consumption and Production

Adrienne Kessler was a highly successful hairstylist in Hollywood's motion picture industry. After being overexposed to toxic hair chemicals, which led to an autoimmune disorder, she realized that both her health and the health of the planet were equally important. Motivated by this vision, she started Leaf'd in 2019—an online marketplace that curates all types of products including home essentials, kitchen products, health and beauty aids, women's and men's fashions, food, and kid's as well as pet's products.[1] You may be thinking "not another online marketplace," but think again! This one is very different. Every single product sold on the platform is ethically and sustainably sourced.

There are many companies today that spend a lot of money advertising that their products are environmentally friendly or sustainably sourced when, if you dig deep, you find the opposite. This practice, called greenwashing, leads to a false sense that something is environmentally friendly when it is not.[2] For example, consider bamboo clothing that is packaged in a plastic container. Bamboo as a textile is very eco-friendly because bamboo is a regenerative resource, but the plastic is not biodegradable.

Vendors, those selling products on the Leaf'd platform, are vetted to ensure rigorous sustainability standards are met.[3] To qualify as a vendor, products must meet at least one of the following criteria as explained on their vendor application form:

- Products are sourced or made with sustainable or recycled materials.
- Company is committed to improving social and environmental impact.
- Company is committed to the elimination of toxic and hazardous substances from products and operations.
- Company honors the increase of efficiency by minimizing use of raw materials, energy, and water, or minimizing pollution and waste.
- Management of waste disposal and/or usage is environmentally responsible.
- Environmental impact is low throughout production process.
- Products encourage low or zero-waste living.

Vendors first apply for approval status. Once approved, their products are listed on the Leaf'd platform. Customers buy directly through the Leaf'd website and Leaf'd ensures that the vendor's proceeds are deposited in the appropriate vendor's PayPal account after deducting a small fee. A fee is only collected if the products sell; there is no cost to list products on the site once approved. It's a win-win for both vendors and customers. Customers have access to a dedicated marketplace, and vendors are able to reach a larger customer base than they would be able to on their own.

With a small leadership team of six people, empowerment at Leaf'd is less about the team, who are already intrinsically motivated by the cause, and more about the empowerment of the company's customers and vendors. What's so interesting about Leaf'd is how it empowers its customers to make sustainable and ethical choices with confidence because the products have gone through a rigorous vetting process. Leaf'd also empowers vendors to produce sustainable products and find their target customers.

Critical Thinking Questions

1. Who are the customers of Leaf'd? And how are they empowered and motivated?

2. Do you believe that other organizations can empower and motivate customers? How?

3. Have you ever felt empowered and/or motivated by a business, either as an employee or as a customer? If yes, how?

MOTIVATION AND EMPOWERMENT IN BUSINESS

Leaf'd is a great example of a company that takes a holistic approach to motivation and empowerment. Not only does Leaf'd foster a motivational culture within its own team, but it also empowers its customers and vendors (who are also customers) to make sustainable and ethical choices.

Motivation is the forces from within individuals that stimulate and drive them to achieve goals.[4] These forces can be internal or external. Internal motivational forces are the feelings, values, and desires that drive us toward the attainment of our professional and personal goals. External motivational forces are factors outside our control that can drive us to perform well or perform poorly. For example, some studies measuring the total motivation of employees during the COVID-19 pandemic found that the people who were forced to move from the office to working from home were the least motivated, and the most likely to experience inertia, emotional pressure, and economic pressure.[5] Lack of interaction with colleagues, a decline in purpose due to an inability to experience the impact of their work on clients, and loss of potential through lack of access to mentors and managers also contributed to decreased work performance and low motivation. Yet other research found working from home can increase quality of life and productivity.[6] Different and even conflicting research results suggest that the factors that drive one's motivation can vary from person to person. In business, it is important to recognize these forces and put measures in place to motivate employees and ourselves with the goal of achieving specific individual and organizational objectives.

The Motivation Process

Our motivation process is shaped by tension created from an unsatisfied need. For example, you may have an unsatisfied need to achieve a high grade on an exam, which creates tension. The demand to satisfy this need and relieve the discomfort drives you to study hard, which helps you to attain your goal, thus reducing tension. Whatever your intended goal, you would not be able to achieve it without going through the motivation process as illustrated in Figure 13.1.

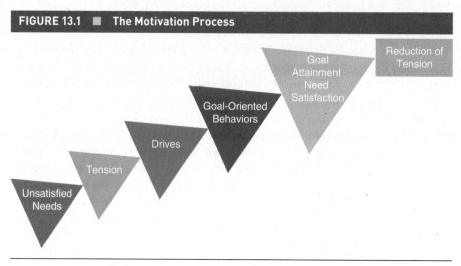

Source: Neck, C., Houghton, J., & Murray, E. (2020). *Organizational behavior* (2nd ed.). SAGE.

Empowerment

Empowerment and motivation are intertwined; each informs the other. If you feel empowered, you may be more motivated. If you are motivated, you may feel a greater sense of empowerment. Empowerment plays a crucial role in building successful customer and employee relationships. The Leaf'd case demonstrates how the company empowers its employees, customers, and the community by promoting and making sustainable and ethical choices, in addition to empowering its vendors to produce products that make a positive impact on the planet.

Empowerment occurs at two levels: the organizational level and the individual (employee) level. Organizational empowerment encourages individuals, teams, or departments to participate in independent decision making and sharing responsibilities at work. By increasing the degree of autonomy (self-direction) and self-determination (sense of control on the job), people are better able to represent their interests and those of the organization.[7] In other words, empowerment at the organizational level involves helping employees to have more control over performing their jobs in terms of what tasks they do and how they do them.

Empowerment applied to an organizational level then leads to greater individual or psychological empowerment. Psychological empowerment is the extent to which employees feel a sense of personal fulfillment and intent when carrying out tasks, together with a belief that their work contributes to some larger purpose. When employees are empowered, they are more likely to be more motivated toward achieving their goals. Both empowerment and motivation lead to overall employee engagement, thereby increasing productivity and morale.

The key to empowering people is to understand what motivates them in the first place. Take millennials, for instance. Studies show that millennials are the least engaged group in the workplace (29%), often regarded as "lazy" and "complacent," with a tendency to hop from one job to another. But this is not the case. Millennials actively look for challenging, meaningful work and if they don't get it, they will seek to find it elsewhere.[8] Giving millennials the opportunities to work on bigger, more complex, purpose-driven projects helps to motivate and empower them to achieve company goals. On the other hand, Gen Zers are thought to be slightly less purpose driven and value job security and financial stability. They are very entrepreneurial, like to work independently, and are extremely competitive. Thus, while millennials are empowered and motivated by purpose-driven projects, Gen Zers are more motivated by financial rewards and healthy competition. Later in this chapter empowerment is discussed in further detail. For now, let's explore the different theories of motivation.

INTRINSIC MOTIVATION

Over the last few decades, a growing number of motivational theories have sprung up, but despite the enormous amount of motivation research, there is no single theory that has been universally accepted. There are two different categories of motivational theories: intrinsic and extrinsic. Let's focus first on the intrinsic side of motivation.

Intrinsic motivation is the performance of tasks for our own, innate satisfaction rather than for some type of reward.[9] For instance, staying late at work because you enjoy your job, participating in sports for the excitement of playing, or cooking because of the pleasure of making a meal are all examples of intrinsic motivation.

Intrinsic motivation consists of two main mechanisms: need for competence and need for self-determination.

Need for competence is the desire we may have to stretch and exercise our capabilities. For example, researchers at Massachusetts General Hospital discovered that older adults who still function to high academic, physical, and professional standards—known as "superagers"—tend to challenge themselves mentally and physically in comparison with their peers.[10]

Intrinsic motivation may be the reason why Jean Kops pursued a degree at the University of Nebraska at the age of 87.

Associated Press/Jenna Vonhofe

Need for self-determination describes the aspiration we may have to be in control of our own growth and development rather than being dependent on external influences. Self-determined people feel competent enough to complete a task, the autonomy to carry out a task, and connected enough to others to achieve the task. Studies show that autonomy, resulting from self-determination, in the workplace leads to higher productivity and greater job satisfaction.[11] Music streaming service Spotify is a good example of a company that is creating an environment that encourages self-determination. Each team, called "squads," is accountable for their own products and how they perform but are also expected to help each other progress. This environment builds communication and increases trust between teams.[12]

Most motivation researchers focus on the idea that motivation is based on different needs that motivate people and the behavioral outcomes of fulfilling those needs. As a result, all theories related to intrinsic motivation emphasize how positive behavioral changes occur when certain needs are met.

Then, when needs are met, we are motivated to sustain our positive behavior leading to better overall work performance. Let's look at seven intrinsic motivation theories.[13]

Maslow's Hierarchy of Needs

Psychologist Abraham Maslow introduced one of the most popular needs theories in 1943, called the **hierarchy of needs theory**, which proposes that people are motivated by five levels of individual needs: physiological, safety, love/belonging, esteem, and self-actualization.[14] Figure 13.2 illustrates Maslow's hierarchy pyramid.

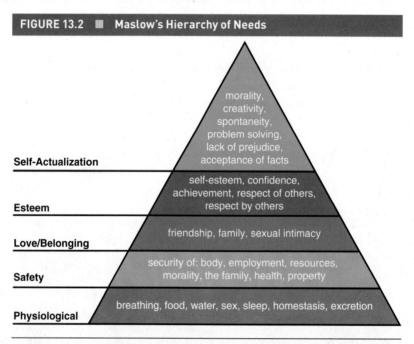

FIGURE 13.2 ■ Maslow's Hierarchy of Needs

Self-Actualization: morality, creativity, spontaneity, problem solving, lack of prejudice, acceptance of facts

Esteem: self-esteem, confidence, achievement, respect of others, respect by others

Love/Belonging: friendship, family, sexual intimacy

Safety: security of: body, employment, resources, morality, the family, health, property

Physiological: breathing, food, water, sex, sleep, homestasis, excretion

Source: Factoryjoe. (2009, June 29). *Maslow's hierarchy of needs.* Wikimedia Creative Commons. Licensed CC BY-SA 3.0. https://commons.wikimedia.org/wiki/File:Maslow%27s_Hierarchy_of_Needs.svg

Maslow's theory holds that each need must be satisfied before moving up the pyramid to satisfy the next need as depicted in Figure 13.2. For example, the physiological needs to breathe, eat, and drink must be satisfied before moving to safety needs such as looking after our families or getting a job. Successfully accomplishing the lower-level needs leads to the achievement of higher-level needs such as gaining confidence, self-esteem, and finally self-actualization, the point where we realize our full potential.

Though Maslow's theory is useful for identifying categories of needs, it has been challenged by a number of scientists who have questioned the validity of the hierarchy of needs and their order of importance.[15] For example, according to the hierarchy, people who reach self-actualization won't be as concerned with gaining the respect of others. Researchers have also argued against the step-by-step sequence of Maslow's hierarchy, proposing that people may be motivated to satisfy these needs in a number of different ways, or even simultaneously. More recently, in 2018, Facebook challenged Maslow's theory by asking: "If Maslow was around today, what would he identify as the main motivators?" Researchers found that its employees were motivated by three main factors: career (work drives independence and promotes learning and development); community (groups support feelings of connection and belongingness); and cause (missions and goals to do good are a valuable source of pride).[16] Although Maslow's theory continues to be challenged by researchers, it is still a source of fascination, as the Facebook study demonstrates.

ERG Theory of Motivation

Proposed by Clayton Alderfer in 1969 as a modification to Maslow's theory, the **ERG theory of motivation** sets out three categories of human needs related to human behaviors: existence needs (E), relatedness needs (R), and growth needs (G).[17] Existence needs are similar to Maslow's physiological and safety needs; relatedness needs reflect Maslow's love/belonging needs; and growth needs focus on our need for personal fulfillment, self-development, and accomplishment, similar to Maslow's esteem needs and self-actualization needs.

Although Alderfer also used a hierarchical structure to demonstrate the different levels of needs, he believed that different levels of needs can be pursued simultaneously, moving up and down within the hierarchy depending on how well a particular need is satisfied at the moment. ERG theory has received more support from researchers than Maslow's hierarchy of needs, but further research needs to be carried out to fully test the validity of Alderfer's model.

Herzberg's Two-Factor Theory

Developed by psychologist Frederick Herzberg in the 1950s, the two-factor theory (also referred to as motivation-hygiene theory, or dual theory) explores the impact of motivational influences on job satisfaction.[18] Through his research involving interviews with hundreds of workers, Herzberg concluded that two factors influence employee behavior: hygiene factors and motivator factors (see Figure 13.3).

Hygiene factors are sources of job satisfaction such as salary, status, and security. If employees considered any of these factors to be poor or below average, then the rate of job dissatisfaction was higher. Motivator factors are sources of job satisfaction, such as recognition, achievement, status, responsibility, and opportunity for advancement. When these motivators are absent, employees experience a certain ambivalence toward their roles; however, if motivators are effective, then employees are highly stimulated and satisfied with their roles. Herzberg believed that managers needed to address the hygiene factors first to satisfy employees before moving on to the next step of using motivators to meet their higher-level needs.

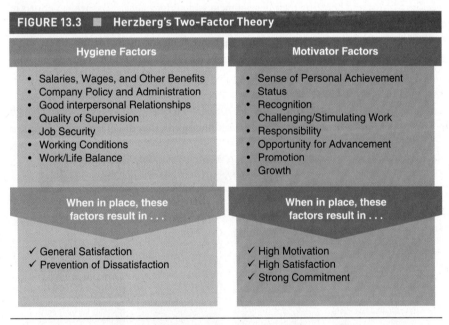

FIGURE 13.3 ■ Herzberg's Two-Factor Theory

Source: Based on Herzberg, F., Mausner, B., & Snyderman, B. (1959). *The motivation to work* (2nd ed.). Wiley; Herzberg, F., One more time: How do you motivate employees? *Harvard Business Review* 81, no. 1 (January 2003): 87–96.

Over the years, Herzberg's two-factor theory has received a number of criticisms for being too narrow in scope. Some theorists have questioned Herzberg's assumption that satisfied employees are more productive. Others have argued that what motivates one person might not necessarily motivate another. The theory has also been criticized for not accounting for individual differences, meaning that some individuals may respond differently to hygiene or motivator factors.

Despite these criticisms, Herzberg's two-factor theory has been an important influence on the motivational techniques employed by managers with their workforce, particularly in the areas of job security, job enrichment, and job satisfaction.[19]

McClelland's Acquired Needs Theory

Developed by psychological theorist David McClelland in 1990, the acquired needs theory holds that our needs are shaped over time and formed by our life experiences and cultural background. McClelland classified needs into three main categories: need for achievement, need for affiliation, and need for power.[20] Although McClelland believed that in each of us, one of these needs is the dominant motivator, he also believed that all three, in particular the need for achievement, can be learned through training.

Need for achievement is the desire to excel. People who are achievement oriented are generally positive in nature, and tend to set their own goals, thrive on feedback, and take ownership of their work. High achievers do well in challenging environments but may lose motivation in routine roles. Actor Emma Stone is a good example of a high achiever. She has starred in a plethora of acting roles over the years and has won numerous awards for her work. Furthermore, Stone maintains her positive outlook by practicing self-compassion, meditation, and self-kindness to combat her personal struggles with anxiety and stress.[21]

Need for affiliation is the desire to belong to a group and to be liked. Generally, people who possess this need as a dominant motivator like to belong to a certain social group. They tend not to make good managers because they like to maintain the status quo for fear of falling out of favor with their colleagues. Without daily contact with others, people with strong affiliation needs might lose motivation, which may lead to job dissatisfaction.

Need for power is the desire to control and influence the behavior of others. There are two types of power. Institutional power is the power an individual exerts for the good of the organization and its employees. Former CEO of Popeyes, Cheryl Bachelder, used her institutional power by putting her employees' needs first and boosting their development and performance.[22] Bachelder's efforts resulted in a massive turnaround for Popeyes, which was sold in 2017 to Restaurant Brands International Inc. for $1.8 billion. Personal power is power focused on controlling and manipulating others for personal gain. Former Uber CEO Travis Kalanick is a good example of someone who used his personal power to harm the company. Complaints about Kalanick's infamous sexist "bro" culture led to his subsequent dismissal from the company he originally founded.[23]

Figure 13.4 compares theories from Maslow, Alderfer, Herzberg, and McClelland. Though these famous theorists all agree that we are motivated by fulfilling needs, they disagree on what those needs are.

FIGURE 13.4 ■ Comparison of Maslow, Alderfer, Herzberg, and McClelland

Maslow's Need Hierarchy	Alderfer's ERG Theory	Herzberg's Theory	McClelland's Acquired Needs
Self-Actualization	Growth	Motivators	Need for Achievement
Esteem			Need for Power
Love/Belonging	Relatedness		Need for Affiliation
Safety	Existence	Hygienes	
Physiological			

Equity Theory

First introduced by psychologist J. Stacey Adams in 1963, the concept of equity theory holds that motivation is based on our perception of how fairly we are being treated in comparison with others.[24] In other words, people may be more motivated when they perceive their treatment as being equal to others or fair but demotivated if they consider their treatment to be unfair or not up to the standards that others receive. According to this theory, our perception of what is fair depends on the O/I ratio, where O equals outcomes like salary, job security, employee benefits, recognition, and status, and I equals inputs like our effort, loyalty, time, tolerance, experience, and ability (see Figure 13.5).

People tend to compare their own perceived O/I ratio to their perceptions of the O/I ratio of referent others, or people whose situation is comparable to their own. As long as the ratios are similar there is no problem, but people who perceive the other person's ratio as greater than their own will feel an inequity. For example, if you discover that a coworker's salary is higher than your own, even though you have exactly the same role, then you may experience a sense of unfairness.

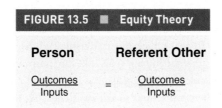

FIGURE 13.5 ■ Equity Theory

Person		Referent Other
$\dfrac{\text{Outcomes}}{\text{Inputs}}$	$=$	$\dfrac{\text{Outcomes}}{\text{Inputs}}$

Expectancy Theory

Introduced by Yale school of management professor Victor Vroom in 1964, expectancy theory holds that individuals are more likely to be motivated and perform well if they expect to receive desired rewards.[25] Vroom's theory explores the motivation of individuals to maximize satisfaction and minimize dissatisfaction. In this context, motivation is a function of an individual's beliefs concerning effort-to-performance relationships (expectancy), work–outcome relationships (instrumentality), and the desirability of various work outcomes (valence). The theory is summarized in Figure 13.6.

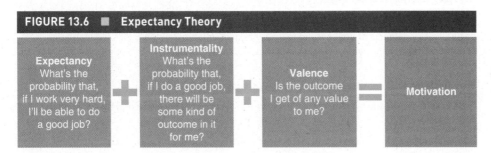

FIGURE 13.6 ■ Expectancy Theory

Expectancy · What's the probability that, if I work very hard, I'll be able to do a good job? **+** Instrumentality · What's the probability that, if I do a good job, there will be some kind of outcome in it for me? **+** Valence · Is the outcome I get of any value to me? **=** Motivation

Expectancy is the probability that the amount of work effort invested by an individual will result in a high level of performance. In other words, it could be phrased as, "What's the probability that, if I work very hard, I'll be able to do a good job?" It is measured in a range from zero to +1. If someone believes strong effort will not result in a higher performance level, their expectancy is zero; however, if the person believes a good effort *will* lead to high performance, expectancy is +1. For example, if you work hard, you will expect to reach the required goals.

Instrumentality is the probability that good performance will lead to various work outcomes. Another way of saying this is, "What's the probability that, if I do a good job, there will be some kind of outcome in it for me?" It can range from –1 to +1. An instrumentality of +1 would apply to people who believe that their performance would make an outcome likely, whereas people who think their performance will not result in outcomes would have an instrumentality of –1. For example, if you hit all your performance targets, you will expect to receive rewards in the form of pay or promotion or recognition.

Valence is the value individuals place on work outcomes. Phrased a different way, "Is the outcome I get of any value to me?" Valences range from –1 to +1 and are positive or negative depending on the nature of the outcome. For example, if you work long hours and prefer extra time off to a cash bonus, then you may see this as a negative outcome.

Managers can use expectancy theory as a motivator by bringing the three elements together. When employees are reassured that their efforts will result in a higher performance (expectancy), know they will be given some form of award for their hard work (instrumentality), and realize they will earn types of awards that they value (valence), then they are more likely to thrive in the workplace. Studies have shown that instrumentality, valence, and expectancy are key components of entrepreneurial motivation when starting a new venture, and closely related to the intentions, efforts, and behaviors over time that will eventually lead to company success.[26]

Goal-Setting Theory

Setting goals is an essential part of achieving personal, professional, and organizational success. Goal-setting theory, first proposed by researchers Locke and Latham, suggests that human performance is directed by conscious goals and intentions. Goal-setting in the workplace is a powerful way to motivate employees. The Entrepreneurial Mindset Activity describes how meaningful goals can set employees on the right path to goal achievement. Melanie Perkins, CEO and cofounder of online design platform Canva, believes that setting big goals is key to motivating her employees: "One of the most important things is to be able to set big goals that inspire and motivate your team. I think it's easier to attract great people when you set out to achieve something that's crazy huge, because great people like great challenges. It's also essential to set a clear direction for the company and frequently talk about the future. If everyone knows where you are trying to get to, I think there's less debate about the small things that don't matter."[27]

ENTREPRENEURIAL MINDSET ACTIVITY

S.M.A.R.T. Goal Setting

Setting meaningful goals can motivate yourself and groups in the right direction. One of the most popular methodologies of goal setting is to create goals that match the S.M.A.R.T. definition: specific, measurable, achievable, relevant, and time-bound goals. Below is an explanation of S.M.A.R.T goals:

Specific: Make your goals specific and narrow for more effective planning

Measurable: Define the evidence that will prove you are making progress and that your goal is trackable

Attainable: Make sure you can reasonably accomplish your goal within a certain time frame

Relevant: Ensure your goals align with your values and long-term objectives

Time-based: Set a realistic, ambitious end-date for task prioritization and motivation

Developing S.M.A.R.T. goals is essential to leaders, managers, and even entrepreneurs. There is too much work that needs to be done not to set goals. Productivity is important to business progress and to our own morale and motivation.

Your mindset activity is to set six S.M.A.R.T. goals. These goals can be around school work or other activities in your life. Remember, each needs to be specific, measurable, achievable, relevant, and time-bound. Three should be short-term goals (within 6 months) and three should be longer-term goals (within 3 years). Each goal must pass the five tests presented by the S.M.A.R.T. goal-setting rubric.

Here's an example to get you started:

Example 1

I will obtain a job as a staff accountant in an accounting firm within 3 months after graduating with my bachelor of science in business administration.
- **Specific:** The goal of becoming a staff accountant is well-defined.
- **Measurable:** Success can be measured by the number of applications, interviews, and job offers.
- **Achievable:** The goal setter will have the appropriate degree for the job.

- **Relevant:** The goal setter is planning to get a job in the accounting industry after getting a business degree.
- **Time-based:** The goal setter has set a deadline to achieve their objective within the 3 months following graduation.

Critical Thinking Questions

1. How does each goal fulfill the requirements of the five S.M.A.R.T. goal-setting pillars?
2. Which is easier to create: short-term or long-term goals? Why?
3. Which of the five characteristics of S.M.A.R.T. goals is the most difficult to create?

Now that we have explored intrinsic motivation theories, let's find out more about extrinsic motivation and its impact on motivation at work.

EXTRINSIC MOTIVATION

Although intrinsic motivation refers to behavior that derives from internal rewards (fulfilling our needs), extrinsic motivation refers to behavior driven by external rewards such as money, fame, grades, paid vacation, benefits, and praise.[28]

An extreme example of an extrinsic award is the enormous bonuses awarded to certain CEOs. A recent study of the top 350 public firms in the United States showed that in 2021, America's CEOs made almost 351 times more than their average employees' salaries.[29] Some of the top-paid CEOs include Chad Richison at Paycom Software ($211 million), Lawrence Culp Jr. at General Electric ($73 million), Mike Sievert at T-Mobile ($54.9 million), Brian Niccol at Chipotle ($38 million), and David Zalsav at Discovery ($37.7 million).

Extrinsic rewards are usually financial or tangible rewards to motivate and incentivize employee performance. Let's explore two sources of extrinsic motivation: financial and nonfinancial.

Financial Sources of Extrinsic Motivation

Pay-for-perfomance is standard in business, and is based on the belief that you will get paid more for greater levels of performance. This also assumes, sometimes falsely, that we are all motivated by money. We will explore the nonfinancial sources of motivation a little later, but let's explore some of the most well-known financial, pay-for-performance systems.

Seniority-Based Pay

Seniority-based pay is a type of extrinsic reward where employees receive guaranteed wages and salary increases based on time spent with the organization. Once popular, particularly in Japan, seniority-based pay has mostly been phased out but still exists in European countries Belgium, Bulgaria, and Slovenia.[30]

Job Content–Based Pay

Job content–based pay is based on an evaluation of a job's worth to the organization and its relationship to other jobs within the organization.[31] While this is one of the most common methods of rewarding employees, research conducted by staffing firm Robert Half found that 46% of workers still believe they are underpaid; 37% of those respondents earned more than $100,000.[32]

Skill-Based Pay

Skill-based pay rewards employees for the acquisition of new skills that lead to enhanced work performance.[33] Global professional services firm Aon has suggested that more companies should offer current employees bonuses for acquiring new skills to reduce the expense and pressure of hiring new talent.[34]

Performance-Based Pay

Performance-based pay is a financial incentive awarded to employees for meeting specific goals or objectives. There are two levels of performance-based pay: individual-level performance-based pay and organization-level performance-based pay.[35]

Individual-level performance-based pay includes piece rate pay, merit pay, and bonus pay.

- Piece rate is a pay plan in which workers are paid a fixed sum for each unit of production completed. For instance, tree farms often pay workers for the amount of fruit they pick rather than paying them an hourly or daily rate.

- Merit pay links pay increases directly to performance. In other words, it rewards performance by increasing the employee's salary on a long-term basis. It may have been used for decades, but studies show that merit pay doesn't work in the teaching industry. For instance, teachers who are awarded small bonuses when their students achieve high test scores do not tend to view it as an incentive; rather, it has a negative impact on teacher morale, attraction, and retention.[36]

- Bonus pay rewards employees for good performance in addition to their base salary. Many top companies in the U.S. pay out bonuses as part of their compensation schemes. Maryland real estate company St. John Properties made headlines in 2019 for giving its employees a surprise bonus averaging $50,000 each at the company's annual holiday party.[37]

A worker like this apple picker, who earns piece rate pay, is paid for the amount of fruit picked rather than an hourly or daily rate.

Tim Leedy/MediaNews Group/Reading Eagle via Getty Images

In addition to the individual-level performance-based financial incentives, there are organizational-level incentives where if the company performs well, employees will be financially rewarded for being a part of the company. There are three types of organization performance-based plans:

- Gain sharing is a system whereby managers agree to share the benefits of cost savings with employees in return for their contribution to the company's performance.[38]

- Profit sharing is a pay system in which the organization shares its profits with employees.[39] Retail corporation Target is an example of a company that offers a profit-sharing system. The program is available to employees as soon as they complete 1,000 hours of service.[40]

- Employee stock ownership plans (ESOPs) allow employees to purchase company stock, often at below-market price, as one of their benefits.[41] In 2021, San Francisco–based resource recovery company Recology, which provides composting, recycling, and disposal programs serving 150 communities across Oregon, Washington, and California, is a company that offers such an ESOP. In fact, Recology won The ESOP Association's Company of the Year Award for its commitment to "employee participation, wealth creation, individual dignity and worth."[42]

As previously stated, money is not the only extrinsic motivator. Many are motivated by nonfinancial incentives we discuss next.

Nonfinancial Sources of Extrinsic Motivation

Though money is the most common motivator, it's certainly not always the most effective one. A company can get really creative with its nonfinancial awards and these can provide significant value to employees, especially in new and growing companies that may not have enough cash to reward employees financially. Let's talk about some of the most common nonfinancial extrinsic motivators.

Awards and Recognition

Trophies, certificates, T-shirts, parties, and email announcements are all examples of awards and recognition that cost the company very little money but can inspire and motivate employees. For instance, a manager publicly praising a presentation made by an employee to the rest of the company can be a powerful motivator as it creates a sense of accomplishment and gives the employee the impression that the work they are doing is valuable, recognized and has meaning.

Job Enrichment

Job enrichment is about giving an employee more authority and challenge without changing their title or their manager. The company is saying, "You are a wonderful employee and doing a great job, and we think you can handle more challenge, control, and authority in your role." Here, no money is given, but the employee feels incredibly valued and sees the new challenge as motivating rather than as additional work.

Training and Development

The ability to build our skillset, increase knowledge, and continuously learn can be very motivating to some. Companies often identify high-potential employees and future managers and pay for them to attend executive education programs offered through universities. For example, Babson College in Massachusetts works with many larger companies to deliver entrepreneurial leadership programs to its high-potential employees. Being chosen to attend is a signal that says, "You are doing great work and we want to support your development in this company. We see you holding very important leadership positions in the future."

ETHICS IN BUSINESS

Is Minumum Wage Ethical?

You just found out you won the Entrepreneur of the Year award. Your low carb cereal company has taken off. You have record sales, and you just hired your 100th employee. But all is not great. One of your new employees (a driver who delivers the cereal to grocery stores) just sent you an email asking for a wage increase. You are following the government guidelines of paying at least the minimum per hour wage, but it is not meeting "human decency" requirements, as it does not equate to a "living wage" or fulfill their most basic needs. What should you do?

Critical Thinking Questions

1. Is paying only minimum wage unethical? Why or why not?
2. What is your response to the employee?
3. What stakeholders beyond the employee are impacted by your decision? How are they impacted? Is the impact small enough to justify an increase in pay?

Source: Hubbard, K. (2017). The ethics of wages. *Saint Anselm College Center for Ethics in Business and Governance.* Retrieved from https://www.anselm.edu/ethics-governance/blog/ethics-wages

COMBINING BOTH INTRINSIC AND EXTRINSIC MOTIVATORS

As this chapter highlights, there are two types of motivation: extrinsic and intrinsic. Bestselling author Daniel Pink explores how extrinsic and intrinsic motivation can be combined to improve business results using the following four steps:[43]

1. **Baseline rewards**

    It was once commonly thought that money is the biggest motivator for employee and company performance. But this is not always the case. Companies are responsible for providing **baseline rewards**, first level employee rewards such as salary, contract, and benefits. Rewards perceived by employees to be unfair are likely to have a negative impact on morale and work performance, leading to a drop in motivation. In this instance, there is very little evidence of an interaction between intrinsic or extrinsic motivation at play. Pink advises that organizations should pay people enough to remove the focus on money altogether.

2. **"If, then" rewards**

    As soon as baseline rewards have been agreed to, employees might be offered a "carrot and stick" proposal for motivation, called **"if, then" rewards**; these are second level employee rewards received by employees when they reach a certain target. In other words, employees will receive a reward when they reach some prespecified goal, quota, or target. For example, *if* employees working in a call center hit their monthly sales targets *then* they will receive a cash bonus. "If, then" rewards may boost motivation in the short term but can also negatively impact intrinsic motivation in the long term. In our call center example, you may rush to meet your sales targets, but this daily pressure could become too stressful and exhausting as time goes on. In addition, rewards tend to narrow our focus, causing us to ignore everything else until the goal has been achieved. Research shows that extrinsic rewards are effective for algorithmic tasks such as manufacturing or simple computer programming, where there is a set process to follow. However, extrinsic rewards are ineffective for tasks that require flexible problem solving, creativity, and conceptual understanding.

3. **Goals and intrinsic rewards**

    Pink describes in step 2 the negative impact associated with extrinsic rewards in relation to a narrowed focus toward tasks. In fact, research shows that short-term goals accompanied by a substantial extrinsic reward can encourage unethical behavior. For example, a college student on a scholarship may need to get an A on their next exam to secure a B in the course. Anything lower than a B will guarantee that the student will lose the scholarship. On the day of the exam, the student is not prepared and resorts to cheating to secure an A. The reward in this scenario is the scholarship, but the behavior is not only unethical but could lead to expulsion as well as loss of the scholarship.

Other examples relate to retailer Sears, which implemented a sales quota on auto repair staff; the employees began overcharging customers and completing unnecessary repairs. And when Ford imposed strict deadlines on the production of the model Ford Pinto, employees took some shortcuts, omitted safety checks, and ended up releasing an unsafe vehicle on the road. As Pink said, "The problem with making extrinsic reward the only destination that matters is that some people will choose the quickest route there, even if it means taking the low road."

In contrast, intrinsic motivation ignites positive behavior because the reward in the internal feeling relates to the task itself. Employees who are encouraged to continuously learn gain satisfaction by helping customers, and feel a sense of fulfillment by exceeding their own expectations. They feel much happier in their roles, and as a consequence rarely feel the need to take shortcuts and behave unethically.

4. **When do rewards (extrinsic rewards) work?**

Extrinsic rewards work for routine (algorithmic) tasks that require little exploration and creativity. Because these tasks tend to be fairly boring or monotonous, there is unlikely to be any real intrinsic motivation in the first place. Yet these routine tasks still need to be carried out, and employees still need to be motivated enough to complete them to the best of their ability. Pink suggests the following three ways that managers can motivate their employees using extrinsic tasks:

a. **Explain why the task is necessary**

Routine computer tasks like data entry are unlikely to appeal to many people, but if a manager explains why it needs to be done, and the positive impact your work has on the company, then you are more likely to be invested in the task.

b. **Acknowledge that the task is boring**

Managers can be upfront about how dull the task is and empathize with their employees about the monotony of the activity. This will encourage workers to feel that the managers are supportive of their efforts.

c. **Allow people to complete the task their own way**

When it comes to boring tasks, managers might offer people the option to do the tasks their own way. For example, in a data entry task, employees could be given a deadline to deliver yet the freedom to reach that deadline however they may choose, through flexible working hours or otherwise. Extrinsic rewards should only be offered when the task is complete.

Extrinsic rewards often work best for monotonous jobs that don't involve a lot of creativity such as folding napkins. Many would find it difficult to be intrinsically motivated by such mundane tasks.

Mark Leffingwell/Digital First Media/Boulder Daily Camera via Getty Images

Motivation for Ourselves

Professor of psychology Edward Deci from the University of Rochester believes that motivation goes beyond trying to get one person to do something; rather, motivation is something that we do for ourselves.[44] A study of fund-raisers at the University of Michigan explains this theory.[45] Researchers divided work-study students into three groups. Each group was given a common task with the same information: to make calls to University of Michigan alumni to raise money for the school. The only differentiating aspect of the task was what happened 5 minutes before they started making the calls. Each group was given something to read: Group 1 was given neutral information to read; group 2 was given letters from previous call center employees who gave positive feedback on their experiences of working there; and group 3 was given letters from people who had directly benefited from the fund-raising and had succeeded in their chosen careers as a result. Researchers found that the third group performed twice as well as the other two groups in terms of weekly pledges and donations. By explaining to people the purpose behind what they are doing, they are more likely to be motivated into performing at a higher level.

The next section explores how empowering employees can lead to positive change in organizations.

MOTIVATION THROUGH EMPOWERMENT AND SELF-LEADERSHIP

Earlier in this chapter the concept of empowerment was explored as a pathway to employee satisfaction and engagement. Research shows that employees who feel empowered at work tend to demonstrate higher job performance, job satisfaction, and commitment to the organization.[46] Other benefits of empowerment include higher-quality service, speedier problem resolution, and greater levels of accountability and ownership.[47] A study by leadership development company Zenger Folkman found that people who feel less empowered tend to exert less effort. Only 4% of employees made more effort when empowerment was low, but 67% worked harder when empowerment was high.[48]

Many of today's successful organizations cultivate an environment focused on empowering employees. For example, low-cost retail company Sam's Club implemented an empowerment plan that included significant salary raises, a concerted effort to uncover and resolve employee pain points and frustrations, and an increase in technology to make the transaction processes smoother. The results? A dramatic increase in staff retention rates, a big improvement to the bottom line, and a rise in customer satisfaction.[49] In another example, global animal-health company Zoetis empowered employees during the COVID-19 pandemic by enabling them to make difficult decisions under guidance, and ensuring they felt supported and heard by holding weekly check-ins.[50] This approach united employees in working toward the same goals, leading to the successful roll-out of the largest product in Zoetis's company history, released in the middle of the pandemic.

Table 13.1 lists some examples of how organizations and managers can foster this culture of empowerment.

TABLE 13.1 ■ How Organizations Empower Employees
● Offer ongoing training to empower employees in customer service, problem solving, and conflict resolution
● Give access to company data and information to support employee decision making
● Supply mentors to guide employees and give them advice and direction
● Provide tools and equipment to ensure employees can do their jobs properly
● Set clear boundaries to ensure employees understand their levels of empowerment
● Exhibit trust in employees to allow them to make their own decisions
● Give decision-making power to front-line employees who are dealing with day-to-day issues
● Place employees in roles that play to their strengths

Source: Adapted from Lotich, P. (2019). 13 characteristics of empowered employees. *Thriving small business.* https://thethrivingsmallbusiness.com/employee-empowerment/

Although research shows that empowered employees tend to be more creative, helpful, and trusting of their leaders, there are times when empowerment does more harm than good. For example, one study found that some employees who had been given extra responsibility and decision-making powers felt pressured and stressed rather than empowered.[51] It is important for managers to understand the limitations of empowerment and build a trusting relationship with employees to ensure they are comfortable with additional responsibilities.

Self-Leadership as a Key Empowerment Strategy for Managers

Employees can learn to practice self-leadership, a process through which people intentionally influence their thinking and behavior to achieve their goals and objectives.[52] In other words, people can deliberately guide themselves toward attaining favorable outcomes. Business people who are self-leaders have the ability to empower others to engage in self-leadership, by leading others to lead themselves in order to perform at the highest levels. Self-leadership strategies are generally divided into three categories: behavior-focused strategies, natural reward strategies, and constructive thought strategies.[53]

Behavior-focused strategies increase our self-awareness and help manage our own conduct. They include self-observation, self-reward, and self-cueing strategies.

- Self-observation involves analyzing our own behaviors to identify those that need to be adjusted, enhanced, or eliminated altogether. For example, observing how many times a day you check your social media and direct messages is an example of self-observation. You might find you are checking your social media so often that it is distracting you from doing your homework. You identify this behavior as something that needs to be changed in order to make better grades in your classes.

- Self-reward helps us to motivate ourselves and improve performance by mentally praising our own achievements and giving ourselves positive feedback and corrections. For example, you might say, "When I finish my homework for this class, I can play a video game."

- Self-cueing strategies, such as writing to-do lists or keeping an efficient record of information, can help to focus our attention on assigned tasks.

Natural reward strategies is a self-leadership process that can help us to find pleasure in certain aspects of our roles, leading to an enhanced sense of competence, self-discipline, and application. For example, if you are given a particularly tedious and boring assignment, you could decide to complete the assignment while playing music that you enjoy in the background, as long as the music did not make you lose focus. Even external reward strategies can make a difference in the way we work. For example, adding personal touches to your desk can have a calming effect when work becomes frustrating.

Constructive thought pattern strategies focus on the modification of certain key mental processes. That is, the more positive and optimistic our thinking patterns, the better our work performance. Mental practice, imagining successful completion of an event before you physically complete the event, is one strategy we can use to shape our thought processes by visualizing the successful attainment of the goal before we begin. This is a common technique among top athletes; for example, former professional basketball player Michael Jordan once said, "I visualized where I wanted to be, what kind of player I wanted to become. I knew exactly where I wanted to go, and I focused on getting there."[54]

Motivating and empowering employees isn't easy, especially when people tend to respond differently to certain motivational or empowerment strategies. Successful organizations explore the key drivers for their employees and foster a culture of autonomy and trust that encourages people to take ownership of their roles.

13.1 Compare and contrast motivation and empowerment and discuss the roles of both in business today.

Motivation is the forces from within individuals that stimulate and drive them to achieve goals. These forces help to drive us toward the attainment of our professional and personal goals. The motivation process is shaped by unsatisfied needs and the resulting tension. Empowerment refers to measures designed to increase the degree of autonomy and self-determination in people and in teams in order to enable them to represent their interests and those of the organization in a responsible and self-determined way. When employees are empowered, they are more likely to be more motivated toward achieving their goals.

13.2 Explain the meaning of intrinsic motivation and detail various intrinsic theories of motivation.

Intrinsic motivation is the performance of tasks for our own innate satisfaction rather than for some type of reward. Intrinsic motivation consists of two main mechanisms: need for competence and need for self-determination. The main intrinsic motivational theories are: Maslow's hierarchy of needs, Alderfer's ERG theory, McClelland's need theory, and Herzberg's two-factor theory. Hierarchy of needs theory proposes that people are motivated by five levels of individual needs: physiological, safety, love/belonging, esteem, and self-actualization needs at the top. ERG Theory of Motivation sets out three categories of human needs related to human behaviors: existence needs (E), relatedness needs (R), and growth needs (G). Herzberg's two-factor theory (also referred to as motivation-hygiene theory, or dual theory) explores the impact of motivational influences on job satisfaction. McClelland's acquired needs theory holds that our needs are shaped over time and formed by our life experiences and cultural background.

13.3 Describe the concept of extrinsic motivation and explore various extrinsic theories of motivation.

Extrinsic motivation refers to behavior that is driven by external rewards such as money, fame, grades, paid vacation, benefits, and praise. There are several types of extrinsic rewards used by organizations to motivate employees: seniority-based pay, job content–based pay, skill-based pay, and performance-based pay.

13.4 Explore how intrinsic and extrinsic motivation can be combined to achieve superior results in businesses.

Extrinsic and intrinsic motivation can be combined to improve business results using different types of rewards. Studies have also shown that motivation goes beyond trying to get one person to do something; rather, motivation is something that we do for ourselves.

13.5 Evaluate how empowerment helps to motivate others and how encouraging self-leadership is a key empowerment strategy for managers.

Organizations can empower others by giving them more autonomy in decision making, providing access to company data and information, setting boundaries to ensure employees understand their levels of empowerment, and trusting them to allow them to make their own decisions. Self-leadership is a process through which people intentionally influence their thinking and behavior to achieve their objectives. Self-leadership strategies are generally divided into three categories: behavior-focused strategies, natural reward strategies, and constructive thought strategies.

BUSINESSES DISCUSSED IN THIS CHAPTER

Organization	UN Sustainable Development Goals
Canva	7. Affordable and Clean Energy 12. Responsible Consumption and Production
Facebook	13. Climate Action
Leaf'd	12. Responsible Consumption and Production
Popeyes	12. Responsible Consumption and Production
Sam's Club	12. Responsible Consumption and Production 13. Climate Action
Spotify	8. Decent Work and Economic Growth 10. Reduced Inequality 12. Responsible Consumption and Production
St. John Properties	12. Responsible Consumption and Production 13. Climate Action
Target	12. Responsible Consumption and Production 13. Climate Action
Uber	11. Sustainable Cities and Communities 13. Climate Action

KEY TERMS

Acquired needs theory (p. 274)

Baseline rewards (p. 280)

Behavior-focused strategies (p. 283)

Bonus pay (p. 278)

Constructive thought pattern strategies (p. 283)

Employee stock ownership plans (ESOPs) (p. 279)

Equity theory (p. 274)

ERG theory of motivation (p. 272)

Expectancy theory (p. 275)

Expectancy (p. 275)

External motivational forces (p. 269)

Extrinsic motivation (p. 277)

Gain sharing (p. 278)

Goal-setting theory (p. 276)

Hierarchy of needs theory (p. 272)

Hygiene factors (p. 273)

Instrumentality (p. 275)

Internal motivation forces

Intrinsic motivation (p. 271)

Job content–based pay (p. 277)

Job enrichment (p. 279)

Merit pay (p. 278)

Motivation (p. 269)

Motivator factors (p. 273)

Natural reward strategies (p. 283)

Need for achievement (p. 274)

Need for affiliation (p. 274)

Need for competence (p. 271)

Need for power (p. 274)

Need for self-determination (p. 271)

Organizational empowerment (p. 270)

Performance-based pay (p. 278)

Piece rate (p. 278)

Profit sharing (p. 279)

Psychological empowerment (p. 270)

Self-leadership (p. 283)

Seniority-based pay (p. 277)

Skill-based pay (p. 277)

Two-factor theory (p. 273)

Valence (p. 275)

"If, then" rewards (p. 280)

BUSINESS CASE 13.2: PIPS REWARDS—NEW YORK, NEW YORK

SDG 3:   Good Health and Well-Being

Known as a "currency of good," PIPs, or Positive Impact Points, are offered through the PIPs Rewards App, which uses action-tracking tools and machine learning to capture and reward healthy choices and behaviors to drive engagement and motivate behavioral change—to essentially develop healthy and Earth-friendly habits. President of PIPs Rewards, Wendy Gordon, and her cofounders, David Sand, Evan Sable, and Yaniv Eyny, began PIPs Rewards with one simple question: "Could we create a mobile platform that was sufficiently engaging to change our everyday actions, from the way we got to work or school to the container in which we carried our coffee?"

The PIPs App is built on the 3 R's of habit formation: reminder, routine, and reward, and a little gamification for an element of fun and play. The concept of "PIP'n" is making healthier dietary choices such as buying fresh, organic food from companies that use sustainable means of production, being more physically active by doing more exercise, and/or being environmentally conscious by recycling or conserving energy. So small actions like biking, recycling, and volunteering can all earn points and these points start to add up to positive change and unlocking rewards. The list of positive activities can be created with its clients, typically universities, and rewards range from tuition assistance to food credits to students donating to charitable organizations to gift cards for sustainable retailers such as Patagonia. Each action is worth a certain amount of PIPs. For example, taking public transit one day instead of driving in a car might earn the user 50 PIPs, and PIPs accumulate even faster when this is carried out on a daily basis. The founders believe that if everyone includes PIP'n in their daily lives, the differences to personal and communal health will be significant.

PIPs Rewards is a subsidiary of the PIPs Education Fund (PEF), a nonprofit organization based in New York City that supports low-income students in paying for higher education in a way that benefits themselves and the community. PIPs started a program in June 2021 called PIPs for School (P4S) Scholars where students in college or college-bound with financial need are invited to participate in PIPs Rewards. These selected P4S Scholars have a year to earn up to 100,000 PIPs that can be cashed in for $1,000 in grant money that is paid directly into the student's college account. As one PS4 Scholar noted, "When you become conscious of what you are doing and the impact it has, it motivated you to keep on doing it."

PIPs has also partnered with ThinkHumanTV, a platform developed by social entrepreneurs, artists, and scientists from Columbia, University of Pennsylvania, and Stanford. The platform promotes socioemotional skill development (also known as emotional intelligence) for young people. An example of the platform's work includes a browser extension that operates on streaming platforms such as Netflix and Disney. Viewers who sign on to the program earn PIPs by reflecting on the emotional states (expressed by posture, facial expression, and tone of voice) of the characters from movies and shows, such as *Never Have I Ever, Orange Is the New Black*, and *Cobra Kai*, among others. The idea is to motivate the individual by engaging them on an emotional level through content they enjoy, with the goal of teaching them the language they need to describe emotional experiences. ThinkHuman founders believe that the higher emotional knowledge they gain, the more likely young people will be able to manage relationships, experience less anxiety and depression, and improve academically. The PIPs Rewards provide ThinkHuman users with more motivation to contribute on a societal and environmental level.

Ultimately, PIPs Rewards focuses on changing behaviors that are self-nurturing, planet-protecting, and socially conscious, comprising what it calls a "360 degree cycle of good."

Critical Thinking Questions

1. Do PIPs Rewards rely more on intrinsic motivation or extrinsic motivation? Explain your answer.

2. As a college student, would you be motivated by and engaged with PIP'n?

3. What are the 3 R's of habit formation? In what way have you used these in your life without knowing it?

References

Clear, J. (2018). *Atomic habits: An easy & proven way to build good habits & break bad ones*. Penguin.

W, Gordon. (2021, November 18). *Students credit PIPs for increased sense of agency*. PIPs Rewards-Medium. https://pipsrewards.medium.com/students-credit-pips-for-increased-sense-of-agency-b02fc4b2f8c1

PIPs Rewards. (2019). *Our story*. https://www.pipsrewards.com/ourstory

These digital blueprints for a hospital are rendered with technology by Autodesk. This technology allows architects and engineers to update plans in real-time at the job site.

Andrew Harrer/Bloomberg via Getty Images

 **COMMUNICATION IN BUSINESS**

<table>
<tr><td colspan="2">LEARNING OBJECTIVES</td></tr>
<tr><td>14.1</td><td>Define communication and explain its importance in the workplace.</td></tr>
<tr><td>14.2</td><td>Discuss the various forms of communication.</td></tr>
<tr><td>14.3</td><td>Explore barriers to effective communication.</td></tr>
<tr><td>14.4</td><td>Illustrate the types of communication networks in organizations.</td></tr>
<tr><td>14.5</td><td>Discuss the importance of effective cross-cultural communication in the workplace.</td></tr>
</table>

BUSINESS IMPACT CASE 14.1: AUTODESK—SAN RAFAEL, CALIFORNIA

SDG 11: Sustainable Cities and Communities

You might have never heard of Autodesk, but you've probably been affected by its software. Autodesk is a design, engineering, and construction software company that makes software for people who make things. As its website states: "If you've ever driven a high-performance car, admired a towering skyscraper, used a smartphone, or watched a great film, chances are you've experienced what millions of Autodesk customers are doing with our software."[1] This $2.5 billion company now has its eyes on the evolution of "smart cities."

Smart cities use digital technology across all functions in an urban area including government, building, health care, mobility, infrastructure, technology, energy, and citizens.[2] The idea is that smart cities will make urban living more efficient, cheaper, less wasteful, and even more social by connecting people, data, and technology. The emergence of smart cities around the world is a result of internet connectivity, data analytics, and the prolific use of smartphones. It's about using data to improve lives, and Autodesk's software is helping different cities become smarter in different ways.

How smart cities communicate across city functions is not that different from how people communicate within business. Autodesk discusses three approaches to smart cities.[3] The first approach is centralized, where everything is connected. An example is Singapore's GovTech Agency that is tasked with implementing all of the city's digital initiatives, from public transit to a portal for public-sector workers. The second approach is called less formal because smart cities are emerging more organically out of necessity rather than strategy. Autodesk points to Nairobi, Kenya, as a prime example.[4] Mobile phone usage has increased from 14% in 2005 to 95% today. Given the amount of data generated from smartphone usage, including city apps, Nairobi is better able to assess the needs of its citizens—especially as they relate to transportation and mobility. The third and final type of approach is experimental. In a very entrepreneurial way, cities are trying new things to see what works before making significant investments. Boston, as an example, has tried several applications for reporting potholes, paying for parking tickets and meters, and even erecting solar-powered park benches that charge mobile devices.

Autodesk is connecting its customers through its process called BIM, which stands for Building Information Modeling. BIM creates 3D models of any new building or infrastructure project. It helps city designers better prepare their cities for the future because BIM not only models new projects but connects all phases, including planning, designing, building, and operating. BIM itself is a smart tool that collects data through all phases, creating efficiencies, cost-savings, and less waste in the future as well.

The future is definitely smart, but the concept of smart cities continues to evolve. Smart cities are simply about connecting people to technology in order to get data to improve services and protect the future. In short, smart cities involve using technology to help cities communicate with their residents and residents communicate with the cities in which they reside.

Critical Thinking Questions

1. Think about your own city or town that you are currently living in. How smart is it? Is it communicating with you? Are you communicating with it? How?

2. Do you think the city you are living in now is a "smart city"? Why or why not?

3. How does the concept of a "smart city" help protect the future of the planet?

THE ROLE OF COMMUNICATION

Autodesk highlights the importance of communication when connecting people, data, and technology to create smart cities. Today, everything communicates with everything else, and technology has enabled us to do this. The car dealership communicates with our cars. Our cars communicate with our smartphones. Our smartphones communicate with the lights in our home. Everything is communicating with everything, and it can be overwhelming at times. But let's take a step back and just think about what basic communication is. Communication is the act of transmitting information, thoughts, and processes through various channels.[5] When we take technology out of the equation, communication is about people (not things) transmitting knowledge and exchanging information back and forth, which is the focus of this chapter.

Strong communication skills are essential in business. Think about it. Our ability to communicate in clear and creative ways is one thing that makes us uniquely human. How we communicate, then, can be a differentiator in business. Studies show that people in the workplace spend up to 80% of their time communicating.[6] This could involve anything from having a quick chat with your work colleague when you arrive to work in the morning, sending off a few emails, making some calls, texting within a work team, or attending meetings with colleagues or customers. Because we spend such a large percentage of time communicating, it makes sense that we should do it effectively—and most employers agree. For instance, the IBM Institute for Business Value recently surveyed approximately 5,670 executives across 48 countries to learn more about the skills needed to execute business strategies. Among the most in-demand skills were the ability to communicate effectively in a business environment.[7]

Communication is also important to employees. In a recent survey of 11 million employees, effective communication was the second most important reason they gave for staying with an organization (the first was a change in pay). In fact, other studies have found that regular communication between managers and employees leads to higher engagement, productivity, and performance, and better staff retention. The most effective managers make an effort to communicate with their employees daily, return employees' calls or messages within 24 hours, and invest in them as people by taking an interest in their lives outside of work.

During the COVID-19 pandemic, the way we communicated with each other rapidly changed. For many of us, our in-person interactions shifted to online communication or wearing masks inside when social distancing was not a possibility. Although most people have adapted quickly to these changes, there are challenges and limitations to some of these methods of communication, which we will explore later in the chapter.

In order to better develop our own communication skills, let's first understand the general structure of communication processes.

The Communication Process

The Shannon-Weaver communications model is a useful way to understand how communication works. It was created in 1947 by mathematician Claude E. Shannon, which was later developed further by Warren Weaver. The Shannon-Weaver model (see Figure 14.1) is the cornerstone of communication models and is still in use today.[8]

The process relies on the interaction between eight main components: sender, message, receiver, encoder, decoder, channel, feedback, and noise. The sender or source of the message is the person who shares

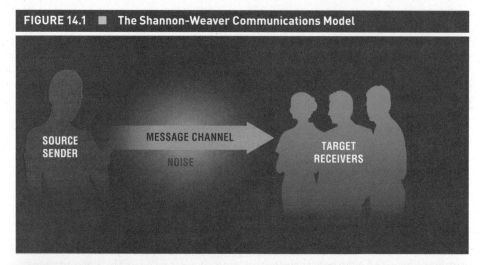

FIGURE 14.1 ■ The Shannon-Weaver Communications Model

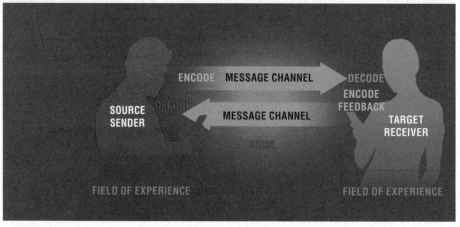

Source: Edwards, A., Edwards, C., Wahl, S.T., & Myers, S. A. (2020). *The communication age: Connecting and engaging* (3rd ed.). SAGE.

information. When the sender transmits information through a communication channel (such as face-to-face conversations, phone, email, instant messaging, and so on), it is encoded into understandable language through written, oral, or electronic means. The message is then interpreted by the receiver into a perceived meaning. The receiver then provides feedback to the sender to confirm that the message has been received and understood. One of the main interruptions to the communication process is noise. Noise could be anything from poor cell phone reception, background noise such as construction work, or complex or difficult language that might distort the meaning of what is being said. The removal of any noise is essential for clear communication between sender and receiver. The next section explores different types of communication.

FORMS OF COMMUNICATION

As recently as 30 years ago, there were only a few forms of communication available to us. Thanks to the rapid rise of technology, there are vast amounts of channels to send and receive messages. Types of communication are generally split into two main categories: face-to-face (F2F) communication and virtual communication (see Figure 14.2). Additionally, communication can be received and sent through verbal and nonverbal means.

Face-to-Face Communication

When we talk to people face to face, verbal and nonverbal communication happens.

Verbal communication is the exchange of information, ideas, and processes through speech, either one on one or as a group. In the workplace, we regularly communicate orally through telephone conversations, presentations, meetings, speeches, personal discussions, conferences, and video or web

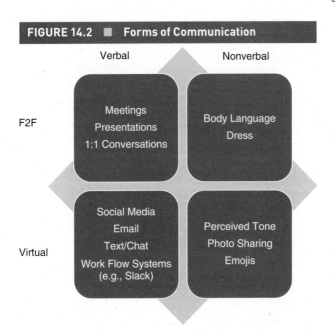

FIGURE 14.2 ■ Forms of Communication

	Verbal	Nonverbal
F2F	Meetings Presentations 1:1 Conversations	Body Language Dress
Virtual	Social Media Email Text/Chat Work Flow Systems (e.g., Slack)	Perceived Tone Photo Sharing Emojis

conferences. Swedish climate activist Greta Thunberg's speech addressing world leaders at the United Nations' Climate Action Summit in New York City in 2019 is an example of oral communication.

There are advantages and disadvantages of verbal communication. Talking to people is a great way to network and build relationships. It also provides an excellent forum for immediate and spontaneous feedback. However, sometimes the immediate nature of verbal communication may lead to rash responses delivered before thinking, and because there is no formal documentation of the communication, it can also lead to forgetfulness or misunderstandings.

Swedish climate activist Greta Thunberg (in pink, right) engages in face-to-face verbal communication at the 2019 UN Climate Action Summit to bring attention to her cause.

LUDOVIC MARIN/AFP via Getty Images

Nonverbal communication is the transmission of wordless behaviors and actions between people. Examples of nonverbal cues during face-to-face interaction include facial expressions, eye gaze, gestures, tone of voice—the way we walk, stand, dress, and position ourselves.[9] Body language in the workplace plays a huge part in how we are perceived. For example, crossing your arms during a conversation may give the impression that you're defensive, insecure, or resistant to open discussion. Research has shown that 70% of interpersonal communication is conveyed through nonverbal cues.[10] This is why nonverbal communication is so important to achieving effective communication in the workplace. Table 14.1 outlines some effective ways to communicate nonverbally as supported by scientific studies.

TABLE 14.1 ■ Effective Ways to Communicate Nonverbally
● **Maintain eye contact** More than 40% of our attention during a conversation is focused on the speaker's eyes. Make sure you look someone in the eye when you're talking to them.
● **Stand up straight** Slouching, looking at the ground, and hunching your shoulders make you look insecure and incompetent. Standing straight with your shoulders back gives the impression of confidence.
● **Use gestures** Hand gestures are a good way to emphasize your points and build a relationship with your listener.
● **Be aware of your facial expressions** Facial expressions are one of the first things people notice when they're talking to someone. Start every conversation with a clear mind, and try to be mindful of how your thoughts might be represented in your facial expressions.
● **Don't forget to smile** Not only does smiling make you more likeable, but studies show that it can also lift the moods of others around you.

There are advantages and disadvantages of nonverbal communication. It can be an important way of interacting with others by reinforcing the verbal message through eye contact, vocal tone, and posture. However, because we are usually unaware of the nonverbal messages we are sending, we are at risk of unintentionally conveying the wrong message, which, in turn, may give the wrong impression. There can also be confusion and discrepancies between the nonverbal cues we convey and the words we are saying. For example, you might tell your manager that you are happy to work late but defensive body language such as folded arms, downcast eyes, or legs crossed away from your manager will suggest otherwise.

Health care workers rely on positive nonverbal communication, such as smiling and direct eye contact, to show empathy to their patients. Research shows that patients who receive high nonverbal support demonstrate a greater tolerance for pain and recover more quickly. Showing nonverbal communication was particularly challenging for health care workers during COVID-19, when face masks and personal protective equipment interfered with nonverbal communication by suppressing facial expressions and body movements. Health care workers worked hard to overcome this obstacle by communicating with compassion, kindness, and empathy.[11]

Virtual Communication

Verbal and nonverbal communication also take place when we communicate virtually.

Virtual communication is the verbal exchange of information through email, videoconferencing, blogs, fax, instant messaging, texting, and social networking (Twitter, Snapchat, Slack, Viber, LinkedIn, Facebook, YouTube, Pinterest, Instagram, Zoom, and more). Despite the number of tools available, studies show that emails and texts make up 75% of all electronic communications between workers.[12] During COVID-19, more than half of global organizations increased their use of virtual communication channels, with live chat, email, and video the most popular choices for staying connected with their employees.[13] Table 14.2 lists some tips for videoconferencing etiquette.

There are advantages and disadvantages to virtual communication. We know that virtual communication is the best way of instantly reaching a large audience from anywhere in the world. However, written messages are also subject to misinterpretation, technical problems, and privacy breaches by hackers. Although almost 30% of our day is devoted to writing and responding to emails or other text-based communication, this form of communication is not for everyone. When Suzy Batiz, founder of bathroom spray Poo-Pourri, realized how much time and energy she was spending on writing and reading emails, she stopped, and told her team to communicate verbally instead. Batiz said, "I communicate best in person, so I've asked my team to pop in face-to-face if they have quick questions, which saves emails and improves communication."[14]

TABLE 14.2 ■ Video Conferencing Etiquette
1. Mute yourself when not speaking.
2. Be on time.
3. Ensure your technology works correctly.
4. Use technology to fully engage remote participants.
5. Choose the proper software and hardware.
6. Wear work-appropriate clothing.
7. Frame the camera correctly.
8. Have the right light.
9. Look into the camera.
10. Pay attention.

Source: Hart, M. (2020). *Video conferencing etiquette: 10 tips for a successful video conference.* Owllabs.com. https://resources. owllabs.com/blog/video-conferencing-etiquette

ENTREPRENEURIAL MINDSET ACTIVITY

Connect to a Great Communicator

We often see classmates, professors, celebrities, politicians, online personalities, and others who do a fantastic job communicating to their audience. Those still learning to be great communicators, speakers, and presenters can recognize this talent when they see it. While it is a great idea to pay close attention to these great communicators, those still improving their skillsets can go a step further. Your mindset activity is to locate two great communicators and then go out of your way to connect and network with them. The first should be someone whose style of personal communication strikes you as highly effective and talented, such as a great presenter to a class or a great lecturer. The second should be a person who has found great ways to communicate and spread messages on social and digital platforms; digital communication has become relevant in all fields and will continue to gain importance.

To complete this activity successfully, simply find a way to introduce yourself to each of these communicators. By engaging in this networking activity, you hone your ability to reach out to new people and network, and you gain two potential mentors and leaders who can share their best practices and advice with you. One day when you become a great communicator yourself, you can pass the favor on to another student who is in the process of studying your ability. There are digital platforms like LinkedIn that have made it very easy to find and reach out to peers and leaders, but nothing beats an in-person introduction. In the long run, every connection you meet could play an important role in your career or life, so it is great practice to begin finding people from whom you can learn and build a valuable relationship.

Critical Thinking Questions

1. What is one benefit of connecting to a couple of great communicators?
2. What did you learn from your connections about how to be a more effective communicator?
3. How can you practice your communication skills? Will your practice be different if you are communicating face to face or virtually?

BARRIERS TO EFFECTIVE COMMUNICATION

Every day, our ability to communicate is hampered by obstacles that impede our ability to transmit and receive messages accurately. **Barriers to communication** are obstacles that interrupt the flow of conveying and receiving messages. The most significant consequences of poor work communication include stress, miscommunication, conflict, delays, failure to complete a project, low morale, missed goals, and slower career progression.[15] It is essential that we understand the barriers that impede our communication so we can learn to overcome them. A survey from The Economist Intelligence Unit studying the effects of communication breakdowns at work across U.S. companies provides some insights into the causes and impacts on working life.[16] Let's take a look at the three of the most common barriers to communication reported by the survey together with some possible solutions (see Table 14.3 for a full list of the causes of poor communication).

1. **Different communication styles**

   According to the study, almost a third of millennials claim that they use social media and instant messaging at work every day; whereas only 12% of baby boomers use the same mode of communication. According to Medium.com, Gen Zers are more likely than any other generation to rank social media as one of their most used communication methods.[17] As mentioned earlier, because of the lack of body language and tone, instant messaging like texting or email and using social media to communicate can often lead to misinterpretation.

   Solution: To bridge the gap between generations, baby boomers could make an effort to use modern technology, and Gen Zers and millennials could try picking up the phone or engaging in more face-to-face interaction (especially when delivering emotional messages).

2. **Unclear responsibilities**

   Over one third of respondents said they had an unclear understanding of their roles and responsibilities, and almost 50% admitted they had limited understanding of the tasks and actions they needed to undertake following a meeting. In other words, the results of this survey suggested that managers did not effectively communicate responsibilities to the employees. Without a clear outline of their goals and duties, employees will struggle, which leads to poor performance and lack of productivity.

   Solution: The fewer people there are in the meeting room (eight or less) the more effective the meeting will be. Reducing the number of attendees provides better opportunities to define tasks and action items for everyone involved.

3. **Time pressures**

   The pressure of looming deadlines and quick work turnarounds can cause a high level of stress. This stress can impact our ability to think clearly and make rational decisions as well as our ability to communicate calmly and effectively. Emotions are heightened under stress and pressure, so we are more at risk of saying something we did not intend to say.

   Solution: If you're struggling to cope with stressful time pressures, then try and practice some exercises to control your anxiety. This involves anything from taking a break from whatever you're doing to focusing on your breathing until you feel calm enough to return to the task.

TABLE 14.3 ■ Causes of Poor Communication
● Different communication styles
● Unclear responsibilities
● Time pressures
● Lack of strong leadership
● Personal differences among colleagues
● Client demands
● Corporate culture
● Ineffective tools/technologies
● Financial pressures
● Use of jargon

Source: The Economist—Intelligence Unit. Communication barriers in the modern workplace. (2018). *The Economist.* https://eiuperspectives.economist.com/sites/default/files/EIU_Lucidchart-Communication%20barriers%20in%20the%20modern%20workplace.pdf

Listening

One of the chief barriers to communication is not really listening to what the other person is saying. Listening is the active effort to understand, learn, and derive information from others. Not paying attention can lead to misunderstandings that can create tension and potentially damage working relationships. If you don't listen, it simply creates a bad impression. The ability to listen is one of the most important skills you can have in business. Andrew Glincher, CEO and managing partner of law firm Nixon Peabody, learns and obtains information by listening. Glincher says, "I ask a lot of questions and really focus on the response. I don't learn much from what comes out of my mouth."[18] If you think you're a good listener, then you're probably in the minority. Research shows that the average speech rate is 150 words per minute, but we can only process about 35% of this communication.[19] It also doesn't help that humans have an average 8-second attention span, which means our minds tend to wander pretty quickly.[20] Without our full attention, messages get lost, or only half-remembered.

There are several different poor listening behaviors commonly practiced:

Defensive listening: a type of listening that occurs when the receiver of the message takes general statements as a personal attack. Rather than listening, the receiver is planning their reply.[21]

Offensive listening: a type of listening when the receiver tries to find fault in what is being said.[22]

Selective listening: a type of listening when the receiver only hears what they want to hear and ignores everything else being said.[23]

Pretending listening: a type of listening when the receiver is pretending to listen out of politeness rather than making an effort to understand or really converse with the sender.[24]

They might be common, but these types of listening behaviors are ineffective and even harmful to relationships. However, there is one type of listening that dramatically improves our ability to communicate. This type of listening is called active listening.

Active Listening

Active listening is the act of concentrating on the true meaning of what other people are saying. Studies show that active listeners have healthier relationships with others, are more productive, and have lower stress levels. It takes effort, persistence, and training to become an active listener.[25]

Many of us have a tendency to listen out of politeness rather than curiosity. If you have ever come away from a conversation without learning something interesting, then you weren't really listening. You can train yourself to listen by being curious. Hal Gregersen, executive director of the MIT Leadership Center, advises: "Each day, ask yourself, 'What am I going to be curious about?" This question keeps your mind open and interested during your interactions.[26]

Another barrier to effective listening is our tendency to enter a conversation with our own agenda, which also prevents us from listening effectively. Controlling your agenda involves quieting down your mind and really listening to what others are trying to say. If we don't turn off our agendas, we run the risk of missing out on important information.

Interrupting the speaker, agreeing or disagreeing too quickly without fully understanding what is being said, and second-guessing what the other person is about to say are also examples of poor listening. Although it is tempting to jump in with your own opinions before the speaker has finished, a key part of active listening is to wait until you are sure it is your turn to respond. Repeating back to the speaker or paraphrasing what you have heard is another useful way to ensure the message is being communicated and understood by each party. This also signals to the person that you are conversing with that you are, in fact, listening!

Active listening involves truly concentrating on what other people are saying, periodically paraphrasing what you hear, and waiting to speak until it is your turn to respond.

iStockphoto.com/fizkes

One of the best ways to improve your listening skills is to ask more questions than giving answers. Asking questions is a great way to give people the opportunity to share their own viewpoints and opinions. Try for a 2:1 ratio of listening to talking; in other words, listen twice as much as you talk. Scott Eblin, author of *Overworked and Overwhelmed: The Mindfulness Alternative,* believes that keeping track (via note-taking) of how much we talk in meetings versus how much we listen is a useful way to calculate our talk/listen ratio. Table 14.4 offers seven tips for becoming a better listener.

TABLE 14.4 ■   Tips for Becoming a Better Listener
1. Listen with purpose
2. Have a goal but not an overly prescribed agenda
3. Probe to learn more interesting information
4. Analyze how much time you spend talking versus listening
5. Paraphrase what you are hearing during the conversation
6. Don't interrupt; wait your turn to talk
7. Don't look around while listening

ETHICS IN BUSINESS

Fired for Posting on Facebook?

When do or should your personal social media posts impact your job? Here's the situation. A college employee posts inappropriate comments using hate speech related to women and abortion on their personal Facebook page. The post goes viral. Two days later, the employee is fired. The college claimed the post was threatening, condoning violence, and did not represent the college's values and culture. Those against the firing, including a human rights organization, claimed the firing was against the employee's First Amendment right to free speech.

Critical Thinking Questions

1. Should an employee be fired for posting on personal social media accounts if their comments do not align with the organization's values?
2. Should everything you write, say, or record online be protected by the First Amendment right to free speech?
3. If your job requires an online presence, how should you separate personal and professional posts?

COMMUNICATING IN ORGANIZATIONS

There is no doubt that communication between people can be complex and is often the cause of conflicts and misunderstandings. In this section, we explore how the different directions of communication affect the functioning of organizations.

Three Directions of Communication

The flow of communication in an organization can move in three main directions depending on how an organization is structured.[27] (See Figure 14.3.) Recall that we discussed different organizational structures in Chapter 9.

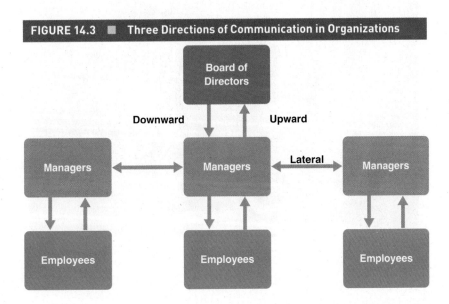

FIGURE 14.3 ■ Three Directions of Communication in Organizations

Downward Communication

Downward communication sends messages from the upper levels of the organizational hierarchy to the lower levels. An announcement about a new company acquisition sent as a message from senior levels to the rest of the staff would be an example of downward communication.

There are advantages and disadvantages of downward communication. Downward communication is a useful way to explain goals, ensure employee compliance and discipline through positive influence, improve efficiencies through the delivery of instructions and information, and boost transparency in relation to organizational performance, strategies, developments, and goals. However, a failure to transmit messages effectively from the upper levels down to the lower levels can cause confusion, distrust, and anxiety among employees throughout the company.

Upward Communication

Upward communication sends messages from the lower levels of the organizational hierarchy to the higher levels. Some examples of upward communication include suggestion boxes, employee satisfaction surveys, meetings with upper-level management, and focus groups.

There are advantages and disadvantages of upward communication. Upward communication builds trust and fosters good relationships between the upper and lower levels; provides an opportunity for staff to introduce their own thoughts, give feedback, and share ideas with senior management; and boosts confidence and morale among employees when their feedback is heard and applied. However, when lower-level employees do not communicate effectively with senior management or withhold information, then it can cause an inaccurate representation of what is really going on.

Lateral Communication

Lateral communication sends messages between and among similar levels across organizations. Two managers discussing an upcoming presentation is an example of lateral communication.

There are advantages and disadvantages of lateral communication. Lateral communication can be an effective way for people from different departments to communicate the information they need quickly and accurately. It can also encourage cooperation and collaboration between people across an organization. However, disadvantages include lack of managerial control, potential interpersonal conflict, and lack of discipline when too many participants collaborate at once.

Lateral communication is taking place in this advertising agency meeting for a CoverGirl campaign.

Associated Press/Kathy Willens

Formal and Informal Networks

Regardless of the direction of the flow of communication within organizations, most messages are sent through two main communication networks: formal and informal.[28]

Formal networks transmit the messages established and approved by executive management. Messages sent through formal lines of communication could be notification of policies and procedures to the rest of the staff. For example, when a CEO needs to tell employees about a new privacy policy, management could send the information in the form of an email.

In contrast, **informal networks** handle the unofficial sharing of information between employees and across company divisions. Members of informal networks may organize casual team events, create a union, or share their opinions of their bosses. One of the main forms of informal networks is the **grapevine**, the unofficial line of communication between individuals or groups.[29] Grapevines can be a useful method of communicating messages openly, quickly, and efficiently in person, and obtaining immediate feedback. Yet, in this system, word spreads rapidly, often leading to misinformation, distorted meaning, and rumor. Modern-day grapevines like social media posts or tweets have often resulted in termination. For instance, emergency room nurse Katie Duke was fired for using an insensitive caption on an Instagram post of a photo of a messy, empty trauma room previously used to treat a patient who had suffered serious injuries.[30]

Grapevines also give rise to **gossip chains** where employees spread information about other employees that may be true, false, or misleading—but likely should not be shared.[31] The receiver of the gossip either chooses to keep it confidential or passes it on to someone else. For example, in the instance of an employee getting fired, one employee might spread gossip to others to share their thoughts about the underlying reasons for the termination. True or false, the information moves very quickly and can be damaging to an organization and/or to an individual employee(s) regardless of management's efforts to confirm or deny the rumors.

How To Control Gossip

Studies show that as much as 90% of conversations and 15% of emails qualify as gossip.[32] Not all gossip is bad; it is a good way for people to air their grievances and frustrations to others who often make us feel better. However, spreading assumptions that are simply untrue can be damaging to a company and its employees. Although it is unrealistic to stop gossip altogether, it can be controlled by applying the following strategies:

- *Be honest and open:* If something major is about to happen (the shutting down of an office location or a merger with another organization), communicate quickly and clearly to those affected by using hard facts before they create their own version of the truth. Breaking unpleasant news is never easy, but better to defuse the panic before it begins.

- *Ask for opinions:* The only way to really understand what your people are talking about is to ask them. For instance, a plan to terminate one team member can cause widespread panic amongst the rest of the team if it is not handled properly. Showing concern by asking those affected questions before, during, and after the termination process is a great way of acquiring feedback, gauging morale, and preventing negativism.

- *Encourage social gatherings:* The more you get to know someone as a person rather than just a coworker, the less likely you are to gossip negatively about them. For example, creating opportunities to build positive relationships through company events and outings, introducing creative icebreakers at the start of team meetings, or holding one-on-one meetings with different colleagues in informal settings (such as a coffeehouse or restaurant).

Successful organizations actively control rumors and gossip through effective, honest, and consistent communication.[33]

CROSS-CULTURAL COMMUNICATION

In a globalized world, a large portion of business people will be required to communicate with workers from many different types of cultures. Research shows that effective cross-cultural communication, a field of study that explores how people from different cultures communicate, has been linked to positive financial performance, increased creativity, enhanced productivity, and innovation.[34] Building trust is key to effective cross-cultural communication. Studies show that smart executives do three things to establish trust:[35]

1. **Start with the right mindset**

   Business people understand that the process of building trust takes time, effort, and patience. They also take the time to absorb the implications of a high-trust culture and a low-trust culture. Typically, the U.S. is considered to be a high-trust culture, while countries like Argentina and Brazil are lower-trust cultures. High-trust cultures are characterized by interpersonal trust among members being relatively high whereas low-trust cultures involve conditions of low interpersonal trust. This is important to know, especially when it comes to people from high-trust cultures working in low-trust environments, who may become frustrated at the time it takes for trust to be established. Similarly, people from low-trust cultures might find it difficult to connect with people from high-trust cultures because of their different approach.

2. **Learn about different cultural backgrounds**

   Business people build trust by making the effort to learn about their colleagues' different cultural backgrounds. Some of this research involves establishing the level of trust in a culture (see above), the degree of performance expectation, and whether they have come from a hierarchical or autocratic culture. They also learn from the people in a particular culture how they build trust themselves. For instance, in a hierarchical culture, employees may feel reluctant to engage in open communication with their managers because they are used to a more top-down working environment.

3. **Understand the different factors central to building trust**

Finally, people who successfully build cross-cultural trust understand two main factors: whether trust is based on results, or whether it relies on a person's character. For example, in a high-trust culture like the U.S., workplace trust is generally based on results—an employee who completes projects and meets deadlines is more likely to be given more assignments because they are more trusted. In other cultures, trust might be built on character. For example, in Arab countries, most of the large organizations are family-owned because familial relationships are considered the most trustworthy.

The ability to communicate across different cultures is essential to building trust in organizations. Yet, all too often, employees at all levels lack the necessary preparation when it comes to communicating with and across different cultures, which can create barriers to cross-cultural communication.

As companies grow increasingly diverse, learning how to communicate cross-culturally is becoming more and more important. One important aspect of cross-cultural communication is learning about different cultural backgrounds.

Luis Alvares/DigitalVision/via Getty Images

Barriers to Cross-Cultural Communication

For cross-cultural teams to be successful, they must commit to open communication. But it isn't easy with so many barriers in the way. Let's take a look at some of the most common barriers to cross-cultural communication.

Ethnocentrism

One of the biggest obstacles to cross-cultural communication is ethnocentrism, the tendency to believe your culture or ethnicity is superior to everyone else's.[36] This can lead to friction between team members, especially when team members who are part of marginalized populations feel ignored, disparaged, or not taken seriously. Anxiety, uncertainty, stereotyping, and ethnocentrism are caused by lack of cultural knowledge and poor intercultural communication skills.[37]

If you think you might be an ethnocentric, consider learning more about language and culture to educate yourself. Some organizations offer cross-cultural training for employees who regularly communicate with people from different countries. If you show a genuine interest in people who come from a different country or culture, they will feel more appreciated and will likely be open to building a trusting relationship with you. A good start is simply asking, "What do you love most about your country?" The conversation is likely to flow from there.

Informal Language

Informal language can further complicate our communication with members of other countries.[38]

Slang, an informal language applied in a particular context or group, is not usually appropriate in business communication, as it has the potential to cause great confusion. For example, you may not get an enthusiastic response for calling someone a "jock" in the United Kingdom, given that "jock" is often used as derogatory slang for somebody from Scotland.

Euphemisms, mild words or expressions used in place for those considered to be too blunt or harsh, can also hamper cross-cultural communication. Popular business euphemisms such as "Let's circle back," or "We don't have the bandwidth," can be difficult to understand for people who have English as a second language.

Proverbs, or wise sayings, are also common to many different cultures. Common proverbs used in a U.S. business environment include: "A bad workman always blames his tools," and "Better late than never." Once again, this sort of language has the potential to cause confusion and even exclude people.

To avoid challenges and confusion, carefully consider the type of language you use when communicating with people from different cultures. If informal language is pretty typical in your organization, then take the time to explain what it means to minimize confusion.

Participation Norms

People from different cultures participate in team discussions in different ways. For example, team members from the U.S. or Australia are more likely to put forward their ideas than teammates from Japan, who might only speak up after the more senior colleagues in the room have shared their thoughts.

Useful methods to give everyone a fair chance of participating include: going around the table at least once; asking open-ended questions to encourage exploration of thoughts and ideas; keeping your own thoughts to yourself at first; or even applying the "four-sentence rule" (to limit the amount of air-time taken up by the more talkative team members).

Conflict

Healthy conflict is important between team members, but some people find it uncomfortable to engage in. For instance, people from Asian cultures, where "saving face" is paramount, are less willing to voice their disagreement for fear of upsetting group harmony. In contrast, people from Latin and Middle Eastern cultures may raise their voices and show passion to make a point.

To encourage healthy debate, you can appoint somebody neutral to control the discussion or by asking all the team members to offer the pros and cons of the points being made to open up the opportunity for people to argue both sides in the way they feel most comfortable.

Constructive Criticism

Constructive criticism is crucial to the successful operation of cross-cultural teams. Feedback is an important way to solve problems relating to anything from work performance, punctuality, and behavior. The context of a country's culture can impact the type of feedback given. In a low-context culture, communication takes place through explicitly spelled out and defined words, and listeners interpret spoken or written words as they are. Germany, Sweden, and the United States are generally classified as low-context cultures. On the other hand, in a high-context culture, nonverbal cues and unspoken background information are used along with explicit verbal expressions for successful communication. Therefore, listeners are often expected to understand spoken and written words based not only on the meaning of the words but also on voice tone, gesture, and context. People from high-context cultures choose more nuanced language when giving feedback, whereas people from low-context cultures prefer to use very direct language.[39]

With so many potential obstacles to avoid, communicating with different cultures can seem a daunting prospect. The more knowledge and understanding we have, the smoother and more successful communication will be.

IN REVIEW

14.1   Define communication and explain its importance in the workplace.

Communication is the act of transmitting information, thoughts, and processes through various channels. Effective communication conducted through regular meetings between managers and employees leads to higher engagement, productivity, and performance, and better staff retention. The Shannon-Weaver communications model is a useful way to understand how the process of communication works. The process relies on the interaction between eight main components: sender, message, receiver, encoder, decoder, channel, feedback, and noise.

14.2   Discuss various forms of communication.

Types of communication are generally split into two main categories: face-to-face communication and virtual communication. When we talk to people face to face or virtually, two forms of communication take place: verbal and nonverbal communication.

Verbal communication is the exchange of information, ideas, and processes through speech, either one on one or as a group. Nonverbal communication is the transmission of wordless behaviors and actions between people. Virtual communication is the verbal exchange of information through email, videoconferencing, blogs, fax, instant messaging, texting, and social networking.

14.3   Explore barriers to effective communication.

Barriers to communication are obstacles that interrupt the flow of conveying and receiving messages. Three of the most common barriers include different communication styles, unclear responsibilities, and time pressures. One of the chief barriers to communication is not really listening to what the other person is saying. Listening is the active effort to understand, learn, and derive information from others. Communication can be improved by active listening, which is the act of concentrating on the true meaning of what other people are saying. It takes effort, persistence, and training to become an active listener.

14.4   Illustrate the types of communication networks in organizations.

The flow of communication in an organization can move in three main directions, depending on how an organization is structured: downward communication, which sends messages from the upper levels of the organizational hierarchy to the lower levels; upward communication, which sends messages from the lower levels of the organizational hierarchy to the higher levels; and lateral communication, which sends messages between and among similar levels across organizations.

14.5   Discuss the importance of effective cross-cultural communication in the workplace.

Cross-cultural communication is a field of study that explores how people from different cultures communicate. Building trust is key to effective cross-cultural communication. Barriers to cross-cultural communication include: ethnocentrism, high-context and low-context cultures, informal language, participation norms, conflict, and constructive criticism.

BUSINESSES DISCUSSED IN THIS CHAPTER

Organization	UN Sustainable Development Goal
Autodesk	11. Sustainable Cities and Communities
Nixon Peabody	7. Affordable and Clean Energy
	8. Decent Work and Economic Growth
	15. Life on Land
Poo-Pourri	3. Good Health and Well-Being
	12. Responsible Consumption and Production

KEY TERMS

Active listening (p. 295)

Barriers to communication (p. 293)

Communication (p. 289)

Cross-cultural communication (p. 299)

Defensive listening (p. 295)

Downward communication (p. 297)

Electronic communication (p. 292)

Ethnocentrism (p. 300)

Euphemisms (p. 301)

Formal networks (p. 298)

Gossip chains (p. 298)

Grapevine (p. 298)

High-context cultures (p. 301)

Informal networks (p. 298)

Lateral communication (p. 298)

Listening (p. 295)

Low-context cultures (p. 301)

Nonverbal communication (p. 291)

Offensive listening (p. 295)

Pretending listening (p. 295)

Proverbs (p. 301)

Selective listening (p. 295)

Shannon-Weaver communications model (p. 289)

Slang (p. 301)

Upward communication (p. 297)

Verbal communication (p. 290)

Virtual communication (p. 292)

BUSINESS CASE 14.2 ALLBIRDS—SAN FRANCISCO, CALIFORNIA

SDG 5:   Gender Equality

Allbirds was founded in 2016 after its founder, Tim Brown, realized there was a lack of sustainable footwear options. As a former professional soccer player, Tim had been sponsored by major sneaker brands, so he was keenly aware of how pervasive synthetic materials were in the footwear market. As a native New Zealander, Tim was familiar with the versatility of merino wool, so Tim teamed up with Joey Zwillinger, an engineer and sustainability expert in the U.S., and the two began working on a sustainable, comfortable shoe, launched as the Wool Runners, made out of New Zealand merino wool. The comfortable and sustainable shoes were an instant success, and Allbirds quickly became one of the fastest-growing shoe companies in the world. Just 2 years after launch, Allbirds sold its one millionth pair of shoes. It could be argued that effective communication is one of the keys to Allbirds' success.

Early on, customers reported that wool, although comfortable and cozy, was not necessarily the ideal fabric for warmer months and climates. Allbirds listened to its customers and began expanding its search for sustainable materials. Today, the Allbirds product lines include shoes made from a variety of sustainable materials designed to keep feet cool, including eucalyptus, plant leather, sugar cane, and other recyclable, renewable materials in addition to merino wool.

Listening to customers has always been part of Allbirds's direct-to-customer (DTC) model. The company primarily uses social media platforms like Instagram to gather customer feedback and new product ideas. According to Tim, only "a small amount" of sales come from social media advertising, and most of the company's success can be attributed to word of mouth among consumers. Like other direct-to-consumer brands, Allbirds obtains most of its website traffic directly from search results.

While Allbirds's DTC model has been extremely successful in the United States, the company had to change its approach when launching in other countries, since customer behavior and expectations can vary significantly by culture. For example, Allbirds had to relinquish control over its distribution model and partner with Alibaba Tmall in order to establish itself in China. According to Christina Fontana, head of fashion and luxury at Tmall, "One of the biggest mistakes brands make is not studying and understanding the Chinese consumer. . . . Brands also need to communicate the core value of [their] brand to Chinese consumers. And never underestimate how much communication is necessary to do that."

Allbirds's message of minimalist design worked well in the United States, but it did not translate as well to the China market, where tastes differed. The company quickly learned that Chinese customers were less attracted by the sustainability message. When Allbirds started communicating that the wool upper part of the shoe was produced at the same factories as luxury Italian brands, Chinese customers paid attention and paid for the product!

Though Allbirds modified its brand messaging for China, its internal focus on building a simplistic, fashion-forward shoe using sustainable materials never wavered.

Consequently, in its 2020 Sustainability Report, Allbirds outlined its strategic priorities to "reverse climate change through better business." At the foundation of those strategic priorities are fair labor, diversity, and gender equality. As part of its commitment to gender equality, Allbirds outlined the following initiatives:

- Conduct wage analysis for all manufacturing and supplier partners
- Ensure proper channels exist for the supply chain and factory workers to voice concerns
- Create programs across the employee life cycle to cultivate a culture that increases diversity, equity, inclusion, and belonging
- Foster a sense of belonging through international communications where "all birds feel welcomed, included, and proud to work at Allbirds"
- Support employee resource groups for women, LGBTQ+ employees, parents, and multicultural employees

Allbirds acknowledges that it has more work to do when it comes to gender and racial diversity at upper levels of leadership within the company. Currently, only 31% of Allbirds leadership is female globally, and only 26% are people of color in the United States. Allbirds is committed to increasing both percentages to 40% by 2025.

Critical Thinking Questions

1. What role has communication played in Allbirds's success in the footwear industry?

2. How did Allbirds adjust its communication when expanding into China?

3. What are some initiatives that Allbirds could undertake to promote gender equality?

References

Allbirds. (2021, September 10). *2020 sustainability report.* Allbirds. https://cdn.allbirds.com/image/upload/v16251 61698/marketing-pages/Allbirds_Sustainability_Report_2020.pdf

Allbirds. (n.d). *Our story.* Allbirds. https://www.allbirds.com/pages/our-story

Allbirds. (n.d). *Sustainable practices: Renewable materials.* Allbirds. https://www.allbirds.com/pages/renewable-materials

Butler-Young, S. (2020, January 23). *For comfort brand Allbirds, an entry into China has meant being a bit . . . uncomfortable.* Footwear News. https://footwearnews.com/2020/business/retail/allbirds-tmall-china-alibaba-120290 9449/

Gainnoulis, S., Strang, E., & Mack, B. (2018, April 13). *Wool for the trees.* Idealog. https://www.pressreader.com/new-zealand/idealog/20180413/page/82/textview

Sentence, R. (2021, February 9). *How Allbirds has been successful in both the west and China.* Econsultancy. https://econsultancy.com/how-allbirds-has-been-successful-in-both-the-west-and-china/

Similarweb. (2022, May). *Allbirds.com.* Similarweb. https://www.similarweb.com/website/allbirds.com/#demo graphics

Stern, J. (2018, November 27). *In the elevator with Allbirds CEO Tim Brown: These shoes might be edible.* [Video]. The Wall Street Journal. https://www.wsj.com/video/series/in-the-elevator-with/in-the-elevator-with-allbirds-ceo-tim-brown/65922B58-8F17-4F13-927B-E48D29840CA0

BLOCK 5
PERFORMANCE

15 BUSINESS OPERATIONS

15.1   Define operations and its critical role in running an efficient business.

15.2   Describe product operations and the importance of maintaining quality in the production process.

15.3   Identify various production methods used in operations.

15.4   State the various quality control methods used in production.

15.5   Discuss the role of service operations in building a quality customer experience.

15.6   Explore digital operations as the next frontier in operations for all types of companies.

15.7   Evaluate the role of supply chain management in operations.

BUSINESS IMPACT CASE 15.1: STARBUCKS—SEATTLE, WASHINGTON

SDG 6:   Clean Water and Sanitation

Starbucks is a global brand known for its streamlined operations and consistent, quality service. As a massive coffee chain with 15,000 stores across 50 countries, Starbucks is rated by research firms as operating one of the most efficient and profitable supply chain operations of any Fortune 500 company.[1] Founded in Seattle, Washington, in 1971, it has grown to become the most dominant brand in its industry, and its rise to dominance has been partially attributed to its world-class attention to operations management.

Starbucks's operations revolve around digital technology, centralized systems, waste reduction, and sustainable, diverse supplier ecosystems. For example, its logistics and shipping network spans six continents as well as multiple distribution centers throughout the United States, Europe, and Asia. To keep efficiency levels high throughout its disparate, global operations, Starbucks leadership employs a single scorecard, based on a set of metrics, by which it rates and scores its own facilities.[2] Metrics used by operations teams track safety statistics, delivery, and fulfillment rates, total costs, and total savings. By leveraging advanced information technology (IT) systems to track these metrics, Starbucks can notice changes, threats, mistakes, and identify innovative ideas for operational and efficiency improvements. At the end of the long Starbucks supply chain is a cup of coffee: one that provides the same taste produced with the highest-quality controls on any given day at any given location, across its more than 30,000 stores worldwide.

Given the global scope of the company, Starbucks has launched a number of initiatives to make a positive impact on the world throughout its supply chain. With a commitment to sustainability, Starbucks launched the Ethos Water Fund to address global water shortages. Over 1 billion people still do not have access to clean drinking water.[3] Starbucks donates 5 cents for every bottle of Ethos water sold to fight global water challenges. Five cents may not sound like a lot, but it adds up quickly. Since launching the Ethos water brand, the Starbucks Foundation has granted more than $12 million to support clean water, sanitation, and hygiene education programs in struggling countries. The program has positively impacted more than 500,000 people so far.

In addition to the Ethos fund, Starbucks actively pursues renewable energy sources in an effort to boost operational and global sustainability. The company sets self-imposed guidelines such as serving drinks in reusable or recycled containers.[4] As a massive organization, slight changes to its operations have large effects over time, and Starbucks produces large amounts of plastic, paper, and pollutant waste, something that the company is actively trying to address through its sustainability goals, even when those changes come at a significant financial cost. Because of the size of Starbucks's operations and supply chain networks, implementing ambitious goals like these takes a highly advanced and well-run team of departments and leaders.

Starbucks has laid the groundwork to make these changes by being efficient and adaptive, continuously finding as many ways as it can to grow the company while recognizing its role in helping humanity.

Critical Thinking Questions

1. What are some of the metrics Starbucks tracks in order to ensure its supply chain operations are running smoothly and efficiently?

2. What is one of the programs Starbucks created to make sustainable, positive impacts on the global community?

3. Supply chain management will be defined later in this chapter, but after reading about Starbucks, what do you think a supply chain is?

THE OPERATIONS BEHIND RUNNING A BUSINESS

The opening case illustrates Starbucks's commitment to efficiency and sustainability through its business operations. Operations refers to the wide range of activities that businesses engage in to keep a company running and earn a profit. In other words, operations are the internal engine that powers companies and includes everything from invoicing clients, as in the case of a law firm, to a consumer products company manufacturing products, like Procter & Gamble, that are shipped around the world to retailers, such as Target. Smooth-running, efficient operations are essential for all companies and critical for business success. For Starbucks, business operations involves leveraging digital technology, centralized systems, waste reduction, and an integrated, transformative supply chain, which has allowed the company to grow and adapt while simultaneously making a positive impact on the environment and the global community. Today, Starbucks has continued to respond to consumer desire for convenience and seamless delivery by integrating more digital initiatives into its operations, such as Pickup—an app that enables mobile ordering, payment, and delivery.[5]

Operations managers are key personnel in upper-level management. They seek to maximize productivity and efficiency by empowering employees to achieve company-wide goals. Operations managers are also responsible for monitoring the company's production processes to reduce the costs of materials, labor, and technology, in addition to eliminating costs that may add little to no value to the completed product. For example, when Jag Bath joined as CEO of on-demand food delivery service Favor with the goal to grow and scale the business, he had to make some tough operations decisions.[6] Although Favor remained popular in Austin, Texas, it lacked the funding to compete effectively against other companies in most of the cities into which it had expanded. Jag made the difficult decision to close down operations in all markets except in Texas to save time, effort, and capital involved in running the business outside Austin. Jag said, "It was the hardest decision I've ever made. You worry a lot about the people you have to let go, but you also worry about the people who stay, because you have to continue to motivate them." By doubling down in Texas and solely focusing on Texas markets, Favor was able to create a more efficient operations system, which allowed it to expand its delivery coverage in Texas. Thanks to this strategy of "thinking small," Favor became profitable within a year, has 300 employees, and operates in 130 markets (all in Texas).

Converting Inputs Into Outputs

For a company to compete successfully within an industry, it must convert resources into goods or services as efficiently as possible. Typically, an operations manager directs this process by transforming inputs into outputs, also known as the production process (see Figure 15.1). For example, Starbucks's inputs include human resources (people), facilities and processes (roasting plants, warehouses), technology (data and digital technology), raw materials (coffee beans), and other materials (paper cups, stone cups, lids), which are converted into outputs such as goods (a cup of high-quality, fair-trade coffee and other products) and services (retail and café space) to meet customer desires and demands.

Companies like Starbucks must work hard to continually improve their production processes by focusing on quality, and eliminating or reducing costs without sacrificing that quality.

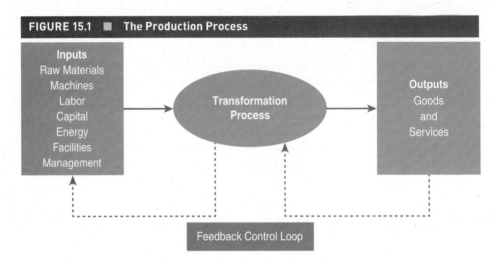

FIGURE 15.1 ■ The Production Process

How Operations Function in Different Industries

The type of operations depends on the industry in which a business is operating. The following are some examples of how operations function in different industries:[7]

Retail Business Operations

In a retail business, the primary focus is to ensure there is enough product in stock for customers, with items priced appropriately for the target market. From an operations perspective, this involves managing and optimizing inventory to analyze the items that are selling well, or not selling at all, and consider price adjustments. Many companies use operations software programs to manage inventory in real time. Such software is often integrated into the POS (Point of Sale) system, which is the modern-day version of the cash register.

Restaurant Business Operations

Like retail businesses, food businesses also need to focus on inventory as part of their operations. But unlike most retail businesses that sell "things," restaurants sell food and beverages, so there is an even greater need to keep track of food costs, reduce food waste, and ensure timely delivery of fresh food so that high-quality meals are served to customers. Restaurant operations generally involve purchasing, preparation, and pricing, in addition to training staff to provide the best customer experience at your restaurant.

Service Company Business Operations

Service companies such as airlines, banks, or accounting firms provide services instead of selling physical products. They divide their operations into two main areas: client-facing and business-related. Operations for the client-facing side might involve figuring out how to optimize your client interactions; for instance, improving the customer experience by eliminating any unnecessary or unwanted notifications from the company. For the business side, operations might involve investigating how business processes impact the services offered and the projects bring managed, and finding solutions to any problems. An example of an operational concern in this instance would be client projects that are consistently coming in over budget. One way to address this concern is to review the processes used to calculate the budget at the beginning of the project and make the necessary adjustments. Part of Starbucks's client-facing service operations is to create a positive experience for its customers by fostering a welcoming atmosphere, providing digital solutions such as ordering on the Starbucks app, and offering new options beyond the standard coffee drinks.[8]

Product Business Operations

Companies that make physical products such as cars, furniture, computers, and so on, focus on adding efficiencies to their operations wherever possible. This might involve assessing how goods are purchased, stored, manufactured, and delivered to customers and finding ways to improve certain processes such as eliminating bottlenecks, improving transportation, and negotiating better terms from suppliers. A **supplier** is an individual or an organization that provides particular types of goods. A reason why so many U.S. companies are manufacturing in China, Mexico, and other countries is that the cost of labor is significantly lower, which allows these companies to price their products lower in the U.S. market. Apple, for example, designs its products in California, but they are assembled in China. The workforce available in China can assemble 500,000 iPhones per day, which is not possible in the United States. For example, Apple's assembly factory in Zhengzhou, China employs 230,000 people.[9]

Digital Business Operations

Digital companies focus on using technology to create digital products such as websites, apps, and other tools. Operations in digital companies tend to focus on monitoring processes and software used for coding products, and streamlining collaboration between teams to ensure everything is running smoothly and efficiently.

Although some companies just focus on product, others on services, and others on digital, the growing trend for larger companies is to focus on all three types of operations for overall efficiency. The following sections explore product operations, services operations, and digital operations in greater depth.

PRODUCT OPERATIONS

During the production process managers must continually schedule and monitor activities to ensure the smooth running of operations. **Product operations** is an operational function that sits at the intersection of manufacturing, marketing, sales, and product development, and helps to improve the go-to-market and customer experience.

Product operations, and the role it plays, varies from business to business, but in this section we are going to focus on the manufacturing and production aspects of operations. Other sections in this chapter will focus on the customer side. In the case of manufacturing companies, product operations has an area called **production control,** which is the task of coordinating people, materials, and machinery to provide maximum production efficiency. By creating a well-defined set of procedures, operations managers will be able to solicit and respond to feedback and make adjustments where needed. There are five main steps in the production control process: production planning, routing, scheduling, dispatching, and follow up.

Step 1: Production Planning

Production planning is the stage of production control that determines the amount of resources (raw materials, staff, and equipment) required by an organization to fulfill sales orders and produce a certain output. Production planning is particularly important in the food industry, where more than 1 billion tons of food are wasted every year.[10] Efficient planning can help reduce food waste by matching the quantity of food to customer demand.

Production planning is important in the food industry to prevent waste. However, restaurant owners could never have planned for the initial COVID-19 pandemic lockdowns, which caused many restaurants to donate or toss food they could no longer serve.

Joe Raedle/Getty Images News/via Getty Images

Step 2: Routing

Routing is the second stage of production control that determines the sequence of work throughout the facility and makes decisions about who will perform each task at what location. Think of routing as simply the most efficient way of getting from point A to B to C and so on in the production process.

Routing choices depend on two factors: the type of good or service, and the type of facility layout. Efficient routing procedures help to boost productivity and reduce costs. For example, awning manufacturer Rader Awning & Upholstery, based in New Mexico, automated some of its routing operations by using value-stream mapping—a process that provides a visual representation of all the steps in a work process—to automate some of its operations. This new process allowed Rader Awning & Upholstery to evaluate how orders were routed from sales to manufacturing over 2 days. Thanks to the insights generated by value-stream mapping, the company was able to correct inconsistencies, which led to enhanced productivity, less production defects, and fewer installation corrections.

Step 3: Scheduling

Scheduling is the third stage of production control where managers develop timetables specifying how each operation in the production process takes place and when employees perform what tasks. Efficient scheduling ensures that production meets prescribed deadlines, resources are used effectively, and delivery dates are met.

Step 4: Dispatching

Dispatching is the fourth step of the production control process in which the operations manager instructs each department on the type of work that needs to be done and the amount of time allowed for its completion. Amazon runs one of the most efficient dispatching systems in the world. As soon as an order is received, it is picked up in one of the company's vast warehouses and placed on a conveyor belt where it is scanned, weighed, and labeled. Depending on the delivery location, the item may be transported by truck or plane. Amazon also has teams of drivers on the ground to support the delivery of products. The industry giant is constantly exploring ways to improve the dispatching process, including the use of drones to fly packages directly to customers' homes.

Step 5: Follow Up

The final step in the production control process is the follow-up stage, where managers and employees or team members exchange feedback, trouble-shoot problems, and discuss potential solutions.

TYPES OF PRODUCTION METHODS

Operations managers use different types of production methods to determine how and where goods are produced. The type of production method depends on the type of product being manufactured and the amount of raw materials involved. There are various types of production methods: make to order, mass production, mass customization, continuous production, lean manufacturing, agile manufacturing, and additive manufacturing.

Make to Order

Make to order is a type of production method where the product is made only after an order has been placed. This method is typically used by companies that make low-volume, expensive, highly customized products. Sometimes producing these products requires a lot of skill, mainly because the work is more manual than mechanical. For example, motorbike manufacturer Harley-Davidson provides customers with a unique product by offering a service that gives them the opportunity to customize their bikes and accessories. Similarly, but on the lower-cost end, bag company Timbuk2 allows customers to customize backpacks and messenger bags using different colors and fabrics.

Harley-Davidson allows customers to customize their bikes, like this V-Twin motorcycle.

Robert Nickelsberg/Archive Photos/via Getty Images

Mass Production

Mass production is a type of production method in which large quantities of standardized products are made at a low cost, using assembly lines or other automated technology. Goods are made based on forecasting models designed to anticipate inventory need in order to fulfill projected sales. Ford

famously adopted a mass production process in its car manufacturing process by creating an assembly line composed of multiple work stations. Workers each had their own specialized tasks to complete before the product was moved on to the next station. Mass production requires huge initial investment up front, but it is an efficient method of producing large volumes of products that are exactly the same. However, unlike the make to order method, there is no room for customization. Mass-produced products are all around us. Technology, like your smartphone to the computer you may be using to read this book, is a product of mass production. Food such as the popular snack Cheeze-Its, to the soda you grab out of your refrigerator, is mass produced. The shirt you might have bought at The Gap, socks at Target, and the sneakers you wear around town are all mass produced. Most everyday items are mass produced.

Ford engages in mass production in its car manufacturing process. An assembly line like this one in Chicago consists of multiple work stations.

JIM YOUNG/AFP via Getty Images

Mass Customization

Mass customization is a type of production method in which high quantities of customized products are made at a low cost. Companies liaise with customers to find out their customization specifications and then manufacture the products as inexpensively as possible. They may also use this method to mass produce a product first and then customize it according to customer demands. For example, sports footwear giant Nike offers a "Nike by You" service that allows its customers to customize some of its footwear, and M&Ms manufactured by confectionery company Mars Inc. offers a service where customers can design their own M&Ms by choosing their own colors, messages, and patterns.

Continuous Production

Continuous production is a type of production method where products made from basic materials are continuously processed, 24/7, all year round. Although continuous production and mass production are often confused, there is an important difference between the two methods: In mass production, humans and machines work alongside each other, whereas in continuous production, most of the work is conducted by machines. A good example of continuous production is beer brewing. Basic raw materials such as wort (a combination of malt extract and water) is input continuously into the machines and beer flows out the other end. This is an efficient way to manufacture goods; as the machines run continuously, it saves on the cost and energy associated with repeatedly shutting down and resetting them. It also saves on the cost of labor because production is mostly carried out by machines. However, unlike other production methods, continuous production does not allow for any customization, which could be a disadvantage in today's customer-driven markets.

Lean Manufacturing

Lean manufacturing is the implementation of best practices to eliminate inefficiencies and waste while increasing profit.[11] Table 15.2 defines eight types of waste in lean manufacturing: transport, inventory, motion, waiting, overproduction, overprocessing, defects, and unutilized talent. The main principles of the lean approach include using flexible and up-to-date technology, educating employees on the lean methodology and philosophy, training employees in all areas, instilling a sense of commitment, and shifting cultural values to embrace the lean model. In a lean company, there is a strong emphasis on quality.[12]

TABLE 15.2 ■ The Eight Wastes of Lean Manufacturing

Transport	Inventory	Motion	Waiting
Time and resources wasted when moving products unnecessarily	Waste associated with surplus products and materials	Time and effort wasted by unnecessary movement of workers from one place to another	Waste of time due to workers waiting for others to complete their step in the process
Overproduction	**Overprocessing**	**Defects**	**Unutilized Talent**
Waste left over from companies producing higher quantities of products than customers demand	Time wasted by work that is done before it is needed	Mistakes and errors in products that fail to meet customer expectations, resulting in waste	Talent waste due to failure to utilize workers' talents, skills, and knowledge

Source: Adapted from Skhmot, N. (2017). The 8 wastes of lean. *The Lean Way.* https://theleanway.net/The-8-Wastes-of-Lean

Agile Manufacturing

Agile manufacturing is closely related to lean manufacturing. Although the terms "*lean* and *agile* tend to be used interchangeably, there is an important difference: Lean manufacturing focuses on streamlining processes to reduce waste to create more value for the customer, while agile manufacturing is a business approach that creates value for customers by rapidly responding to changes.[13]

Agile manufacturing originated from the world of software development in 2001 by a group of software engineers who created a manifesto designed to unearth improved methods of developing software. The ideas they outlined have since been applied to many different types of industries to create more value for the customer through the use of technology. An agile approach has become essential for companies competing in a constantly evolving environment. Companies need to adapt to new technology to keep up with changing customer needs and market fluctuations.

Toyota was one of the first organizations that successfully applied the lean model in its manufacturing process, and those principles have greatly influenced the agile approach. Toyota has not only eliminated waste but has made processes more flexible, efficient, and error-free by ensuring continual quality checks of its products. For example, Toyota staff members are given full authority to halt operations during the manufacturing process if they find a problem. The process resumes only when the problem is addressed, preventing potential quality issues.[14]

Additive Manufacturing

Additive manufacturing (also known as 3D printing) is the process of using technology by adding layers of materials to create 3D objects. For example, car manufacturer General Motors (GM) is integrating 3D printing technology in its operations to boost production speed and agility. Audley Brown, GM director of Additive Design and Materials Engineering, said, "Compared to traditional processes, 3D printing can produce parts in a matter of days versus weeks or months at a significantly lower cost."[15]

During the COVID-19 pandemic, large and small industrial companies used additive manufacturing to design products to support the health care industry, including concrete isolation rooms for people to isolate in the absence of hospital space, contactless door openers to prevent the transmission of the virus, and supplying emergency respirators to hospitals for COVID-19 patients.[16]

ETHICS IN BUSINESS

The Manufacturing Quandary: Produce at Home or Abroad?

You've been making really cool backpacks by hand for friends and family. The fabrics you use are from sustainable sources, and your designs are trendy and attract a lot of attention. You've decided to take the plunge and start a real business, but you need to figure out how you can get more bags produced rather than using family and friends sewing in your basement! Advisers have encouraged you not to manufacture in the United States because of high costs. You could consider manufacturing your backpacks in a different country, where the costs of production would be significantly less as the cost of labor is much lower. For example, 1 hour of manufacturing labor in the United States can average $20 per hour, but the cost of labor in China is $6.50 per hour, Mexico $4.82 per hour, and Vietnam $2.99 per hour.[17] However, you have concerns about the quality of the production, and the working conditions for employees in some of these manufacturing facilities. You know that some countries use child labor, impose long working hours, and have harsh working conditions. You are also aware that many of your competitors manufacture their products overseas as well.

Critical Thinking Questions

1. As founder of your company, is it ethical to have your company's products produced in a country where the workers are making very low wages and working under very poor conditions?
2. Given that many of your competitors produce backpacks overseas, how would you compete if you chose to manufacture your products in the United States? What benefits might you enjoy over your competition?
3. What's your decision and why?

QUALITY CONTROL

Throughout the entire production process, operations managers are directly involved in efforts to ensure that goods successfully meet specifications and that quality standards are maintained. Quality refers to the degree to which the characteristics of a product or service satisfies a specific set of expectations (from a customer perspective) or specifications (from the manufacturing perspective). For example, when you buy a smartphone, you expect to use it to make calls, email, use social media, and so on.

When some of these functions don't work, you question the quality of the product. Similarly, when you go to a restaurant, you expect to be served in a reasonable amount of time. When the wait time goes on too long, you are likely to conclude that you're the recipient of poor-quality service.

Poor-quality products and services can have a detrimental impact on any business, resulting in lost revenues and a damaged reputation. When customers lose confidence in a company, they will simply move elsewhere to buy their goods. South Korean carmaker Hyundai suffered severe blows to its reputation following allegations of a number of safety defects flagged by a whistleblower.[18] These safety lapses led to a recall of over 240,000 vehicles. Samsung Securities auto analyst Eim Eun-young said, "[Hyundai's] . . . reputation is already seen at the rock bottom in South Korea, so I am not sure whether there is room for a further fall." Companies like Hyundai need to work hard to address quality concerns if they are to win back customer confidence.

The concept of Total Quality Management (TQM) has been a mainstay philosophy in business operations. TQM is based on the principle that employees at all levels (from entry-level hourly workers to top executives) be committed to maintaining high standards of work in every aspect of a company's operations. There are several popular methods connected to the TQM philosophy that companies employ to monitor, evaluate, and ensure high levels of quality throughout their operations. These are: continuous improvement, statistical quality control, and Six Sigma and Lean Six Sigma.

Continuous Improvement

Continuous improvement is the ongoing improvement of the design, production, and delivery of a company's products and services. St. Mary's General Hospital in Kitchener, Ontario (Canada), successfully created a culture of continuous improvement by engaging front-line nurses to identify and resolve problems, and selecting board members who were fully committed to continuous improvement. Thanks to these measures, the number of patients who fell out of bed or while walking dropped by 80% in a year and St. Mary's is considered to be one of the highest-performing hospitals in Canada for patient safety.[19]

Statistical Quality Control (SQC)

Statistical quality control (SQC) is the use of statistics taken from samples from production runs for the sole purpose of determining production quality. This could be a sample of chocolate, water, frozen pizza, shampoo, lotion, toothpaste—you name it! SQC is mostly used in the manufacturing industry to gauge the effectiveness of the output of manufacturing processes. Managers applying SQC study a variety of charts, graphs, and other methods to analyze statistical information to ensure that quality is maintained within the standard range of acceptability.

Assume you run a gluten-free cookie business and you advertise 50 chocolate chips in every chocolate chip cookie. How can you test to determine whether this goal is being met? You could use a statistical process control method called a sampling distribution. On a periodic basis, you would take a sample of cookies off the production line and measure the amount of chocolate chips in each cookie. Then you'd record that amount on a control chart designed to compare actual quantities of chips with the desired quantity (50 count). If your chart shows that several samples in a row are low on chocolate chips, you'd shut down the production line and take corrective action.

Six Sigma and Lean Six Sigma

Many service and manufacturing organizations also adopt the principles of Six Sigma, a business management strategy designed to analyze the causes of defects, using statistical methods. Originally introduced by Motorola and popularized by GE, the Six Sigma philosophy has become a standard in TQM and adopted by many companies.

Six Sigma also promotes the five-step methodology of define, measure, analyze, improve, and control (DMAIC), a data quality-driven strategy used to improve processes (see Table 15.1).[20] Amazon, Ford, and 3M are just a few examples of organizations that use Six Sigma methodology to ensure the highest level of quality operations.

TABLE 15.1 ■ DMAIC Methodology

1. *Define.* Identify the problem and analyze customer feedback and requirements to understand the types of improvements that need to be made.

2. *Measure.* Evaluate the process by using maps or charts to analyze the frequency of the problem.

3. *Analyze.* Investigate the process to determine the underlying causes of the problem and develop theories to explain the reasons behind the problem.

4. *Improve.* Find ways to improve the process by brainstorming solutions, running experiments for positive change, and collecting data to confirm an improvement.

5. *Control.* Sustain the improvement by creating a plan to continuously measure the newly implemented solution to ensure standards are kept at an acceptable level.

Source: De Mast, J., & Lokkerbol, J. (2012). An analysis of the Six Sigma DMAIC method from the perspective of problem solving. *International Journal of Production Economics, 139*(2), 604–614.

Lean Six Sigma is a combination of lean manufacturing (discussed earlier in this chapter) and Six Sigma. This approach focuses on problem-solving by eliminating waste while also improving processes. Akron-Canton Regional Foodbank, based in Ohio, used Lean Six Sigma methodology to improve its donations processes.[21] Before Lean Six Sigma, it was taking an average of 92 days for donations to make it into the hands of the needy. After applying the methodology, the time was reduced to 39 days. Although this is a huge improvement, the Akron-Canton staff are still striving to do better, particularly by applying new measures to the sorting, inspecting, packing, and delivering processes.

SERVICE OPERATIONS

Service operations is an operational function intended to support the customer support team, customer experience team, and customer success team by developing strategies designed to attract, engage, and delight customers. The function also includes providing tools and systems to customer support departments that enable them to monitor customer feedback, track customer engagement, and offer a positive customer experience. Most companies have sales and marketing teams, but not all companies have a service operations department, particularly small and mid-sized companies. Yet a service operations team is essential for operational quality.

Key roles in a service operations team include data analysts, customer operations strategists, and customer analysts who work alongside internal team members to ensure the organization is prepared to deliver the best customer experience.[22] The following section outlines more service operations roles and responsibilities.

Measure Customer Feedback

Service operations teams can measure customer feedback through a variety of surveys, such as an NPS (Net Promoter Score) survey—a one-question survey that measures customer loyalty and satisfaction by assessing how likely customers are to recommend your business to a friend. A typical question would be, "On a scale of zero to 10, how likely is it that you would recommend [Company Name] to a friend or colleague?"[23] Depending on the score given by the customer, they will be labeled either a promoter (high score), passive (middle score), or detractor (low score). Then subtracting the promoters from the detractors gives you the NPS, which is a more refined understanding of loyalty and even perceived quality. NPS ranges from +100 to ‾100. Above 0 is good, above 20 is favorable, above 50 is excellent, and above 80 is world class. Apple, for example, has one of the highest NPSs at 61![24,25]

NPS is just one way to capture customer feedback. Sending out more in-depth surveys, conducting interviews, monitoring reviews online, and hosting focus groups are all ways to gather feedback. Keep in mind, however, measurement without action is not good operations. Data are only useful if they produce information that is usable! We will focus more on data in Chapter 16.

Report on Customer Data

Service operations teams are responsible for developing new and managing existing customer data, and reporting on these data to enable the organization to make strategic decisions. A customer service report includes data such as average response times to customer queries, the number of service requests from customers, the length of time it takes to handle those requests, and NPS scores. When used effectively, customer service reports can improve a company's response times, enhance customer loyalty, and identify opportunities for further staff training.[26]

Manage Technology

Technology is one of the main methods used by companies to communicate with their customers. Service operations teams work closely with front-line customer service teams to ensure internal systems and processes are running smoothly and make sure that external technology tools such as chat platforms, self-service support, and messaging are operating at peak efficiency levels. For example, German bike manufacturer Canyon Bicycles supports customers who speak different languages by connecting them with salespeople on chat platforms who speak in the customers' preferred language.[27]

Strategize Positive Customer Experience

Service operations teams give a lot of attention to understanding and managing the customer journey. By understanding every interaction a customer has with the company, teams can work to provide a better overall customer experience from beginning to end. Some organizations create a customer journey map, a visual representation that captures customer experience across multiple touchpoints of the business. This method allows companies to connect to customers on an emotional level and provide the optimal customer experience by addressing and resolving key pain points. Figure 15.2 illustrates a retail customer journey map showing each stage of the buying process and identifying pain points along the way.

Support Customer Onboarding

Customer onboarding is the process of welcoming new customers to your business by guiding them through their purchases and addressing any queries or concerns. Service operations teams work closely with customer success teams and sales operations to provide the necessary information to build a long-term relationship with new customers. As part of its customer onboarding process, graphic-design site Canva asks new users their reasons for using the site by presenting different categories such as Teacher, Student, Small Business, Large Company, and so on. Once users make their selection, Canva provides them with the most relevant tools, support, and templates for their design project, enabling them to get started instantly.[28]

DIGITAL OPERATIONS

The rise of the digital economy has provided organizations with the opportunity to build innovative new products, services, and experiences to keep up with evolving customer demand. Digital services have become an integral part of our daily lives, influencing everything from how we buy, sell, work, learn, and much more. An essential part of operations for all organizations is to build teams focused on developing long-term relationships with customers by listening and responding to their needs, creating new and innovative methods to enhance their experience, and engaging them as long-term customers. Digital operations is the concept of digitizing and integrating business processes across the organization to improve customer and employee experience.[29] It plays a key role in accelerating organizational agility by providing the necessary tools and technologies to quickly adapt to market changes. Companies with agile, intelligent, digitally enabled processes have a greater ability to improve the user experience, optimize the customer journey, compete more effectively, deliver better outcomes, and achieve higher growth.

FIGURE 15.2 ■ Retail Customer Journey

Need — "I need to make a purchase."

Research — "I looked up options online, but I think I need to go into the store to decide."

Go to store — "The store was pleasant to visit."

Purchase — "This met my price expectations." "The cashier wasn't very helpful."

Usage — "This product has met my expectations."

Support — "I'm so glad you answered my phone call and questions about the product."

Repeat Purchase — "I need to purchase again."

Google, Amazon, Facebook, and Netflix are among the organizations that have reshaped their digital strategies to develop more agile ways of working to respond faster to customer needs than their competitors.[30] Though the concept of digital operations is still new and emerging, all companies, whether product or service, will have digital operations in the future. Table 15.3 offers guidance in the form of questions for any business trying to increase its operational efficiencies through digitization.

TABLE 15.3 ■ Questions to Guide Digital Operations

1. How can our digital operations improve the customer experience?

2. How can we improve our employee experience by automating mundane tasks, thereby improving productivity?

3. How can we use digital operations for innovation?

4. How might our digital operations help us stay agile and lean? How can we embrace and not fear technology to improve our business performance?

5. What is the first area of our business that can and should be digitized?

Digital Transformation

Recent changes in work patterns such as hybrid working, remote working, and the rise of new technological tools and devices have driven many organizations to create digital transformation strategies to keep up with ever-changing customer needs, stay relevant, and keep ahead of the competition. Digital transformation is the process of integrating digital technology into all areas of a business to improve operational efficiency and deliver value. A recent study reported that nearly 80% of Fortune 500 companies named digital transformation as their biggest priority in 2021.[31] Swedish furniture giant IKEA is a good example of a company that is prioritizing its digital transformation efforts. For example, as part of its digital transformation strategy, it created a "Shop & Go" feature in the IKEA app, which allows customers to use their own mobile device to scan and pay for their items, enabling them to save time by skipping the checkout line in the store.[32]

Digitization and the Employee Experience

Although many organizations focus on the customer experience as part of their digital transformation strategy, employee experience is equally important to the success of the transformation. According to recent research, organizations that focus on employee experience achieve twice as much customer satisfaction and generate higher profits than those that don't.[33] The employee experience is the journey workers take through each stage of a particular company and the perceptions they have about their experiences at work. Shifting employee expectations and the drive to attract, engage, and retain talent have encouraged many organizations to adopt an employee-first approach as part of their digital transformation strategy.

The digital employee experience involves ensuring employees have the most up-to-date communication and collaboration technology they need to function in their roles, whether they are in the office or working remotely; the ability to access internal company information when they need it, such as HR policies and payment information, and the capacity to link with social media to share or post company updates, where permitted. According to industry thought leaders, taking an employee-centric approach is key to business growth, staff retention, and productivity.[34]

Now that you have a good foundation related to the fundamentals of business operations, this last section brings everything together as a chain of activities from beginning to end—from raw material to customer purchase. This is referred to as supply chain management. As we stated earlier, digital transformation involves integrating digital technology into all areas of a business, and that includes integration into a company's supply chain, a critical component of a business's success.

SUPPLY CHAIN MANAGEMENT

As we discussed previously, a supplier is an individual or an organization that provides particular types of goods to a business. A supply chain is a network between a company and its suppliers to produce and distribute a product.[35] Therefore, supply chain management (SCM) is the facilitation and coordination of the flow of goods and services from production to the delivery of the final product.[36] Everything we have discussed in this chapter is connected to the supply because the supply chain is at the heart of an organization's operations. Today's customers are more demanding than ever before and expect to be able to instantly access products and services and receive them just as quickly. Companies rely on suppliers to produce and deliver high-quality goods to customers as efficiently and cost-effectively as possible. Both suppliers and purchasers must work together in order to meet these goals.

The COVID-19 pandemic disrupted thousands of supply chains due to multiple lockdowns, staff shortages, and staff resignations that stalled the flow of materials and goods, prompting many businesses operating in a variety of different industries to rethink their approach to SCM. Findings from a recent survey found that more than 60% of supply chain executives plan to strengthen their supply chains by increasing investment in AI and robotic automation, focusing on reskilling and retraining workers, and boosting collaboration with suppliers and customers.[37]

Supply chain disruptions happen for a number of reasons. The COVID-19 pandemic caused supply chain disruptions in certain products such as toilet paper, leading to empty shelves.

Lindsey Nicholson/Universal Images Group via Getty Images

Supply chain managers are responsible for coordinating with the key companies in the supply chain such as logistics teams, suppliers, retailers, distributors, and consumers (see Figure 15.3). Logistics is the process of planning and organizing the movement of goods from their point of origin to their final destination. For instance, a manufacturing supply chain might include a flow of goods from the supplier to the manufacturer, which the manufacturer delivers to the warehouse; from the warehouse, the goods are delivered to retail stores and then finally sold to consumers. Often, these points in the supply chain are linked by systems to monitor stock such as barcodes or tracking devices so that all parties can assess the level of inventory available and locate the goods at any given time.

FIGURE 15.3 ■ Example of a Supply Chain

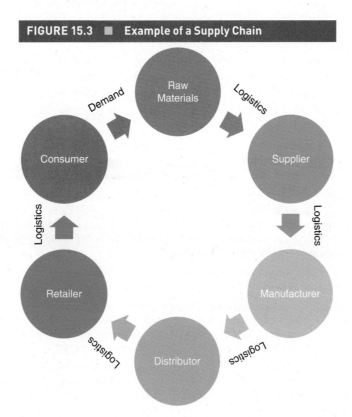

Both SCM and operations management are essential for organizational success. Without suppliers, companies would not have the materials to produce products or services. Although both functions are closely linked, there is a key difference between SCM and operations management: SCM mainly focuses on what happens outside the company in relation to how materials are acquired and how products are delivered, while operations management is concerned with the internal business operations that drive the development of these products and services. Working closely together, SCM and operations management have the ability to boost profits by reducing costs, improving efficiency, and meeting customer demand. But how well the supply chain works really depends on the relationship between the company and its suppliers. This is why choosing the right supplier is so important. Table 15.4 outlines some tips for choosing suppliers.

TABLE 15.4 ■ Tips for Choosing Suppliers

1. **Do your homework**. Make sure you research your suppliers before you agree to work with them. This may involve providing them with a list of your requirements, timelines, and overall business needs.

2. **Use multiple suppliers**. Never rely on just one supplier for your business because you will have no backup if there is a disruption in the supply chain. Having more than one supplier reduces dependency and balances out the level of risk.

3. **Communicate with suppliers.** The key to building a successful relationship with suppliers is to maintain consistent communication. Where possible, suppliers should be included in your company's planning meetings so they are aware of their role in the strategic process. This is also a good way of building trust, which is key to a positive professional relationship.

4. **Monitor supplier performance.** It is very important to measure your suppliers' performance to ensure they are meeting your company's expectations. In some cases, corrective action will be necessary, but if mistakes continuously occur, then you may need to consider replacing them.

5. **Look for new suppliers**. Although you may be satisfied with your supplier, make sure you still identify other potential suppliers every 2 or 3 years. This gives you the opportunity to learn about what others are doing in the industry (new technical innovations, etc.) and gives your current suppliers a chance to preserve the business.

Source: Adapted from Bucciarelli, P. (2019). What is supply chain management (SCM)? *Small Business Development Center at Duquesne University.* https://www.sbdc.duq.edu/Blog-Item-A-Supply-Chain-Primer-for-the-Entrepreneur

Recall that Starbucks, featured in our opening case, has developed a highly efficient supply chain that spans across multiple countries all over the world. This is because Starbucks has managed to build a good relationship with its suppliers to meet the demands of its customers and ensure it has the right product, in the right quantity, at the right price. Table 15.5 outlines how the Starbucks supply chain works from bean to cup.

TABLE 15.5 ■ Starbucks's Supply Chain: Bean to Cup

- Sourcing: Starbucks sources its coffee beans from almost 30,000 coffee farms all over the world in countries such as Brazil, Colombia, and Mexico and as far-flung as Saudi Arabia, Kenya, and Tanzania. Suppliers must adhere to the Starbucks standards known as Coffee and Farmer Equity (CAFE) and Coffee Sourcing Guidelines (CSG). These standards prohibit suppliers from using forced or child labor and instructs farms to implement safe work conditions.

- Supplier relationship management: Starbucks continuously works with its suppliers to ensure that operations are running smoothly and that each coffee bean is produced at the highest quality.

- Manufacturing and distribution: Starbucks runs highly efficient manufacturing and distribution processes. The raw beans from the suppliers are sent to one of Starbucks's storage facilities (there are six in total), where they are roasted and packaged. The beans are then dispatched to a Starbucks distribution center, then sent to regional warehouses where they are delivered to retail stores.

- Delivery and sale: Starbucks makes 70,000 deliveries every week all over the world. Its ability to keep up with cutting-edge technology is a huge part of its success. For example, customers use the Starbucks app to order, pay, and find their closest Starbucks store.

ENTREPRENEURIAL MINDSET ACTIVITY

Operations and Quality Management

Large companies, especially customer packaged goods (CPG) companies, which provide us with the products we use every day, undergo constant quality management exercises and manage highly complex supply chains across the globe. For example, if you open https://open.sourcemap.com/maps/5ccf7a0d22582a264b622f97 on your web browser, you can see some of the locations that play into the global supply chain map of Starbucks, the largest coffee maker in the world. There are manufacturing, distribution, and retail locations strategically placed to send massive quantities of high-quality products to storefronts, and the same system exists for all products, ranging from Apple iPhones, to Microsoft Xbox gaming consoles. Not only do supply chain management teams need to source and purchase countless raw materials, they must ship them and put them together to make products, and then ship the products to stores or through online commerce so that consumers like us can buy them.

Your mindset activity is to draw a supply chain map for one of your favorite products. Use Figure 15.3 as your guide. The product you choose could be a smartphone, computer, television, a bottle of tea, or even a favorite pair of jeans. Try to think both geographically and operationally: Where do the raw materials come from? To where? How and where is it manufactured? How does it get to the distributor and then the store and then to you? You can draw a map and take notes at the different locations describing some of the operations that take place. Because supply chain management is so intricate, you may not get every detail, but you can at least research a rough timeline, chain of events, and geography so that next time you use your favorite product, you'll be able to imagine the number of people and places that were involved in producing it. Be sure to choose a physical good as opposed to a service like Netflix or Facebook—these have supply chains as well, but they are more unique to a digital infrastructure as opposed to an operational supply chain.

Critical Thinking Questions

1. What product did you choose, and how many different locations and processes did you map out?
2. After doing research on a single product, were you surprised by how many complex activities take place before your purchase, and how do you feel about the price for the product after building a supply chain map for it? Explain your conclusions.
3. As a small exercise, consider that all of the raw materials you thought of also have supply chains of their own. In your opinion, how do so many intricate moving parts around the world manage to successfully work together to create products, when there are so many companies and operations that exist along the way?

IN REVIEW

15.1 Define operations and its critical role in running an efficient business.

Operations management involves overseeing the production process by managing the resources (materials, labor, money, information), people, and machinery in the most efficient way possible while making necessary improvements to support the company's strategic goals. The type of operations depends on the industry in which a business is operating. Different types of operations include retail business operations, restaurant business operations, service company business operations, product business operations, and digital business operations. An operations manager is responsible for monitoring the company's production processes to reduce the costs of materials, labor, and technology, in addition to eliminating costs that may add little to no value to the completed product.

15.2 Describe product operations and the importance of maintaining quality in the production process.

Product operations is an operational function designed to ensure product teams operate as effectively as possible. This function operates at the intersection of manufacturing, marketing, sales, and product development to improve the go-to-market and customer experience. Production control is the task coordinating people, materials, and machinery to provide maximum production efficiency. There are five main steps in the production control process: production planning, routing, scheduling, dispatching, and follow up.

15.3 Identify various production methods used in operations.

Operations managers also use different types of production methods to determine how and where goods are produced, such as: make to order, mass production, mass customization, continuous production, and lean manufacturing.

15.4 State the various quality control methods used in production.

There are a variety of methods businesses use to monitor and control the quality of their products and services. These include continuous improvement, statistical quality control, Six Sigma and lean Six Sigma.

15.5 Discuss the role of service operations in building a quality customer experience.

Service operations is an operational function intended to support the customer support team, customer experience team, and customer success team by developing strategies designed to attract, engage, and delight customers. Service operations roles and responsibilities include measuring customer feedback, managing technology, reporting on customer data, strategizing positive customer experience, and supporting customer onboarding.

15.6 Explore digital operations as the next frontier in operations for all types of companies.

Digital operations is the concept of digitizing and integrating business processes across the organization to improve customer and employee experience. It plays a key role in accelerating organizational agility by providing the necessary tools and technologies to quickly adapt to market changes. Digital transformation is the process of integrating digital technology into all areas of a business to improve operational efficiency and deliver value. Many organizations create digital transformation strategies to optimize the customer and employee experience.

15.7 Evaluate the role of supply chain management in operations.

Supply chain management (SCM) is the handling of the flow of goods and services from the collection of raw materials to the delivery of the final product. Supply chain managers are responsible for coordinating with the key companies in the supply chain such as logistics teams, suppliers, retailers, distributors, and consumers.

BUSINESSES DISCUSSED IN THIS CHAPTER

Organization	UN Sustainable Development Goal
Apple	7. Affordable and Clean Energy 12. Responsible Consumption and Production
Canon Bicycles	11. Sustainable Cities and Communities 13. Climate Action
Canva	7. Affordable and Clean Energy 12. Responsible Consumption and Production
Favor	9. Industry, Innovation, and Infrastructure
General Motors	12. Responsible Consumption and Production
Harley-Davidson	5. Gender Equality 11. Sustainable Cities and Communities 13. Climate Action
IKEA	3. Good Health and Well-Being 11. Sustainable Cities and Communities 12. Responsible Consumption and Production

Organization	UN Sustainable Development Goal
Mars Inc.	3. Good Health and Well-Being 8. Decent Work and Economic Growth 12. Responsible Consumption and Production
Rader Awning	7. Affordable and Clean Energy
Starbucks	6. Clean Water and Sanitation
Toyota	Meets all 17 goals

KEY TERMS

Additive manufacturing (also known as 3D printing) (p. 315)
Agile manufacturing (p. 314)
Continuous improvement (p. 316)
Continuous production (p. 314)
Customer onboarding (p. 318)
Digital operations (p. 318)
Digital transformation (p. 320)
Dispatching (p. 312)
Employee experience (p. 320)
Follow-up stage (p. 312)
Lean manufacturing (p. 314)
Logistics (p. 321)
Make to order (p. 312)
Mass customization (p. 313)
Mass production (p. 313)
NPS (Net Promoter Score) survey (p. 317)

Operations (p. 309)
Operations managers (p. 309)
Production control (p. 311)
Product operations (p. 311)
Production planning (p. 311)
Quality (p. 315)
Routing (p. 312)
Scheduling (p. 312)
Service operations (p. 317)
Six Sigma (p. 316)
Statistical quality control (SQC) (p. 316)
Supplier (p. 311)
Supply chain (p. 320)
Supply chain management (SCM) (p. 320)
Total Quality Management (TQM) (p. 316)
Value-stream mapping (p. 312)
Whistleblower (p. 316)

BUSINESS CASE 15.2: HILTON HOTELS—MCLEAN, VIRGINIA

SDG 6:   Clean Water and Sanitation

With more than 6,500 properties operating in 122 countries and territories, it may be hard to believe that Hilton was ever a one-hotel shop. Hilton was founded in 1919 by American businessman and founder Conrad Hilton, who purchased the Mobley Hotel in Cisco, Texas, with the goal to build a hotel chain that would provide the best customer experience for its guests. Over the years, the company acquired and built more hotels and resorts to become the powerhouse it is today. Today, Hilton employs 141,000 employees and has a net worth of more than $47.3 billion. Its most recent brands include: Motto, a "hostel-style micro-hotel"; Signia, targeted at business travelers; and Tempo, a "lifestyle-first luxury hotel," bringing the total of unique Hilton brands to more than 120.

How does a company grow from being a one-hotel business to owning thousands of properties around the world? For Hilton, strategic operations and supply chain management were and continue to be critical components of its success. Hilton Supply Management (HSM) is the largest end-to-end supply chain provider and manages the operations and procurement for the Hilton portfolio. Unlike other supply chain providers, HSM is focused exclusively on the service and hospitality industry.

Below are some strategies HSM uses to help control quality and drive profitability at its Hilton-branded properties:

- Leverages its size and massive customer base to negotiate the best prices for the 500,000 unique products that it sources from more than 1,200 unique suppliers

- Develops global and regional pricing agreements to offer the best value for customers

- Offers furniture, fixtures, and equipment (FF&E) services to help hotel owners complete hotel renovations within budget

- Provides technology resources like its eProcurement platform and Customer Portal so hotel owners can track operations and supply chain activity in real time

- Builds strong supplier and vendor relationships

HSM is committed to more than just efficiency and quality control. The organization has also pledged to double the number of diverse suppliers, double its social impact investment, and reduce its environmental footprint by half as part of Hilton's Travel with Purpose 2030 Goals. One way Hilton is reducing its environmental footprint is by reducing its water use. Between 2008 and 2022 Hilton reduced its water intensity by 47%, and multiple water-reduction pilots are underway as Hilton continues to determine the best ways its properties can save water. In addition, the company is a signatory to the CEO Water Mandate's UN Water Action Platform and is a member of the California Water Action Collaborative and Ceres Connect the Dots Campaign.

In celebration of its 100th anniversary, Hilton launched the Hilton Global Foundation, a nonprofit that acts as the primary international philanthropic arm for Hilton. The Hilton Global Foundation is aligned with Hilton's Travel with Purpose 2030 Goals and awards grants to nonprofit organizations around the world that are committed to restoring the planet and restoring communities for "future generations of travelers."

Improving society was something extremely important to Hilton founder Conrad. In 1944, he established the Conrad N. Hilton Foundation, an independent family foundation separate from the Hilton corporation. The foundation has awarded more than $2.4 billion in grants to nonprofit organizations working to improve living conditions and reduce poverty throughout the world. One of the foundation's seven programs is focused on developing "reliable, affordable, and safely managed water services" for communities experiencing water-service failures.

Critical Thinking Questions

1. What are some operations and supply chain management strategies that Hilton Supply Management uses to manage costs and quality at its properties?

2. How has Hilton incorporated sustainability and social impact in its operations and supply chain management practices?

3. Have you stayed in a Hilton-brand hotel in the past? What were your thoughts on the quality of the experience?

References

CEO Water Mandate Secretariat. (2017, April 18). *Hilton endorses the CEO Water mandate*. https://ceowatermand ate.org/posts/hilton-endorses-ceo-water-mandate/

Conrad N. Hilton Foundation. (n.d.). *Overview*. Conrad N. Hilton Foundation. https://www.hiltonfoundation.org/about

Conrad N. Hilton Foundation. (n.d.). *Safe water: Developing reliable, affordable, and safely managed water services*. Conrad N. Hilton Foundation. https://www.hiltonfoundation.org/programs/safe-water

Forbes. (2022). *Hilton (HLT)*. https://www.forbes.com/companies/hilton/?sh=113673aa8fc7

Hilton Global Foundation. (n.d.). *2021 annual grants* Hilton Global Foundation. https://hiltonglobalfoundation.hilt on.com/wp-content/uploads/sites/2/2022/04/HiltonGlobalFoundation_2021Grantees_MAPUpdated.pdf

Hilton. (2020). *Hilton 2020 environmental, social and governance (ESG) report*. https://cr.hilton.com/wp-content/uploads/2021/04/Hilton-2020-ESG-Report.pdf

Hilton. (2022a). *Our brands* https://www.hilton.com/en/corporate/#:~:text=For%20nearly%20a%20century%2C %20Hilton,who%20walks%20through%20its%20doors

Hilton. (2022b). *Our journey toward 2030*. https://cr.hilton.com/toward2030/#goals

Hotel Tech Report. (2022, January 26). *Hilton's 18 hotel brands explained*. https://hoteltechreport.com/news/hilton-hotel-brands

Macrotrends. (2022). *Hilton worldwide holdings net worth 2011–2021 | HLT*. https://www.macrotrends.net/stocks/charts/HLT/hilton-worldwide-holdings/net-worth

Associated Press/Gunnar Rathbun

16

DATA MANAGEMENT AND ANALYTICS

16.1 Distinguish between data and information in the production of knowledge.

16.2 Explore the different types of information systems used in modern business.

16.3 Discuss data communication networks and cloud computing.

16.4 Evaluate data security issues in a networked world.

16.5 Discuss business analytics and its related types and components.

BUSINESS IMPACT CASE 16.1: WALMART—BENTONVILLE, ARKANSAS

SDG 1: No Poverty

Today, companies of all sizes collect and analyze huge sums of data every day. Leaders use data-driven insights to drive their plans and decision making, and to identify mistakes and errors. As one of the world's largest employers, with over 2 million employees and over half a trillion dollars in annual revenue, Walmart uses some of the most advanced data analytics processes to guide its decision making. Walmart is considered a world-class benchmark for using data analytics to create operational savings and efficiency. The power of data is undeniable and how to use and interpret that data is considered one of the most essential skills in business today.

With nearly 12,000 stores transacting thousands of unique items per day, Walmart generates unimaginably large sums of data about its products, customers, stores, supply chain operations, logistics, and more. While collecting raw data in all of these areas, it processes, consolidates, and analyzes the data to create valuable information to boost customer satisfaction, sales, and corporate profitability.[1] For example, Walmart uses comprehensive, cutting-edge data analytics to improve store checkouts: "While it is still only testing the process, Walmart is using predictive analytics to anticipate store demand and determine how many associates are needed to man registers. The data also reveals the best form of checkout at each store: traditional stations or self-checkout."

No one likes long lines at the grocery store, so Walmart dynamically adjusts its shifts and self-checkouts based on previous data that show store activity at each location during each hour of the day. Using advanced technology, software, and data analytics teams, Walmart can make informed decisions like this. Another common example is product placement and assortment. Individual shoppers leave an obvious, yet important, trail of data at every location.

By analyzing purchase data, Walmart can create a story of the types of products that are commonly bundled, or purchased together, and the success of new products. In addition, data can be used to predict what will be purchased when, and we aren't just talking about holidays! For example, after analyzing what people purchase before hurricanes in the southern part of the United States, Walmart learned that customers stocked up on strawberry Pop-Tarts. Upon learning that strawberry Pop-Tart sales increase by seven times, the company made sure to order additional inventory when hurricanes approached the region.[2] Walmart data teams analyze purchase data like these and more to identify needs in inventory and product placement in stores. In a store as large as a Walmart, the physical location of a product in the store can heavily impact its sales performance and lead to higher profitability and spending from customers.

Walmart's brand is based on providing the lowest prices for everyday items from groceries to lawn care to personal-care products to clothes. If you have ever entered a Walmart store, you can understand why they are called "superstores" given their size and breadth of product offerings. Core to its vision, even since its founding in the 1960s, is the reduction of poverty by giving customers access to affordable products.[3] The impact of such low prices is debated. Walmart makes both positive and negative impacts on poverty through its massive, low-priced grocery stores. On the positive side, there are obvious benefits to eliminating poverty by providing employment and supplying the lowest-cost food and household furnishing available for anyone who chooses to walk in the door.

On the negative side, there may be hidden costs to Walmart's low-price strategy. According to Forbes research,[4] for example, one of the methods Walmart uses to keep prices low is to pay relatively low wages or hire for only part-time work, thus leaving some of its employees struggling to make living wages without benefits of health care. In fact, some studies have found many Walmart employees must collect Medicaid and Supplemental Nutrition Assistance Program (SNAP) "food stamps" in addition to their wages to get by. Furthermore, suppliers are pressed to tighten margins to keep costs down.

Recently, however, in light of the COVID-19 global pandemic, Walmart increased hourly wages for employees to between $15–$19 per hour, an average increase of $2 per hour. While minimum wage in the United States is $7.25 per hour, Walmart is paying significantly above the minimum required by federal law.

Regardless of your opinion on the debates surrounding Walmart and its role in working to reduce poverty, it is undeniable that its size makes a big impact on the world. Walmart has made a commitment to end hunger by making substantial investments to improve access to healthier foods for more vulnerable populations, especially the poor.[5] It donates unsold food—720 million pounds of food in 2019, of which 55% was fruits, vegetables, and meat—and is working throughout its entire supply chain for positive impact. The company funds training for farmers around the world, embraces small-scale food entrepreneurs, and supports women and indigenous farmers.

Critical Thinking Questions

1. How is Walmart using data to increase revenues?

2. Is Walmart a force against poverty or is it a force contributing to poverty? Back up your opinion with data.

3. Consider some data that you may have at your home, dorm, or apartment. For example, perhaps you record your fitness workouts daily in terms of calories burned, or distance you biked or ran. What can you learn from this data?

DATA AND INFORMATION

The Walmart case study demonstrates how large retailers use raw data to optimize the customer experience and generate valuable information about its products, stores, and supply chain operations.[6] Data are a set of facts and statistics used by businesses to analyze or calculate something. Data are meaningless without information, which is data that have been transformed into a type of useful form to support planning and decision making. For example, temperature readings count as data, but when those readings are organized and analyzed to inform about global warming, then that is information.[7] "Data" and "information" are often used interchangeably, but there are some important distinctions (see Table 16.1).

TABLE 16.1 ■ Differences Between Data and Information	
Data	**Information**
• Individual numbers, facts, or statistics	• Outcome of analyzing data
• Raw form of knowledge	• Perception of the raw pieces of data (e.g., "there is meaning behind the numbers")
• Little meaning without interpretation	• Has meaning in context (e.g., Walmart selling Pop-Tarts during hurricane season)
• Simple yet chaotic in quantity	• Patterns found in the chaos that lead to insights

Big Data Versus Small Data

Data can be "big" or "small." Big data are large volumes of structured and unstructured data that flow into an organization on a daily basis. For example, Netflix uses big data for targeted advertising by analyzing past search and watch data to give the company an insight into customer preferences.[8] But it's not just large companies that use big data—small businesses can benefit from it, too. For example, the Point Defiance Zoo & Aquarium in Tacoma, Washington, analyzed climate data from the National Weather Service to predict the number of visitors to the zoo on certain days.[9] This allowed managers to make preparations for bad weather when attendance would likely be lower, such as the number of employees needed to work at the zoo on those days.

In contrast, small data are more bite-sized pieces that are more accessible, informative, and actionable. Some big companies use small data to give them more insight into their customers. Lego is a good example of an industry giant that used small data to revolutionize the company. Because of the results generated by big data, Lego management originally considered making Lego bricks bigger, concluding that children didn't have the patience or stamina for more time-consuming projects. Yet, when Lego executives observed children playing with Lego, they discovered the opposite: Children were more likely to persevere with small pieces to create a Lego build.[10] In this context, the small data were the observations made through spending time with the customers.

Danish company Lego used small data to determine that children enjoyed playing with small Lego pieces.

Jessica Christian/The San Francisco Chronicle via Getty Images

User-Generated Data

Generating data is not just for different types of organizations—anybody with online access can do it. User-generated content (UGC) is any type of content such as text, videos, reviews, and blogs that can be created by people outside the business.[11] Over 80% of young adults today believe that positive UGC is a good indicator of the quality of a brand. Instagram is one of the most powerful platforms for sharing UGC, with an average of 60 million images uploaded every day. Engaging in UGC helps businesses connect more intimately with their customers and broaden their online presence. For example, San Francisco–based online vacation rental marketplace Airbnb shares UGC such as Instagram posts from all over world and engages with its followers by asking questions and making suggestions. Airbnb simply "regrams" posts from customers celebrating where they are staying. This encourages followers to check out Airbnb accommodations for potential stays throughout their journey. By using UGC as a form of marketing, Airbnb has succeeded in strengthening its online community by building a base of loyal followers. James McClure, general manager of Airbnb in northern Europe, said, "Your community, your customers, are the best marketing asset you have."[12]

INFORMATION SYSTEMS

Data are kept in information systems. All businesses use information systems, from retailers tracking their biggest-selling products to hotels establishing their levels of customer loyalty. An information system (IS) is the combination of technologies designed to collect, process, store, and distribute information for decision making and controlling company-wide activities.[13] In most large organizations, the information system is operated by a senior management team that includes a chief information officer (CIO) and chief technology officer (CTO). Recall from Chapter 9 that a CIO is an executive officer who oversees the planning, development, and implementation of technology inside the organization, and a CTO is an executive officer who is responsible for technology creation and design, anticipating customer needs, and focusing on emerging technologies. Table 16.2 outlines the role of information systems managers.

TABLE 16.2 ■ Information Systems Managers' Tasks
● Understanding the technological and organizational needs of the company
● Keeping up-to-date with current and emerging technology
● Collecting the appropriate data
● Researching ways in which systems can improve productivity
● Using technology to convert data into information
● Directing the flow of information to the right people
● Recognizing that information needs vary according to different levels, operational units, and functional areas

Source: Pearlson, K. E., Saunders, C. S., & Galletta, D. F. (2019). *Managing and using information systems: A strategic approach* (7th ed.). John Wiley & Sons.

Information officers share their findings across an **enterprise resource planning (ERP)** system, which provides a flow of information to include accounting, manufacturing, customer relationship management, sales, and service.[14] Within health care, the system holds data from across all the departments, such as medical records, inventory, billing, HR, and staff scheduling.

Organizations need information systems to enable their employees to carry out tasks effectively and efficiently. Without them, managers would not be able to implement the necessary controls to assess organizational performance.

Information systems managers derive most of their data from **databases**, which are an organized collection of data that can be accessed by various people in the organization.[15] To enable data analysis, information systems managers may use a **data warehouse**, which is a centralized database where data are collected and organized to provide meaningful analysis. Turning raw data into useful information would not be possible without **data mining**, which is the process of analyzing large amounts of data to generate information that can be used by an organization to predict future behavior.

Types of Information Systems

While information systems officers at the higher levels of management typically use ERP to share information, there are other systems that can be used by different levels of managers to support their roles. For example, lower level managers tend to use operations support systems, which are a set of programs that monitor, control, analyze, and manage an information network. Operations support systems usually fall into two categories: transaction processing systems and process control systems.

A **transaction processing system (TPS)** is an information processing system that records the daily business transactions of an organization at the operational level. Examples of TPS include payroll, stock control, airline reservations, and booking systems. Lower level managers can also use **process control systems,** which is an information processing system that monitors and controls physical processes by using sensors to collect data for analysis. For example, in food preparation, the data collected by the process control system can indicate when adjustments are needed or alert the operator when necessary.

Mid and upper level managers may use different types of information systems than lower level managers. Typically, there are four different types of information systems to support decision-making activities: management information systems, decision support systems, executive information systems, and expert systems.

A **management information system (MIS)** aids organizations in running more efficiently by incorporating people, technology, and information systematically.[16] The system records the operational activities such as staffing, financial costs, and workload.

A **decision support system (DSS)** is a computer-based information system that helps organizations with their decision-making processes.[17] In some clinics, DSSs aid doctors in making more accurate diagnoses. Such systems contain detailed health data, such as types of diseases and conditions. When the doctor enters certain criteria, such as age, weight, gender, and symptoms, the system produces a list of options, based on probability, as to what could be the issue with the patient.

An executive information system (EIS) is an information support system that supports senior management needs by providing access to strategic information relevant to organizational goals. For example, in an airline company, an EIS might be used to give senior managers a complete overview of an airplane's safety record.

An expert system is an information support system that uses artificial intelligence to mimic the thinking of human experts to solve complex problems. Expert systems have been used to improve health care and are advancing all the time. For example, machine learning startup Curai, based in Palo Alto, California, is using artificial intelligence to increase the accuracy of medical diagnoses by gathering data through an app that connects patients, providers, and health coaches. Patients can use the app to input information about their own health, chat with providers, and access health records. The app then offers the providers suggestions for diagnosis and treatment based on the algorithms generated by the underlying system. With over 200,000 deaths in the U.S. every year attributed to incorrect diagnoses, the Curai model has the potential to make a big difference. Curai cofounder Xavier Amatriain said, "In five years, we see ourselves serving millions of people around the world, and providing them with great-quality, affordable healthcare." . . . "We feel that we not only have the opportunity, but also the responsibility, to make this work."[18]

DATA COMMUNICATION NETWORKS

In addition to using systems to process information, companies use networks to communicate and share information inside and outside the organization. This is made possible by data communication networks, which refers to the transmission of digital data from one computer to another using a variety of wired and wireless communication channels. Though wired networks are still used today, cloud computing has allowed us to be networked wirelessly in ways we could not have imagined just 15 years ago.[19]

Cloud Computing

Cloud computing is a segment of IT services that uses remote services hosted on the internet to store and manage data rather than using local services or personal devices.[20] Cloud computing services are divided into three main categories, often regarded as the building blocks of modern computing: infrastructure as a service (IaaS), platform as a service (PaaS), and software as a service (SaaS).[21]

Large rooms of servers are used to make cloud computing possible. Cloud computing saves companies money, provides users with access to resources, and reduces the number of IT staff.

iStock.com/jeffbergen

Infrastructure as a service (IaaS) is the largest segment of cloud computing where customers pay for access to software applications and databases provided by third parties. Popular services include customer relationship management and enterprise resource planning software (ERP). Recall that ERP is a process used by organizations to integrate important parts of the business, such as finance, HR, sales, manufacturing, and so on. Seattle-based web hosting company Hostwinds offers 24-hour support for website hosting services for individuals and businesses of all sizes.

Platform as a service (PaaS) is a model that provides customers with access to hardware and software tools for application development. Through PaaS, users can build apps with the support of code without needing to build their own infrastructure and operating systems. As Jim Deters, founder of Denver-based education company Galvanize, put it, "Two guys in a Starbucks can have access to the same computing power as a Fortune 500 company."[22]

Software as a service (SaaS) is a model that provides customers with software that can be accessed over the web. These are usually subscription-based services that can be accessed by simply logging in. This is a better model for organizations, as it dispenses with the need for manual software installation on a machine or server. Gmail, cloud file storage company Dropbox, and online questionnaire and survey company SurveyMonkey are good examples of SaaS providers.

Moving IT functions to the cloud has a number of advantages: It saves on costs, as you only pay for storage and system time; it provides access to resources, software, and applications; and it reduces the number of information technology staff. However, there are also some disadvantages of cloud computing, including possible disruptions to internet service, security risks, and unreliability of service provider systems.

The Internet

Though we use the internet every day, we often forget that it's a network—the world's largest network. The **internet** is a global network consisting of smaller, interconnected networks linking millions of computers together. The internet has vastly impacted how businesses communicate with their employees, customers, clients, and other parties. Tools like Zoom and Skype allow companies to share information through video meetings with people in different locations all over the world. Email and social media have also enabled quick communication between parties. Table 16.3 outlines more ways that businesses use the internet.

TABLE 16.3 ■ How Businesses Use the Internet
Buying and selling products and services
Sharing information with employees
Staff training using online training videos
Researching the competition
Engaging with customers through social media and email
Marketing and advertising
Providing online payment services
Utilizing online systems to support production

Companies called internet service providers link to the internet infrastructure to connect users to the internet through paid subscriptions, enabling them to communicate with others through text, email, video calling, and so on. They also connect users to third-party providers, allowing them access to a wide variety of information, including newspaper and magazine articles and financial information. Comast, AT&T, and Charter are among the biggest internet service providers in the U.S.

The World Wide Web

The World Wide Web ("the web") is a subset of the internet that allows access to an interconnected system of web pages. Whenever a page is visited on the web a special protocol is used known as hypertext transfer protocol (HTTP). HTTP is a set of rules that defines how documents, images, videos, and sounds are transferred by the user.

Users can navigate through internet resources through hypertext, a feature of computer programming that contains links to information. To view web pages from anywhere on the internet, users have access to a web browser, a software application that locates information from other parts of the web and transmits it to a computer, smartphone, or other mobile device. Web browsers allow users to shop online, upload pictures, play games, and much more. Although the web would not exist without the internet, it's the web that provides the multimedia material accessed every day by millions of users.

The Intranet

While the internet is a globally connected public network accessible to anybody, an intranet is a computer network for sharing information only available to employees working within an organization. The intranet is protected by a firewall, a type of software that blocks unauthorized access to the network.

Extranet

An extranet is an intranet that securely shares information with certain outside parties, such as suppliers, partners, vendors, or a particular set of customers. The George Washington University, based in Washington, D.C., allows students to access its extranet to complete their application forms for undergraduate and graduate programs. It also allows them to upload their résumés, transcripts, and letters of recommendation. Today, many universities connect to a common extranet called the Common Application, where college applicants can use the same application to apply to multiple colleges and universities.

DATA SECURITY ISSUES[23]

Conducting business over the internet presents some unprecedented challenges, particularly in the area of security. During the COVID-19 pandemic, the number of cyberattacks grew at an alarming rate as organizations rapidly deployed remote systems to support employees working from home. Cybercriminals exploited security vulnerabilities, causing disruption by stealing data and generating profits.[24] A variety of cybersecurity threats pose significant risks for organizations. These include ransomware, malware, social engineering, and piracy.

Ransomware is a type of malicious software (or malware) used by an attacker to gain access to a victim's computer files, lock them, and then demand a ransom to unlock them.[25] The University of Utah experienced a ransomware attack when hackers exposed a vulnerability in the servers, which compromised the personal information of students and faculty. The university paid the ransom, which amounted to almost $500,000, but it is still working on recovering some stolen files.

Malware, also known as malicious software, is any file or program used to wreak havoc on computer systems, such as worms (replicates itself and spreads from computer to computer), viruses (codes that corrupt the system and destroy data), Trojan horses (a type of code that can take control of your computer), and spyware (software that steals data and sensitive information).[26] Emotet is a Trojan that has been classified by the U.S. Department of Homeland Security as one of the most destructive forms of malware in the world as it is the cause of financial information theft, stealing bank logins and digital currencies.[27]

Social engineering is the act of tricking users into divulging sensitive information. The most common social engineering attacks come in the form of phishing, a cybercrime in which fraudulent emails designed to resemble legitimate institutions are sent to users to extract sensitive information such as banking and credit card details, passwords, or log-in information.[28] According to Small Business Trends, one in 99 e-mails is a phishing attack, costing a midsized business an average of $1.6 million in damages.[29]

Piracy is the illegal copying or distribution of copyrighted content such as music or software. The theft of digital products over the internet not only cheats the individuals and organizations that create them, but also reduces sales and negatively impacts the bottom line. Recent statistics show that the United States had the highest number of visits to piracy sites, with just over 17 billion visits in 2018.[30]

Colonial Pipeline was forced to temporarily pause operations because of a cyberattack that affected its systems. The company delivers fuel to customers on the East Coast.

Associated Press/Mike Stewart

Protecting Against Cybercrime

Due to the growing threats to cybersecurity, organizations need to put protective measures in place to prevent attacks on sensitive information and reassure their customers that they are safe to make online purchases. To reduce the risks of online threats, most companies install firewalls to prevent unauthorized access to computer networks.

Another effective method for keeping information secure is encryption—the process of encoding information to hide its true meaning. Only individuals (or computers) with a secret code (or key) have the ability to decode it. A commonly used encryption scheme is a secure sockets layer (SSL), which is designed to ensure privacy and data integrity by establishing a link between a server and a client. Often, the user receives a digital certificate of authenticity, issued by a certificate authority (CA)—an organization that validates identities and lets users know who they are communicating with online.

BUSINESS ANALYTICS

Many companies like Walmart, featured in our business impact case, make huge investments in the technology that gathers and processes data, but for these data to be useful for decision making, companies employ business analytics. Business analytics[31] is the process of collecting, processing, and exploring business data based on statistical analysis and past history to generate actionable insights. The goal of business analytics is to find the data most useful to problem-solving and to leverage that data to increase efficiency, productivity, and profitability. Business analytics is a subset of business intelligence, which is a technology-driven process for identifying actionable raw data that support decision making. Simply put, business intelligence explores *what* has happened in the past, and business analytics establishes *why* it happened and develops models to create predictions and recommendations for future events, such as Walmart having more strawberry Pop-Tarts in inventory during hurricane season.

Consider this example of harnessing business analytics to enhance sports performance. The Louisiana State University football team worked with a startup called Perch, a technology-enabled consumer products company that uses business analytics to collect data through velocity-based training.[32] This method of training involves examining how fast the athlete is lifting the weight on the bar as opposed to the traditional method of training where the amount of weight on the bar is the key metric. Data are gathered in the weight room through a camera that monitors a player's movements by measuring bar speed based on the amount of weight on the bar and the number of repetitions or "reps" performed by the athlete. The data provide the coaches and trainers with real-time feedback on the player's performance. Former head coach Ed Orgeron noticed an improvement in team performance within a few weeks of this new approach to training: "I think our guys are stronger and quicker and faster," he said. Orgeron also mentioned that the players seemed to be suffering fewer injuries than in prior years.

The Louisiana State University Tigers football team has used business analytics to collect data that provide coaches and trainers with real-time feedback on a player's performance.

Photo by Steve Limentani/ISI Photos/Getty Images

Types of Business Analytics[33]

There are four types of business analytics used by companies to gain insights that can lead to better solutions, new ideas, process improvements, and better decision making. These are: descriptive analytics, diagnostic analytics, predictive analytics, and prescriptive analytics. Each type is explored using an example based on the rates of website traffic in an organization.

Descriptive Analytics

Descriptive analytics interpret historical data to summarize what has happened in the past or is happening currently. It is the most common and simplest form of analytics and uses data aggregation and data mining techniques to provide accessible and understandable data to members across the organization, including managers, investors, and shareholders. For example, a sales report might show information on new clients, the number of successful sales, or the number of customers in a certain demographic. Armed with this information, companies can identify strengths and weaknesses to provide insight into customer behavior and design strategies to improve customer service. Figure 16.2 illustrates the decrease in website traffic in quarter 3 of the first year. This provides enough information to run a descriptive analysis to find out what happened.

Diagnostic Analytics

While descriptive analytics summarizes what has happened in the past, diagnostic analytics focuses on past performance to figure out how and why it happened. Diagnostic analytics helps businesses to determine the factors that contribute to an outcome using correlations. For example, a website analysis report tracked over the course of a year would help a company understand the reasons for increases or decreases in site visitors. Figure 16.2 illustrates some of the reasons for the fall in website traffic, citing a search engine algorithm update, a decrease in published web content, and heavy losses in backlinks (the links created when one site links to another).

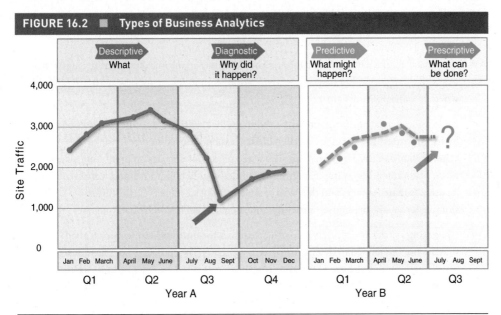

FIGURE 16.2 ■ Types of Business Analytics

Source: Adapted from Pickell, D. (2019). 4 types of data analytics your business can benefit from. *Learning Hub.* https://learn.g2.com/types-of-data-analytics

Predictive Analytics

Predictive analytics focuses on making predictions about the future using statistical techniques such as data mining, predictive modeling, and machine learning. Although predictive analytics is used to predict future outcomes, it cannot anticipate whether events will actually occur. Rather, it focuses on the likelihood of an event and helps companies prepare for certain eventualities. Figure 16.2 outlines some predictions of what web traffic could look like over the next few quarters based on the information generated by the diagnostic analysis.

Prescriptive Analytics

Finally, **prescriptive analytics** builds on predictive analytics by providing recommendations for best actions to drive desired outcomes to satisfy business objectives. It depends on a strong feedback system and constant analysis to continually learn about the correlations between actions and outcomes. As new or additional data become available, they are automatically adjusted by computer programs to calculate certain probabilities much faster than humans ever could. Artificial intelligence streamlines the four types of business analytics enabling organizations to jump from one to the other depending on different scenarios. Figure 16.2 illustrates some suggestions to boost the number of site visitors by posting more content and increasing the level of email marketing.

Components of Business Analytics[34]

Regardless of type used, business analytics is made up of many various components, including data aggregation, data mining, association and sequence identification, forecasting, optimization, and data visualization.

Data Aggregation

Data aggregation is the process of collecting data before analysis and cleaning the data to avoid duplication of data or inaccurate, incomplete, and unusable data. Data can be aggregated from two main areas of data: **transactional data**, which is the information captured by an organization's transactions such as banking records, sales records, etc.; and **volunteered data**, which is data shared by the consumer or by an authorized third party in paper or digital form, such as personal information.

Data Mining

Recall that data mining is used to identify previously unrecognized trends and patterns by searching through vast amounts of data. Table 16.4 describes 10 examples in which data mining is used in real life. Data mining exploits three main statistical techniques to clarify information:

- **Classification** is a data mining function that identifies items in a data set and assigns them to specific categories. For instance, classification techniques are used by banks to establish whether loan applicants are safe or risky.

- **Regression** is a data mining function used to predict continuous numeric values based on historical patterns. Both classification and regression are used in prediction analysis, but classification assigns data into categories while regression focuses on predicting a range of numerical values. For example, regression would be used to predict house value based on location, square footage, and the price of similar homes; whereas classification would be more suitable for separating houses into different categories such as lot size, crime rates, and so on.

- **Clustering** is a data mining function that searches for similarities in groups (called "clusters") that are not predefined to determine patterns based on the characteristics found in the data. This function might be used by marketing departments to identify similarities between groups of customers based on their past purchases.

TABLE 16.4 ■ Ten Examples of Data Mining In Real Life

Mobile Service Providers: Data mining is used by mobile service providers such as broadband, phone, and gas providers to predict churn and devise marketing strategies to prevent customers from moving to other vendors. Data mining tools analyze huge chunks of data such as email, bills, texts, and other data that tell the provider if the customer is looking to switch vendors and enable the company to offer incentives to stay.

Retail Sector: By using data mining to analyze the purchase history of customers, supermarkets and other retail companies can assess the buying preferences of customers. Supported by these results, the companies can design promotions and marketing campaigns offering special discounts on some of these products.

Artificial Intelligence: Data mining is used in artificial intelligence systems to provide patterns analyzed from large data sets. These patterns help companies to offer personalized recommendations to online customers. Amazon is a good example of a company that uses artificial intelligence on mined data that suggest different products to customers based on past purchasing history.

E-commerce: Many e-commerce sites, such as Amazon and Flipkart, use data mining from their customers' purchasing history to offer cross-selling and upselling of their products to their customers through the "People also viewed" and "Frequently bought together" functions on their sites.

Science and Engineering: Through data mining, vast amounts of data are collected and stored, allowing scientists and engineers the opportunity to explore new results and experiment with the process to monitor systems, find faults, and improve performance. Data mining is often used in scientific fields of study such as astronomy, geology, satellite sensors, etc.

Crime Prevention: Data mining supports agencies by providing patterns and trends in the data and predicting future events. These data allow police to assess the areas more prone to crime, the amount of police needed to patrol the area, the most likely demographic to be involved in the crime, etc.

Research: Researchers use data mining tools to explore the correlations between certain factors. For example, environmental researchers might use data mining to investigate the relationship between air pollution and diseases such as asthma among people in certain areas.

Farming: Supported by data mining results, farmers can estimate the amount of water required to generate the necessary amount of vegetables in a harvest.

Dynamic Pricing: Data mining helps companies to charge customers based on supply and demand. For instance, ride hailing company Uber charges its customers the service providers to estimate demand and adjust prices.

Transportation: Transportation companies use data mining to monitor the movement from warehouses to different outlets and explore product loading patterns.

Source: Adapted from Software Testing Help. (2022, July 16). *Data mining examples: Most common applications of data mining.* https://www.softwaretestinghelp.com/data-mining-examples/

Text mining, a form of data mining, is the process of collecting high-quality information from text (words) to create meaningful insights. The information gathered from social media sites, blog comments, and call center scripts can be used to develop new products, improve customer service, and assess competitor performance. For example, fashion retailer H&M used text mining from social media to gain a better understanding of what its customers were looking for, and customized ads to attract new customers.[35]

Association and Sequence Identification

Association and sequence identification is a component of business analytics that focuses on understanding different types of consumers to reveal patterns in buying behavior. Association identifies the groups of consumers who tend to buy products that are associated with each other, like shampoo and conditioner. In the sequence identification, consumers are identified by the sequence on buying, such as booking an airline ticket, followed by booking a cab to the airport, and then booking a hotel room.

Forecasting

Forecasting is the process of using historical data to predict future events and outcomes. For example, a beverage company could analyze seasonal sales trends from the last 10 years to predict how many units it expects to sell. This information will help it to buy the right materials, hire the right people, and make the right decisions, thereby saving money and boosting profitability.

Optimization

Optimization is the process of identifying best-case scenarios and actions to make the business more efficient and cost-effective. For example, retailers might use optimization to anticipate surges in demand for their products so they can increase production, and also create sales, promotions, new product launches, and discounts based on business analytics.

Data Visualization

Data visualization is the graphic representation of data to generate new information and insights. This visual form allows organizations to explore and analyze the data to initiate new business goals, improve customer relations, and boost revenues. Figure 16.1 illustrates the shopping activity at a retailer on a particular day.

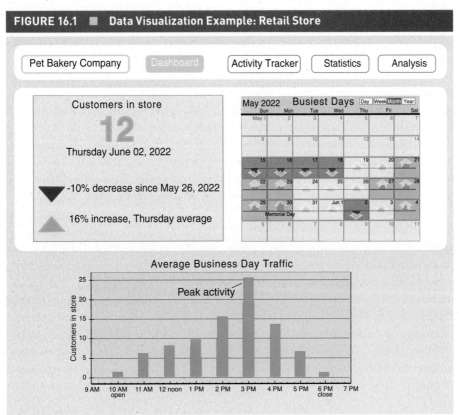

FIGURE 16.1 ■ Data Visualization Example: Retail Store

ENTREPRENEURIAL MINDSET ACTIVITY

Show Me the Data

Business analytics is about using real-time (or as close to it as possible) data to make decisions and leverage those data to identify new opportunities. In this activity, it's time for you to collect data on how businesses collect and use data! You are to identify three startup companies in three different industries and answer the questions below.

> What data does the company use most?
> How does it get the data?
> What systems does it use to analyze the data?
> A few guidelines before you get started:

- You may not use any of the examples used in this chapter.
- A startup company is defined as a company that is 5 years old or less.
- "Data" for this activity cannot be financial data such as sales and expenses.
- Don't depend on what you read on the internet. Pick up your phone and call some startups. It's a great way to build your network.

Critical Thinking Questions

1. What surprised you most about the type of data collected and used by the startups?
2. Were there differences in data collection and use across industries?
3. Who was responsible for *collecting* the data? Who *used* the data?

Challenges Presented by Business Analytics

Business analytics will only be successful if everyone in the organization fully supports its implementation and execution. The following sections outline some of the challenges presented by business analytics.

Executive Distrust

Although many companies depend heavily on business analytics, some organizations have struggled getting buy-in from upper management. This is because some senior level executives still view data analytics with a degree of distrust, especially when they are more comfortable making decisions based on intuition, their own collected data, and experience. Or, perhaps, they just don't like what the data are saying! Gut instinct and intuition have their place: Evidence shows that managers who spend too much time analyzing the data may be at risk of losing touch with their own instincts. Masayoshi Son, founder of SoftBank, a Japanese multinational holding company, credits his intuition for his ability to size up an opportunity, and Starbucks founder Howard Schultz has relied on his gut instinct to guide him on making decisions about entering seemingly impenetrable markets.[36] Upper level managers may be more inclined to adopt business analytics when it is presented as a trial project to prove its ability to make accurate predictions that support existing company strategies. To be truly effective, business leaders need to balance data analytics with intuition to make important decisions.

Poor Collaboration

Synchronized teams across different departments are key to the successful implementation of analytics-driven initiatives. Lack of collaboration can lead to poor communication, undefined goals and expectations, and incorrect requirements. This only fuels the distrust of business analytics and creates the risk that analytics won't provide the necessary information, leading to the potential abandonment of the project itself. According to recent research conducted by Forbes, 70% of leaders believe that implementing a successful analytics strategy depends on close collaboration between IT and business units.[37] However, only 15% agreed that these two groups collaborated well. The study showed that analytics teams in technology and other business units such as operations, marketing, and HR must work together to promote the use of analytics across the organization.

Lack of Commitment

Lack of commitment is one of the greatest threats to the successful adoption of business analytics. The upfront cost of analytics software packages tends to be high, and it takes time before organizations see meaningful results. It is essential for businesses to commit during this crucial period and trust that data usefulness will improve over time. However, many businesses lose trust in the technology's capability to generate the results they are looking for, and abandon the initiative altogether. Setting realistic timelines for results is a useful way to manage expectations.

Low-Quality Data

Low-quality data can lead to inaccurate analysis and poor decision making. Business analytics implementations often fail because the data have become compromised through lack of integrated systems, human error in data entry, and outdated data. According a recent Gartner study, poor-quality data cost the average business $14 million every year and seriously impact their ability to achieve their data-driven goals. Data need to be cleaned, assessed, and scored for quality before using for decision-making purposes. The company's own technological infrastructure must also be appraised to ensure it has the ability to support new analytics requirements.[38]

ETHICS IN BUSINESS

The Ethics of Bad Data

You are the founder and CEO of a pharmaceutical startup. Your main goal is to develop a cure for a deadly neurological disease commonly found in young infants. Your drug shows promise, but it needs to be approved by the United States Food and Drug Administration (FDA). You are also aware that competitors are also developing drugs to cure this disease, and being first to get the drug approved would be a major competitive advantage. During early testing of the drug, you realize that the data are not leaning your way and more testing will be required, resulting in additional costs and loss of time. You are considering manipulating some of the data in order to get the required FDA support. You don't think this is a bad thing, given you truly believe in the drug and its ability to cure this deadly infant disease, and you feel that future data would support you—if you had the time and money to collect these data. What do you do? By not manipulating the data, your chances of being first to the market are impossible, and your company could go under. However, if you get caught, you could go to jail. Also, many babies could be harmed by being given a drug deemed safe due to manipulated data.

Critical Thinking Questions

1. In terms of making an ethical decision, do you think the outcome of a decision is more important than the process used to make that decision? In other words, do you agree with the statement that the ends justify the means?
2. When does unethical behavior turn into illegal behavior?
3. As an employee of the company above, if your company manipulated data would it be unethical for you to stay quiet about this?

Source: Roland, D. (2019, September 14). The startup that manipulated data to get a miracle drug on the market. *The Wall Street Journal.* https://www.wsj.com/articles/the-startup-that-manipulated-data-to-get-a-miracle-drug-to-market-11568433625

IN REVIEW

16.1 Distinguish between data and information in the production of knowledge.

Data are a set of facts and statistics used by businesses to analyze or calculate something. Data are meaningless without information, which is data that have been transformed into a type of useful form to support planning. Data can be "big" or "small." Big data are large volumes of structured and unstructured data that flow into an organization on a daily basis, and small data are volumes of data that are small enough in volume to be accessible, informative, and actionable. Managers derive most of their data from databases, which are organized collections of data that can be accessed by various people in the organization for decision-making purposes.

16.2 Explore the different types of information systems used in modern business.

Data are kept in information systems. By definition an information system is technology used to collect, process, store, and distribute information for decision-making purposes or controlling business activities. There are various types of information systems: management information systems, decision support systems, executive information systems, and expert systems.

16.3 Discuss data communication networks and cloud computing.

Companies use data communication networks to share information inside and outside the organization. A data communication network relates to the transmission of digital data from one computer to another using a variety of wired and wireless communication channels. Though wired networks are still used today, cloud computing has allowed us to be networked wirelessly in ways we could not have imagined just 15 years ago. The internet (including the World Wide Web), intranets, and extranets are all examples of data communication networks.

16.4 Evaluate data security issues in a networked world.

A variety of cybersecurity threats pose significant risks for organizations. These include ransomware, malware, social engineering, and phishing. Ransomware is a type of malicious software (or malware) used by an attacker to gain access to a victim's computer files, lock them, and then demand a ransom to unlock them. Malware is any file or program used to wreak havoc on computer systems. Social engineering is the act of tricking users into divulging sensitive information through phishing, a cybercrime in which fraudulent emails designed to resemble legitimate institutions are sent to users to extract sensitive information such as banking and credit card details, passwords, or log-in information. Piracy is the illegal copying or distribution of copyrighted content such as music or software.

16.5 Discuss business analytics and its related types and components.

Business analytics is the process of collecting, processing, and exploring business data based on statistical analysis and past history to generate actionable insights. It is a subset of business intelligence, which is a technology-driven process for identifying actionable raw data that support decision making. Business analytics is made up of many various components, including data aggregation, data mining, text mining, association and sequence identification, forecasting, optimization, and data visualization. There are four types of business analytics: descriptive analytics, diagnostic analytics, predictive analytics, and prescriptive analytics.

BUSINESSES DISCUSSED IN THIS CHAPTER

Organization	UN Sustainable Development Goal
Curai	3. Good Health and Well-Being
George Washington University	4. Quality Education
Lego	4. Quality Education 12. Responsible Consumption and Production
Netflix	12. Responsible Consumption and Production
Point Defiance Zoo & Aquarium	13. Climate Action
Starbucks	6. Clean Water and Sanitation 11. Sustainable Cities and Communities
Walmart	1. No Poverty
Zoom	9. Industry, Innovation, and Infrastructure

Association and sequence identification (p. 339)

Big data (p. 330)

Business analytics (p. 335)

Business intelligence (p. 335)

Certificate authority (p. 335)

Classification (p. 338)

Cloud computing (p. 332)

Clustering (p. 338)

Data (p. 329)

Data aggregation (p. 337)

Data communication networks (p. 332)

Data mining (p. 331)

Data visualization (p. 339)

Data warehouse (p. 331)

Databases (p. 331)

Decision support system (DSS) (p. 331)

Descriptive analytics (p. 336)

Diagnostic analytics (p. 336)

Encryption (p. 335)

Enterprise resource planning (ERP) (p. 331)

Executive information system (EIS) (p. 332)

Expert system (p. 332)

Extranet (p. 334)

Firewall (p. 334)

Forecasting (p. 339)

Hypertext (p. 334)

Information (p. 329)

Information system (p. 330)

Infrastructure as a service (IaaS) (p. 333)

Internet (p. 333)

Internet service providers (p. 333)

Intranet (p. 334)

Malware (p. 334)

Management information system (MIS) (p. 331)

Operations support systems (p. 331)

Optimization (p. 339)

Phishing (p. 334)

Piracy (p. 335)

Platform as a service (PaaS) (p. 333)

Predictive analytics (p. 337)

Prescriptive analytics (p. 337)

Process control systems (p. 331)

Ransomware (p. 334)

Regression (p. 338)

Small data (p. 330)

Social engineering (p. 334)

Software as a service (SaaS) (p. 333)

Text mining (p. 339)

Transaction processing system (TPS) (p. 331)

Transactional data (p. 337)

User-generated content (p. 330)

Volunteered data (p. 337)

Web browser (p. 334)

World Wide Web (p. 334)

BUSINESS CASE 16.2: OVERSTORY—AMSTERDAM, THE NETHERLANDS

SDG 15: Life on Land

Businesses are inundated with huge volumes of data every day. Although data are essential to every company today, they are meaningless unless they can be processed into information useful for decision making. Processing data into information is a science and, in the case of Overstory, data are used to predict and prevent natural disasters.

Dutch satellite vegetation platform Overstory provides businesses and government agencies with environmental insights designed to prevent wildfires, preserve precious land-based resources, and avoid large-scale power outages. Its mission is "to become the standard in planet intelligence. Monitoring all natural resources on Earth in real-time." At any given time there are over 2,500 satellites orbiting the Earth, and over 600 of these are collecting data and images of our planet. Cofounder Indra den Bakker says, "We take data from different providers, we process it with our machine learning algorithms, then we share the insights, alerts or data layers with our customers."

As the Earth grows warmer, regional climates are changing around the world, reversing patterns in some areas while exacerbating existing patterns in others. Consider the western part of the United States, for example. In 2021, California, Oregon, and Nevada experienced their hottest summer on record, while Washington and Arizona had their second hottest. Although this region has typically experienced high temperatures and periods of drought, the temperature has risen significantly in recent years leading to longer periods of drought that resulted in a prolonged wildfire season and water shortages. Fighting these fires costs billions each year in firefighting resources and loss of property. Satellite imagery enables Overstory to provide real-time, actionable data about regional vegetation and report detailed information about tree species, height, vitality, and density to identify areas susceptible to wildfires, enabling its clients to take preventative action.

A lesser-known reason why wildfires ignite are trees growing into or falling on power lines. In California alone, 1,500 wildfires have ignited due to the collision between trees and power lines. The Overstory platform alerts utility companies, one of its primary customers, to trees that are at risk of causing a fire. With its AI technology and satellite imaging, Overstory can easily identify tree height, location, and health. Utility companies can then hire crews to prune or cut down trees. Traditionally, utility companies rely on antiquated, inefficient, and often inaccurate methods of data collection. "Most utilities go out by foot to manually monitor and manage vegetation near power lines," explains Indra den Bakker, founder and CEO of Overstory. "Bigger utility companies might have their own helicopters and drones, but that is still not efficient or scalable because networks on the grid are so large." Overstory's data analytics, on the other hand, can scan an entire utility grid every single day to help companies take preemptive action to eliminate risks of fire or power outage—and at a fraction of the amount it would cost the utility companies to carry out this assessment themselves, and with a lot more accuracy. Cutting down or pruning one tree can save an entire forest.

Critical Thinking Questions

1. The chapter discusses various types of business analytics. Which type do you think best describes what Overstory does? Explain your response.

2. Individual companies, such as utility companies, hire Overstory for its data. It would make sense from an ethical perspective (greater good to the greatest amount of people) that perhaps entire industries or even governments hire Overstory, given the benefits of Overstory's data (such as preventing forest fires). Do you agree or disagree?

3. Overstory has currently chosen to focus on utilities as its primary customer. Can you think of other uses of this technology that could help both business and the environment?

References

Canon, Gabrielle. (2021, December 25). What the numbers tells us about a catastrophic year of wildfires. *The Guardian.* https://www.theguardian.com/us-news/2021/dec/25/what-the-numbers-tells-us-about-a-catastrophic-year-of-wildfires

CTVC. (2020, September 28). *Indra den Bakker (Overstory).* https://climatetechvc.org/indra-den-bakker-overstory/

Overstory. (n.d). *About Us.* https://www.overstory.com/about-us

John, St., & Jeff. (2020, September 3). AI startups raise funding to help utilities de-risk dangers of climate change. Green Tech Media. https://www.greentechmedia.com/articles/read/how-artificial-intelligence-can-help-utilities-de-risk-the-dangers-of-climate-change

TechLeap. (2020). Overstory: Helping the planet can be a scalable business. *TechLeap.* https://www.techleap.nl/blog/overstory-helping-the-planet-can-be-a-scalable-business/

17 ACCOUNTING BASICS

LEARNING OBJECTIVES

17.1   Define accounting and discuss its purpose in business.

17.2   Identify the nine most common branches of the accounting discipline.

17.3   Discuss the three major financial statements.

17.4   Explore the connections between an income statement, a balance sheet, and a statement of cash flows.

17.5   Use the six most important ratios to analyze the financial performance of a company.

BUSINESS IMPACT CASE 17.1: PORTFOLIA—SAN MATEO, CALIFORNIA

SDG 5:   Gender Equality

Most high-growth businesses need funding from external sources. For many entrepreneurs this comes in the form of equity investment, where investors invest cash in a business with expectations that they will receive some type of return on their investment at an undetermined period of time in the future. Over the years, venture capitalists have invested in young startups from Google to Amazon to Facebook and, through their investments, have arguably changed the business world. An underlying problem, however, is that venture capital funding has traditionally gone to men 97% of the time even though women-owned businesses account for 42% of all business in the U.S., employing 9.4 million and generating $1.9 trillion in revenues.[1] Additionally, mostly men are investing. Of the women who have the ability to invest in new businesses, only 1% do so.[2]

To combat the gender imbalance of both investors and investment in women-owned business, venture capitalist Trish Costello started Portfolia in 2014. Portfolia designs investment funds for primarily women investors. According to Trish, "Women for the first time control the majority of wealth in this country, and we know that when they invest, they back highly innovative but overlooked entrepreneurs and add tremendous value. Our aim is to make it as easy and seamless as possible for women to exercise their financial power for both returns and impact."[3]

Courtesy of Trish Costello

The concept, though inherently complicated, is made simple for investors. Portfolio creates a fund around a particular focus such as women's health and identifies three to four lead partners who will make the investment decisions. The lead partners are investors themselves and have the requisite investment knowledge and experience to make decisions related to the best companies to invest in. Portfolio then opens the fund to new investors who can invest a minimum of $10,000. These investors do not have any decision-making authority; they are trusting the lead investors to make decisions in the best interest of the fund.

By law, a fund can only have up to 249 accredited investors—those who have more than $1 million net worth or an annual income greater than $200,000. Once the fund raises money from accredited investors, Portfolia's "lead partners" in the fund do the actual investing. These lead partners have the expertise and knowledge to conduct the appropriate due diligence and make investment decisions. The lead partners invest in 10 companies over a 12–18 month period to create a diversified, yet focused, portfolio.

Portfolia launched its first fund in 2015 and today is raising money for its 10th fund, called FemTech II, which seeks to invest in companies on women's health issues including female-focused cancers, menopause, and aging, and issues that may affect women differently such as mental health, heart disease, and pain management.

Trish is changing the world of investment and startups one fund at a time. As she notes, "If women want specific companies in the world that address their needs, the only way to do that is for women to become the investors."[4] Since 2014 she has worked to build a very successful and accessible investment platform for women. She has been named one of the 100 most powerful women in business by *Entrepreneur* magazine, and Portfolia was named a most innovative company in 2019 by the Stevie Awards—premier awards for women in business.

Critical Thinking Questions

1. Think about the proportion of funding going to start male-owned businesses versus female-owned businesses. Does the percentage surprise you? Why or why not?

2. How is Portfolia supporting gender equality?

3. Look up Portfolia online and see the types of businesses that are being funded. Can you identify any commonalities across their investments?

ACCOUNTING IS THE LANGUAGE OF BUSINESS

Accounting is often referred to as "the language of business." This phrase was coined by Warren Buffet, the chair and CEO of American multinational conglomerate holding company Berkshire Hathaway. Buffet is thought to have used the phrase when giving advice to a 17-year-old intern during a CNBC interview. He believes that accounting should be studied the same way as a foreign language, and once absorbed, can be a key factor to success in the business world.[5]

By definition, accounting is a process of recording, sorting, retrieving, and reporting financial data. Having accounting processes in place helps managers and business owners answer three fundamental questions:

- Is the business profitable?

- Is the business financially healthy?

- Does the business have enough cash to operate and meet financial obligations?

And these questions and others can be answered from reports generated from accounting data; these reports are called financial statements.

Not every student of business needs to be an accountant, but every business student needs to understand the numbers that the discipline of accounting produces. Your ability to read the numbers is a critical business skill, and that's the focus of this chapter—understanding the language of accounting and interpreting the numbers that accounting produces. For example, say you wanted to start a T-shirt printing business. You decide to invest $10,000 of your own money to get the business off the ground. You run the business for a month and want to find out how much you have made and if you have anything left out of the original investment. If you have carefully recorded the business transactions over the month, you will know that you have used $3,000 out of the $10,000 investment to buy printing equipment and cover other expenses, which means you have $7,000 remaining. You have also made $5,000 in sales to your customers, leaving you with $12,000 in cash. Yet your profit so far is only $2,000. Oh, by the way, you may have to pay taxes on that profit! This is accounting in its simplest form, but the more your business grows, the more complex it will become.

Accounting is a process of recording, sorting, retrieving, and reporting financial data. Understanding the language of accounting is a critical business skill.

cofotoisme/iStockphoto.com

Many businesses fail because of poor accounting systems. Without understanding when cash comes in, when cash goes out, how much you can pay employees, and when bills are due, you just can't run a sustainable business. But this information is not only important to business owners, managers, and employees; the purpose of accounting is bigger than that. Financial information is important to many other users—some required by law and some required for decision-making purposes. The purpose of accounting is illustrated in Figure 17.1.

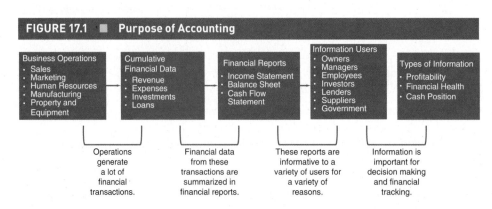

FIGURE 17.1 ■ Purpose of Accounting

Users of Accounting Information

The information users (as depicted in Table 17.1) are both internal to the organization and external. Companies have different types of users. For example, the main users in Portfolia are the **investors**—people who spend their money to invest in and support new ventures with the expectation of receiving a financial return. Portfolia investors look at financial statements as part of their due diligence as to whether they should make a decision to invest or not. **Due diligence** is a rigorous process that involves evaluating an investment opportunity prior to actually making the investment. This may include interviewing founders, reviewing current and past financial statements, analyzing the industry, reviewing market segments, and looking at other investments that may have been made.

Internal users are owners, managers, and employees.[6] Owners need financial information to assess overall performance and guide their decision making; managers need financial information to evaluate the quantity of supplies purchased, the amount of cash held in the company, and if certain goals have been met; and employees need financial information to ensure that the company is profitable enough to pay salaries and benefits and offer opportunities for career development.

External users include outside investors, lenders, suppliers, and the government. Investors use financial information to calculate the company's level of profitability or potential for profitability and chances of success; lenders such as banks and financial institutions need financial information to establish the company's ability to pay back their debts; suppliers need to know about a company's finances to understand whether the company will pay their bills when due; and the government is interested in the company's financial information for taxation and regulatory purposes.

Every user needs financial information to understand more about the position and direction of a company. Though the focus of this chapter is on understanding the basics of accounting that all students of business should learn, the field of accounting is quite broad, requiring different areas of knowledge and specialization. In the next section we introduce the nine most common branches of accounting.

TYPES OF ACCOUNTING

Business owners need to be familiar with the two main types of accounting: financial accounting, which has an external focus; and managerial accounting, which has an internal focus. Each serves a different purpose in the organization.[7]

- **Financial accounting** is the process of recording the financial transactions and developing financial statements used for financial analysis and external reporting. In the case of large, public companies, they are required to use generally accepted accounting principles (GAAP) issued by the Financial Accounting Standards Board (FASB). The main goal of GAAP is to ensure consistency across financial statements in terms of definitions, methods, and assumptions in recording and reporting accounting information.

- **Managerial accounting** is a branch of accounting that relates to the identification, measurement, analysis, and interpretation of accounting information so that it can be used to help managers make informed operational decisions. Unlike financial accounting, managerial accounting focuses on internal reporting to support decision making.

Accountants were a valuable resource for many struggling small businesses seeking advice on how to stabilize, reimagine, or reposition their operations during the COVID-19 pandemic. Nick Swedberg, a partner at accountancy firm Boyum Barnescheer in Minnesota, worked through some creative ideas with the owner of a Mexican restaurant to figure out a way to keep the business afloat during lockdown. Following some careful financial analysis, Swedberg found that the costs of a pivot would be minimal and potentially beneficial to the business. As a result, the restaurant turned half the space into a market where customers could purchase the ingredients they needed to make Mexican meals at home, giving the restaurant a much-needed revenue boost.[8]

Though financial and managerial accounting are the two most discussed branches of accounting, Table 17.1 gives an overview of seven additional branches of accounting. If you are studying business at a business school, there is probably a course offered in most of these types of accounting.

TABLE 17.1 ■ Branches of Accounting	
Branch	**Focus**
Financial Accounting	Recording financial transactions to produce financial statements
Managerial Accounting	Interpreting financial data to make better operating decisions
Cost Accounting	Primarily used to record and analyze manufacturing costs and how they can be better managed
External Auditing	Examination of financial statements by an independent party with the purpose of expressing an opinion as to fairness of presentation and compliance with GAAP
Internal Auditing	Examination of accounting procedures and controls inside an organization to ensure compliance with laws and achieve greater efficiency in data collection and overall operations
Tax Accounting	Financial reporting required by tax authorities as well as helping business better plan for tax implications
Fiduciary Accounting	Accounting related to estates and trusts, which are not businesses
Behavioral Accounting	Looks at how accounting systems impact employee behavior
Forensic Accounting	Focuses on financial investigations related to fraud and other illegal activity

Cash Basis Accounting and Accrual Basis Accounting

Within the realm of financial accounting, businesses use one of two financial reporting methods—cash or accrual (see Table 17.2). **Cash basis accounting** is an accounting method that *records* cash as income when it is received and expenses as they are paid.[9] For example, if you invoice a client for $5,000 in early January and you receive the payment in mid-February, you would record the income as received in February. The same concept would apply to your expenses. Cash basis accounting can be used for companies that earn less than $5 million per year and is often the accounting method of choice for small businesses so they know how much cash is in the bank at all times. Although it is a simple method of monitoring cash flow, it doesn't account for all incoming revenue or outgoing expenses, or for the company's liabilities, which may lead you to believe that you have more cash than you actually do.

For example, let's go back to that T-shirt business example at the start of the chapter. You may order $3,500 of colored, blank T-shirts in April. Each T-shirt costs $7, so you purchased 500 units. This is an expense. But you may not design, silk-screen, and sell these until May. If you sell each T-shirt for $25 starting in May and you sell out in the same month, your revenue is 500 units x $25 or $12,500. Now, if you are using cash basis accounting, the expense would be recorded in April when you paid for the T-shirts and the revenue would not be recorded until May when you sold the T-shirts. The issue is that your books would show a $3,500 loss for April but a $12,500 profit for April. However, the actual profit is really $9,000 over the 2 months, yet using a cash basis makes it a bit more difficult to calculate. However, in a simple business like this and many other small businesses, cash on hand is more important than understanding profit, so using a cash basis is simpler and clearer.

Accrual basis accounting is an accounting method that records income when earned, such as when the product is delivered or service is rendered and expenses when they are billed and before money changes hands.[10] In the most basic terms, revenue and expenses are recognized and recorded when they occur. But with cash basis, as discussed above, nothing is documented or recorded until cash is received or paid. For example, if you bill $10,000 income in early January, you would record that as income in your January account statement, even if the $10,000 does not reach your bank account until mid-February. Under GAAP guidelines most large companies with sales over $25 million are required to use the accrual basis accounting method when reporting financial performance. Unlike cash basis accounting, accrual basis accounting provides a more accurate picture of income and expenses, and therefore profit, over a certain period of time. This helps companies assess customer activity and preferences and enables them to plan for the future. However, there are some drawbacks. Accrual basis accounting is a more complex method of accounting than cash-basis accounting and can be expensive to implement. While it offers a better long-term view of finances, it does not provide a fully realistic picture unless carefully monitored; for instance, your company financial reports may show a large amount of revenue, but your bank account could be empty.

TABLE 17.2 ■ Cash and Accrual Accounting

Cash Accounting	Accrual Accounting
Records income when cash has been received	Records income when it is earned
Records expenses as they are paid	Records expenses when they are billed and will actually be paid at some point in the future
Taxes are not paid on cash that has not been received	Taxes paid on money that is due
Easier to track cash flow and recognize potential cash shortages before they happen	More accurate picture of profitability in the long term
Mostly used by small businesses that do not have much inventory	Mostly used by large companies with revenue over $25 million and publicly traded companies

Source: McCool, C. (2020). Cash basis accounting vs. accrual accounting. *Bench.* https://bench.co/blog/accounting/cash-vs-accrual-accounting/#:~:text=The%20difference%20between%20cash%20and%20accrual%20accounting%20lies%20in%20the,billed%20(but%20not%20paid); and Morah, C. (2020, March 7). Accrual accounting vs. cash basis accounting: What's the difference? *Investopedia.* https://www.investopedia.com/ask/answers/09/accrual-accounting.asp

THE THREE MAJOR FINANCIAL STATEMENTS[11]

Financial statements (see Table 17.3) provide a window into the financial health and performance of a company. Every business person needs to understand the three essential financial statements: an income statement, a balance sheet, and a cash flow statement. The **income statement** (or profit and loss statement) is a financial report that measures the financial performance of your business on a monthly or annual basis. It shows sales and expense-related activities that result in profit or loss over a set period of time. The **balance sheet** is a financial report that shows what the company owes, and what it owns, including the shareholders' stake, at a particular point in time. The **cash flow statement** is a financial report that details the inflows and outflows of cash for a company over a set period of time. Each statement examines the company from a slightly different perspective, yet together they provide a holistic economic view of the company.

In the following sections, we will take a closer look at each of these three financial statements.

TABLE 17.3 ■ The Financial Statements

Business Question	Financial Statement	Time Period Covered
Is the business profitable?	Income Statement	Period of time. Example: 1st quarter, Month of January 2022, or Year 2022.
Is the business financially healthy?	Balance Sheet	Snapshot at a point in time. Example: As of December 31, 2022.
Does the business have enough cash to operate and meet financial obligations?	Statement of Cash Flows	Snapshot at a point in time. Example: As of December 31, 2022.

The Income Statement

The income statement measures the financial performance of your business on a monthly or annual basis. It subtracts the COGS (cost of goods sold) and expenses (administrative, marketing, research, and other operating expenses) from the total revenue to give you a net income figure, which will be either a profit or a loss. Using Table 17.4 as a guide and assuming revenue of $10,000 as an example, let's explore the different line items of the income statement in further detail.

TABLE 17.4 ■ The Income Statement	
Revenue	$10,000
(-) Cost of Goods Sold	$4,000
Gross Profit	**$6,000**
Operating Expenses	
(-) Sales, General and Administrative	$2,000
(-) Marketing	$1,000
(-) Research and Development	$500
(-) Depreciation and Amortization	$250
Operating Profit	**$2,250**
(-) Interest Expense	$100
(-) Taxes	$675
Net Income	**$1,475**

First, revenue is recorded on the income statement when the company makes a sale of a product or service and then delivers to the customer, thereby creating an obligation for the customer to issue payment to the company. It is important to note that there is a difference between a sale (revenue) and an order (bookings). An order may or may not become a sale. Orders become sales only when the product is shipped to and accepted by the customer. A sale is recorded on the income statement, while an order might only show up in a backlog—orders that have been received but not delivered to the customer. Also, the revenue number should be expressed net of any discounts offered. Table 17.5 explains the distinctions between revenue, bookings, and backlogs.

TABLE 17.5 ■ Revenue, Bookings, and Backlog	
Revenue = Sale	Shown on the income statement net of any discounts when a customer receives and accepts an order.
Bookings = Order	An order is a promise to purchase, which does not show up on the income statement until the customer receives and accepts the product or service.
Backlog = Orders – Revenue	Orders that have been received but not delivered to the customer.

COGS represents the total cost to manufacture a product. Costs are expenditures of raw materials, labor, and manufacturing overhead used to produce a product. For a service business, COGS may include the cost-of-service staff and associated overhead.

There are three types of margins that can be calculated from the income statement: gross margin, operating profit, and net income. Subtracting COGS from revenue leaves you with the gross margin (also known as operating profit). A high gross margin percentage that remains consistently high over time can be an indicator of the company's long-term competitiveness. It also shows that the company has sufficient funds for sales, marketing, product development, and other operating expenses.

Cost of goods sold (COGS) includes expenditures of raw materials, labor, and manufacturing overhead used to produce a product. For example, this may include the amount spent on labor at the Woolrich Inc. woolen mill in Woolrich, Pennsylvania.

Luke Sharrett/Bloomberg via Getty Images

Operating expenses are the expenditures that the company makes to generate income. These expenditures generally include sales, general, and administrative (SG&A); research and development (R&D); and marketing expenses. These expenses directly lower income.

The income statement also reflects depreciation and amortization of your company's assets. Depreciation is the decrease of the value of physical assets over time. In others words, it is the cost of wear and tear of your physical assets such as machinery, equipment, and the building in which you operate. Amortization is the decrease of the value of intangible assets over time. It works similarly to depreciation; the main difference is that amortization relates to intangible assets such as patents, trademarks, copyrights, and business methodologies. Amortization matches the useful life of an intangible asset with the revenue it generates.

If you have studied accounting in the past, you might hear depreciation referred to as a "noncash" expense that is usually ignored when calculating free cash flow or EBITDA (Earnings Before Interest, Taxes, Depreciation, and Amortization). This is an accepted practice, but it avoids the obvious, which is that equipment and buildings eventually need to be replaced. From a short-term perspective, depreciation is a noncash charge to earnings, but in the long term, someone has to write a check for replacement.

The second of the three margins to monitor is operating profit, which is the amount left over from gross margin once all operating expenses are subtracted.

Sometimes there are other expenses, and interest expense is the most common. Interest expense is the cost related to borrowing money, like the cost of keeping a bank loan. Taxes are the last expense item before net income. This line item captures federal, state, and sometimes municipal taxes due for the period. Sales taxes are not recorded here.

The third margin item is net income (also referred to as profit margin), which indicates what is left after other expenses have been subtracted from the operating profit such as interest and taxes. It is important to note that there is a difference between income and cash; for instance, it is quite possible for a company to have positive net income but have a negative cash flow, which causes it to struggle to pay its bills. We will explore this concept in more detail later.

The income statement alone does not reveal much about a company's long-term viability or financial health. It tells you little about how and when the company receives cash or how much it has on hand. For an accurate picture of financial health, the balance sheet and cash flow statements also need to be analyzed.

The Balance Sheet

The balance sheet (see Table 17.6) is a statement that shows a "snapshot" at a particular point in time of what the company has today (assets), how much it owes (liabilities), and what it is currently worth (shareholder equity). Numbers in Table 17.7 are for illustrative purposes only.

TABLE 17.6 ■ The Balance Sheet Equation		
What You Own	**=**	**What You Owe + What You Are Worth**
Assets	**=**	**Liabilities + Shareholder Equity**

Both sides of this equation must always balance.

As explained in Table 17.7, the balance sheet gets its name from a basic equation, which must be equally balanced.[12]

TABLE 17.7 ■ The Balance Sheet			
Assets (what the business owns)		**Liabilities (what the business owes)**	
Current Assets		Current Liabilities	
Cash	$36,000	Accounts Payable	$68,000
Inventory	$128,000	Accrued Expenses	$88,000
Accounts Receivable	$43,000	Short-Term Debt	$25,000
Prepaid Expenses	$16,000	Other Current Liabilities	$0
Fixed Assets		**Long-Term Debt**	$200,000
Property, Plant, and Equipment	$601,000	**Shareholder Equity** (what the business is worth)	
Accumulated Depreciation	($8,000)	Retained Earnings	$335,000
		Capital Stock	$100,000
Total Assets	**$816,000**	**Total Liabilities and Shareholder Equity**	**$816,000**

Assets include cash, machines, inventory, buildings, and what you are owed and what you have the right to collect. **Current assets** include cash and other assets such as inventory, accounts receivable, and prepaid expenses that can be converted into cash within a year. Cash usually includes both cash and cash equivalents, or short-term, low-risk investments. Inventory represents what the company has to sell, as well as materials that are to be made into products. There are three basic types of inventory: raw materials, which include any goods or components used in the manufacturing process; work-in-process (WIP) or semifinished products, which are partially assembled items awaiting completion; and finished goods, which are ready to be sold (see Figure 17.2).

Accounts receivable refers to money owed to the company for goods or services provided and billed to a customer. When the company ships a good or provides a service to a customer on credit and sends a bill, the company has the right to collect this money. **Prepaid expenses** represent payments the company has already made for services not yet received. These are usually things like insurance, deposits, and prepayment of rent. Prepaid expenses are considered current assets because the company has already paid for these services and will not have to use cash to pay for them in the near future.

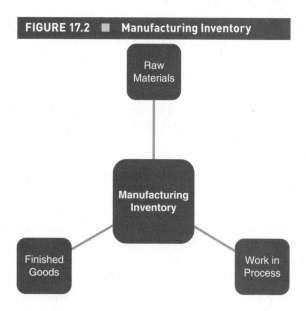

FIGURE 17.2 ■ Manufacturing Inventory

Fixed assets might also appear on the balance sheet as property, plant, and equipment (PP&E). These are productive assets that are not intended for sale and are used over time to produce goods, store them, ship them, and so on. This commonly includes land, buildings, equipment, machines, furniture, trucks, autos, and other goods that have a useful life of 3 to 5 years, although the life of some assets, such as land and buildings, could be much longer. These assets are reported at cost minus accumulated depreciation. Recall that depreciation is an accounting convention that appears on the income statement and represents the decline in value of the asset, due to age, wear, and the passage of time. Accumulated depreciation is the sum of all the depreciation charges taken since the asset was acquired.

Finished goods, which are ready to be sold, are one form of inventory. These tires at a Continental Tire Sumter plant distribution warehouse are considered finished goods.

Luke Sharrett/Bloomberg via Getty Images

Other Types of Assets

"Other assets" is a catchall category that includes items such as the value of patents, goodwill, and intangible assets. **Goodwill** represents the price paid for an asset in excess of its book value. You will see this on the balance sheet when the company has made one or more large acquisitions. **Intangible assets** represent the value of patents, software programs, copyrights, trademarks, franchises, brand names, or assets that cannot be physically touched. One important note is that only items that have been purchased can appear here. For instance, companies are not allowed to create a value for things like a brand name and place it on the balance sheet.

Another type of asset includes long-term investments, which refers to assets that are more than 1 year old and are carried on the balance sheet at cost or book value with no appreciation. Examples of long-term investments include cash, stock, bonds, and real estate. It is possible that the assets are worth much more, or much less, than the original cost, but the convention is to carry them at cost.

Liabilities and Shareholder Equity

Let's turn our attention to the other side of the balance sheet: liabilities and shareholder equity. Liabilities are economic obligations of the company, such as money it owes to lenders, suppliers, and employees.

Current liabilities are bills that must be paid within 1 year of the date of the balance sheet. They are organized based on who is owed the money. Accounts payable is money owed by a business to its suppliers. Accrued expenses are costs incurred by the company for which no payment has been made. For example, wages and taxes may be indicated on the balance sheet to be paid at a future date, but that payment hasn't occurred just yet. Short-term debt is the portion of long-term debt that must be paid within a year. A common example of short-term debt is money owed to lenders such as bank loans. Other current liabilities are short-term liabilities that do not fall into a specific category; these will include sales tax, income tax, and so forth.

Long-term debt is an obligation for debt that is due to be repaid in more than 12 months. Bank loans, finance, and leasing obligations are all examples of long-term debt.

Shareholder equity represents the money that has been invested in the business plus the cumulative net profits and losses the company has generated. This is a liability that is not usually repaid over the normal course of business. Subtracting what the company owns (total assets) from what it owes (total liabilities) provides the percentage of its value to the owners, or its shareholders' equity.

There are two main components of shareholder equity. One component is retained earnings, capital stock, which represents the original amount the owners paid into the company plus any additional paid-in capital to purchase stock in the company.

Shareholder equity increases when the company makes a profit (increase in retained earnings) or sells new stock to increase the capital stock. If the company has a loss, which lowers retained earnings, or pays a dividend, which also lowers retained earnings, these actions will result in a decrease in shareholder equity.

The Cash Flow Statement

The cash flow statement tracks the movement of cash into (cash inflows) and out of (cash outflows) the company over a period of time. Cash inflows include sales, returns on investments, and financing; while outflows include payment to suppliers, wages and salaries, and dividends to shareholders (see Table 17.8). A typical small business may have cash inflows primarily from sales or maybe a bank loan. It gets quite a bit more complicated for a very large company with lots of business units and transactions.

The cash flow statement is like a cash register for the company. It shows the cash available at the beginning of the period—in other words, cash already in the register. It also shows cash received during the period such as cash from the sale of a product or service, or cash received from investments, borrowing, or the sale of assets, minus the cash paid out in the period. This is cash actually paid out to support operations necessary to make and sell a product or service, or cash used to pay down loans, taxes, or the purchase of assets. This, then, leaves you with cash at the end of the period. Only cash transactions affect cash flow and are considered on the cash flow statement.

Cash flow statements are generally divided into two basic parts: cash generated from operations or profit-making activities, and cash generated from investment and financing activities. The first examines the profit-making inflows and expense outflows, while the second examines inflows and outflows of cash related to the purchase and sale of assets, and financing activities such as bank borrowing and stock sales. Together they form the full picture of cash moving through the company (see Table 17.8).

TABLE 17.8 ■ Cash Flow Statement	
Net Income	**$50,000**
(+) Depreciation and Amortization	$1,000
(+) Sources: Decrease in Assets or Increase in Liabilities	$12,000
(-) Uses: Increase in Assets or Decrease in Liabilities	($15,000)
Increase/(Decrease) Cash from Operations	**$48,000**
(-) Net Property Plant and Equipment	($8,000)
Increase/(Decrease) Cash from Investments	**$40,000**
(+) Increase in Net Borrowing	$0
(+) Sale of Stock	$0
(-) Paying of Dividends	$0
Increase/(Decrease) Cash from Financing	**($4,000)**
Increase/(Decrease) in Cash	**$36,000**
(Should be equal to cash on the Balance Sheet)	

The first line of the cash flow statement is net income. The first thing to do when examining cash flow is to add back depreciation and amortization that appear on the income statement. As you may recall, these are considered "noncash" charges related to the declining value of tangible and intangible assets. So, even though a write-down, or charge, may appear on the income statement, no cash actually left the company. Because we want to determine only cash in this statement, we add back both depreciation and amortization expenses.

The next step is to examine the changes in the balances of current assets and current liabilities on the balance sheet. If a current asset balance increases, we are using cash. If a current asset balance decreases, we are adding cash. Conversely, an increase in a current liability balance adds cash, while a decrease in a current liability balance uses cash (see Table 17.9).

TABLE 17.9 ■ Cash Inflows and Outflows	
Cash Inflows	**Cash Outflows**
Loans	Payments to Suppliers
Sales	Wages and Salaries
Interest	Dividends to Shareholders
Shares	Taxes on Profits
Receipts from Debtors	Loan Payments

Initially, it is best to understand the inflows and outflows of cash related to the operating activities of the company by determining the sources (inflows) and uses (outflows) associated with current assets and current liabilities to arrive at the degree of cash flow from operations.

Next, we shift our focus to cash changes stemming from investment and financing activities. One option might be simply to stockpile cash on the balance sheet, but this isn't the most productive use of cash. Another option might be to return cash to shareholders in the form of dividends, or to pay down any debt that the company may have amassed. And still another option might be to invest in productive assets such as machinery and equipment, or to acquire all or part of another business. This may show up as a separate line item in the cash flow as "Investments in Fixed Assets," or something similar.

Finally, you must examine cash inflows and outflows from financing activities such as selling stock, borrowing, or paying dividends. Borrowing money increases the amount of cash on hand. Conversely, paying down your debt lowers the amount of cash on hand, while the sale of stock by a company increases the amount of cash coming into the company.

Adding the cash flow from operations to the cash flow from investing and financing leaves us with either a cash increase or decrease for the period. If a company has either cash in the bank or access to additional cash, it can withstand negative cash flow for several periods. It is good business practice to strive to achieve profits and convert those profits into cash.

Net Income Versus Cash Flow

Although net income (or profit) and cash flow are both crucial to the success of the business, there are important differences between the two.

Net income, as it appears on the income statement, is determined by accounting principles and includes accruals and noncash items such as depreciation and amortization. In other words, there are items on the income statement that determine net income for a period that do not represent actual cash coming in or going out of the company for that period. For instance, in respect of how revenue is recorded on the income statement, the credit sales are captured as an obligation to pay (asset) in the balance sheet as an account receivable. Even though no cash has changed hands, the revenue on the income statement still reflects the sale. This treatment also applies to expenses and capital expenditures on the income statement.

Cash flow, in contrast, deals only with actual cash transactions. A company's operating policies, production techniques, and inventory and credit-control systems will influence the timing of cash moving through the business; and this is what the entrepreneurial manager must master in order to convert profit into cash.

CONNECTING THE THREE STATEMENTS[13]

The power of financial statements lies in the linkages. It is important to understand how the three financial statements are linked to one another and how decisions related to the operations of a company will impact its financial performance. A company's pricing and credit policies will have a direct impact on revenue, an income statement item; and accounts receivable, a balance sheet item. Although each financial statement provides a different view of the company, each statement is also related to the other.

For instance, net income on the income statement is added to retained earnings on the balance sheet. The ending cash balance on the cash flow statement is equal to the cash on the balance sheet. Every business person needs to understand how cash and goods and services flow into and out of the company.

Figure 17.3 shows what happens when a sale is made, the product or service is delivered, and the cash is collected. When a sale is made and the product or service is accepted by the customer, revenue on the income statement increases. Assuming that credit is extended for the sale, accounts receivable on the balance sheet also increases. Once the obligation to pay is met by the customer, accounts receivable decreases and the amount paid becomes a cash inflow on the cash flow statement. Additionally, when a sale is made, the value of the product is moved from inventory (a balance sheet item) to cost of goods (an income statement item).

As with the *sales* cycle explained above, these types of connections between the various statements can be charted in similar fashion for the *expense* cycle, the purchase of fixed assets, and investments. When you understand how cash moves through the company, you begin to understand how policies related to credit, inventory, and payables can affect the time it takes for cash to be converted into products and returned back to the company at a profit.

FIGURE 17.3 ■ Income Statement/Balance Sheet/Cash Flow Statement

Income Statement

Revenue	$$$$
(-) Cost of Goods	$$
Gross profit	$$
(-) Sales, General and Administrative	$
(-) Marketing	$
(-) Research and Development	$
(-) Depreciation and Amortization	$
Operating profit	$$
(-) Interest Expense	$
(-) Taxes	$
Net Income	$$

When a sale is made, Revenue increases on the Income Statement and an obligation to pay is incurred by the customer, which increases Accounts Receivable on the Balance Sheet.

When a sale is made, the value of the product is moved from Inventory on the Balance Sheet to Cost of Goods on the Income Statement.

Balance Sheet

Assets (What You Own)		Liabilities (What You Owe)	
Current Assets		Current Liabilities	
Cash	$$	Account Payable	$$
Inventory	$$	Accured Expenses	$$
Accounts Receivable	$$	Short-Term Debt	$$
Prepaid Expenses	$$	Other Current Liabilities	$$
Fixed Assets		**Long-Term Debt**	
Property, Plant and Equipment	$$	**Shareholders' Equity (What You Are Worth)**	
Accumulated Depreciation	$$$	Retained Earnings	$$
		Capital Stock	$$
Total Assets	$$$$	**Total Liabilities and Shareholders' Equity**	$$$$

When Net Income on the Income Statement increases, Retained Earnings on the Balance Sheet increases. The opposite is also true. A decrease in Net Income will decrease Retained Earnings.

Cash Flow Statement

Net Income	$$$
(+) Depreciation and Amortization	$
(+) Sources: Decrease in Assets or Increase in Liabilities	$
(-) Uses: Increase in Assets or Decrease in Liabilities	$
Increase/(Decrease) Cash from Operations	$$$
(-) Net PP&E	$
Increase/(Decrease) Cash from Investments	$$
(+) Increase in Net Borrowing	$
(+) Sale of Stock	$
(-) Paying of Dividends	$
Increase/(Decrease) Cash from Financing	$$
Increase/(Decrease) in Cash	$$
(Should be equal to cash on the Balance Sheet)	

When the customer pays for the product or service, Accounts Receivable on the Balance Sheet decreases while a receipt of cash is recorded on the Cash Flow Statement.

ENTREPRENEURIAL MINDSET ACTIVITY

Forecast Your Own Idea

Think about a new small business idea. Maybe it's a food truck, a car-washing business, a T-shirt printing company, or a dog-walking business. When you have an idea, work to create a pro-forma income statement. Unlike what's been discussed in this chapter, a pro-forma income statement means "projected" or "estimated." In other words, you are forecasting what your sales and expenses could be to determine if the business could be profitable. Create a pro-forma income statement for 1 month of operations.

● What are your sales?
● What is the cost of sales?

- What are your expenses?
- What is your potential net income?

Critical Thinking Questions

1. Are you more or less profitable than you thought you would be?
2. What would happen if you created the pro forma income statement for a year? Would there be changes based on seasons or months or years?
3. How did you estimate your sales? How confident are you in your sales numbers?

ANALYZING PERFORMANCE: RATIO ANALYSIS[13]

The financial statements allow business people to perform financial analysis such as changes from one period to another or comparison to similar companies in the industry and forecasting. This type of analysis is called ratio analysis. By definition, ratio analysis allows you to compare performance over time as well as compare your performance to others in the same industry or sector. The most important ratios discussed next are calculated from the company's income statement and balance sheet. Calculating and understanding the most important ratios will help you better answer the key questions with which we started off this chapter: Is the business profitable? Is the business financially healthy? And does the business have enough cash to operate and meet its financial obligations?

The Six Most Important Financial Ratios

We are going to discuss the most common ratios used in financial analysis: how to calculate, what questions each one answers, and how to interpret (see Table 17.10 for an overview).

TABLE 17.10 ■ Six Most Important Financial Ratios At-a-Glance			
Ratio	Calculation	Question Answered by the Ratio	Where Do You Get the Data?
Gross Margin Percentage	Gross Profit/Revenue	How much profit are we making on each unit sold?	Income Statement
Profit Margin	Net Income/Revenue	What percentage of revenue is pure profit after accounting for all expenses?	Income Statement
Return on Equity	Net Income/Shareholder's Equity	How well is the business doing at generating profit with investors' money?	Income Statement and Balance Sheet
Debt to Equity	Total Liabilities/Total Equity	What percentage of financing comes from bank loans vs. investors?	Balance Sheet
Quick Ratio	(Cash + Short-term Investments + Current Receivables) / Current Liabilities	Can the business pay off its current liabilities within 90 days if needed?	Balance Sheet
Current Ratio	Current Assets/Current Liabilities	Can the business pay off its current liabilities?	Balance Sheet

Ratio #1 Gross Margin Percentage

Calculation: Gross margin percentage = gross profit/sales

As you read earlier, gross profit is the company's net sales revenue minus the costs of goods (COGS) sold. For instance, if you sell $1,000 in T-shirts and they cost you $750 to produce (COGS), then your gross profit is $250. Gross margin percentage is the gross profit divided by sales. In this example, it would be $250/$1,000, which is equal to a gross margin percentage of 25%. One way to interpret this number is that for every $1 you earn in revenue, $0.25 is available to spend on operating expenses. A common question may now arise: Is 25% a good gross margin? There are a few considerations in answering this question. First, the higher the ratio the better, because higher ratios mean more money is available to spend on operating expenses. Second, you want to compare your gross margin percentage to similar companies in your industry. For example, your mother has a friend who lives in another state and is running a booming sock business. After a conversation with your mother's friend, you learn that her gross margin is 42%. You also learn you have similar operating expenses. So why is her gross margin so much higher? In this scenario, it's because your COGS are much higher, so the best way to increase your gross margin is to reduce your cost of goods sold. Can you source your T-shirts from another supplier at a lower cost? Keep in mind that the higher your gross margin, the more able you will be to pay operating expenses such as payroll, marketing, rent, internet, and other expenses.

Ratio #2: Profit Margin

Calculation: Profit margin = net income/revenues

Profit margin is a profitability ratio that measures the amount of net income as a percentage of sales. Profit margin is also referred to as return on sales, and this terminology makes a lot of sense. Think about it this way: For every sale the company makes, what's the return to us? Let's consider the T-shirt company at the end of the year. The company sold $350,000 in T-shirts; COGs were $200,000; and operating expenses totaled $175,000. Net income for the year in this scenario is $25,000 ($350,000 − $200,000 − 125,000). The profit margin is then $25,000/$350,000, which is 7%. Similar to the gross margin discussed above, there are different considerations to know if this number is good. A positive profit margin indicates that the business is able to cover its expenses. To increase the margin even further, however, reduce your operating expenses. Keep in mind that this calculation does not factor in costs that are out of your control such as interest, taxes, and dividends. But it will tell you the overall profitability of a business and give you a clear indication of EBIT (earnings before interest and taxes).

Ratio #3: Return on Equity

Calculation: Net income/shareholder's equity

Return on equity (ROE) is a financial ratio that demonstrates how successful a company is at managing the capital contributed by shareholders. As an investor or shareholder you want to ensure that your money is being used in the most efficient way possible in order to generate as much profit as possible. If investors aren't happy, this is not a good sign! If the company has a low return on equity, meaning it isn't making money, then there is little point in investing.

This ratio uses net income from the income statement and shareholder's equity from the balance sheet. The higher the ratio the better, but what ratio is expected varies by industry. For example, at the time of this writing, the average ROE in the auto industry was 4.5%, but the average ROE in computer services was 13.5%.[14] So let's say you wanted to invest in a computer software company and have narrowed it down to two companies. Company A has an ROE of 16% and Company B has an ROE of 10%. These ratios compared to the industry average ROE of 13.5% may steer you to opt for Company A.

It's important to note that ROE can also be negative when calculated. If your calculation generates a negative ROE, then the company is not profitable—the net income is negative. Many new businesses operate at a loss for the first few years, so ROE may not be indicative of performance in this case.

Ratio #4: Debt-to-Equity Ratio

Calculation: Debt-to-equity ratio = total liabilities/total equity

Debt-to-equity ratio measures the degree of debt owed by the company, and the amount of equity financed by people outside the company. It is calculated by dividing total liabilities by total equity. A higher debt-to-equity ratio indicates that financing comes from places such as banks and other creditors that must be paid back as opposed to financing through investors and shareholders. Thus, a lower debt-to-equity ratio signals greater financial health, given total liabilities are lower. For example, if a company was looking for additional financing from a bank and the bank noticed a high debt-to-equity ratio, it may be less likely to issue additional loans simply because the company is already leveraged. Leverage in a business sense means that the company is financing its activities more through borrowed funds such as loans, which increases a company's liabilities. As noted with other ratios, determining an acceptable debt-to-equity ratio is often industry-specific.

The ratio is a useful way to find out whether the company is operating at a level of acceptable risk. Generally, companies aim for a ratio of one-to-one or below. For example, a ratio of .5 indicates a company has half the amount of liabilities than it does equity; a ratio of 1 means it has an equal amount of each; and a ratio of 1.5 means it has 50% more liabilities than equity. Overall, the lower the ratio, the less risk involved and indicates the company is not overly leveraged.

Ratio #5: Quick Ratio

Calculation: Quick ratio = liquid assets/current liabilities

Quick ratio is a financial ratio that measures liquidity. Liquidity in business refers to how fast a business can convert its assets into cash. Liquidity is important for three primary reasons. Let's say a business has a bad quarter or year in terms of sales, so there is less cash to cover expenses and other financial obligations. Having liquid assets available (such as accounts receivables, cash in other accounts, or investments) can help the business weather unpredictable times and pay its short-term liabilities. The quick ratio is calculated by dividing liquid assets by current liabilities and indicates if the company can pay down short-term liabilities, those coming due within 90 days. A higher quick ratio signals that business operations are making enough profit to cover short-term obligations, which is a very good thing!

Companies with a quick ratio greater than 1 translates as having more quick or liquid assets than current liabilities and have a higher chance of getting a loan than companies with weak ratios. If a company doesn't have enough current assets to cover its current liabilities, it is usually a sign of impending trouble.

Ratio #6: Current ratio

Calculation: Current ratio = current assets/current liabilities

Current ratio is another liquidity ratio that assesses whether the company has enough current assets to pay its short-term liabilities. It is similar to quick ratio (see #5) except that instead of measuring liquid assets, it includes all current assets such as cash, accounts receivable, and inventory and compares them to current liabilities stated on the balance sheet. The current ratio is an important measure because it signals if a business can pay off current liabilities—those due within 1 year.

Unlike quick ratio, liquidating inventory is not a speedy process, as it involves the selling of a company's assets to generate enough cash to pay off the debt. A business with a higher rate of inventory may be more suitable for a current ratio, while quick ratio may be more appropriate for companies with a slower rate of inventory. Additionally, a higher current ratio for an inventory heavy company, such as an auto dealership or clothing store, is favorable because the company is able to fulfill its short-term financial obligations and pay all borrowers on time and as expected. In this sense, the current ratio is also referred to as an efficiency ratio because it signals how efficient the company is at turning over its inventory.

A high current ratio for a high-inventory business like a fabric store is desirable. Current ratio assesses whether the company has enough current assets to pay its short-term liabilities.

Mariusz Szczawinski/Alamy Stock Photo

ETHICS IN BUSINESS

Cooking the Books

In accounting, there is a fine line between ethical and legal dilemmas. A common issue in business is called "cooking the books," a slang term meaning that the financial records look better than they actually are. This practice involves using fake or made-up numbers rather than actual numbers. Additionally, it could include simply leaving out important information such as not reporting an asset or listing a liability. Companies do this for a variety of reasons. A small business owner may want to underreport income so as to avoid paying taxes. A large public company may misstate earnings, given the pressure to meet projected earnings expected by stockholders.

More recently, companies have been cooking the books by faking products. One such case is Theranos, a biotech company founded in 2003 claiming that it had revolutionary blood-testing technology. A small drop of blood could be inserted into a Theranos machine and the machine would conduct countless blood tests in minutes at a fraction of the cost of traditional tests. The company raised more than $700 million in investment over its 15-year existence. In 2015, *The Wall Street Journal* reported that Theranos had grossly exaggerated its product capabilities. Imagine that you worked at Theranos and found out that the product did not work, or really didn't exist. Would you say anything?

Critical Thinking Questions

1. How is "cooking the books" unethical?
2. If you knew the company was selling a fake product, as with Theranos, would you say anything?
3. How does not understanding accounting and financial statements contribute to fraudulent behavior?

Sources

Tun, Z. T. (2019, August 27). Theranos: A fallen Unicorn. *Investopedia*. https://www.investopedia.com/articles/investing/020116/theranos-fallen-unicorn.asp

Kenton, W. (2020, August 6). Cook the books. *Investopedia*. https://www.investopedia.com/terms/c/cookthebooks.asp

IN REVIEW

17.1   Define accounting and discuss its purpose in business.

By definition, accounting is a process of recording, sorting, retrieving, and summarizing financial data. Having an accounting process in place helps managers and business owners understand whether a business is profitable, financially healthy, and if it has enough cash to operate and meet financial obligations.

17.2   Identify the nine most common branches of the accounting discipline.

Business owners need to be familiar with the two main types of accounting: financial accounting, which has an external focus; and managerial accounting, which has an internal focus. Each serves a different purpose in the organization. The nine common branches of the accounting discipline include financial accounting, managerial accounting, cost accounting, external auditing, internal auditing, tax accounting, fiduciary accounting, behavioral accounting, and forensic accounting.

17.3   Discuss the three major financial statements.

There are three essential financial statements: an income statement, a balance sheet, and a cash flow statement. The income statement (or profit and loss statement) is a financial report that measures the financial performance of your business on a monthly or annual basis. It shows sales and expense-related activities that result in profit or loss over a set period of time. The balance sheet is a financial report that shows what the company owes, and what it owns, including the shareholders' stake, at a particular point in time. The cash flow statement is a financial report that details the inflows and outflows of cash for a company over a set period of time.

17.4   Explore the connections between income statement, balance sheet, and statement of cash flows.

Although each financial statement provides a different view of the company, each statement is also related to the other. For instance, a company's pricing and credit policies will have a direct impact on revenue, and income statement item, and on accounts receivable, a balance sheet item.

17.5   Use the six most important ratios to analyze the financial performance of a company.

Managers use ratio analysis to compare performance over time as well as compare performance to others in the same industry or sector. There are six most important key ratios: gross margin percentage, profit margin, return on equity, debt to equity, quick ratio, and current ratio.

BUSINESSES DISCUSSED IN THIS CHAPTER

Organization	UN Sustainable Development Goal
Portfolia	5. Gender Equality

KEY TERMS

Accounting (p. 347)

Accounts payable (p. 356)

Accounts receivable (p. 354)

Accrual basis accounting (p. 350)

Accrued expenses (p. 356)

Amortization (p. 353)

Backlog (p. 352)

Balance sheet (p. 351)

Capital stock (p. 356)

Cash basis accounting (p. 350)

Cash flow statement (p. 351)

Current assets (p. 354)

Current liabilities (p. 356)

Current ratio (p. 362)

Debt-to-equity ratio (p. 362)

Depreciation (p. 353)

Due diligence (p. 349)

Financial accounting (p. 349)

Fixed costs

Goodwill (p. 355)

Gross margin percentage (p. 361)

Income statement (or profit and loss statement)
 (p. 351)

Intangible assets (p. 355)

Interest expense (p. 353)

Investors (p. 349)

Liabilities (p. 356)

Long-term debt (p. 356)

Long-term investments (p. 356)

Managerial accounting (p. 349)

Net income (p. 353)

Net Operating Margin Percentage

Operating expenses (p. 353)

Operating leverage

Operating profit (p. 353)

Other current liabilities (p. 356)

Prepaid expenses (p. 354)

Profit margin (p. 361)

Quick ratio (p. 362)

Ratio analysis (p. 360)

Retained earnings (p. 356)

Return on equity (p. 361)

Shareholder equity (p. 356)

Short-term debt (p. 356)

Variable costs

BUSINESS CASE 17.2: ACCENTURE—DUBLIN, IRELAND

SDG 9: Industry, Innovation, and Infrastructure

When you think of innovation, what comes to mind? Perhaps Tesla, SpaceX, or medical breakthroughs by pharmaceutical companies. You may not immediately think of a company like Accenture, a management consulting and technology firm headquartered in Dublin, Ireland, which has its origins in accounting. Accenture began as the business and technology consulting division of highly successful accounting firm Arthur Andersen, founded in the early 1950s. It eventually split off from the accounting firm as Andersen Consulting, and the name changed to Accenture in 2001. Today, the company has a strong focus on innovation; even its name stresses innovation, as it is derived from "accent on the future."

Ranked #258 on Fortune's Global 500 list, Accenture is a multinational company with $44 billion in annual revenue. It focuses on multiple industries and has 674,000 employees with offices in 200 cities across 50 countries. With a whopping 8,200 patents, the company has a bold purpose: "To deliver on the promise of technology and human ingenuity. We help our clients become the next and best versions of themselves." Aligning with this purpose is its sustainability promise, "to embed sustainability into everything we do, with everyone we work with, creating both business value and sustainable impact, enabled by technology and human ingenuity."

Accenture is an expert when it comes to financial and accounting processes. For example, it teamed with the global energy company, British Petroleum (BP), to consolidate and run its finance and accounting function across Europe and North America, resulting in a reduction of BP's financial operating costs by 35% (even though work volumes doubled). The company is also an innovator when it comes to financial operations. Specifically, it offers services that help clients transform their finance operations "from a transactional service to a strategic asset with a data-driven, intelligent operating model." Accenture is investing $3 billion over the next 3 years to enable its clients to become cloud-first businesses, helping them store more of their information, including accounting related data, on the cloud. Accenture explains that this will help banks improve scalability, efficiency, agility, and security. Another huge innovation Accenture is proposing in the world of accounting and finance is the use of artificial intelligence (AI). AI can be used to improve the accuracy and efficiency of routine processes and administrative tasks, allowing workers to spend more time on tasks that are complicated and require judgment and imagination. Banks also can use AI to engage with, advise, assist, and sell to customers in a much more personalized way. In 2020, Accenture partnered with hotel group NH Hotels, which had over time expanded to operating across 28 countries. NH Hotels handled over $70 million a month across 20 million individual payments. When Accenture analyzed NH Hotels's finances and accounting areas, it discovered it could standardize processes by using more automation and artificial intelligence to better manage costs and improve productivity and service quality. With consulting help from Accenture, NH Hotels improved its productivity by 45%.

Accenture has its eye on what it sees as the next big disruption in all business sectors—quantum computing. "Quantum computers solve many problems exponentially faster and with less energy consumption than classical, or binary, computers. To understand why, imagine a two-dimensional maze. . . . If the maze comprises 256 possible paths, the classical computer has to run through the maze about 128 consecutive times (on average, half of a maze's paths must be tried to find the right one). A quantum computer, however, is able to work with all 256 paths at once." Quantum computers are great for running simulations and data analyses.

The financial services industry is one strategic area that is actively exploring quantum computing technologies. With the ability to more effectively analyze large or unstructured data sets, financial institutions can make better investment decisions and improve customer service through timelier or more relevant offers.

In a recent Accenture survey of 250 business leaders in the New York metropolitan area from companies with $500 million or more in annual revenue, 97% of those surveyed see the usage of quantum computing as a driver of business growth because of its promise to businesses to better optimize investment strategies, improve encryption, and discover better products for unique customers. They also strongly believed the technology would improve efficiencies and effectiveness internally within their businesses. Partnerships are one way industries are seeking to jumpstart their integration of quantum computing, and Accenture is positioning itself to be just such a partner. In 2021, Accenture announced it was partnering with IonQ, which is designing the hardware for quantum computing. "Accenture's experience and skills in quantum, coupled with its ability to design and create customized industry solutions tailored to IonQ's quantum computing technology, will help more companies innovate and become quantum ready."

Critical Thinking Questions

1. How do you think Accenture's focus on innovation affects its day-to-day operations?

2. Accounting and innovation are two terms you don't often hear together. How does Accenture involve both of these concepts?

3. How is quantum computing different from traditional forms of computing we are familiar with today?

References

Accenture. (2017). Finance and accounting business process services (BPS) delivers business value. [Presentation]. https://www.accenture.com/_acnmedia/pdf-4/accenture-finance-and-accounting-bpo-infographic.pdf

Accenture. (2020, December 17). New York's quantum opportunities top $300B. https://www.accenture.com/us-en/insights/technology/new-york-quantum-opportunities

Accenture. (2021, September 14). *Accenture and IonQ collaborate to accelerate quantum computing into the enterprise.* https://newsroom.accenture.com/news/accenture-and-ionq-collaborate-to-accelerate-quantum-computing-into-the-enterprise.htm#:~:text=Accenture%20and%20IonQ%20Collaborate%20to%20Accelerate%20Quantum%20Computing%20into%20the%20Enterprise,-content&text=NEW%20YORK%3B%20Sept.,organizations%20globally%20and%20across%20industries

Accenture. (2022a). About us. https://www.accenture.com/us-en/about/company-index

Accenture. (2022b). The Accenture sustainability value promise. https://www.accenture.com/us-en/about/sustainability/sustainability-value-promise

Accenture. (2022c). Business process services. https://www.accenture.com/us-en/services/business-process-services/intelligent-finance-accounting

Accenture. (2020d). The cloud imperative for the banking industry. https://www.accenture.com/us-en/insights/banking/cloud-imperative-banking

Accenture. (2022e). NH Hotels: Building 5-star finance operations. https://www.accenture.com/us-en/case-studies/operations/nh-hotels-builds-5-star-finance-operations

Forbes. (2022a). *Accenture (ACN).* https://www.forbes.com/compndersenenture/?sh=68aa43d548d6

Fortune. (2022b). Global 500 Accenture. https://fortune.com/condersenenture/global500/

InformationWeek. (2000). Andersen consulting changing name to Accenture. https://www.informationweendersendersen-consulting-changing-name-to-accenture-/d/d-id/1009400

McKinsey. (2020, December 18). How quantum computing could change financial services. https://www.mckinsey.com/industries/financial-services/our-insights/how-quantum-computing-could-change-financial-services https://hbr.org/2022/01/quantum-computing-for-business-leaders

Ruane, J., McAffe, A., & Oliver, W. D. (2022, January–February). Quantum computing for business leaders. *Harvard Business Review.* https://hbr.org/2022/01/quantum-computing-for-business-leaders

Associated Press/Amy Sussman

18   FINANCIAL MANAGEMENT

LEARNING OBJECTIVES

18.1   Explain the role of financial management and its purpose in a business.

18.2   Explore two aspects of financial planning—budgeting and forecasting.

18.3   Differentiate between equity and debt financing.

18.4   Illustrate the cash conversion cycle and how it helps understand cash flow.

18.5   Contrast the three types of internal financial controls.

BUSINESS IMPACT CASE 18.1: WW INTERNATIONAL— NEW YORK, NEW YORK

SDG 3:   Good Health and Well-Being

Jean Nedetch was overweight most of her life and tried every diet in the book. After entering a 10-week program offered by a clinic in New York City, she lost 20 pounds. She invited a group of friends over to her apartment in Queens, New York, who also wanted to lose weight. Using similar principles from the clinic program Jean experienced combined with weekly weigh-ins and a reward structure, the original Weight Watchers program was born.[1] The New York City home soon became the first group meeting of what would become Weight Watchers. One of the group's participants, Al Lippert, encouraged and helped Jean turn her weight-loss methodology into a business. The company was officially founded in 1963 in Queens, went public in 1968, sold to the H. J. Heinz company for $71 million in 1999, and then acquired by a German investment company in 2001 for $735 million.[2] Today, the company is one of the most widely used weight loss programs in the world and had $1.2 billion in revenue in 2021.[3]

Weight Watchers rebranded itself in 2018 to WW International to focus less on weight loss and more on overall health and wellness. Though one might think that WW stands for Weight Watchers, it does not. The new WW stands for "Wellness that Works."[4] Today, WW has both a studio business and a digital business.

The digital business is a subscription-based mobile app where members track food, activity, water intake, and sleep. It also allows you to quickly scan bar codes of purchased food items, read expert content, get a coaching session, develop healthy habits, and calculate how many days you have been in a "healthy eating zone." It develops weekly food plans, and even offers recipes based on what's currently in your refrigerator. The physical weekly weigh-in that the original Weight Watchers was known for is now a virtual weekly check-in where you track your weight, assess progress, and set future goals. Within the app is a social media platform where members can connect, build community, and support other WW members.

WW also has 3,000 brick-and-mortar studios in the United States that primarily conduct workshops. The workshops are run by a WW coach who is an expert in nutrition, wellness, and weight loss. A workshop can be characterized as a support group where you do a weigh-in but also work with other members to reach similar goals around health and wellness. For some, the digital method may not be sufficient and having a physical support group can help with accountability and goal attainment.

WW's stock return over the last few years has averaged close to 9% for investors, a very strong return. Oprah Winfrey bought a significant stake in the company in 2015 because she saw WW as having a role that "goes far beyond a number on a scale."[5] The emphasis on health and wellness during a time when obesity in the U.S. is a significant problem was purpose-driven and signaled WW's proactive rather than reactive approach to weight management and overall well-being.

The growth of WW is attributed to many factors. As Amy O'Keefe, the company's CFO, said about its early 2021 performance, "We had a strong finish to a year with unique challenges, driven by the growth of our Digital business with fourth quarter Digital end-of-period subscribers up 24% year-over-year. Our attractive Digital business model, the continued shift in subscriber mix and strong cost discipline enabled us to expand adjusted gross margin to over 61% in the quarter. We ended 2020 well-positioned to navigate a dynamic environment and drive cash flow and shareholder value." [6]

That's CFO speak for we are doing a good job, meeting the needs of our customers, controlling expenses, and staying relevant in a very busy market space—even during a pandemic where the business model shifted to 100% digital.

Critical Thinking Questions

1. Oprah Winfrey bought a significant stake in WW in 2015. Do some research on your own: How did this affect WW stock price at the time?

2. Do you see WW growing in the future? Why or why not?

3. Is the studio business relevant today? Or should WW focus mainly on the digital side of the business?

FINANCIAL MANAGEMENT OVERVIEW

Earlier in the book we defined management as a process of organizing, planning, controlling, and leading (see Chapter 11). As such, **financial management** is organizing, planning, controlling, and leading the financial activities of a business to ensure the effective acquisition and utilization of financial resources for efficient operations and future growth. WW International has built financial success by rebranding itself from a weight loss company to one that promotes overall health and wellness through both a studio-based and digital-based business model.

During the COVID-19 pandemic, WW pivoted to a virtual-only model, launching 20,000 virtual workshops globally led by fully trained coaches. By making good financial management decisions such as adapting to new markets and changes, and keeping up to date with technological shifts, WW has successfully attracted high-profile investors, increased shareholder value, and attracted millions of customers.

Three Types of Financial Management Decisions

Financial management includes three types of decisions—financing decisions, investment decisions, and dividend decisions (see Figure 18.1).

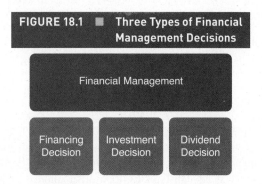

FIGURE 18.1 ■ Three Types of Financial Management Decisions

Financial Management

Financing Decision | Investment Decision | Dividend Decision

In general, **financing** is acquiring the money you need to start, operate, or expand a business. So, financing decisions involve identifying sources of capital, allocating the funds to support investment decisions, determining the duration of the investment, and assessing the amount of return.[7] There are two types of financing decisions: financial planning decisions involve predetermining the amount of funds available to invest; and capital structure decisions involve identifying the sources of capital to meet the long-term needs of the business.

Investment decisions relate to the decisions managers make to select the amount of investment available within different investment opportunities.[8] There are two types of investment decisions: long-term investment decisions (or capital budgeting) and short-term investment decisions. Long-term investment decisions involve committing funds for a long period of time, such as investing in a building or land, or buying new machinery; while short-term investment decisions (or working capital decisions) mean investing funds for a short period of time, such as in savings accounts, government bonds, cash, and bank deposits.

Every company must make investment decisions. A startup company like Boston-based Iterators may decide to make a long-term investment in office space and machinery, or to use a shared office space.

David L. Ryan/The Boston Globe via Getty Images

Dividend decisions relate to the portion of a company's earnings that will be distributed as a dividend to shareholders. These are often complex decisions, as managers need to balance the needs of the company, which needs to retain some of the profit to operate, with the requirements of shareholders, who often demand a higher dividend.

Financial Management Functions

Finance managers follow several core financial management functions to increase organizational and operational efficiency and to ensure that the organization is meeting its planned goals and objectives (see Figure 18.2).

Estimate Required Capital

Capital is the amount of money a business has to pay for its ongoing operations, such as working capital introduced in Chapter 17. Financial managers must evaluate the amount of capital needed to meet the daily requirements of the organization, safeguard funds for potential growth and expansion, and ensure that it has enough liquidity to weather unpredictable times and pay short-term liabilities.

Determine Capital Structure

Once the capital requirements have been evaluated, financial managers need to determine the best plan for maximizing shareholder value while minimizing the cost of capital. They establish the capital structure by assessing the amount of debt and equity capital and using financial ratios to analyze the financial health of the company.

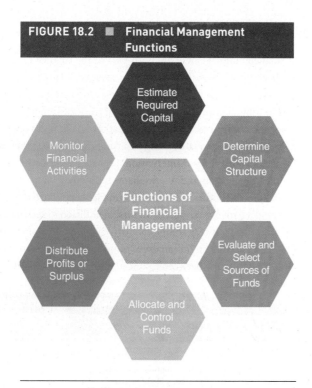

FIGURE 18.2 ■ Financial Management Functions

Estimate Required Capital

Monitor Financial Activities

Determine Capital Structure

Functions of Financial Management

Distribute Profits or Surplus

Evaluate and Select Sources of Funds

Allocate and Control Funds

Source: Azam, G. (n.d.). What is financial management and example? Explain its functions and importance. *Startup Plan.* https://startu-paplan.com/what-is-financial-management/

Evaluate and Select Sources of Funds

A key part of the finance manager role is to explore different methods of raising capital for the organization. This involves evaluating internal resources or looking at potential sources outside the business to establish the source that raises funds at the least cost for the company. The most common sources of funds include using working capital, securing a loan or line of credit, raising funds from investors (called equity), and selling existing assets (such as property and equipment).

Allocate and Control Funds

The financial manager assesses the amount of funds required in each financial area of the business and allocates them accordingly. This amount can increase or decrease, depending on the financial decisions made by the organization.

Distribute Profits or Surplus

When the organization starts to make a profit, financial managers need to decide what part of the earnings should be retained and what part should be distributed. Some organizations might allocate a portion of the earnings to shareholders as dividends, and retain some of the profits to invest in expansion and modernization plans.

Monitoring Financial Activities

Financial managers are responsible for overseeing the company's financial activities and analyzing financial data to ensure legal requirements are being met. They use these data to create ideas on how to optimize the organization's financial position through the maximization of profits.

In this chapter, we will be focusing primarily on financing and investment decisions. These are the types of decisions businesses make every day to meet needs such as buying supplies, paying for utilities, and paying salaries to their employees. Financial management is the function that ensures that every single department within a business is allocated with enough funds, and a budget, to stay on track.

How Financial Management Is Different From Accounting

While accounting and financial management are both part of the finance function, there are several key differences that set them apart.[9] Where financial management focuses on managing the finances and resources of an organization to achieve financial objectives and plan for future growth, accounting focuses on measuring, recording, identifying, and reporting the past financial transactions of a company using standard procedures and rules. As noted in Chapter 17, the main objective of accounting is to report on the financial position of a company using past financial transactions based on the Generally Accepted Accounting Principle (GAAP) and International Financial Reporting Standards (IFRS) prepared according to accounting standards and requirements set by the Financial Accounting Standards Board (FASB) and other regulatory bodies. This information is then reported to external users such as creditors, suppliers, shareholders, investors, and regulators, in addition to internal users such as managers and other employees. Accounting is very compliance driven, whereas financial management is more strategic—using the data from accounting to analyze, project, plan, and identify new opportunities. Table 18.1 outlines more key differences between financial management and accounting.

TABLE 18.1 ■ Differences Between Financial Management and Accounting		
	Financial Management	**Accounting**
Definition	Organizing, planning, controlling, and leading the financial activities of a business to ensure the effective utilization of financial resources for efficient operations	Recording, sorting, retrieving, and summarizing financial data
Objective	Strategic use and acquisition of financial resource to optimize profit	Recording financial information and producing financial statements
Importance	Helps make key business decisions on future growth and management of current assets and liabilities	Summarizes the financial health of the business
Purpose	Strategic	Tactical
Time focus	Future oriented	Past oriented
Leadership position in the company	Chief financial officer	Controller

The Role of a CFO in a Business

Financial management also enables financial managers such as the CFO to provide data to create a long-term vision and strategy, supports decisions on where to invest, and offers insights on how to fund investments.[10] Recall from Chapter 9 that the CFO is an executive officer who is responsible for the financial operations of a company including forecasting, planning, and analysis. CFOs' duties include tracking cash flow, monitoring financial risk, planning financial strategy, and analyzing the company's strengths and weaknesses with a view to providing corrective action.[11] The CFO of WW International is Amy O'Keefe. Part of her role is to oversee global finance and accounting for WW and driving business growth and maximizing profitability in line with WW's digital transformation strategy.[12]

To give you a better idea of the CFO's role, let's consider a beverage company that produces organic teas. The CEO wants to introduce a new product: a cider drink made with apple cider vinegar because of its purported health benefits. The CFO will be called upon to assess the cost of producing the new product and identify how the new product will be funded (bank loan, etc.). Once the funds are acquired, the CFO will allocate a sufficient amount to manufacture the new cider drinks as cost-effectively as possible. Once the cider drinks are made and sold, the CFO analyzes the financial data and decides whether the product is profitable enough to allocate additional money toward producing more cider drinks. The CFO will also decide on the portion of profits that will be distributed as dividends to the company's shareholders. If the product sells well, the CFO may see an opportunity to allocate some of the profit to produce a variation of the cider drink, perhaps by adding honey and turmeric as additional ingredients.

During this entire process, the CFO needs to make sure the project stays within budget and meets sales forecasts. If performance is not going as planned, the CFO will need to make adjustments and, at worst, recommend that the new product be terminated.

Differences Between CFOs and Controllers

Most large companies have a CFO and a controller, although smaller companies may combine these two roles. A controller is a company executive who is responsible for the organization's compliance and reporting of accounting tasks and activities and usually reports to the CFO. Depending on the company, a controller's duties could include payroll processing, financial reporting, and data collection, and they may support the CFO in preparing operating budgets. Table 18.2 lists some differences between CFOs and controllers, although there may be some overlap in certain duties.

TABLE 18.2 ■ Differences Between a CFO and Controller	
CFO	**Controller**
Responsible for forecasting, planning, and analysis	Responsible for compliance and reporting
Tracks company growth, formulates high-level strategies, and develops action plans for improvement	Prepares financial reports like income statements and balance sheets
Main focus is financial planning	Main focus is accurate financial reporting
Analyzes financial reports	Produces financial reports
Monitors cash flow	Controls cash flow
Looks to the future "Big Picture Thinking"	Reports on the present

As Table 18.2 demonstrates, financial planning plays a large part in the role of the CFO. The next section describes financial planning in further detail.

FINANCIAL PLANNING

Financial planning is the process of forecasting future financial results and making decisions about how best to use the company's financial resources to achieve its short- and long-term goals.[13] As financial planning involves looking into the future, it requires both a creative and an analytical mindset.

Financial planning includes both budgeting and forecasting. Though some may use these interchangeably or together, there are differences.

Budgeting is the part of the financial plan that outlines what the company will likely earn and spend for an upcoming period of time—usually a year, but it also can be done monthly or quarterly. Then, throughout the year, the budget is compared to actual performance. The difference between the budget and actual performance for any given expense or income item is called the variance. Let's go back to the apple cider drink example. For the first three months, $50,000 was budgeted for marketing, but the company actually ended up spending $60,000. The variance here is +$10,000. A part of financial management is understanding the source of the variance and to determine if more money should be budgeted for marketing in the future or if the additional $10,000 was an anomaly and one-time expense. Budgeting, as in this example, is a great way to monitor progress.

Table 18.3 gives an example of an annual budget for a business called Paws Rehab & Swim Clinic that provides physical therapy (PT) and hydrotherapy for dogs that suffer from physical injuries, neurological disorders, and arthritis. In addition to receiving hands-on physical therapy from certified clinicians, dogs can swim in a heated pool or walk in an underwater treadmill. Pet owners can also buy products related to rehabilitation such as special harnesses, educational toys, eating bowls, and supplements.

TABLE 18.3 ■ Annual Business Budget: Paws Rehab & Swim Clinic			
Category	Budget Amount (at beginning of the year)	Actual Amount (at year end)	Variance
Income			
Physical therapy sessions	$ 122,000	$ 125,035	$ 3,035
Swim sessions	$ 85,000	$ 83,240	$ (1.760)
Product sales	$ 7,250	$ 7,578	$ 328
Total Income	$ 214,250	$ 215,853	$ 1,603
Expenses			
Rent	$ 31,200	$ 31,200	$ -
Insurance	$ 21,696	$ 21,696	$ -
Payroll	$ 55,200	$ 55,200	$ -
Payroll taxes	$ 8,832	$ 8,832	$ -
Merchant account fees	$ 8,570	$ 8,634	$ 64
Marketing	$ 5,500	$ 6,820	$ 1,320
Inventory purchase	$ 10,875	$ 10,920	$ 45
Subscriptions	$ 100	$ 75	$ (25)
Professional services (CPA + payroll)	$ 2,330	$ 2,450	$ 120
Loan payments	$ 2,700	$ 2,700	$ -
Office supplies	$ 2,500	$ 2,125	$ (375)
Pool supplies	$ 1,400	$ 1,475	$ 75
Pool repair	$ 750	$ 250	$ (500)
Rehabilitation supplies	$ 600	$ 624	$ 24
Utilities (water, electricity)	$ 7,200	$ 7,326	$ 126
Internet and phone	$ 1,680	$ 1,680	$ -
Travel	$ 1,750	$ -	$ (1,750)
Shipping	$ 250	$ 125	$ (125)
Meals and entertainment	$ 3,000	$ 3,521	$ 521
Miscellaneous	$ 1,100	$ 644	$ (456)
Total Expenses	$ 167,233	$ 166,297	$ (936)
Income Expenses	$ 47,017	$ 49,556	$ 2,539

From the above budget the CFO or financial manager can see that, all in all, most things came in fairly close to budget. The increase in PT sessions offset the decrease in swim sessions. More was spent on marketing, so it's likely the CFO needs to address this with the marketing team because the increase in marketing may have worked, given the increase in sales. Travel was zero because planned travel to a conference didn't happen during the year. For each line item, the manager would look to see variances, try to explain them, and that information would help inform the following year's budget.

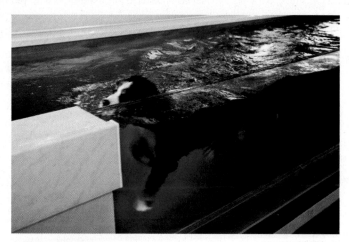

Injured and rehabilitating dogs can swim in underwater treadmills like this one to engage in canine hydrotherapy.

Arterra/Universal Images Group via Getty Images

Budgets can be simple, such as the one in Table 18.3, or more complicated. It all depends on the size and scope of the organization. A small company may have a budget (as above), but a larger company with many departments may have a budget for each department that feeds into the larger company budget. If Paws Rehab & Swim Clinic has multiple locations in a state or around the country there would be a budget created for each location.

Budgeting is often confused with forecasting because both partially deal with historical data or past company performance while also trying to project cash inflows and outflows. Whereas budgeting is more short-term and used for monitoring purposes, financial forecasting is an estimate of future revenue and expenses for an extended period of time (typically 3–5 years). Forecasting can be helpful for making decisions on such things as big expenditures (new equipment or acquisitions), new product introductions, and geographic expansion. Thus, the main difference between a budget and a forecast is that the budget lays out the plan for the direction in which the company plans to go in the short term, while a forecast is a prediction of what the company will actually achieve.[14] Table 18.4 outlines the main differences between a budget and a forecast.

TABLE 18.4 ■ Differences Between a Budget and Forecast	
Budget	**Forecast**
What the business is likely to earn and spend for a year—heavily based on historical data	Prediction of what the business will actually achieve given financial goals and strategy
Represents future results, financial position, and cash flows during a certain period of time	Limited to revenue and expenses
May be updated once a year depending on management requirements	Updated regularly—monthly/quarterly
Compared to actual results to determine variance	No variance analysis
Results may trigger changes in performance-based compensation paid to employees	Changes in forecast have no impact on performance-based compensation paid to employees

Source: The difference between a budget and a forecast. (2021, April 19). *Accounting Tools.* https://www.accountingtools.com/articles/what-is-the-difference-between-a-budget-and-a-forecast.html

ENTREPRENEURIAL MINDSET ACTIVITY

Business Budgeting Turns Personal

A lot of what you learn in this chapter about financial management can be applied to your own life. Personal finance has a lot of parallels to business finance. In this mindset activity, you will create an

The Budget Template

Category	Annual Budget Amount
Income	
Current job	
Other sources of income	
Total Personal Income	
Expenses	
Big purchase (laptop/car/home electronics)	
Car payments	
Clothes	
Credit card payment	
Tuition	
School supplies (textbooks, other)	
Groceries	
Gym membership	
Haircuts	
Health care	
House supplies	
Internet or WiFi	
Meals out and entertainment	
Online subscriptions (e.g., Netflix)	
Cell phone	
Rent/mortgage	
Ride share	
Student loan payment	
Utilities	
Home or renters insurance	
Other	
Total Personal Expenses	
Personal Profit (Income – Expenses): Cash left over for an entrepreneurial opportunity!	

annual budget for yourself with a goal of assessing if you have cash available for an entrepreneurial opportunity of your choice. Your goal is to determine if, after accounting for all personal expenses, you will have enough cash to test out some type of entrepreneurial activity. This may be creating or testing out a new product idea, traveling to visit and learn from an entrepreneur, volunteering in a startup, selling a product at a local farmer's market . . . the opportunities are only limited by your own imagination. Below is a personal budget template to help you get started, but there are many free templates online that you can use; we suggest the budget template in Google Sheets. You must create the budget for a full year. An annual budget will give you a better view of your personal finance situation.

Critical Thinking Questions

1. Is there enough money left over to test your new business idea?
2. Are there any expenses that could be reduced or eliminated for you to have more money available for your opportunity?
3. Did anything in your personal budget surprise you, and why?

EQUITY AND DEBT FINANCING

Regardless of the type and size of business, there are many factors around financing that need to be taken into account. Financing is the activity of acquiring the money you need to start, operate, or expand a business.[15] For example, every business needs capital (financial resources) to produce goods and services. Capital can mean money, labor, office space, tools, equipment, machinery, and factories. There are two main methods for companies to raise capital: equity financing and debt financing. Most companies use a combination of both types of financing.

Equity Financing[16]

Equity financing is the method of acquiring capital through the sale of shares of stock in exchange for cash. This is a popular choice for startup companies that need capital to produce and sell their products and services and run the business. Equity financing comes from many different sources: friends and family, investors, or through an initial public offering (IPO), which is the process private companies undertake to offer shares to the general public. In May 2021, The Honest Company, an eco-friendly consumer products company founded by actor Jessica Alba—selling products such as eco-friendly diapers and natural skincare, bath, and home-cleaning products—launched an IPO raising over $400 million in capital.[17]

The idea behind equity is similar to splitting a pie. When you are the only owner of the company, you own 100% of a small pie. When someone invests in your company to help start it or enhance growth, then your pie becomes bigger. As you need to give away equity in exchange for the investment, the company is no longer fully yours. However, if the company does well, then your smaller slice of the bigger pie will be much larger than the original smaller pie you had without investment.

There is no magic formula telling you how much equity to keep or give away. For example, before launching the IPO for The Honest Company, it was estimated that Jessica Alba owned 15–20% of the company she founded. Although this may not sound like a lot, the company was also valued at $1 billion, which made Alba worth about $200 billion—a pretty lucrative slice of pie.[18]

The Honest Company, founded by Brian Lee and Jessica Alba, launched an IPO that raised over $400 million.

J. Emilio Flores/Corbis via Getty Images

However, splitting the pie starts before investment, if there is a team involved. And splitting the pie in an early-stage company represents a unique challenge because what you are splitting is rather worthless.[19] The founders agree to a percentage of ownership of something that doesn't really exist, and the question becomes, How do you determine who should get what percentage of the pie in the beginning? Does everyone get an equal share? Entrepreneur Mike Moyer, who wrote the book *Slicing the Pie*, uses a common example of four students working on a venture in an entrepreneurship course. They split the "equity" four ways, and each gets 25%. They even incorporate the business. The class ends and one student really takes the idea forward and the other three are slackers, yet they all want to keep their 25% stake in the company. What do you do? Legally, they may have a right to that 25%, but it's not really the right thing. Moyer says new entrepreneurs make two mistakes: "The first is to divide the pie *before* you build the company. This is quite common, and founders often wind up where my hapless student did. The other mistake is dividing up the pie *after* you build the company, which often leads to internal battles that can cripple a startup team."[20] Moyer suggests creating a process for allocating equity based on contribution, including time, money, intellectual property, and other resources. This will help later when formal financing, such as what we talk about next, is warranted.

Stages of Equity Financing for Business Startups

There are several stages of investment,[21] but for the purposes of this chapter we focus on the initial stages of equity financing usually provided to young companies: seed-stage financing, startup financing, and early-stage financing. **Seed-stage financing** usually consists of small or modest amounts of capital provided to potential business owners to prove a concept. **Startup financing** is the money provided to entrepreneurs to enable them to implement their idea by funding product research and development; and **early-stage financing** consists of larger amounts of funds provided for companies that have a team in place and a product or service tested or piloted, but as yet show little or no revenue. Before The Honest Company did its IPO in May 2021, the company had seven rounds of funding from seed to startup to early- and even late-stage funding. Its first round of early-stage funding was received in 2011 for $6 million. Additional early-stage financing was received through 2012, $21 million, and 2013, $25 million. All financing was used to build and grow the company as it worked toward its 2021 IPO.[22]

One of the most important factors to consider when you are seeking investment is to find investors who are most suitable for your stage of the company. Timing is also a factor. There is no use trying to raise funds when the venture is down to its last dollar. For one thing, it can take at least 6 months to raise money; in addition, a desperate early venture may give away far too much equity to investors, which can seriously dilute the position of its founders.

As the business grows and starts to take in more revenue, entrepreneurs may seek second-stage or later-stage financing. Even further down the road, a profitable company looking to expand and go public through an IPO may seek investment through the third or mezzanine stage of financing. Finally, entrepreneurs may need bridge financing to cover the expenses associated with the IPO. These stages are displayed graphically in Figure 18.3.

Forms of Early-Stage Equity Financing

Depending on the stage of their venture, business owners have several equity financing options available to them. As we discussed earlier, those starting a business looking to raise initial funds tend to turn to friends and family.

However, new business owners seeking more formal financial capital to fund a growing business may choose to seek an **angel investor**—investors who use their own money to provide funds to young startup private businesses run by entrepreneurs who are neither friends nor family.[23] Entrepreneurs may choose to seek a **venture capitalist (VC)** who is a professional investor who generally invests in early-stage and emerging companies because of perceived long-term growth potential.

Angel investors and VCs tend to be looking for the same types of opportunities, but there are differences between them, as illustrated in Table 18.5.

Seed-stage and startup entrepreneurs tend to seek out angel investors when they are initially trying to grow and scale the organization. VCs also invest in startups, but they are more likely to invest in companies in the early to third stage of business.

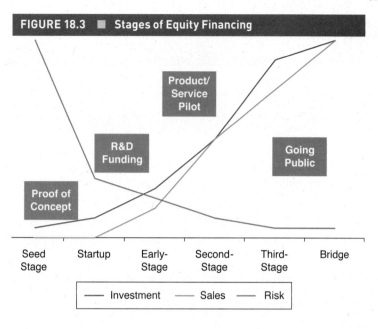

FIGURE 18.3 ■ Stages of Equity Financing

Source: MaRS Startup Toolkit. (n.d.). *Stages of company development: Angel, seed and venture capital investors.* MaRS DD. https://www.marsdd.com/mars-library/angel-investors-seed-or-venture-capital-investors-that-depends-on-your-stage-of-company-development/

TABLE 18.5 ■ The Differences Between Angels and VCs

Angels	VCs
Individuals worth more than $1 million	Funds consisting of limited partnerships
Invest from $25k to $100k in personal funds	Invest from $500,000 upwards in VC funding
Fund seed or early-stage companies	Fund from early- to late-stage companies
Carry out informal due diligence	Conduct formal due diligence
Responsible for own decisions	Decisions made with committee
Exit with returns on personal investment	Exit with returns to fund's partners

Source: Adapted from Adams, P. (2014, January 12). How do angel investors differ from venture capitalists? Retrieved from http://www.rockiesventureclub.org/colorado-capital-conference/how-do-angel-investors-differ-from-venture-capitalists/

Table 18.6 lists some other factors and key questions that investors take into account when making the decision to invest.

TABLE 18.6 ■ Factors That Investors Take Into Account

Factor	Key Questions
Market conditions	Is the market ready for your product/service? Is the market size big enough? Is the market reachable?
Competition	Who are the competitors in your industry? How does your product compare with similar items in the market? Is there a unique and compelling competitive advantage?
Market opportunity	What is the opportunity for your product? How many customers? What is the proof that there is a market?

(*Continued*)

TABLE 18.6 ■ Factors That Investors Take Into Account (Continued)

Factor	Key Questions
Founders	Are they experienced in the industry? Have they done startups before? Can the investor work with them? Are they coachable?
Social proof	Is there evidence that others believe in the founders' vision as much as they do? Does the company have a board of advisers? What are their customers saying about the business?
Value add	How much value can investors bring to your business through their expert advice and guidance?
Potential for return	If an investor puts in $1 today, what will they get in 5 years? 10 years? Does the potential return match the potential risk?

Sources: What investors look for before investing in a small business. (n.d.). *Accion.* Retrieved from https://us.accion.org/resource/7-things-investors-look-investing/; Newlands, M. (2014). 5 things investors want to know before signing a check. *Entrepreneur.* Retrieved from https://www.entrepreneur.com/article/234536; What investors look for. (n.d.). *Fundable.* Retrieved from https://www.fundable.com/learn/resources/guides/investor/what-investors-look-for; Harroch, R. (2015). 20 things all entrepreneurs should know about angel investors. *Forbes.* Retrieved from http://www.forbes.com/sites/allbusiness/2015/02/05/20-things-all-entrepreneurs-should-know-about-angel-investors

Debt Financing

Debt financing is the method of borrowing funds and paying it back with interest to the lender.[24] Unlike equity financing, there is no obligation to sell a portion of the company to secure capital, which means the owners have full control of the business. Another benefit to debt financing is that the relationship with the lender ends once the loan is paid back. Finally, the interest on the funds is tax deductible. However, there are some downsides, too. As anyone who has been in debt knows, this method of financing depends on your ability to pay back the loan in the future—and when you're running a business, things can go wrong: The economy or market could take a downturn, or your company could run into unforeseen difficulties, which limits its capacity to grow. This is why careful consideration must be made when choosing the right type of financing for your company. Table 18.7 lists some of the differences between debt and equity financing.

TABLE 18.7 ■ Debt Versus Equity Financing

Debt Financing	Equity Financing
Company borrows funds from lenders	Company gives up portion of business to investors
Debt must be paid back to lender	No guarantee that investor will be paid back
Lenders have no ownership over the business or any say in how the business is run	Investors have voting rights and need to be consulted on major business decisions
Lenders have a legal right to be repaid	No legal obligation to pay dividends
Payment on interest over a fixed period of time	Investors are repaid in the form of a return subject to the performance of the company
Interest is tax deductible	Dividends are not tax deductible

Credit Scores. A credit score is a number between 300 and 850 that provides an overview to lenders of the borrower's creditworthiness. The higher the score, the more chance you have of securing a loan. Your credit score also impacts the interest rate and the length of time the bank gives you to pay back the loan. You can view your credit scores through several credit bureaus like Experian, TransUnion, and Equifax. Although most traditional banks prefer to see scores in the 700s, some will consider lower scores (around 680). Online lenders and other alternative financing providers will go even lower. We will explore these types of loans in the next section.

Credit History. In addition to your credit scores, lenders will analyze your credit history including your credit usage. This demonstrates to lenders the length of your credit history, the age of the accounts, and how you have managed both business and personal credit.

Cash Flow. A cash flow loan is a type of loan used by small businesses to cover day-to-day operations. Lenders also need to verify that you have a steady stream of income that will enable you to make periodic payments on your business loans. Your credit profile also plays a big part in being approved. Some lenders will approve your application within minutes for amounts up to $100,000, but you will need to pay a minimum of 25% APR, which could go as high as 90%. Examining your cash flow will give them a good idea as to whether you can make those payments in the future. Most lenders will require at least 3 months of bank statements before they agree to give you a loan, or even a credit card. They may also ask you about unpaid invoices or to provide a prediction of what your financial situation might be in 2 years' time.

Time in Business. Many traditional lenders prefer to loan to businesses with a few years of experience and a proven track record. This makes it trickier for startups to secure loans from major lenders, but some online lenders only require a year in business. Idea-stage startups have the most difficult time acquiring a loan because they have no performance history, which makes them a bigger risk for lenders, but these types of startups have the option of a business credit card (see "Types of Business Loans") if they are struggling to obtain a loan.

Collateral. If your credit score isn't high enough, many traditional lenders will ask for collateral for business loans as security. Using collateral to secure a loan is called asset financing, which is a way to borrow money or get a loan by using existing assets as security against business loans from a lender. A lot of money can be tied up in buildings, inventory, and equipment, so businesses might use them as collateral to take out a loan in order to acquire the cash to pay for operations or to purchase additional assets. Typically, the amount loaned depends on the value of the assets. Asset financing is often used as a short-term funding solution—to acquire the extra cash to pay employees, suppliers, or to invest in company growth. It is easier to access than traditional bank loans and is often used by startups. However, there is also the risk that you will lose your assets if the business falters. For startups that may not have business assets just yet, collateral could be the form of personal assets such as using your home and taking out a mortgage on your home. Of course, this is a risky strategy because if the startup fails, and many do, you will likely default on your loan and lose your home. In other words, the bank will take your home to cover the amount of money loaned to it.

Loyalty. Major lenders, credit unions in particular, are more likely to approve loans when you have banked with them for a number of years. For example, many banks approved the Paycheck Protection Program (PPP) coronavirus loan (introduced in 2020 to help small businesses keep employees on the payroll) to their long-standing customers before considering applicants from unfamiliar businesses. Loyalty can also result in more favorable business terms for small businesses.

Types of Business Loans[25]

There are a variety of loans available to businesses, but it is essential to review each option to choose the right type of financing to meet your business needs. The average interest rate for a business loan varies depending on your qualifications as a borrower, the type of loan you're applying for, and which lender you select. Loans from traditional lenders, such as banks or credit unions, can have annual percentage rates (APRs) ranging from 3% to 7%, while alternative or online loans can have APRs ranging from 7% to more than 100%.[26] The most common type of business loans include: business term loans, commercial mortgage, equipment lease, line of credit, business credit cards, SBA loans, and microloans.

Business Term Loan

A business term loan is a traditional bank loan where you can obtain funds to support your business needs if you fulfill the strict criteria. Depending on the agreement, the business term loan will be set at a fixed interest rate and will require the borrower to repay the loan in line with a monthly or quarterly schedule. Loans can run from 1–20 years.

Commercial Mortgage

A commercial mortgage is similar to a home mortgage, but the commercial mortgages are used for businesses that are looking to expand into a different location. Businesses with a poor credit history will often be required to personally guarantee the loan, meaning they will need to pay it back if the business fails.

Equipment Lease

Equipment lease is a type of financing whereby businesses lease equipment with payments spread over a set amount of time. Once the lease has run out, you have the option either to return the equipment or purchase the equipment by paying off the remaining value. It's worth noting that although the lease payments are lower than the cost of buying the equipment outright, you will be charged interest on those payments.

Line of Credit

Working capital is the financial heart of day-to-day business operations. It is the money used by companies to pay for daily expenses such as inventory and overhead expenses. Working capital is really the amount of cash a business can safely spend. It's calculated by taking current assets and subtracting current liabilities. Recall from our discussion on financial statements in Chapter 17 that current assets are those that can quickly be converted to available cash to be spent immediately. This includes cash already in the bank, account receivables that can be collected, and inventory that can be sold. A line of credit can be used to increase the amount of working capital a company has when it doesn't want or have time to convert existing assets to cash.

Line of credit works similarly to a credit card: You can borrow a certain amount of money and only pay interest on the amount you have used, as long as you stay within your credit limit. Different from a loan, you only pay back when you use it. Let's say you have a limit of $20,000 on a credit card—this is a line of credit. You don't have to pay your credit card bill until you have a balance. A line of credit, however, is usually larger than what a credit card will allow, and it also has a more favorable interest rate. An interest rate on a business credit card could be anywhere from 13–25%. A typical interest rate for a line of credit is likely to be lower—as low as 5%—but also depends on your credit score. This is a popular choice for businesses but can be difficult for which to qualify. Banks require a steady flow of income and revenues and a healthy credit history before they approve the line of credit.

Business Credit Cards

Business credit cards are credit cards that are intended for business use rather than personal use, and act as a less formal and often more expensive line of credit. Younger businesses often use business credit cards as a short-term funding solution to acquire the capital they need to start and grow their business. It is often easier to qualify for a business credit card than a traditional bank loan or line of credit. Rates of up to 25% apply to loans between $1,000 and $25,000 and applicants can find out if they're qualified for the credit card within a period of 3 weeks.

SBA Loans

SBA is the Small Business Association in the U.S. It offers SBA loans to small businesses with lower rates and better terms than traditional loans and offers amounts ranging between $50,000 and $5 million. Depending on the type of loan you need for your business, the approval process can take weeks or even months. The SBA has also been known to come to the relief of small business owners in need. For example, during the COVID-19 pandemic, the SBA's American Rescue Plan offered over $415 billion in emergency relief aid that impacted over 6 million small businesses.[27]

Microloans

Microloans are very small, short-term loans. They are often made to entrepreneurs in developing countries to help them cover the costs of starting a business. For example, a microloan can be used to buy a goat in Africa that will be used to generate milk that will be sold in a village. Or a microloan could be used to buy beads that will then be converted to jewelry by local artisans and sold in city markets. Kiva is a nonprofit organization headquartered in San Francisco that offers loans for as little as $25 to low-income entrepreneurs with limited or no access to traditional finance. The loans are funded by lenders who choose whom to back by browsing through hundreds of entrepreneurs profiled on the Kiva website. Kiva does not charge interest or take a cut of the loan—the entire amount goes to the entrepreneur. When the entrepreneur repays the loan, the lender has the option to use the money to offer another loan to support a different entrepreneur.[28]

Although Kiva does not charge interest on the loans, in some developing countries microloans may have extraordinary interest rates because such loans do not require collateral or a decent credit history, or any credit history at all. Because of the risk involved in loaning money to unqualified borrowers, rates and costs will be far higher than traditional bank loans. Generally, microloans, with low interest rates like with Kiva, are a useful way for people to acquire the funds they need to get their startup off the ground. However, they do need to be paid back within quite a short time frame, and some lenders specify how the money should be spent: for example, on equipment purchases.

Small companies, like this cement stone manufacturer in Mongolia, have been able to invest in startup materials and expand production using microloans.

Thomas Koehler/Photothek via Getty Images

Paying Back a Business Loan

Borrowing money costs money, and the cost of a loan is often underestimated. Before acquiring a business loan, it's worth doing a few quick calculations to check if you will be able to pay back the loan when the time comes. The following example illustrates how loan payments work for businesses.

Darius has a lawn and landscaping business that focuses on using the most eco-friendly treatments available. He has been in business for 3 years, and his business grows every year. In order to expand on his mission of eco-friendliness he now wants to invest in battery-powered equipment such as battery-powered lawn mowers, blowers, edgers, etc. Based on his business plan, he estimates that he will need approximately $50,000 to make the conversion to 100% battery-powered equipment. A bank has agreed to loan Darius $50,000 at 6% interest to be paid back over 5 years (60 months). What is the monthly loan payment Darius will have to make? And what is the total cost of this loan? Using a business loan calculator such as Bankrate.com (see https://www.bankrate.com/calculators/business/business-calculator.aspx) you can plug in all the information. Let's assume the following:

Loan amount: $50,000

Length of loan: 5 years or 60 months

Interest rate: 6%

The easy way to calculate the monthly payment is to use an online calculator such as the Bankrate.com calculator. Simply plugging in the key variables of loan amount, length of loan, and interest rate will quickly calculate monthly payments of $966.64. There is always a cost to borrowing money that is determined by the interest rate and length of loan. By multiplying the monthly payment by number of months in the loan you can see the cost of the loan.

$$\text{Cost of loan} = (\text{monthly payment x number of monthly payments}) - \text{loan amount}$$
$$\text{Cost of Darius's Loan} = (\$966.64 \times 60) - \$50,000$$

For Darius, the cost of his loan is $7,998.40. He will spend this amount in order to receive the $50,000 loan. It's also the total interest he paid over the life of the loan. $50,000 is what is called the principal, or the total amount borrowed minus interest.

Now, what's behind the Bankrate.com calculator number? The formula to determine your monthly loan payments looks like the following:

$$\text{Loan Payment(P)} = \text{Amount of Loan(A)/Discount Factor(D)}$$

We know that A is $50,000, but we now need to calculate the Discount Factor, which is calculated as follows:

$$D = \{[(1 + r)^n]-1\}/[r(1 + r)^n]$$

r is the interest rate divided by 12 payments per year. In our example r = .06/12 = .005.

n is the number of total payments. Since our loan is for 5 years, the total number of payments is 12 x 5 or 60 payments.

Now we have all of the information for the Loan Payment (P) formula. Let's start with the discount factor calculation first.

$$D = \{[(1 + .005)^{60}]-1\}/[.005(1 + .005)^{60}]$$
$$D = 51.726$$
Let's now go back to the original formula of P = A / D
$$P = \$50,000/51.726$$
$$P = \$966.63$$

So, again, the monthly loan payment is $966 and some change. We are one cent off here compared to the Bankrate.com online calculator, but that's simply due to rounding.

Darius has a decision to make. Can he afford the monthly payments, given his monthly cash flow? If no, maybe he could talk to the bank and ask for a longer payback period; however, if he gets a loan for longer than 5 years the cost of the loan, assuming the same interest rate, will increase. He also needs to look at his projected cash flow as well. Perhaps shifting to battery equipment and marketing this shift to his current and potential customers will help increase his business, which would then bring in more revenue that can help pay his monthly loan expense.

Business loan payments must be made on time. Not doing so can lead to financial penalties and also harm the credit reputation of the business leading to decreased chances of getting additional loans in the future. So it's important to thoroughly understand and consider the average number of days it takes to sell inventory, the amount of time given to pay for the inventory, and the length of time it takes for customers to pay and have inventory converted to cash. This is called the cash conversion cycle, and understanding this cycle helps determine if a business has the ability, or lack thereof, to meet loan payment obligations.

THE CASH CONVERSION CYCLE[29]

Cash is used to purchase materials, which are then made into products. This creates obligations to make payments to certain suppliers of those materials, which is captured on the balance sheet in accounts payable. These products are stored, which appears on the balance sheet as inventory, and are eventually sold and delivered to customers. Then the company has the right to collect cash for the selling price of the products, which appears on the balance sheet in accounts receivable. Once collected, this cash has now returned to the company. You hope that this journey produces more cash that is returned to the hands of the company. This journey is called the **cash conversion cycle (CCC)**, and it refers to the number of days a company's cash is tied up in the production and sales process. In other words, CCC is the number of days it takes to convert a transaction from sale to cash in the bank. CCC can be calculated using the equation shown in Figure 18.4.

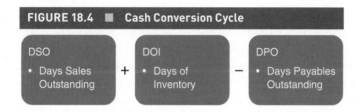

FIGURE 18.4 ■ Cash Conversion Cycle

Calculated in days, this equation shows how long the journey is for cash from the point of leaving the company to the point of return.

Days sales outstanding (DSO) is a measure of the number of days that it takes to collect on accounts receivable. Remember, if you do business in cash, then your DSO is zero, but if you sell on credit, then this will be a positive number. DSO is calculated using the following equation:

DSO = Average Accounts Receivable/Revenue per day

Average Accounts Receivable = (Beginning Accounts Receivable + Ending Accounts Receivable)/2

Revenue per day = Revenue/365

Days of inventory (DOI) is a measure of the average number of days it takes to sell the entire inventory of a company. DOI is calculated using the following equation:

DOI = (Average Inventory)/COGS per day

Average Inventory = (Beginning Inventory + Ending Inventory)/2

COGS per day = COGS/365

Days payable outstanding (DPO) is a measure of the number of days it takes you to pay your bills. DPO is calculated using the following equation:

DPO = Average Accounts Payable/COGS per day

Average Accounts Payable = (Beginning Accounts Payable + Ending Accounts Payable)/2

COGS per day = COGS/365

To calculate CCC, you need to include several items from the financial statements. From the income statement you need revenue and COGS. From the balance sheet, you need beginning and ending inventory, accounts receivable, and accounts payable.

Note that because balance sheet items capture a snapshot in time, you want to use an average over the period of time that you are investigating. So if you are looking at 1 year, then you need to look at the ending period for the current year and the same ending period for the previous year.

Let's use an example to explore this equation in more detail. Suppose you are making men's shirts and selling them through a retail channel. The DOI is 80 days. You purchase enough cotton material to make a shirt. This purchase creates an obligation for the shirt maker to pay (account payable) for this material in 30 days (DPO). The raw material arrives (inventory) and the manufacturing process begins.

At the end of 80 days, the completed shirt is sold to the retailer (DOI). The retailer now has an obligation to pay the shirt maker (account receivable) and takes 40 days to pay for the completed shirt. This means that from the time cash left the shirt maker 30 days after the purchase of raw material, it took 90 days for cash to make its way back to the shirt maker. In this case the formula would be:

$$CCC = DSO + DOI - DPO$$
$$= 80 + 40 - 30$$
$$= 90$$

Figure 18.5 illustrates this process. The CCC, or days that it takes for cash to return to the business, must be funded. Any increase in sales usually results in an increase in working capital necessary to support this higher level of sales. Therefore, you must be able to fund the growth of the company.

As a stand-alone number the CCC doesn't tell you much. Like many other metrics and ratios it must be compared over time and to other competitors in the industry. In general, a decreasing CCC is a good thing, while a rising CCC should motivate you to look a little more deeply into the management policies of the business to try and find the cash necessary to fund the company.

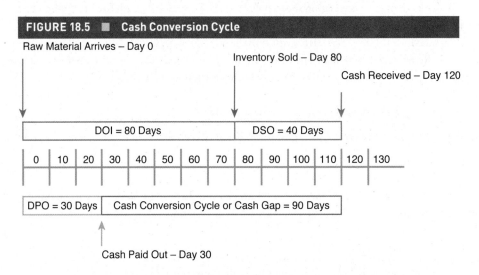

FIGURE 18.5 ■ Cash Conversion Cycle

INTERNAL FINANCIAL CONTROLS

Financial controls are designed and implemented based on the size, industry, and resources of an organization. **Internal financial controls** are the procedures, policies, and processes by which an organization manages its financial resources.[30] They are designed to identify errors in financial reporting as well as prevent fraud. For example, a smaller business may use financial controls that track and monitor daily activities, whereas a multinational corporation may have a wider range of financial controls in place to manage risk, prevent and detect errors, and safeguard assets. Businesses lose up to $4 trillion annually due to internal fraud. **Internal fraud** is the misuse or misapplication of business resources, especially financial resources and assets, by company employees or managers.[31] Every business, big or small, needs to have the appropriate internal controls in place to protect against fraud, and ensure that these policies and procedures are adhered to and communicated effectively to all employees.

Types of Internal Financial Controls[32]

There are three major types of financial controls: detective internal controls, preventative internal controls, and corrective internal controls (see Figure 18.6).

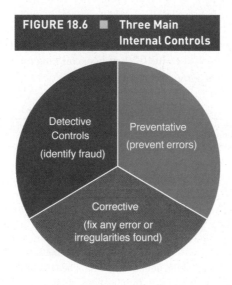

FIGURE 18.6 ■ Three Main Internal Controls

Detective Internal Controls

A detective internal control is a type of internal control designed to highlight discrepancies and iden-tify problems after they have occurred. It is commonly used for quality control, legal compliance, and to prevent fraud. Counting inventory, internal audits, or surprise cash counts are all examples of detective internal controls. Counting inventory shows whether any theft has taken place; conducting an internal audit ensures the safety of assets; and a surprise cash count is an effective way of highlight-ing discrepancies in the cash balance while also determining whether cashiers are doing their jobs efficiently or not.

Preventative Internal Controls

A preventative internal control is a type of internal control created to prevent errors or fraud from occurring in the first place. These are the types of controls that every employee is expected to adhere to on a daily basis. There are three main examples of preventative internal controls: separation of duties, controlling access, and double entry accounting.

- Separation of duties (also known as segregation of duties) involves splitting tasks among multiple people to protect against internal fraud. This is common practice in an accounting department. For instance, one person may book an invoice, which is passed onto another person for review and approval, before being passed to another person to make the payment. By not having one person in control of the whole process, there is less chance of deceit. Job rotation is another example of separation of duties, where personnel are transferred regularly to different departments to ensure that they do not have access to data for long periods of time. Rotating people around an organization helps to prevent against theft and other illegal activities.

- Controlling access is a feature that denies people access to certain parts of an accounting system unless they have the right password.

- Double entry accounting is a system of bookkeeping where every entry to an account requires a corresponding entry to a different account. In other words, it is a method of tracking the money that goes in and out of a company. It is a useful method of ensuring that the books are always balanced.

Corrective Internal Controls

A corrective internal control is a type of internal control that is put in place to correct the errors identi-fied by the detective internal controls to prevent them from occurring. Examples of corrective controls include policies and procedures for reporting mistakes so they can be corrected as soon as possible;

incorporating these policies and procedures into employee training so they know how to correct the errors and to prevent employees from repeating the same mistakes. Data backups that safeguard data in the event of a disaster, physical audits (such as handcounting money), and revision of policies and procedures are all examples of corrective internal controls.

ETHICS IN BUSINESS

Are You an Insider or an Outsider?

You work for and own stock in a large company. The company has been working on a revolutionary new product for the past 5 years that could have a major impact on your industry. Your company's stock price has increased substantially over the past year in anticipation of the product launch. You just learned that a competitor is going to introduce a similar product before yours. Your company is trying to keep this news from the public for the time being, but you are considering selling your stock. Yet you are concerned about the ramifications of insider trading, which is the trading of a company's securities by individuals with access to confidential or material nonpublic information about the company. What do you do?

Critical Thinking Questions

1. If you sell your stock based on this news, is this considered insider trading?
2. Do your own research. What are the risks/consequences of employee insider trading?
3. Why does public information cause the price of stock to rise and fall?

IN REVIEW

18.1   Explain the role of financial management and its purpose in a business.

Financial management is the organizing, planning, controlling, and leading the financial activities of a business to ensure the effective utilization of financial resources for efficient operations. Financial management activities include three types of decisions—financing decisions, investment decisions, and dividend decisions—and follows several core financial management functions to increase organizational and operational efficiency.

18.2   Explore two aspects of financial planning—budgeting and forecasting.

Financial planning is the process of forecasting future financial results and making decisions about how best to use the company's financial resources to achieve its short- and long-term goals. Budgeting is the part of the financial plan that outlines what the company will likely earn and spend for an upcoming period of time, whereas financial forecasting looks a few years out and focuses primarily on the major expense and income areas.

18.3   Differentiate between equity and debt business financing.

Equity financing is the method of acquiring capital through the sale of shares of stock in exchange for cash. Startup companies often use equity financing to raise the capital to produce and sell their products and services and run the business. Equity financing can come from many different sources: friends and family, investors, or through an initial public offering (IPO). Debt financing is the method of borrowing funds and paying them back with interest to the lender. Unlike equity financing, there is no obligation to sell a portion of the company to secure capital, which means the owners have full control of the business.

18.4   Illustrate the cash conversion cycle and how it helps understand cash flow.

The cash conversion cycle (CCC) refers to the number of days a company's cash is tied up in the production and sales process. It can be calculated through an equation illustrated in the text (Figure 18.4).

18.5 Contrast the three types of internal financial controls.

Internal financial controls are the procedures, policies, and processes by which an organization manages its financial resources. They are designed to identify errors in financial reporting as well as prevent fraud. There are three major types of financial controls: detective internal controls, preventative internal controls, and corrective internal controls.

BUSINESSES DISCUSSED IN THIS CHAPTER

Organization	UN Sustainable Development Goal
Google	12. Responsible Consumption and Production 14. Life Below Water 15. Life on Land
Honest Company	3. Good Health and Well-Being 12. Responsible Consumption and Production
Kiva	1. No Poverty 2. Zero Hunger 3. Good Health and Well-Being 4. Quality Education 5. Gender Equality 6. Clean Water and Sanitation 7. Affordable and Clean Energy 8. Decent Work and Economic Growth
WW International	3. Good Health and Well-Being

KEY TERMS

Accounting (p. 372)
Angel investor (p. 378)
Asset financing (p. 381)
Budgeting (p. 373)
Business credit cards (p. 382)
Business term loan (p. 381)
Business loan payments (p. 384)
Capital (p. 370)
Cash flow loan (p. 381)
Cash conversion cycle (CCC) (p. 385)
Commercial mortgage (p. 382)
Controller (p. 373)
Controlling access (p. 387)
Corrective internal control (p. 387)
Days of inventory (DOI) (p. 385)
Days payable outstanding (DPO) (p. 385)
Days sales outstanding (DSO) (p. 385)
Debt financing (p. 380)
Detective internal control (p. 387)
Dividend decisions (p. 370)
Double entry accounting (p. 387)

Early-stage financing (p. 378)
Equipment lease (p. 382)
Equity financing (p. 377)
Financial forecasting
Financial management (p. 369)
Financial planning (p. 373)
Financing decisions
Financing (p. 377)
Internal financial controls (p. 386)
Internal fraud (p. 386)
Investment decisions (p. 370)
Line of credit (p. 382)
Microloans (p. 382)
Preventative internal control (p. 387)
SBA loans (p. 382)
Seed-stage financing (p. 378)
Separation of duties (p. 387)
Startup financing (p. 378)
Variance (p. 373)
Venture capitalist (VC) (p. 378)
Working capital

BUSINESS CASE 18.2: AGBIOME—RESEARCH TRIANGLE PARK, NORTH CAROLINA

SDG 17:   Partnership for the Goals

Agriculture is a $5 trillion global industry forecasted to substantially increase as the world's population expands. By 2050, the agriculture industry must produce enough to feed a projected 9.7 billion people. Growth and innovation are essential for the agriculture sector to meet this demand. Investors are taking notice of opportunities to improve the productivity of the agriculture industry. In 2021, venture capitalists invested $10.5 billion across 751 deals in agtech startups. These startups focus on solutions that improve crop yields, increase efficiency, drive profitability, and as a result, contribute to food security throughout the world. However, between 20–40% of crops around the world are lost to pests every year. The United Nations estimates that plant diseases account for $220 billion in economic costs annually, and invasive insects cost around $70 billion.

AgBiome, an agricultural biotechnology company based in North Carolina, develops products to address the threat of insects and disease on the global food supply. The privately held company creates products aimed at improving crop productivity. AgBiome's team of scientists identify microbiomes—or the community of fungi, bacteria, and viruses living in or on a plant—that help keep it healthy and resistant to disease. An article in North Carolina's *Herald Sun* compared this microbiome in plants to the organisms that live in human intestines to help with digestion. AgBiome aims to create a suite of products that replace synthetic chemicals and reduce the number of crops lost to disease each year. For example, its Howler and Theia fungicide products target diseases like powdery mildew that devastate high-value fruit and vegetable crops.

The company was founded in 2012, but it did not launch its first commercial fungicide product until 2020. It was support from outside investors that contributed to the success AgBiome is seeing today in its first commercial products. In its early days, AgBiome secured funding from both venture capitalists and equity ownership partners. In 2014, AgBiome ended its first series of investments with $17.5 million. Investors grew more confident in AgBiome as it gained financial support from other industry leaders. As one executive from AgBiome investor Polaris Partners noted, "[I]t is gratifying to see that each of these well-positioned investors sees promise in AgBiome." Two years later, the company secured its second round of financing—$34.5 million—from organizations like the Bill & Melinda Gates Foundation and the University of Texas Investment Management Company.

In 2021, AgBiome announced it received an additional $116 million in funding from new and existing investors. The company boasts its Howler fungicide product demonstrated 10 times sales growth in 2020, and it is positioned to expand into insecticides and herbicides by 2025. AgBiome plans to use the capital to hire more employees, expand its portfolio of products, and continue building partnerships throughout the world. The chair of the AgBiome board, Marijin Dekkers, said in a press release, "[T]his significant fundraising will allow AgBiome to rapidly accelerate its mission to feed the world responsibly by both discovering and developing its own products as well as by identifying strategic acquisition growth opportunities."

For example, AgBiome's continued grant from the Bill & Melinda Gates Foundation will help farmers in sub-Saharan Africa. AgBiome has identified microbial strains that protect maize, sorghum, banana, and yam crops from disease and insects. It plans to continue the second phase of its research in the field conditions of sub-Saharan Africa in 2022. Partnerships with organizations like the Bill & Melinda Gates Foundation bring AgBiome one step closer to production-ready, sustainable pest control solutions to increase the income of smallholder farmers in Africa.

Critical Thinking Questions

1. Why is sound financial management so important for a company like AgBiome that secures grants from other organizations?

2. What aspects of financial management might be affected when a company like AgBiome participates in partnerships?

3. How might AgBiome have an impact on sustainability not just through its product development but also through its financial management?

References

AgBiome. (2014, November 17). AgBiome backed by world-leading agribusiness companies. *AgBiome*. https://blog.agbiome.com/agbiome-backed-by-world-leading-agribusiness-companies

AgBiome. (2015, August 20). AgBiome secures $34.5 million series B financing. *AgBiome*. https://blog.agbiome.com/agbiome-secures-34-5-million-series-b-financing

AgBiome. (2021, September 14). AgBiome raises $116 million led by Blue Horizon and Novalis Lifesciences. *AgBiome*. https://blog.agbiome.com/agbiome-raises-116-million-led-by-blue-horizon-and-novalis-lifesciences

AgBiome. (2022, January 26). AgBiome receives grant to continue developing effective crop protection solutions for farmers in sub-Saharan Africa. *AgBiome*. https://blog.agbiome.com/agbiome-receives-phase2grant

Food and Agriculture Organization of the United Nations. (2019, April 3). New standards to curb the global spread of plant pests and diseases. *United Nations*. https://www.fao.org/news/story/en/item/1187738/icode/

Gaston, L. (2016, July 28). Press release: AgBiome awarded grant from Bill & Melinda Gates Foundation. *Bill & Melinda Gates Foundation Strategic Investment Fund*. https://sif.gatesfoundation.org/news-and-updates/press-release-agbiome-awarded-grant-bill-melinda-gates-foundation/

Goedde, L., Horii, M., & Sanghvi, S. (2015). Global agriculture's many opportunities. *McKinsey & Company*. https://www.mckinsey.com/~/media/McKinsey/Industries/Private%20Equity%20and%20Principal%20Investors/Our%20Insights/Global%20agricultures%20many%20opportunities/Global%20agricultures%20many%20opportunities.ashx

Hall, C. (2021, September 14). AgBiome lands $116M for safer crop production technology. *TechCrunch*. https://techcrunch.com/2021/09/14/agbiome-lands-166m-for-safer-crop-protection-technology/

Oleniacz, L. (2013, September 1). Agricultural biotech startup AgBiome gears up. *The Herald Sun via AgBiome Blog*. https://www.agbiome.com/agricultural-biotech-startup-agbiome-gears-up/

PitchBook. (2022). 2021 annual agtech report: VC trends and industry overview. *PitchBook*. https://pitchbook.com/news/reports/2021-annual-agtech-report

The World Bank. (2022, April 1). Agriculture and food. *The World Bank*. https://www.worldbank.org/en/topic/agriculture/overview

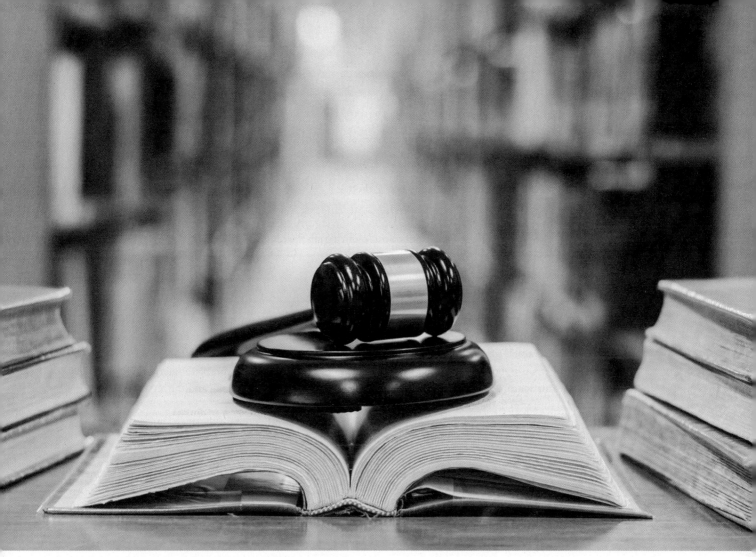

APPENDIX A:
NAVIGATING LEGAL AND IP
ISSUES IN BUSINESS

With Contributions from Richard Mandel, JD

LEARNING OBJECTIVES
A.1   Discuss why understanding business law is essential.
A.2   Explain the most common types of legal structures available to businesses.
A.3   Define Intellectual Property (IP) and the role it plays in business.
A.4   Assess the global impact of IP theft.
A.5   Describe the common IP traps experienced by businesses.
A.6   Explain the legal requirements of hiring employees.

LEGAL CONSIDERATIONS

Business law is a collection of legal requirements that involves protecting rights, maintaining orders, resolving disputes, and establishing a set of generally accepted standards. Every business, large or small, is responsible for complying with the legal regulations applied to its respective business practices. Some functions of business law include: shareholder and employee rights, workplace safety, environmental regulations, payment rules (salary, compensation, and working overtime), and the regulations related to the formation of new businesses.[1]

The legal side of business may not sound as exciting as other parts of business, but seeking expert legal advice is essential. Most business owners either lack the skills to understand the legalities of setting up a business or neglect the legal side altogether. Facebook cofounder Mark Zuckerberg made several big legal mistakes in his early startup stage, including setting up Facebook with the wrong business structure, which we talk about a little later.[2]

Legal costs vary widely, depending on the type of business you are setting up. A simple, home-based cupcake-baking business may cost only a few hundred dollars in legal fees, whereas a larger, more complex enterprise is likely to cost a good deal more. In general, a business attorney will charge at least $200 per hour, but a simple startup business may only need 1 or 2 hours of work to draw up the required documents. Some legal practices provide a free 1-hour consultation for new clients and/or payment plans for startups. Before you decide on a lawyer, do some research and compile a list of four or five possible candidates, their qualifications, and their rates. Like anything else worthwhile that you need to buy for your business, it pays to shop around.

Of course, there are a wide range of free resources regarding legal issues and documents available online to business owners looking for advice. However, be careful using these resources, as they may not be strictly accurate or relevant to the type of business you are trying to set up. Using certain sites online (see Table A.1) is a good way to gather research and identify the type of legal counsel you might need. Although legal advice can be expensive, the expense far outweighs the risk of attempting to do it all yourself with free, potentially inaccurate information online.

Legal support for business people is provided by law schools all over the United States. For example, second- and third-year law students at Santa Clara University in California provide affordable legal services to entrepreneurs looking to set up a business or for advice on the legal issues that may arise from running a business.[3] Law school websites can also be useful for legal information, as they may provide certain forms or documentation for no charge. Washburn University of Law, in particular, offers a wide range of forms and information, which can be accessed for free.[4]

The U.S. government also provides resources for entrepreneurs. One such resource is the United States Patent and Trademark Office (USPTO), which provides a pro bono or no-fee legal program to support business owners. The Small Business Administration also sponsors the SCORE association, a network of volunteer business counselors throughout the United States and its territories trained to serve as counselors, advisers, and mentors to aspiring entrepreneurs and business owners. These resources can be incredibly useful in learning the different legal requirements for your venture. Armed with this information, you will have a better chance of finding the right legal help when the time comes.

TABLE A.1 ■ Useful Online Legal Resources	
Docracy	Free, open-sourced site for contracts and other legal documents. Documents are free to download and edit. https://www.docracy.com/
LegalZoom*	Provides legal services to help start and run a business as well as file trademark applications. https://www.legalzoom.com/
NOLO*	Offers low-cost DIY kits for setting up business entities. https://www.nolo.com/
Quora	A question-and-answer website on thousands of topics but also a good place to ask legal questions. There is an area devoted to startup law. https://www.quora.com/topic/Startup-Law-1
Rocket Lawyer*	Helps you draft legal documents to start a business, manage employees, or rent property. https://www.rocketlawyer.com/
Startup Company Lawyer	Good sources for answers to frequently asked legal questions such as "When do I need to incorporate a company?" and "What state should I incorporate in?" and "What type of entity should I form?" http://www.startupcompanylawyer.com/
U.S. Small Business Administration	A comprehensive site for business people that offers free guides for legal compliance in starting and running a business. https://www.sba.gov/
United States Patent and Trademark Office	You can learn about patent and trademark basics, search existing patents, and register trademarks. https://www.uspto.gov/

Note: The authors are not advocating or promoting any paid services. We have no relationship with any site promoting products for a fee.

The best lawyers not only will be able to provide legal counsel but will also add value for many years as your business grows.[5] They will have experience with early-stage startups, know the industry, and be up front with their fee structure. They may also have an impressive list of contacts, which can be very useful in connecting you with investors and advising you on fundraising. What's more, a good lawyer will be a person you can actually relate to. The best way to hire legal experts is the same way you would hire an employee. When the time comes, ask yourself, "Is this the right person to advise and represent my company?"

TYPES OF LEGAL STRUCTURES

Every business has a legal structure, and there are various structures based on size, purpose, and number of employees. The type of structure affects the authorities you need to notify regarding your business, tax, and other contributions you may have to pay; the records and documentation you will need to maintain; and how decisions are made about the business.

As legal structures vary from state to state (and country to country), it is essential that business owners do as much research as possible before deciding on a particular form of organization. Depending on your situation, there are several structures to choose from, and it is important to understand the differences among them. If, after researching the question, you are still not sure which one best suits your business, then paying a few hundred dollars for a legal consultation can be a worthwhile investment. Let's examine some of the most common legal structures used by businesses in the United States.

Sole Proprietorship

A sole proprietorship is a business owned by one person who has not formed a separate entity to run it. This is the simplest and most inexpensive form of legal structure for startups, but it is rarely the correct choice. It means the business is completely managed and controlled by you, the owner, and that you are entitled to all the profits your business makes. However, it also means you are personally exposed to all the risks and legal responsibilities or liabilities of the business. But many large organizations began as sole proprietorships; for example, eBay was a sole proprietorship owned by founder Pierre Omidyar for 3 years before he joined with other partners.[6]

The main reason why sole proprietorship is the most common choice of business structure is that forming a sole proprietorship is quite simple. In many jurisdictions and industries, there is no legal filing at all to set yourself up as a business owner.[7] If your business is in an industry and/or a location where licenses or permits are necessary, you may just need to pay a nominal fee to obtain the right license or permit. For example, for a painting business you might need a home improvement contractor license; for any retail business you will likely need a sales tax permit. Because you and your business are treated as one entity, you have to file only one personal tax return outlining your income and expenses. (You do, however, have to use a separate form, Schedule C, to report your business income.)[8] The business's income is added to whatever other income you (and your spouse) may have and is taxed at your personal income tax rate after a 20% deduction is allowed.

However, as previously mentioned, you are also held personally liable for any debts the business incurs (see Figure A.1). There can be quite a lot of pressure to running a sole proprietorship, especially when it comes to fulfilling all your financial obligations. For example, say you have borrowed money to run your business, but you lose a major customer, which leaves you unable to repay the loan. Or say an employee of yours is involved in an automobile accident while on the job and injures another driver; you, as sole proprietor, are fully responsible for dealing with the injured person's claims. Either of these scenarios could potentially mean having to sell personal assets such as your car, your investments, or even your house to raise the money. You could even be driven to personal bankruptcy. Some of the other business structures we will discuss provide at least a minimal level of protection against such personal losses.

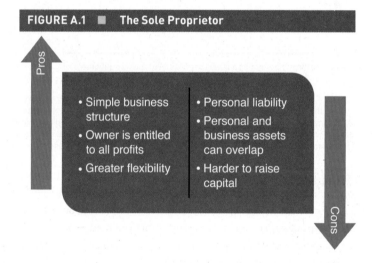

FIGURE A.1 ■ The Sole Proprietor

Pros

- Simple business structure
- Owner is entitled to all profits
- Greater flexibility

- Personal liability
- Personal and business assets can overlap
- Harder to raise capital

Cons

General Partnership

A **general partnership** involves two or more people who have made a decision to share ownership, management, as well as profits and losses of a business. Like a sole proprietorship, setting up a general partnership is relatively low cost and straightforward. As each partner reports profits and losses on individual tax returns rather than corporate returns, a process called pass-through taxation, taxes are also paid at your personal income tax rates (after the previously mentioned 20% deduction).

For example, say you and your business partner decide to open a café. To qualify for general partnership legal status, you and your partner must be involved in the business and contribute toward setting up and paying the costs of running the café. You and your partner will split the profits and losses between you.

Although partnership arrangements can be quite flexible, it is wise to have a formal agreement drafted by a legal expert to lay out the terms of the partnership. Typically, this agreement will cover the percentage of shares you are each entitled to, your individual rights and duties, and the consequences of one of you leaving the business for any reason.

Sharing the burden of running the business with someone else can be a great asset to a startup. However, like the sole proprietorship legal structure, in a general partnership each partner is still personally liable for the company's financial obligations. In a worst-case scenario, this means that if one partner is responsible for running the company into the ground, the other partner will still be liable. And if the offending partner cannot pay, the other partner would be liable for the full amount. Therefore, before entering into a general partnership, it is essential that the partners know each other well and establish a high degree of trust.

C Corporation

A C corporation (sometimes known as a "C-corp") is a separate legal entity created by the state government and owned by an unlimited number of shareholders. This means that the corporation, not the shareholders, is legally liable for its actions. The most money that shareholders can lose is their personal investment—the value of their stock.

Another advantage to the C corporation is transferable ownership, which means it can issue shares of stock to investors in exchange for capital. In addition, because the corporation is a separate entity, it benefits from continuous existence, which means that it will still survive after the demise of its owners. This allows the corporation to plan for the future.

Many people believe that corporations, business entities owned by their shareholders, are so complex that they are reserved for larger, more established businesses with numerous employees. In reality, however, corporations normally are not very time-consuming or expensive to set up. Many corporations are owned by only one or a few stockholders who elect themselves as directors and officers.

An alleged disadvantage is double taxation: The corporate profit is taxed twice—first on the profit it makes, and second, the shareholders are taxed on the dividends. However, in a startup, corporate profits are often paid out to the owners as additional compensation (which means that corporate tax is eliminated on nonexistent corporate profits). Otherwise, these profits are often retained to fund the growth of the startup, thus eliminating any current tax on dividends (the sum of money paid to shareholders from company profits) and leaving only the corporate tax at a rate calculated without adding the income of stockholders and their spouses.

S Corporation

An S corporation (sometimes known as an "S-corp") is a corporation whose stockholders elect special treatment for income tax purposes. For all other purposes, it is identical to a C corporation. In order to qualify as an S-corp, the corporation must be a U.S. domestic corporation. In addition, it must have no more than 100 shareholders, who in most cases must be individual U.S. citizens or legal immigrants (not corporations, partnerships, or trusts), and all of whom must own only one class of common stock (ordinary shares).

Unlike the C-corp, the S-corp does not have to deal with double taxation, as there is only one level of tax to pay. Similar to a partnership, the income and losses are passed through to the company's shareholders' tax returns and taxed at the individual rates, after a 20% deduction. This is especially attractive for corporations expecting to lose money in the short term, as such losses will offset other income earned by shareholders, acting as a so-called "tax shelter." S-corps, as they grow, often switch to C-corp status because their S-corp status restricts the number and types of shareholders permitted. Another reason for switching to C-corp status is the fact that an S-corp's future retained earnings would be taxed to stockholders as so-called "phantom income"—earnings are taxed but not received by the individual.

Limited Liability Company

A limited liability company (LLC) is a business structure that combines the pass-through taxation aspects of a partnership with the limited liability benefits of a corporation without being subject to the eligibility requirements of an S corporation.

This means that profits and losses are reported on individual tax returns in the same manner as other pass-through entities; therefore, double taxation does not apply, and there is potential tax sheltering from losses while personal assets are protected. Modern limited liability company statutes allow LLCs to have continuous existence, similar to corporations. And just as with partnerships and corporations, it is advisable for the LLC's owners (called "members") to enter into ownership agreements, often contained within an operating agreement that serves the combined purposes of bylaws and stockholder agreements in corporations. LLCs are rapidly replacing S corporations as the entity of choice for many startup businesses.

Benefit Corporation

A **benefit corporation** (sometimes known as a B-corp) is a form of organization certified by the nonprofit B Lab, which ensures that strict standards of social and environmental performance, accountability, and transparency are met. B Lab certification ensures that the for-profit company fulfills its social mission. It is available to businesses operating as any one of the business entities mentioned above (not just corporations).

In addition to the B Lab certification, many states have enacted statutes creating a new form of business entity, also called a B or Benefit corporation, that is not subject to the fiduciary obligations of other business corporations. Most business corporations must justify all their actions as contributing ultimately to increased shareholder wealth.[9]

On the contrary, a statutory B corporation declares in its charter one or more social benefit goals. This protects it and its managers from lawsuits from shareholders claiming that the company is spending more time or resources on social issues than on maximizing profit.

A statutory B corporation is similar to a corporation, as it also has shareholders and employees. However, the main difference lies in the fact that managers in a statutory B corporation are held responsible for ensuring the right balance is met between pure profit and its declared social benefit goals.

The principal types of legal structures we have described are summarized in Table A.2.

TABLE A.2 ■ Types of Legal Structures				
Business Entity	**Structure**	**Liability**	**Taxation**	**Notes**
Sole Proprietorship	One owner	Unlimited	Pass-through	
General Partnership	Two or more partners	Unlimited, joint and several	Pass-through	
C Corporation	Stockholders, directors, officers	Limited	Taxable entity	Potential double tax on dividends
S Corporation	Stockholders, directors, officers	Limited	Pass-through	Subject to eligibility requirements
Limited Liability Company (LLC)	Members, optional board of managers	Limited	Pass-through	May elect to be taxable entity
Benefit Corporation (under corporate law)	Stockholders, directors, officers	Limited	May be either C-corp or S-corp, if eligible	Charter sets forth social purpose(s)

Not-for-Profit Entities

Not-for-profits are not technically a different form of business entity. **Not-for-profit** is a tax status available to corporations, LLCs, trusts, and other structures that meet specific criteria set out in the Internal Revenue Code.

All not-for-profits are exempt from income tax on their profits (so-called "surplus"), and some are also eligible to receive donations that are tax deductible to their donors. Only those companies described in Section 501 of the tax code are eligible; these include charitable organizations, business leagues, civic leagues, labor organizations, chambers of commerce, social clubs, fraternal organizations, cemetery companies, and the like.

Those also eligible to receive tax-deductible contributions are the smaller list of organizations in Section 501(c)(3), including religious, educational, scientific, and charitable institutions. One important condition applicable to all not-for-profits, however, is that none of the organization's earnings are permitted to benefit individuals. In other words, although not-for-profits can pay reasonable compensation to employees, they cannot have shareholders; all profit must be reinvested in the business and used for the organization's exempt purpose.

INTELLECTUAL PROPERTY (IP)

Intellectual property (IP) is intangible personal property created by human intelligence, such as ideas, inventions, slogans, logos, and processes. IP law includes the copyright, trademark, trade secret, and patent protections for physical and nonphysical property that is the product of original thought and that can, in some sense, be owned. IP is a valuable asset for which business owners need to create an IP strategy that supports and evolves with the business. Intellectual property rights legally protect inventions.[10] IP is the backbone of innovation all over the world because it plays a significant role in economic growth and development.

Examples of companies that depend on intellectual property.

©iStockphoto.com/AnatoliiBabii

Many startups are dependent on IP protection, regardless of industry or line of business; from manufacturing to tech enterprises to restaurants, IP protection is essential to the survival of small businesses. Without it, powerful companies like Amazon, Google, eBay, or Staples would never have gotten off the ground.[11]

Small businesses are becoming increasingly dependent on protecting their IP in order to bring their products and services to market. In fact, protecting IP has become more important to entrepreneurs than ever before.[12] The late Steve Jobs realized the importance of protecting IP early on: "From the earliest days at Apple, I realized that we thrived when we created intellectual property. If people copied or stole our software, we'd be out of business."[13]

IP is one of the most valuable assets for startups when it comes to transforming ideas and innovations into real market value. If the IP is usable and owned by the startup, investors will be more comfortable in investing, and it can increase the valuation of the new venture. Protecting your IP also prevents competitors from trying to copy your products and services.

However, IP law can be complex, confusing, and entirely misunderstood. In the flurry of setting up new ventures, many business people neglect the issue of IP protection and fail to seek advice from experts. Yet, if the IP protection isn't in place, the whole venture can collapse.

Determining IP ownership is not straightforward. For instance, say you create IP for a venture while still employed at another company, or when you have just left a job. In many employment contracts and under the law of most jurisdictions, the rights to inventions that substantially relate to the employee's old job description belong to the company.[14] This means that your IP is owned by your former employer—not you. It is fundamental in the early stage of a startup that you seek legal advice from an IP attorney and review employee contracts and applicable law to determine whether there is anything that might prevent you from obtaining IP ownership.

Furthermore, a startup may use an independent contractor or a third party to help develop an innovation or trademark. Without a formal agreement in place, that third party may have a right to a portion of any IP that results from their contribution, even though they may have been paid to create it. Table A.3 outlines some more resources for IP information.

Finally, be aware of the relationship between IP and hackathons—events where software and hardware developers intensively collaborate to generate new ideas and inventions. A number of popular innovations, such as the ideas for Twitter and GroupMe, arose from hackathons.

When organizations hold internal hackathons whose participants are their own employees, they automatically own the IP of whatever creative innovations arise. However, taking part in an external hackathon is not so clear-cut, especially if you are already an employee at a tech organization. Developing a proof-of-concept prototype at a hackathon and then disclosing and sharing the idea in public at the hackathon could destroy any chance of patenting it in the future. Even worse, with so many people involved, it is not clear who can claim IP ownership of the innovation.[15] Similar issues can arise in the context of group projects in college classwork. In summary, it behooves you as a business person to educate yourself about IP and to seek legal guidance whenever appropriate.

TABLE A.3 ■ Resources for IP Information	
U.S. Patent and Trademark Office	The site offers a wealth of information about patents, trademarks, and IP law and policy. https://www.uspto.gov/
U.S. Copyright Office	The authoritative source for information about copyright. https://www.copyright.gov/
World Intellectual Property Organization (WIPO)	An all-encompassing site to help navigate the world of copyright, patent, trademarks, and industrial designs. https://www.wipo.int/about-ip/en/
Managing Intellectual Property	A source of the latest news and updates on IP-related issues around the globe. https://www.managingip.com
LegalTemplates	Download free nondisclosure agreement template. https://legaltemplates.net
Pat2PDF	A web-based tool that finds patents and downloads them as PDFs. https://www.pat2pdf.org/
Inventors Digest	An online hub loaded with inventor and IP developer news, as well as IP trends and tips. Referred to as the magazine for "idea people." https://www.inventorsdigest.com/
PatentWizard	Designed by a patent attorney, the site helps you take the critical first steps toward filing an early provisional patent. https://www.neustelsoftware.com/patentwizard/

The Four Types of Intellectual Property

IP is an essential asset to a company, as it provides opportunities for others to invest or collaborate and allows the founders to license, exchange, or even franchise their IP. In order to protect their IP, business people need to be very knowledgeable about the different types during the early days of their business. There are four types of IP that fall under the protection of U.S. law: copyright, trademark, trade secrets, and patent.[16]

Copyright

Copyright is a form of protection provided to the creators of original works in the areas of literature, music, drama, choreography, art, motion pictures, sound recordings, and architecture. It is important for tech entrepreneurs to be aware that computer code is classified as a literary work for purposes of copyright protection.[17] Another crucial thing to remember is that copyright does not protect ideas; it protects the tangible expression of the idea, such as written materials or recordings. Generally, U.S. copyright lasts for the duration of the author's life plus 70 years.

Copyright infringement cases can prove costly. For example, over the years British singer and songwriter Ed Sheeran has faced several million-dollar lawsuits for alleged copyright infringement. In 2022, Sheeran won a copyright lawsuit over the alleged infringement of his hit single "Shape of You," the most streamed song in Spotify's history. Sheeran was accused of copying another artist's song to create this hit music. The lawsuit was estimated to cost around nearly $4 million in legal fees.[18]

Some limited uses of copyrighted material are allowed without the permission of the copyright owner; this is called "fair use." Generally, it must be shown that the work is of a type meant to be copied, the use is for a noncommercial purpose, it constitutes only a small portion of the work, and/or it won't have a negative effect on the market for the work. Fair use is a "gray area" in U.S. law; there are no absolute rules or boundaries around what is and is not fair use.

Trademark and Service Mark

Any word, name, symbol, or device used in business to identify and promote a product is a trademark; its counterpart for service industries is the service mark. Although the law affords some limited protection to trademarks without registration, a federally registered trademark generally lasts 10 years and, if still in use, can be renewed every 10 years thereafter. Trademarks and service marks are the legal basis of most branding campaigns. Multimillion-dollar Swedish oat milk company Oatly took legal action against UK-based, family-run company Glebe Farm Foods for alleged trademark infringement, accusing the smaller company of attempting to pass off its oat drink "PureOaty" as an Oatly product, and causing confusion to buyers by producing packaging in similar font and colors. In 2021, the court ruled in favor of Glebe Farm Foods, stating there was no likelihood of confusion between Glebe Farm Foods' product and any of the Oatly trademarks.[19]

Trade Secret

A trade secret is any confidential information that provides companies with a competitive edge and is not publicly known or accessible, such as formulas, patterns, customer lists, compilations, programs, devices, methods, techniques, or processes. Trade secrets last for as long as they remain secret; they are protected from theft under federal and state law. Companies can protect their trade secrets by having their employees and contractors sign nondisclosure, work-for-hire, and noncompete agreements or clauses. Famous examples of trade secrets allegedly include the recipe for Coca-Cola's beverages, KFC's ingredients, and the formula for WD-40.[20]

Patent

A patent is a grant of property rights on inventions through the U.S. government. It excludes others from making, using, selling, or importing the invention without the patent owner's consent. In order to be granted a patent, the product or process must present a new or novel way of doing something, be nonobvious, or provide some sort of solution to a problem. The duration of a patent is generally 20 years from the filing date of application, and it can be costly to file for a patent.

In the United States, the invention must not have been made public in any way before 1 year prior to the filing application date (the 1-year grace period does not exist in most other countries). Laws of nature, physical phenomena, mathematical equations, scientific theories, the human body or human genes, and abstract ideas cannot be patented. However, it is possible for a mobile app to be patented if it meets the criteria of the USPTO.

It is important to remember that although copyright protects artistic expression and trademark protects brand, there is no way to protect or patent an idea. Of course, the whole innovation must begin with an idea, but an idea must be turned into an invention before it can qualify for patenting.[21] This does not necessarily mean creating a prototype, but you must be able to meaningfully describe the invention, how it is made, and how others could use it.

Nondisclosure Agreement

A business can protect its IP through a nondisclosure agreement (NDA) or confidentiality agreement, which is a legal contract that outlines confidential information shared by two or more parties.[22] This means that neither party has the right to share this information with competitors, the general public, or anyone else outside those involved in the agreement.

In general, you will come across several situations where you will be required to share confidential information with another person or company, or they may want to share confidential information with you. When should you ask them to sign an NDA? When should you sign one when asked? Usually, when either of you have something of value to share about your business and you want to make sure the other party does not steal it. Table A.4 outlines some guidelines for when an NDA is required.

However, NDAs should not be used when you just have a half-baked idea with no resources. If you place an NDA in front of someone, especially an early investor, they may not sign it.

Although you may not need an NDA in the very early stages of your business when you haven't really cemented your idea yet, when the right time comes, NDAs are essential to entrepreneurs, especially to protect against the growing threat of IP theft.

TABLE A.4 ■ Guidelines for When to Use an NDA	
1. When talking to your competitors	In some situations, you will likely find yourself in conversation with your competitors. Without an NDA in place, they could copy your business and you could copy theirs. Signing a mutual nondisclosure agreement is the best way to protect both parties.
2. When disclosing patent information	If you have invented something and patented the information, never disclose the patent information to outsiders until after the NDA has been signed by all parties involved.
3. When discussing trade secrets	Always use an NDA to protect your trade secrets, and even then, make sure that you only disclose them on a need-to-know basis with people you trust the most.[23]
4. When taking on a partner or an investor	When you're considering taking on a new partner or investor, make sure the information you share, such as business financials, personal information, and so on, is protected by an NDA. Bear in mind, however, that most investors will refuse to sign NDAs for startups in the very early stages.
5. When discussing the sale or licensing of a product or technology	When in discussions about licensing or selling your product, you need to make sure that the potential buyer does not disclose the details of your product or, indeed, any information about your company to a competitor. A signed NDA will protect all sensitive company information.
6. When employees have access to confidential and proprietary information	Without a strong NDA in place, there is nothing to stop your employees from accessing valuable information (client lists, supplier agreements) and using these data to set up a competing business after they have left your company. Make sure that every employee signs an NDA at the time of hire.
7. When sharing business information with a prospective buyer	If you are considering selling your business, then you will need to disclose every single detail of your financial and operations information to that acquiring company. An NDA will ensure all your information stays protected.[24]

GLOBAL IP THEFT

Any business that has a trademark, trade secret, patent, or copyright is dependent on IP protections. Consider this scenario: You have just launched a T-shirt business with a trademarked brand, and sales are really taking off. A few months later, you come across another website set up in a different country that is selling counterfeit versions of your T-shirts for a fraction of the price. You start losing sales, your brand becomes tainted, investors think twice about investing in your company, and your reputation becomes damaged—and all because someone has stolen your unique trademark and copied it for financial gain.

Millions of people all over the world violate IP laws every day. Global online piracy is rife in the area of digital content such as movies, music, software, games, and e-books. Recent statistics show that the United States had the highest numbers of visitors to media piracy sites, with more than 12 billion visits, followed by Russia with 8 billion visits, and then China with nearly 7 billion visits.[25] Ignoring copyright by downloading your favorite song from a peer-to-peer website without paying for it is similar to going into a music store and stealing a CD, yet people who would otherwise characterize themselves as law-abiding do it all the time. IP theft costs the United States between $225 and $600 billion every year, and it has a huge negative impact on legitimate businesses.[26]

Why does IP protection sometimes fail? IP rights are territorial, which means that although your rights may be protected in the United States, they are not necessarily protected in other countries. Countries such as the United States impose strict IP laws, but countries like China and India have a rich history of IP rights violations.

Nevertheless, there is still a strong market for counterfeit goods in the United States. In 2021, U.S. Customs and Border Protection officials seized a container carrying more than 13,000 items containing counterfeit goods. Bags, clothing, and accessories bearing counterfeit logos, including Gucci and Louis Vuitton, were among the most counterfeited items.[27]

Thousands of counterfeit Rolex watches were seized during an investigation in Philadelphia.

AP Photo/Nati Harnik

Major corporations can afford to wage massive legal battles and get compensation for IP theft, but how can a startup or a small business protect its IP in different territories? Entrepreneurs who are seeking to sell their innovations abroad must first conduct a search to ensure their company's name and brand can be used in the foreign country. Then, they must register for local IP ownership in that country or extend U.S. registrations to foreign countries at the beginning of the process. Also, it would be wise to seek proper IP counsel to protect IP rights abroad.

Finally, don't depend wholly on your patent for your business strategy. Building customer relationships, promoting your trademarked brand, providing quality products and services, and implementing rapid innovation will also help you defend your business against the effects of IP theft.

COMMON IP TRAPS

IP can be a minefield, and many inventors fall into common traps that hamper the potential of exciting innovations.[28] Patenting can cost thousands of dollars, and some inventors find that they earn less than the cost of registering the patent. In a classic example, Robert Kearns, the inventor of the intermittent windshield wiper, sued car manufacturers Chrysler and Ford for copying the technology he had patented. Following a court battle that spanned decades, Kearns was finally granted a total of $40 million in compensation, which may sound like a lot, but it is nothing in comparison to what Kearns would have made if he had been credited with his invention from the beginning. Let's explore the common IP pitfalls and how business people can avoid them.

Publicly Disclosing Your Innovation

You might be bursting to tell the world about your discoveries, but don't. Disclosing your new product or service in public before you have filed a patent application means that in most countries you will not be permitted to patent it at all. (We've mentioned the 1-year grace period in the United States.) For example, a professor at Imperial College London, Robert Perneczky, discovered a protein that had the potential to significantly improve the chances of spotting the onset of Alzheimer's disease. However, Perneczky failed to qualify for a patent because of a detailed article he had written about his discovery that had been published in an academic journal. Because Perneczky's idea had been disclosed to the public, he was prevented from patenting it.

It is impractical to avoid disclosing anything at all about your discoveries, but try to refrain from revealing every single step. One way of protecting your IP that works in the United States is to file a provisional patent application before you make your idea public. This secures your rights as the inventor and gives you 12 months to complete the research and develop your idea into a working prototype. However, you will have to file a full patent application as soon as the 12 months are up; otherwise, the knowledge it holds will become publicly available. Also, your invention cannot have changed substantially from the date of the initial filing. Bear in mind that the United States has changed from being a "first to invent" to a "first to file" country, which means that if an inventor waits too long to file a patent application, they may lose out to someone else who is working on a similar innovation.

Failure to Protect Product and Processes

As Robert Kearns learned, it is easy for innovations to be copied by others. This is why it is important for entrepreneurs to ensure their products and processes are fully protected. Some inventors and other scientists protect their products by building unique markers into them; for example, a unique chemical "thumbprint" can reveal through a simple test whether someone else has copied their product. Another option some use is to license their innovation to a larger organization that has all the tools already in place to protect and commercialize the invention. The inventor then profits through a stream of royalties.

The intermittent windshield wiper was created by Robert Kearns, who sued Chrysler and Ford for copying his invention.

©iStockphoto.com/deepblue4you

Inability to Determine Originality

Entrepreneurs often build on existing products, tools, and techniques to create their innovations. However, the outcome must be considered both novel and useful if it is to qualify for IP protection. This means ensuring that products and services contain enough features to significantly improve the way they are used by others, with the intention of solving a problem. For example, when Jeffrey Percival and his research team developed the Star Tracker 5000—a low-cost device that determines a space rocket's altitude and tracks stars—the concern was it was not original enough, as it was mostly formed of standard components. To make his product more original, Percival added an algorithm that rapidly transmits digitized images. By enhancing the features of the product, Percival was able to patent the Star Tracker 5000 and license it to NASA for its space missions.

Failure to Assign Ownership

In the early stages of a startup, a number of people may be formally involved in contributing to the innovation process. This is why it is best to make formal agreements regarding IP ownership prior to any further development, in order to decide who owns and controls the innovation and who doesn't. Ownership can even vest in people you haven't paid, people you have paid but who haven't signed a formal assignment of ownership, or people who have otherwise made a valuable contribution to the innovation.

For example, InBae Yoon invented a medical device called the trocar, used to withdraw fluid from a body cavity, which he subsequently licensed to a larger organization. However, Yoon had originally collaborated with electronics technician Young Jae Choi to create the product. Yoon failed to pay Choi for his work or obtain an assignment of his rights. Some years later, a competitor discovered the technician's involvement, amended the patent to assign him partial ownership, and won a court case to secure a separate licensing agreement with Choi to allow them to use the product. The same kinds of problems can arise with people who may have coauthored copyrighted material or helped to design a logo for a company's trademark.

Failure to Protect IP in Global Markets

As we mentioned earlier, IP rights are territorial, which means that although your rights may be protected in the United States, they are not necessarily protected in other countries. For example, in China, Apple Inc. lost a court battle with Chinese technology firm Proview International Holdings, which claimed it owned the iPad trademark in the Chinese market.[29] The case seriously threatened Apple's ability to sell the iPad in China. Apple finally agreed to pay $60 million in 2012 to settle the 2-year dispute.

Innovators hoping to sell in other countries need to get the right legal advice and carry out due diligence before even starting their business, to understand how to navigate any obstacles up front. Otherwise, they risk running into some major difficulties along the way.

HIRING EMPLOYEES

There will likely come a time when you need to hire employees when your business takes off. Yet there's more to the hiring process than interviewing and selecting the best person for the job. As an employer, you need to understand federal and state labor laws in order to protect both your business and your employees. In this section, we describe some of the regulatory steps you need to consider when hiring your first employee.[30]

Equal Employment Opportunity

Employers in the United States need to be aware that federal laws prohibit discriminating against employees on the basis of race, sex, creed, religion, color, national origin, or age. Workers with disabilities are also protected, though employers can refuse to hire on the basis of a disability if it prevents the worker from fulfilling job tasks. Some states forbid discrimination on the basis of sexual orientation.

Globally, the rules are not the same. For example, the 2021 global rights index provided by the International Trade Union Confederation (ITUC) shows the level of inequality in other countries is rising, particularly since the onset of the COVID-19 pandemic, with some countries launching attacks on employees who want the right to strike, and the right to create and join a trade union. The report showed that Bangladesh, Brazil, Colombia, Egypt, and Turkey are among the worst countries in the world for equal opportunities and workers' rights.[31]

Employer Identification Number

Before you hire your first employee, make sure you get an employer identification number (EIN). You will need to use this on documents and tax returns for the IRS. It is also necessary when reporting employee information to state agencies. There is also a regulatory requirement to register your newly hired employee with your state directory within 20 days of the hire date. Even if you are a sole proprietor, you need an EIN, and you can apply for it online.

Unemployment and Workers' Compensation

Register with your state's labor department to pay state unemployment compensation taxes, which provide temporary relief to employees who lose their jobs. Depending on the size of your business, most states will require you to register for workers' compensation insurance to protect against any work-related injuries. (Some states make exceptions for very small businesses.)

Withholding Taxes

To comply with IRS regulations, you will need to withhold part of your employees' income and keep records of employment taxes for at least the most recent 4 years. You will need to report these wages and taxes every year. There may also be a requirement to withhold state income taxes, depending on the state in which your employees are located.

Employee Forms

Make sure you set up personnel files containing important documents for each employee you hire. Each employee must fill out a W-4 form that lets you, as the employer, know how much money to withhold from their paychecks for federal tax purposes. You can ask employees to fill out this form once unless they wish to change the withholding amount at some point in time. This form does not have to be filed with the IRS. The Form 1-9 is another form you need to complete within 3 days of hiring your new employee; this requires employers to verify the new employee's eligibility to work in the United States. In addition, you must file IRS Form 940 every year to report federal unemployment tax, which provides payment of unemployment compensation to employees who have lost their jobs.

Benefits

As an employer, you will need to decide what sorts of benefits you will provide your employees. The law requires you to pay and withhold Social Security taxes and an additional rate for Medicare, and to pay for unemployment insurance. Businesses with more than 50 employees must also provide family and medical leave and health insurance. In a few states, employers must provide a certain number of paid sick days. You are not required by law to provide life insurance, retirement plans, or paid vacation leave, but by offering a competitive benefits package, you will have a better chance of attracting and retaining high-caliber employees. If you choose to provide these optional benefits, be aware that they are subject to many regulations; consultation with an accountant experienced in such benefits is a worthwhile investment.

Safety Measures

All employers have a responsibility to their employees to maintain a safe and healthy workplace environment. This means training employees to do their jobs safely, ensuring the workplace is free from hazards, maintaining safety records, and reporting any serious accidents at work to government administrators. You should also have provisions in place such as medical treatment and rehabilitation services to support employees who are injured on the job.

The key to complying with legal requirements is being organized. Maintaining payroll records, filing tax returns on time, keeping your employees informed, and ensuring you are up to speed with federal reporting requirements go a long way toward running an efficient business. Table A.5 outlines 10 steps to setting up a payroll.

TABLE A.5   ■   Ten Steps to Setting Up a Payroll
1.   Get an Employer Identification Number (EIN)
2.   Find out whether you need state or local tax IDs
3.   Decide if you want an independent contractor or an employee
4.   Ensure new employees return a completed W-4 form
5.   Schedule pay periods to coordinate tax withholding for IRS
6.   Create a compensation plan for holiday, vacation, and leave
7.   Choose an in-house or external service for administering payroll
8.   Decide who will manage your payroll system
9.   Know which records must stay on file and for how long
10.   Report payroll taxes as needed on a quarterly and annual basis

Source: U.S. Small Business Administration. (n.d.). *Hire and manage employees.* Retrieved from https://www.sba.gov/business-guide/manage-your-business/hire-manage-employees

Hiring a Contractor or an Employee?

When hiring people, it is important to distinguish between contractors and employees.[32] Many startups and small businesses use independent contractors because of the advantages they bring. For example, it generally saves money to hire contractors because they don't require contributions toward health care, compensation insurance, or any other benefits. In addition, there can be cost-saving benefits when it comes to office space and equipment, as contractors will usually provide their own.

Furthermore, working with independent contractors gives employers greater flexibility in hiring and letting go of workers. For example, you could hire contractors for a specific project, and then let them go when the job is finished. Equally, if you do not like their work, you never have to see them again. There can also be valuable cost savings in hiring contractors who are experts in their field and are ready to hit the ground running, which means saving time and money on training.

Independent contractors are not protected by the same laws as employees, which means there is less chance of dealing with the same legal claims that could be brought by employees. However, there are some disadvantages to hiring independent contractors. Because contractors have autonomy in what, when, and how they perform their job duties, you may feel you have less control over them. Also, independent contractors may be present for only a short period of time before leaving again, which might be disruptive to the other employees.

Finally, it is important to be aware that the classification of workers as independent contractors or employees is not your choice. The classification is dictated by the facts of the relationship. State and federal agencies are very strict on workers who are classified as contractors versus employees, and you may risk facing government audits as a result.

Misclassifying independent contractors and employees could have costly legal consequences. For example, if the individual you thought you were hiring as an independent contractor actually meets the legal definition of an employee, you may need to pay back wages, taxes, benefits, and anything else an employee would receive in your company—health insurance, retirement, and so on. Table A.6 outlines some of the main differences between employees and contractors.

Whether the person you hire is a contractor or an employee depends on all of the factors listed above, but the most significant factor is the amount of control the employer has over the work being done.[33] For example, if you expect the person to show up at the same time every day and work a set period of hours, and you expect to closely oversee their duties, then you will have hired an employee rather than retained a contractor.

TABLE A.6   ■   Differences Between Employees and Contractors

Employee	Contractor
Duties are dictated or controlled by others	Decides what, when, and how duties are performed
Works solely for employer	Provides services to other clients
Uses tools or materials provided by employer	Supplies own tools or materials
Working hours set by employer	Sets own working hours
Tax, benefits, and pension paid by employer	Pays own tax, benefits, and pension
Expenses paid for by employer	Pays own expenses
Tasks must be performed by the employee	Can subcontract work to others
Employer provides annual and personal leave	Not provided with annual and personal leave
Paid regularly (weekly, monthly, etc.) as per employee contract	Provides an invoice when work is performed and the task is completed
Provided with training	Does not receive training

Source: U.S. Small Business Association. Hire a contractor or an employee. https://www.sba.gov/content/hire-contractor-or-employee. Retrieved August 2, 2015.

Compensating Employees

It is often the case that a startup's need for additional employees outstrips the company's ability to pay in cash. When faced with this resource constraint, business owners often come up with alternative ways to compensate employees, such as giving them flexible hours, additional days off, and small perks such as gift cards or a lunch paid for by the company.

Compensation in the Form of Equity

Business people often attempt to obtain services from employees and contractors in exchange for a share of the business, which is called equity. This raises two legal issues.

First, in the context of issuing shares to friends and family, issuance of shares to employees and contractors risks noncompliance with securities laws. Although the workers are not investing cash in the business, their time and labor is considered an investment under the law, triggering the protection of securities regulation. Therefore, just as much care must be paid to having the right processes in place when issuing shares to employees and contractors as when issuing shares to traditional investors.

Second, it is important to note that income tax is triggered any time an individual receives any form of property in exchange for performing services, not just when they are paid in cash. Therefore, the receipt of shares as compensation for work can result in an unexpected tax bill. This may not seem much of a problem in the early days of a startup when the shares may not be worth very much, but it could become an issue later on.

However, if the shares are subject to a vesting schedule, meaning that there is a preset period of time until the shares of stock can be sold, the problem becomes magnified. In this situation the tax may not apply until the shares have vested (when, it is hoped, they will have greatly increased in value). This same problem exists when founders' stock is made subject to a vesting schedule, since by doing so, you are tying the retention of stock to the performance of services. There are tax techniques available to mitigate, and in some cases eliminate, this unwelcome tax issue, so be sure to consult competent tax professionals before agreeing to pay compensation in the form of equity.

Unpaid Internships

The thought of receiving the services of enthusiastic young interns looking for work experience rather than financial compensation can be very attractive to the resource-constrained startup. However, bear in mind that such arrangements may be illegal. The Fair Labor Standards Act provides a minimum wage, overtime pay, and other protections to most workers. Putting an intern to work in your business might require compliance with these requirements. The U.S. Department of Labor has adopted a "primary beneficiary" test, allowing this practice if the benefits of the internship flow primarily to the intern and not to the employer. The Department of Labor has published a list of seven factors it will consider in determining the "primary beneficiary," including whether the internship is tied to the intern's formal education program and the extent to which the intern's work complements, rather than displaces, the work of paid employees.[34]

IN REVIEW

A.1 Discuss why understanding business law is essential.

Business law is a collection of legal requirements that involves protecting rights, maintaining orders, resolving disputes, and establishing a set of generally accepted standards. Every business, large or small, is responsible for complying with the legal regulations applied to their respective business practices.

Taking legal considerations into account may add value to the firm. Whether it is a lawyer, free website content, or some form of legal expert, obtaining competent legal advice will certainly help improve the performance of the venture.

A.2 Explain the most common types of legal structures available to businesses.

The most common types of legal structures are sole proprietorship, general partnership, C corporation, S corporation, limited liability company (LLC), limited partnership, limited liability partnership (LLP), and benefit corporation. In addition, most of these business structures can be run as a not-for-profit, provided the company complies with IRS section 501(c).

A.3   Define intellectual property (IP) and the role it plays in business.

Intellectual property (IP) is intangible personal property created by human intelligence, such as ideas, inventions, slogans, logos, and processes. The four main types of IP are copyright, trademark/service mark, trade secret, and patent. It behooves entrepreneurs to understand IP because startups are, by definition, innovative and likely to involve the creation of IP. One way for a startup to protect its IP is through a nondisclosure agreement (NDA) or confidentiality agreement, which is a legal contract that outlines confidential information shared by two or more parties.

A.4   Assess the global impact of IP theft.

Any business that has a trademark, trade secret, patent, or copyright is dependent on IP protections. Millions of people all over the world violate IP laws every day by ignoring copyright. IP theft costs the United States between $250 and $600 billion every year.

A.5   Describe the common IP traps experienced by businesses.

Business entrepreneurs often make mistakes in the following areas:

- Public disclosure of an invention or innovation;
- Failure to protect products, processes, brands, and so on;
- Inability to determine originality;
- Failure to allocate ownership; and
- Failure to protect IP in global markets.

A.6   Explain the legal requirements of hiring employees.

Legal requirements related to hiring employees include registering employees with the state labor department, keeping records of employee tax history, preparing the appropriate legal documentation, and complying with safety regulations.

KEY TERMS

Business law (p. 394)

Benefit corporation (B-corp) (p. 398)

C corporation (C-corp) (p. 397)

Copyright (p. 401)

General partnership (p. 396)

Intellectual property (IP) (p. 399)

Limited liability company (LLC) (p. 397)

Nondisclosure agreement (NDA) (p. 402)

Not-for-profit (p. 398)

Patent (p. 401)

S corporation (S-corp) (p. 397)

Sole proprietorship (p. 395)

Trade secret (p. 401)

Trademark (p. 401)

APPENDIX B: PUTTING IT ALL TOGETHER

THE BUSINESS IMPACT PROJECT

A business is an entity that is engaged in commercial, industrial, or professional activities that produce and/or sell goods or services for the creation of economic and social value. Economic value relates to the profitability of the business and its ability to generate revenue, pay expenses, and generate positive net income. Social value encompasses the positive impact a business can have on society including its employees, customers, and communities in which the business operates. Social value also includes the effect business can have on the environment such as issues related to sustainability and climate. Given that businesses should exist to generate economic and social value, it can be said that businesses should measure performance by evaluating their contribution to people, planet, and profits.

Throughout this book, we have given you examples of businesses of all shapes and sizes. But one thing every chapter-opening Business Impact case and end-of-chapter case has in common is that each business is creating economic and social value at the same time. From Patagonia's work on climate change to Tesla on clean energy to Little Cocoa Bean's emphasis on responsible consumption and production of food, these businesses are not only profitable and entrepreneurial, they are also socially relevant and acting as business change agents.

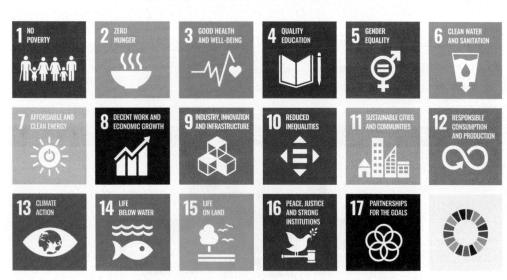

The UN's Sustainable Development Goals

Source: United Nations. (2022). *Sustainable Development Goals*. United Nations Sustainable Development; United Nations. https://www.un.org/sustainabledevelopment/sustainable-development-goals/. The content of this publication has not been approved by the United Nations and does not reflect the views of the United Nations or its officials or member states.

Chapter 1 introduced you to the 17 UN Sustainable Development Goals as a guide for the sustainability of the planet *and* a source of exponential business opportunities—as you can see from the examples throughout the book. Focusing on people, planet, and profit is not just a nice way to do business in today's world; it's the right way to do business in today's increasingly entrepreneurial environment. Research has suggested that businesses focusing on generating social and economic value concurrently outperform those that simply focus on generating economic value. As a result, paying attention to social and environmental issues is not only good for the world but also impacts business performance in five areas: sales, new business opportunities, employee engagement, operational efficiencies, and financial return.[1]

1. Sales: Consumers are more likely to pay more for products from companies that are socially responsible. It is reported that 90% of customers are willing to switch brands to support a cause and are also willing to boycott brands that impact people or the environment negatively.

2. New business opportunities: By focusing on social and environmental needs, new opportunities arise. It may be a new product or an existing product in a new market. Research suggests that more environmentally sustainable companies are four times as likely to be considered an innovation leader in their industry.

3. Employee engagement: Meaning and purpose is a powerful driver for the current generation of employees and entrepreneurs. Employees report greater job satisfaction and employers report higher employee engagement, greater ability to attract top talents, and retain that talent. Additionally, entrepreneurs focusing on social value report experiencing meaningful work experiences.

4. Operational efficiencies: Companies that have moved to more sustainable as well as ethical business practices have found increases in productivity and decreases in materials used—both of which contribute to a reduction in operating expenses.

5. Financial return: Data have proven that publicly traded companies with strong corporate social responsibility programs have better stock performance than their competitors. Additionally, social-focused investors, called impact investors, are targeting all sizes of companies. As a result, startups and growth companies that focus on social and environmental issues have greater access to capital.

The Business Impact Slide Deck

The five areas above align with the five building blocks that created the structure of the book (Table B.1) and were introduced in Chapter 1.

TABLE B.1 ■ Building Blocks of Successful Businesses

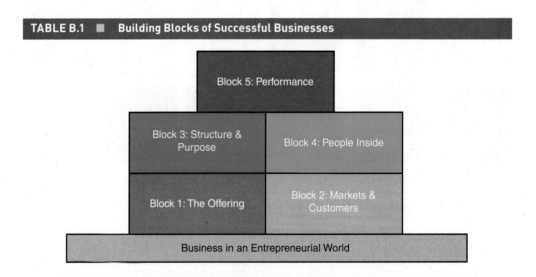

Business Building Blocks	Chapters
The Offering	3. Business Creation
	4. Business Models
	5. Business Strategy for Competitive Advantage

Markets and Customers	**6.** Marketing and Sales
	7. Customer Behavior and Market Segments
Structure and Purpose	**8.** Organizational Structure and Design
	9. Organizational Mission and Culture
People Inside the Business	**10.** Management and Leadership
	11. Human Resource Management
	12. Motivation and Empowerment
	13. Communication in Business
Performance	**14.** Operations and Quality Management
	15. Data Management and Analytics
	16. Accounting and Financial Statements
	17. Financial Management

As you work through each chapter in the book, the *business impact project (BIP)* is where you put your knowledge into action to better understand and connect with a business you are curious about, admire, want to potentially work for, already work for—or perhaps you are a super fan of its products. Regardless of the business you choose for this experience, the business must connect to one or more of the UN Sustainable Development Goals—just as the opening chapter stories and end-of-chapter cases connect to them.

When starting a big project, sometimes it's easier to start at the end. What's the deliverable when you finish the project? By the end of this experience you will have a *business impact deck (BID)*, which is a PowerPoint (or equivalent) presentation that depicts the five building blocks of the company of your choice, its impact related to the UN SDGs, as well as two to four potential entrepreneurial opportunities that the company should pursue in the future. These opportunities are uncovered as you research the five building blocks, learn more about the company, the industry in which it competes, and the customers it currently serves and could serve in the future. These entrepreneurial opportunities could be new products, services, processes related to how work is done, new initiatives inside the company, or new projects to benefit the community served by the company.

Table B.2 addresses suggested questions to be answered for each block as well as other required components for the project. We say *suggested* questions, because not all questions will likely be answered in your deck; therefore, it's up to you to critically think about what should or should not be included in order to present a compelling story of the company of your choice, its impact, and future potential opportunities. The length or number of slides needed for an effective BID may be determined by your course instructor; the table below is just a guideline.

TABLE B.2 ■ Business Impact Deck Guidelines

BID Component	Questions to Be Answered	Suggested Number of Slides
Introduction	What is the company? Where is it located? What UN SDG is it connected to, and how? Why should society care about this company? What made you choose this company?	1–3
The Offering	When was the company founded? What is its startup story? What does it sell? How would you describe its business model? Who is its competition?	2–4

(Continued)

TABLE 8.2 ■ Businee Impact Deck Guidelines *(Continued)*		
BID Component	**Questions to Be Answered**	**Suggested Number of Slides**
Markets and Customers	What is the marketing mix (4Ps)? How does the company find customers and make sales? What market segments does the company engage with? What is its ideal customer in each segment?	3–6
Structure and Purpose	What type of structure is used by the company? Is there an organizational chart you can show? What is the mission of the company? How would you describe the company culture? Are there unique elements of the company that contribute to its culture?	3–4
People Inside the Business	How many employees does the company have? What do employees like most about working there? What motivates them? What does leadership look like in this company? Who is the most admired leader in the company? Why? Who is the most admired manager in the company? Why? What forms of communication are most used in the business? What is the coolest job in the organization?	3–6
Performance	What does operations look like in this business? How is quality measured? Does it collect customer data? How is it used? Does it practice business analytics? In what way? How does data inform decision making? What data are most valuable? What is the company's annual revenue? What are its gross margins? Is the company profitable? What are the most important financial ratios to this business? Calculate them. Is accounting done in-house or is it outsourced? What type of financial planning is done?	5–7
Overall Business Impact	What impact is this company making on the world? How is it positively impacting people, planet, and profits as well as generating economic and social value at the same time?	2–5
Entrepreneurial Opportunities	Now that you have critically evaluated this company, what two to four new entrepreneurial opportunities should it consider pursuing, and why? For each opportunity, what is it, who is the customer, and why should the company pursue it? Opportunities could be new products, services, processes related to how work is done, new initiatives inside the company, or new projects to benefit the community served by the company.	2–4
Your Summary and Reflection	Think about what you learned through this process. What do you know now that you did not know before? What surprised you the most about the company studied? What do you want to learn more about? Would you work for this company?	1–2

Researching Your Chosen Company

The business impact project requires a great deal of research to produce a high-quality business impact deck. Figure B.1 illustrates four types of data that can be used in your research, and each has a different data source.

FIGURE B.1. ■ Types of Research Data		

	QUANTITATIVE Numeric based, hard data, empirical	*QUALITATIVE* Text based, soft data, exploratory
PRIMARY *Data collected in real time for a specific purpose. Data did not exist previously.*	*Surveys* *Experiments* *Counting and/or Measuring Any Type of Collected Data*	*Interviews* *Observations* *Focus Groups*
SECONDARY *Available data that currently exists. Data has already been collected and used by others.*	*Public Financial Statements* *Market Research Reports* *Databases*	*Company Websites* *Annual Reports* *Published News Articles* *Videos*

Both primary and secondary data should be used in your project. Primary data are data that you collect on your own while secondary data are data that are already available. Quantitative data are numbers and used to count, measure, and analyze. Qualitative data are text and used to categorize or describe. For example, if you google "number of employees at Patagonia 2022," you might immediately find the number 2,677. This is secondary data, but it's also quantitative because it is numerical. If you peruse Patagonia's website to find a report or article on Patagonia's initiatives around climate change, this is also secondary data, but it's qualitative given that its describing the company's initiative. However, if in the report there are numbers and graphs based on the warming of the planet, this is quantitative data! You can have both in one source. If you decide to interview a few employees at Patagonia to get their perspective on the company's culture, this would be qualitative and primary. You collected the data. And if that interview led you to an opportunity to create a survey to reach many more employees to measure and analyze employee satisfaction, this would be quantitative and primary. Again, you collected the data.

At a minimum, your project should include quantitative secondary data, qualitative primary data, and qualitative secondary data. Your local or school library and the internet can be very useful for secondary data. Because internet searches sometimes produce unreliable sources, it is best to start with your library to see what is available to you. Libraries often have easy access to databases at no cost to you that are not available for free online.

Summary of Deliverable Expectations

- Combination of primary and secondary data is used. Primary data will likely come from interviews and observations rather than focus groups, surveys, or experiments.

- All sources should be cited on the slide in which the information is used or in slide notes. If the number of references is large, then a slide can be added at the end of the deck with a list of references.

- Instructors can assign preferred style for references. Our example uses APA style.

- Slides should include pictures and graphics rather than text only. Students are strongly encouraged to use the slide notes feature to write a type of presentation script that elaborates on the slide content.

BUSINESS IMPACT DECK EXAMPLE

A sample BID and presentation with notes can be found online at the student resource site for this title. The company used in the example is Unilever and the BID was produced by undergraduate student at Babson College, Alexandra Douglas.

GLOSSARY

7S's hypercompetition model: A framework that guides companies to continuously create competitive advantages in disruptive environments

Ability diversity: The representation of people with different levels of mental and physical abilities within an organization

Absolute advantage: The ability of a country or business to produce certain products more efficiently than its competitors

Absolute quota: The maximum number of specific goods permitted to enter a country during a specific time period

Accounting: A process of recording, sorting, retrieving, and summarizing financial data

Accounting: Focuses on measuring, recording, identifying, and reporting the past financial transactions of a company using standard procedures and rules

Accounts payable: Money owed by a business to its suppliers

Accounts receivable: Refers to money owed to the company for goods or services provided and billed to a customer

Accrual basis accounting: An accounting method that records income and expenses where they are billed and earned before money changes hands

Accrued expenses: Costs incurred by the company for which no payment has been made

Acquired needs theory: A theory that holds that our needs are shaped over time and formed by our life experiences and cultural background

Action plan: The specific action, people, and resources needed to accomplish a goal

Active listening: The act of concentrating on the true meaning of what other people are saying

Additive manufacturing: (Also known as 3D printing) The process of using technology by adding layers of materials to create 3D objects

Adhocracy culture: A type of corporate culture based on the ability to adapt quickly to changing conditions by challenging assumptions and taking risks

Administrative managers: Oversee the day-to-day management of operations and workers

"Ad valorem" tariff: A tax paid based on a proportion of the value of imported goods

Advertising business model: The amount of revenue gained through advertising products and services

Affinity bias: The tendency to be drawn to others because they share similar interests, experiences, and backgrounds

Affirmative action: Proactive steps taken by organizations to counteract discrimination against minorities, including women

Age diversity: The inclusion of people of all different ages within the workplace

Ageism: The tendency to have negative feelings toward others based on their age

Ageism: Discrimination based on someone's age; one of the most common forms of discrimination at work

Aggregator business model: A model whereby the company connects vendors and buyers on the same platform and sells its services under its own brand

Agile manufacturing: A business approach that creates value for customers by rapidly responding to changes

Ambiguity: Relates to the future being unknowable, very unclear, and vague. Ambiguity can create both complexity and uncertainty

Amortization: The decrease of the value of intangible assets over time

Anchor bias: The tendency to hold on to a preexisting piece of information to make decisions

Angel investor: A type of investor who uses their own money to provide funds to young startup private businesses run by entrepreneurs who are neither friends nor family

Annual performance review: Identifies goal achievements, areas for improvement, performance issues, and opportunities for career progression

Artificial intelligence (AI): The capability of a machine to imitate intelligent human behavior

Asset financing: A way to borrow money or get a loan by using existing assets as security against a business loan from a lender

Association and sequence identification: A component of business analytics that focuses on understanding different types of consumers to reveal patterns in buying behavior

Attribution bias: The tendency to negatively interpret the behavior of another based on prior interactions rather than making an effort to understand that person

Authority: The legitimate right to give orders and make decisions

B2B businesses: Sell their products and services directly to the decision makers in another business

B2C businesses: Sell their products and services to customers for personal use

Backlog: Orders that have been received but not delivered to the customer

Balance of payments: A record of international trade and the flow of financial transactions made between a country's residents and the rest of the world

Balance sheet: A financial report that shows what the company owes, and what it owns, including the shareholders' stake, at a particular point in time

Barriers to communication: Obstacles that interrupt the flow of conveying and receiving messages

Baseline rewards: First level employee rewards such as salary, contract, and benefits

Beauty bias: The tendency to treat attractive people more favorably because they are perceived to be more successful, competent, and qualified

Behavior-focused strategies: Strategies that involve analyzing our own behaviors to identify those that need to be adjusted, enhanced or eliminated altogether

Behavioral segmentation: Divides markets based on customer behaviors and decision-making patterns

Benefit corporation (B-corp): A form of organization certified by the nonprofit B

Lab, which ensures that strict standards of social and environmental performance, accountability, and transparency are met

Benefit corporation, or B Corp: A form of organization certified by the nonprofit B Lab for for-profit companies that ensures that strict standards of social and environmental performance, accountability, and transparency are met

Benefit corporation: (Sometimes known as a "B-corp") A form of organization certified by the nonprofit B Lab, which ensures that strict standards of social and environmental performance, accountability, and transparency are met

Big data: Large volumes of structured and unstructured data that flow into an organization on a daily basis

Birth stage: (Nonbureaucratic) The stage in the organizational life cycle when the organization is first created

Board of directors: A group of people elected by company shareholders to monitor the actions of the organization

Bonus pay: A type of payment plan that rewards employees for good performance in addition to their base salary

Broadcast advertising: A form of advertising that includes television and radio

Budgeting: The part of the financial plan that outlines what the company will likely earn and spend for an upcoming period of time

Bureaucracy: A system characterized by formalized rules and regulations, specialized routine tasks, division of labor, and centralized authority

Business analytics: The process of collecting, processing, and exploring business data based on statistical analysis and past history to generate actionable insights

Business credit cards: Credit cards issued in the name of a business that are intended for business use rather than personal use, and acts as a less formal and often more expensive line of credit

Business ethics: Behaviors based on accepted standards in the business context and often relate to such issues as corporate governance, bribery, discrimination, and improper use or reporting of financial resources

Business intelligence: A technology-driven process for identifying actionable raw data that support decision making

Business law: A collection of legal requirements that involves protecting rights,

maintaining orders, resolving disputes, and establishing a set of generally accepted standards

Business law: A collection of legal requirements that involves protecting rights, maintaining orders, resolving disputes, and establishing a set of generally accepted standards

Business Model Canvas (BMC): A one-page plan that divides the business model's four parts into nine components to further understand how to create, capture, and deliver value

Business model: the rationale of how a new business venture creates, delivers, and captures value

Business plan: A lengthy written document that articulates the entrepreneur's vision for the future by outlining the core business objectives and how they are to be achieved over a certain period of time

Business plan: A written document that describes the actions and goals needed to support organizational strategy

Business strategy: A plan of action that helps companies develop a path to compete in an industry

Business term loan: A traditional bank loan where you can obtain funds to support your business needs if you fulfill the strict criteria

Business: An organization that is engaged in commercial, industrial, or professional activities that produce and/or sell goods or services for the creation of economic and social value

Buyer persona: A fictional representation of the idea customer

Buyer's dissonance: A condition of remorse or regret shortly after buying a product

Buying process: The sequential steps a customer follows to find the right product or service

Business loan payments: A type of loan where the principal plus interest accrued is spread equally over an equal number of payments

C corporation (C-corp): A separate legal and taxable entity created by the state government and owned by an unlimited number of shareholders.

C corporation: (Sometimes known as a "C-corp") A separate legal and taxable entity created by the state government and owned by an unlimited number of shareholders.

Capability: A bundle of resources combined that when used can lead to competitive advantage

Capital stock: The original amount the owners paid into the company plus any additional paid-in capital to purchase stock in the company

Capital: The amount of money a business has to pay for its ongoing operations

Cash basis accounting: An accounting method that records income when it is received and expenses as they are paid

Cash flow loan: A type of loan used by small businesses to cover day-to-day operations

Cash flow statement: A financial report that details the inflows and outflows of cash for a company over a set period of time

Cash conversion cycle (CCC): The number of days it takes to convert a transaction from sale to cash in the bank

Centralization: An organizational structure that gives top-level managers the authority to make decisions on behalf of the entire company

Certificate authority: An organization that validates identities and lets users know who they are communicating with online

Chain of command: A flow of authority and power from the highest to the lowest levels of the organization

Chief executive officer (CEO): The highest-ranking person of a company who is responsible for making major decisions, creating a corporate vision, and communicating with the board of directors about company strategy

Chief financial officer (CFO): An executive officer who is responsible for the financial operations of a company and for cash flow, financial risk, and financial strategy

Chief information officer (CIO): An executive officer who oversees the planning, development, and implementation of technology inside the organization

Chief marketing officer (CMO): An executive officer who is responsible for marketing strategies in relation to the company's products and offerings that are designed to deliver value for target customers, clients, or other businesses

Chief technology officer (CTO): An executive officer who is responsible for technology creation and design, anticipating customer needs, and focusing on emerging technologies

Circular structure: An organizational structure that depicts higher-level employees at the center of the circle and lower-level employees on the outer rings, designed to encourage a free flow of information between all parts of the organization by illustrating that all divisions are part of the same whole

Clan culture: A family-like or tribe-like type of corporate environment that emphasizes consensus, teamwork, collaboration, participation, and the commonality of goals and values

Classification: A data mining function that identifies items in a data set and assigns them to specific categories

Clearance sales: A type of sales promotion where goods are sold at a discount to get rid of surplus stock

Cloud computing: A segment of IT services that uses remote services hosted on the internet to store and manage data rather than using local services or personal devices

Clustering: A data mining function that searches for similarities in groups (called "clusters") that are not predefined to determine patterns based on the characteristics found in the data

Commercial mortgage: A mortgage that is similar to a home mortgage but used for businesses that are looking to expand into a different location

Commercial: The selling of goods or services

Communal culture: A type of organizational culture where employees tend to think alike, are happy to share knowledge, and have a clear focus on the direction of the task

Communication skills: The ability to give and receive information

Communication: The act of transmitting information, thoughts, and processes through various channels

Comparative advantage: The ability of a nation to produce a product at a lower opportunity cost compared to another nation

Competing values framework (CVF): A means to identify, measure, and change culture

Competitive advantage: A position of superiority or top performance created by showcasing characteristics that are not easily copied or bought elsewhere

Competitive advantage: Refers to those factors that lead to a business outperforming its rivals/competitors

Competitive environment: The need to understand how businesses compete in an industry and the different ways in which they compete; something that is called strategy

Competitive parity: Describes the average capabilities of a company in a particular area as compared to other companies in the same industry

Competitive pricing: A pricing strategy that involves setting prices based on what the competition is charging

Competitive profile matrix (CPM): A tool that allows you to compare your business to competitors so that your strengths and weaknesses (and theirs) are revealed

Complexity: Means there are a lot of moving parts involved

Conceptual or abstract skills: The ability of a manager to visualize the entire organization and think through complex systems and problems

Confirmation bias: The tendency to seek out information to support our views while dispensing information that does not

Constructive thought pattern strategies: Strategies that focus on the modification of certain key mental processes

Consumer behavior: The actions and decision-making processes people go through when purchasing or investing in a product or service

Consumers: People who use the product or service

Content marketing: The process of planning, creating, distributing, sharing, and publishing content to engage, attract, and retain a target audience

Continuous improvement: The ongoing improvement of the design, production, and delivery of a company's products and services

Continuous production: A type of production method where products made from basic materials are continuously processed, 24/7, all year round

Controller: A company executive who is responsible for the organization's compliance and reporting of accounting tasks and activities and usually reports to the CFO

Controlling access: A feature that denies people access to certain parts of an

accounting system unless they have the right password

Controlling: The process of monitoring activities such as company and regulatory policies, measuring results, comparing them with goals, and correcting performance when necessary

Copyright: A form of protection provided to the creators of original works in the areas of literature, music, drama, choreography, art, motion pictures, sound recordings, and architecture

Copyright: A form of protection provided to the creators of original works in the areas of literature, music, drama, choreography, art, motion pictures, sound recordings, and architecture

Corporate entrepreneurship (also known as intrapreneurship): A process of creating new products, ventures, processes, or renewal within large corporations

Corporate social responsibility (CSR): The way in which companies conduct business that is sensitive to social, cultural, economic, and environmental issues

Corporation: A business entity owned by its shareholders

Corporation: A business entity owned by its shareholders

Corrective internal control: A type of internal control that is put in place to correct the errors identified by the detective internal controls to prevent them from occurring

Cost focus strategy: A strategy used by organizations to gain competitive advantage by keeping costs and prices lower than their rivals and charging a low price while targeting a narrow market where products meet a very specific need; often referred to as a "niche" market

Cost leadership strategy: A strategy used by organizations to seek competitive advantage and gain market share by producing a product or service at the lowest possible cost, resulting in offering low-priced products

Cost structure: Represents all the expenses required to run the company and how those costs impact pricing

Cost-plus pricing: A pricing strategy that involves determining the costs of making your product and adding a markup to determine a selling price

Critical success factors: Internal and external factors required by businesses to perform at the highest levels in an industry

Critical thinking: The use of intelligence, knowledge, and skills to question and carefully explore situations and arrive at thoughtful conclusions based on evidence and reason

Cross-cultural communication: A field of study that explores how people from different cultures communicate

Cross-selling: The practice of selling an extra product in conjunction with a primary product. One of the most common cross-selling promotions is "buy 2, get 1 free"

Cultural awareness: The understanding that our own culture (customs, social behaviors, attitudes, and values) differs from others

Cultural competence: The set of values, behaviors, attitudes, and practices that enables individuals and organizations to interact effectively with people across different cultures

Culture: The values and beliefs that create an environment that is unique to that business

Current assets: Cash and other assets such as inventory, accounts receivable, and prepaid expenses that can be converted into cash within a year

Current liabilities: Bills that must be paid within 1 year of the date of the balance sheet. They are organized based on who is owed the money

Current ratio: A financial ratio that assesses whether the company has enough current assets to pay its short-term liabilities

Customer onboarding: The process of welcoming new customers to your business by guiding them through their purchases and addressing any queries or concerns

Customer segments: Involve identifying the company's target customers

Customer value proposition (CVP): Explains how your products and services can help customers do something more inexpensively, easily, effectively, or quickly than before

Customer-centric selling: A sales technique that uses empathy through every stage of the sales process

Customer: Someone who pays for a product or service

Customers: The people who buy and use our products and services

Customers: The people who populate the segments of a market that your offering is serving

Daily deal: (Also known as a flash sale) A type of sales promotion strategy that offers products at a discount from anywhere between 24 and 72 hours

Data aggregation: The process of collecting data before analysis and cleaning the data to avoid duplication of data or inaccurate, incomplete, and unusable data

Data communication networks: Refers to the transmission of digital data from one computer to another using a variety of wired and wireless communication channels

Data licensing/selling model: A model that generates revenue by selling or licensing high-quality, exclusive, valuable information to other parties

Data mining: The process of analyzing large amounts of data to generate information that can be used by an organization to predict future behavior

Data visualization: The graphic representation of data to generate new information and insights

Data warehouse: A centralized database where data are collected and organized to provide meaningful analysis

Data: A set of facts and statistics used by businesses to analyze or calculate something

Databases: Organized collections of data that can be accessed by various people in an organization

Days of inventory (DOI): Number of days that it takes to collect on accounts receivable

Days payable outstanding (DPO): Number of days it takes you to pay your bills **Days sales outstanding (DSO):** A measure of the number of days that it takes to collect on accounts receivable

Debt financing: Financing method where funds are borrowed and paid back with interest to the lender

Debt-to-equity ratio: The degree of debt owed by the company, and the amount of equity financed by people outside the company

Decentralization: An organizational structure where middle managers and lower-level employees are permitted to make decisions and suggestions, rather than just the top-level management

Decision makers: Customers similar to economic buyers who have even more authority to make purchasing decisions, as they are positioned higher up in the hierarchy

Decision support system (DSS): A computer-based information system that helps organizations with their decision-making processes

Decision-making skills: The ability to choose between possible solutions to a problem to select the best outcome

Decisional roles: Managers are responsible for making judgments and decisions based on available information and analysis of the situation

Deep-level diversity: Verbal and nonverbal behaviors that lie beneath the surface

Defensive listening: A type of listening that occurs when the receiver of the message takes general statements as a personal attack

Delegation: The process of transferring authority and responsibility to others to carry out certain tasks and activities

Deliberate practice: Defined as carrying out carefully focused efforts to improve performance

Demand: The prospective customers' desire for the goods and services available

Demographic segmentation: Divides a market by demographic factors such as age, education, income, gender, occupation, ethnicity, family size, and nationality

Departmentalization: A process of grouping activities into different types of departments within the overall organizational structure

Depreciation: The decrease of the value of physical assets over time

Descriptive analytics: The interpretation of historical data to summarize what has happened in the past or is happening currently

Design pathway: A pathway that is used to help uncover high-value opportunities by focusing on unmet needs of customers—specifically, latent needs

Design thinking: A nonlinear problem solving method that requires talking with and observing customers to identify needs, quickly developing prototypes to test new ideas, and get ongoing feedback from those you are designing for to ensure you are meeting the needs identified

Detective internal control: A type of internal control designed to highlight discrepancies and identify problems after they have occurred

Diagnostic analytics: Focuses on past performance to figure out how and why it happened

Differentiation focus strategy: A strategy used by organizations to achieve competitive advantage by providing better-value products or services to a narrow or niche target market

Differentiation strategy: A strategy used by organizations to seek competitive advantage by providing goods and services that are significantly different from the competition

Digital operations: The concept of digitizing and integrating business processes across the organization to improve customer and employee experience

Digital transformation: The process of integrating digital technology into all areas of a business to improve operational efficiency and deliver value

Direct distribution channels: The distribution of the product directly from the manufacturer to the consumer

Directional plan: A general, flexible plan that provides guidelines for an organization's long-term goals

Directive leadership: A style of leadership in which leaders provide specific, task-focused directions, giving commands, assigning goals, implementing guidelines, closely supervising employees, and ensuring individuals follow rules

Disabilities: Physical or mental impairments that substantially limit one or more of an individual's major life activities

Dispatching: The third step of the production control process, in which the operations manager instructs each department on the type of work that needs to be done and the amount of time allowed for its completion

Disruptive business model: A model that creates new markets by addressing unmet needs by improving or changing an existing business model

Disruptive innovation: An innovation that either disrupts the existing market by displacing established companies or creates an entirely new market segment

Distributor: A type of business model where the company buys products from manufacturers and resells them to retailers or the public

Diversity: The presence of differences within a given setting

Dividend decisions: The portion of a company's earnings that will be distributed as a dividend to shareholders

Division of labor: The level to which jobs are divided into specific tasks

Divisional structure: An organizational structure that groups employees by products and services, by geographic regions, or by customers

Double entry accounting: A system of bookkeeping where every entry to an account requires a corresponding entry to a different account

Downward communication: Sends messages from the upper levels of the organizational hierarchy to the lower levels

Dual-purpose: Companies that build economic and social value into their core mission

Due diligence: A rigorous process that involves evaluating an investment opportunity prior to actually making the investment

Early-stage financing: A type of financing that consists of larger amounts of funds provided for companies that have a team in place and a product or service tested or piloted, but as yet show little or no revenue

Economic buyers: The customers who have the ability to approve large-scale purchases

Economic value: The profitability of the business and its ability to generate revenue, pay expenses, and generate positive net income

Effectuation pathway: A pathway that is used to apply to what you have (skills, knowledge, abilities) to uncover an opportunity that uniquely fits with the entrepreneur

Effectuation: The idea that the future is unpredictable yet controllable

Effectuation: The idea that the future is unpredictable yet controllable

Electronic communication: The exchange of information through email, videoconferencing, blogs, fax, instant messaging, texting, and social networking

Embargo: A trade restriction imposed by the government of the exchange of goods or services with a particular country or countries

Emotional value: The value derived from how a product makes the customer feel

Employee development programs: Programs that offer personal and professional growth for employees

Employee development: The process of helping employees learn the skills necessary to carry out future roles

Employee experience: The journey workers take through each stage of a particular company and the perceptions they have about their experiences at work **Employee stock ownership plans (ESOPs):** A type of payment plan that allows employees to purchase company stock, often at below-market price, as one of their benefits

Empowering leadership: A style of leadership in which leaders encourage followers to take ownership of their own behaviors and work processes and provide them with the support and resources to achieve their goals

Encryption: The process of encoding information to hide its true meaning

End users: The customers who will actually use your product

Enterprise resource planning (ERP): A system that provides a flow of information to include accounting, manufacturing, customer relationship management, sales, and service

Entrepreneurial mindset: The ability to quickly sense, take action, and get organized under uncertain conditions in order to find or create opportunities

Entrepreneurial: A way of thinking and acting that combines the ability to find or create new opportunities with the courage to act on them

Entrepreneurs inside: Employees who think and act entrepreneurially within different types of organizations

Equipment lease: A type of financing whereby businesses lease equipment with payments spread over a set amount of time

Equity financing: The method of acquiring capital through the sale of shares of stock in exchange for cash

Equity theory: A theory that holds that motivation is based on our perception of how fairly we are being treated in comparison with others

Equity: Ensures that processes and programs are impartial, fair, and provide equal access to new opportunities in order to enhance the success of all employees

ERG theory of motivation: A theory that sets out three categories of human needs related to human behaviors: existence needs, relatedness needs, and growth needs

Ethical culture: A type of organizational culture where senior people lead by example by behaving in an ethical manner and ensuring, through clear communication and training workshops, that their employees do the same

Ethical dilemma: A situation in which a difficult choice has to be made between two courses of action, either of which entails transgressing a moral principle

Ethics: The moral principles that guide our behavior, and those behaviors are based on accepted standards of what actions are right and wrong

Ethnocentrism: The tendency to believe your culture or ethnicity is superior to those of everyone else

Euphemisms: Mild words or expressions used in place for those considered to be too blunt or harsh

Evaluation: The stage in the buying process where customers consider and compare alternative possibilities to ensure they are making the right decision

Exclusive distribution: A distribution strategy under which a company sells its products through just one outlet

Executive information system (EIS): An information support system that supports senior management needs by providing access to strategic information relevant to organizational goals

Expectancy theory: A theory that holds that individuals are more likely to be motivated and perform well if they expect to receive desired rewards

Expectancy: The probability that the amount of work effort invested by an individual will result in a high level of performance

Expert system: An information support system that uses artificial intelligence to mimic the thinking of human experts to solve complex problems

Exporting: The sale of domestic products to foreign customers

External motivational forces: Factors outside our control that can be negatively and positively impacted by external events

External strategic analysis: An objective evaluation of the world in which a business operates

Extranet: An intranet that securely shares information with certain outside parties, such as suppliers, partners, vendors, or a certain set of customers

Extrinsic motivation: Behavior that is driven by external rewards such as money, fame, grades, paid vacation, benefits, and praise

Family enterprise: A business that is owned and managed by multiple family members, typically for more than one generation

Fear of failure: The disposition to avoid failure and/or the capacity for experiencing shame or humiliation as a result of failure

Financial accounting: The process of recording the financial transactions and developing financial statements used for financial analysis and external reporting

Financial forecasting: An estimate of future revenue and expenses for an extended period of time, typically 3 to 5 years

Financial management: The organizing, planning, controlling, and leading the financial activities of a business to ensure the effective acquisition and utilization of financial resources for efficient operations and future growth

Financial managers: Maintain the financial health of an organization by providing financial guidance and support

Financial planning: The process of forecasting future financial results and making decisions about how best to use the company's financial resources to achieve its short- and long-term goals

Financial statements: Reports generated from accounting data

Financial viability: The revenue and cost structures a business needs to meet its operating expenses and financial obligations

Financing decisions: Identifying sources of capital, allocating the funds to support investment decisions, determining the duration of the investment, and assessing the amount of return

Financing: The activity of acquiring the money you need to start, operate, or expand a business

Find pathway: A pathway that focuses first on identifying a problem and developing a business to solve that problem

Firewall: A type of software that blocks unauthorized access to the network

First-line managers: People who direct daily activities for producing goods and services

First-line managers: People who direct the day-to-day operations and activities

Five forces model: An external strategic analysis tool to help companies analyze the potential attractiveness of an industry and establish whether it is worth entering or remaining in

Fixed costs: Set expenses that are not linked to sales and production

Fixed mindset: The belief that people perceive their talents and abilities as set traits

Follow-up stage: The stage where managers and employees or team members exchange feedback, trouble-shoot problems, and discuss potential solutions

Forecasting: The process of using historical data to predict future events and outcomes

Formal networks: Transmit the messages established and approved by executive management

Formalization: The process of determining an organization's policies, procedures, and rules, usually in writing

Fragmented culture: A type of organizational culture where employees tend to keep to themselves, avoid socializing, and work as individuals rather than as part of a team

Franchise: A type of license purchased by an individual (franchisee) from an existing business (franchisor) that allows the franchisee to trade under the name of that business

Franchising business model: A type of business model based on the franchisor helping the franchisee by providing support in marketing, operations, and financing

Free samples: A sales promotion strategy where small portions of new products are introduced to customers for free

Freemium business model: A type of business model that involves mixing free (mainly web-based) basic services with premium or upgraded services

Freshwatching: An approach that involves focusing on other companies, often from outside your own business or industry, to ignite new ideas

Functional structure: An organizational structure that groups employees according to the tasks they perform for the organization, such as marketing, finance, and human resources

Functional value: The value derived from the problem it solves

Gain sharing: A system whereby managers agree to share the benefits of cost savings with staff in return for their contribution to the company's performance

Gender bias: The tendency to prefer one gender over another gender

Gender diversity: The equal representation of both men and women in the workplace

General partnership: A business owned by two or more people who have made a decision to comanage and share in the profits and losses

General partnership: A business owned by two or more people who have made a decision to comanage and share in the profits and losses

Geographic segmentation: Divides the market based on geographical location, climate, or population density

Gig economy: A labor market characterized by picking up short-term, flexible, freelance work known as gigs

Global dexterity: The ability to adapt your behavior to be effective when interacting with other cultures without losing your sense of self in the process

Global trade: The exchange of goods and services between countries has led to an exponential rise in the value of goods exported throughout the world

Goal-setting theory: A theory suggesting that human performance is directed by conscious goals and intentions

Goodwill: The price paid for an asset in excess of its book value

Gossip chains: Where employees spread information about other employees that may be true, false, or misleading—but should not likely be shared

Grapevine: The unofficial line of communication between individuals or groups

Grit: The quality that enables people to work hard and sustain interest in their long-term goals

Gross margin percentage: The gross margin divided by sales, which gives you the percentage of sales remaining after deducting COGS

Growth company: A business that increases its annual revenue faster than its competitors in the same industry or market

Growth mindset: The belief that abilities can be developed through dedication, effort, and hard work

Guerilla advertising: A form of advertising that focuses on personally interacting with a target group by promoting products and services through surprise or other unconventional means

Habit: A sometimes unconscious pattern of behavior that is carried out often and regularly

Height bias: The tendency to judge a person who is significantly shorter or taller than the "normal range"

Hierarchy culture: A type of organizational culture based on clearly defined corporate levels and structures where employees are primarily guided by processes, rules, and procedures

Hierarchy of needs theory: A theory that proposes that people are motivated by five levels of individual needs: physiological, safety, love/belonging, esteem, and self-actualization needs at the top

High-context cultures: Communication is more subtle and nuanced, with most messages conveyed through body language and nonverbal cues

Holacracy: A company structure that distributes decision-making authority to self-managed, "boss-less" teams or "circles"

Horizontal organizational structure: (Also known as flat structures) A company structure that focuses on teamwork and collaboration to work on shared tasks to achieve collective goals

Human resource management: The practice of recruiting, hiring, deploying, and managing an organization's employees

Human resources managers: Oversee the human resources department and ensure HR teams carry out their functions and tasks

Hygiene factors: Sources of job satisfaction such as salary, status, and security

Hypercompetition: Characterized by intense competitive action and rapid innovation in an industry forcing competitors to respond quickly

Hypertext: A feature of computer programming that contains links to information

Idea classification matrix: A framework that helps entrepreneurs to identify and rate the ideas that can be converted to innovations or significant improvements as sources of new business opportunities

"If, then" rewards: Second level employee rewards received by employees when they reach a certain target

Implicit bias: A set of positive or negative stereotypes that someone may unconsciously hold toward a person or group

Import quota: A type of trade restriction that sets a limit on the quantity of particular goods being imported into a country during a given period of time

Importing: The buying of products overseas and reselling them in one's own country

In-app advertising: A form of advertising where companies place ads or run campaigns inside mobile apps to attract new app users and maximize revenue

Inbound selling: A sales technique that prioritizes the needs, challenges, goals, and interests of individual buyers to help guide them through the decision-making process

Inclusion: The practice of ensuring that people feel a sense of belonging in the workplace and are welcomed

Income statement (or profit and loss statement): A financial report that measures the financial performance of your business on a monthly or annual basis

Indirect distribution channels: The distribution of products through the use of an intermediary, such as a wholesaler, before they are sold through a retailer

Industrial activities: The manufacturing of goods

Industry: A grouping of similar companies based on their primary business activities

Influencers (or opinion leaders): Customers with a large following who have the power to influence our purchase decisions

Infographics: Visual images of information and data designed to present an easy-to-understand overview of a particular topic

Informal networks: Handle the unofficial sharing of information between employees and across company divisions

Information search: Collecting information on the products or services identified in the need recognition stage

Information system: The combination of technologies designed to collect, process, store, and distribute information for decision making and controlling company-wide activities

Information: Data that have been transformed into a type of useful form to support planning

Informational roles: Require managers to gather, assess, and communicate information to individuals and teams in support of the organization's values, mission, vision, and goals

Infrastructure as a service (IaaS): The largest segment of cloud computing where customers pay for access to software applications and databases provided by third parties

Infrastructure: The key resources (people, technology, products, suppliers, partners, facilities) that an entrepreneur must have to drive the value proposition

Instrumentality: The probability that good performance will lead to various work outcomes

Intangible assets: The value of patents, software programs, copyrights, trademarks, franchises, brand names, or assets that cannot be physically touched

Intellectual property (IP): Intangible personal property created by human intelligence, such as ideas, inventions, slogans, logos, and processes

Intellectual property (IP): Intangible personal property created by human intelligence, such as ideas, inventions, slogans, logos, and processes

Intellectual property: A category of property created by human intelligence that includes ideas, inventions, slogans, logos, designs, and symbols

Intensive distribution: A distribution strategy under which a company sells through as many locations or outlets as possible

Interest expense: The cost related to borrowing money, as in interest on a bank loan

Internal financial controls: The procedures, policies, and processes by which an organization manages its financial resources

Internal fraud: The misuse or misapplication of business resources, especially financial resources and assets, by company employees or managers

Internal motivation forces: Feelings, values, and desires that drive individuals toward the attainment of their professional and personal goals

Internal strategic analysis: An objective evaluation of an organization's internal environment to identify its strengths and weaknesses

Internet service providers: Link to the internet infrastructure to connect users to the internet through paid subscriptions, enabling them to communicate with others through text, email, video calling, and so on

Internet: A global network consisting of smaller, interconnected networks linking millions of computers together

Interpersonal roles: Require managers to build relationships with the people they work with and act as a public symbol for the many people they represent**Intranet:** A computer network for sharing information that is only available to employees working within an organization

Intrinsic motivation: The performance of tasks for our own, innate satisfaction rather than for some type of reward

Investment decisions: The decisions managers make to select the amount of investment available within different investment opportunities

Investors: People who spend their money on financial schemes with the expectation of receiving a profit

Job analysis: The process of gathering and analyzing information about the content and the human requirements of jobs, as well as the context in which jobs are performed

Job content–based pay: A type of pay that is based on an evaluation of a job's worth to the organization and its relationship to other jobs within the organization

Job description: The duties and responsibilities of a position

Job enrichment: The process of building motivators into a job to make it more interesting and challenging

Job specification: The qualifications—skills, knowledge, and abilities—needed to perform the job

Joint promotions: A promotional strategy whereby two companies join together to promote their products and services

Key metrics: Data that show how the company measures success by tracking its overall performance

Key partners: A company's partners such as suppliers, distributors, and other business associates

Key resources: The physical, intellectual, human, and financial assets at a company

Large businesses: Organizations with more than 500 employees

Latent needs: Needs we have that have yet to surface

Lateral communication: Sends messages between and among similar levels across organizations

Leadership: The process of influence aimed at directing behavior toward the accomplishment of objectives

Leading: The process of motivating and communicating with people to achieve goals

Lean manufacturing: The implementation of best practices to eliminate inefficiencies and waste while increasing profit

Liabilities: Economic obligations of the company, such as money it owes to lenders, suppliers, and employees

Licensing business model: A way of earning revenue by giving permission to other parties to use protected intellectual property (copyrights, patents, and trademarks) in exchange for fees

Limited liability company (LLC): A business structure that combines the taxation advantages of a partnership with the limited liability benefits of a corporation without being subject to the eligibility requirements of an S-corp

Limited liability company (LLC): A business structure that combines the taxation advantages of a partnership with the limited liability benefits of a corporation without being subject to the eligibility requirements of an S-corp

Limited-time offer: A type of sales promotion strategy that involves providing products or services at a discount, deal, or for free over a limited period

Line of credit: A type of loan that allows you to borrow a certain amount of money and only pay interest on the amount you have used, as long as you stay within your credit limit

Listening: The active effort to understand, learn, and derive information from others

Logistics: The process of planning and organizing the movement of goods from their point of origin to their final destination

Long-term debt: An obligation for debt that is due to be repaid in more than 12 months. Bank loans, finance, and leasing obligations are all examples of long-term debt

Long-term investments: Assets that are more than 1 year old and are carried on the balance sheet at cost or book value with no appreciation

Low-context cultures: Communication is explicit, clear, precise, and conveyed through the spoken or written word

Machine learning: A branch of AI; it is the science of getting computers to act without being explicitly programmed

Make to order: A type of production method where the product is made only after an order has been placed

Malware: Any file or program used to wreak havoc on computer systems; malicious software

Management information system (MIS): Aids organizations in running more efficiently by incorporating people, technology, and information systematically

Management: The process of working with people and organizational resources to achieve goals efficiently and effectively

Manager: A person responsible for supervising employees and directing resources in order to achieve goals

Managerial accounting: A branch of accounting that relates to the identification, measurement, analysis, and interpretation of accounting information so that it can be used to help managers make informed operational decisions

Managerial roles: Organizational expectations that determine the actions of managers

Market culture: A type of organizational culture that emphasizes competitiveness not only between the organization and its market competitors but also between employees

Market segmentation: The process of dividing a target market into approachable groups based on wants, needs, common interests, common behaviors, and demands

Market: A place where people can sell goods and services (the supply) to people who wish to buy those goods and services (the demand)

Marketing managers: Responsible for helping the organization promote and sell its products and services to customers

Marketing mix: A framework that helps define the brand and differentiate it from the competition

Marketing: The process of attracting people to the goods and services on sale

Mass customization: A type of production method where high quantities of customized products are made at a low cost

Mass production: A type of production method in which large quantities of standardized products are made at a low cost,

using assembly lines or other automated technology

Matrix organizational structure: A company structure that combines functional and divisional reporting lines to create a grid, or matrix

Maturity stage: The stage in the organizational life cycle where the organization becomes very bureaucratic and mechanistic

Mechanistic model: A formalized structure based on high centralization and departmentalization

Mercenary culture: A type of organizational culture where making money is the top priority

Merit pay: Links pay increases directly to performance

Microloans: Short-term loans with a relatively low interest rate

Micromarkets: The markets within the larger market

Mid-size businesses: Organizations with between 100 and 500 employees

Middle managers: Report to upper management and direct the work of first-line managers; they are also responsible for divisions or departments

Middle managers: People who report to upper management and direct the work of first-line managers; they are also responsible for divisions or departments

Midlife stage: The stage in the organizational life cycle where the organization is growing in the marketplace, and becoming larger in size

Mindset: A set of beliefs and attitudes that help people make sense of the world around them

Mission statement: A short statement defining what an organization is, why it exists, and its reason for being

Mission-driven content marketing: A type of marketing that incorporates the company's core values that aligns with its audience's interests

Motivation: The forces from within individuals that stimulate and drive them to achieve goals

Motivator factors: Sources of job satisfaction, such as recognition, achievement, status, responsibility, and opportunity for advancement

Multinational corporation (MNC): A company that operates in its own country as well as

other different countries around the world is known as a multinational coporation

Multinational corporation: A business with operations in multiple countries that sells products and services to customers all over the world

Mystery offers: Special offers that evoke curiosity by including a surprise

Myths: Narratives based on true events that are repeated to emphasize an important component of an organization's culture

N.E.A.T. selling: A sales technique based on a particular framework

Name bias: The tendency to prefer certain types of names over others

Natural reward strategies: Rewards that help us to find pleasure in certain aspects of our roles, leading to an enhanced sense of competence, self-discipline, and application

Need for achievement: The desire to excel

Need for affiliation: The desire to belong to a group and to be liked

Need for competence: The motivation we derive from stretching and exercising our capabilities

Need for power: The desire to control and influence behavior of others

Need for self-determination: The feeling of motivation we get from being in control of our own growth and development rather than being dependent on external influences

Need recognition: (Also called problem recognition) Occurs when a customer identifies an unmet need and recognizes the need for a product or a service

Net income: Indicates what is left after all costs, expenses, and taxes have been paid

Net Operating Margin Percentage: A profitability ratio that indicates the amount of net income or profit generated as a percentage of revenue

Network structure: An organizational structure on which organizations work together to provide goods and services

Networked culture: An organizational culture characterized by a high degree of trust between employees and a willingness to communicate and share information

Nondisclosure agreement (NDA): A legal contract that outlines confidential information shared by two or more parties

Nondisclosure agreement (NDA): A legal contract that outlines confidential information shared by two or more parties

Nonprofit organization: A business that is exempt from paying tax, with the expectation that any generated profit will be reinvested in the business and never paid to owners

Nontraditional candidates: People without degrees, people from different educational backgrounds, people with no employment experience, and people with criminal records

Nonverbal bias: An unconscious bias whereby nonverbal communication attributes such as body language negatively influence our perception of others

Nonverbal communication: The transmission of wordless behaviors and actions between people

Not-for-profit: A tax status granted to companies performing functions deemed by Congress to be socially desirable that exempts them from income tax and, in some cases, allows them to receive tax-deductible donations

Not-for-profit: A tax status granted to companies performing functions deemed by Congress to be socially desirable that exempts them from income tax and, in some cases, allows them to receive tax-deductible donations

NPS (Net Promoter Score) survey: A benchmark that measures customer loyalty and satisfaction by assessing how likely customers are to recommend your business to a friend

Offensive listening: A type of listening when the receiver tries to find fault in what is being said

Offering: Addresses products and services, business models, and how they connect products and services to customers via marketing and sales

Offering: What you are offering to a particular customer segment, the value generated for those customers, and how you will reach and communicate with them

Onboarding: The process of equipping workers with the skills, knowledge, and behaviors to transition into an organization

Online advertising: Involves advertising through the internet

Operating expenses: The expenditures that the company makes to generate income

Operating leverage: A key financial ratio that is used to measure the percentage of fixed costs relative to variable costs

Operating profit: The amount left over from revenue once all costs and expenses are subtracted

Operational plan: Focuses on particular procedures and processes required to keep the organization running smoothly

Operations managers: Oversee day-to-day operations and ensure processes and procedures are being applied by employees

Operations managers: Manager responsible for monitoring the company's production processes to reduce the costs of materials, labor, and technology, in addition to eliminating costs that may add little to no value to the completed product

Operations support systems: A set of programs that monitor, control, analyze, and manage an information network

Operations: The processes used to get the daily work done, and the data collected from this work and your customers to better inform decision making

Operations: Refers to the wide range of activities that businesses engage in to keep a company running and earn a profit

Opportunity: A way of generating value through unique, novel, or desirable products, services, and even processes that have not been previously exploited in a particular context

Optimization: The process of identifying best-case scenarios and actions to make the business more efficient and cost-effective

Organic model: A less formalized structure based on decentralization and cross-functional teams

Organization: A group of people formed and structured in a certain way to achieve goals

Organizational chart: A graphic representation of the structure that communicates how a company is organized

Organizational culture: A pattern of shared norms, rules, values, and beliefs that guides the attitudes and behaviors of its employees

Organizational empowerment: The situation where organizational encourage individuals, teams, or departmentsto participate in independent decision-making and sharing responsibilities at work

Organizational structure: Determines the flow of work and outlines how tasks are directed to achieve organizational goals

Organizational structure: A system that coordinates the people, tasks, and activities necessary to carry out a particular purpose

Organizing: The process of orchestrating people, structure, actions, resources, and decisions to achieve goals

Other current liabilities: Short-term liabilities that do not fall into a specific category; these will include sales tax, income tax, and so forth

Outbound sales: A traditional sales approach that involves pushing your sales message onto large groups of people who may or may not be interested in your product

Outdoor advertising: Also known as out-of-home (OOH), a type of advertising that targets customers when they are away from home

Patent: A grant of exclusive property rights on inventions through the U.S. and other governments

Patent: A grant of exclusive property rights on inventions through the U.S. and other governments

Penetration: A pricing strategy that initially uses low prices to attract customers to a new product or service in an effort to tempt customers away from the competition

People: The employees who work in and on a business

Performance appraisal: An assessment of an employee's performance; also provides the employee with feedback necessary to improve performance

Performance review: The final stage of a traditional performance management process where goal achievements, area of improvements, performance issues, and opportunities for career progression are identified

Performance-based pay: A financial incentive awarded to employees for meeting specific goals or objectives

Person-organization fit (P-O fit): The compatibility between employees and organizations

PESTLE analysis: An external strategic analysis tool for assessing the environment based on six factors external to the business: political, economic, social, technological, legal, and environmental

Phishing: A cybercrime in which fraudulent emails designed to resemble legitimate institutions are sent to users to extract sensitive information

Piece rate: A pay plan in which workers are paid a fixed sum for each unit of production completed

Piracy: The illegal copying or distribution of copyrighted content such as music or software

Place: Where the product is actually distributed to a target market

Planning: A type of management function that involves setting goals for the future, designing appropriate strategies, and choosing the right resources to achieve organizational goals and objectives

Platform as a service (PaaS): A model that provides customers with access to hardware and software tools for application development

Podcast: A digital audio file that can be downloaded from the internet

Positive organizational culture: A type of organizational culture where employees are active in decision making, encouraged to collaborate, rewarded for achieving goals, and kept informed of the organization's vision and direction

Post-purchase evaluation: The final stage of the buying process where the customer considers the value and usefulness of the purchase and how satisfied they are with the product or service

Practices: Activities within an organization that occur frequently and give an indication of the type of organizational culture in an organization

Predictive analytics: Focuses on making predictions about the future using statistical techniques such as data mining, predictive modeling, and machine learning

Prepaid expenses: Payments the company has already made for services not yet received

Prescriptive analytics: Provides recommendations for best actions to drive desired outcomes to satisfy business objectives

Pretending listening: A type of listening when the receiver is pretending to listen out of politeness rather than making an effort to understand the sender

Preventative internal control: A type of internal control created to prevent errors or fraud from occurring in the first place

Price skimming: A pricing strategy that involves setting a product at a high price when it enters the market before gradually lowering it as the market evolves

Price: The amount that the customer is expected to pay for the product, its perceived value, and the degree to which the price can be raised or lowered depending on market demand and how competitors price rival products

Print advertising: A type of advertising that is printed in hard copy such as ads in magazines, newspapers, brochures, leaflets, and flyers

Process control systems: An information processing system that monitors and controls physical processes by using sensors to collect data for analysis

Process-based organizational structure: A company structure designed around systems, processes, tasks, and knowledge

Product operations: An operational function that sits at the intersection of manufacturing, marketing, sales, product development and helps to improve the go-to-market and customer experience

Product placement advertising: The promotion of brands and products within the context of a TV show or a movie

Product: Anything tangible or intangible (such as a service) offered by the company

Production control: The task coordinating people, materials, and machinery to provide maximum production efficiency

Production planning: The stage of production control that determines the amount of resources (raw materials, staff, and equipment) required by an organization to fulfill sales orders and produce a certain output

Professional activities: Activities that require trained or certified skills

Professional business model: A type of business model that provides professional services on a time and materials contract

Profit margin: A profitability ratio that measures the amount of net income as a percentage of sales; also known as return on sales

Profit sharing: A pay system in which the organization shares its profits with employees

Profit: The amount of money gained after selling goods and services and paying expenses associated with operating the business

Promotion: Any type marketing communication used by companies to inform target customers about their offering

Protectionism: A set of government policies designed to defend domestic industries against foreign competition

Proverbs: Wise sayings common to many different cultures

Psychographic segmentation: Divides the market into the psychological aspects of behavior such as values, opinions, personality traits, attitudes, lifestyle, hobbies, beliefs, fears, and interests

Psychological empowerment: The extent to which employees feel a sense of personal fulfillment and intent when carrying out tasks, together with a belief that their work contributes to some larger purpose

Public relations: A type of communication process used to protect, enhance, or build reputations through the media

Public service advertising (PSA): A type of advertising intended to inform or educate rather than sell a product or service

Purchase decision: The point in the buying process at which the customer decides to move forward with the purchase

Quality: The characteristics of a product or service that bear on its ability to satisfy stated or implied needs

Quick ratio: A financial ratio that measures liquidity and assesses whether the company has enough liquid assets to pay its short-term liabilities

Ransomware: A type of malicious software (or malware) used by an attacker to gain access to a victim's computer files, lock them, and then demand a ransom to unlock them

Ratio analysis: A method that allows you to compare performance over time as well as compare your performance to others in the same industry or sector

Recommenders: People who may evaluate your product and tell the public about it

Recruiting: The process of identifying suitable candidates and encouraging them to apply for openings in the organization

Regression: A data mining function used to predict continuous numeric values based on historical patterns

Relational skills: The ability to collaborate and communicate with others

Resource-based view: A theoretical framework that helps businesses identify sources of competitive advantage

Resource: Something that adds value

Responsibility: The personal obligation to perform tasks and reach specified goals

Retailer: A person or business that sells products directly to the public either from a store or a website

Retained earnings: The cumulative amount of profit retained by the company and not paid out in the form of dividends to owners

Return on equity: A financial ratio that demonstrates how successful a company is at managing the capital contributed by shareholders

Revenue model: The way in which the company generates revenue and earns a profit

Rituals: Activities and ceremonies that celebrate important occasions and accomplishments within an organization

Routing: The second stage of production control that determines the sequence of work throughout the facility and makes decisions about who will perform each task at what location

S corporation (S-corp): A type of corporation that is eligible for, and elects, special taxation status

S corporation: (Sometimes known as an "S-corp") A type of corporation that is eligible for, and elects, special taxation status

Sales channels: How the company reaches its customers

Sales cycle: A set of specific actions followed by salespeople to close a sale

Sales: The activities that lead to the selling of goods and services

Sanitary embargo: A trade restriction enforced to protect people, animals, and plants

SBA loans: A type of loan that offers small businesses lower rates and better terms than traditional loans

Scenario planning: A strategic planning method for managing uncertainty that makes assumptions and predictions about different future circumstances (called scenarios) that could occur, and then identifies responses and creates contingency plans for when or if such scenarios actually happen

Scheduling: The third stage of production control where managers develop timetables specifying how each operation in the production process takes place and when workers should perform it

Search pathway: A pathway that is used when entrepreneurs are not quite sure what type of venture they want to start but engage in active search to discover new opportunities

Seasonal deals: A sales promotion strategy that involves selling off company stock at a discount

Seed-stage financing: A type of financing that usually consists of small or modest amounts of capital provided to entrepreneurs to prove a concept

Selection process: The process of gathering information on candidates, evaluating their qualifications, and choosing the best candidate for the job

Selective distribution: A distribution strategy under which a company sells through just a few select businesses who specialize in more expensive products

Selective listening: A type of listening when the receiver only hears what they want to hear

Self-leadership: A process through which people intentionally influence their thinking behavior to achieve their objectives

Seniority-based pay: A type of extrinsic reward where employees receive guaranteed wages and salary increases based on time spent with the organization

Separation of duties: (Also known as segregation of duties) The action of splitting tasks among multiple people to protect against internal fraud

Serial entrepreneur: An individual who has started multiple businesses

Serial entrepreneurs (also known as habitual entrepreneurs): People who come with continuous ideas and start several businesses, either simultaneously or consecutively

Serial entrepreneurs: Entrepreneurs who start several businesses, either simultaneously or consecutively

Service operations: An operational function intended to support the customer support team, customer experience team, and customer success team by developing strategies designed to attract, engage, and delight customers

Sexual orientation: Refers to a person's sexual identity and the gender(s) to which she or he is attracted

Shannon-Weaver communications model: A theory of communication that breaks human communication down into eight main components: sender, message, receiver, encoder, decoder, channel, feedback, and noise

Shareholder equity: Represents the money that has been invested in the business plus the cumulative net profits and losses the company has generated

Shareholders: Individuals or companies that own shares of stock in a corporation

Short-term debt: The portion of long-term debt that must be paid within a year

Simple structure: A common organizational structure used in small businesses where decision making is centralized with one single person

Situational leadership: A style of leadership where leaders adapt their leadership style based on the types of people they are leading and the requirements of the task

Six Sigma: A business management strategy designed to analyze the causes of defects, using statistical methods

Skill-based pay: Rewards employees for the acquisition of new skills that lead to enhanced work performance

Skills: The talents or abilities that enable a person to complete a particular task, interaction, or process effectively and efficiently

Slang: An informal language applied in a particular context or group, is not usually appropriate in business communication, as it has the potential to cause great confusion

Small businesses: Organizations that have fewer than 100 employees

Small data: A volume of data that are small enough in volume to be accessible, informative, and actionable

SNAP selling: A sales technique that focuses on how customers make decisions and influences them positively to encourage them to feel as though they have made a decision by themselves

Social engineering: The act of tricking users into divulging sensitive information

Social entrepreneurship: The process of sourcing innovative solutions to social and environmental problems

Social media advertising: A form of online advertising that allows companies to attract target audiences while they are engaging with posts or stories on their preferred social media platforms

Social media contest: A sales promotion strategy that involves running an online contest to attract a larger audience

Social value: The positive impact a business can have on society including issues related to employee diversity, equity, inclusion, as well as issues related to environmental sustainability and global challenges

Software as a Service (SaaS): A distribution model in which companies offer their applications, software, and platforms to customers over the internet

Software as a service (SaaS): A model that provides customers with software that can be accessed over the web

Sole proprietorship: A business owned by one person who has full exposure to its liabilities

Sole proprietorship: A business owned by one person who has full exposure to its liabilities

Solution: How the company intends to meet the customers' needs

Span of control: The number of subordinates for whom managers are directly responsible

Specialty promotion: Use of free merchandise give-aways to celebrate or promote a brand, company, or product

SPIN selling: A sales technique based on four stages of questions designed to engage prospects with a goal of making a sale

Spiritual culture: A type of organizational culture that focuses on opportunities for employees to grow and find purpose in the workplace by carrying out meaningful tasks that contribute to the good of society as a whole

Stakeholders: People who have an interest in or are affected by a business such as customers, employees, suppliers, and local communities

Startup financing: The money provided to entrepreneurs to enable them to implement their idea by funding product research and development

Startup: A newly formed business with limited or no operational history

Statistical quality control (SQC): The use of statistics taken from samples from production runs for the sole purpose of determining production quality

Strategic embargo: A trade restriction that forbids the exchange of military goods with a country

Strategic human resource planning: The process of developing a plan for satisfying the organization's human resource needs in order to help the company achieve its mission and related goals

Strategic plan: A broad, long-term plan that helps to define the entire organization's strategic mission and goals, and the actions needed to achieve them

Subscriber specials: Discounts given to subscribers

Subscription business model: A type of business model that involves charging customers to gain continuous access to a product or service and earns money through repeat purchases

Supplier: An individual or an organization that provides particular types of goods

Supply chain management (SCM): The facilitation and coordination of the flow of goods and services from production to the delivery of the final product

Supply chain: A network between a company and its suppliers to produce and distribute a product

Supply: The sellers who compete for customers in the marketplace

Surface-level diversity: Describes the more obvious differences between us, such as age and generation, race and ethnicity, gender and sexual orientation, and physical and/or mental ability

Sustainable Development Goals (SDGs): A set of 17 goals created by the United Nations for achieving a thriving, inclusive, and sustainable society by 2030

SWOT analysis: A method of assessing an organization's strengths, weaknesses, opportunities, and threats (abbreviated as SWOT)

Symbols: Objects that convey meaning to others about an organization's culture

Tactical plan: Supports a strategic plan by transforming it into a specific plan by applying it to particular parts of the organization

Tagline: A short, memorable phrase or motto to convey purpose or value of a brand or product

Talent management: A function of HRM and can be defined as the processes involved in managing the flow of well-qualified employees into an organization and through various positions within the organization

Target market: A group of specific people who are most likely to buy the company's products and services

Target market: A group of specific people who are most likely to buy the company's products and services

Tariff rate quota: A two-tiered quota system that allows a specified quantity of product to be imported at a lower tariff rate

Tariff: A tax or duty paid on imported goods

TEA: The percentage of the population of each country between the ages of 18 and 64 who are either an early entrepreneur (setting up a business) or owner-manager of a new business (up to 3 years old)

Technical skills: The abilities and knowledge to perform job-specific tasks

Technology adoption life cycle: A model that describes the process of acceptance of a new innovation over time, according to defined adopter groups

Text mning: The process of collecting high-quality information from text to create meaningful insights

The Halo effect: The tendency to ascribe positive attributes to a person after learning something impressive about them

The Horns effect: The tendency to view another person negatively after learning something "unsavory" about them

Time-management skills: The ability to manage time effectively

Top managers: People who set the organization's direction and make decisions that affect everybody

Top managers: People who set the organization's direction, develop strategic plans, and make decisions that affect everybody

Total leverage: A financial ratio that measures the level of operating and financial leverage held by a company

Total Quality Management (TQM): An operations management philosophy based on the principle that employees at all levels (from entry level hourly workers to top executives) be committed to maintaining high standards of work in every aspect of a company\'s operations

Trade embargo: A trade restriction that bans the exports or imports of certain goods and services to or from one or more countries

Trade restriction: A government policy that limits the flow of goods and services between countries

Trade secret: Confidential information that provides companies with a competitive edge and is not in the public domain, such as formulas, patterns, compilations, programs, devices, methods, techniques, or processes

Trade secret: Confidential information that provides companies with a competitive edge and is not in the public domain, such as formulas, patterns, compilations, programs, devices, methods, techniques, or processes

Trade surplus: When a nation imports more than it exports

Trademark: Any word, name, symbol, or device used in business to identify and promote a product. Its counterpart for service industries is the service mark

Trademark: Any word, name, symbol, or device used in business to identify and promote a product. Its counterpart for service industries is the service mark

Training: The process of teaching new or existing employees the skills necessary to carry out their roles and improve current job performance

Transaction processing system (TPS): An information processing system that records the daily business transactions of an organization at the operational level

Transactional data: The information captured by an organization's transactions such as banking records, sales records, etc.

Transactional leadership: A style of leadership in which leaders use rewards and punishment as motivation

Transformational leadership: A style of leadership in which leaders create visions to motivate, inspire, and stimulate employees

Transient advantage: A strategy that assumes competitive advantages are temporary and requires continuous innovation to maintain any type of competitive positioning

Two-factor theory: (Also referred to as motivation-hygiene theory or dual theory) A theory that explores the impact of motivational influences on job satisfaction

Uncertainty: The degree that the future is unknown

Upskilling: The process of equipping workers with the necessary skills or abilities to move into a new role within the organization rather than terminating workers and recruiting new people with a different skill set

Upward communication: Sends messages from the lower levels of the organizational hierarchy to the higher levels

User-generated content: Any type of content such as text, videos, reviews, and blogs that can be created by people outside the business

Utility and usage business model: A type of business model that charges customers fees on the basis of how often goods or services are used

Valence: The value individuals place on work outcomes

Value proposition: Explains the uniqueness of a company's offering suggesting why a customer should choose your company over the competition

Value statements: Statements that inform an organization's employees and customers about its priorities and goals

Value-based pricing: A pricing strategy based on the customers' perceived value of the product or service

Value-stream mapping: A process that provides a visual representation of all the steps in a work process

Values: Underlying desires and core beliefs that shape an identity of an organization, and act as a good guide for how employees are expected to behave

Variable costs: Costs that fluctuate depending on a company's rate of production

Variance: The difference between the budget and actual performance for any given expense or income item

Venture capitalist (VC): A type of professional investor who generally invests in early-stage and emerging companies because of perceived long-term growth potential

Verbal communication: The exchange of information, ideas, and processes through speech, either one on one or as a group

Vertical organizational structure: A traditional company structure based on a chain of command where leaders sit at the top of the hierarchy and pass down orders to lower-level workers

Video marketing: The use of videos to market or promote a product or service

Virtual communication: The verbal exchange of information through email, videoconferencing, blogs, fax, instant messaging, texting, and social networking

Virtual organizational structure: A company structure where employees are geographically spread and tend to communicate by phone, email, and the internet

Vision statement: A short statement that describes the current and future organizational goals

Vision: A mental image that describes what an organization wants to become

Volatility: The pace of change

Volunteered data: Data shared by the consumer or by an authorized third party in paper or digital form, such as personal information

VRIO analysis: A four-question framework to assess whether a resource is valuable, rare, and inimitable, and if the business is organized enough to capture value from that resource

VUCA: An acronym that stands for volatility, uncertainty, complexity, and ambiguity

Web browser: A software application that locates information from other parts of the web and transmits it to a computer, smartphone, or other mobile device

Whistleblower: A person who reports another person or organization for engaging in illegal, unethical, or other significant types of wrongdoings

Working capital: The money used by companies to pay for the day-to-day operations such as inventory and overhead expenses

Workplace diversity: The degree to which an organization values the differences and similarities between people in relation to age, gender, religion, race, ethnicity, sexual orientation, skills, and backgrounds

World Wide Web: ("the web") A subset of the internet that allows access to an interconnected system of web pages

Youth stage: The stage of the organizational life cycle where growth and expansion take place

ENDNOTES

FRONT MATTER

1. Business leaders at UN forum challenged to invest in a more sustainable future for all. (2018, April 4). *UN News*. https://news.un.org/en/story/2018/04/1006531

2. Companies can create 380 million jobs by integrating sustainable development goals into business strategies, secretary-general tells international employers summit | Meetings coverage and press releases. (2020). *UN.org*. https://www.un.org/press/en/2020/sgsm20226.doc.htm

3. Deloitte. (2019). *Welcome to generation Z*. https://www2.deloitte.com/content/dam/Deloitte/us/Documents/consumer-business/welcome-to-gen-z.pdf

CHAPTER 1

1. Leighton, M. (2019). Patagonia just won the United Nations' top environmental honor for entrepreneurial vision—here is why we're not surprised. *Business Insider*. https://www.businessinsider.com/patagonia-un-champions-of-the-earth-award-2019.

2. In climbing, a *piton* is a metal spike that is driven into a crack or seam in the climbing surface with a climbing hammer, and which acts as an anchor either to protect the climber against the consequences of a fall or to assist progress in aid climbing.

3. Patagonia. (2017). Beginnings and blacksmithery. https://www.patagonia.com.au/pages/company-history

4. Aten, J. (2021, December 24). Patagonia's 5-word explanation of why it's closing its stores and giving employees a week off is the best I've seen yet. *Inc.com*. https://www.inc.com/jason-aten/patagonias-5-word-explanation-of-why-its-closing-its-stores-giving-employees-a-week-off-is-best-ive-seen-yet.html

5. Lexico. https://www.lexico.com/en/definition/corporation

6. Ryan, K. J. (2020). 7 innovative start-ups to watch in 2020. *Inc*. https://www.inc.com/kevin-j-ryan/innovative-startups-to-watch-in-2020.html

7. The 100 largest companies in the world by market value 2019. (2020). *Statista*. https://www.statista.com/statistics/263264/top-companies-in-the-world-by-market-value/

8. P&G website. https://www.pgcareers.com/about-us

9. Bear Mattress 2019 Inc 5000 rank. (n.d.). https://www.inc.com/profile/bear-mattress

10. Biswas, S. (2019). Forever 21, teen-focused retailer, files for bankruptcy. *The Wall Street Journal*. Retrieved from https://www.wsj.com/articles/forever-21-teen-focused-retailer-files-for-bankruptcy-11569811923

11. Osterwalder, A., & Pigneur, Y. (2010). *Business model generation: A handbook for visionaries, game changers, and challengers*. Wiley.

12. Naturebox website. https://naturebox.com/aboutus

13. Unilever puts vitality at core of new mission. (2004). https://www.unilever.com/news/press-releases/2004/04-02-12-Unilever-puts-vitality-at-core-of-new-mission.html

14. Brooks, R. (2018). Workplace spotlight: What Google gets right about company culture. *Peakon*. https://peakon.com/us/blog/workplace-culture/google-company-culture/

15. Fink, L. (2018). A sense of purpose: Larry Fink's annual letter to CEOs. https://www.blackrock.com/hk/en/insights/larry-fink-ceo-letter

16. Pontefract, D. (2019). Decoding Black Rock chairman Larry Fink's letter to CEOs on the importance of purpose. *Forbes*. Retrieved from https://www.forbes.com/sites/danpontefract/2019/01/26/decoding-blackrock-chairman-larry-finks-letter-to-ceos-on-the-importance-of-purpose/#31448a512995

17. Gharib, S. (2019). Aflac CEO on leadership: Take care of your people. They'll take care of your business. *Fortune*. https://fortune.com/2019/10/10/aflac-ceo-on-leading-leadership/

18. Frauenheim, E. (2018). Why companies that give back also receive. *Fortune*. https://fortune.com/2018/02/09/bank-of-america-giving-back/

19. Brown, M. M. (2019). Purpose-driven business in action. *Lead Change*. https://www.smartbrief.com/original/2019/10/leadership-good

20. Chen, C. (2019). How REI has managed to lead with its values and still turn a profit. *Business Insider*. https://www.businessinsider.com/rei-company-values

21. REI. (2021). REI co-op COVID-19 health & safety standards. REI. https://www.rei.com/newsroom/article/may-2020-health-and-safety-fact-sheet

22. Business leaders at UN forum challenged to invest in a more sustainable future for all. (2018). *UN News*. https://news.un.org/en/story/2018/04/1006531

23. Vali, N. (2017). More than philanthropy: DGS are a $12 trillion opportunity for the private sector. *Our Perspectives—United Nations Development Programme*. https://www.undp.org/content/undp/en/home/blog/2017/8/25/More-than-philanthropy-SDGs-present-an-estimated-US-12-trillion-in-market-opportunities-for-private-sector-through-inclusive-business.html

24. Giddens, M. (2018). The SDGs are an opportunity, not just a challenge. *Forbes*. https://www.forbes.com/sites/michelegiddens/2018/05/24/the-sdgs-are-an-opportunity-not-just-a-challenge/#31a2e2433ef5

25. SDGs: An opportunity for business (2017). *LexisNexis blog*. https://sdgresources.relx.com/articles-features/sdgs-opportunity-business

26. Jacobs, E. (2021, December). The future of work. *Financial Times*. https://www.ft.com/content/7202c5d4-fbc9-4ad7-93c2-cb05e6b582e9

27. Mulcahy, D. (2017). *The gig economy: The complete guide to getting better work, taking more time off, and financing the life you want* (p. 2). Amacom.

28. Henderson, R. (2021, December 10). How COVID-19 has transformed the gig economy. *Forbes*. https://www.forbes.com/sites/rebeccahenderson/2020/12/10/how-covid-19-has-transformed-the-gig-economy/?sh=2c51e7b36c99

29. Zgola, M. (2021, August 12). Council post: Will the gig economy become the new working-class norm? *Forbes*. https://www.forbes.com/sites/forbesbusinesscouncil/2021/08/12/will-the-gig-economy-become-the-new-working-class-norm/?sh=1a43b824aee6

30. Istrate, E., & Harris, J. (2017). The future of work: The rise of the gig economy. *NACo*. https://www.naco.org/featured-resources/future-work-rise-gig-economy

31. Nicholson, C. (n.d.). A.I. wiki: A beginner's guide to important topics in AI, machine learning, and deep learning. *Pathmind*. https://pathmind.com/wiki/ai-vs-machine-learning-vs-deep-learning

32. What is machine learning? A definition. (2017). *Expert System*. https://expertsystem.com/machine-learning-definition/

33. Manyika, J., & Sneader, K. (2018). AI, automation, and the future of work: Ten things to solve for [Blog post]. *McKinsey & Company*. https://www.mckinsey.com/featured-insights/future-of-work/ai-automation-and-the-future-of-work-ten-things-to-solve-for

34. Meister, J. (2019). The future of work: The rise of workers who self automate their jobs. *Forbes*. https://www.forbes.com/sites/jeannemeister/2019/05/07/the-future-of-work-the-rise-of-workers-who-self-automate-their-jobs/#261650ad3c23

35. Manyika & Sneader (2018). AI, automation, and the future of work.:

36. McConaghy, T. (2019). 3 ways we can maximize AI's impact on meeting the UN sustainable development goals. *ITU News*. Retrieved from https://news.itu.int/3-ways-we-can-maximize-ais-impact-on-meeting-the-un-sustainable-development-goals/

37. Aoun, J. E. (2017). *Robot-proof: Higher education in the age of artificial intelligence*. MIT Press.

38. Harari, Y. N. (2015). *Sapiens: A brief history of humankind*. HarperCollins.

39. What is Social Responsibility (SR)? ASQ. (2022). Asq.org website: https://asq.org/quality-resources/social-responsibility

40. Santa Clara University. (2020). What is ethics? https://www.scu.edu/ethics/ethics-resources/ethical-decision-making/what-is-ethics/

41. Business Ethics: Fair business policies within controversial subjects. (2022). *Investopedia*. https://www.investopedia.com/terms/b/business-ethics.asp

42. *Oxford English Dictionary*.

CHAPTER 2

1. Amazon staff. (n.d.). Thousands of Amazon sellers convene at Acclerate 2001. *Amazon*. https://www.aboutamazon.com/news/small-business/thousands-of-amazon-sellers-convene-at-accelerate-2021

2. Ibid.

3. Ibid., and Kaziukenas, J. (2019, January 21). Amazon merchants selling more than $1 million a year. *Marketplace Pulse*. https://www.marketplacepulse.com/articles/amazon-merchants-selling-more-than-1-million-a-year

4. Moon, M. (October 6, 2021). Amazon opens its first 4-start store outside the US. *Endgadget*. https://www.engadget.com/amazon-first-4-star-store-outside-us-100545112.html

5. Amazon. (October 21, 2021). Today at Amazon accelerate: Amazon launches new tools to Empower American small businesses to growth their export sales. https://press.aboutamazon.com/news-releases/news-release-details/today-amazon-accelerate-amazon-launches-new-tools-empower

6. Ibid.

7. Ann Clark Cookie Cutters. (n.d.). About us. https://www.annclarkcookiecutters.com/category/about-ann-clark-cookie-cutters

8. Amazon. (October 21, 2021). Today at Amazon Accelerate: Amazon launches new tools to Empower American small businesses to growth their export sales. https://press.aboutamazon.com/news-releases/news-release-details/today-amaz

on-accelerate-amazon-launches-new-tools-empower

9. Friedman, T. L. (2006). *The world is flat: A brief history of the twenty-first century*. New York: Farrar, Straus and Giroux.

10. Worldwide export trade value 1950–2020. Statista. (2020). https://www.statista.com/statistics/264682/worldwide-export-volume-in-the-trade-since-1950/

11. Lesley, L. (2021, December 27). Effects of climate change taking root in the wine industry—*60 Minutes*. From Cbsnews.com website: https://www.cbsnews.com/news/wine-industry-climate-change-60-minutes-2021-12-26/

12. Kassam, A. (2014, July 7). Airbnb fined €30,000 for illegal tourist lets in Barcelona. *The Guardian*. https://www.theguardian.com/technology/2014/jul/07/airbnb-fined-illegal-tourist-lets-barcelona-catalonia

13. McClanahan, (2021, September 22). Barcelona takes on Airbnb. *New York Times*. https://www.nytimes.com/2021/09/22/travel/barcelona-airbnb.html

14. 5 things to know when expanding a business internationally. (2020, September 23). *Wolterskluwer*. https://www.wolterskluwer.com/en/expert-insights/5-things-to-know-when-expanding-a-business-internationally

15. Reynolds, K. (2017, January 6). 11 biggest challenges of international business in 2017. *Hult International Business School*. https://www.hult.edu/blog/international-business-challenges/

16. Which products and companies rely on protective tariffs? (2022). *Investopedia*. https://www.investopedia.com/ask/answers/051315/what-are-examples-products-and-companies-rely-protective-tariffs-survive.asp

17. Tariffs, embargoes, quotas & policy. (2022). *Shmoop*. https://www.shmoop.com/international-trade/tariffs-embargoes-quota-policy.html

18. Batabyal, A. A. (2018, March 15). What is a tariff? An economist explains. *The Conversation*. https://theconversation.com/what-is-a-tariff-an-economist-explains-93392

19. News, B. (2020, January 16). A quick guide to the US–China trade war. *BBC News*. https://www.bbc.com/news/business-45899310

20. Countries sanctioned by the U.S. and why. (2022). *Investopedia*. https://www.investopedia.com/financial-edge/0410/countries-sanctioned-by-the-u.s.---and-why.aspx

21. Bashir, N. (2020, July 20). Hong Kong's new national security law explained. *CNN*. https://edition.cnn.com/2020/07/20/uk/uk-hong-kong-extradition-gbr-intl/index.html

22. What are embargoes, and do they actually work? *ThoughtCo*, https://www.thoughtco.com/what-is-an-embargo-definition-examples-4584158; https://www.facebook.com/thoughtcodotcom. (2019).

23. Ibid.

24. Import Quotas. (2020, July 5). *WallStreetMojo*. https://www.wallstreetmojo.com/import-quotas/; Batabyal, A. A. (2018, March 15). What is a tariff? An economist explains. *The Conversation*. https://theconversation.com/what-is-a-tariff-an-economist-explains-93392

25. Boyce, P. (2020, November 7). Comparative Advantage definition. *Boycewire*. https://boycewire.com/comparative-advantage-definition/

26. Ibid.

27. Ibid.

28. Ibid.

29. How we operate around the world. (2016, September 27). *Walmart*. https://corporate.walmart.com/how-we-operate-around-the-world

30. https://www.facebook.com/economicshelp.org. (2019, May 21). Benefits of being a multinational company—Economics help. *Economics Help*. https://www.economicshelp.org/blog/147528/economics/benefits-of-being-a-multinational-company/

31. Impact of multinational companies on host countries—Super Business Manager. (2022 *Superbusinessmanager*. https://www.superbusinessmanager.com/impact-of-multinational-companies-on-host-countries/

32. L'Oréal. (2021, June 27). L'Oréal for Youth: A global program in favor of youth employment. *L'Oréal*. https://www.loreal.com/en/articles/commitments/loreal-for-youth-program/

33. Seah, L. (2021). The importance of cultural awareness in international business. *Airswift*. https://www.airswift.com/blog/importance-of-cultural-awareness

34. Sainato, M. (2020, September 12). US corporations continue sending jobs abroad during pandemic. *The Guardian*. https://www.theguardian.com/business/2020/sep/12/us-corporations-sending-jobs-abroad-offshoring-pandemic

35. Balch, O. (2021, February 12). Mars, Nestlé and Hershey to face child slavery lawsuit in US. *The Guardian*. https://www.theguardian.com/global-development/2021/feb/12/mars-nestle-and-hershey-to-face-landmark-child-slavery-lawsuit-in-us

36. Amed, I. (2020, December 10) How can a garment be cheaper than a sandwich? *New York Times*. https://www.nytimes.com/2020/12/10/opinion/covid-fashion-industry-worker-exploitation.html

37. McDonaldization and why sociologists are not lovin' t. *ThoughtCo*. https://www.thoughtco.com/mcdonaldization-of-society-3026751; https://www.facebook.com/thoughtcodotcom. (2020).

38. Laville, S. (2020, March 30). Report reveals "massive plastic pollution footprint" of drinks firms. *The Guardian*. https://www.theguardian.com/environment/2020/mar/31/report-reveals-massive-plastic-pollution-footprint-of-drinks-firms

39. Pegg, D., & Evans, R. (2020, January 31). Airbus to pay record £3bn in fines for "endemic" corruption. *The Guardian*. https://www.theguardian.com/business/2020/jan/31/airbus-to-pay-record-3bn-in-fines-for-endemic-corruption

40. Multinational corporations in developing countries—The Borgen Project. (2020, September 13). *The Borgen Project*. https://borgenproject.org/multinational-corporations-in-developing-countries/

41. Kapner, S. (2021, December 23). Tiffany's new French owner brings a makeover—and a culture clash. *The Wall Street Journal*. https://www.wsj.com/articles/tiffanys-new-french-owner-brings-a-makeoverand-a-culture-clash-11640264191

42. How to bridge the culture gap and be an international team player. (2017, October 12). *The University of Queensland*. https://business.uq.edu.au/article/2016/06/how-bridge-culture-gap-and-be-international-team-player

43. Ibid.

44. Ibid.

45. Abadi, M. (2017, November 17). 6 American work habits people in other countries think are ridiculous. *The Independent*. https://www.independent.co.uk/news/business/american-work-habits-us-countries-job-styles-hours-hoilday-a8060616.html

46. How to bridge the culture gap and be an international team player. (2017, October 12). *The University of Queensland*. Retrieved from Uq.edu.au website: https://business.uq.edu.au/article/2016/06/how-bridge-culture-gap-and-be-international-team-player

47. Denboba, D., U.S. Department of Health and Human Services, Health Services and Resources Administration (1993). MCHB/DSCSHCN Guidance for Competitive Applications, Maternal and Child Health Improvement Projects for Children with Special Health Care Needs.

48. DMIS Model—IDRInstitute. (2021, April 19). Intercultural Development Research Institute. *IDR Institute*. https://www.idrinstitute.org/dmis/

49. Jackson, T. (2002). The management of people across cultures: Valuing people differently. *Human Resource Management, 41*(4), 455–475.

50. Indonesian culture: Do's and Don'ts. *Culture Atlas*. https://culturalatlas.sbs.com.au/indonesian-culture/indonesian-culture-do-s-and-don-ts

51. Hofstede, G. (1985). The interaction between national and organizational value systems. *Journal of Management Sudies, 22*(4), 347–357; Hofstede, G. (1984). The cultural relativity of the quality of life concept. *Academy of Management Review, 9*(3), 389–398; Mathiaszyk, L. P., & Volkmann, C. K. (2016). Is managers strategy culture sound? International differences in strategy choice. In *Academy of Management Proceedings, (2016)*1, 16494. (Briarcliff Manor, NY 10510: Academy of Management).

52. Hofstede, G. (1993). Cultural constraints in management theories. *Academy of Management Perspectives, 7*(1), 81–94.

53. Meyer, E. (2014). Navigating the cultural minefield. *Harvard Business Review, 92*(5), 119–123.

54. Hall, E. T. (1976). *Beyond culture*. New York: Anchor Press–Doubleday

55. Gupta, S. (2019, December 27). Book review: The Culture map by Erin Meyer—The eight scales of culture deploy yourself. Sumit Gupta. Leadership for the 21st century—productivity, wellbeing, and meaning—together. https://www.deployyourself.com/book-review/the-culture-map-erin-meyer-eight-scales/

56. Molinsky, A. (2013). *Global dexterity: How to adapt your behavior across cultures without losing yourself in the process.* Harvard Business Review Press.

57. Rockson, T. (2016, September 8). Dissecting the cultural code of China with Andy Molinsky. *HuffPost.* https://www.huffpost.com/entry/dissecting-the-cultural-c_b_11910694

58. Molinsky, A. (2017, September 5). Want to boost your cultural intelligence? Do this 1 thing first. *Inc.* https://www.inc.com/andy-molinsky/want-to-boost-your-cultural-intelligence-do-this-1.html

59. Cliffe, S. (2015, October). Companies don't go global, people do. *Harvard Business Review, 93*(10), 82–84.

60. Ibid.

CHAPTER 3

1. Jerry was the country director for Save the Children (U.S.) in Bangladesh, Philippines, Vietnam, Egypt, and most recently, Burma. He was a Peace Corps volunteer and country director in Rwanda, Mauritania, Nepal, and the Philippines, as well as assistant dean and student adviser at the Harvard Business School.

2. Save the Children. (n.d.). https://www.savethechildren.net/about-us/who-we-are

3. Kien, V. D., Lee, H. Y., Nam, Y. S., Oh, J., Giang, K. B., & Minh, H. V. (2016). Trends in socioeconomic inequalities in child malnutrition in Vietnam: Findings from the Multiple Indicator Cluster Surveys, 2000–2011. *Global Health Action, 9*(1), 29263.

4. Heath, C., & Heath, D. (2007). *Made to stick: Why some ideas survive and others die.* Random House. See excerpt from https://www.fastcompany.com/1514493/switch-dont-solve-problems-copy-success

5. Corbett, A. (2020, September). We need entrepreneurial leaders now

more than ever. *EntrepreneurEurope.* https://www.entrepreneur.com/article/355760

6. Espindola, D. (2019, April). Technology is exponential but humans are linear. *Intercepting Horizons.* https://www.interceptinghorizons.com/post/technology-is-exponential-but-humans-are-linear

7. Dweck, C. S. (2016). Mindset: The new psychology of success. Random House.

8. Bronson, P. (2007, August 3). How not to talk to your kids. *New York Magazine.* http://nymag.com/news/features/27840/

9. Warby Parker. https://www.warbyparker.com/history

10. Dweck, C. (2010). How can you change from a fixed mindset to a growth mindset? *Mindset.* http://mindsetonline.com/changeyourmindset/firststeps/

11. Atkinson, J. W. (1966). Motivational determinants of risk-taking behavior. In J. W. Atkinson & N. T. Feather (Eds.), *A theory of achievement motivation* (pp. 11–30). John Wiley & Sons.

12. Perkins-Gough, D. (2013, September). The significance of grit: A conversation with Angela Lee Duckworth. *Educational Leadership, 71*(1), 14–20. http://www.ascd.org/publications/educational-leadership/sept13/vol71/num01/The-Significance-of-Grit@-A-Conversation-with-Angela-Lee-Duckworth.aspx

13. Sarasvathy, S. D. (2009). *Effectuation: Elements of entrepreneurial expertise.* Elgar.

14. Seth, S. (2019). World's top 10 serial entrepreneurs. *Investopedia.* https://www.investopedia.com/articles/personal-finance/083115/worlds-top-10-serial-entrepreneurs.asp

15. Ibid.

16. Sarasvathy, S. D. (2009). *Effectuation: Elements of entrepreneurial expertise.* Elgar.

17. Ibid and Sarasvathy's principles for effectuation. https://innovationenglish.sites.ku.dk/model/sarasvathy-effectuation/

18. Read, S., Sarasvathy, S., Dew, N., & Wiltbank, R. (2016). *Effectual entrepreneurship.* Routledge.

19. Terracycle. https://www.terracycle.com/

20. Baron, R. A., & Henry, R. A. (2010). How entrepreneurs acquire the capacity to excel: Insights from research on expert performance. *Strategic Entrepreneurship Journal, 4,* 49–65.

21. Clear, J. (n.d.) The beginner's guide to deliberate practice. *James Clear.* https://jamesclear.com/beginners-guide-deliberate-practice

22. Wasserman, N. (2014, August 25). How an entrepreneur's passion can destroy a startup. *The Wall Street Journal.* http://online.wsj.com/articles/how-an-entrepreneur-s-passion-can-destroy-a-startup-1408912044

23. McMullen, J. S., & Shepherd, D. A. (2006). Entrepreneurial action and the role of uncertainty in the theory of the entrepreneur. *Academy of Management Review, 31*(1), 132–152.

24. Giles, S. (2018, May 9). How VUCA is reshaping the business environment, and what it means for innovation. *Forbes.* https://www.forbes.com/sites/sunniegiles/2018/05/09/how-vuca-is-reshaping-the-business-environment-and-what-it-means-for-innovation/#430c215aeb8d

25. Leonhard, G. (2016). *Technology vs. humanity.* Fast Future Publishing.

26. McMullen, J. S., & Shepherd, D. A. (2006). Entrepreneurial action and the role of uncertainty in the theory of the entrepreneur. *Academy of Management Review, 31*(1), 132–152.

27. Kraaijenbrink, J. (2018, December 19). What does VUCA really mean? *Forbes.* https://www.forbes.com/sites/jeroenkraaijenbrink/2018/12/19/what-does-vuca-really-mean/#637ecde17d6

28. Shaw, C. (2013, September 9). Dealing with ambiguity: The new business imperative. *Beyond Philosophy Blog.* https://beyondphilosophy.com/dealing-with-ambiguity-the-new-business-imperative/

29. Giles, S. (2018, May 9). How VUCA is reshaping the business environment, and what it means for innovation. *Forbes.* https://www.forbes.com/sites/sunniegiles/2018/05/09/how-vuca-is-reshaping-the-business-environment-and-what-it-means-for-innovation/#430c215aeb8d

30. UNC Executive Development. (2017). The origins of VUCA. *UNC Executive Development Blog.* http://execdev.ken

an-flagler.unc.edu/blog/the-origins
-of-vuca

31. WHO Coronavirus (COVID-19) Dash-
board. (2022). *Who.int*. https://covid19
.who.int/

32. Rumsfeld. D. (2002, February 12).
DoD news briefing—Secretary
Rumsfeld and General Myers. *U.S.
Department of Defense*. https://archiv
e.defense.gov/Transcripts/Transcrip
t.aspx?TranscriptID=2636

CHAPTER 4

1. Hathaway, I. (2016). What startup
accelerators really do. *Harvard Business Review, 7*(1). https://hbr.org/201
6/03/what-startup-accelerators-re
ally-do

2. Dullea, S. (2019, July 19). A decade of
impact: A note from the MassChallenge CEO. https://masschallenge.or
g/article/a-decade-of-impact-a-note
-from-the-masschallenge-ceo

3. Freight Farms. https://www.freightfa
rms.com/home#mission

4. Weber, J. (2019, November 6). Ginkgo
Bioworks CEO wants biology to manufacture physical goods. *Bloomberg
Businessweek*. https://www.bloombe
rg.com/news/features/2019-11-06/gi
nkgo-bioworks-ceo-wants-biology-t
o-manufacture-physical-goods

5. Small Business & Entrepreneurship
Council. (n.d.). Facts and data on
small business and entrepreneurship. Retrieved on March 25, 2020,
from https://sbecouncil.org/about-u
s/facts-and-data/

6. Lauckner, S. (2019, September 5).
How many small business are in the
U.S.? *Fundera*. https://www.fundera.
com/blog/small-business-employm
ent-and-growth-statistics

7. Ghosh, I. (2021, May 5). How has the
pandemic affected America's small
businesses? *World Economic Forum*. h
ttps://www.weforum.org/agenda/20
21/05/america-united-states-covid
-small-businesses-economics/

8. Bosma, N., Hill, S., Ionescu-Somers,
A., Kelley, D., Levie, J., & Tarnawa, A.
(2020). *Global entrepreneurship monitor: 2019/2020 global report*. Global
Entrepreneurship Research Association: London Business School, 24.

9. United States Economy Profile.
(2021). *Global Entrepreneurship Monitor*. https://www.gemconsortium.org
/economy-profiles/
united-states-2

10. Brockhaus, R., & Horowitz, P. (1986).
The psychology of the entrepreneur.
In D. Sexton & R. Smilor (Eds.), *The
art and science of entrepreneurship*
(pp. 25–48). Ballinger.

11. Sarasvathy, S. D. (2008). *Effectuation:
Elements of entrepreneurial expertise*.
Edward Elgar.

12. Ibid.

13. Brown, P. (2013, November 6).
Entrepreneurs are "calculated" risk
takers—The word that can be the difference between failure and success.
Forbes. www.forbes.com/sites/actio
ntrumpseverything/2013/11/06/entr
epreneurs-are-not-risk-takers-they
-are-calculated-risk-takers-that-on
e-additional-word-can-be-the-differ
ence-between-failure-and-success/

14. Schlesinger, L., Kiefer, C., & Brown,
P. (2012). *Just start: Take action,
embrace uncertainty, create the future*.
Harvard Business School Press.

15. Costello, C., Neck, H., & Williams, R.
(2011). *Elements of the entrepreneur
experience*. Babson Entrepreneur
Experience Lab. http://elab.business
innovationfactory.com/sites/default
/files/pdf/BabsonBIF-eLab-NVE-V1
-2012rev.pdf

16. Rosen, A. (2015, May 7). *Why collaboration is essential to entrepreneurship*.
https://www.entrepreneur.com/artic
le/245599

17. Spors, K. K. (2007, January 9). Do
start-ups really need formal business plans? *The Wall Street Journal*. h
ttp://www.wsj.com/articles/SB11683
0373855570835

18. Costello, C., Neck, H., & Williams, R.
(2011). *Elements of the entrepreneur
experience*. Babson Entrepreneur
Experience Lab. http://elab.business
innovationfactory.com/sites/default
/files/pdf/BabsonBIF-eLab-NVE-V1
-2012rev.pdf

19. Covin, J. G., & Miles, M. (1999). Corporate entrepreneurship and the
pursuit of competitive advantage.
*Entrepreneurship: Theory and Practice,
23*(3), 47–63.

20. DSM. https://www.dsm.com/corpora
te/about/businesses/dsm-venturin
g.html

21. Costello, C., Neck, H., & Dziobek,
K. (2012). *Entrepreneurs of all kinds:
Elements of the entrepreneurs inside

experience*. Babson Entrepreneur
Experience Lab. http://elab.business
innovationfactory.com/sites/default
/files/pdf/babsonBIF-elab-EI-V2-20
12rev.pdf

22. Partridge, A. (2019, May 9). A 40-year
IBM vet talks spurring innovation for
decades. *Westchester Magazine*. https
://westchestermagazine.com/public
ations/a-40-year-ibm-vet-talks-spu
rring-innovation-for-decades/

23. Judd, R. J., & Justis, R. T. (2007).
Franchising: An entrepreneur's guide
(4th ed.). Cengage Learning.

24. Entrepreneur Franchise 500. (2019).
Entrepreneur. https://www.entrepren
eur.com/franchises/500/2019

25. Number of francise establishments
in the U.S. from 2007 to 2020. (n.d.).
Statista. https://www.statista.com/st
atistics/190313/estimated-number
-of-us-franchise-establishments-si
nce-2007/

26. U.S. Small Business Administration.
(n.d.). Buy an existing business or
franchise. https://www.sba.gov/cont
ent/buying-existing-business

27. Ruback, R., & Yudkoff, R. (2017). Buy-
ing your way into entrepreneurship.
Harvard Business Review, January–
February, pp. 149–153.

28. Neck, H. M., Brush, C., & Allen,
E. (2009). The landscape of social
entrepreneurship. *Business Horizons,
52*, 13–19; Mair, J., & Marti, I. (2006).
Social entrepreneurship research: A
source of explanation, prediction and
delight. *Journal of World Business, 41*,
36–44.

29. B Lab. (2019). About B Corps. https://
bcorporation.net/about-b-corps

30. Clifford, C. (2012, June 11). B Corps:
The next generation of company.
Entrepreneur. www.entrepreneur.co
m/blog/223762

31. Seventh Generation B Impact Report.
Certified B Corporation. https://bcorp
oration.net/directory/seventh-gen
eration

32. Seventh Generation. (2018, November 7). Journey to a more sustainable,
equitable planet: Seventh Generation's 2025 Goals. https://www.seven
thgeneration.com/blog/journey-mor
e-sustainable-equitable-planet-seve
nth-generations-2025-goals

33. Eileen Fisher B. Impact Report. (n.d.).
Certified B Corporation. https://bcorp

oration.net/directory/eileen-fishe r-inc

34. Habbershon, T. G., Williams, M., & MacMillan, I. C. (2003). A unified systems perspective of family firm performance. *Journal of Business Venturing, 18*, 451–465.

35. SCORE. (2018, March 14). Family-owned businesses created 78% of new U.S. jobs and employ 60% of the workforce. https://www.prnewswire. com/news-releases/family-owned-b usinesses-create-78-of-new-us-job s-and-employ-60-of-the-workforce -300613665.html

36. L.L. Bean company information. (n.d.). https://www.llbean.com/llb/sh op/516920?nav=ln-516919

37. Seth, S. (2019, September 16). World's top 10 serial entrepreneurs. *Investo-pedia.* https://www.investopedia.com /articles/personal-finance/083115/ worlds-top-10-serial-entrepreneu rs.asp

38. Jaume, J. (2012, November 13). 8 tech innovations and gadgets that never took off. *Brandwatch.* https://www.br andwatch.com/blog/8-tech-invent ions-and-gadgets-that-never-took -off/

39. Armitage, H. (2017, August 11). 10 inventions no one thought would be a success. *Culture Trip.* https://thecultu retrip.com/north-america/usa/articl es/10-inventions-no-one-thought-w ould-be-a-success/

40. Lanthier, K. (2020, April 3). Sending an air hug. *Babson Thought & Action.* h ttps://entrepreneurship.babson.edu/ sending-an-air-hug/

41. Baron, R. A. (2006). Opportunity rec‍ognition as pattern recognition: How entrepreneurs "connect the dots" to identify new business opportunities. *Academy of Management Perspectives, 20*, 104–119.

42. Fiet, J. O. (2000). The theoretical side of teaching entrepreneurship. *Journal of Business Venturing, 16*, 1–24; Fiet, J. O. (2002). *The systematic search for entrepreneurial discoveries.* Quorum Books.

43. Berger, S. (2018, October 22). How this 22-year-old with Down syndrome built a multimillion-dollar business off his love of crazy socks. *CNBC: Make It.* https://www.cnbc.com/2018 /10/22/22-year-old-with-down-syn drome-founded-johns-crazy-sock s.html

44. Bygrave, W. (2005). *Jim Poss. Babson College case study #130-C04-A-U.* Case Centre.

45. Bigbelly Blog. (2019, December 12). Big Belly solar partners with McCar-thy Capital to accelerate growth. http s://blog.bigbelly.com/big-belly-solar -partners-with-mccarthy-capital-to -accelerate-growth

46. Cohen, D., Pool, G., & Neck, H. (2020). *The IDEATE method.* SAGE.

47. Bike-powered pastry shops. (n.d.) *Trendhunter.* https://www.trendhunte r.com/trends/pief-paf

48. Suzanne-Mayer, D. (2019, April 26). Lyft, grocery trucks trying to solve the problem of food deserts. *The Takeout.* https://thetakeout.com/lyft -grocery-trucks-trying-to-fix-food-d eserts-1834330376

49. Beth Israel Deaconess Medical Center. (2019, July 22). Widespread aspirin use despite few benefits, high risks. *ScienceDaily.* www.sciencedaily .com/releases/2019/07/1907221821 26.htm

CHAPTER 5

1. Kavilanz, P. (2019, June 21). How he got 200,000 people to buy ugly fruits and vegetables. *CNN.* Retrieved from https://www.cnn.com/2019/06/17/su ccess/imperfect-produce/index.html

2. Ibid.

3. Feeding America (n.d.). How we fight food waste in the US. Retrieved from https://www.feedingamerica.org/our -work/our-approach/reduce-food -waste

4. Gingiss, D. (2019, April 28). How Imperfect Produce turned ugly fruit and vegetables into marketing per-fection. *Forbes.* Retrieved from https: //www.forbes.com/sites/dangingiss /2019/04/28/how-imperfect-produc e-turned-ugly-fruit-and-vegetables -into-marketing-perfection/#41447 f576d73

5. Crawford, E. (2019, October 7). Imperfect Produce becomes Imper-fect Foods as it expands offerings across categories and distribution. *Food Navigator USA.* https://www.foo dnavigator-usa.com/Article/2019/10 /07/Imperfect-Produce-rebrands-ex pands-offerings-distribution

6. Kavilanz, P. (2019, June 21). How he got 200,000 people to buy ugly fruits and vegetables. *CNN.* Retrieved from https://www.cnn.com/2019/06/17/su ccess/imperfect-produce/index.html

7. Osterwalder, A., & Pigneur, Y. (2010). *Business model generation: A hand-book for visionaries, game changers, and challengers.* Wiley.

8. Ovans, A. (2015, January 23). What is a business model. *Harvard Business Review.* Retrieved from https://hbr.or g/2015/01/what-is-a-business-mo del

9. Magretta, J. (2002. May). Why busi-ness models matter. *Harvard Busi-ness Review.* Retrieved from https://h br.org/2002/05/why-business-mode ls-matter

10. Johnson, M., Christensen, C., & Kagerman, H. (2008, December). Reinventing your business model. *Harvard Business Review,* 1–11; Oster-walder, A., & Pigneur, Y. (2010). *Busi-ness model generation: A handbook for visionaries, game changers, and chal-lengers.* Wiley.

11. Ung, E. (2019, April 10). Seeing beauty in "ugly" vegetables, cofounders find business model for reducing food waste. *Forbes.* Retrieved from https: //www.forbes.com/sites/colehaan/2 019/04/10/seeing-beauty-in-ugly-ve getables-cofounders-find-business -model-for-reducing-food-waste/#4 9c705475a3c

12. What are some examples of a busi-ness model? (n.d.). *Aha!* Retrieved from https://www.aha.io/roadmappi ng/guide/product-strategy/what-a re-some-examples-of-a-business -model

13. Morin, C. (2020, January 29). Pata-gonia's customer base and the rise of an environmental ethos. *CRM.org.* Retrieved from https://crm.org/articl es/patagonias-customer-base-and-t he-rise-of-an-environmental-ethos

14. Chouinard, Y. (2018, July 18). Patago-nia in the making: My founder story. *Branding Strategy Insider.* Retrieved from https://www.brandingstrategyi nsider.com/brand-patagonia-a-fou nders-story-and-strategy/#.XqL1Zl NKhBw

15. BrainStation Blog. (2019, May 28). How organizations are using data for social good. Retrieved from https://b rainstation.io/blog/how-organization s-are-using-data-for-social-good

16. This section draws heavily from Osterwalder, A., & Pigneur, Y. (2010).

Business model generation: A hand-book for visionaries, game changers, and challengers. Wiley.

17. Lokitz, J. (2019, November 2). How to use the Business Model Canvas for innovation. *Design a Better Business*. Retrieved from https://designabetter business.com/2017/11/02/how-to-us e-the-business-model-canvas-for-i nnovation/

18. Ibid.

19. Ibid.

20. Wood, M. (2020, January 31). Why your company needs a disruptive business model. *Fundera*. Retrieved from https://www.fundera.com/blog /disruptive-business-model

21. Ibid.

22. Much of this section is sourced from Moore, R. (2019, June 4). 11 disruptive innovation examples (and why Uber and Tesla don't make the cut. *OV Blog*. Retrieved from https://openviewpart ners.com/blog/11-disruptive-innov ation-examples-and-why-uber-and -tesla-dont-make-the-cut/#.Xqnm A6hKj-h

23. Material in this section is sourced from Bhadana, R. (2019, July 21). What is a disruptive business model? *Feedough*. Retrieved from https://ww w.feedough.com/what-is-disruptive -business-model/

CHAPTER 6

1. Bansal, T. (2021, December 10). How green is Tesla, really? *Forbes*. https:/ /www.forbes.com/sites/timabansal/ 2021/05/13/how-green-is-tesla-real ly/?sh=521b02631576

2. Reed, E. (2019, August 21). How to buy a Tesla. *Smart Asset*. https://smartas set.com/investing/how-to-buy-ates la#:~:text=Tesla%20offers%20two% 20ways%20to,buy%20it%20on%20t he%20spot

3. Rowland, C. (2018). Tesla, Inc.'s generic strategy and intensive growth startegies. *Panmore Institute*. http://panmore.com/tesla-motors-i nc-generic-strategy-intensive-grow th-strategies-analysis#:~:text=(Pri mary%20Strategy).-,Tesla%2C%20 Inc.,cars%20in%20the%20United% 20States

4. Daley, B. (2019, November 18). Tesla's business strategy is not chaotic—it's brilliant. *The Conversation*. https://the conversation.com/teslas-busines s-strategy-is-not-chaotic-its-brillia nt-127153

5. Dow, J. (2020, February 26). How to buy a Tesla in 2020: Everything you need to know. *Electrek*. https://electr ek.co/2020/02/26/how-to-buy-a-tesl a-everything-you-need-to-know/

6. Tesla. https://www.tesla.com/about

7. Anderson, G. (2020, November 17). Chipotle's digital-only location antici-pates new era for quick-serve res-taurants. *Forbes*. https://www.forbes .com/sites/retailwire/2020/11/18/chi potles-digital-only-location-anticipa tes-new-era-for-quick-serve-restau rants/?sh=2a01603e58d8

8. Duff, V. (n.d.). Difference between industry & market analysis. *Chron*. ht tps://smallbusiness.chron.com/diffe rence-between-industry-market-an alysis-41062.html

9. Watkins, M. D. (2007, September 10). Demystifying strategy: The what, who, how, and why. *Harvard Business Review*. https://hbr.org/2007/09/dem ystifying-strategy-the-what

10. Porter's generic strategies: Choosing your route to success. (n.d.). *Mind-Tools*. https://www.mindtools.com/p ages/article/newSTR_82.htm#:~:tex t=According%20to%20Porter's%20G eneric%20Strategies,Cost%20Lead ership%2C%20Differentiation%20an d%20Focus

11. Porter, M. E. (1985). *The competitive advantage: Creating and sustaining superior performance*. Free Press. (Republished with a new introduction, 1998).

12. Reed, E. (2019, August 21). How to buy a Tesla. *Smart Asset*. https://smartas set.com/investing/how-to-buy-a-tes la#:~:text=Tesla%20offers%20two% 20ways%20to,buy%20it%20on%20t he%20spot

13. Symonds, M. (2012). Stuck in the middle? Take the flexible approach. *Forbes*. https://www.forbes.com/site s/mattsymonds/2012/02/24/stuck-i n-the-middle-take-the-flexible-appr oach/#15676a222ebd

14. Wilson, M. (2019, July 22). Arby's is betting $3.9 billion that customers don't want fake meat. *Fast Company*. h ttps://www.fastcompany.com/90370 906/arbys-is-betting-customers-do nt-want-fake-meat

15. Martin, M. (2019, December 3). How Porter's five forces can help small

businesses analyze the competition. *Business News Daily*. https://www.b usinessnewsdaily.com/5446-porter s-five-forces.html

16. Ibid.

17. Frue, K. (2016, November 21). PESTLE analysis of Coca Cola. *Pestle Analysis*. https://pestleanalysis.com/ pestle-analysis-of-coca-cola/

18. Tarver, E. (2019, September 24). Why the "share of Coke" campaign is so successful. *Investopedia*. https://ww w.investopedia.com/articles/market s/100715/what-makes-share-coke-c ampaign-so-successful.asp#:~:text =Coca%2DCola%20empowered%20c onsumers%20to,in%20the%20hands %20of%20customers.&text=Consum ers%20shared%20more%20than%2 0500%2C000,Facebook%20followers %20that%20same%20year

19. All, R., & Luther, D. (2020, May 14). Scenario planning: Strategy, steps and practical examples. *Brainyard/ Oracle Institute*. https://www.netsuite .com/portal/business-benchmark-b rainyard/industries/articles/cfo-cen tral/scenario-planning.shtml

20. Mariton, J. (2020, March 9). What is scenario planning and how to use it. *SME*. https://www.smestrategy.net/ blog/what-is-scenario-planning-an d-how-to-use-it

21. Wilksinson, A., & Kupers, R. (2013) Living in the futures. *Harvard Busi-ness Review, 91*(5), 118–127.

22. Valentin, E. K. (2001). SWOT analysis from a resource-based view. *Journal of Marketing Theory & Practice, 9*(2), 54–68.

23. Barney, J. B. (2001). Is the resource-based "view" a useful perspective for strategic management research? Yes. *Academy of Management Review, 26*(1), 41–56.

24. Jurevicius, O. (2013). Resource based view. *Strategic Management Insight*. h ttps://strategicmanagementinsigh t.com/topics/resource-based-view .html

25. Powell, T. C. (2003). Varieties of com-petitive parity. *Strategic Management Journal, 24*(1), 61–86.

26. Ibid.; Smith, R. (n.d.). Explaining the VRIO framework. *Clear Point Strategy*. https://www.clearpointstrategy.com /vrio-framework/

27. Jurevicius, O. (2013). Competitive profile matrix. *Strategic Management*

Insight. https://strategicmanagement insight.com/tools/competitive-profil e-matrix-cpm.html

28. Ibid.

29. Mui, C. (2012, January 18). How Kodak failed. *Forbes.* https://www.forbes.c om/sites/chunkamui/2012/01/18/ho w-kodak-failed/#1bcc7e9f6f27

30. D'aveni, R. A. (2010). *Hypercompeti- tion.* Simon and Schuster; Rifkin, G. (1996, April 1). The art of hypercom- petition. *Strategy + Business.* https:// www.strategy-business.com/article/ 14886?gko=73753

31. d'Aveni, R. A. (1995). Coping with hypercompetition: Utilizing the new 7S's framework. *Academy of Manage- ment Perspectives, 9*(3), 45–57.

32. Maier, E. (2013, June 11). Transient advantage. *Guidewire.* https://www.g uidewire.com/blog/general-interest /transient-advantage#:~:text=As%2 0a%20textbook%20definition%2C%2 0Transient,advantages%20are%20of ten%20short%20lived.&text=Instead %20of%20building%20one%20advan tage,the%20velocity%20of%20comp etitive%20advantage

33. Dyrda, L. (2020, January 6). 15 things to know about Amazon's healthcare strategy heading into 2020. *Becker's Healthcare Review.* https://www.beck ershospitalreview.com/healthcare-i nformation-technology/15-things-t o-know-about-amazon-s-healthcar e-strategy-heading-into-2020.html

34. McGrath, R. G. (2013). Transient advantage. *Harvard Business Review, 91*(6), 62–70.

35. Maier, E. (2013, June 11). Transient advantage. *Guidewire.* https://www.g uidewire.com/blog/general-interest /transient-advantage#:~:text=As%2 0a%20textbook%20definition%2C%2 0Transient,advantages%20are%20of ten%20short%20lived.&text=Instead %20of%20building%20one%20advan tage,the%20velocity%20of%20comp etitive%20advantage

36. McGrath, R. G. (2013). Transient advantage. *Harvard Business Review, 91*(6), 62–70.

37. The 50 best workplaces for innova- tors. (2019, August 5). *Fast Company.* https://www.fastcompany.com/bes t-workplaces-for-innovators/2019

38. Ibid.

39. Iqbal, M. (2022, June 30). Zoom Revenue and Usage Statistics.

BusinessofApps. Retrieved from https ://www.businessofapps.com/data/zo om-statistics/

40. Yuan, E. (2020, February 26). Zoom's commitment to user support and business continuity during the Coro- navirus outbreak. *Zoom Blog.* https:// blog.zoom.us/zoom-commitment-us er-support-business-continuity-duri ng-coronavirus-outbreak/

41. Aten, J. (2020, March 26). Zoom became the most important app in the business world overnight. Here are five reasons. *Inc.* https://www.inc .com/jason-aten/heres-how-zoom-b ecame-most-important-app-in-worl d-its-really-quite-simple.html

42. Wertz, J. (2019, January 30). Why stealth mode could be the best growth tactic for your business. *Forbes.* https://www.forbes.com/sit es/jiawertz/2019/01/30/stealth-mod e-best-growth-tactic-startup-busin ess/#244c9ef11240 and https://www. fireflyon.com/

43. Lambert, F. (2019, December 28). 5 things Tesla is bringing to market in 2020. *Electrek.* https://electrek.co/20 19/12/2For example, 8/5-things-tesl a-bring-market-2020/

44. LeBeau, P. (2020, February 10). Tesla's competitors play catch-up on electric batteries. *CNBC.* https://ww w.cnbc.com/2020/02/10/teslas-co mpetitors-play-catch-up-on-electri c-batteries.html

45. Rifkin, G. (1996, April 1). The art of hypercompetition. *Strategy + Busi- ness.* https://www.strategy-business .com/article/14886?gko=73753

46. Ibid.

CHAPTER 7

1. About Us—4ocean. (2022). https:// www.4ocean.com/pages/about

2. Ibid.

3. Our Impact—Every pound pulled is documented and tracked—4ocean. (2022). https://www.4ocean.com/pag es/our-impact

4. Schulze, A. (n.d.). I've spent most of my life out on the water. *Oceano- graphic.* https://www.oceanographic magazine.com/features/4ocean-gu atemala/

5. Hart, M. (n.d.). What's the difference between sales and marketing? A

simple & easy primer. *HubSpot.* https ://blog.hubspot.com/sales/sales-an d-marketing

6. Hart, M. (n.d.). Cost-pus pricing: What is it and when to use it. *HubSpot.* https://blog.hubspot.com/sales/cos t-plus-pricing

7. Dholakia, U. M. (2018, July 12). When cost-plus pricing is a good idea. *Har- vard Business Review.* https://hbr.or g/2018/07/when-cost-plus-pricing-i s-a-good-idea

8. Kocak, Y. (2018, October 18). Compet- itive pricing: Definition, advantages, and disadvantages. *Prisync.* https://p risync.com/blog/competitive-pricin g-advantages-vs-disadvantages/#re al-life-competitive-pricing

9. Dawson, T. (2020, May 5). How Star- bucks uses pricing strategy for profit maximization. *Price Intelligently.* https ://www.priceintelligently.com/blog /bid/184451/how-starbucks-uses-p ricing-strategy-for-profit-maximiz ation

10. Dawson, T. (2020, May 11). Price skimming: Definition, pros and cons, strategy, and examples. *Price Intel- ligently.* https://www.priceintelligent ly.com/blog/bid/183669/ride-the-de mand-curve-price-skimming-and-y our-pricing-strategy

11. 5 of the best penetration pricing examples. (n.d.). *Intelligence node.* ht tps://www.intelligencenode.com/bl og/5-best-penetration-pricing-exa mples/

12. Stephen Fry's exclusive sleep story. (2020, July 17). *Calm blog.* https://blo g.calm.com/blog/stephen-fry-slee p-story-blue-gold

13. 3 types of sites that have qual- ity AdSense revenue. (n.d.). *Good AdSense.* https://www.google.com/in tl/en_uk/adsense/start/resources/ 3-types-of-sites/

14. Thacker, A. (2021, June 11). A primer on social media advertising products. *Linkedin.* https://www.linkedin.com/ pulse/product-primer-social-media- advertising-adi-thacker/; Newberry, C., & McLachlan, S. (2020, September 9). Social media advertising 101: How to get the most out of your ad budget. *Hootsuite.* https://blog.hoot suite.com/social-media-advertising /; Newberry, C. (2021, November 2). How to advertise on TikTok in 2022: An 8-step guide to using TikTok ads. *Hootsuite.* https://blog.hootsuite.com /tiktok-advertising/

15. Statista Research Department. (2022). U.S. social media ad spend 2022. *Statista*. https://www.statista.com/statistics/736971/social-media-ad-spend-usa/

16. Tak, C. (2021, March 5). What is in-app advertising? *AppLovin*. https://www.applovin.com/blog/what-is-in-app-advertising/

17. Zantal-Wiener, A. (n.d.). What is guerilla marketing? 7 examples to inspire your brand. *HubSpot*. https://blog.hubspot.com/marketing/guerilla-marketing-examples

18. Local & national TV advertising costs & how to advertise 2019. (2019). *Fit Small Business*. https://fitsmallbusiness.com/tv-advertising/#:~:text=For%20local%20television%20stations%2C%20advertisers,for%20upward%20of%20%245.25%20million

19. Data report: FIFA World Cup ad cost analysis. (2019). *SQAD*. https://sqad.com/news-room/sqad_reports/data-report-fifa-world-cup-ad-cost-analysis/#:~:text=2018%2D2019%20ANALYSIS&text=Fox%20charged%20%24506%2C605%20for%20a,2018%20men's%20World%20Cup%20finals

20. Epstein, A. (2020, April 1). Celebrities are warning us about coronavirus. We ranked their best and worst PSAs. *Quartz*. https://qz.com/1829339/all-the-celebrity-coronavirus-psas-ranked/

21. Trendjackers Team. (2017). 7 genius examples of product placement in TV & cinema. *Trendjackers*. https://trendjackers.com/7-genius-examples-of-product-placement/ and https://chrisdeblasio.com/2019/09/12/13-genius-examples-product-placement-tv-shows-movies/

22. Hsu, T. (2019, December 22). Future product placement in films and television will be tailored to individual viewers, say marketing executives. *Independent*. https://www.independent.co.uk/news/business/product-placement-future-film-tv-individual-viewers-direct-marketing-a9257046.html

23. Keskin, S. (2019, October 15). 7 tried-and-tested sales promotion examples that'll skyrocket your sales. *Sleeknote*. https://sleeknote.com/blog/sales-promotion-examples

24. Winkler, N. (2020, July 21). Ultimate flash sale ecommerce guide: How to sell over $3 billion on autopilot. *Shopify Plus*. https://www.shopify.com/enterprise/flash-sale

25. 9 sales promotion examples. (2019, March 1). *ThriveHive*. https://thrivehive.com/sales-promotion-examples/

26. Ibid.

27. 10 social media contest trends making waves in 2019. (2019, June 4). *ShortStack*. https://www.shortstack.com/blog/social-media-contest-trends/

28. Ibid.

29. Bernazzani, S. (n.d.). 18 examples of successful co-branding partnerships. *HubSpot*. https://blog.hubspot.com/marketing/best-cobranding-partnerships

30. Wynne, R. (2016, January 21). Five things everyone should know about public relations. *Forbes*. https://www.forbes.com/sites/robertwynne/2016/01/21/five-things-everyone-should-know-about-public-relations/#1829aaac2a2c

31. Hellmann's presents The Restaurant With No Food, making the best out of waste. (2019, May 21). *Social samosa*. http://www.socialsamosa.com/2019/05/hellmanns-the-restaurant-with-no-food/

32. Blair, I. (n.d.). Content marketing 101: A primer (part 2 of 2). *Build Fire*. https://buildfire.com/content-marketing-101-primer-part/#:~:text=Content%20marketing%20is%20a%20new,a%20successful%20digital%20marketing%20strategy

33. Dyakovskaya, A. (2017, June 22). The value of mission-driven content marketing. *NewsCred Insights*. https://insights.newscred.com/mission-driven-content-marketing/

34. This section is based on Baker, K. (2020). The ultimate guide to content marketing in 2020. *HubSpot*. https://blog.hubspot.com/marketing/content-marketing

35. French, K. (n.d.). 5 brands doing infographic marketing that will make you jealous. *Column Five Media*. https://www.columnfivemedia.com/5-brands-doing-infographic-marketing-the-right-way

36. Dyakovskaya, A. (2017, June 22). The value of mission-driven content marketing. *NewsCred Insights*. https://insights.newscred.com/mission-driven-content-marketing/

37. Gotter, A. (2018, July 9). B2B and B2C marketing: What's the difference? *Disruptive Advertising*. https://www.disruptiveadvertising.com/marketing/b2b-and-b2c/#:~:text="B2B"%20stands%20for%20"business,makers%20in%20any%20particular%20business.&text=B2C%20businesses%20sell%20products%20and%20services%20to%20customers%20for%20personal%20use

38. Ibid.

39. Conley, M. (n.d.). 10 examples of B2C campaigns that B2B marketers can learn from. *HubSpot*. https://blog.hubspot.com/agency/b2c-campaigns-b2b-marketers-learn

40. Prater, M. (n.d.). The sales cycle: The backbone of a successful sales effort. *HubSpot*. https://blog.hubspot.com/sales/sales-cycle

41. Rackham, N. (2020). *SPIN®-selling*. Routledge.

42. Bosschem, J. (2017, December 1). Sales techniques: 5 highly effective modern sales methods. *Teamleader*. https://blog.teamleader.eu/sales-marketing/sales-optimisation/sales-techniques

43. Das, S. (2020, February 4). Using N.E.A.T. selling methodology in your sales process. *Salesmate*. https://www.salesmate.io/blog/neat-selling-methodology-in-sales-process/

44. Burnam, E. (2019, April 9). What is inbound sales? *New Breed +*. https://www.newbreedmarketing.com/blog/what-is-inbound-sales#:~:text=Inbound%20sales%20is%20a%20sales,through%20the%20decision%2Dmaking%20process

45. This section is based on Wellington, E. (2019, November 19). The 5 key principles of customer-centric selling. *HelpScout*. https://www.helpscout.com/blog/customer-centric-selling/

CHAPTER 8

1. Mixtroz transforms corporate events—and their business model—to meet the needs of a virtual world. (n.d.). *Google startups*. https://startup.google.com/stories/mixtroz/

2. 6 questions with founder of innovative Mixtroz app. (2019, November 21). *Alabama.com*. https://www.al.com/business/2019/11/6-questions-with-founder-of-innovative-mixtroz-app.html

3. Mixtroz transforms corporate events—and their business model—to meet the needs of a virtual world.

(n.d.). *Google startups*. https://startup.google.com/stories/mixtroz/

4. Nijssen, E. (2014). *Entrepreneurial marketing: An effectual approach* (p. 29). Routledge.

5. Leonard, K. (2019, March 27). How to do a market segment analysis. *Chron*. https://smallbusiness.chron.com/market-segment-analysis-58771.html

6. Brunsman, B. J. (2017, March 23). P&G launches ad campaign to remedy bias against African-Americans. *Cincinnati Business Courier*. https://www.bizjournals.com/cincinnati/news/2017/03/23/p-g-launches-ad-campaign-to-remedy-bias-against.html

7. Scocco, D. (2006). Users, purchasers and influencers [Blog post]. *Innovation Zen*. http://innovationzen.com/blog/2006/12/06/users-purchasers-and-influencers

8. Blank, S., & Dorf, B. (2012). *The startup owner's manual* (pp. 87–88). K&S Ranch.

9. Blank, A. (2019, November 18). Why Taylor Swift is so influential (and how you can increase your influence). *Forbes*. https://www.forbes.com/sites/averyblank/2019/11/18/why-taylor-swift-is-so-influential-and-how-you-can-increase-your-influence/?sh=6079feb31020

10. Blank, S. (2017). Everything you ever wanted to know about marketing communications [Blog post]. *Steve Blank*. https://steveblank.com/2017/04/05/everything-you-ever-wanted-to-know-about-marketing-communications/

11. Stewart, D. W. (2018). *A primer on consumer behavior: A guide for managers*. Business Expert Press.

12. Magids, S., Zorfas, A., & Leemon, D. (2015, November). The new science of customer emotions: A better way to drive growth and profitability. *Harvard Business Review*, 66–76.

13. Kozomos, K. (2021, January 14). Top WD-40 uses. *WD-40*. https://wd40.co.uk/tips-and-tricks/uses-for-wd40/

14. Pedersen, L. (2019) *Forging an iron clad brand: A leader's guide*. Lioncrest.

15. What we do. (n.d.). *Consumer Reports*. https://www.consumerreports.org/cro/about-us/what-we-do/index.htm

16. Jones, S. (2014). The six stages of the consumer buying process and how to market to them. *Business 2 Community*. https://www.business2community.com/consumer-marketing/six-stages-consumer-buying-process-market-0811565

17. Market segmentation: Types, benefits and best practices. *Qualtrics*. https://www.qualtrics.com/experience-management/brand/what-is-market-segmentation/

18. Thomas, S. R. (2020, June 23). 4 types of market segmentation with real-world examples. *Yieldify*. https://www.yieldify.com/blog/types-of-market-segmentation/

19. Virag, J. (n.d.). Market segmentation: The no-nonsense guide. *Nutshell*. https://www.nutshell.com/blog/market-segmentation/

20. Ibid.

21. Mialki, S. (2020, Sept 10). Defining behavioral segmentation with 7 examples. *Instapage*. https://instapage.com/blog/behavioral-segmentation

22. Section is sourced from market segmentation: Types, benefits and best practices. *Qualtrics*. https://www.qualtrics.com/experience-management/brand/what-is-market-segmentation/; Dontigney, E. (2019, January 11). The advantages of marketing segmentation. *Chron*. https://smallbusiness.chron.com/advantages-marketing-segmentation-67156.html

23. Carman, A. (2020, April 3). Why Zoom became so popular. *The Verge*. https://www.theverge.com/2020/4/3/21207053/zoom-video-conferencing-security-privacy-risk-popularity

24. Michels, D. (2020, September 3). 6 reasons why Zoom is winning the video race. *No Jitter*. https://www.nojitter.com/video-collaboration-av/6-reasons-why-zoom-winning-video-race

25. Ibid.

CHAPTER 9

1. The Zappos Family core values. (2022). *Zapposinsights.com*. https://www.zapposinsights.com/about/core-values

2. Henshell, A. (2017, October 13). How 4 top startups are reinventing organizational structure. *Process.st*. https://www.process.st/organizational-structure/

3. Holacracy & self-organization (2014). *Zapposinsights.com*. https://www.zapposinsights.com/about/holacracy

4. Groth, A. (2013, December 30). Zappos is going holacratic: No job titles, no managers, no hierarchy. *Quartz*. https://qz.com/161210/zappos-is-going-holacratic-no-job-titles-no-managers-no-hierarchy/

5. Chander, A. D., Jr. (1988). Origins of the organization chart. *Harvard Business Review, 66*(2), 156–157.

6. This discussion is based on Bonoma, T. V., & Lawler, J. C. (1989). Chutes and ladders: Growing the general manager. *MIT Sloan Management Review, 30*(3), 27–37.

7. Shepard, J. M. (1969). Functional specialization and work attitudes. *Industrial Relations: A Journal of Economy and Society, 8*(2), 185–194.; Jagoda, A. (2013). Deskilling as the dark side of the work specialization. *International Journal of Academic Research, 5*(3), 331–334.

8. Owen Nieberding, A. (2014). Employee engagement and other bonding forces in organizations. *Consulting Psychology Journal: Practice and Research, 66*(4), 320–323; Price, J. L. (1968). The impact of departmentalization on interoccupational cooperation. *Human Organization, 27*(4), 362–368; Yeh, D., & Jeng, J. H. (2002). An empirical study of the influence of departmentalization and organizational position on software maintenance. *Journal of Software Maintenance and Evolution: Research and Practice, 14*(1), 65–82.

9. Davis, S. M. (1974). Two models of organization: Unity of command versus balance of power. *Sloan Management Review (pre-1986), 16*(1), 29–40; Wren, D. A., Bedeian, A. G., & Breeze, J. D. (2002). The foundations of Henri Fayol's administrative theory. *Management Decision, 40*(9), 906.

10. Davis, S. M. (1974). Two models of organization: Unity of command versus balance of power. *Sloan Management Review (pre-1986), 16*(1), 29–40; Fayol, H. (1949) *General and industrial management* (C. Storrs, Trans.). Sir Isaac Pitman & Sons; Wren, D. A., Bedeian, A. G., & Breeze, J. D. (2002). The foundations of Henri Fayol's administrative theory. *Management Decision, 40*(9), 906.

11. Hirsch, L., & Cullen, T. (2018, August 6). PepsiCo's Indra Nooyi to step

down after 12 years as CEO, President Ramon Laguarta to succeed her. *CNBC*. https://www.cnbc.com/2018/08/06/pepsicos-indra-nooyi-to-step-down-after-12-years-as-ceo-president-ra.html

12. Trentman, N. (2019, November 27). GE's new CFO has an $8 million incentive to stay. *The Wall Street Journal*. https://www.wsj.com/articles/ges-new-cfo-has-an-8-million-incentive-to-stay-11574897316

13. Dua, T. (2018, June 19). The 25 most innovative CMOs in the world in 2018. *Business Insider*. https://www.businessinsider.com/most-innovative-cmos-2018-5?r=US&IR=T

14. Krigsman, M. (2020, February 25). CIO strategy: Become a transformational chief information officer. *ZDNet*. https://www.zdnet.com/article/cio-strategy-become-a-transformational-chief-information-officer/

15. Enterprise Management 360. (2018, August 6). Top 10 CTOs ruling the world of tech. https://www.em360tech.com/tech-news/top-10-ctos-tech/

16. Raimondi, A., & Zenios, S. (2020, January 8). The role of COO is evolving, and it's more important than ever. *Quarts at Work*. https://qz.com/work/1781215/how-the-role-of-coo-is-changing/

17. Ouchi, W. G., & Dowling, J. B. (1974). Defining the span of control. *Administrative Science Quarterly, 19*(3), 357–365.

18. Riegel, D. (2019, August 15). 8 ways leaders delegate successfully. *Harvard Business Review*. https://hbr.org/2019/08/8-ways-leaders-delegate-successfully

19. Fayol, H., & Storrs, C. (1949). *General and industrial management* (Constance Storrs, Trans.). Sir Isaac Pitman & Sons.

20. Ibid.

21. Loehr, A. (n.d.). Should your organization be decentralized? *Anne Loehr Blog*. https://www.anneloehr.com/2018/07/19/should-your-organization-be-decentralized/

22. Peters, G. (1988). Organisation as social relationship, formalisation and standardisation: A Weberian approach to concept formation. *International Sociology, 3*(3), 267–282.

23. Gingiss, D. (2019, October 7). 6 customer service tenets used by Amazon to create effortless experiences. *Forbes*. https://www.forbes.com/sites/dangingiss/2019/10/07/6-customer-service-tenets-used-by-amazon-to-create-effortless-experiences/#7e39dd1a3fc5

24. Pesico.com. https://www.pepsico.com/about/about-the-company

25. Simpson, R. L. (1959). Vertical and horizontal communication in formal organizations. *Administrative Science Quarterly, 76*(5), 188–196; Aoki, M. (1986). Horizontal vs. vertical information structure of the firm. *The American Economic Review, 76*(5), 971–983.

26. Henshall, A. (2017). How 4 top start-ups are reinventing organizational structure. *Process.st*. https://www.process.st/organizational-structure/

27. Sobiya. (n.d.). Network organizational structure: Examples, definition, advantages & disadvantages. *Advergize*. https://advergize.com/business/network-organizational-structure-examples-definition-advantages-disadvantages/

28. Vasquez, M. (2019, March 6). Organizational chart: Holocratic style in practice. https://www.youtube.com/watch?v=tzSwQPI4ZCQ

29. Martinez, L. (2021). COVID-19 reveals why flat organizations thrive: Steal their secrets. *Great Place to Work®*. https://www.greatplacetowork.com/resources/blog/covid-19-puts-a-spotlight-on-why-flat-organizations-thrive

30. Courtright, J. A., Fairhurst, G. T., & Rogers, L. E. (1989). Interaction patterns in organic and mechanistic system. *Academy of Management Journal, 32*(4), 773–802; Gillen, D. J., & Carroll, S. J. (1985). Relationship of managerial ability to unit effectiveness in more organic versus more mechanistic departments. *Journal of Management Studies, 22*(6), 668–676; Zanzi, A. (1987). How organic is your organization? Determinants of organic/mechanistic tendencies in a public accounting firm. *Journal of Management Studies, 24*(2), 125–140; Dust, S. B., Resick, C. J., & Mawritz, M. B. (2014). Transformational leadership, psychological empowerment, and the moderating role of mechanistic–organic contexts. *Journal of Organizational Behavior, 35*(3), 413–433.

31. Toren, N. (1976). Bureaucracy and professionalism: A reconsideration of Weber's thesis. *Academy of Management Review, 1*(3), 36–46; Walton, E. J. (2005). The persistence of bureaucracy: A meta-analysis of Weber's model of bureaucratic control. *Organization Studies, 26*(4), 569–600; Weiss, R. M. (1983). Weber on bureaucracy: Management consultant or political theorist? *Academy of Management Review, 8*(2), 242–248.

32. Ibid.

33. Sisney, L. (2019, February 26). The top 10 signs it's time to change your organizational structure. *Organizational Physics*. https://organizationalphysics.com/2019/02/26/the-top-10-signs-its-time-to-change-your-organizational-structure/

34. Market Insider. (2018, December 11). Braidio acquires InnoStreams to create workstream intelligence for agile enterprises. https://markets.businessinsider.com/news/stocks/braidio-acquires-innostreams-to-create-workstream-intelligence-for-agile-enterprises-1027797942

35. Foster, W. (2020, March 18). How to manage a remote team. *Zapier*. https://zapier.com/learn/remote-work/how-manage-remote-team/

36. Kimberly, J. R., & Miles, R. H. (1980). *The organizational life cycle*. Jossey-Bass.

37. Ward, M. (2017, May 25). Mark Zuckerberg returns to the Harvard dorm room where Facebook was born. *CNBC Make It*. https://www.cnbc.com/2017/05/25/mark-zuckerberg-returns-to-the-harvard-dorm-where-facebook-was-born.html

38. Influencer Marketing Hub. (2020, February 3). The incredible rise of TikTok. https://influencermarketinghub.com/tiktok-growth/

39. Evans, D. (2019, October 12). Apple's newest iPhone relies on cameras to hide its lack of innovation. *CNBC*. https://www.cnbc.com/2019/10/12/apples-newest-iphone-lacks-innovation.html

CHAPTER 10

1. Berger, S. (2018, October 23). How this 22-year-old with Down syndrome build a multimillion-dollar business off his love of crazy socks. *CNBC*. https://www.cnbc.com/2018/10/22/22-year-old-with-down-syndrome-founded-johns-crazy-socks.html

2. John's Crazy Socks. (2022). About Us. https://johnscrazysocks.com/pages/our-story

3. Berger, S. (2018, October 23). How this 22-year-old with Down syndrome build a multimillion-dollar business off his love of crazy socks. *CNBC*. https://www.cnbc.com/2018/10/22/22-year-old-with-down-syndrome-founded-johns-crazy-socks.html

4. Kraaijenbrink, J. (2019, November 8). How to bring sustainability to the masses: Tony's Chocolonely's impact strategy. *Forbes*. https://www.forbes.com/sites/jeroenkraaijenbrink/2019/11/08/how-to-bring-sustainability-to-the-masses-tonys-chocolonely-impact-strategy/#6a682d02712a

5. Cronin, M. X. (2021, February 28). John's Crazy Socks donates $1,000 for Covid-19 frontline workers at Good Samaritan Hospital. *John's Crazy Socks*. https://johnscrazysocks.com/blogs/news/john-s-crazy-socks-donates-1-000-for-covid-19-frontline-workers-at-good-samaritan-hospital

6. Perry, T. (2019, October 7). Dick's CEO reveals he destroyed $5 million worth of assault weapons after store-wide ban. *Good*. https://www.good.is/dicks-ceo-admits-it-destroyed-5-million-worth-of-assault-weapons-after-banning-from-stores?utm_source=The+Upworthiest&utm_campaign=95410f48b4-EMAIL_CAMPAIGN_2019_07_22_07_15_COPY_01&utm_medium=email&utm_term=0_78f827fba6-95410f48b4-238665857;%20aso%20see%20link%20below%20supporting%20Dick%E2%80%99s%20focus%20on%20health%20and%20well%20being%E2%80%A6one%20of%20UN%20Sustainability%20goals:%20%20https://sustainablebrands.com/read/marketing-and-comms/top-5-companies-that-effectively-amplified-their-impact-in-2018

7. Sterling, D. (2019, October 18). This is what I learned as a millennial managing other millennials. *Fast Company*. https://www.fastcompany.com/90418313/this-is-what-i-learned-as-a-millennial-managing-other-millennials

8. Lavoie, A. (2017, March 21). How to engage employees through your company vision statement. *Entrepreneur*. https://www.entrepreneur.com/article/290803

9. Forsey, C. (n.d.). 18 core company values that will shape your culture & inspire your employees. *HubSpot*. https://blog.hubspot.com/marketing/company-values

10. Castrillon, C. (2021, December 29). Why 2022 is the year of workplace culture. *Forbes*. https://www.forbes.com/sites/carolinecastrillon/2021/12/29/why-2022-is-the-year-of-workplace-culture/?sh=4627aa5c1bbb

11. Schuneman, F. (2019, March 14). The importance of workplace culture. *Invista*. https://www.invistaperforms.org/the-importance-of-workplace-culture/

12. Colvin, G. (2017, June 11). Inside Wells Fargo's plan to fix its culture post-scandal. *Fortune*. https://fortune.com/2017/06/11/wells-fargo-scandal-culture/

13. The Startups Team. (2019, June 20). The best and worst company culture examples. *Startups.com*. https://www.startups.com/library/expert-advice/best-worst-company-culture-examples

14. Semarjian, M. (2019, October 17). How this founder built one of the happiest companies during the recession. *Entrepreneur*. https://www.entrepreneur.com/article/340380

15. Hartnell, C. A., Ou, A. Y., & Kinicki, A. (2011). Organizational culture and organizational effectiveness: A meta-analytic investigation of the competing values framework's theoretical suppositions. *Journal of Applied Psychology, 96*(4), 677–694.; Quinn, R. E., & Rohrbaugh, J. (1983). A spatial model of effectiveness criteria: Towards a competing values approach to organizational analysis. *Management Science, 29*(3), 363–377.

16. Based on the competing values framework in Cameron, K., & Quinn, R. (2011). *Diagnosing and changing organizational culture* (3rd ed.). Jossey Bass.

17. Workpop. (2017, November 21). 6 ways to create a competitive work culture that's team first (and not me first). *Inc*. https://www.inc.com/workpop/6-ways-to-create-a-competitive-work-culture-thats-team-first-and-not-me-first.html

18. Grensing-Pophal, L. (2018, April 12). 4 distinct types of corporate culture—which is yours? *HR Daily Advisor*. https://hrdailyadvisor.blr.com/2018/04/12/4-distinct-types-corporate-culture/

19. Hartnell, C. A., Ou, A. Y., & Kinicki, A. (2011). Organizational culture and organizational effectiveness; Quinn and Rohrbaugh. A spatial model of effectiveness criteria.

20. Laschinger, H. K. S., Wong, C. A., Cummings, G. G., & Grau, A. L. (2014). Resonant leadership and workplace empowerment: The value of positive organizational cultures in reducing workplace incivility. *Nursing Economics, 32*(1), 5–44.

21. Torman, M. (2019, October 2). Zoom employees the happiest in the U.S. *Zoom Blog*. https://blog.zoom.us/wordpress/2019/10/02/zoom-employees-happiest/

22. Zoom. (2021, January 22). Zoom: A best place to work in 2021! *Zoom*. https://blog.zoom.us/zoom-best-place-to-work-2021/

23. Goffee, R., & Jones, G. (1998). *The character of a corporation: How your company's culture can make or break your business*. HarperCollins.

24. Kenyon, J. (2019, January 14). When it comes to creating a great company culture, think back to college. *Entrepreneur*. https://www.entrepreneur.com/article/326167

25. Goffee, R., & Jones, G. (1998). *The character of a corporation: How your company's culture can make or break your business*. HarperCollins.

26. Lareau, J. (2019, October 6). GM's ignition switch crisis created culture shift to spot defects. *Detroit Free Press*. https://www.boston.com/cars/car-news/2019/10/06/gms-ignition-switch-crisis-created-culture-shift-to-spot-defects

27. Goffee, R., & Jones, G. (1998). *The character of a corporation: How your company's culture can make or break your business*. HarperCollins.

28. Sullivan, M. (2018, October 25). 10 ways to get axed in Netflix's cutthroat work culture. *Fast Company*. https://www.fastcompany.com/90257371/10-ways-to-get-axed-in-netflix-cutthroat-work-culture

29. Goffee, R., & Jones, G. (1998). *The character of a corporation: How your company's culture can make or break your business*. HarperCollins.

30. Ruiz-Palomino, P., Martínez-Cañas, R., & Joan, F. (2013, August). Ethical culture and employee outcomes: The mediating role of person-organization fit. *Journal of Business Ethics*,

116(1), 173–188; Meinert, D. (2014, April). Creating an ethical culture. *Human Resource Management, 59*(4), 22–27.

31. Blue California News Center. (2021, February 23). Blue Shield of California named one of the world's most ethical companies for fifth consecutive year. https://news.blueshieldca.com/2021/02/23/blue-shield-of-california-is-named-one-of-the-worlds-most-ethical-companies-for-fifth-consecutive-year

32. Fawcett, S. E., Brau, J. C., Rhoads, G. K., Whitlark, D., & Fawcett, A. M. (2008). Spirituality and organizational culture: Cultivating the ABCs of an inspiring workplace. *International Journal of Public Administration, 31*(4), 420–438.

33. McLaughlin, C. (2009). Spirituality and ethics in business. *The Center for Visionary Leadership.* http://www.visionarylead.org/spirituality-in-business.html

34. Gardner, W. L., Reithel, B. J., Cogliser, C. C., Walumbwa, F. O., & Foley, R. T. (2012). Matching personality and organizational culture: Effects of recruitment strategy and the Five-Factor Model on subjective person–organization fit. *Management Communication Quarterly, 26*(4), 585–622.

35. Wasserman, T. (2019, October 11). Half of millennials and 75% of Gen Zers have left their job for mental health reasons. *CNBC @ Work.* https://www.cnbc.com/2019/10/11/mental-health-issues-cause-record-numbers-of-gen-x-z-to-leave-jobs.html

36. Klara, R. (2018, August 2). Move over, pink Cadillac—Mary Kay is rewarding sales reps with Mini Coopers now. *Adweek.* https://www.adweek.com/brand-marketing/move-over-pink-cadillac-mary-kay-is-rewarding-sales-reps-with-mini-coopers-now/

37. Downes, S. (2020, January 15). If your team constantly checks email and slack after hours, you might need to set a formal policy. Here's why. *Inc.* https://www.inc.com/sophie-downes/after-hours-work-communication-rules-ceo-survey.html

38. West. M., & Judson, K. (2017, August 26). Want to strengthen workplace culture? Design a ritual. *HuffPost.* https://www.huffpost.com/entry/want-to-strengthen-workpl_b_11730914

39. Ewoldt, J. (2015, October 2). Did someone really return a set of tires to Nordstrom? *Star Tribune.* https://www.startribune.com/did-someone-really-return-a-set-of-tires-to-nordstrom/330414071/

CHAPTER 11

1. Based on an interview conducted by Heidi Neck with Tracy Skelly on September 27, 2021, via Zoom.

2. Mintzberg, H. (1973). *The nature of managerial work.* Harper & Row.

3. Asseo, L. (2019). How women can empower themselves to be strong leaders. *Swaay.* Retrieved from https://www.swaay.com/women-leaders

4. Reints, R. (2018, September). Domino's ends 100 years of free pizza campaign after 350 people get logo tattoos. *Fortune.* Retrieved from https://fortune.com/2018/09/12/dominos-pizza-tattoos/

5. Sharma, G. (2018, August). 4 strategies to help improve your customer service standards. *Social Media Today.* Retrieved from https://www.socialmediatoday.com/news/4-strategies-to-help-improve-your-customer-service-standards/529799

6. Cremades, A. (2018). How to create a business plan. *Forbes.* Retrieved from https://www.forbes.com/sites/alejandrocremades/2018/07/24/how-to-create-a-business-plan/#64d9c0d37391

7. World Health Organization. Retrieved from https://www.who.int/sdg/global-action-plan

8. The North Face. Retrieved from https://www.thenorthface.co.uk/about-us/careers/employees.html

9. 16 best eco-friendly wordpress themes for 2020 [Blog post]. *HubSpot.* Retrieved from https://blog.hubspot.com/website/best-environmental-wordpress-themes

10. Taylor, B. (2019, December). To build a strong culture, create rules that are unique to your company. *Harvard Business Review.* Retrieved from https://hbr.org/2019/12/to-build-a-strong-culture-create-rules-that-are-unique-to-your-company

11. Marks, O. (2021, September 7). "If you have inner strength, you can achieve whatever you want": *Vogue* meets Emma Raducanu, the British teen taking tennis by storm. *Vogue.* Retrieved from https://www.vogue.co.uk/arts-and-lifestyle/article/emma-raducanu-interview

12. Hess, A. (2019) The 25 most in-demand technical skills of 2019, according to LinkedIn. *CNBC Make It.* Retrieved from https://www.cnbc.com/2019/01/08/the-25-most-in-demand-technical-skills-of-2019-according-to-linkedin-.html

13. McDowell, E. (2019). The 45 most beloved CEOs in America, according to employees. *Business Insider.* Retrieved from https://www.businessinsider.com/best-ceos-ranking-glassdoor-companies-employees-2019-7?r=US&IR=T#24-brad-jackson-slalom-22

14. Coleman, B. (2019). 6 ways real leaders lead as taught by CBS's "Undercover Boss." *Inc.* Retrieved from https://www.inc.com/bernard-coleman/6-ways-real-leaders-lead-as-taught-by-cbs-undercover-boss.html

15. See, for example, Dwyer, C. P. (2017). *Critical thinking: Conceptual perspectives and practical guidelines.* Cambridge University Press; Lack, C., & Rousseau, J. (2016). *Critical thinking, science, and pseudoscience: Why we can't trust our brains.* Springer.

16. Plummer, M. (2019, October). A short guide to building your team's critical thinking skills. *Harvard Business Review.* Retrieved from https://hbr.org/2019/10/a-short-guide-to-building-your-teams-critical-thinking-skills

17. Lui, J. (2019). The 10 most in-demand soft skills to master if you want a raise, promotion or new job in 2020. *CNBC Make It.* Retrieved from https://www.cnbc.com/2019/11/21/10-top-soft-skills-to-master-for-2020-if-you-want-a-raise-promotion-or-new-job.html

18. For a review of leadership research, see House, R. J., & Aditya, R. N. (1997). The social scientific study of leadership: Quo vadis? *Journal of Management, 23*(3), 409–473; Jago, A. G. (1982). Leadership: Perspectives in theory and research. *Management Science, 28*(3), 315–336.

19. Monarth, H. (2019). 3 reasons why leading with fear is a terrible idea. *Fast Company.* Retrieved from https://www.fastcompany.com/90429748/3-reasons-why-leading-with-fear-is-a-terrible-idea

20. Huffington, A. (2018, January). Stop rewarding a culture of burnout. *National Retail Federation.* Retrieved from https://nrf.com/blog/arianna-huffington-stop-rewarding-culture-burnout

21. Flybits named winner in Institute for Sustainability's smart wayfinding competition. *Flybits.* Retrieved from https://www.flybits.com/about-us/press-release/flybits-named-winner-institute-sustainabilitys-smart-wayfinding-competition/

22. Schwantes, M. (2019). If you haven't learned these 6 leadership lessons, you're limiting your success. *Inc.* Retrieved from https://www.inc.com/marcel-schwantes/if-you-havent-learned-these-6-leadership-lessons-youre-limiting-your-success.html?cid=hmhero

23. Hersey, P., Blanchard, K. H., & Johnson, D. E. (2007). *Management of organizational behavior* (Vol. 9). Prentice Hall; Blanchard, K. H., Zigarmi, D., & Nelson, R. B. (1993). Situational Leadership® after 25 years: A retrospective. *Journal of Leadership Studies*, *1*(1), 21–36; Luo, H., & Liu, S. (2014). Effect of situational leadership and employee readiness match on organizational citizenship behavior in China. *Social Behavior and Personality: An International Journal*, *42*(10), 1725–1732; Guilherme, T., & Flavio, F. (2017); Implementation of lean manufacturing and situational leadership styles an empirical study. *Leadership and Organisation Development*, *38*(7), 948–959.

24. World Economic Forum (2020). Diversity, Equity and Inclusion 4.0: A toolkit for leaders to accelerate social progress in the future of work. Retrieved from https://www.weforum.org/reports/diversity-equity-and-inclusion-4-0-a-toolkit-for-leaders-to-accelerate-social-progress-in-the-future-of-work

25. University of Michigan (n.d.). Defining DEI. Retrieved from https://diversity.umich.edu/about/defining-dei/

26. Foma, E. (2014). Impact on workplace diversity. *Review of Integrative Business & Economics Research*, *3*(1), 402–410.

27. Goldin, C., & Rouse, C. (2000). Orchestrating impartiality: The impact of "blind" auditions on female musicians. *The American Economic Review*, *90*(4), 715–741.

28. Heinz, K. (2021, August 10). What does diversity, equity and inclusion mean in the workplace? *Built In.* Retrieved from https://builtin.com/diversity-inclusion/what-does-dei-mean-in-the-workplace

29. Ferdman, B. M. (2013). Frameworks for understanding inclusion. In B. M. Ferdman & B. R. Deane (Eds.), *Diversity at work: The practice of inclusion.* Jossey-Bass.

30. O'Donovan, D. (2018). Diversity and inclusion in the workplace. In C. Machado & J. P. Davim (Eds.), *Organizational Behavior and Human Resource Management*, pp. 73–108, Springer International Publishing.

31. T. Barnes (2018, May 29). Starbucks closes 8,000 stores to give staff diversity training amid race storm. *Independent* https://www.independent.co.uk/news/world/americas/starbucks-stores-closed-diversity-training-racial-bias-philadelphia-arrests-racist-a8374426.html

32. Ibid.

33. Ibid.

34. 10 companies with effective DE&I policies. (2021, January 21). *Comparably.* Retrieved from https://www.comparably.com/news/10-companies-with-effective-dei-policies/

35. Pedulla, D. (2020, March 20). Diversity and inclusion efforts that really work. *Harvard Business Review.* Retrieved from https://hbr.org/2020/05/diversity-and-inclusion-efforts-that-really-work

36. Powerful ways to promote diversity, equity and inclusion in the workplace. (2021, May 12). *InStride.* Retrieved from https://www.instride.com/insights/diversity-equity-inclusion-in-the-workplace/

37. Ibid.

38. Ibid.

39. Ibid.

40. Ibid.

41. Ibid.

CHAPTER 12

1. JetBlue's award-winning employer-sponsored college degree program, JetBlue Scholars, reaches a milestone—250 degrees conferred. (2019). *JetBlue.com.* http://www.mediaroom.jetblue.com/investor-relations/press-releases/2019/12-04-2019-194804610#:~:text=Nearly%20700%20JetBlue%20crewmembers%20are,bachelor's%20degree%20through%20JetBlue's%20model

2. JetBlue adds Peirce College to its JetBlue Scholars employer-sponsored college degree program. (2021, April 30). *Businesswire.* https://www.businesswire.com/news/home/20210430005454/en/JetBlue-Adds-Peirce-College-to-its-JetBlue-Scholars-Employer-Sponsored-College-Degree-Program

3. Airway News. (2014, May 7). Inside JetBlue University. *Forbes.* https://www.forbes.com/sites/airchive/2014/05/07/jetblue-university/?sh=5f13820e196b

4. Stewart, G., & Brown, K. (2019). *Human resource management* (4th ed.). Wiley.

5. How important is job satisfaction in today's workplace?. (2019). *Villanova University.* https://www.villanovau.com/resources/hr/importance-of-job-satisfaction-in-the-workplace/

6. Stewart, G., & Brown, K. (2019). *Human resource management* (4th ed.). Wiley.

7. Gartner survey shows global talent shortage is now the top emerging risk facing organization. (2019, January 17). *Gartner.* https://www.gartner.com/en/newsroom/press-releases/2019-01-17-gartner-survey-shows-global-talent-shortage-is-now-the-top-emerging-risk-facing-organizations

8. Gillett, R. (2017, September 20). Trader Joe's was voted one of the best places to work—and a former employee says the reason is the managers. *Business Insider.* https://www.businessinsider.com/why-employees-love-working-at-trader-joes-2017-9; Speizer, I. (2004). The grocery chain that shouldn't be. *Fast Company.* https://www.fastcompany.com/48666/grocery-chain-shouldnt-be

9. Miller, C., & Yar, S. (2019, September 20). Young people are going to save us all from office life. *New York Times.* https://www.nytimes.com/2019/09/17/style/generation-z-millennials-work-life-balance.html

10. Phillips, P. (2019, October 16). The evolving role of HR in a gig economy. *Forbes.* https://www.forbes.com/sites/forbeshumanresourcescouncil/2

019/10/16/the-evolving-role-of-hr-i n-a-gig-economy/#3c2c182761a3

11. Kaminski, S. (2022, January 4). 5 HR challenges (and solutions) for 2022. *BenefitsPRO*. https://www.benefitsp ro.com/2022/01/04/5-hr-challenge s-and-solutions-for-2022/?slreturn= 20220217171149

12. Jaiswal, A., Arun, C. J., & Varma, A. (2022). Rebooting employees: Upskilling for artificial intelligence in multinational corporations. *The International Journal of Human Resource Management, 33*(6), 1179–1208.

13. How to build a successful upskilling program. (2022, January 18). *Harvard Business Review*. https://hbr.org/202 2/01/how-to-build-a-successful-ups killing-program

14. Hunt, V., Layton, D., & Prince, S. (2015, January 1). Why diversity matters. *McKinsey & Company*. https://w ww.mckinsey.com/business-functio ns/organization/our-insights/why-di versity-matters#

15. Nkomo, S. M. (1988). Strategic planning for human resources—let's get started. *Long Range Planning, 21*(1), 66–72.

16. Job analysis. (n.d.). *University of Nebraska–Lincoln human resources*. h ttps://hr.unl.edu/compensation/nuva lues/jobanalysis.shtml/

17. Jacobson, N., Trojanowski, L., & Dewa, C. S. (2012). What do peer support workers do? A job description. *BMC Health Services Research, 12*(1), 205.

18. Arthur, D. (2012). *Recruiting, interviewing, selecting & orienting new employees*. AMACOM.

19. Zaballero, A. G., & Kim, Y. (2012). Theoretical frameworks and models supporting the practice of leveraging workforce diversity. In C. L. Scott & M. Y. Byrd (Eds.), *Handbook of research on workforce diversity in a global society: Technologies and concepts* (pp. 463–480). Business Science Reference/IGI Global.

20. Harrison, D. A., Price, K. H., Gavin, J. H., & Florey, A. T. (2002). Time, teams, and task performance: Changing effects of surface-and deep-level diversity on group functioning. *Academy of Management Journal, 45*(5), 1029–1045.; Wang, J., Cheng, G. H. L., Chen, T., & Leung, K. (2019). Team creativity/innovation in culturally diverse teams: A

meta-analysis. *Journal of Organizational Behavior, 40*(6), 693–708.

21. Wang, J., Cheng, G. H. L., Chen, T., & Leung, K. (2019). Team creativity/innovation in culturally diverse teams: A meta-analysis. *Journal of Organizational Behavior, 40*(6), 693–708.

22. McNiff, S. (2020, July 16). Many older Americans face ageism every day, survey finds. *US News & World Report*. https://www.usnews.com/news/he alth-news/articles/2020-07-16/man y-older-americans-face-ageism-eve ry-day-survey-finds

23. Cook, L. (2018, December 21). Ageism in the workplace "starts at 40" for women. *Financial Times*. https://www .ft.com/content/e4141576-04eb-11e 9-99df-6183d3002ee1

24. Cilluffo, A., & D'Vera, C. (2019, April 11). 6 demographic trends shaping the U.S. and the world in 2019. *Pew Research Center*. https://www.pewre search.org/fact-tank/2019/04/11/6-d emographic-trends-shaping-the-u-s -and-the-world-in-2019/

25. Byars-Winston, A., Fouad, N., & Wen, Y. (2015). Race/ethnicity and sex in US occupations, 1970–2010: Implications for research, practice, and policy. *Journal of Vocational Behavior, 87*, 54–70; Humes, K., & Hogan, H. (2015). Do current race and ethnicity concepts reflect a changing America? In G. F. Koeske (Ed.), *Race and social problems* (pp. 15–38). Springer.

26. 10 companies around the world that are embracing diversity in a BIG way. (n.d.). *socialtalent*. https://www.socia ltalent.com/blog/recruitment/10-co mpanies-around-the-world-that-ar e-embracing-diversity

27. Roh, H., & Kim, E. (2016). The business case for gender diversity: Examining the role of human resource management investments. *Human Resource Management, 55*(3), 519–534.

28. 2022 State of the Gender Pay Gap Report. (2022, March 15). *Payscale*. ht tps://www.payscale.com/research-a nd-insights/gender-pay-gap/

29. Treisman, R. (2022, February 22). The U.S. national women's soccer team wins $24 million in equal pay settlement. *NPR*. https://www.npr.or g/2022/02/22/1082272202/women-s occer-contracts-equal-pay-settlem ent-uswnt#:~:text=The%20U.S.%20n ational%20women%E2%80%99s%2

0soccer%20team%20wins%20%242 4%20million%20in%20equal%20pay %20settlement&text=via%20Getty% 20Images-,Members%20of%20the% 20World%20Cup%2Dwinning%20U.S .%20women%E2%80%99s%20team %20take,July%202019%20in%20Ne w%20York

30. Huber, C., & O'Rourke, S. (2017). How to accelerate gender diversity on boards. *McKinsey Quarterly, 1*, 116–120.

31. Jackson, A. E. (2020, June 5). Amazing companies that champion LGBTQ equality hiring now. *Glassdoor*. https:/ /www.glassdoor.com/blog/companie s-lgbtq-equality/

32. Liptak, A. (2020, June 16). Civil rights law protects gay and transgender workers, Supreme Court rules. *New York Times*. https://www.nytimes.c om/2020/06/15/us/gay-transgende r-workers-supreme-court.html

33. Telwatte, A., Anglim, J., Wynton, S. K., & Moulding, R. (2017). Workplace accommodations for employees with disabilities: A multilevel model of employer decision-making. *Rehabilitation Psychology, 62*(1), 7–19.; Cleveland, J. N., Barnes-Farrell, J. L., & Ratz, J. M. (1997). Accommodation in the workplace. *Human Resource Management Review, 7*(1), 77–107.

34. Winiarski, D. (2019, October 29). Hiring the disabled is good for business. *TLNT*. https://www.tlnt.com/hiring-t he-disabled-is-good-for-business/

35. Jerdee, C. (2019, April 23). What companies gain by including persons with disabilities. *World Economic Forum*. ht tps://www.weforum.org/agenda/201 9/04/what-companies-gain-includin g-persons-disabilities-inclusion/

36. Miller, C. (2019). Affirmative action and its persistent effects: A new perspective. *California Management Review, 61*(3), 19–33; Selmi, M. (2002). The price of discrimination: The nature of class action employment discrimination litigation and its effects. *Texas Law Review, 81*, 1249.

37. U.S. Equal Employment Opportunity Commission. (n.d.). https://www.eeo c.gov/overview

38. Flynn, K. (2020, June 11). Refinery29 is reeling from claims of racism and toxic work culture. *CNN Business*. htt ps://edition.cnn.com/2020/06/11/me dia/refinery29-workplace-culture/i ndex.html

39. Schawbel, D. (2012, August 15). The power within: Why internal recruiting and hiring are on the rise. *Time*. http://business.time.com/2012/08/15/the-power-within-why-internal-recruiting-hiring-are-on-the-rise

40. Venneri, A. (2018, January 18). Social recruiting is growing. Are you prepared? *Forbes*. https://www.forbes.com/sites/gradsoflife/2018/01/18/social-recruiting-is-growing-are-you-prepared/#6c0413f29cae

41. Simon, R. (2020, January 25). The company of second chances. *The Wall Street Journal*. https://www.wsj.com/articles/the-company-of-second-chances-11579928401?mod=hp_listc_pos2

42. Peter, A. (2020, February 12). The Body Shop will start hiring the first person who applies for any retail job. *Fast Company*. https://www.fastcompany.com/90462746/the-body-shop-will-start-hiring-the-first-person-who-applies-for-any-retail-job

43. Farr, J. L., & Tippins, N. T. (Eds.). (2013). *Handbook of employee selection*. Routledge.

44. Arnold, J. T. (2010). Ramping up onboarding. *HRMagazine, 55*(5), 75–78.; Snell, A. (2006). Researching onboarding best practice: Using research to connect onboarding processes with employee satisfaction. *Strategic HR Review, 5*(6), 32–35.

45. Carucci, R. (2018, December 3). To retain new hires, spend more time onboarding them. *Harvard Business Review*. https://hbr.org/2018/12/to-retain-new-hires-spend-more-time-onboarding-them

46. Statista Research Department. (2022, February 7). Training industry in the U.S. (2021). *Statista*. https://www.statista.com/topics/4896/training-industry-in-the-us/#dossierKeyfigures

47. Forray, J. M. (2010). Management and leadership development. *Academy of Management Learning & Education, 9*(1), 145–147.

48. Employee training and development is the biggest HR focus area in 2019. (2019, January 7). *PayScale*. https://www.payscale.com/compensation-today/2019/01/employee-training-development

49. Manyika, J., Lund, S., Chui, M., Bughin, J., Woetzel, J., Batra, P., Ko, R., & Sanghvi, S. (2017, November 28). Jobs lost, jobs gained: What the future of work will mean for jobs, skills, and wages. *McKinsey & Company*. https://www.mckinsey.com/featured-insights/future-of-work/jobs-lost-jobs-gained-what-the-future-of-work-will-mean-for-jobs-skills-and-wages

50. Roberts, G. E. (2003). Employee performance appraisal system participation: A technique that works. *Public Personnel Management, 32*(1), 89–98.

51. Wigert, B., & Mann, A. (2017, September 25). Give performance reviews that actually inspire employees. *Gallup*. https://www.gallup.com/workplace/236135/give-performance-reviews-actually-inspire-employees.aspx

52. Luckwaldt, J. H. (2018, December 26). 95 percent of managers hate performance reviews. So why are we still doing them? *PayScale*. https://www.payscale.com/career-news/2018/12/95-percent-of-managers-hate-performance-reviews-so-why-are-we-still-doing-them

53. Wigert, B., & Mann, A. (2017, September 25). Give performance reviews that actually inspire employees. *Gallup*. https://www.gallup.com/workplace/236135/give-performance-reviews-actually-inspire-employees.aspx

54. Brower, C., & Dvorak, N. (2019, October 11). Why employees are fed up with feedback. *Gallup*. https://www.gallup.com/workplace/267251/why-employees-fed-feedback.aspx

55. Ibid.

56. Mady, E. (2019, November 5). How to have difficult conversations with your employees. *Fast Company*. https://www.fastcompany.com/90426470/how-to-have-difficult-conversations-with-your-employees

57. 4 companies winning with feedback in the workplace. (2020, March 3). *Partners in Leadership*. https://www.partnersinleadership.com/insights-publications/companies-that-understand-importance-of-feedback-in-the-workplace/

58. Levitsky, A. (2019, October 17). Job hopping: This is how long employees typically stay at Tesla, Apple, Facebook, Cisco, Nvidia, Oracle and more. *Silicon Valley Business Journal*. https://www.bizjournals.com/sanjose/news/2019/10/17/tech-employers-longest-tenure-tsla-aapl-csco-intc.html?ana=yahoo&yptr=yahoo

59. Berger, L. A., & Berger, D. R. (2008). *The compensation handbook* (6th ed). McGraw Hill.

60. Haileyesus, S. (2019, October 20). 75% of your employees may not plan to stay for more than 5 years. *Small Business Trends*. https://smallbiztrends.com/2019/10/2019-employee-retention-statistics.html

61. 2019–2020 Aflac WorkForces Report. (2022). *Aflac*. https://www.aflac.com/business/resources/aflac-workforces-report/default.aspx

62. The employee experience: 4 ways to attract, engage, & retain talent in today's competitive market. (2019). *ExecuSearch Group*. https://www.execu-search.com/~/media/Resources/pdf/eBook-2019-hiring-outlook

63. Croswell, A. (n.d.). 10 companies with great learning and development programs. *Culture Amp*. https://www.cultureamp.com/blog/10-companies-with-great-learning-and-development-programs/

64. Hall, J. (2020, July 22). Why you should start considering universities for long-term partnerships. *Inc.* https://www.inc.com/john-hall/how-to-create-a-successful-partnership-with-a-university.html

65. Elliot, C. (2018, June 11). These companies have the best customer service. *Forbes*. https://www.forbes.com/sites/christopherelliott/2018/07/11/these-companies-have-the-best-customer-service-heres-why/#439a751cb80a

66. Thottam, I. (2016). 10 companies with awesome training and development programs. https://www.monster.com/career-advice/article/companies-with-awesome-training-development-programs

67. Davidson, P. (2019, October 20). More employees offer flexible hours but many grapple with how to make it succeed. https://www.usatoday.com/story/money/2019/10/20/flexible-hours-jobs-more-firms-offer-variable-schedules/4020990002/

68. Toh, M., & Wakatsuki, Y. (2019, November 18). Microsoft tried a 4-day workweek in Japan. Productivity jumped 40%. *CNN Business*. https://www.cnn.com/2019/11/04/tech/microsoft-japan-workweek-productivity/index.html

69. Kelly, J. (2021, December 10). Interest and excitement about the adoption

of a four-day workweek is picking up speed. *Forbes*. https://www.forbes.com/sites/jackkelly/2021/10/29/interest-and-excitement-about-the-adoption-of-a-four-day-workweek-is-picking-up-speed/?sh=7328439a2c47

70. Manganaro, J. (2019, October 22). The price tag of financial stress. *Planadviser*. https://www.planadviser.com/price-tag-financial-stress/

71. Employers offering financial wellness programs double in recent years. (2019, September 19). *Businesswire*. https://www.businesswire.com/news/home/20190919005032/en/Employers-Offering-Financial-Wellness-Programs-Double-Years

72. Williams, G. (2022). 13 Companies That Offer Unlimited Vacation Days. *US News & World Report*. Retrieved from https://money.usnews.com/careers/slideshows/companies-that-offer-unlimited-vacation-days?slide=2

73. Friedman, E. (2020, April 6). Top five issues facing human resources in 2020. *Forbes*. https://www.forbes.com/sites/forbeshumanresourcescouncil/2020/04/06/top-five-issues-facing-human-resources-in-2020/#40141b8948d5=

74. Meister, J. (2022, January 8). Top ten HR trends for the 2022 workplace. *Forbes*. https://www.forbes.com/sites/jeannemeister/2022/01/05/top-ten-hr-trends-for-the-2022-workplace/?sh=3eeb23bb3006

75. Meister, J. (2022, January 8). Top ten HR trends for the 2022 workplace. *Forbes*. https://www.forbes.com/sites/jeannemeister/2022/01/05/top-ten-hr-trends-for-the-2022-workplace/?sh=3eeb23bb3006

76. Shellenbarger, S. (2019, October 28). Does your boss have your back when a loved one dies? *The Wall Street Journal*. https://www.wsj.com/articles/does-your-boss-have-your-back-when-a-loved-one-dies-11572255002

CHAPTER 13

1. Sustainable marketplace Leaf'd plans to tackle climate change head on. (2018). *Yahoo.com*. https://www.yahoo.com/now/sustainable-marketplace-leaf-d-plans-172000979.html?guccounter=1&guce_referrer=aHR0cHM6Ly93d3cuZ29vZ2xlLmNvbS8&guce_referrer_sig=AQAAAIQcyRgMi6aCu7s-UCNYoEevLbfToIBLJLxYDvADycNVf0g1L_hXrAgfNtR_M44eiV3ZH-2IP48xyof2MTMc9aY1lI4hACT9rbmPiBsEpJNbuyw6It5tFQoH567YXyemTAdeXWISS2LKVXLS19GPvgBRLssD5M7JhYK-LZMBlVZ6

2. Delmas, M. A., & Burbano, V. C. (2011). The drivers of greenwashing. *California Management Review, 54*(1), 64–87.

3. Kessler, A. (2022, January 31). *Leaf'd eco friendly marketplace*. Leafd Marketplace. https://leafd.com/

4. Refer to the following for an overview of work motivation theory: Grant, A. M., & Shin, J. (2012). Work motivation: Directing, energizing, and maintaining effort (and research). In R. M. Ryan (Ed.), *Oxford handbook of motivation* (pp. 505–519). Oxford University Press; Kanfer, R. (2012). Work motivation: Theory, practice, and future directions. In S. W. J. Kozlowski (Ed.), *The Oxford handbook of organizational psychology* (Vol. 1, pp. 455–495). Oxford University Press; Kanfer, R., Frese, M., & Johnson, R. E. (2017). Motivation related to work: A century of progress. *Journal of Applied Psychology, 102*(3), 338–355.

5. McGregor, L., & Doshi, N. (2020, April 9). How to keep your team motivated, remotely. *Harvard Business Review*. https://hbr.org/2020/04/how-to-keep-your-team-motivated-remotely

6. Surprising working from home productivity statistics (2022). (2022, January 2). *Apollo Technical LLC*. https://www.apollotechnical.com/working-from-home-productivity-statistics/#:~:text=Several%20studies%20over%20the%20past,and%20are%2047%25%20more%20productive

7. Empowerment: What's it about and who benefits? (n.d.). *Windsor Group*. https://www.windsor-group.com.au/our_news/what-is-meant-by-empowerment/

8. Levy, A. (2017, April 13). Millennials aren't entitled, they're empowered. *Forbes*. https://www.forbes.com/sites/forbescoachescouncil/2017/04/13/millennials-arent-entitled-theyre-empowered/#428403814289

9. Deci, E. L. (1975). *Intrinsic motivation*. Plenum; Hagger, M. S., Koch, S., & Chatzisarantis, N. L. D. (2015, January). The effect of causality orientations and positive competence-enhancing feedback on intrinsic motivation: A test of additive and interactive effects. *Personality and Individual Differences, 72*, 107–111.

10. Sun, F. W., Stepanovic, M. R., Andreano, J., Barrett, L. F., Touroutoglou, A., & Dickerson, B. C. (2016). Youthful brains in older adults: Preserved neuroanatomy in the default mode and salience networks contributes to youthful memory in superaging. *Journal of Neuroscience, 36*(37), 9659–9668.

11. Cooper, B. (2016, May 4). The key to happiness at work isn't money—it's autonomy. *Quartz*. https://qz.com/676144/why-its-your-call-is-the-best-thing-you-can-say-to-keep-employees-happy/

12. Stevenson, M. (2018, May 8). Autonomous leadership and ways to encourage autonomy in the workplace. *HR Exchange Network*. https://www.hrexchangenetwork.com/hr-talent-management/articles/autonomous-leadership-and-ways-to-encourage

13. Kanfer, R., Frese, M., & Johnson, R. E. (2017). Motivation related to work: A century of progress. *Journal of Applied Psychology, 102*(3), 338–355.

14. Maslow, A. H. (1943). A theory of human motivation. *Psychological Review, 50*(4), 370–396.

15. Wahba, M. A., & Bridwell, L. G. (1976). Maslow reconsidered: A review of research on the need hierarchy theory. *Organizational Behavior and Human Performance, 15*(2), 212–240; Harrigan, W. J., & Commons, M. L. (2015). Replacing Maslow's needs hierarchy with an account based on stage and value. *Behavioral Development Bulletin, 20*(1), 24–31.

16. What Facebook has learned about motivation in the modern workplace. (n.d.). *IDEOU*. https://www.ideou.com/blogs/inspiration/what-facebook-has-learned-about-motivation-in-the-modern-workplace

17. Alderfer, C. P. (1969). An empirical test of a new theory of human needs. *Organizational Behavior and Human Performance, 4*(2), 142–175; Schneider, B., & Alderfer, C. P. (1973). Three studies of measures of need satisfaction in organizations. *Administrative Science Quarterly, 18*(4), 489–505.

18. Herzberg, F. (2017). *Motivation to work*. Routledge; Holmberg, C., Caro, J., & Sobis, I. (2018). Job satisfaction among Swedish mental health nursing personnel: Revisiting the two-factor theory. *International Journal of Mental Health Nursing, 27*(2), 581–592.

19. King, N. (1970). Clarification and evaluation of the two-factor theory of job satisfaction. *Psychological Bulletin, 74*(1), 18–31; Wall, T. D., & Stephenson, G. M. (1970). Herzberg's two-factor theory of job attitudes: A critical evaluation and some fresh evidence. *Industrial Relations Journal, 1*(3), 41–65; Furnham, A., Eracleous, A., & Chamorro-Premuzic, T. (2009). Personality, motivation and job satisfaction: Hertzberg meets the big five. *Journal of Managerial Psychology, 24*(8), 765–779; Sledge, S., Miles, A. K., & Coppage, S. (2008). What role does culture play? A look at motivation and job satisfaction among hotel workers in Brazil. *The International Journal of Human Resource Management,19*(9), 1667–1682.

20. McClelland, D. C. (1961). *Achieving society*. Simon and Schuster; McClelland, D. C. (1975). *Power: The inner experience*. Irvington; Harrell, A. M., & Stahl, M. J. (1981). A behavioral decision theory approach for measuring McClelland's trichotomy of needs. *Journal of Applied Psychology, 66*(2), 242; Liu, Y. S., & Arendt, S. W. (2016). Development and validation of a work motive measurement scale. *International Journal of Contemporary Hospitality Management, 19*(9), 1667–1682.

21. Ho, L. (2020, July 21). 10 things high achiever do to attain greatness. *Lifehack*. https://www.lifehack.org/articl es/productivity/10-things-high-achie vers-differently.html

22. Bachelder, C. A. (2018). *Dare to serve: How to drive superior results by serving others*. Berrett-Koehler.

23. Bussewitz, C. (2019, December 24). Uber co-founder Travis Kalanick, its former CEO, has cashed out, will resign from board. *Chicago Tribune*. h ttps://www.chicagotribune.com/busi ness/ct-biz-uber-founder-quits-boa rd-20191224-y34p7wdvqzcb7gdjkc3a cea27a-story.html

24. Adams, J. S. (1963). Towards an understanding of inequity. *The Journal of Abnormal and Social Psychology, 67*(5), 422–436; Polk, D. M. (2011). Evaluating fairness: Critical assessment of equity theory. In D. Chadee (Ed.), *Theories in social psychology* (pp. 163–190). Wiley-Blackwell; Ryan, J. C. (2016). Old knowledge for new impacts: Equity theory and workforce nationalization. *Journal of Business Research, 69*(5), 1587–1592.

25. Vroom, V. H. (1964). *Work and motivation*. Wiley.

26. Renko, M., Kroeck, K. G., & Bullough, A. (2012). Expectancy theory and nascent entrepreneurship. *Small Business Economics, 39*(3), 667–684.

27. Kimmorley, S. (2018, January 31). Here's how 12 successful CEOs set their goals for the year. *Business Insider Australia*. https://www.busine ssinsider.com.au/how-ceos-set-goa ls-2018-1

28. Locke, E. A., & Schattke, K. (2018). Intrinsic and extrinsic motivation: Time for expansion and clarification. *Motivation Science, 5*(4), 277–290.

29. Mishel, L., & Kandra, J. (2021, August 10). CEO pay has skyrocketed 1,322% since 1978: CEOs were paid 351 times as much as a typical worker in 2020. *Economic Policy Institute*. https://www .epi.org/publication/ceo-pay-in-20 20/

30. Aumayr-Pintar, C., & Bechter, B. (2019, April 17). Seniority entitlements: A policy of the past, or a fix for the future? *Eurofound*. https://www.e urofound.europa.eu/publications/blo g/seniority-entitlements-a-policy-o f-the-past-or-a-fix-for-the-future

31. Pierson, D. A., Koziara, K. S., & Johannesson, R. E. (1983). Equal pay for jobs of comparable worth: A quantified job content approach1. *Public Personnel Management, 12*(4), 445–460; Adkins, J. L. (1990). Fair pay: The managerial challenge of comparable job worth and job evaluation. *ILR Review, 43*(2), 335–336.

32. 46 percent of workers feel like they're underpaid. But are they? (2018, September 24). *PayScale*. https://www.p ayscale.com/career-news/2018/09/4 6-percent-of-workers-feel-like-they re-underpaid-but-are-they

33. Mitra, A., Gupta, N., & Shaw, J. D. (2011). A comparative examination of traditional and skill-based pay plans. *Journal of Managerial Psychology, 26*(4), 278–296; Murray, B., & Gerhart, B. (2000). Skill-based pay and skill seeking. *Human Resource Management Review, 10*(3), 271–287.

34. Bolden-Barrett, V. (2020, January 14). Complete training, get paid: Aon proposes skill-based compensation. *HR Dive*. https://www.hrdive.com/n ews/complete-training-get-paid-ao n-proposes-skill-based-compensati on/570285/

35. Boachie-Mensah, F., & Dogbe, O. D. (2011). Performance-based pay as a motivational tool for achieving organisational performance: An exploratory case study. *International Journal of Business and Management, 6*(12), 270–285; Van Yperen, N. (2003). The perceived profile of goal orientation within firms: Differences between employees working for successful and unsuccessful firms employing either performance-based pay or job-based pay. *European Journal of Work and Organizational Psychology, 12*(3), 229–243.

36. Greene, P. (2019, February 9). Teacher merit pay is a bad idea. *Forbes*. https://www.forbes.com/sit es/petergreene/2019/02/09/teache r-merit-pay-is-a-bad-idea/#42866 7c44ffb

37. Elassar, A. (2019, December 11). A real estate company surprised employees with $10 million in bonuses at a holiday party. *CNN Business*. https://edition.cnn.com/2019/1 2/10/us/company-10-million-bonuse s-trnd/index.html

38. Arthur, J. B., & Kim, D. O. (2005). Gainsharing and knowledge sharing: The effects of labour–management co-operation. *The International Journal of Human Resource Management, 16*(9), 1564–1582.

39. Florkowski, G. W. (1987). The organizational impact of profit sharing. *Academy of Management Review, 12*(4), 622–636; Magnan, M., & St-Onge, S. (2005). The impact of profit sharing on the performance of financial services firms. *Journal of Management Studies, 42*(4), 761–791.

40. Kramer, J. (2018, May 15). 16 companies that will help you retire a millionaire. *Glassdoor*. https://www.glas sdoor.com/blog/retire-a-millionaire/

41. Jones, D. C., & Kato, T. (1995). The productivity effects of employee stock-ownership plans and bonuses: Evidence from Japanese panel data. *The American Economic Review, 85*(3), 391–414.

42. The ESOP Association. (2022, May 3). 2021 ESOP Company of the year

announced. https://esopassociation.org/articles/2021-esop-company-year-announced

43. Pink, D. H. (2011). *Drive: The surprising truth about what motivates us.* Penguin.

44. Deci, E. (1971). The effects of externally mediated rewards on intrinsic motivation. *Journal of Personality and Social Psychology, 18*, 105–115.

45. Hartman, J. (2019, October 25). Bestselling author Daniel Pink on what really motivates us to change. *Thrive Global.* https://thriveglobal.com/stories/bestselling-author-daniel-pink-on-what-really-motivates-us-to-change/?utm_source=Heleo+Newsletters&utm_campaign=a0b0eb1b96-EMAIL_CAMPAIGN_2019_11_04&utm_medium=email&utm_term=0_85eb2ca8d0-a0b0eb1b96-216967485&mc_cid=a0b0eb1b96&mc_eid=dc9dcd9535

46. Lee, A., Willis, S., & Tian, A. (2018, March 2). When empowering employees works, and when it doesn't. *Harvard Business Review.* https://hbr.org/2018/03/when-empowering-employees-works-and-when-it-doesnt

47. Leonard, K. (2020, July 2). What are the benefits of employee empowerment? *Chron.* https://smallbusiness.chron.com/benefits-employee-empowerment-1177.html

48. Williams, B. (n.d.). The importance of empowering employees. *Primeast Forward Focus.* https://www.forwardfocusinc.com/jumpstart-change/the-importance-of-empowering-employees/

49. Soltes, F. (2020, January 12). Inspiration, empowerment and even better wages at Sam's Club. *National Retail Federation.* https://nrf.com/blog/inspiration-empowerment-and-even-better-wages-sams-club

50. Peck, K., & Malik, A. (2020, August 4). How Zoetis's new CEO reset priorities and empowered employees during the pandemic. *McKinsey & Company.* https://www.mckinsey.com/industries/life-sciences/our-insights/how-zoetiss-new-ceo-reset-priorities-and-empowered-employees-during-the-pandemic

51. Lee, A., Willis, S., & Tian, A. (2018, March 2). When empowering employees works, and when it doesn't. *Harvard Business Review.* https://hbr.org/2018/03/when-empowering-employees-works-and-when-it-doesnt

52. Manz, C. C. (1986). Self-leadership: Toward an expanded theory of self-influence processes in organizations. *Academy of Management Review, 11*(3), 585–600; Stewart, G. L., Courtright, S. H., & Manz, C. C. (2019). Self-leadership: A paradoxical core of organizational behavior. *Annual Review of Organizational Psychology and Organizational Behavior, 6*, 47–67; Neck, C. P., & Houghton, J. D. (2006). Two decades of self-leadership theory and research. *Journal of Managerial Psychology, 24*(4), 270–295.

53. Neck, C. P., & Manz, C. C. (1992). Thought self-leadership: The influence of self-talk and mental imagery on performance. *Journal of Organizational Behavior, 13*(7), 681–699.

54. Jordan, M. (1994). *I can't accept not trying: Michael Jordan on the pursuit of excellence.* Rare Air Limited.

CHAPTER 14

1. Autodesk technology helping AEC address COVID-19. (2020, December 6). *Autodesk.com.* https://www.autodesk.com/company/newsroom/corporate-info

2. Trieu, R. (2016, May 19). What is the future of smart cities? *Redshift.* https://www.autodesk.com/redshift/smart-cities/

3. Autodesk. https://www.autodesk.com/solutions/architecture-engineering-construction/3-approaches-smart-cities

4. APA News. (2018, July 17). Kenya: Mobile phone penetration at 95.1 percent. http://apanews.net/en/news/kenya-mobile-phone-penetration-at-951-percent-report

5. For a general introduction to the field of organizational communication, refer to the following: Hargie, O., & Tourish. D. (2009). *Auditing organizational communication: A handbook of research, theory and practice.* Routledge; Harris, T., & Nelson, M. (2008). *Applied organizational communication: Theory and practice in a global environment* (3rd ed.). Taylor & Francis Group/Lawrence Erlbaum Associates; May, S., & Mumby, D. (2005). *Engaging organizational communication theory and research: Multiple perspectives.* SAGE.

6. Klemmer, E. T., & Snyder, F. W. (1972). Measurement of time spent communicating. *Journal of communication, 22*(2), 142–158.

7. Bersin, J. (2019, October). Surprise! The skills of the future aren't technical: It's time to prioritize gaps in behavioral and leadership skills. *Human Resource Executive.* https://hrexecutive.com/surprise-the-skills-of-the-future-arent-technical/

8. Berlo, D. K. (1960). *The process of communication.* Holt, Rinehart, & Winston; Shannon, C., & Weaver, W. (1949). *The mathematical theory of communication.* University of Illinois Press.

9. Beattie, G. (2004). *Visible thought: The new psychology of body language.* Routledge; Gifford, R. (2011). The role of nonverbal communication in interpersonal relations. In L. M. Horowitz & S. Strack (Eds.), *Handbook of interpersonal psychology: Theory, research, assessment, and therapeutic interventions* (pp. 171–190). Wiley.

10. Advaney, M. (2017). To talk or not to talk that is the question! At least 70 percent of communication is nonverbal. *YouthTime.* https://youth-time.eu/to-talk-or-not-to-talk-that-is-the-question-at-least-70-percent-of-communication-is-non-verbal/

11. Nobilo, B. (2020). Coronavirus has stolen our most meaningful ways to connect. *CNN.* https://edition.cnn.com/interactive/2020/06/world/coronavirus-body-language-wellness/

12. O'Donnell, B. (2017, February). Most U.S. workplaces still use "old-school" tech like email and phone calls to communicate: Old habits die hard. *Recode.* https://www.vox.com/2017/2/22/14671396/modern-workplace-remote-silicon-valley-collaboration-survey-slack

13. Sava, J. (2022, February 21). COVID impact on use of digital communication tools. *Statista.* https://www.statista.com/statistics/1201336/covid-use-adoption-communication-channels/

14. O'Connell, L. (2019, October). Entrepreneur Suzy Batiz prioritizes mental health to achieve business success. *Thrive Global.* https://thriveglobal.com/stories/entrepreneur-suzy-baitz-priorities-mental-health-business-success/

15. Communication barriers in the modern workplace. (2018). *The Economist—Intelligence Unit.* https://eiuperspectives.economist.com/sites/defa

ult/files/EIU_Lucidchart-Communic ation%20barriers%20in%20the%20 modern%20workplace.pdf

16. Ibid.

17. https://medium.com/changing-com munications/across-generations-em ail-remains-a-critical-tool-for-dail y-life-b2143c368470

18. Cutter, C. (2019, October). A law-firm veteran who leads by listening. *The Wall Street Journal*. https://www.wsj. com/articles/a-law-firm-veteran-w ho-leads-by-listening-11561176001

19. Manning, G., Curtis, K., & McMillen, S. (1996). *Building community: The human side of work* (pp. 127–154). Thomson Executive Press.

20. Vozza, S. (2017). 6 ways to become a better listener. *Fast Company*. https:// www.fastcompany.com/3068959/6-w ays-to-become-a-better-listener

21. Benson, K. (2017). How to listen without getting defensive. *The Gottman Institute*. https://www.gottman.com/ blog/listen-without-getting-defen sive/

22. Poor listening habits. (n.d.). *The Executive Advisory*. http://www.theex ecutiveadvisory.com/toolkit/listenin g/poor-listening-habits/

23. Davis, W. (2018). The levels of listening [Blog post]. *England Logistics*. http s://www.englandlogistics.com/the-l evels-of-listening/

24. Ibid.

25. Vozza, S. (2017). 6 ways to become a better listener. *Fast Company*. https:// www.fastcompany.com/3068959/6-w ays-to-become-a-better-listener

26. Ibid.

27. Goris, J. R., Vaught, B. C., & Pettit, J. D., Jr. (2000). Effects of communication direction on job performance and satisfaction: A moderated regression analysis. *The Journal of Business Communication, 37*(4), 348–368; Lunenburg, F. C. (2010). Formal communication channels: Upward, downward, horizontal, and external. *Focus on Colleges, Universities, and Schools, 4*(1), 1–7; Roberts, K. H., & O'Reilly, C. A. (1974). Measuring organizational communication. *Journal of Applied Psychology, 59*(3), 321.

28. Hartman, R. L., & Johnson, J. D. (1990). Formal and informal group communication structures: An examination of their relationship to role ambiguity. *Social Networks, 12*(2), 127–151; Langan-Fox, J. (2001).

Communication in organizations: Speed, diversity, networks, and influence on organizational effectiveness, human health, and relationships. In N. Anderson, D. S. Ones, H. K. Sinangil, & C. Viswesvaran (Eds.), *Handbook of industrial, work & organizational psychology* (pp. 188–205). SAGE.

29. Davis, K. (1953). Management communication and the grapevine. *Harvard Business Review, 31*(5), 43–39; Crampton, S. M., Hodge, J. W., & Mishra, J. M. (1998). The informal communication network: Factors influencing grapevine activity. *Public Personnel Management, 27*(4), 569– 584; Nicoll, D. (1994). Acknowledge and use your grapevine. *Management Decision, 32*(6), 25; Smith, B. (1996). Care and feeding of the office grapevine. *Management Review, 85*(2), 6–7.

30. Morrissey, P. (2020, February). 6 people who were fired for social media posts. *Smith's Lawyers*. https://www. smithslawyers.com.au/post/6-peop le-who-were-fired-for-social-medi a-posts

31. Davis, K. (1953). Management communication and the grapevine. *Harvard Business Review, 31*(5), 43–39; Foster, E., & Rosnow, R. (2006). Gossip and network relationships. In D. Kilpatrick, S. Duck, & M. Foley (Eds.), *Relating difficulty: The processes of constructing and managing difficult interaction* (pp. 161–180). Erlbaum.

32. Bassuk, A., & Lew, C. (2016, November). The antidote of office gossip. *Harvard Business Review*. https://hbr. org/2016/11/the-antidote-to-offic e-gossip

33. Mishra, J. (1990). Managing the grapevine. *Public Personnel Management, 19*(2), 213–228.

34. Hyun, J., & Conant, D. (2019, April). 3 ways to improve your cultural fluency. *Harvard Business Review*. https: //hbr.org/2019/04/3-ways-to-improv e-your-cultural-fluency

35. Mansour, J., & Zaheer, A. (2019, May). How leaders around the world build trust across cultures. *Harvard Business Review*. https://hbr.org/2019/05/ how-leaders-around-the-world-buil d-trust-across-cultures

36. LeVine, R. A., & Campbell, D. T. (1972). *Ethnocentrism: Theories of conflict, ethnic attitudes, and group behavior*. Wiley.

37. Jenifer, R. D., & Raman, G. P. (2015). Cross-cultural communication

barriers in the workplace. *International Journal of Management, 6*(1), 348–351.

38. Ferraro, G., & Briody, E. (2017). *The cultural dimensions of global business*. Routledge.

39. Lee, M. (2019). *High- and Low-Context Cultures and Responsibility for Miscommunication*. Go Philosophy. https: //go-philosophy.com/high-and-low-c ontext-cultures/

CHAPTER 15

1. Hollingsworth LLC. (2017, June 9). *Best supply chains from companies around the world*. https://www.holling sworthllc.com/best-supply-chains-c ompanies-around-world/

2. Sargent, M. (2017, May 10). Supply chain putting the star in Starbucks. *Fronetics*. https://www.fronetics.com /supply-chain-putting-star-starbu cks/

3. Starbucks Stories & News. (2008, March 5). *Ethos Water and H20 Africa join forces to help alleviate the world water crisis*. https://stories.starbuc ks.com/press/2008/ethos-water-an d-h2o-africa-join-forces-to-help-all eviate-the-world-water-cr/

4. Clama, J. (2020, January 21). Starbucks sets new sustainability goals for the decade. *The Verge*. https://ww w.theverge.com/2020/1/21/21075852 /starbucks-sustainability-goals-was te-water-greenhouse-gases-decade

5. World Coffee Portal. (2021, July 28). *Starbucks at 50 Pt.3: New ways of working*. https://www.worldcoffeepo rtal.com/Latest/InsightAnalysis/202 1/July/Starbucks-at-50-Pt-3

6. Foster, T. (2019). This CEO bet big on Texas and helped his food-delivery company finally turn a profit. *Inc. Magazine*. https://www.inc.com/mag azine/201911/tom-foster/favor-jag-b ath-delivery-startup-ceo-texas-com petition-strategy.html?icid=hmside2

7. Kiisel, T. (2015, July 22). What is operations? And why does my business need It? *OnDeck*. https://www.ondeck .com/resources/what-is-operations

8. Stipetic, M., & Grgic, S. (2020, December 13). 8 Starbucks customer experience innovations—how Starbucks became a leader in CX? *SuperSuper*. https://www.supersuperagen cy.com/blog/starbucks-customer-ex perience-cx-innovations

9. Rawson, C. (2012, January 22). Why Apple's products are "Designed in California" but "Assembled in China." *Engadget*. https://www.engadget.com/2012-01-22-why-apples-products-are-designed-in-california-but-assembled.html

10. Depta, L. (2018). Global food waste and its economic impact. *Reset*. https://en.reset.org/knowledge/global-food-waste-and-its-environmental-impact-09122018

11. Barker, R. C. (1994). The design of lean manufacturing systems using time-based analysis. *International Journal of Operations & Production Management, 14*(11), 86–96; Ramesh, V., & Kodali, R. (2012). A decision framework for maximising lean manufacturing performance. *International Journal of Production Research, 50*(8), 2234–2251.

12. Anderson, J. C., Rungtusanatham, M., & Schroeder, R. G. (1994). A theory of quality management underlying the Deming management method. *Academy of Management Review, 19*(3), 472–509.

13. Gunasekaran, A. (1999). Agile manufacturing: A framework for research and development. *International Journal of Production Economics, 62*(1–2), 87–105.

14. Lombardi, S. (n.d.). 4 good examples of companies that use lean manufacturing. *Redefined Impact*. https://refinedimpact.com/4-good-examples-of-companies-that-use-lean-manufacturing/

15. P.M. (2021, January 12). General Motors opens new center dedicated to additive manufacturing. *3D Natives*. https://www.3dnatives.com/en/general-motors-aic-additive-manufacturing-120120217/

16. Amelia, H. (2020, December 30). 3D printing vs COVID-19: The most exceptional initiatives of the pandemic. *3D Natives*. https://www.3dnatives.com/en/3d-printing-vs-covid-19-301220204/

17. Statista. (n.d.). Manufacturing labors costs per hour for China, Vietnam, Mexico from 2016 to 2020. https://www.statista.com/statistics/744071/manufacturing-labor-costs-per-hour-china-vietnam-mexico/

18. Kwaak, J. (2017, May 16). Hyundai whistle-blower, in rarity for South Korea, prompts recall. *New York Times*. https://www.nytimes.com/2017/05/16/business/hyundai-south-korea-whistle-blower-recall.html

19. Chandrasekaran, A., & Toussaint, J. (2019, May 24). Creating a culture of continuous improvement. *Harvard Business Review*. https://hbr.org/2019/05/creating-a-culture-of-continuous-improvement

20. De Mast, J., & Lokkerbol, J. (2012). An analysis of the Six Sigma DMAIC method from the perspective of problem solving. *International Journal of Production Economics, 139*(2), 604–614.

21. Lean Six Sigma. (n.d.). https://goleansixsigma.com/lean-six-sigma-success-stories-in-the-food-industry/

22. Riserbato, R. (2021, July 7). The ultimate guide to service operations in 2021. *Hubspot.com*. https://blog.hubspot.com/service/service-operations

23. Colvin, G. (2020, May 18). The simple metric that's taking over big business. *Fortune*. https://fortune.com/longform/net-promoter-score-fortune-500-customer-satisfaction-metric/

24. Qualtrics. (2021, February 22). What is a Good Net Promoter Score (NPS)? Retrieved August 25, 2022, from https://www.qualtrics.com/experience-management/customer/good-net-promoter-score/

25. Apple NPS Score Benchmarks in 2022 (2022). NPS Benchmarks. Retrieved https://customergauge.com/benchmarks/blog/4-key-ingredients-fuelling-apples-high-net-promoter-score

26. Wojcik, M. (2018, September 24). 9 companies using live website chat in a creative way. *Hubspot.com*. https://blog.hubspot.com/marketing/companies-using-live-chat

27. Calzon, B. (2022, March 15). A guide to customer service data analysis & service reports. *Datapine*. https://www.datapine.com/blog/customer-service-reports/

28. Amaresan, S. (2022, March 24). Smooth user onboarding examples that'll make you jealous. *Hubspot.com*. https://blog.hubspot.com/service/user-onboarding-examples

29. Digital Operations. (2021). *Cognizant.com*. https://www.cognizant.com/us/en/glossary/digital-operations#:~:text=Digital%20operations%20is%20the%20concept,delight%20customers%20and%20improve%20performa

nce; Berry, L. (2021, February 5). How a focus on employee experience can accelerate your digital transformation. *Interact Software*. https://www.interactsoftware.com/blog/employee-experience-digital-transformation/

30. Arundel, T. (2020, July 28). What is digital operations? The core of digital transformation & agility. *Claravine*. https://www.claravine.com/2020/07/28/what-is-digital-operations/

31. Krishanu. (2021, June 14). 4 ways enterprises use digital transformation to enhance productivity. *Replicon*. https://www.replicon.com/blog/ways-enterprises-can-use-digital-transformation-to-enhance-productivity/

32. Stackpole, T. (2021, June 4). Inside IKEA's digital transformation. *Harvard Business Review*. https://hbr.org/2021/06/inside-ikeas-digital-transformation

33. Berry, L. (2021, February 5). How a focus on employee experience can accelerate your digital transformation. *Interact Software*. https://www.interactsoftware.com/blog/employee-experience-digital-transformation/

34. Chapco-Wade-Safina, C. (2021, November 5). The impact of digitalization on the employee experience. *Medium*. https://colleenchapcowadesafina.medium.com/the-impact-of-digitalization-on-the-employee-experience-7d6a510c1535

35. Kenton, W. (2020, July 7). Supply chain. *Investopedia*. https://www.investopedia.com/terms/s/supplychain.asp

36. Janvier-James, A. M. (2012). A new introduction to supply chains and supply chain management: Definitions and theories perspective. *International Business Research, 5*(1), 194–207.

37. Harapko, S. (2021, February 18). How COVID-19 impacted supply chains and what comes next. *Ey.com*. https://www.ey.com/en_gl/supply-chain/how-covid-19-impacted-supply-chains-and-what-comes-next

CHAPTER 16

1. Amato-McCoy, D. (2017). Five ways Walmart uses big data. *Chain Store Age*. https://chainstoreage.com/operations/five-ways-walmart-uses-big-data

2. Overdeep, M. (2019, August 28). You'll never guess what surprising product Walmart stocks up on before big storms. *Southern Living*. https://www.southernliving.com/news/walmart-strawberry-pop-tarts-hurricane

3. Walmart. (n.d.). Business for 2030. http://www.businessfor2030.org/walmart

4. Kestenbaum, R. (2017). Is Walmart good or bad for America? The question may be outdated. *Forbes*. https://www.forbes.com/sites/richardkestenbaum/2017/05/18/is-walmart-good-or-bad-for-america/?sh=48895d8022ae

5. Walmart. (n.d.). Business for 2030. http://www.businessfor2030.org/walmart

6. Much of this section is sourced from Kilby, J., Fox, J. & Lucas, A. (2005). *Casino operations and management* (2nd ed, pp. 183–184). John Wiley & Sons.

7. Data vs. information. https://www.diffen.com/difference/Data_vs_Information for a good chart of comparing examples of data vs information

8. Kopanakis, J. (2018). 5 real-world examples of how brands are using big data analytics. *Mentionlytics*. https://www.mentionlytics.com/blog/5-real-world-examples-of-how-brands-are-using-big-data-analytics/

9. Kelleher, K. (2014). What 3 small businesses learned from big data. *Inc.* /https://www.inc.com/magazine/201407/kevin-kelleher/how-small-businesses-can-mine-big-data.html

10. Dialogue Review. (2019). *Small data is the key to Lego's success*. https://dialoguereview.com/small-data-lego

11. Taylor, V. (2019). 6 best brands that dominate user-generated content on Instagram. *Business 2 Community*. https://www.business2community.com/instagram/6-best-brands-that-dominate-user-generated-content-on-instagram-02252433

12. Shrivastava, T. (n.d.). How AirBnB thrives on user generated content. *Pixlee*. https://www.pixlee.com/blog/how-airbnb-thrives-on-user-generated-content/

13. Saunders, C., & Pearlson, K. (2009). *Managing and using information systems*. Wiley.

14. See for example: Basoglu, N., Daim, T., & Kerimoglu, O. (2007). Organizational adoption of enterprise resource planning systems: A conceptual framework. *The Journal of High Technology Management Research, 18*(1), 73–97; Jacobs, F. R. (2007). Enterprise resource planning (ERP)—A brief history. *Journal of Operations Management, 25*(2), 357–363.

15. This section is sourced from Rainer, R. K., Prince, B., Splettstoesser-Hogeterp, I., Sanchez-Rodriguez, C., & Ebrahimi, S. (2020). *Introduction to information systems*. John Wiley & Sons.

16. See for example: Li, C., Peters, G. F., Richardson, V. J., & Watson, M. W. (2012). *The consequences of information technology control weaknesses on management information systems: The case of Sarbanes-Oxley internal control reports* (pp. 179–203). Mis Quarterly; Călin, O. A. (2018). Management information systems—Activities and elements in decision process. *Hyperion International Journal of Econophysics & New Economy, 11*(1), 191–195.

17. Chatzimouratidis, A., Theotokas, I., & Lagoudis, I. N. (2012). Decision support systems for human resource training and development. *The International Journal of Human Resource Management, 23*(4), 662–693; Piel, J. H., Hamann, J. F., Koukal, A., & Breitner, M. H. (2017). Promoting the system integration of renewable energies: Toward a decision support system for incentivizing spatially diversified deployment. *Journal of Management Information Systems, 34*(4), 994–1022.

18. Kontzer, T. (2020, August 21). Need healthcare? AI startup Curai has an app for that. *NVIDIA*. https://blogs.nvidia.com/blog/2020/08/21/curai-ai-healthcare-app/

19. Ibe, O. C. (2017). *Fundamentals of data communication networks*. John Wiley & Sons.

20. Farsi, M., Ali, M., Shah, R. A., Wagan, A. A., & Kharabsheh, R. (2020). Cloud computing and data security threats taxonomy: A review. *Journal of Intelligent & Fuzzy Systems, 38*(3), 2517–2527.

21. Carey, S. (2018). What's the difference between IaaS, SaaS and PaaS? *Computerworld*. http://staging.computerworld.in/news/whats-difference-between-iaas-saas-and-paas

22. Davies, A. (2021). 10 top PaaS providers of 2021. *Dev Team Space*. https://www.devteam.space/blog/10-top-paas-providers/

23. Patro, S. P., Padhy, N., & Panigrahi, R. (2016). Security issues over e-commerce and their solutions. *International Journal of Advanced Research in Computer and Communication Engineering, 5*(12), 81–85.

24. Interpol. (2022). INTERPOL report shows alarming rate of cyberattacks during COVID-19. https://www.interpol.int/en/News-and-Events/News/2020/INTERPOL-report-shows-alarming-rate-of-cyberattacks-during-COVID-19

25. Fruhlinger, J. (2020, June 19). Ransomware explained: How it works and how to remove it. *CSO*. https://www.csoonline.com/article/3236183/what-is-ransomware-how-it-works-and-how-to-remove-it.html

26. Furhlinger, J. (2019, May 17). Malware explained: How to prevent, detect, and recover from it. *CSO*. https://www.csoonline.com/article/3295877/what-is-malware-viruses-worms-trojans-and-beyond.html

27. Gatefy. (2020, June 18). 11 real and famous cases of malware attacks. https://gatefy.com/blog/real-and-famous-cases-malware-attacks/

28. Ferreira, A., & Teles, S. (2019). Persuasion: How phishing emails can influence users and bypass security measures. *International Journal of Human–Computer Studies, 125*, 19–31.

29. Guta, M. (2019, July 12). 1 in 99 emails is a phishing attack, what can your business do? *Small Business Trends*. https://smallbiztrends.com/2019/07/phishing-statistics.html

30. Statista. (n.d.). Number of visits to media piracy sited worldwide in 2018, but country. https://www.statista.com/statistics/786046/media-piracy-site-visits-by-country/

31. Microstrategy. (n.d.). Business analytics: Everything you need to know. https://www.microstrategy.com/en/resources/introductory-guides/business-analytics--everything-you-need-to-know

32. West, G. (2020, June 3). An inside look at the technology that will help LSU football return to peak physical condition. *Fan Nation*. https://www.si.com/college/lsu/football/how-lsu-use-perch-technology

33. Evans, J. R. (2017). *Business analytics* (3rd ed.). Pearson.

34. Collins, K. M., & Shemko, J. (2008). *Exploring business*. Pearson/Prentice Hall; Hardoon, D. R., & Shmueli, G. (2013). *Getting started with business analytics: Insightful decision-making*. CRC Press; Holsapple, C., Lee-Post, A., & Pakath, R. (2014). A unified foundation for business analytics. *Decision Support Systems, 64*, 130–141.

35. Reports and Data. (2020). Text mining market to reach USD 16.85 billion by 2027. *Global Newswire*. https://www.globenewswire.com/news-release/2020/07/16/2063589/0/en/Text-Mining-Market-To-Reach-USD-16-85-Billion-By-2027-Reports-and-Data.html

36. Stoll, J. D. (2019, October 18). Feel the force: Gut instinct, not data, is the thing. *The Wall Street Journal*. https://www.wsj.com/articles/the-secret-behind-starbucks-amazon-and-the-patriots-gut-instinct-11571417153

37. Insights Team. (2018, August 15). 4 challenges with leveraging analytics and how to overcome them. *Forbes*. https://www.forbes.com/sites/insights-cisco/2018/08/15/4-challenges-with-leveraging-analytics-and-how-to-overcome-them/#5fe7a65e2469

38. Ghosh, P. (2018, January 4). How is bad data crippling your data analytics? *Dataversity*. https://www.dataversity.net/bad-data-crippling-data-analytics/

CHAPTER 17

1. Lesonsky, R. (2020, March 4). The state of women entrepreneurs. *SCORE*. https://www.score.org/blog/state-women-entrepreneurs#:~:text=World%2Dwide%2C%206.2%25%20of,the%20highest%20entrepreneurial%20participation%20rates

2. Stengel, G. (2020, December 2). Funding female founders: If males VCs won't do it, women angels and limited partners will. *Forbes*. https://www.forbes.com/sites/geristengel/2020/12/02/funding-female-founders-if-male-vcs-wont-do-it-women-angels-and-limited-partners-will/?sh=6633352e405f

3. Portfolio. (2019, November 1). Silicon Valley's Portfolio named in Stevie Awards 2019 most innovative companies. *Cision PR Newsire*. https://www.prnewswire.com/news-releases/silicon-valleys-portfolio-named-finalist-in-stevie-awards-2019-most-innovative-companies-300950128.html

4. Thielking, M. (2019, August 14). One health care startup at a time, this venture capitalist wants to harness the investing power of women. *STAT*. https://www.statnews.com/2019/08/14/trish-costello-women-in-investing/

5. Natter, E. (2018, November 5). Why is accounting often referred to as the language of business? *Chron*. https://smallbusiness.chron.com/accounting-referred-language-business-63107.html

6. Users of financial statements. (n.d.). *AccountingVerse*. https://www.accountingverse.com/accounting-basics/users-of-financial-statements.html

7. Material in this section is sourced from various sources. See Carlson, R. (2020, November 30). The 3 types of accounting in small business. *The Balance Small Business*. https://www.thebalancesmb.com/accounting-and-your-business-392932; Hayes, A. (2019, September 30). Behavioral accounting. *Investopedia*. https://www.investopedia.com/terms/b/behavioral-accounting.asp; The 8 branches of accounting. (n.d.). *FreshBooks*. https://www.freshbooks.com/hub/accounting/8-branches-of-accounting

8. Dennis, A. (2021, August). How CPAs helped save businesses during COVID-19. *Journal of Accountancy. A Practice Management Feature*. https://www.journalofaccountancy.com/issues/2021/aug/how-cpas-helped-save-businesses-during-coronavirus-pandemic.html

9. Quickbooks. (2019, May 3). Cash vs. accrual accounting: What's best for your small business? *Intuit Quickbooks*. https://quickbooks.intuit.com/r/bookkeeping/cash-vs-accrual-accounting-whats-best-small-business/

10. Ibid.

11. The section heavily sourced from Santinelli, A. (2020). Supplement A: Financial statements and projections for startups. In H. Neck, C. Neck, & E. Murray (Eds.), *Entrepreneurship: The practice & mindset* (2nd ed., pp. 332–340). SAGE.

1 2 Ibid.

13. This section is compiled from several sources including: Kiyosaki, R. (2019, July 2). 8 key financial ratios to know if a business is healthy or not. *Rich Dad*. https://www.richdad.com/key-financial-ratios; Fuhrmann, R. (2020, August 12). Understanding negative return on equity: Is it always bad? *Investopedia*. https://www.investopedia.com/ask/answers/070914/are-companies-negative-return-equity-roe-always-bad-investment.asp#:~:text=Return%20on%20equity%20(ROE)%20is%20measured%20as%20net%20income%20divided,business%2C%20such%20as%20through%20restructuring; Bloomenthal, A. (2021, February 20). Ratio analysis. *Investopedia*. https://www.investopedia.com/terms/r/ratioanalysis.asp; Financial ratio cheatsheet. (n.d.). *MyAccountingCourse.com*. https://www.myaccountingcourse.com/other/financial-ratio-cheatsheet.pdf; What are financial ratios? (n.d.) *Corporate Finance Institute*. https://corporatefinanceinstitute.com/resources/knowledge/finance/financial-ratios/

14. Return on equity by sector. (2021, January). *New York University Stern School of Business*. http://pages.stern.nyu.edu/~adamodar/New_Home_Page/datafile/roe.html

CHAPTER 18

1. Carroll, C. (2020, November 6). What is Weight Watchers? *Verywell Fit*. https://www.verywellfit.com/weight-watchers-overview-4691074#:~:text=Weight%20Watchers%20started%20in%20the,best%20methods%20for%20losing%20weight.&text=Lippert%20helped%20Nidetch%20to%20do,company%20went%20public%20in%201968

2. Beck, E. (1999, July 23). Heinz sells Weight Watchers interest to ARtal Luxembourg for $735 million. *The Wall Street Journal*. https://www.wsj.com/articles/SB932675635414732326

3. Weight Watchers (WW)—Revenue. (2021). *Companiesmarketcap.com*. https://companiesmarketcap.com/weight-watchers/revenue/#:~:text=Revenue%20in%202021%20(TTM)%3A,that%20were%20of%20$%20241.41%20B

4. Hope, K. (2018, September 24). Weight Watchers drops "weight" from name. *BBC News*. https://www.bbc.com/news/business-45625191

5. Tyko, K. (2020, May 19). WW, formerly Weight Watchers, announces plans to start reopening studios ahead of Oprah event. *USA Today*. https://www.usatoday.com/story/money/2020/05/15/reopening-america-ww-weight-watchers-studios-plans-oprah-covid-19/5197884002/

6. WW International. (2021, February 25). WW announces fourth quarter and full year 2020 results. *Intrado Global News*. https://www.globenewswire.com/news-release/2021/02/25/2182904/0/en/WW-Announces-Fourth-Quarter-and-Full-Year-2020-Results.html

7. Azam, G. (n.d.). What is financial management and example? Explain its functions and importance. *Startup Plan*. https://startupaplan.com/what-is-financial-management/

8. Ibid.

9. Thakur, M. (n.d.). Accounting vs financial management. *EDUCBA*. https://www.educba.com/accounting-vs-financial-management/; and Thakur, M. (n.d.). Accounting vs. financial management. *Wall Street Mojo*. https://www.wallstreetmojo.com/accounting-vs-financial-management/

10. Strutner, S. (n.d.). Financial management explained: Scope, objectives and importance. *NetSuite*. https://www.netsuite.com/portal/resource/articles/financial-management/financial-management.shtml

11. Grant, M. (2021, February 28). Chief financial officer. *Investopedia*. https://www.investopedia.com/terms/c/cfo.asp#:~:text=A%20chief%20financial%20officer%20(CFO,weaknesses%20and%20proposing%20corrective%20actions

12. WW International. (2020, August 4). Amy O'Keefe joins WW International as Chief Financial Officer, Nicholas Hotchkin promoted to Chief Operating Officer. *WW online*. https://corporate.ww.com/news-room/press-releases/news-details/2020/Amy-OKeefe-Joins-WW-International-as-Chief-Financial-Officer-Nicholas-Hotchkin-Promoted-to-Chief-Operating-Officer/default.aspx#:~:text=(NASDAQ%3A%20WW)%2C%20a,of%20North%20American%20operations%20since

13. Hill, B. (n.d.). About business financial planning. *Chron*. https://smallbusiness.chron.com/business-financial-planning-2675.html

14. The difference between a budget and a forecast. (2021, April 19). *Accounting Tools*. https://www.accountingtools.com/articles/what-is-the-difference-between-a-budget-and-a-forecast.html

15. SBA. (n.d.). Financial management for a small business. https://www.sba.gov/sites/default/files/files/PARTICIPANT_GUIDE_FINANCIAL_MANAGEMENT.pdf

16. Much of this section is sourced from Neck, H., Neck, C., & Murray, E. (Eds.). (2021). Chapter 13: Financing for startups. In *Entrepreneurship: The practice & mindset* (pp. 303–306). SAGE.

17. The Honest Company. (2021, May 12). *Profile generated by PitchBook for Samantha Porter, Babson College.* Pitchbook.

18. Çam, D. (2021). Inside Jessica Alba's long and turbulent road to taking The Honest Company public. https://www.forbes.com/sites/denizcam/2021/05/04/inside-jessica-albas-long-and-turbulent-road-to-taking-the-honest-company-public/?sh=140319326be1

19. Moyer, M. (2012). Slicing pie: A guide to dividing up early-stage start-up equity. https://slicingpie.com/slicing-pie-a-guide-to-dividing-up-early-stage-startup-equity/

20. Ibid.

21. Venture capital. (n.d.). *Small business notes*. http://www.smallbusinessnotes.com/business-finances/venture-capital.html

22. The Honest Company. (2021, May 12). *Profile generated by PitchBook for Samantha Porter, Babson College.* Pitchbook.

23. Shane, S. (2008, September). *The importance of angel investing in financing the growth of entrepreneurial ventures* (a working paper for the Small Business Association). http://www.angelcapitalassociation.org/data/Documents/Resources/AngelGroupResearch/1d%20-%20Resources%20-%20Research/19%20Angel_Investing_in_Financing_the_Growth_of_Entrepreneurial_Ventures.pdf

24. Maverick, J. B. (2021, April 26). Equity financing vs debt financing: What's the difference? *Investopedia*. https://www.investopedia.com/ask/answers/042215/what-are-benefits-company-using-equity-financing-vs-debt-financing.asp#:~:text=Debt%20finan cing%20involves%20the%20borrowing%20of%20money%20and%20paying%20it,debt%20financing%20is%20a%20loan

25. Ibid., and Business financing from *Encyclopedia.com*. https://www.encyclopedia.com/finance/encyclopedias-almanacs-transcripts-and-maps/business-financing

26. Song, J. (2021, March 15). Average small business loan interest rates in 2021: Comparing top lenders. *Value Penguin by Lending tree*. https://www.valuepenguin.com/average-small-business-loan-interest-rates

27. The U.S. Small Business Administration. (2022). The U.S. Small Business Administration is delivering support to America's small businesses, helping them recover from the COVID-19 pandemic. https://www.sba.gov/article/2021/nov/24/fact-sheet-us-small-business-administration-delivering-support-americas-small-businesses-helping#:~:text=The%20retooled%20COVID%20EIDL%20Targeted,still%20reeling%20from%20the%20pandemic

28. https://www.kiva.org/about

29. The section is sourced from Santilli, A. (2021). Supplement A: Financial statements and projections for startups. In H. Neck, C. Neck, & E. Murray (Eds.), *Entrepreneurship: The practice & mindset* (2nd ed., pp. 341–342). SAGE.

30. Financial controls. (n.d.). *Corporate Finance Institute*. https://corporatefinanceinstitute.com/resources/knowledge/finance/financial-controls/

31. What is fraud? (n.d.). *Association of Certified Financial Examiners*. https://www.acfe.com/fraud-101.aspx#:~:text=Internal%20fraud%2C%20also%20called%20occupational,executive%20commits%20fraud%20against%20his

32. Thakur, M. (n.d.). Accounting controls. *Wall Street Mojo*. https://www.wallstreetmojo.com/accounting-controls/; The three main internal controls for accounting and how they protect your assets. (n.d.). *Signature Analytics*. https://signatureanalytics.com/blog/the-three-main-internal-controls-for-accounting-and-how-they-protect-your-assets/

APPENDIX A

1. Johnston Thomas Attorneys At Law, PC. (2019, November 14). What is business law and why is it important. https://johnstonthomas.com/what-is-business-law-and-why-is-it-important/

2. Abramowitz, Z. (2015, March 23). How lawyers can add value for startups. *Above the Law.* Retrieved on August 2, 2015, from http://abovethelaw.com/2015/03/how-lawyers-can-add-value-for-startups/

3. Santa Clara University. (n.d.). The Entrepreneurs' law clinic. http://law.scu.edu/elc/

4. Source for legal research on the web. http://www.washlaw.edu/

5. Abramowitz, Z. (2015, March 23). How lawyers can add value for startups. *Above the Law.* http://abovethelaw.com/2015/03/how-lawyers-can-add-value-for-startups/

6. Successful entrepreneurs who started out as sole proprietors. (n.d.). *Gaebler.com.* http://www.gaebler.com/Successful-Entrepreneurs-Who-Started-Out-As-Sole-Proprietors.htm

7. http://www.inc.com/guides/2010/10/how-to-start-a-sole-proprietorship.html

8. http://www.moneyedup.com/2010/08/how-sole-proprietorship-works/

9. See, e.g., California Corporations Code Sections 2500, et seq., and Massachusetts General Laws Ch. 156E.

10. Intellectual property rights for innovative entrepreneurship. (n.d.). *The Innovation Policy Forum.* https://www.innovationpolicyplatform.org/content/intellectual-property-rights-innovative-entrepreneurship

11. Keating, R. J. (2013). *Unleashing small business through IP: Protecting intellectual property, driving entrepreneurship* (p. 36). Small Business & Entrepreneurship Council. http://www.sbecouncil.org/wp-content/uploads/2013/06/IP+and+Entrepreneurship+FINAL.pdf

12. Ibid.

13. Isaacson, W. (2011). *Steve Jobs* (p. 396). Simon & Schuster.

14. McKenna, C. (2015, April 3). Do you really own all your intellectual property? *The National Law Review.* http://www.natlawreview.com/article/do-you-really-own-all-your-intellectual-property

15. Steele, A. (2013, June 11). Who owns Hackathon inventions? *Harvard Business Review.* https://hbr.org/2013/06/who-owns-hackathon-inventions

16. Purvis, S. (n.d.). *The fundamentals of intellectual property for the entrepreneur.* Presentation, U.S. Patent and Trademark Office, Department of Commerce. http://www.uspto.gov/sites/default/files/about/offices/ous/121115.pdf

17. www.copyright.gov/circs/circ61.pdf

18. Khomami, N. (2022, April 6). Ed Sheeran wins court battle over Shape of You plagiarism accusation. *The Guardian.* https://www.theguardian.com/music/2022/apr/06/ed-sheeran-wins-court-battle-over-shape-of-you-plagiarism-accusation

19. PA Media. (2021, August 6). Alt-milk maker Oatly loses trademark case against family-run UK firm. *The Guardian.* https://www.theguardian.com/business/2021/aug/06/alt-milk-maker-oatly-loses-trademark-case-against-family-run-uk-firm

20. Halligan, R. M., & Haas, D. (2010, February 19). The secret of trade secret success. *Forbes.* http://www.forbes.com/2010/02/19/protecting-trade-secrets-leadership-managing-halligan-haas.html

21. Quinn, G. (2014, February 15). Protecting ideas: Can ideas be protected or patented? *IPWatchdog.* http://www.ipwatchdog.com/2014/02/15/protecting-ideas-can-ideas-be-protected-or-patented/id=48009/

22. Twin, A. (2019). Non-disclosure agreement (NDA). *Investopedia.* https://www.investopedia.com/terms/n/nda.asp

23. Ibid.

24. Zwilling, M. (2017). How and when to pitch your idea without a signed NDA. *Inc.* https://www.inc.com/martin-zwilling/how-when-to-pitch-your-idea-without-a-signed-nda.html

25. Stoll, J. (2021, September 23). Global number of visits to media piracy sites by country 2020. *Statista.* https://www.statista.com/statistics/786046/media-piracy-site-visits-by-country/

26. Sherman, E. (2019). One in five U.S. companies say China has stolen their intellectual property. *Fortune.* http://fortune.com/2019/03/01/china-ip-theft

27. Cullinane, S. (2021, December 5). CBP seizes $30 million shipment of fake handbags, clothing, ahead of holidays. *CNN.* https://edition.cnn.com/2021/12/05/us/cbp-counterfeit-handbag-seizure/index.html

28. Most of this section is based on Kotha, R., Kim, P. H., & Alexy, O. (2014, November). Turn your science into a business. *Harvard Business Review, 92*(11), 106–114.

29. Lococo, E. (2012, July 2). Apple pays Proview $60m to resolve iPad trademark dispute. *Bloomberg Business.* http://www.bloomberg.com/news/articles/2012-07-02/apple-pays-60-million-to-end-china-ipad-dispute-with-proview

30. U.S. Small Business Administration. (n.d.). *Hire and manage employees.* https://www.sba.gov/business-guide/manage-your-business/hire-manage-employees

31. International Trade Union Confederation. (2021). The world's worst countries for workers—Executive summary. https://files.mutualcdn.com/ituc/files/ITUC_GlobalRightsIndex_2021_EN_Final.pdf

32. U.S. Small Business Administration. (n.d.). *Hire and manage employees.* Author.

33. See, e.g., Internal Revenue Service Publication 15-A, Employer's Supplemental Tax Guide 2016.

34. Wage and Hour Division (WHD). (n.d.). https://www.dol.gov/whd/regs/compliance/whdfs71.htm

APPENDIX B

1. Dassel, K., & Wang, X. (2016). Social purpose and value creation: The business return of social impact. Deloitte Consulting, LLP. Retrieved from https://www2.deloitte.com/content/dam/Deloitte/uy/Documents/home/social-purpose-and-value-creation.pdf Brieger, S.A., De Clercq, D. & Meynhardt, T. (2021). Doing Good, Feeling Good? Entrepreneurs' Social Value Creation Beliefs and Work-Related Well-Being. Journal of Business Ethics 172, 707–725 (2021).

INDEX

ability, 5, 30–31, 42, 49–52, 54–55, 60, 69–71, 73, 76, 161–62, 228, 230, 233–35, 239, 246–47, 289, 293–95, 322, 340–41, 346–47
  differing, 201–2
ability diversity, 249, 263
accounting, 81, 178, 181, 184–85, 273, 276, 346–51, 360, 363–66, 372, 377
accounts, 354, 358, 362, 364, 381, 385
accrual accounting, 351
accrual basis accounting, 350–51, 364
achievement of long-term goals, 54
achievements, 38, 41, 51, 69, 207, 217, 253–54, 257, 272–74, 283, 285
action plans, 53, 226, 240, 373
actions, entrepreneurial, 57
ADA (Americans with Disabilities Act), 249
adhocracy culture, 208, 211, 215, 217
Administrative Managers, 228, 240
advertising, 89, 91–92, 96, 134–35, 137–39, 146, 150–51, 160, 166, 170–71, 330, 333
advertising business models, 89, 100
Affordable and Clean Energy, 19, 42–43, 80–81, 99–100, 104, 123–24, 148, 169, 195, 262–63, 324–25
aggregator business model, 89, 100
agriculture industry, 390
Amazon, 15, 24–25, 32–33, 62, 67, 166, 312, 316, 319, 338, 346
ambiguity, 38, 57–61, 69
Americans with Disabilities Act (ADA), 249
amortization, 352–53, 357–59, 364
amount of cash on hand, 358
amount of revenue, 86, 89, 91
angel investors, 378–80, 389
annual percentage rates (APRs), 381
appraisals, companies conduct employee, 244, 261
APRs (annual percentage rates), 381
artificial intelligence, 15–16, 18, 20, 101, 246, 332, 338, 365
assets, 9, 114, 354–59, 362–63, 381, 386–87, 400
  productive, 355, 357
audience, 90, 112, 135–36, 139–40, 293
authority, 146, 148, 157–58, 169, 178–79, 181–82, 184, 186, 194, 196, 279
awards, 217, 264–65, 274, 276, 279

balance sheet, 346, 348, 351, 353–62, 364, 373, 385
Ball Corporation, 35
bargaining power of customers, 110, 123
barriers, 28, 57, 237, 239, 288, 293, 295, 300, 302–3

barriers to cross-cultural communication, 300, 302
basic types of leaders, 234, 242
behavioral segmentation, 164–65, 169–70
behavior-focused strategies, 283–85
behaviors, 17–18, 35–37, 40–42, 52–53, 156, 158, 165, 167, 207, 223–24, 230–33, 237–39, 274, 276–77, 283–84
behaviors and attitudes, 52–53
Benefit Corporations, 79, 81, 398, 410
best companies, 82, 206, 347
big data, 330, 341, 343
BIM, 288
birth stage, 193, 196
Block, five, 7
Blockbuster, 96
BMC. *See* Business Model Canvas
BMW, 93–94, 99, 105
bracelets, 130–34, 136
brand awareness, 134, 136, 138–39
branded products, 168
brand loyalty, 165–67
brands, 4–6, 8, 10, 24, 89, 91–92, 102, 130–32, 134–36, 138, 159, 165–67, 171, 303, 401–2
BRT (Business Roundtable), 9–10
budget, 81, 135, 141, 150, 310, 325, 371, 373, 375, 377
budgeting, 81, 207, 368, 373, 375, 388–89
building blocks, five, 411–12
business, 4–21, 23–45, 48–62, 66–76, 78–82, 84–86, 88–95, 104–6, 113–16, 122–23, 141–43, 222–304, 315–20, 339–44, 346–52, 356–66, 368–73, 377–78, 380–86, 393–413
  companies conduct, 16, 18
  digital, 368
  existing, 71–73, 79, 85, 88, 91, 167
  good, 4–5, 16, 18
  startup, 394, 398
  textile, 241
business analytics, 328, 335–37, 339–44
business assets, 381, 396
business communication, 183, 301
business corporations, 398
Business Creation, 63–81, 412
business credit cards, 381–82, 389
business data, 335, 342
business entities, 395, 397–98
business environment, 38, 42, 58, 111, 113, 190, 289, 301
  changing, 85, 185
businesses use, 333, 350
business functions, 81, 179, 192
business growth, 140, 320, 366, 372
business ideas, 13, 95
  new, 13, 79, 168, 377

business impact case, 4, 24, 48, 66, 84, 104, 130, 154, 176, 328, 335
business impact project, 411–12, 414
business intelligence, 335, 342–43
Business law, 394, 409–10
business leaders, 13, 58, 180, 202, 205, 340, 366
business loans, 381, 383
Business Model Canvas (BMC), 84, 92–95, 99–100
Business Model Canvas for innovation, 92–93
business model development, 84, 99
business models, 4, 7, 20, 63, 83–101, 106, 241, 369, 412–13
  existing, 84, 93, 95, 99
business operations, 9, 35, 305–25, 348, 362, 382
  ceasing, 35
business opportunities, 11, 13, 75–76
  new, 74, 77, 224, 411
business owners, 59–60, 151, 184, 194, 348–49, 364, 378, 394–96, 399, 409
business partners, 186, 396
business people, 114, 283, 299, 360, 394–95, 399–400, 404, 409
businesspeople, 38, 40, 50
business performance, 9, 177, 319, 411
business person, 143, 351, 358, 400
business plan, 70, 81, 226, 240, 383
business processes, 9, 124
  integrating, 318, 324
business results, 280, 284
Business Roundtable (BRT), 9–10
business strategy, 103–5, 113, 122, 124, 404
Business Strategy for Competitive Advantage, 63, 105–25, 412
business structures, 26, 396–97, 410
business student, 347
business success, 10, 309
business term loan, 381, 389
business units, 340, 356
business value, 289, 365–66
business world, 346–47
buyer persona, 167, 170
buyers, 8, 89, 91, 96, 108, 110, 140–42, 146, 156–57, 169–70, 401

campaign, 109, 134, 138, 151, 225, 253
candidates, 229, 237, 247, 250, 252–53
capital, 66, 72, 115–16, 309–10, 361, 369–71, 377–78, 380, 382, 388–90, 396–97
  working, 370–71, 382, 386, 389
cash, 346–51, 353–54, 356–60, 362, 364, 370, 376–77, 381–82, 384–86, 388, 409